FRAU OU

NIETZSCHE'S
WAYWARD DISCIPLE

BY RUDOLPH BINION

WITH A FOREWORD BY

WALTER KAUFMANN

PRINCETON, NEW JERSEY
PRINCETON UNIVERSITY PRESS
1968

FOREWORD BY WALTER KAUFMANN

WHEN A research committee asked me long ago whether a comprehensive study of Lou Andreas-Salomé deserved support, the answer was easy to give: Of course. After all, she was a fascinating woman, and her successive friendships with Nietzsche, Rilke, and Freud clearly deserved investigation. Asked many years later to read the manuscript that had grown out of this project, I was astonished by its vastness. Was Lou really *that* important? The brief first chapter reinforced my doubts. For all my admiration for Freud, I do not care for books that substitute psychoanalytical speculations for painstaking scholarship. But the long second chapter, which deals with Lou's encounter with Nietzsche, represents a triumph of sustained research and offers fascinating discoveries of major importance. It also sets the tone for the rest of the book. Rarely has such a comprehensive grasp of all the relevant materials been fused with such a lively mind.

The bulk of this volume is not out of proportion to the importance of its subject, for *Frau Lou* is more significant than Lou's own books. In the case of most biographies the opposite may be taken for granted, but in this case the author's reach exceeds the woman whose biography he offers us—in two ways.

First: not only does he deal with Nietzsche, Rilke, and Freud; we also encounter an amazing array of other German and Austrian writers and scholars. It is scarcely an exaggeration to say that Lou's friendships approximate a Who Was Who of Central European intellectual life during the half-century between 1880 and 1930.

It would have been relatively easy to write a much shorter and rather superficial book, capitalizing on the human interest of brief vignettes of famous people, going along with the fashionable journalistic prostitution of biography and history. In an age in which masses of irrelevant detail so often hide a lack of insight and the absence of all power to interpret, Rudolph Binion offers us a book of stunning richness that throws new light on a great many interesting men.

The whole literature on Lou's troubled relationship to Nietzsche and Paul Rée is dated by *Frau Lou*. Making use of a large quantity of hitherto unpublished documents and letters, Binion proves that Lou, like Nietzsche's sister, falsified the story. That the sister's ac-

v

count was mendacious has been known for a long time, but everyone who discussed this episode without relying on the sister has invariably relied on Lou. Thus Binion makes a major contribution to the study of Nietzsche's life and character.

The point of the book, however, is by no means to turn a widely admired woman into a villain. Binion shows what her relationship to Nietzsche did to Lou, and he shows how it was not by any means, as had been widely supposed, significant for Nietzsche only and at most a passing fancy for Lou. He demonstrates its lasting impact on her life and work, and shows how her fiction and some of her later friendships represent repeated attempts to cope with her rejection by Nietzsche.

What one might take merely for a biography of a woman whose stature does not brook comparison with that of her most famous friends turns out to be a highly sensitive, imaginative, and erudite essay in intellectual history. Even so, the book has another whole dimension; it is also a psychoanalytical study. The author aims to show that the findings of psychoanalysis are fruitful for biographers and intellectual historians who are not in search of shortcuts but who wish to make the most of the abundant documentary materials they have studied.

Often scholars say of some large work that it seems excellent except for those parts in which they are specialists. I am in the happy position of being full of admiration for the long chapter on Nietzsche, in which I have been able to check the evidence. And considering how controversial both Nietzsche and Freud were and still are, I have no qualms about saying that the author's psychoanalytical interpretations strike me as the most controversial part of his book. To this, however, two points must be added.

Probably no previous psychoanalytical biography has been based on such thorough research. So far, criticism of the use of psychoanalytical ideas in such contexts has usually come down to the discovery that the author did not know his subject sufficiently. Professor Binion makes it possible at long last to discuss the problem on a higher level.

Moreover, the introduction of psychoanalysis into a study of Frau Lou is peculiarly pertinent. After all, she herself became a lay analyst, and her friendship with Freud and his dominant influence on her thought lasted far, far longer than her encounters with Nietzsche and Rilke. Readers who find Binion's psychoanalytical terminology and explanations uncongenial ought to keep in mind that Lou herself came to accept these ways of thinking.

Foreword

The final portions of the book are as moving as any. In the last chapter we see the old Lou writing her memoirs, rewriting her life once more, fashioning a final version of events that she could not face as they had actually happened. Then we still get an account of the author's source materials and the obstacles he faced when he visited her archives. It would be a rank abuse of his hospitality to tell this story in the Foreword, but it provides the perfect link between those last years in which Lou tried to forge her myth and this book in which the myth is finally exposed. Only after having read those pages can one fully appreciate Rudolph Binion's immense accomplishment.

Here is scholarship that involves all the excitement of detective work. The central story line is clear and simple: the life of Lou, the development of her mind and myth, the contrast between fact and fancy, the pathology of brilliance. But we are given far more than this. The book is so full of ideas and discoveries that, having finished it once, one turns back to it again and again. For this volume is a rich mine and harbors more treasures than any single reading could bring to light.

Dates are written the day first, then the month in Roman, then the year, thus: 7 VII 1897. Lou's diary entries are cited by their dates preceded by a D, thus: D 7 VII 1897. The formula for a letter, whether published or unpublished, is addresser→addressee, date, thus: Lou→Freud, 27 IX 1912. Correspondents' surnames or full names are used except in Lou's and the following cases: B-H (Richard Beer-Hofmann); CG (Clara Gelzer); Clara (Clara Westhoff Rilke); EK (Ellen Key); Emma (Emma Wilm Flörke); FN (Friedrich Nietzsche); Frieda (Frieda von Bülow); Hanna (Hanna Bormann); Helene (Helene Klots Klingenberg); HVH (Hugo von Hofmannsthal); Ida O (Ida Overbeck); Lisbeth (Elisabeth Nietzsche, later Förster-Nietzsche); MVM (Malwida von Meysenbug); O (Franz Overbeck); RMR (Rainer Maria Rilke). An asterisk signifies an oral source, thus: *Franz Schoenberner.

Lou's works are named when the occasion requires—some in obvious short form—but otherwise cited according to the presumed order of their conception as shown in Table III of the Bibliography, in which case a postfixed colon followed by a number designates a page reference to the corresponding publication in Table II (books being preferred to periodicals in instances of republication): thus 1898a:320 designates page 320 of the first work conceived by Lou in 1898, "Zurück ans All" (not as printed in the periodical *Die Romanwelt* early in 1899 but as reprinted later that year in her *Menschenkinder*). Table III omits some brief book reviews, which are referred to by incomplete titles, thus: "Das Kindlein . . ." As for works other than Lou's, a name followed by a number between commas constitutes a page reference to a publication that is the only one listed in Table IV for the author having that name: thus Dohm, 280, designates page 280 of Hedwig Dohm's delightful polemic against three backtracking feminists, Frau Lou foremost. If the work is not the only one of its author's listed there, the title is given, generally in abbreviated form: thus Rée, *Entstehung*, 50, denotes page 50 of Paul Rée's *Die Entstehung des Gewissens*.

The authors Richard Beer-Hofmann, Elisabeth Förster-Nietzsche, Friedrich Nietzsche, and Rainer Maria Rilke are styled B-H, E F-N, FN, and RMR respectively. Nietzsche's, Rilke's, and Freud's most familiar works are cited by section rather than page for referential convenience, and in English by catchwords in the following cases: FN, *Tragedy* (*The Birth of Tragedy*), *Untimely* (*Untimely Reflections*), *Human* (*Human, All Too Human*), *Dawn* (*Flush of Dawn*), *Science* (*The Gay Science*), *Zarathustra* (*So Spoke Zarathustra*), *Beyond* (*Beyond Good and Evil*), *Genealogy* (*The Genealogy of Morals*), *Ecce* (*Ecce Homo*), *Twilight* (*The Twilight of the Idols*); RMR, *Elegies* (*The Duino Elegies*), *Sonnets* (*Sonnets to Orpheus*), *Malte* (*The Notebooks of Malte Laurids Brigge*); Freud, *Three Essays* (*Three Essays on Sexual Theory*), *Beyond* (*Beyond the Pleasure Principle*), *Discomfort* (*Discomfort in Civilization*), *Outline* (*An Outline of Psychoanalysis*).

As a rule, the source references (numbered consecutively) appear on pp. 511-35 rather than in the footnotes (lettered consecutively), except for those that are bound up with footnote matter. Furthermore, whenever the source of a quotation is indicated in the text proper (as precisely as possible, that is, in the case of undated letters or diary entries), no formal source reference is appended.

PREFACE

S<small>IGNING HERSELF</small> "Frau Lou" to a new acquaintance in her middle years, Lou Andreas-Salomé urged: "Please call me this, as do my friends, instead of the three long names!"[1] The nickname appealed to her in that it was simple but distinctive, girlish and ladylike both, wifely yet not conjugal. And it appealed to her especially just then, when she was thinking hard about what it meant to be a woman. It appeals to me because her trouble in being a woman was at the source—indeed, practically *was* the source[a]—of her whole mental life, which is my subject.

Frau Lou is a psychoanalytic study of a near-mad near-genius of a woman. That woman being Lou Salomé, *Frau Lou* is also a microcosmic study in European culture from the 1880's to the 1930's. Psychoanalytic and microcosmic, *Frau Lou* has little of a typical "life" and less of a typical "life and times." Lou's were times of unprecedented European vitality passing over into unprecedented violence in 1914. And her life in its long heyday was that of a free spirit ranging out from Berlin and, later, Göttingen as far as the Volga and the Atlantic, the Arctic and the Adriatic. Her charmed circle embraced a vast company of cultural notables, over and beyond an intimate company of notables-to-be including Nietzsche, Rilke, and Freud. She was herself a renowned—and a remarkable—woman of letters. She outlived her literary renown but made cultural history behind the scenes through others who responded with éclat to her writings and, more directly, to her prodigious intellect and personality. She can be seen in this perspective through *Frau Lou. Frau Lou*'s subject proper, however, is her psychic convolutions and not her European presence.

A case study though it is, *Frau Lou* has the form of a personal history in that it narrates Lou's inner life along with her outer life. This convenient scheme entails an inconvenience straight off, as baby Lou's anal-sexual cravings are recorded before being duly evidenced. It is also subject to a big qualification. Until far along, the only two terms of Lou's inner life as it is told in *Frau Lou* are its two end terms: infancy and recency. Then it is shown how certain of her bygone adult experiences stacked up in her memory and how

---

[a] Whence her animus against Adler, who told her so (impersonally): see below, pp. 336, 422-23.

she reacted to them several at a time over the years. The experiences
concerned are necessarily chronicled in full detail beforehand. The
decisive one was her encounter with Nietzsche—which was of comparable import for Nietzsche himself, and indirectly for all her men
after him.

Like her inside story, Lou's outside story will come as news. The
reason why is itself a case in point: her accounts of herself, which
have passed for factual, are really fanciful through and through. Yet
she did tell every last truth about herself at least once in some misleading context or other; therefore I have torn many a telltale phrase
of hers out of context for use against her with a clean scholar's—
if not gentleman's—conscience. The pattern of her distortions, and
with it the proof of them, will emerge in due course.

Psychoanalytic from the first, my investigative method became—
in Freud's word—"metapsychological" toward the last under pressure
from my material. That is, in order to make sense of Lou's mental
acts I had to ignore her own sense of them in the final reckoning.
The result was a few discoveries affecting the science of mind and
suggestive of a science of history; "Beyond *Frau Lou*" reviews these
in conclusion. They amount to a merest beginning along new lines.
Even so, they are my justification for exhibiting Lou at fuller length
than, to judge conventionally, her standing in cultural history war-
rants.

Translating Lou was troublesome, for as she grew older her style
carried the weight of her arguments more and more. Academic at
first—even in her fiction—it acquired sonorous modulation and
intricate articulation in her middle years. Then it went the way of
compact allusiveness, as if aiming to compress all of Creation into
a single, pious syllable. Tractable as is German diction, Lou strained
it baroquely in the end. This compelled me to strain English even
harder in order to convey her message intact. I moreover found best
reason to quote her at her worst, for then her latent texts were most
legible—especially when she was either solecistic or silly, which she
rarely was. A select sample of her late prose is therefore in order:
one appears with a parallel translation in Appendix A.

Appendix B contains miscellaneous addenda to the footnotes.
And the Bibliography, besides cataloguing sources, retraces the course
of my research.

It is my pleasure to express my gratitude herewith to all the persons and institutions that assisted me along that course as indicated
in the Bibliography, and to Professors Marc Raeff, Richard Hofstadter,
and Michael Stocker and Miss Marie Lindahl for other documentary

Preface

services rendered. I am also beholden to the American Council of Learned Societies for having financed my year of research abroad, and to the Council for Research in the Social Sciences and other agencies of Columbia University for having defrayed many additional expenses involved in the preparation of this book. I wish furthermore to thank Mrs. Patricia Dreyfus for an expert first typing job with marginalia to match; Miss Theda Shapiro for a masterly final typing job in the course of which she continually exacted needful rewordings and frequently contributed points of substance; Miss Amy Hackett for a pioneering draft of Appendix A and for counsel on feminism in the Germanies; Professor Carolyn G. Heilbrun and Mr. Timothy Wright for strenuous efforts to turn my final copy into literature; Professor and Mrs. Richard Schoenwald for a rigorous once-over; and Professor Walter Kaufmann for invaluable advice at the publication stage.

Finally, my wife was my indispensable assistant throughout, particularly with Lou's fiction: my debt to her is inexpressible.

RUDOLPH BINION

November 1967

xi

CONTENTS

FOREWORD BY WALTER KAUFMANN   v

KEY TO THE REFERENCE MATTER   viii

PREFACE   ix

Part One: Childhood

I   FATHER AND FATHER-GOD   5

II   GOD'S VICAR, GILLOT   14

III   AFTER GILLOT   21

Part Two: Youth

I   THE UNHOLY TRINITY   35

II   FROM PILLAR TO POST   58

III   "A PITY FOREVER"   81

IV   LOU WITHOUT NIETZSCHE   112

V   THE WAYWARD DISCIPLE   141

Part Three: Womanhood

I   RITES OF LOVE   175

II   SUPER-LOU AND RAINER   212

III   RUSSIA IN, RAINER OUT   266

IV   IDLY BUSY   305

Part Four: Maturity

I   AT FREUD'S ELBOW   335

II   A PERSONALIZED FREUDIANISM   340

III   THEORIZING FOR FREUD   347

IV   LIVING FOR FREUD   366

V   ASIDE FROM FREUD   400

Part Five: Old Age

I   REVAMPING THE PAST   461

II   "HOMECOMING"   481

III   A RETROSPECT   491

BEYOND *Frau Lou*   493

BIBLIOGRAPHICAL NOTES   511

APPENDIX A: LOU'S "LITERARY EXPRESSION"   537

APPENDIX B: MISCELLANY   543

BIBLIOGRAPHY   557

INDEX   577

To redeem the past,
transforming every "so it was"
into a "so did I wish it":
to me,
redemption would mean no less.
FRIEDRICH NIETZSCHE

PART ONE · CHILDHOOD

SIEGFRIED WILM, a Hamburg baker's son faced with conscription in 1813, fled with a Danish bride to Saint Petersburg. There he made a fortune as a sugar refiner. He was fitfully unmaking it when, in his prime, he took a knife to his son on orders from God to destroy all survivors of the Neva floods. His wife disarmed him, then kept him under guard in a back room, addressing "diary pages" to him regularly until his death and even afterwards "on remembrance days, anniversaries, children's birthdays"—not excluding "the very day" of her remarriage.[1/a]

In 1844 the Wilms' daughter, Louise, then twenty-one,[b] married Gustav Ludwig Salomé, aged thirty-seven.[c] Gustav was a Baltic German of Huguenot extraction[d] who, after a military schooling in Petersburg, distinguished himself at twenty-four for valor in storming Warsaw.[e] He soon rose to general, then turned state official.[f] Louise was handsome, high-strung, and chilly.[g] Gustav, still handsomer, was a suave and affectionate tyrant. The two were as one in their pietism. Pietism in fact (French, Dutch, German, English) bound the whole foreign colony of Petersburg together as a "city unto itself."[2] So did

[a] On the Wilms generally: *Franz Schoenberner, whose mother—daughter of Siegfried's son, Eduard—kept a family log. (The information here supersedes Schoenberner, 42 and *passim.*) *Franz Schoenberner: Siegfried had one son and one daughter—but see below, pp. 9, n. *s*, 11 n. *x*.

[b] Granting her dates of birth (7 II 1823) and marriage (XII 1844) as in Pfeiffer, *Leben*, 294—where, however, Gustav's birth is misdated. (All dates are given New Style.)

[c] Gustav was born on 23 VII 1807.

[d] Gustav's parents were Karl Salomé of Magdeburg (9 III 1764 to 5 IX 1821) and Katherine Elisabeth Salomé *née* von Oding (1 XII 1775 to 31 VII 1831). (They were not royalist émigrés from revolutionary France as in 1931a:73, Hermann, etc.—nor was Gustav born noble.) Rilke, who dabbled in genealogies, discovered a possible ancestor of Gustav's in André Salomé, late sixteenth-century notary and memorialist of Les Baux (Avignon), whence the Huguenots were evicted in 1621 (RMR→Lou, 23 X 1909).

[e] In IX 1831.

[f] Gustav Karlovitch Salomé appears in the Calendar-Address book for the Czar's Central Administration through the 1850's as "state councilor" and thereafter as "actual state councilor" in charge of military accounts. Given his high functions, he ought normally to have been ennobled; available records evidence no such ennoblement, however—which in any case would hardly have extended to Lou.

[g] On Louise Wilm Salomé see especially Lou→Caro [6? VI 1898] (draft?). Her handwriting, incidentally, consisted of erratic, violent, giddily slanted strokes and gaudy curlicues.

the colonists' passion for their cosmopolis, their patronizing love for the Russian people, and their contempt for the autocratic Czarist regime—which they loyally served.[h] The Salomés moved seasonally between the General Staff Building (a majestic multiple dwelling across from the Winter Palace) and a private estate in nearby Peterhof (the Czar's summer residence), with time out for trips West. Seconded by a multinational liveried staff of domestics complete with French governess and Russian nurse,[3] they raised four children under the scrutiny of an Evangelical god akin to Gustav: stern, with grace in reserve. Their fourth—an only daughter, named Louise and called Lelia—was born on February 12, 1861.

Little Lelia was wretched amidst plenty as only a human being can be. Her trouble was psychic growing pains which fortunately can, and unfortunately must, be traced to their crude source. This was a craving for her father excited by excretion and attended by darkling visions of reentering his bowel-womb to repossess his penis. Her purest joy was pain at his hands[i]: she would cry or soil herself or otherwise misbehave so as to be spanked by him. As her courtship hardly came off at that, she made excuses for him: he could spare little time from his high charges, and her mother saw to it that he spared still less affection. Consoling herself with "intimate . . . wishing"[j] accompanied by intimate doing, she lost control of both and fell prey to fears lest—in her pristine perspective—her old severance from him were still to come.

At length Lelia renounced her father[k] and her naughtiness both. It remained for her to incorporate a love-image of him into her inchoate self; this she did by a pathological detour stretching the whole of her prolonged childhood. First she withdrew into a solitary playworld laid out alternatively on the Peterhof lawn or beneath the grand piano in the Petersburg salon. Her father played along with her—originally

---

[h] On the Salomés' Petersburg milieu see Podach, *FN und LS*, 133; Schoenberner, 42; 1901a:21-23.

[i] On embracing her once, Lou later recollected, he burnt her with a cigarette. She howled, he covered her with kisses, and the sight of "honest-to-goodness tears in his steel-blue eyes"(1913c:457) struck her dumb with delight. Fictionally she commented: "I would now gladly let my arm be burnt off if only he would kiss me that way again" (1893g:70). Be the story true or false, the moral is the same.

[j] 1913c:450 (which concerns "that tenderness my father's mouth and eyes had for me—joined, though, to an incontestable plenitude of power both pleasing and· paining").

[k] Perhaps after witnessing the "primal scene," related in 1897j (melodramatically) and D [early II 1913] (contradictorily: as if she both did and did not understand what was going on). She was to represent herself repeatedly in her fiction as an orphan after the age of five or so.

in the guise of a pair of leather bellows, then as a toy pet amidst other, brotherly toy pets or a porcelain doll beside her baby doll. At last he rejoined her as the household god intimately giganticized, with grandfatherly visage vanishing heavenward above a huge cloak of invisibility that concealed "a thousand"[4] "impressively large folds and pockets" filled with "toys of all descriptions."[5] Originally a nocturnal apparition, her "very earliest and best friend"[6] was soon available at all hours to take her up fondly beneath his nether garments. There she would appropriate "the objects in his pockets, which indulged every childish wish beyond all measure,"[7] and would impart her fancies to him in the past tense, ever and again adjoining an "as you know" with a thrill of delight, for that way, by his very silence, he would not only endorse them each in turn but, so to speak, return them "as if new."[8] A god all her own, he maintained secret rapport with her even while standing formal attendance at family prayers, but especially inside that "single room of the house admitting a single person at a time and offering a single seat, where she was mistress over her most intimate action or inaction and where she might lock herself in without locking the Good Lord out."[9] By his grace she was mistress over the whole visible world besides, which together they might extinguish at will; yet she was pleased to feel tiny and helpless over against him. Their realm, secure against intrusion, was off limits to her elders. More, her rejection of parental standards was his own: he was a god "who neither bids nor forbids, only condones."[10] Thus patronized, she came to be at home in make-believe.[*l*] One of her later storybook accounts of her childhood reads: "When lying was in order—something no one and hence she alone could know—she went about it eagerly."[11] Indeed, she was thrashed for it again and again. But her father's rod was one of the few hard facts with whose hardness she had no quarrel; and if his strokes now felt punitive rather than voluptuous, she now had a father-god only too willing to commiserate over the sore spot.[*m*]

This transfer of affection from her real father to his idealized,[*n*]

[*l*] Among her earliest memories was that of having refrained from opening an exploding bonbon so as to be able to imagine its contents lovelier than by her father's warning they really were (1893g:70; 1913c:457-58).

[*m*] For this division of labor, see 1909a:chapter I; 1913c:460. In a later, fictional version (1919d) she devises him to thrash her father for having thrashed her, then intercedes for clemency, thereby doing unto others . . .

[*n*] Idealized through being maximally permissive and powerful, available and affectionate—but also grandfatherly, which to her connoted age-old and hence imperishable. Additionally on this last point: her father was over 53 years her senior, the household god was patriarchal, and her mother called the household faith "*altväterlich*" (Louise Salomé→Caro [early 1879]). Her maternal grandfather was no less her god's *proto*prototype, as will emerge.

endopsychic counterpart was, then, her first step toward identifying with him[o]: so far so healthy. The next big step, however, the identification itself, was delayed for years and years, during which her interest remained withdrawn from reality. In these conditions, her ego firmed as it had first formed: as wildly self-aggrandizing and self-indulgent on the infantile premise that thought is omnipotent.[p]

Before her puberty, Lelia's psychosis—for such it was—evolved nonetheless toward its eventual undoing. In a first innovation, she took over from her god to the extent of preparing her tales by day for recitation to him (and retroaction by him) at night; thus she exercised divine auditory discretion part-time—however tentatively—while talking directly to herself. Next she stood in for him by day as humankind's maker and providence in that she concocted a whole slew of personages with interlocking fates for her nightly reports. She would take off from strangers observed in the city streets, joining this one's head to that one's shoulders or calling this older one that younger one at a later age. And she would lose sight of the pedestrian originals as she spun out fates within her "second world" till the oldest spinnings became "primal," "immemorial," "reality" itself.[12] "Likely my memory would gradually have gone lame from all this arbitrary devising and disposing," she later judged, "had not the divine memory reassured me."[13] In drawing on actual people for her personages, she was opening up her "second world" to the first. Yet beneath the surface, her personages were still mostly herself and her father, their fates still determined by her old father-romance. Her youngest brother, Jenia (Eugene), who was three years her senior,[q] was represented more currently in her "second world," though even his basic identity there was an archaic one: that of her son by her father.[14]

Jenia alone of Lelia's brothers was ever her playmate. In her days of toy animals and dolls he would even outplay her—and clean up afterwards, ranging the menagerie within its small-scale kennels, stalls, and sties, and taking the dolls to bed with him. About this introversive, effeminate boy "there was *from the first* a wholly mad nervousness."[15] He fast learned to brutalize his mother, and the mere sight of his father would drive him into solitary "fits of rage."[16]

[o] Pursuant to her unseemly old scheme of penetrating his bowels and appropriating his penis. The libidinal force of her addiction to make-believe (to affirming what was not) was itself penis-envy: see Lou→Freud, 19 x 1917.

[p] Of her original erotic motives, one had been sublimated portentously: her anal procreativity, displaced upwards into her tales twice told: above, p. 7. Note her god's minimal coproductive role (cf. 1899a: below, pp. 234ff., 240ff.).

[q] Born 29 i 1858.

Roba (Robert) and Sasha (Alexander)—respectively nine and twelve years older than Lelia—were more civil, but also more remote; both left home, moreover, by the time Lelia was ten. But whether her family circle numbered five or three, Lelia was "bitterly lonely among them all and given to absolute fantasy as her sole joy."[17] "Squarely averse" to Christmases and birthdays,[18] she saw the gifts bestowed on her then as sly demands on her to "be good."[19] As against her native willfulness she taught herself to "be good" with every inner reservation—to take on the "protective coloring"[20] of her environment and pass unnoticed. Her environment met her half way: a "little English private school"[21] which she entered at age eight was most undemanding,[r] and her parents early conceded her the status of hopeless fantast to be humored and not crossed. "Probably rarely has a girl had everything so much her own way," averred her mother.[22]

It was within her "second world" that Lelia gradually took full cognizance of the first. She began in earnest following a humiliation: her cousin Emma[s] interrupted her in the midst of a tall tale before their four parents to call her a liar.[23] She thereupon schooled herself with a vengeance in observing and recounting fact—by way of acquiring a final right to fable. There were thenceforth two moments to her singular evening prayers: the moment of fact and the moment of fancy. Distinct, successive moments at first, the two eventually merged to the effect that she would recast her experiences even while scrupulously respecting their material constituents. She thus acquired a phenomenal grasp of reality in the service of a deep antagonism toward it—or in fact alienation from it, for her grudging acknowledgment of reality lacked all elementary inner conviction.[t] She would stalk, shadow, and scrutinize the same Petersburg strangers day after day, intent on descrying the veriest truth about them even while concocting fates for them. Then she would turn her day into words— "and for the very same reason for which I took the utmost care to avoid omitting or underrating even the tiniest bit of reality, I abandoned myself for the rest all the more candidly to my imaginings,

[r] She may have learned English there, though: she later read it fluently without having been otherwise exposed to it.

[s] Emma Wilm, later Flörke (see the dedication of *Im Zwischenland*)—*not* a daughter of Eduard Wilm, who settled in Germany at mid-century and lost touch with his sister Louise (*Franz Schoenberner—but cf. above, p. 5 n. *a*). Incidentally, no relative of Lou's on her father's side ever came into her correspondence or reminiscences, though Gustav's brothers Karl Heinrich (1800-1870) and Georg (1810-1881) and his nephew Karl Friedrich (1819-1882: presumably son to Gustav's brother Peter Franz, 1796-1828) all raised families in Petersburg with German wives.

[t] See 1900d:79-80 for her poignant sense of what she was missing.

certified trustworthy by God the way any everyday fact had to be."[24] Even so, she could no longer believe in her personages except by virtue of their foothold in the "first world"—of "that fragment of reality through which I held firmly to sights actually seen."[25] Accordingly she reasoned that they followed her to Peterhof for the summer in the guise of flowers brought by Petersburg vendors (whereupon they each acquired a distinctive fragrance for the winter months)— though again, "the imaginary people thereby grew only the more genuine, 'real,' whereas a shadow of suspicion fell upon the plants."[26] Fittingly, springtime reminded her in after years of her swaying back and forth on a yellow balcony at Peterhof to the rhythm of the chaffinch's quaver while viewing a lilac blossom alternately from afar as if "from 'another' world," then from "almost inside" as if "taken up" into this world.[27] Her own existence came in for as much doubt as anything else's, if not more: she would spend hours playing with masks before the mirror and mimicking others so as to become solid like them. At least her self-identification with her father-god advanced inasmuch as her fates game, on being transplanted to Peterhof, "underwent an enlargement: it was henceforth to encompass all of nature as well as all of mankind."[28]

Puberty gave such new vigor to Lelia's old daughterly craving that her fantasy god ceased to serve his purpose. She anthropomorphized him increasingly; his "invisibility" only grew the more "visible."[29] Hitherto latent, her resentment of his immateriality now burst into the open, there to vie with her affection for him. The showdown came one early spring night after a farmhand from Peterhof reported that a couple to whom he had denied shelter in her garden playhouse at her behest had since shrunk away on the spot, leaving only some black buttons and a battered hat frozen round with tears. She saw the joke, yet besought her god to pronounce it such with the word "Snowmen!" A calvary ensued in the deathly stillness; by about the ninth hour her god was no more.[u] "The impression was left of a demise, an abandonment, not of any doubting his existence or disloyalty on my part. He withdrew as does childhood into the never-was, in a riddlesome, dreamlike way."[30]

Her mourning was gloomy, "hypertense,"[31] fearful, guilt-ridden. Godforsaken, she felt "self-abandoned,"[32] cut off within a spiritually vacant universe of discrete parts. Her mirror image assumed sharp

---

[u] She had begun fancying herself Jesus even before her calvary. The snow couple signified—beyond her own parents, who had no right of entry into her Peterhof den of fables—Joseph and Mary as in the Austrian folk song "Wer Klopfet An?" She outdid Jesus in that she dismissed her mother along with her earthly father—and before the nativity at that.

contours before which she felt "shut out of house and home."[33] After having scorned her parents since her god's appearance, she took remorseful heed of them upon his disappearance, considering that they too had suffered cosmic loss, if unknowingly. Her god paid her a frightful return visit in disguise when she fretted lest she had tried him with a presolved riddle at the devil's instigation: the *"deus inversus"*[34] held out to her "his hindside, blackened ('backbitten' by [love] itself)."[35/v] Without him[w] she had to bear alone the "whole earthly burden"[36] of spinning out the "numberless fates."[37] The threads having lost their godgiven lustre, she spun them the swifter. The tangle grew such that she took to noting names and dates soon joined by lines to symbols which at length she herself could barely decipher. Down with the measles, she brooded over "my responsibility for all my people, not knowing what should become of them were I to die."[38] Back up, she turned her notes into prose "with the concerned feeling of a mother of man"[39]: her first diary. By then she could do without her god, however mournfully. Yet her take-over from him was neither final nor full. Of her former affection for him, only some of that originally paid him for his lofty generative and regulative functions had reverted to herself, and this insecurely. The rest fell back upon the Evangelical god. He, churchlier than ever, now exacted strictest piety from her. Covertly, though, she fancied herself both his virgin bride and especially his son, whose faith had been solely a love bond and whom he had let down—only to raise up in the end.

Autistic as ever, "awkward" and "shy"[40] to boot, Lelia kept to herself throughout adolescence. She went to no parties, not even Jenia's. Her one confidante her own age was her cousin Emma, who would daydream with her about true love. A "pert" flouter of Petersburg-German mores, Emma opted for a Russian love life—only to fall in love with Jenia, then marry a German lovelessly, whereupon her "life-line . . . sank into the banal."[41] Lelia's only other intimate was an uncannily clever and charming maiden aunt named Caro,[x] who won her heart by treating her as the special girl she knew herself to be. In Caro's vocabulary,[42] "freedom" meant acting out of deep "unconscious" "needs" governing the mind and will. A woman's innermost need was to "snuggle up" to someone both physically and mentally. The rationale of mind, however, was to "stand alone." Thus a woman had to choose between "freedom" and "independence"—be-

[v] Cf. Jahweh atop Sinai; also above, p. 7, on Lou's early vision of entering into her god the anal way. In 1919d a phallic hallucination follows her fit of anal diabolism—exposing her original project (above, p. 6).

[w] Or rather within him: see preceding note.

[x] Apparently Lelia's mother's sister (as in 1919g)—but see above, p. 5 n. *a*.

tween fulfilling her innermost need and having a mind of her own. A capable woman would choose "independence" unless "confronted by a whole *man*" so masterful and intelligent that to submit to him would mean not to "bow down and surrender" but the opposite—in which case she would suffer in proportion to her strength of mind before accepting her "destiny" and settling into "the sweetness of peace, of leaning on him and looking up to him." "Independence" had won out with Caro, who felt "often drawn afar. I have such a sense of unfulfillment," she told Lelia, "that at times it drives me wild. Yet I am so old already. At my age others grow peaceful, but in me the wildness will not abate." Her precepts read as if they had been written just for Lelia. Perhaps they were; in any event Lelia shortly made them her own.

Lelia "learned nothing"[43] at her gymnasium, the German Lutheran Petrischule, where at sixteen she still wrote like a whimsical child of ten. Her German teacher commented on a fantastical little poem by her entitled "An die Winne [=Wonne]" (To Joy): "Not on the assigned topic,"[44] and on her second prose composition of that same year, 1876-1877: "Much affectation and phrase-making"—then belatedly recognized her first, an encyclopedia-style essay on Schiller, as plagiarism.[45] Lelia had meanwhile blacked out the marginalia on the second and inscribed a passing grade over the failing one, but to no avail: she might continue her studies as auditor only. Her one good subject had been French—the Salomés' social language. Her very worst had been Russian. Only at about this time did she first meet Russian Russians socially—on a family jaunt to the Urals, where Roba was serving as engineer. Her father had long since taught her that Russians were lovably spiritual-sensual, violent-submissive, profound-naïve, rascally-guileless; she now kept at his own loving distance from them. Photos out of those years show Lelia lank and boyish in build, with a high arched forehead, wavy light hair, full wide lips, and big, deep-set, shy eyes.

Just after Lelia turned seventeen, her father died at seventy.[v] Her nursling's jealous hate for her mother revived in all its ferocity; it was to rage for years. And her religiosity turned urgent and heretical again. At sixteen she had begun training under Hermann Dalton at the family church (the German Evangelical Reformed) to be confirmed in a year's time, but because of her father's fatal illness the rite was postponed until her eighteenth birthday. She had copied out the catechism in an exquisite hand; now, converting her heartache into a headache, she filled the margins of her copy with a sniping critique

[v] On 23 ɪɪ 1878.

of church dogma amounting to a Lutheran demand for direct access to a more personal god.[z] Caro, then residing in Berlin, came to Petersburg for the funeral and stayed to absolve Jenia of guilt over recent spats with his father[46] and to restrain Lelia from doing "something really rash."[47] That summer Lelia visited Berlin and opened her heart to Caro about God and her loneliness. Caro saw to the root of her malaise: Lelia wanted her god here and now as well as on high and in eternity. Caro also saw which way the solution lay. She advised Lou to go hear a sermon by a preacher new to Petersburg: Hendrik Gillot.

[z] E.g. on Christ's seeking not to damn but to save, "He should note the church's intolerance"; on suffering as going without one's rightful possessions, "Often we suffer most for want of what we have no right to possess"; on each Christian sect as seeing the same Christ and the same gospels through its own particular shade of colored glasses, "Then it is most reasonable to belong to *no* sect. Why purposely put on distorting glasses when one—thank God!—has his two good eyes and his human reason?"

13

ENDRIK GILLOT was an ultraliberal pulpit orator attached to the Dutch legation in Petersburg, hence independent of the local church authorities. He preached at a Dutch Evangelical Reformed chapel on the Nevsky Prospect—in German as a rule. He would begin his sermons with a brief prayer, then take off from a line in the Bible or even in Goethe or Kant to lecture on the history or the philosophy of religion. He saw four typical historic stages to religion: first, "natural powers are represented as gods"; next, "the gods are dissociated from the natural powers"; then comes "a philosophic-theoretical age during which faith comes to be seen as a cure-all and fanaticism arises"; finally, the religion spreads abroad, "all obstacles notwithstanding." According to Gillot, Judaism passed into its fourth, Christian stage through the person of Jesus. After having regarded himself as just another Jewish prophet, Jesus came to see blessedness in the very striving for blessedness, whereupon he declared that the kingdom of heaven was within us and he its messiah. After his death, however, his disciples did not feel all that blessed, so the belief arose among them that salvation was not here and now, but hereafter. Yet Christ's whole message, Gillot added, was simply the "final flowering" of the Judaic one that there is a spiritual point to life: to be a Christian meant no more—but no less—than to take the spiritual as a standard for the physical life.[a]

Constructions like Gillot's were rife since Herder and Hegel had made history progressional and Baur and Strauss had made Jesus historical.[b] Even so, the elders of evangelical Petersburg did not deem the pulpit a proper platform for them. But since the young mostly rallied to Gillot, his every sermon was soon "a big and controversial event."[48] He cut an appropriately impressive figure with his commanding manner, flaxen locks, overly fine, sensual mouth, and eyes of a demonic apostle. In the fall of 1878, he was forty-two and married, with two children Lelia's age.

Whatever his merits as preacher or scholar, Gillot proved himself in Lelia's case a thaumaturgical molder of the mind and healer of the soul—with, to be sure, the benefit of having won her whole heart in

---

[a] From a résumé of Gillot's preachings prepared by Lou from memory in 1883 or 1884.

[b] Gillot's own construction owed much to Otto Pfleiderer, on whom he had written a book published in 1872.

should not restrict his instruction to religion and preparation for confirmation," she told Lou, "seems to me self-evident, given his whole nature and purpose."[64] On Lou's account, though, Caro balked at his "frightful thoroughness": "You say that brainwork does you no harm, that it is better than harassing thoughts. You may be right about that, but still you ought not to overdo it, to ask too much of yourself. . . . Please, my dear Lou, listen to me and do not run yourself down."[65]

Caro was "quite tense over how the conference will turn out"[66]—and not Caro alone. To their astonishment the two conferrers struck it off so well together that, as Lou overheard through the keyhole,[j] her education was left entirely in Gillot's hands. Another few weeks and the Gillots had arranged with the Salomés to spend the summer near them in Rongas, Finland. Caro, who had earlier rejoiced that Lou was "soon off to Finland, where the lessons will cease for a few months so you can get over the excitement" and "maybe also draw closer to Mama,"[67/k] now grew alarmed, for Lou's health was fast declining. "Your assurances to the contrary notwithstanding, I believe that you overestimate your strength. You say your bodily disorder is a consequence of sleeplessness, but the case is one of reciprocal action: the sleeplessness comes from excessive nervous irritation and mental strain, and it produces physical fatigue in its turn. This must not continue; if by now it is not better, you must discuss it with your Mama after all and take something for it. Though on the one hand it pleases me for your sake that Gillot will be living in your vicinity in Finland so you will be able to reach him whenever your head and heart are too full, on the other hand it would have been much more to my liking had the real lessons been eliminated altogether this summer. Now, maybe Mama too will want that, and you will only celebrate a 'story hour' with Gillot from time to time."[68]

Whatever Mama may have wanted, Lou drove herself all summer long. Her physical symptoms worsened. As for her mental ones: ". . . even here," she recollected in Rongas years later, "my full time still went into the fantasy-work of tireless inner recounting and fabling."[69] Gradually, though, Gillot did bring her interest round from his subjects as his to his subjects as such, then finally as hers: the following winter found her preparing to study comparative religion at the University of Zurich after her confirmation. Meanwhile, even as she was idealizing Gillot—unknowingly "creating him for myself" in the image of her childhood god, and "by the same method" at that[70]

---

[j] Pfeiffer, *Leben*, 289 (*Lou in old age). Despite appearances, this confirms 1893g:65, in which the conference is arranged by Erik unbeknown to forthright little Ruth, who walks in on it unsuspectingly.

[k] Caro had added, with evident sincerity: "which would so please me."

—she suddenly realized that she had created his divine prototype long before. She forthwith took her initial "god-creation"[71] for the pure type of all "god-creations." Her religiosity went undiminished, since she was unable to discern the father-phantom haunting it from the first. She afterwards noted: "Disbelief struck my heart lightninglike —or rather my reason, which compelled my heart to give up the faith to which it clung with childlike ardor."[72] But the renunciation never went that deep even after Rongas, where her heart prompted a supplication in verse to the omnipresent god to show her where to find him again.[l] This supplication bespoke the nostalgia for narcissism that was hers at the very height of her Gillot romance—a nostalgia already manifest in her "longing for solitude and peace"[73] while planning her summer's studies beside Gillot.

In her work for Gillot, that nostalgia ran a progressive course. From her zeal in learning his subjects to her thrill at suggesting texts for his sermons (and sitting at his desk on the sly?[74]) she was already taking over from him. Actually she was aiming beyond him from the very outset: by reason of his Western cultural orientation, which was known to her in advance, she saw him obscurely as her "de-Russification"[75] before even having set eyes on him—as her portal westward from her parental to her ancestral homeland. In those days, "under unstable Alexander II," as she later discovered, ". . . the spirit of revolt, which had found its first program in that of the Narodniki, the 'populists,' was brewing and fermenting" even in foreigners' Petersburg, and "it was hardly possible to be young and alive without being gripped by it."[76] Lou, however, was preclusively gripped by her infantile father complex, still unresolved. Before supplanting Gillot completely, she needed first to establish herself as his virtual daughter-wife—all else and others be damned. Such was the "instinctual *must* not amenable to reason"[77] of her Gillot days, later dignified by her variously as an inner summons to knowledge or freedom or integrity.

Gillot lent her encouragement. He embraced her freely, called her "my girl,"[m] took fondest pains with her. She caught an "undertone" of restrained erotism in his conversation with her,[78] and gave Caro to understand that "a conflict of feelings" was "raging within him."[n]

[l] Here I am taking the exquisite *"Du heller Himmel über mir . . ."* as per 1931a:22 for authentic in this ambiguous point, but in the version putatively just recollected in Rongas as of D 6 VIII 1900 the poetess calls on bright heaven to show her the way back to her *self* (1931: *"Zeig mir den Weg, so heiss ersehnt,/wo ich Dich wiederfinde"* as against 1900: *"Such' mir die Heimat, heiss ersehnt,/wo ich mich selber finde"*). See further below, p. 280.

[m] At all odds Lou→Gillot, 26 III 1882, copy, is signed: *"Ihr Mädel."*

[n] (Caro→Lou, 5 VI 1879: "How well I can think myself into him, and

Not content with encouragement, she took it out on herself in sleeplessness, loss of appetite, bleeding lungs, an aching heart,[o] and fits of deathly gloom. At length, overstrained and overwrought, she recoiled before what she all at once took to be his low designs on her behind his ecclesiastical front. Actually she recoiled before her own designs on him. All reality briefly "sank back into the unreal."[79] Early in 1880 she went abroad with her mother to convalesce from nervous exhaustion.

There was a regressive motive to Lou's insistence on being confirmed by Gillot: she would be restored to the holy spirit by its surrogate. There was also an epithalamic symbolism to it, with Gillot himself as that holy spirit.[p] But above all, as it turned out, there was her most progressive variety of narcissism. The ceremony took place on a late May morning of 1880 in the village church of Sandpoort, near Haarlem, Gillot traveling specially from Petersburg to join Lou and her mother. Lou chose the consecration text, which sounded duly baptismal and nuptial as well as redemptive: the Lord's words to Israel, "Fear not, for I have chosen[q] you; I have called you by name, you are mine." Her prayer thereafter ran: "You bless me, for I do not leave you,"[80] and before she had finished praying, Gillot had lapsed in her sight "from a god to his priest, to him who consecrated me unto everything high and beautiful toward which I was striving."[81] Her ideal had come apart from him, leaving her "aware that I wished, and ought, to live for it *alone, without him*."[82] By the same token, that moment of "purely felt childlike rapture"[83] vindicated "a self-created and self-sanctified duty and morality"[84] commanding compliance on pain of "self-despisal and self-annihilation"[85]—"a power remolding life," overwhelming her whole person and at the same time arousing it "to heightened productivity so that it can create God and law beyond itself": to "self-divinization."[86]

Lou had become one with her father-god at long last—nearly all of an instant, and more or less definitively. She had yet to settle with

---

how heavily he must suffer from a conflict of feelings raging within him. For they are sure to be raging, as his is such a passionate nature. But what strength of will this man must possess!")

[o] Her persistent eye- and headaches seem to have been primarily hysterical too (even though the eyestrain was real). So was a lisplike misspelling—and doubtless mispronunciation—not manifest before or later: she regularly wrote *sch* for *sp*. Other than this, her loss of appetite was her first and last oral symptom.

[p] The confusion is clearer from the German, "*heiliger Geist*"—also holy *mind*.

[q] In German, "*erwählt*"—hence not "redeemed" as in the Standard Edition (Isaiah 43:1).

Gillot in his own right—thenceforth a mere memory, but a live one: that of a nasty philanderer in nimbus. She wasted away only the faster, even as her gloom turned into "full joy and life-affirmation."[87] Meanwhile her confirmation, that "leave-taking" from Gillot,[88] was also a leave-taking from religious faith as far as she ever knew. God's vicar had consecrated her to a none-too-holy spirit all fresh and unfamiliar: her own.

$\mathfrak{F}$OR ONE LONG, decisive moment, Lou's Gillot romance had drawn her attention away from her self and her past. It left her supremely capable of coping with actualities on her own terms—that is, in the service of her predilection for pliant phantasms. Her ego's crucial new assets were Gillot's ethic of self-regard and his rationalistic bent. She turned each to extremest account. Of the first she made a sacred egoism—a licence to affirm herself before the world at large, even against it if need be. The second she applied to comprehending the world's purposes in basic accord with her own. She was to theorize with a passion, continually and sublimely: in the whole history of thought there are few men and no women to match her on these counts. Her interest went first, like Gillot's, to religion and philosophy; then behind these to psychology, and beside them to science and art, but never away from them for long.

No less vital than Gillot's legacy, the memory of him kept acting on her—and she on it. And such was the force of the precedent she set with him that for years to come she could love only "god-men" like him[89] and could indulge her love only in pseudoremembrance. She would alternate between her daughter-role and her father-role—between the girlish-submissive and the manly-masterful stance, between courting god-men and copying them, between outgoing and ingoing affectivity.[r] As for her brother-men—Jenia's breed—she would just play with them.

Her aspirations—intellectual as well as erotic—were one at their source,[s] and that daughterly one found clearest voice in her statements about ultimates. To her thesaurus of father-words belonged all her equivalents for God: "Life," "Reality," "Nature," "Mind," and "Ideal," plus anything "divine" or "eternal" or "creative" or "primal" or "quintessential," together with variants galore, including many a drastic compound toward the last ("life-totality," "the all-extant-and-inclusive," "the ever-proto-initial").[t] These cognates had diverse

[r] Her stock term for her resumption of her father-role was "homecoming"—once styled "loss of God" (1913c:465). Concerning this pattern: as per 1897k: 1213, the more Jesus is reverenced the less the father is and vice versa.

[s] D [late VIII 1882]: all her goals came down to a single one "by natural necessity."

[t] In fact every nominalized adjective of Lou's coinage commencing with "Ur-" or "All-" or "Ewig-" was a father-word. Her father-thesaurus was surely among the richest on record, what with its numberless words to be found

ancillary meanings within her father-complex, and sometimes no meaning outside it. They all entered her vocabulary as palest honorific abstractions; the concretion came later if ever. And differentiate them though she might in use, all would merge on the highest conceptual levels,[u] which thus rejoined the lowest.

Spinoza aiding, "Nature" was already hugely significant for Lou when, in her twenties, she learned to love scenic beauty, then animals, then natural history. At length she would bare her feet on entering a meadow or forest "the way a Moslem does on entering a temple,"[90] and would enter as if for "a short stroll into childhood."[91] Once inside, she would feel bound to "every living thing," "*identical* with everything,"[92] "thrust into that summit of unity . . . an *unio mystica*"[93] —and this in "rapturous gratitude, as for a gift of God containing everything straight off"[94] or else (without the *as*) for a reminder of original intimacy, of "something 'superhumanly' true."[95] By then she was responsive to the signs of the seasons—especially of spring, which she would meet "frolicsome and silly as a calf."[96] She would record the weather just as, to her "consolation," she learned that Tolstoi did: "perpetually, as if he quite personally were raining, blowing, or shining."[97] And she opened her diary ever and again to beast and bush,[v] and took counsel with them at big reunions about whether her experience away from them "had not been too petty or jumbled measured against the fate of the seasons."[98/w] Despite some motherly, even grandmotherly, tenderness for the human breed specifically,[x] she professed indiscriminate love for "the creature, who, un-

---

nowhere else. Its appendices contained "creation" as her self-constitutive act (adjectival form: "childlike"—which, however, also meant Lou-like), "kneeling" as her share in this act, "all joy" or "all fulfillment" as the holy orgasm, "Woman" as herself vis-à-vis her father, and "home" (sometimes written "mother-darkness") as the father-womb.

[u] What all our primal symbols for the fullness of Being mean is "always Life: even 'God' is only the final stress on them" (1913c:467—repeating a 1912 note on Vaihinger); whatever we have succeeded in analyzing we call *real* "in an act of metaphor by which we as it were speak of 'Reality' so as not to speak of 'God' (that is, of quintessences)" (D [late spring 1913]); " 'divine' . . . this word, in any sense of it, *always* means to us at once most intimate *and* most surpassing" (1931a:198); etc.

[v] Even in recollections of childhood—of which D VI 1917 (on the Petersburg-Peterhof seasonal migrations) is supremely lovely. Nature came off shorter, if still grandly, in Lou's works proper—after only a brief, spectral showing in 1883a and hardly more of one till roughly 1897e. Many of her men helped turn her attention to the natural world (Rée, Andreas, Ledebour, Zemek)—which, though, her mother loved extravagantly as of 1931a:65-66.

[w] She also took counsel in reverse: "What bush and tree relate, what they experience, always affects me strongly, opens my ears, makes me reminiscent" (D I 1912).

[x] Sisterly only to fool Freud: see below, p. 380.

banal, need come in no special edition to inform us about Being, which is the same for all of us."[99]/[*y*] Likewise, sharply as she might tell men apart, she insisted that she could not love a man for any- thing personal about him—could not love him, that is, according to the "creative . . . divine . . . mode of affection,"[100] which she saved for herself.

"Life" meant only *father* to Lou deep down, and she would rejoice in it devoutly for all the pain it might bring[*z*]—a hedonism posited as heroism. Fast upon exalting life she would exult in our "identity" with it.[101] She warranted that behind the scenes *it* really lived *us*.[102] She vowed to "love and honor" it, calling mere "resignation" a "breach of faith"[103/*a*]—for "to love life," she averred, "is the only tried and proven way of being spared by death."[104] She gave no pub- lic notice of her repeated mortal quarrels with it. These were muted quarrels with her god-men—were, that is, one self-repeating quarrel. Her reconcilements did tend toward "resignation": a resignation to her father's *no*. Her outbursts of renewed optimism were the shriller for her dread lest that *no* be life's last word to her: her dread of death.

Her clearest post-infantile cry for her father was most clearly a cry for life eternal as well. It sounded first as a self-ashamed whisper in womanhood about absorption of and by the cosmos, then as the ecstatic undertone to her late-life message[*b*] of an indefeasible bond among all living things.[*c*] Correspondingly, she lent coition a "primal religious sense: that we wed ourselves to reality"[105] and considered

y She called love of humanity "often only a conceptual game, a moral bug- bear or the like, but often too just what enables us to speak of creatural love as a strong emotional tug toward each and every animal, compassion with it, joy in it," deriving from "our basic unity with it" (D [III?] 1918). Our way back to pristine love of nature, she maintained, passed through self-love, this being an approach "from the other side" (D IX 1912). Her ambivalence toward mankind cries out of D 13 VI 1903: "Perhaps as God I would torture my people. But only the quite strong and perfect! Toward all others I would be overflowingly good—as to dogs and little birds. As for the strong and per- fect, such would be my way of wedding them, of nearing them, of becoming one with them."

z On Freud's account she was to add the proviso that the pain be merely mental.

a But also calling her love of life "innate"—which was chronologically close to true.

b Appropriated from an outgoing junior god-man, Beer-Hofmann, but also from Nietzsche before him: see below, pp. 260-63, 478.

c With the megalomaniacal term of the reciprocal absorption played down in the latter case—except when she went rapturous, as when she noted that, while watching a girl amidst playmates in a pastoral landscape, she was as if wafted aloft within a "love that feels out toward all this like an 'I love you, you are I, I am you' and would wish to partake of it all ever farther and deeper" (D VI 1917).

that religious parlance expresses, perforce symbolically, a forefeeling of cosmic fulfillment. Even the religious genius, she added, wrongly takes his symbols at face value (as if Mohammed fresh from his cave might have announced, inspired and inspiring: "There is one 'God,' as it were, and Mohammed is, so to say, his 'prophet' "). Again and again she half affirmed the cosmic proposition desymbolized—though symbol or no it was nonsense, since *ex hypothesi* the experience negates the would-be experient.[d]

Concerning the genesis of the gods she was on both sides of her cosmic paradox by turns: they were now idealized parental images, now idealized self-images. Meanwhile, her sometime transcendent god survived in her writings not only in immanent disguise but also variously through equivocation[e] or by undrawn logical inference[f] or on ironical sufferance[g] or as " 'God.' "[h] She was unshy about even "the divine," however, calling it "the embracing power of the 'primal' "[106] and the like. Her diction, solemn enough in her cosmology, went outright Biblical when she dealt with love or childbirth. She observed the Christian feast days twice over (first by the Russian, then by the Western calendar)—especially Easter, when God had repented of his nonexistence. She never flatly asserted that God was not, except with the force of a rebuke. Her explicit complaints against a godless world were that there was no refuge from transience in it and beauty of soul went unseen. As she herself once remarked: could the pious but say what they mean, they would talk straight out of childhood.[107]

Overtly too, the intellectual expression of Lou's longing for her father took a regressive course over the years as she glorified childhood ever more, her own in particular. She became a connoisseur of childhood under a poetic licence. She depicted the whole of it, then eventually infancy alone, as a paradise of self-world unity lost through the intrusion of self-consciousness. She maintained that she herself had consented to grow up only on the self-given assurance that she

[d] That is, in Lou's case the experient would have had to be, not Lou, but Lou-plus-the-cosmos.

[e] E.g. D [1913?] note on Bonus: religion always "supplies something of the very substance of life (or: receives it—for the two are really one and the same)."

[f] See especially 1894b (below, pp. 187-88).

[g] E.g. Lou→RMR, 17 II 1919 (in hard times): God should be more considerate of us, just as "we on our side are after all fond of him even without requiring that he exist."

[h] Except in quoting or ironizing, the adult Lou never did write simply "God," though I am often constrained to translate as if she did. The closest she came was the playful "*der Gott*" or the semiadjectival prefix "*Gottes-*."

would thereby grow back down—that all moving ahead in life "only leads deeper and deeper into the center whence it issued."[108/i] She related her own childhood ever anew, until it grew into a prodigious myth to know which was incumbent on all who knew her. To a dying friend she avowed: "For most people childhood is the best of times when they think back on it, but for me it was the worst."[109] Otherwise she outdid "most people" far and away, what with ever so gracious parents and gallant brothers—only to stop and wonder once how in all Eden she could then have been so wretched.[110] Of her Gillot romance she made an object lesson on the typically feminine,[111] of her childhood faith a school for "life-confidence"[j] as well as a model for the historic development of religions. She continually spoke of her private god, rather than of her belief in him, as having come and gone —and this with slight saving irony, if any.[k] Mental symptoms are all preelaborated subjunctively, in the mood of wishing or fearing; her childhood ones were postelaborated in the same mood. She never once dared look behind them[l]; indeed, what she was nostalgic for in childhood was just that uninhibited consorting with a god who was not.

Her master medium for self-disclosure was literature. Seen from close up, her literary production was of three sorts: fiction, nonfiction, and—in between—false self-accounting. Seen through, it was all one distorted *journal intime*, with the distortions largely wishful— as in her old reports to her god. Gillot had induced her to separate fable from fact again as after Emma's offense,[m] except on her subject of subjects: herself. Anything she told about herself as fiction was eligible for retelling as nonfiction,[n] only not right away. And her first

[i] ". . . and all 'progress,' when genuine, is only another word for eternity."

[j] 1913c quixotically praised her childhood faith for having "prevented my becoming aware of the rift or conflict within myself" (1913c:460—a plug for neurosis), precluded the anxiety and self-estrangement that might have resulted from her stern moralistic upbringing (*ibid.*, 461—an all too drastic prophylactic), and served as a bridge from fantasy to reality (*ibid.*— though especially vice versa). 1920b:365n. repated 1883a to the effect that every child grows up with the help of some pious invention (as if hers were thus normal) which dissolves for emotional reasons that are the more rationalized the older the child is at the time.

[k] E.g. D III 1923: her god was no less real than the outside world is anyhow.

[l] 1913c:457: should she ever make out her god's human prototype—assuredly *not* her father—she would "confess it faithfully." 1914a:251 treated of her god-fantasy implicitly as a revival of the nursing situation, 1920b:365 of her fixation on it explicitly as a reservoir of self-world identity destined to ease the pain of learning to be discrete, etc. But see below, p. 366 n. *f*.

[m] See above, p. 9.

[n] By virtue of her divine imprimatur on her tales, but also of the ambiguity inherent in their having been semiautobiographic.

direct report of an experience was never more than misleading, if never less—line for line and all in all. The final sense of the departures from reality was the same for her self-accounts as for her tales: that her father's big *no* had never been. But in a tale she might go the limit straight off, whereas in a first report she would only stretch the truth as far as she could without its snapping. Her stretching device par excellence was equivocal wording[o]: the truth could still be read into every line. Otherwise she would shift the literary focus away from those facts due for future replacement, or else blur or etherize or simply delete them. So adroit was she at all this that again and again she took herself in and, forgetting what had been what, followed a fictional lead into outright misstatement. Real as was this forgetting, just as deliberate was the prior misleading. But cynical it was not, for her very own construction on an experience was just what she called *her experience*[p]—and she got no back talk from her lordly conscience. Thus her self-accounting was a running fusion of desire and reality, of fiction and nonfiction, of art and life,[q] at the same time as it was a continual expulsion of unpleasant truths from consciousness into unconsciousness and admission of pleasant untruths by way of return.

Lou did not care much for her fiction, perhaps rightly on the balance; or even for her essays, utterly wrongly. Her self-accounts, though, mattered vitally to her. For all her would-be spontaneity, she lived her life as a memoir-to-be, with due reluctance to break it off before she could round it out. She was readying it for reception by a new eternal judge and lover predesignate: posterity.[r] And she spared no cosmetic pains on what were to be her documental remains,

[o] Akin to her equivocations about " 'God.' "

[p] *"Erlebnis"* as against *"Erfahrung"* (below, p. 465). Cf. 1894c:231-32 ("surely one had the right to construe one's own life as prettily as one liked").

[q] This despite her own dictum that art stands "irremediably" (literally: "incurably") apart from life (D [17-20 VIII 1913])—by which she nominally meant that the "repressed complexes" embodied by an artist in his work were at a far cry from his surface subject matter and surface wish to reach a public. That her self-accounting was a compromise between desire and reality was itself a prominent theme of her self-accounting—one always worded, however, so as to sound hyperscrupulous or hyperbolical.

[r] She once aptly termed her original motive for writing (referring to her first notes on her personages) an impulse "to make markings by which life is remembered" in default of God (1911a:88)—"life" here falling clearly within her "second" (fantasy) world. Her diaries abound in remarks patently meant for posterity, including parenthetical identifications of things familiar to herself and premonitions or resolutions interpolated after having been realized. She moreover left behind evidence against almost all of her autobiographic felonies—as if to be found out and punished by posterity for fibbery as she had formerly been by her real father.

periodically emending old diaries and even letters received, besides just cutting out passages or pasting them over, or else effacing them— some transparently, others stroke by stroke with awesome finality.

The diary was the generic form of Lou's literary output. Into her regular or special diaries went self-depictions, characterizations of close acquaintances, philosophical musings, miniature book and play reviews, an occasional poem or fable, travel notes, and personal chronicles.[8] Multiplex, her diaries were only the more monographic, their basic subject being the riches and beauties of her day-by-day inner life.[t] Entries were all duly preelaborated,[u] then predrafted,[v] then traced out in a proud hand[w]—and then periodically purged of anything shoddy or autobiographically obsolete. Those most characteristically hers would back away from an adventitious starting point up to a lofty perspective on all Creation by way of finely articulated, richly modulated literary focal lines converging for a rhetorical about-face that would resound like a Gloria. And yet the image of her addressee was "already extinguished even as it still shone upon her— was now only glow and consecration upon her earth: now but part of her own beauty"; or so she wrote of her grandmother's diary pages,[112] from which hers descended.[x] In conversation too she would start out calling a spade a spade and end up calling it heavenly.[113]

Lou was literary full-time. Her inner monologue was a running repetition of what had "*already* been thought," as if she "were playing the thought through again" in order to fix it "as does a 'thought-concurring' pen more naturally." Before even having a feeling she would "clothe it inwardly in mute words": time and again she caught herself laughing or crying "*clearly* as a mere *effect* of the words

[8] These last were compiled from daily records—only irregularly, it would seem, after 1900. Their stock items were weather, health, mood, readings, writings, encounters—generally noted in cursory style. They were (self-)misleading through misplaced emphasis, omission, mere naming of persons, and the like.

[t] A conversational remark she made on the need for a god to behold beauteous inner lives prompted the essaylet with which her second series of regular diaries began in 1900: see below, p. 282.

[u] Whole lines in some revert to her letters of days or weeks earlier.

[v] Remnants of drafts have survived for many an entry, while residual edges of excised pages frequently disclose prior versions of entries in the same ink.

[w] Splendid except for some youthful curlicues and lapses—and for her feeble old-age calligraphy. Lou→Tönnies (7-)13 xii 1904, draft, urged undecipherable Tönnies to take example from her "scrawl"—after Rilke had done just that (see below, p. 215). Yet she fairly regularly left quotation marks and especially parentheses open (or else, having opened a parenthesis in midsentence, closed it *after* the period, as follows). As she was delinquent this way rather the more in the case of neatly transcribed pages, the delinquency seems to have signified: *See! I do just toss off copy.*

[x] On her fear lest her maternal grandparents' madness was hereditary, see 1904a:26, 45-47.

27

found," so that "the only authentic joy or sorrow" ever to come through was the bit that might have "mixed in" without her noticing.[v] Her fiction specifically came of daydreaming, which she reproved as naughty when not literarily disciplined.[z] But besides her daydreaming, every current of her thought *"already"* thought was channeled pen-and-inkward—in voluptuous anguish.[a]

With sheaves of notes on her personages and a misbegotten poem behind her, she was already an author at heart when she first set eyes on Gillot (so much so that she was to represent herself as having won his affection, sight unseen, through her writing[b]). Gillot made her an author otherwise. The whole tenor and tone and form of her prose— hyperrational, sacral, schoolgirlish—bore his tutorial impress. And no wonder, for her self-identification with him as heir to her own earthly, then heavenly, author held fastest at her writing desk even while she vented her daughterly craving there. She was daughterly as of old in the very act of reporting and the latent stuff of her reports, fatherly as of old in positing the facts of Creation and contriving fates—but now also in authoring herself anew through her self-accounting.[c] Fictionally too she fathered herself—now knowingly, now unknowingly—in a whole line of homologous heroines[d] who

[v] D I 1919—which adds that, if ever caught short of words, she was stricken with "composure," the affect being discharged somatically.

[z] D VI 1917—which notes the several gradients between passive, self-indulgent fantasy and its purposive control.

[a] Like most men so motivated, Lou suffered from lifelong constipation. She was literarily most inspired during menstruation, which, she claimed, rendered her clever (Lou→Frieda [1900?]). For the anal-sexual sense of her menses see e.g. D 19 I 1901: "what is written of an enchanted princess in some tale or other holds in my case on these days every month: that flowers and jewels come out of her mouth every time instead of words"—an analogy followed by associations (with a button box and a woman's innermost jewelry) subsequently submitted by her as typically anal. For her phallic pens, see D Pentecost 1911: her "memories and associations" were influenced by her continual mental interaction with her pens—an "accompaniment [to writing] as gentle and necessary as organ activity, as heartbeat, and in all its unspeakable exteriority perhaps akin to this deepest interiority and to its rhythms. For who knows his own limits?" On the reactive side, she would mutilate her favorite books, wishing to possess their "enchanted contents" disincarnate, "sustained on thin air" (D VII 1917).

[b] See 1893g: Lou's "An die Winne" enthralls Erik (Gillot) before he knows its author. *Lou in old age (Pfeiffer, *Leben*, 289): on the strength of her letter requesting an interview, Gillot spread out his arms to embrace her at her first appearance.

[c] And this by a fusion of subjectivity and objectivity—something even Spinoza's god could not effect locally.

[d] Her female characters not immediately autobiographic stood for herself as her mother or as some other self-identified person in her life, while those immediately autobiographic often came in pairs, confusingly—as spiritual twins by contrast (the cousins in 1898a, the sisters in 1899f), by closeness

displayed her own dearest features scaled bigger than life and whom she wordily fondled from head to foot: all exude her arrant self-delight. Invariably childlike, they were more and more often children over the years—and like the autobiographic Lou-child, the Lou-heroine as child came in for a double dose of doting. Here was Lou's infantile wish come nearly true: herself as her own child. She even celebrated herself loving herself as her own child, for such was the sense of that hallowed image of hers out of the narcissist looking glass: a mother clutching to her breast a piece of her own person mannishly borne and bred by her.[e]

Like her authoring little Lous, her coddling them was maternal as well as autoerotic, of course, but primarily paternal: she did unto them on paper as she had wanted her father to do unto her off paper. Within her father-identity, her erotic interest went preeminently to childlike reeditions of herself—beyond the literary ones, to flesh-and-blood "daughters" (as she called them) when she was old and bold enough. Early aware of hermaphroditism in humans, namely herself, she came to champion bisexual practice[f]—though this nominally for men in particular, women having a supposed equivalent in maternity.[114] She left Petersburg sedulously "girlish, even childlike,"[115] yet set on doing whatever men did and nothing else, from scholarship and letters[g] on down. To her sexual ambitendency was due her penchant for ambiguity but also, on the level of conviction, a *parti pris* for dualism. In her books, "a positive duality" was "to our human way of seeing simply everywhere at work where life is astir,"[116] and try as the monist might to screen it with words, these would disserve him in so far as they made sense.[117] "A" duality meant pretty nearly *any* such: spirit/flesh, ego/sex, active/reactive, objective/

---

plus contrast (the sisters in 1896c), or by closeness that turns into contrast (the sisters in 1900b). Male characters not simply her father (herself as her father) were god-men or brotherly substitutes for these. As a rule, my explications of Lou's fiction will deal only with proximate latent identities of character and situation, the deeper-lying ones having been monotonously Oedipal.

[e] See below, p. 551. Lou regarded child-bearing and -rearing as the most masculine of all feminine doings (D [17-21 x 1913]; etc.) and ordinarily employed "beget" ("*zeugen*") for "bear."

[f] D I 1915 argued that there is more psychic energy left over from erotic for cultural uses in a happy homosexual household.

[g] Few universities in western Europe then admitted women, and an ambitious woman of letters still had good reason to use a male pseudonym, whatever her real reason. It held preeminently for those days of feminist challenge to the traditional division of labor between the sexes that, many as were the grounds for approving a woman who went into studies or letters, there was ever only one for her going. On Lou's own view of her work as man's work, see below, p. 241, etc.

subjective, analysis/synthesis—not, however, life/death. But her preferred vital twosome was masculine/feminine, of which in her usage the others amounted to mere variants. Though each pair worked at cross purposes here and now, she held, each was at one in its final aim.[118]/[h] And so was her personality in its integral tendency a neuter composite as problematic here and now as parallels converging.[i]

Sharp about erotism from the first, Lou was dull to the last about her own case of it: "Nothing like repression even tempts me," she assured her diary[119]/[j]—coquettishly. That mistress of subterfuge well knew how to swell a truth about herself beyond recognition, concealing other truths in the process. Responsive to the magic of words, especially words of her own, she advertised her egoism out of the need to fortify her ego and professed fatalism as a preventive against guilt over misconduct toward others.[k] She went sorry lengths to prove herself ruthless and remorseless—not quite successfully.[l] She claimed to be deaf to the world's injunctions and prohibitions, but was alert to them for purposes of defiance. By way of amends for her childhood she demanded pure joy from life—and she thanked life insistently for spoiling her, yet spent half her days sulking.[m]

Her power of rationalization protected her inwardly as she strove to master the man's world that was hers. Her chief means to its mastery was one hardly distinguishable from that power of rationalization: her rational power. Through all her self-deception and self-projection her thought ran ahead of her, as of her times. And its circle was cosmic if self-enclosed, its vitality that of its sexiest beginnings.[n]

[h] In the same vein, D [late spring 1913] solemnly vindicated ambivalence against reaction formations for expressing contrary impulses simultaneously rather than consecutively.

[i] But anticipated literarily in that she increasingly eschewed regular masculine or feminine nouns for neuter ones specially fashioned out of adjectives ("*das Physische*"), of verbs ("*das Immer-Wieder-Zurückkehrende*"), or of prepositions ("*das Abseits-vom-Leben*").

[j] ("*nichts Verdrängliches*") Cf. 1913c:461 on life's "most vital" gift to her.

[k] As per 1927a:80, Rilke was "too fatalistic to harbor guilt-conflicts" (knew guilt only over not producing). Lou's philosophical *idée fixe*, fatalism, was also fixed to her anality (D III 1923: "outer" experience actualizes an "inner" aptitude for experience) and to her deficient sense of reality (D [16 XI 1912]: for as much as matters, our lives are lived out "behind a curtain").

[l] E.g. D I 1915 on her belated, vacillating guilt over "having had to be brutal." Cf. 1913c:466 for a decorous boast of callousness.

[m] There was no discernible regularity to her moping, nor was it discernibly contingent on outer circumstances (not even the weather: D 8 VII 1894: "Splendid weather. Melancholy"; D 21 VII 1894: "Foul weather. Melancholy") except when it took a suicidal turn after breaks with god-men.

[n] Cf. 1913c:465-66: nothing so resembled her childhood joy in God as her youthful joy in knowledge, which itself derived from an early curiosity about sex.

Her very aloofness from circumstances, a legacy of her long years of introversion, was itself an asset once she was set on imposing herself. And this she was after leaving Gillot, with an ambition to match her self-will, for with her god in hiding, her only way to fulfillment passed through this world.

That way was her very own. She was the shriller about her independence for having an adverse party to shout down: her femininity. She construed life for her sex in her Aunt Caro's terms, as a perpetual forced option between being a person and being a woman, between self-assertion and dedication,[o] between an aspiration to self-development and an atavistic yen to be brutalized by men.[p] Her having grown up an alien grandee's daughter contributed to her sovereign detachment and self-assurance; but of the Salomés' cultural anomalism, their social status, and their secure fortune, she drew the greatest spiritual capital from this last. Her strict autonomy took subsidizing for granted; what was real about her "life-confidence" was negotiable against her father's estate; her ideal of personal authenticity meant owing no one anything; her clean conscience was a solvent conscience. The dream world of her formative years was a leisure-class prerogative. She left home as frugal and industrious as any Baltic German, and with the cosmopolitan styling, the inbred distinction, the poise and bearing befitting the cultivated milieu from which, shut up though she was in her portable playroom, she after all did learn to walk and talk.[q] With these advantages went a worthy physique, which most eased her way among men. She was tall and "very well proportioned"[120] (if somewhat skeletal in her early youth), "with an ancient Roman facial expression,"[121] bright blue eyes, and—her two points

[o] These two antitheses so formulated by Stöcker, "L A-S" (1931).

[p] This last formulation accords with Heine, "L A-S," 81. This theme of love as the destructive antithesis to woman's professional and mental independence pervades Lou's tales of the 1890's, often luridly. 1909b:47-48 spelled it out: even the healthiest woman "runs a zigzag course between sexual and individual life," stunting herself now as person, now as woman.

[q] I can go no farther—if even this far—toward validating the common claim that background shapes the mind and character. It is suggestive that Lou's contemporary critics usually referred her turn of mind and pen back to social, cultural, and ethnic determinants that simply were not hers—in particular aristocratic, Russian, and Jewish. Perhaps she might as well have been a Basque peasant's or Welsh fisherman's daughter for all the real difference it would have made to her mentality and personality. Her father was higher and mightier than most, but he need not have been for her father romance to have had the same outcome: witness Jesus. Of her few hundred thousand surviving words about her childhood, moreover, only a few hundred touch on its larger setting (cultural, social, ethnic, geographic, political), and this on the basis not of recollection or even pseudorecollection, but of reconstruction from later-life readings and impressions.

of greatest vanity, to judge by her gushing compliments to her hero-ines—auburn hair (worn long, at first with bangs[r]) and a supple gait.

Nor did it spoil the effect that she was as disorderly about her body as she was orderly about her mind. For her mind was her charm center. From that center—captivating beyond compare, stimulating beyond compare—emanated the fascination that she held for all who knew her, herself included. From near that center issued her potent sex appeal—that of a vestal virgin combined with a she-Narcissus. She unsettled record numbers of both sexes and all ages. But even before being disconcerting, she was disarming. Indeed, she struck all comers as guilelessness personified: it took a green-eyed humbug with a blind spot for genius, Nietzsche's curse of a sister, to see behind her seeming candor—at second glance. She got her own wild way with the world continually—or almost. Already in her youth she reached an eager reading public; brilliant brother-men attended her; she knelt to true god-men, discerned with a sure flair ascribable to her long intimacy with their original. Reality jolted her now and again but never forced a showdown. And its astonishing readiness to meet her freakish demands upon it, despite her deep disrespect for it, is what kept her sane.

Lou was already as cerebral, bewitching, and heartless as ever she was to be when in the late summer of 1880, after a brief return to Petersburg, she again went West with her mother—for further medical treatment and to study at the University of Zurich.

---

[r] She later removed the bangs from photos that she then had rephotographed (one faces Pfeiffer, *Leben*, 92); the retouched originals are still in Loufried.

PART TWO · YOUTH

*L*OU SALOMÉ spent the academic year 1880-1881 as an auditor[a] at the University of Zurich. She lived just outside of town with a family of sometime Petersburg Germans named Brandt and, to her undisguised vexation, her mother. On campus she listened longest to Andreas Ludwig Kym, a Spinozist who treated by turns of psychology, of "logic in conjunction with metaphysics," and of philosophy since Ionia, all with impressive system and scope. She heard little worth noting from Richard Avenarius, famed for his approach to pure experience called "empiriocriticism," who lectured topically yet fitfully on psychology one term and on logic the next, refuting predecessors at every turn.[b] Only with the sixty-one-year-old theologian Alois Biedermann did she establish personal rapport. "From the very start of our acquaintance," Biedermann was to affirm, "I took a heartfelt interest in this unusual girl's spiritual life, and she met me with a confidence the full value of which I knew and which I was at pains to deserve and repay by seeking to exert as healthy and sober an influence on the direction of her mental aspirations as I knew how."[1]

From his dais Biedermann pointed the way Lou was eager to go. He began his courses by writing "X" for the unknowable stimulus to religious experience; he shortly wrote that same "X" for the unverifiable object of religious experience, only to wind up writing "God" instead for simplicity's sake. This sleight of hand did not detract from his neo-Hegelian teachings about "the inner laws by which religion develops" from sensuality to saga to anthropomorphism to mythology and so on up (laws of dialectical interplay between "outer occasion" and "inner causality-drive," complete with individual reenactments of the historic scenario). Yet his rationalizations of religion did distract from the factual matter of his "theological encyclopedia"[c] shot

---

[a] As *"majorenne Zuhörerin"* ("adult auditress")—which was all that, without a baccalaureate, she qualified to be.

[b] But his lectures may have been more valuable—even to her—than appears from her severely mutilated notes (in which, typically, he countered Kant's view that time and space are never experienced by affirming that, since motion is experienced, time and space must be too). She never mentioned Avenarius or Kym in writing. Avenarius was then thirty-seven, Kym fifty-eight. Kym's *Metaphysische Untersuchungen* (Munich, 1875) was on her shelves at her death.

[c] A course title of his. (Lou also took his "Dogmatics.")

through with religion's symbolic truth as against its literal falsehood, with a "subjective phenomenology of religion" by the terms of which "man's raising himself above his natural self unto an unknown god" was the psychological equivalent to revelation, and with definitions of religion as "man's revolt against his dependency on nature, which he has a holy right to transcend," or as "a coming to consciousness of the human mind's sovereign claim against its finite conditionality," or as "the striving to attain freedom" or "the relating of the infinite to the human" or "the synthesis of two moments: that of the finite mind's relating itself to what is essentially different from itself, and vice versa." To that "central question of philosophy with respect to religion"—namely, "whether an objective truth underlies the religious supposition of a divine relationship to the human mind and, if so, whether the human mind is capable of grasping it"—Biedermann's answer was the ingeniously evasive one that "the religious supposition" affects minds just the same whether it be disclosure or delusion.[d]

Biedermann's deft double talk gave Lou a new agnostic lease on religiosity: following Biedermann, she reverenced religion itself ever afterwards for enfolding and somehow transcending "all of the impulses of mental life." And so affectionately did she learn from Biedermann that in time she mistook formulations of his for ones of her own. Her favorite passage of his historical survey (to judge by the underlinings in her notes) bore on the "symbolical nature religions," in which "the divine so to say shimmers through natural objects. Vital natural impulses are the contents of divine representations, while their form is anthropomorphic in the broadest sense." Concerning Biedermann's contention that anthropomorphism followed from man's conceiving his relationship to God by analogy with his worldly relations she noted: "Man's instinctively worshipping divinity in bodily form provides a kind of hint at divine *immanence* within such form as against the afterworld theory." About Biedermann's point that "never is a god worshipped in natural-sensual form without something divine and supernatural being sensed in and behind him" she remarked: "That is also why there are no *idols* in religion but only *gods*, for an idol is merely something onesidedly *despiritualized*." That nascent piety "expresses itself negatively in astonishment and dread, and in a feeling of dependency to be defended against, but also positively as a sense of freedom, as an awakening to self-consciousness," set her wondering: "Isn't it as if the mind were naïvely astonished at this intimation of its own greatness?" And she commented at large in her Biedermann notebook: "The expression

[d] Quotations are from Lou's class notes.

36

'father' can come to men's lips in all religions at their best"; and again: "To die authentically means to triumph over death." She meanwhile defended the orthodoxy of pure reason against Kant: "In the religious act we cannot *imagine* God except personally, indeed according to our own personality. But we can *think* him absolutely. Light falls into a room in the form of the opening through which it enters. But as thought abstracts from our individual definiteness, which conditions the religious act, it grasps God's formal absoluteness." She quarreled more headily with Baur for overstating the difference between Judaism and Paulinism and with Keim for considering that Jesus meant more by "son of God" than by "son of man"— this as she excerpted and summarized a full dozen Hegelians young and old in addition to Hegel himself. Not once, though, did she so much as name either of the two masters for whose disciple she might have been mistaken in future years: Feuerbach, for whom the gods were merely what men would like to be, and Schleiermacher, for whom the final sense of piety was coalescence with God.[e] Beyond her course readings she took on the *Rig-Veda* and the pre-Socratics, Confucius and the *Tao-teh-king*, Jakob Böhme and Moses Mendelssohn, Goethe and Hugo.

Extracurricularly, Lou entered a literary circle formed around the elderly professor-poet Gottfried Kinkel. At the end of the summer of 1881[f] she sent Kinkel six poems with a request for criticism and, if he saw fit, a good word to a magazine. All six had some pure ring of poetry to them along with their singsong bombast about "depth" and "strength" and "fate" and "torment" and "struggle" and "triumph." One, then titled "To Pain,"[2/g] was memorable. In it the poetess apostrophized life as an enigmatical friend to whose bosom she, combatively flushed, would yet cling though he should have nothing left for her but pain. Lou was herewith seemingly saying a brave, trite yea to life despite her sufferings. But in fact she was jubilating on a fever pitch while wasting away. For a second message sounded through her stanzas *sotto voce*—one of "joy through the

---

[e] She subsequently mentioned Feuerbach slightingly (1898i: 385; 1899d:121), Schleiermacher never.

[f] Kinkel was then sixty-six. Lou and her mother were conceivably in Petersburg earlier that summer, for the date 6/7 ix 1881 is inscribed on a dagger-shaped breastpin bestowed upon General Salomé's widow by the Czar fifty years after the storming of Warsaw (Pfeiffer, *Leben*, 294).

[g] Later retitled by Lou "Life Prayer," by Nietzsche "Prayer to Life" and then "Hymn to Life." And later reworked: Nietzsche's first transcript (below, p. 85 n. *e*) differs from Lou's 1881 copy; Lou's 1883a:187 version was adapted from Nietzsche's own adaptation of ix 1882 (below, pp. 86 n. *f*, 120 n. *h*), and the 1935a:47 one, presented as her first, was new.

voluptuousness of pain."[h] Goethe had taught her that the gods give their darlings all sorrows, like all joys, unendingly—not, however, that the darlings were grateful for both. For once she did not kneel or swoon in her reverence, but declared: "With all my might I clasp thee round." This declaration apart, she was to rewrite "To Pain" in substance repeatedly, yet scoff at it as in substance cheap and puerile.[3/i] Returning it along with her other verse, Kinkel gave her many pointers, some praise, and two evidently futile leads on publication.[4]

Lou's letter to Kinkel had also been a leave-taking. In the course of her year's hard studies, her chronic complaints (primarily coughing, heartache, and bleeding lungs) had taken so sharp a turn for the worse that in later years she wrote of "the way after the break with Gillot I *fell* ill in full joy and life-affirmation."[5/j] Zurich was too damp and cold for her—perhaps also too provincial—so her mother conducted her southward from one health resort to another. In January 1882, she reached Rome, the Brandts assisting her mother as chaperons. She had prevailed upon Kinkel beforehand for a note of introduction to the celebrated idealist Malwida von Meysenbug.[6]

Malwida von Meysenbug must have been most winning in person, given the illustrious company she kept as against the precious, vacuous words she wrote. With Kinkel and all the ardent youth of Europe she had been an 1848er, militating loftily for social democracy and popular education. Prussian *Realpolitik* had not brought her down to earth but frightened her farther up. She turned crusading "anti-materialist," professedly for serious scientific reasons[7] which, however, she kept to herself. She was an eager friend, hostess, and patroness to whatever reformers or revolutionaries, whatever scholars or artists, were assimilable without protest to her philosophical party. Her three-volume *Memoirs of an Idealist* was a bestseller in 1876. The early 1880's found her drifting from social concern toward a cult of exquisiteness: she was to devote the long twilight of her life to extremest moral and esthetic refinement. In January 1882, at the age of sixty-five, she inhabited a splendid villa overlooking the Eternal City and gathered pure-, high-minded youngsters about her in a "Roman club" for preassigned philosophical discussions, poetry readings, and cultural outings, relieved by occasional tea-time cau-

[h] To quote D [late VIII 1882]—which, however, denied that her heroic self-sacrifice to knowledge was a pursuit of such pain-fed joy.

[i] (This, though, in a Freud context: below, p. 476.)

[j] (Italics added.) What began with the break was her elation; the bodily symptoms carried over, then—conceivably in consequence of a small-scale inexplicit romance with Biedermann—worsened.

series or soirées without agenda. She saw herself as taking a courageous new stand on human relations, one "as far from the unrestraint of nihilism as from old-world prudery."[8] In fact she was the apostle of a new-world prudery of which a typical clause intended for young ladies ran: "Associating with noble men is enjoyable and beneficial so long as it does not cross the tender bounds within which the will is as yet up to no mischief and so long as the tone is set by spiritual interests cultivated within free, friendly encounters having to be veiled from no human eye."[9]

All Lou's representations of early 1882 were as if calculated to please Malwida von Meysenbug. She declared herself an idealist of Malwida's own persuasion—which, for all she then knew, she was. She told of a long, lonely struggle for enlightenment against her own religious prepossessions—one that had climaxed in a break with the faith out of inner rectitude. Likewise, her quarrels with her mother were resistance to retrograde constraint, her ailments were martyr's scars, her coming West was a self-exile. Most to the point, she had been cured of sex for life on spying Gillot's low designs through his lofty declarations—and somehow it seemed touching rather than suspicious that she nonetheless carried his portrait and memory close to her heart. She also gave herself out as an aspirant authoress—as indeed she was, though her main concern was to gain entrée among the cultural élite on whatever credentials. She won over Malwida straightaway. By mid-February she was in on all Malwida's regular gatherings and many a special one—escorted to and fro by her mother or a Brandt or some squire of Malwida's choosing. "Your poems touched me deeply," Malwida wrote her in mid-March. ". . . They disclose what I behold with ever purer delight: your inner life, which is meant for blossoms so noble that you must keep it most holy. . . . Yours is a great task: we shall yet speak much of it."[10] Solicitude for Lou's health came next, and by spring Malwida's motherly fondness was as pronounced as her rarefied discourse could accommodate. "In a long time I have not felt such deep affection for a young girl," she declared.[11/k] And no wonder, for in Lou she saw not only "a lofty, pure apostle of our new faith" but "my own youth resurrected."[12]

In early 1882 the Roman club counted only girls. Malwida, however, held that the sexes "should associate openly and freely in spiritual regions, should strive, learn, enjoy together, as against associating in the way that conduces be it only to a playing with feelings or

---

[k] Specifically, not since that felt for her foster daughter, Olga Monod-Herzen.

at all odds a sort of momentary excitation as did the earlier mode of association."[13] Accordingly, odious as she found the moral philosophy of her dear young friend Paul Rée, she prevailed upon him to expound it to her girls and discuss it with them when he turned up at her Villa Mattei in mid-March.[14/l]

Paul Rée, a Schopenhauer adept in his student days, took a doctorate at Halle in 1875 with a dissertation on Aristotle's *Ethics* and that same year brought out an anonymous collection of psychologistic bons mots: *Psychologische Beobachtungen.* In 1877 he came into his own as Positivist, Utilitarian, and Darwinist all in one with an account of how conscience must have originated: *Der Ursprung der moralischen Empfindungen.* Here he followed the master Positivist, Auguste Comte, at least as far as to see man as not only strongly selfish, but weakly selfless too. So did Darwin in *The Descent of Man.* But Rée could not follow Darwin on conscience pangs as mere unsatisfied selflessness[m]; for Rée they were rather self-reproaches over misdeeds. Selfless deeds, he reasoned, must at first have been called good *to others*, then just *good* for short, until at length the utilitarian ground for lauding them was forgotten. A community, he pursued, would habituate its members, especially juniors, to regret committing such acts as it found displeasing, until in time its disapprobation came to be felt as *due*: ergo conscience.[n]

Since publishing this all too neat a priori scheme, Rée had been grounding it for an empirical sequel—with time out to try outdoing Hume's denial of apriority.[o] The scheme withstood years of relentless research and reexamination[p]—which of itself puts Rée in the best scientific company.[q] October 1877 found him studying "every con-

[l] Rée left Genoa for Rome on 13 III 1882 and possibly went to Malwida's that very evening.

[m] Rightly—for, on Darwin's premises, unsatisfied selfishness should give rise to even stronger guilt feelings, whereas to my knowledge only Lou ever complained of such.

[n] Omitting Rée's collateral theory of habituation, which involves the unexamined, untenable Darwinist premise of the inheritability of acquired moral attitudes.

[o] Rée→FN, 10 X 1877, mentions an essay (perhaps the basis for Rée, *Philosophie*, 139-73) extending Hume's argument that causes can be known only a posteriori to the conclusion that causality is itself an a posteriori concept (as Hume well knew).

[p] Except that between Rée→FN, 10 X 1877, and Rée's reply to FN→Rée [15 IV 1879] Rée came to decide that punishment derived from the struggle against vengeance rather than from vengeance itself. For two subsequent minor revisions (due to Nietzsche and Tönnies respectively) see below, pp. 87 and 116.

[q] Including Darwin's own—but, whereas Darwin modified away his theory ("natural selection from random variations") once it was published after twenty years of verification, Rée staunchly stood by his to the last.

ceivable criminal code and primitive people" to discover how this or that act came to be deemed punishable.[15] Twenty months later he boasted "proof from German, Greek, Roman, Russian law, in the highest degree historical," for his thesis that conscience derived from utility and habituation: utility for keeping the peace, as it turned out, and habituation through sanctified fines and punishments for breaking the peace such that in due course the very disposition to break it was felt as *guilty*, then as *evil*. "The work is ready in rough outline," he added, "only even now I cannot make up my mind to fill in any more of it considering how many books there are that could still benefit it."[16]

His thoroughness amounted to a mental block: he was to deal with the same problem in the same terms the rest of his philosophical life. Those terms were as rigorous as they were simplistic: unable to solve his problem, he yet elucidated it marvelously. His formal prose was styleless in its utter parsimony and clarity—the painstaking reverse of his letters, which rambled on and on through blurs and smudges. Only rarely did he as theorist look from moral beginnings to moral ends; then singlemindedness gave way to cross purposes. Generally he seemed to endorse social utility, which in its native England tended to mean scrapping any rule of right without a clear utilitarian point to it and especially any prohibition not needed to keep people from imposing upon each other too crudely or from harming themselves unintentionally. But then his aphoristic master, La Rochefoucauld, had pointed him the way to a "scientific misanthropy," as he called it: man being simply the wiliest and vainest beast of prey, moral progress was a matter of curbs on egoism and scruples over egoism. Rée was given to facile pessimism besides. "However life may be," he once remarked, "it is bad, so it doesn't much matter whether it's this way or that."[17] In this vein he deemed that few men were ever happy, and then only momentarily; and that furthermore, as between practicing virtue or vice conscientiously, compassion was about as painful as remorse, besides which neither of these counted felicifically for as much as temperament or health or circumstances anyhow. This said, he unutilitarianly rated knowledge highest among human values just because it was least animalic.[18/r] Yet he also held self-interest to be after all the self's only interest; thus moral courage meant making a standard of one's own wants and needs. Along this same line, his fixed idea was that if once we realized how the bad conscience began it would end. Or more fully and exactly: to realize that "evil"

r Here he was perhaps following the scholastic lead of Utilitarianism's prodigal son, John Stuart Mill.

meant merely "not beneficial to others" and that moreover the will was unfree would mark an end of moral suffering except for that faint malaise due to unsatisfied selflessness which Darwin mistook for bad conscience.

Unlike, say, Feuerbach's view of religion as simply a corrigible intellectual error, Rée's comparable view of the bad conscience was not even naïve, for Rée never thought better of it despite his own abiding sense of unworthiness. In truth he stressed ego as the big fact of life in the secret hope of making it such in his own case. "His is indeed a rare, good nature," wrote Malwida von Meysenbug, "capable of noblest dedication and as such the shining refutation of his own theories."[19] The refutation went farther than Malwida saw, for Rée was good only in spite of himself: he often broke into impish malevolence, then followed through with brooding. He was ordinarily deep in the doldrums, but emerged at times for a round of fun. Those who hardly knew him knew a hearty, cocky chap, with quick wits and a sharp tongue, dead set on not seeming eager to please. Eager to please he desperately was, however, even as he loathed most everything about himself—beginning with his being a Jew, which he was "to his morbid and boundless sorrow."[20] Try as he might (he even dressed and walked like a priest)[s] he could only half hide the taint from his intimates, who took him for a half Jew.[t] His very physique repelled him, with some good cause: squat and graceless, it was topped off by a huge head embossed with blackest wiry clumps of hair and with massive features of which the elephantine eyes alone were sightly. On one count, though, he took unfailing pride in himself, anti-Semitic Jew and fanatical freethinker though he was: his unbiased mind. His home was a manor named Stibbe, near Tütz in West Prussia, acquired some years earlier by his father, lately deceased; it now belonged to his elder brother, Georg, and was run by his mother. Rée was motherly toward his mother and filial toward his brother. Sex "disgusted" him.[21] In March 1882 he was thirty-two and in high spirits.

Rée delighted Lou. She jumped to his conclusions such as they were[u] (to Malwida's endless annoyance[v]). Worse, she promptly

---

[s] Tönnies, "Rée," 673: children crowded round him to kiss his hand.

[t] Rée is given diversely as Jewish through his father, his mother, or both. Lou herself occasionally represented him as only half Jewish (including fictionally in 1895f); however, Lou→Tönnies, 1 XII 1904, emphatically declared him a full-blooded Jew (contradicting Tönnies, "Rée," 671). Whether he was one or not, he evidently thought he was, which comes to the same.

[u] Rée→FN, 20 IV 1882: Lou "hears everything through and through, so that she almost exasperatingly always knows in advance what is coming and where it is leading."

[v] MVM→Lou, 25 V [1882]: "Rée led you into error because your reason

proposed they set up their own housekeeping salon. She took him out of her way home from Villa Mattei via the Coliseum, where she assured him beguilingly by moonlight that she was out for comrade-ship, not romance. Infatuated, Rée sent for help from his one close friend, Friedrich Nietzsche.

Rée had first met Nietzsche in 1873 through a common friend, the classicist and Kantian Heinrich Romundt, on arriving for a summer in Basel,[w] where Nietzsche was professor and Romundt was visiting him. Nietzsche was then twenty-eight, Rée twenty-three. With an old classmate of Nietzsche's, the dilettante Carl von Gersdorff, Rée attended Nietzsche's course on the pre-Platonic philosophers. Between lectures the three enjoyed some talk and even some silence together.[x] Subsequently Nietzsche read Rée's "*educative* maxims" in manuscript without comment—only to dub them such upon their publication,[y] in a message at which Rée leapt for joy "like a satyr."[22] A correspondence ensued, and in September 1876 a reunion. The two were both just then positivistically surmounting Schopenhauer's influence, Nietzsche in his *Human, All Too Human* and Rée in his derivation of conscience. So congenial did Nietzsche find Rée both philosophically and personally[z] that, after "enjoying the lovely autumn" for some days with him near Montreux,[23] Nietzsche took him along on a win-ter's sick leave spent in Sorrento with Malwida von Meysenbug—by her gracious provision.[a] There Nietzsche helped enough with Rée's second book for Rée to inscribe a gift copy afterwards: "To the father of this work from its mother, most gratefully."[b] Nietzsche meanwhile

---

discerned an undeniably correct side to his method. But . . . his view is also basically false. Valuable as he is to me as a human being, just as repugnant is he to me as a theorist." See also MVM→Lou, 5 VII 1882, on Lou's "over-rapid conversion to materialism" by Rée.

[w] FN→Rohde, 5 V 1873: "A friend of Romundt's has arrived here for the whole summer, a very thoughtful and gifted person, Schopenhauerian, named Rée."

[x] FN→Rée, 22 X 1875—after a bon mot of Rée's.

[y] *Ibid.* Cf. FN→Rohde, 8 XII 1875: "Dr. Rée, quite devoted to me, has brought out an extraordinary little book, *Psychologische Beobachtungen*, anonymously; he is a moralist with the keenest vision—quite a rarity among Germans."

[z] FN→Lisbeth and Franziska Nietzsche, 11 IX 1876: "He and I enjoy each other greatly"; etc.

[a] FN→MVM, 26 IX 1876: "Rée will come with me but of course lodge sepa-rately"; Rée of course lodged at Malwida's Villa Rubinacci. A student of Nietzsche's was a third guest (Albert Brenner, who died two years later). The men occupied the downstairs, Malwida the upstairs. Malwida cooked. As a rule, all worked mornings, walked afternoons, and convened evenings in the salon, where Rée mostly read aloud. Richard and Cosima Wagner, then still Nietzsche's friends, were nearby till XI 1876.

[b] FN→Rée [late] VI 1877 jocularly disclaimed this paternity.

commended it as "likely to mark a decisive turning point in the history of moral philosophy."[24]

It did, for it had aroused a dormant interest of Nietzsche's own in the same subject: he developed into a genealogist of morals in point-by-point opposition to Rée.[c] Already in *Human, All Too Human*, which appeared a year later, a critique of Rée's theses was implicit. Conscience, it ran, was not self-reproach over misdeeds, since a conscience could be good as well as bad and since the worst conscience might well go with the best conduct. Besides, if the good was once the useful, how did its usefulness ever come to be forgotten? Counter-theses there were too, deriving mostly from Bagehot as against Darwin.[d] Thus the ferment of moral evolution was a tension, not between selflessness and selfishness, but between bondage to custom and defiance of custom, between the herd-instinct and individualism. The more ancient a code of custom, the more vital it seemed to the herd, hence the more wicked its violation—though it well might consecrate values predating selflessness (for example, piety). Yet within the herd—and here Nietzsche began speaking on his own—sets of values varied, primarily as between the masters' set, based on the power of retaliation, and the slaves' set, based on impotence and consequent rancor.

By 1882 Nietzsche had conceived a whole host of additional counter-theses still uncoordinated. Thus "justice" was originally neither communal nor authoritarian nor purposeful, nor did it enter into the

[c] In IV 1862 Nietzsche noted that humankind's "conscience, sense of duty" might form "out of external impressions" and "become the property of all" (*HKG:W*, II, 56-57); a notation on remorse as preposterous followed in XI 1862 (*ibid.*, 143); then six years later another (based on Schopenhauer) about persons rather than deeds as guilty (*ibid.*, V, 177)—all of which evidences an early interest in the subject of his future *Genealogy* but hardly anticipates its contents. His *Tragedy* (completed 1871), in which rationality thwarts instinctuality at a historic juncture, is no prestatement of his later thesis either, but at the outside a barest prefiguration of it. According to Nietzsche's archivists, however (below, pp. 164ff.), Nietzsche spent his entire life working out his puerile preconceptions—and as concerns moral evolution even scholarly Sonns, 22ff., agrees. Like many a lesser thinker, Nietzsche himself made it a point of honor to have had the selfsame leading ideas all along (if also to have renewed himself continually)—whence his misleading preface to his *Genealogy*. (This was, incidentally, his only way of misrepresenting the past apart from projecting backwards his current feelings toward persons.) That Rée's work on a subject of prior interest to him set him slowly elaborating a theory of his own by contrariety is the core of truth to *Genealogy*, Preface: 4 (on Rée's *Ursprung*): "Perhaps I have never read anything to which I have said *no* to myself sentence by sentence, conclusion for conclusion, in such measure yet utterly without vexation or impatience."

[d] Bagehot's *Physics and Politics* appeared in 1875. FN→Rée [early] VIII 1877 mentions conversations on Bagehot and Darwin with the editor of *Mind*, George Croom Robertson.

makings of conscience. Rather, it arose out of anger over default among equals in strength: punishing was the creditor's compensatory pleasure. Vengeance,[e] deterrence, redressing wrongs, protecting society: all were *post hoc "justi*fications" of punishment. The sting of conscience was that of retaliatory aggression deflected inward; the voice of conscience was that of parental authority internalized.[25/f] Gods were not natural forces divinized to the end of sanctifying official penalties, as Rée had it; they were tribal fathers to whom, by reason of the pain of being moral, a bad debt was felt to be owing—and growing. Moreover, religion did not merely underwrite official morality, but often enough rewrote it. For morality was transcending itself continually: today's virtues were yesterday's vices. Yet its superseded clauses were not dead letter; rather, they held force of law in man's instinctual underworld, apt of an instant to subvert the moral instruction of a lifetime. Nietzsche too viewed the bad conscience as mankind's mortal ailment, and at first he too saw a quick individual remedy in the correction of certain intellectual errors, notably God and free will. He soon looked instead to a gradual ascendancy of mankind's "intellectual conscience," newly emergent, over mankind's moral conscience, still at loggerheads with the herd-instinct. By 1882 he was dimly envisioning an inversion of values by "free thinkers" (who would repent of their compassion, rancor, and remorse) preliminary to a transvaluation of values by a new, higher species of moral man.

Even discounting his countertheses, Nietzsche's whole use of his subject differed from Rée's. As Lou was to put it on short acquaintance, Nietzsche's interest began where Rée's left off—with "practical morality."[26/g] Or again, "the Rée egoist" and "the hero" personified the two philosophies respectively.[27/h] For Nietzsche made a virtue of virtue, gaging men's worth by the weight of principle they bore; and he rejoiced that bestiality had been intellectualized over the ages (much as he deplored the priestly, then metaphysical turn taken by its intellectualization). But on Rée's premises, moral progress really meant only a painful confusing of instinctual issues. Rée harked back to premoral man, Nietzsche forward to postmoral man—to a final,

---

[e] After Sorrento, Rée ceased deriving justice from vengeance: above, p. 40 n. *p.*

[f] Alexander Bain, *The Emotions and the Will* (1859), had likewise derived conscience ontogenetically from parental commands—but via habituation, not introjection.

[g] (Original in italics.)

[h] Lou here also had Rée's egoist tell himself "as, to Malwida's horror, he marches into the 'final consequences': 'Our only aim is a snug, happy life' "—a real, but on the balance weak, practical tendency of Rée's philosophy.

as against primal, innocence to be achieved through self-mastery and self-knowledge. For only Nietzsche's thinking, not its purport, was bold. Rée's irreverent philosophy was one long writ of impeachment against a tyrannical conscience—his own. Nietzsche's hortatory philosophy summoned men—meaning himself—by some wizardry to banish inhibitions by way of gaining rather than losing self-control. Each bore the marks of a pressing personal alternative: melancholia and paranoiac megalomania respectively. Nietzsche furthermore had not turned positivist for good and all, like Rée, but only *en passant*, as he well knew, and then only halfway—in respect of man's past, that is, but not of man's future. By 1882 he was putting systems behind him so as to think freely. Yet all along, even as he played up Rée, he played down their differences. In *Human, All Too Human* he called Rée "a master of soul-searching"[28] and again "one of the boldest and coldest thinkers."[29] Of this work he told Rée: "To you it *belongs*, to the *others* it is a gift."[30/i] Subsequently he added: "Long live Réealism and my good friend!"[31/j]

The good friends had parted in Sorrento most reluctantly—Rée leaving in mid-April 1877 to seek a lectureship in Zurich, then in Jena, and Nietzsche, detained by illness, only in early May, to wend a valetudinarian way back over the Alps to Basel. Two years later Nietzsche was released from his university duties with a decent allowance because of his health. Subject to dire headaches, eyeaches, and nausea since 1873, with ever rarer interludes of euphoric relief, he suffered the worse for imagining his father's fatal "softening of the brain" to be hereditary.[k] In July and August of 1879 he thought of setting up with Rée in Berlin,[32] then in September declined Rée's visit while at his mother's and sister's in Naumburg,[l] only to exclaim in October: "I have had to give up many a wish but never yet that of our *living together*—my 'garden of Epicurus'!"[33] In January 1880, Rée came to Naumburg after all, bringing Nietzsche five days of "too great heart's refreshment"[34]—yet in August 1881 was turned away with his mother from the itinerant philosopher's summer retreat of Sils-Maria in the Engadin ("6000 feet beyond man and time"[35]) by a message reading: "I . . . need *absolute solitude*, not as a luxury but

---

[i] He was returning Rée's compliment of ten months earlier: see above, p. 43 and n. *b*.

[j] FN→Rée [late] VII 1878 had coined the term *"Réealismus."*

[k] See FN→Brandes, 10 IV 1888 (below, p. 150 n. *a*), etc.—and Blunck, 31-32, for the contrary medical evidence. Nietzsche's father died at thirty-five-and-three-quarters, when Nietzsche was an Oedipal four-and-three-quarters. (To compound the trauma, Nietzsche's younger brother died shortly afterwards.)

[l] FN→o, 29 IX 1879: "I won it over myself to say no. Excuse me if I am proud of this measure of renunciation."

as the condition for my *perhaps* enduring life another few years. . . .
Oh my dear friend Rée, let us remain *together* at the heights of bold
thinking and clear seeing, soar with each other through past and future, and, in the joy of this nearness, be lenient with fate for keeping
us separated."[36]/m As Nietzsche had just told his sister: "I regard as
an enemy anyone who interrupts my Engadin summer work—that
is, my carrying out *my task*, my 'one thing needful.' "[37]/n

Nietzsche's distress on Rée's account, while quite sincere, was only
the outside story. The inside story was released to Malwida years
afterwards, with a vengeance: " 'He's a poor fellow, one must push
him along'—how often have I told myself this when his miserable,
dishonest way of thinking and living revolted me. I have not forgotten
the fury I felt in 1876 as I heard he would come along to you in Sorrento. And . . . in Sils-Maria I became *ill* at my sister's news that he
wanted to come up."[o] On the outside, meanwhile, Nietzsche overrated Rée far more than was even his fond wont with friends. For
Rée had no notion of Nietzsche's mind beyond the narrow range of
his own: all Nietzsche was contained for him in Nietzsche's Réealis-
tic sentence, "Every word is a prejudice."[38] And even within that narrow range Nietzsche was Rée's master. When Rée's mischief was
suspected behind *Human, All Too Human*, Nietzsche declared
amusedly: "He did not have *even the slightest* influence on the conception of my 'philosophy *in nuce*,' which was ready and in large
measure already down on paper when I made closer acquaintance
with him in the fall of 1876."[39]/p By mail Nietzsche would exchange
compliments with Rée but not ideas—for all Rée's trying.

Rée's own ambivalence was subtler at this stage. He mothered
Nietzsche, nursed him, read to him to spare his eyes,[q] but then stole
his symptoms[r] ("our ailments are of a kind," he declared[40])—whereas Nietzsche's worst attacks followed upon meetings with Rée. Rée's
jealousy was not just morbid: Nietzsche—so brilliant and learned,

---

[m] Nietzsche was just then entertaining a vision of the "eternal recurrence."
[n] He added: "I owe it to Dr. Rée not to say no" (this just before saying no).
[o] FN→MVM, VIII 1883. Cf. FN→MVM [12 v 1887]: "There, in the Sorrento
solitude, Brenner and Rée were *too much* for me."
[p] Cf. Gast, Introduction, x (Nietzsche dictated *Human* to him in v, vi, vii, and
ix 1876).
[q] Already in Basel (FN→Lisbeth and Franziska Nietzsche, 11 ix 1876:
"Rée reads much aloud to me"; etc.) and systematically in Sorrento.
[r] First Rée developed eyeache in 1877. Then Rée→FN, x 1879: "I have
had a headache now for some fourteen months without even a minute's let-
up." Reciprocal solicitude filled Rée's subsequent correspondence with Nietzsche. Rée also urged dietary counsel on Nietzsche through Naumburg, including at least one raw steak daily (Rée→Nietzsche [i or ii] 1880, Rée→Lisbeth
[i or ii] 1880); Nietzsche would take none of it. Rée once sailed to the United
States for a salt-water cure (summer-autumn 1880).

with such fine features and manners, a professor at twenty-four and ex-professor at thirty-four, a prodigious author and peerless conversationalist—put him to shame in almost everything close to his heart. Only as stylist did he so much as fancy himself Nietzsche's match. And Nietzsche agreed, wrongly—though here in fact was the one foolproof point of sympathy between them. Both were precisionists with the pen, with a like penchant for epigram. Nietzsche's prose was not lost to theory, however, but bacchanalianly live with it. It reveled in his thinking as he himself did; and amidst his solitude, his thinking ran riot with him. Timid as *he* was, *it* knew no taboos, so that he took wicked delight in it—while also shuddering at it as, beginning in August 1881, he conceived in turn the "eternal recurrence,"[s] the "overman," and the "transvaluation of values." He had ceased heeding outside voices by then, but had only just begun harkening to inner ones: the perfervid prophecy of dread nihilism lay years ahead.

And then it was that Nietzsche chose to "return 'to men,' " as he put it[41]—to come down from the mountain so as "to become human again," like his Zarathustra in *The Gay Science*,[42] then in preparation. He spent the winter 1881-1882 in Genoa expecting Rée.[t] Rée spent it mostly between his mother's sickbed in Stibbe and Nietzsche's mother and sister in Naumburg—spent it, that is, mostly at the universities of Leipzig and Halle consorting with friends and devotees of Nietzsche such as Romundt and Gersdorff. At last he deposited his mother with Nietzsche's and left for Genoa in early February, bearing Nietzsche a typewriter from Naumburg: it collapsed on the way. To his joy, he found Nietzsche hale and hearty as a stripling.[43] A week later Nietzsche wrote home: "With Dr. Rée's visit so far, as was to be expected, all has *not* gone well. The first day, best of spirits; the second endurable only with the help of restoratives; exhaustion the third, fainting in the afternoon; the attack came that night; the fourth in bed; the fifth up again, only to lie down again in the afternoon; the sixth and till now, perpetual headache and weakness. In brief, we have still to *learn* how to be together. It is in fact *all too pleasant* being with Dr. Rée; there could hardly be more delightful company. But I am unused to good things."[44] As for the typewriter, one week of repairs and it was, "strange to say, better than before," Rée told Nietzsche's sister, Lisbeth; ". . . I could almost have kissed

---

[s] To go by FN, *Ecce*, "So Spoke Zarathustra," 1—though Pythagoras's theorem to the same effect was previously cited in FN, *Untimely*, "On the Uses and Drawbacks of History for Life."

[t] FN→Rée [6 XI 1881]: "I thought the *start* of November would bring us together"; FN→Gast, 25 I 1882: "nothing has kept me in Genoa but my family's announcement that Dr. Rée's visit is near to hand"; etc.

it"—for Nietzsche "placed the highest hopes" in it,[45] being by then, in his own recurrent phrase, "seven-eighths blind." The two friends did learn how to be together even unto walking and talking themselves weary without aftereffects. Between times they went to see Sarah Bernhardt, who, overplaying Camille, burst a blood vessel on stage—"an unbearable impression."[46] And "we were two days in Monaco," wrote Nietzsche to his disciple, copyist, and friend, the composer Peter Gast, "I rightly without gambling."[47] By March 13, when Rée left for Rome, the two philosophers had agreed to bathe somewhere together later that summer and even to tour Africa together in 1883. From Rome, Rée gave Lisbeth his word that, after the first bad days, Nietzsche's health had been up to par "except for a *one*-day attack the day of my departure."[48] As for Rée himself: "The days in Genoa on which I was not ill belong to the loveliest of my life."[49]

Rée also reported to Lisbeth: "Your brother uses the typewriter all the time, only his blind groping for keys does give him lots of trouble."[50] Nietzsche thereupon picked out a rejoinder to Rée's eager tidings of Lou: "What pleasure your letters give me! They draw me in every which way—and to you in the end, come what may. . . . Greet the Russian girl for me, if that makes any sense: I am greedy for souls of that species. In fact, in view of what I mean to do these next ten years, I need them! Matrimony is quite another story. I could consent at most to a two-year marriage, and then only in view of what I mean to do these next ten years."[51] And no sooner had the typewriter delivered itself of this Nietzschean jest than it "refused to go on performing—wholly enigmatically. Everything is in order," Nietzsche noted, "only *no* letter is to be made out."[52]

Well before then, Lou was already counting Nietzsche in on her projected residential salon by reason of Rée's and Malwida's respective versions of him as the veriest positivist and veriest idealist.[u] Lou's project was designed to distress her mother, who, distressed, wrote to Gillot begging him to intercede. It was also designed to scandalize Malwida, who, scandalized, admonished Lou that there was no pretending sex and convention did not exist. And it was designed to entice Rée: so pointedly did Lou put it across to him after hours that in undue course, as Malwida later told her, "Rée came to me in greatest commotion and said he had to depart, it was necessary for *him* and for *you*. I gave him a rather stern talking-to, urging him not to disturb a solemn mental relationship right off in this way. Seemingly

---

[u] See Binder, 79, on Malwida's never having understood Nietzsche beyond his sometime enthusiasm for human enlightenment.

this succeeded in calming even him, and, when I spoke to you, *you* seemed to me so ingenuous that I set my mind completely at rest."[53/v] Her mind incompletely at rest, Malwida wrote to caution Rée against "doing certain things. It is always dangerous to tempt fate: that way one lays oneself open to mishaps, and what could at present and in memory remain pure and beautiful turns discordant and turbid."[54]

Just about then Gillot sent advising Lou none too hopefully against carrying on as if her latest brazen daydream were a matter of her free self-development—which he had intended as a "transition" anyhow.[55] Ho! she retorted, he should be *proud* of her "in that I am not in the least merely indulging a fantasy, but shall actualize it . . . through persons who seem to have been hand-picked by you, as they are almost bursting with brains and acumen"—through "Rée, Nietzsche, and others." From Gillot, she added, she expected not strange advice, but "*the* confidence that, whatever I might or might not do, it remains within the compass of that which is ours in common. . . . Such confidence ought to have been mine as naturally and surely as head, hands, or feet ever since the day I became what I have become through you: your girl." And: "Just what do you mean by 'transition'? If some new ends for which one must surrender that which is most glorious on earth and hardest won, namely freedom, then may I stay stuck in transition forever, for *that* I will not give up. Surely no one could be happier than I am now, for the gay fresh holy war likely about to break out does not frighten me: quite the contrary, let it break. We shall see whether the so-called 'inviolable bounds' drawn by the world do not just about all prove to be innocuous chalk-lines." To Gillot's "transition" Lou had addended in the back of her mind: *to marrying me*—or perhaps in the front of her mind for an instant, with a smile. With her manifesto of emancipation she was at bottom declining an imaginary proposal. Yet she was playing for one at the same time, as already through her escapade with Rée. For she told Gillot coquettishly: "The main thing (and that is humanly for me only Rée) one knows straight off or else not at all. He too is not completely won over yet, he is still somewhat perplexed, but in our walks by night between 12 and 2 in the Roman moonlight, when we emerge from gatherings at Malwida von Meysenbug's, I put it to him with increasing success."[56]

Lou followed through at Villa Mattei with what Malwida subsequently recalled to her as "your *very* embarrassed confession of the walks, which really looked like something meant to be kept secret but

---

v Conceivably Rée's commotion was anti-matrimonial, as Nietzsche's response to it (above, p. 49) suggests.

told to me because of conscience pangs (this time probably not in-ured)."[57] To Malwida, Rée's taking Lou home was of itself "painful in the thought that it might displease your mama: I did not want her to think that at my place any but the most noble emancipation was encouraged."[58] As for his taking her home on foot after midnight, arm in arm: what if someone had recognized them?! "And what would Rée have done had an officer or anyone else been unpleasant to you—fought a duel?!!"[59] Malwida's ulterior scruples were superflu-ous: Lou was *only* flirting. This she went on doing, with new success —until, as Malwida later related to her, "Rée came to me a second time in *greatest* excitement, repeated over and over that he was leav-ing the next day, and requested me to tell you that his mother was ill. I refused and finally told him that, if this flight were necessary, then he should go."[60] Malwida had glimpsed a first truth about Lou: she was not unmindful of sex and convention after all. As to that second, unglimpsed truth, Gillot's proposal never ensued. Instead Rée, to his relief, was recast by Lou as big brother under the Brandts' strict sur-veillance; Malwida adjoined a prospective duenna to Lou's phantom salon, by then rather a phantom full-time study group of three, and the colony settled down to wait for the missing third.

Nietzsche was slow about meeting his destiny—unconscionably slow since, as he later related, Rée depicted the Russian girl to him "as if she were almost too good for this world, a martyr to knowl-edge since infancy, renouncing all the joys and comforts of life, in-deed her very health, for the One thing, Truth; consummately self-less, and proved in a long school of sacrifice."[61/w] "Now," Nietzsche added, "someone of this description turns up once in a blue moon, and I would circle the earth to meet him."[62] Perhaps he meant to do just that, Columbus-style, when on March 29 he embarked for Mes-sina on a Sicilian freighter. Yet he had not included even a jest for Lou in a handwritten note of March 23 to Rée: "Many bad days. . . . I am really best off by the sea—only where is the sea spot with shade enough for me? *è una miseria!*" And Rée reported to Lisbeth on April

---

w None of Rée's letters of III-IV 1882 to Nietzsche in Genoa survives. That these were numerous is, however, clear from FN→Rée [21 III 1882], while Rée→FN, 20 IV 1882, drawn on below, p. 52, affords fair evidence that Nietzsche, as just quoted, was hardly exaggerating their tenor—insofar as he meant only letters (in FN→Georg Rée [early VIII 1883], draft, a variant of the line just quoted begins: "[Paul Rée] preached to me," which could signify orally in Rome) and meant letters only from Rée (FN→MVM [early VII 1882], draft: "If you discover [any more] people with this [heroic] way of thinking, give me a sign as you did for the Russian girl," suggests a possible lost letter from Malwida to Messina—the surprise at Nietzsche's arrival in Rome ex-pressed in MVM→Olga Monod-Herzen [late IV] 1882 being in any case im-plausible).

10: "Since a somewhat mysterious card in which he spoke of a sea voyage but without mentioning its goal, I have heard nothing further from him, which is beginning to make me uneasy." Lisbeth supplied his address, and Rée wrote on April 20: "Dear Mr. Messinian! . . . Is it possible! By this step you have above all stricken the Russian girl with astonishment and distress. She has in fact grown so eager to see and speak with you that she wanted to return by way of Genoa, and she was very angry about your being so far away. She is a forceful, unbelievably clever being with the most girlish, even childlike qualities. She would so much like, as she put it, to make a nice year of it at least, meaning next winter. . . . It could really prove too nice."*x* It was not this alluring peril, though, that drew Nietzsche to Rome; rather that same April 20, as Malwida wrote abroad, "the violent sirocco, which he cannot at all stand, drove him away" from Sicily, "which had pleased him infinitely,*y* and he came back to Naples and here on his way to Switzerland."[63] Not until his second day in Rome was he up to seeing Rée and Malwida, and then only briefly. Rée urged Lou upon him this time as, among other things, a ready literary pupil in want of a style and a subject; and Malwida, long since won over again by Lou, urged her upon him as a heroic disciple predestinate. As for Lou, hers was a new pupilage and discipleship *before* first sight—only this time half guarded against.

The first sight was staged by Rée in Saint Peter's. There Lou was struck by Nietzsche's solemn manner—the "cloak and mask," she soon realized, "for an inner life almost never disclosed."[64] His hands "incomparably beautifully and nobly wrought," his "unusually small and delicately shaped ears," his "fine, highly expressive mouth-lines, almost fully concealed by an ample moustache combed over them," his "placid features" in general together with his "gentle laughter," his "noiseless way of talking," his "cautious, wistful gait, shoulders a little bent," his ultra-simple "neat attire," all spoke to her of "discreet solitude. . . . One could hardly imagine this figure amidst a crowd; it bore the stamp of standing aside, of standing alone."[65] His eyes were to her "like the custodians and preservers of personal treasures, of mute secrets meant for no intruding glance. His defective eyesight lent his features a quite special magic in that they did not reflect varying outer impressions but only what was passing through him internally. They looked inwards, yet at the same time into the distance,

---

x Plus more to the same effect—and little else except for a reference to a preceding letter (evidently mailed to Genoa) about the chaperoned *ménage à trois.*

y Cf. FN→Rée [8 v 1882]: "Except for the sirocco I would be in Messina."

well beyond the objects round about him—or better, inwards as if
into the distance."[66/z]

In return, Nietzsche's eyes could barely make Lou out, while to his
ears her voice was somewhat rasping. Otherwise he was pleased
enough with her—if not quite enough to wish to delay his return
north. His own illness delayed it instead. Malwida wrote afterwards:
"He was almost his whole time here in bed and saw nothing of Rome
apart from Villa Mattei and Saint Peter's."[67] Rée agreed to accompany him to the Italian lakes. Lou somehow induced her custodians
to arrange their return trip north accordingly, then pleaded for Rée's
and, through Rée, for Nietzsche's assent. "It is unpleasant to be able
to do nothing but plead in a matter so close to one's heart," she wrote
Rée on April 25. "It now lies primarily with you to shape the next few
weeks most amicably. *Have no fear of painted devils*, see to it that
the trip comes off—*please, please!*" "Most commanding Miss Lou,"
Rée replied, "we leave tomorrow noon, reaching the lakes Saturday
morning [April 29]; Monday in Milan you will find a wire *poste
restante* on our place of sojourn. We shall then travel round the lakes
together. Nietzsche too will remain till then at the lakes. Whether I
shall come as far as Milan to meet you will depend on our location.
Tomorrow morning at about eleven Nietzsche will call on your
mother, and I shall accompany him to pay her my respects. . . .
Nietzsche cannot answer for how he will feel tomorrow, but would like
to introduce himself to your mother before we meet again at the
lakes."

Nietzsche was not fit to leave before another week, within which
he explained to Lou that her chaste *ménage à trois* was not all that
simple even with chaperon, as "I should consider myself duty-bound
to offer you my hand so as to protect you from what people might
say; otherwise etc. etc."[68] He saw part way through her protesta-
tion that marriage was as far from her mind as romance: he egged
Rée on. But Rée feared a *yes* and a *no* equally. "Deep down he is an
unshakable pessimist," Nietzsche commented, "and *how* true to himself he remained in this, against all the arguments of his heart and
my reason, won my great respect in the long run."[69] Between times
Nietzsche presented himself to Lou's mother, who warned him that
Lou's self-accounting was strictly fantastical; he listened with one
sharp ear. Lou's party, bags long since packed, departed on May 3,
Lou bearing introductions from Malwida to idealists all over Europe
but leaving round about Rome the reputation of "a somewhat too

[z] Cf. MVM→Olga Monod-Herzen [late IV] 1882: "One sees in his very beautiful eyes that they have no sight left."

enterprising intellectual adventuress."[70] Nietzsche and Rée followed a day later, rejoining the others in Orta on May 5.

The next day Nietzsche and Lou climbed a nearby mountain sacred to Franciscans, the *monte sacro*. There for the first time Nietzsche thrilled to Lou's responsive intelligence. He spoke to her of the "eternal recurrence," which made self-denial eternally foolish, and of his "son"-to-be, Zarathustra, due to transcend the slave morality of good-and-evil as the historic Zarathustra had transcended the master morality of good-and-bad.[a] Just a few hours on the holy mount and he had dimly conceived the grand design of fashioning her according to his philosophical ideal—of schooling her to be his "heiress" and "successor." Beneath this pedagogical project lay the erotic one of engendering a bride in his own image: thence his constant combination of passion and vagueness about his purpose. The erotism was strictly underlying: Lou was just not his buxom type, a few gallant compliments to come from him notwithstanding. Lou for her part told Rée grandiloquently after her tardy return with Nietzsche: "His very laughter is a deed."[71] And to Malwida she wrote excitedly that his was in truth "a *religious nature*"[72]—which it was, just like her own, even down to his own self-identification with Jesus.[b] She rejoiced as did he in their uncanny affinity, which was the more piquant for her complementary erotism, manifest in her craving for his tutelage. To compound the compatibility, he attracted her sensually. Only there was a catch: her ego was organized against just such intellectual and erotic temptation. Its strongest outside defense was Rée, whose tutorial ideal was her self-development at his side, where she ran no emotional risk. But only well out of Nietzsche's gigantic presence was she ever able to take exception to his proud design on her.

His climb with Lou left Nietzsche an eager party to the plan of working a year at close quarters—if not in shared quarters—with her and Rée.[c] The following afternoon, having arranged with them to rendezvous in Lucerne a week later, he left for a surprise visit to the Overbecks in Basel. Franz Overbeck, professor at Basel[d] and his-

---

[a] Nietzsche also discussed both conceptions with the Overbecks a few days later: Ida O in Bernoulli, *FO und FN*, I, 338, 345. On Zarathustra as Nietzsche's "son," see Ida O, *ibid.*, 338; FN→Lisbeth, 27 IV 1883; FN→Stein, 22 V 1884.

[b] To Lou's early fantasy of having been God's beloved child corresponds a comedy written by Nietzsche at ten in which he (as "Sirenius") is raised to divinity by Jupiter, then has his father (in reality long since dead) and mother wafted to heaven by nymphs [*HKG:W*, I, 329ff.]—Jesus' success story paganized! (Lisbeth, seen weeping at his grave with their parents, is left on earth.) Further, a line from one of his numerous childhood poems about Jesus runs: "He comes from out his father's womb" (*ibid.*, 398).

[c] FN→O, 24 VI 1882, requested a lead on "a place for Miss Lou" (to live), though this perhaps as an aftereffect of his Grunewald fiasco: below, p. 68.

[d] Originally a Petersburg German (like Lou).

torian of the contest between theology and religion, was Nietzsche's loyal friend; his young wife, Ida, was Nietzsche's sagacious confidante. Both wondered at Nietzsche's robustness—at his five days of liveliest talk till midnight, with music between times and "two long sessions at the dentist's . . . all without a real crisis and only one hour's complete prostration."[73] Overbeck reported Nietzsche "full of urgent desire for a new way of life, one taking him away less from men and things."[74] Ida Overbeck later remembered him as then "most excited" and "most hopefully confident."[75] For, she explained, "Nietzsche had given himself to the hope of having found his *alter ego* in Miss Salomé—of working with her, and through her help, toward his goals."[76] And again: "Mentally passionate nonmarital relationship was an ideal always dear to him. Passion there was, but also the desire not to let himself be carried away by it. It reassured him that Rée should be the third in the party, and from Rée's serviceable, selfless nature he expected much."[77] Both Overbecks recognized that, despite his "demand for innermost congruity"[78] and his will "to clasp the girl disciple and now be master at last,"[79] he was not Lou's suitor.

Lou, however, had led him to "fear" lest she had construed his words in Rome about asking her hand as an actual proposal.[80] Already on his way to Basel he had written Rée concerning Lucerne: "I absolutely must speak with Miss Salomé once again, perhaps in the Löwengarten."[81] Lou now misconstrued these words in good faith—all the way from Locarno via Airolo over the San Gottardo through Göeschenen to Lucerne, where on May 13 Nietzsche found her waiting with Rée at the railroad station.[82] Her heart was set on refusing him, so the undeceiving in the Löwengarten came as a shock—whatever she then told him or herself. Still in all, jollity carried the day, and to celebrate the newly constituted "Trinity," as she named it, Lou prevailed upon Nietzsche and Rée to be photographed hauling a cart with her perched atop it, whip in hand.[e]

On the morrow she accompanied Nietzsche on a bittersweet excursion to Tribschen, former home of his sometime friend Richard Wagner.[f] Afterwards she acquainted him with her poem "To Pain."

[e] That this photo was all Lou's idea emerges from Rée→Lou [late v 1882]: the Stibbe doctor would examine her as "*revenge* for the photographing: I shall be as stubborn [about it] as you [were]," and from Rée→Lou [mid-vi 1882]: "Picture arrived yesterday. Nietzsche superb; you and I hideous, can dispute the prize for ugliness between us. You see, Lou, for once you were not right after all." FN→Lou [28 v 1882] was more gallant: "Oh the bad photographer! And yet: what a lovely silhouette atop the rack-waggon!"

[f] 1890a:87. As 1890a was published in Rée's lifetime, the excursion itself is likely factual—but it is less than likely that, once there, Nietzsche sat a while "sunk in memories," then "spoke in a soft voice of bygone days," since FN→ Lou [22 VII 1882] (reproduced in 1890a:83-86, with one excision: see below, p. 157) discussed Wagner quite as a delicate new topic between them.

He was "beside himself" with joy over this "practical echo of his own affirmative thought."[83/g] Weeks later he asserted: "It is among those things which have total power over me: I have yet to be able to read it without weeping, it sounds like a voice for which I have waited and waited since childhood."[h] He presented her in return with his "Schopenhauer as Educator" (the third of his *Untimely Reflections*) by way of fair warning about his pedagogic ideal. He also replaced the motto from Saint Paul on her knick-knack box—"Strive to live quietly and to create and produce with your own hands"[84]—with one he had adopted from Goethe eleven years earlier: "Not in the half but in the whole, in the good and beautiful, resolutely living."

The Trinity settled on a "winter plan" for studying natural science[i] in a university town, provisionally Vienna, and a "summer plan" pursuant to which Lou would gently dispatch her mother, then spend some weeks at Stibbe, some afterwards alone with Nietzsche, and some again vacationing with Nietzsche, Rée, and Rée's mother— with time out to join Malwida at Bayreuth in late July for the world première of *Parsifal*. Nietzsche wrote home on Monday, May 15: "It may sound incredible—but probably I shall come to Naumburg Wednesday." The next morning he departed, halting a few hours in Basel to confer with the Overbecks, whom Lou planned to visit in two weeks.[j] "He charged me," Ida Overbeck later recollected, "with telling Lou about how he was always pursuing only his own mental aims and thinking only of himself"[85]—which was this time unfair warning. Rée meanwhile accompanied the Salomés and Brandts to Zurich, whence he promptly headed for Stibbe after taking leave of Lou in the university's Senatszimmer. He told her subsequently: "You stuck in my memory as much too sick, leaning so far back in your seat that last morning as you spoke of our maybe not seeing each other again."[86]

Sick as Lou was, her morale was sky-high, for her bold, wild Roman dream was, of all things, coming true. She wanted nothing more

[g] So Overbeck related, presumably drawing on remarks passed by Nietzsche in Basel just after the fact.

[h] FN→Gast, 13 VII 1882. Gast had mistaken the poem, transmitted by Nietzsche without explanation, for one by Nietzsche himself (Gast→FN, 16 VII 1882: "not a single word troubled me in this belief").

[i] Natural science was presumably Nietzsche's idea, but 1890a:224 is the sole source for the stock contention that he wanted to study it ten years so as to ground the "eternal recurrence" physically (space and matter finite, time infinite), which is likely as fanciful as the neighboring one (*ibid.*, 224-25) that, cursory study having disclosed the impossibility of ever grounding it, he clung to it only the faster (cf. Schlechta, *Fall*, 30ff.).

[j] FN→O, 15 V 1882: Lou "would like to come to you and your dear wife."

than to cry aloud to this effect, but Nietzsche objected: "I like concealment in life."[87] Rée specified: Nietzsche desired her "very existence" to be kept secret from his mother and sister.[88] Son and twice grandson of preachers, Nietzsche did not ridicule his family on account of its "Naumburg virtue" without also reverencing it on the same account, even unto fantasies of noble lineage: in nothing, declared Overbeck, was his "caprice" more conspicuous.[89] His sister, still his childhood sweetheart, had since *Human, All Too Human* come to idolize his life as against his books,[90] and he cherished her idolatry at heart even as he dreaded her jealousy. But not only in consideration of his family did he treat the Trinity as a daring cabal: he felt it to be one. The key reason was its homosexual tendency—his potentially sharing a woman with Rée. In this respect it was indeed an evil omen, as Ida Overbeck remarked, when Nietzsche fretted to her about having overheard Lou and Rée laugh at him together concerning "I no longer know what book or manuscript of his."[91] At all odds, Rée was already on intimate, "*Du*" terms with Lou in Lucerne behind Nietzsche's (and everyone else's) back—as a "little brother" with his "little sister,"[k] to be sure, yet even fraternally he craved Lou's exclusive affection. Conversely, he wrote back to her on changing trains in Basel: "*Be assured that you are the only person in the world whom I love*"—adding in postscript: "I don't know if Nietzsche is here or not." Rée's aim of turning Lou over to Nietzsche was reversing itself: already he was aiming to turn her against Nietzsche. "Your mind is so pleasant," he told her typically, "in that it does not *weigh down* on one. This Nietzsche's, for instance, does. It presses, oppresses mine; mine breaks down when his is close by."[92] And yet in mid-May 1882 Rée himself hardly sensed that Lou, even in drawing his great friend closer to him than ever, had come between them.

[k] Recurrent terms in their correspondence.

THIS TIME Lou was only two weeks in Zurich. On May 30, 1882, she and her mother left for a Wilm family reunion in Hamburg, arriving June 2. From Vienna, where he was serving a medical internship, Jenia came after them to escort his mother home. The three Salomés quit Hamburg for Berlin sometime before June 13,[1] and on June 19 Lou saw her mother and brother off by sea, then took a night train back to Berlin en route to Stibbe.

All this while, Rée assailed Lou with mail.[m] Of his leaving Zurich he wrote within the hour: "I thought I should expire from pain and longing. But that's all nonsense and childishness (the more since this wistful pain is not without its dash of pleasantness—how come, I don't exactly know: you, my dear Lou, as the better psychologist, will be able to solve this one easily). But what so fearfully disturbs me is your health . . ." From Stibbe on May 18 he telegraphed: "Mama inordinately eager to have you here whenever and as long as you wish. Engadin early July. Don't answer Nietzsche's letter *before* you have mine from here."[n] His from there pressed her to accept his mother's prompt offer of "membership in our family. Nietzsche will ∧ then sooner understand (I shall put my mama's way of seeing things to him shortly too) ~~that~~ if you are not so much with him as with me and —that is, mine ∧ in case you wish to refuse, say, being with him for long, *especially him alone* without his family. Yet it is sad too if I take you away from him altogether—then you won't get to know him—and there is so much to know about him!—and it will be painful for him besides. . . . *Vienna* still holds, naturally with Nietzsche more than

---

[1] A letter to Lou dated 13 VI 1882 expresses tender regret over her having already left Hamburg. (Its author was evidently a boy cousin—and probably the addressee of a surviving fragment [Tegernsee, summer 1884] in which Lou, likening herself to a grandmother counseling youngsters, urged a Hamburg student to master rather than flee his "deepest and holiest dreaming and yearning.")

[m] His letters of those weeks survive only mutilated and defaced, hers not at all (cf. below, p. 132 and n. *e*). His expressed over and again—beyond what follows—peevish uneasiness lest Nietzsche "think I can give him a small fortune and am only being stingy or stubborn if I don't": I could discover no occasion for this (but cf. below, p. 467 n. *w*).

[n] Nietzsche's presumable letter to Lou about the "summer plan" does not survive.

ever. But your home base in non-Russia is, if you please, Stibbe . . ."
Next Rée relayed his mother's proposal for a beach party with Nietzsche to follow Lou's visit, Lou to proceed thereafter to Bayreuth
"or else back to Stibbe or as you will. The main thing: that you come
here as fast as possible so your stay will be good and long, calm, busy,
and fattening." And next: "I prefer not to write Nietzsche after all
that Mama wants to sort of adopt you, as I'm afraid he will see it as
only a trick to keep you from him . . ." Then, in arrears of news
from her, he sent her a telegram marked "urgent" inquiring after her
health; some hours later he learned of its shock effect and explained
apologetically that, in default of a reassuring reply, "I was all ready
to leave for Zurich the same day." To this he added: "I am gradually
getting back into my work on the emergence of conscience in the individual. When you are here, we can work on the religious parts together—unless you have work of your own in mind, as would certainly be better. *Enfin*—there is no hurry about your independent
work . . . seek *not*, and you will find. . . . I am of course indescribably
tense pending your decisions. Already I regret having told you too
emphatically what in my opinion you ought to do. *Heed no one but
yourself* . . ." Again he wrote to Zurich: "I was just thinking (really
I *should* be thinking about 'the emergence of conscience in the individual,' but the cuckoo knows I'm always thinking about Lou) that
I am not so wholly open and honest in my relationship to Nietzsche,
especially since a certain little girl has bobbed up from abroad. . . .
I am and shall remain entirely *your* friend alone; I have no scruples
about behaving a little crookedly, a little falsely, a little mendaciously
and deceitfully toward anyone except you. Out of my friendship to
you I make a cult; I regard as a sin—(what, Mr. Antimoralist?)—
well, I mean: if I did or said anything false, dishonorable, unfriendly,
crooked with respect to you, I would have a feeling just like the one
believers may have after committing a great sin. And from this special uprightness I draw a justification for being false in general. . . .
Not that there has been any misdeed on my part—absolutely not.
It is just a reflexion that passed through my brain and that I noted
maybe only because I am too lazy to work and think intensely . . ."
And again: "The Engadin is *definitely* out. For bathing maybe Warmbrunn in the Riesengebirge (right near here). Mama was there once
and felt so good there. Lovely mountains, small, comfortable, a theater, and amazingly cheap. Also much shade for Nietzsche, if he
wants to come." And then to Hamburg: "It's still Warmbrunn. . . .
But the devil take all plans . . . just come here soon. . . . I have not
corresponded with Nietzsche since writing him at the very beginning

that the first part of our Zulu program could be carried out. Just work it out with him at your discretion as you deem appropriate to his letters . . ." Next Rée announced that, as his foster sister was quartering a sick son at Stibbe for the summer, Warmbrunn was off: "I have also written Nietzsche that we are staying here. . . . I much regret that Nietzsche's plans too are now forever changing. Unfortunately he can't come here—or is this 'unfortunately' a lie? Do you think so? I really don't exactly know. . . . Is it all right under the circumstances for you to stay here till Bayreuth? I must own that (quite apart from my liking it the better the longer you stay) this strikes me as utterly sensible for you too; and Nietzsche will probably also be satisfied if then after Bayreuth you are with him a while longer . . ." And next: "From Nietzsche I had a most amiable letter yesterday—written, though, in illness. He stated rather unhappily that his health made a summer in Thuringia impossible, that he wants to go to Berchtesgaden provided you can be with us till Bayreuth. I gave him this assurance from the heart . . ." And finally: "Are we really going to see each other again—or have I only dreamed it! Come soon, lovely reality, to your nameless P."

All this same while, Nietzsche's letters as against Rée's were lovely, dark, and deep.[o] To Lou in Zurich he wrote in due course: "Here in Naumburg I have so far been wholly silent about you and *us*. That way I remain more independent and can serve you better.—The nightingales sing the whole night through before my window.—Rée is from head to toe a better *friend* than I am or can be: mark well the distinction!—When I am all alone I often, very often, speak your name and—to my greatest pleasure!" And to Rée in Stibbe: "I have hired a bankrupt old tradesman to write two hours a day while my sister dictates from my manuscript [*The Gay Science*] and I listen and correct: the only role I can now play.—I have been *taciturn* and shall remain so—you know *what about*. It is necessary.—One cannot be *friends* more wonderfully than we are now, can one? My dear old Rée!"[p] Dictation apart, Lisbeth was—as she told Ida Overbeck—"quite crazy with joy" to see her brother "so well and so fabulously jolly. We were alone the first five days, as Mama was still away on her spring trip, and we laughed so much that the maid, who knew Fritz only from his last stays here, which were so unfavorable, hardly trusted her eyes and ears that it was the same Herr Professor."[93]

<hr>

[o] FN, *Beyond*, 290: "Every deep thinker is more afraid of being understood than of being misunderstood."

[p] Similarly FN→o, 23 v 1882: "With regard to Lou, deep silence. It is *necessary*.—Her visit to Mrs. Rée is now certain, to judge by Rée's last card."

On May 28, with Lou just due to quit Zurich, Nietzsche sent her "my latest plan for speaking with you": once she reached Berlin, he would move to the Grunewald forest nearby so they might meet *when* we, when *you*, wish," and where she might join him after Stibbe. "For, honestly, I should *very much* like to be all alone with you as soon as possible. Such solitary beings as I must first slowly *get used to* those dearest to them: be considerate of me in this—or rather a little obliging! But should it please you to travel further, we can find another forest hermitage not far from Naumburg (in the neighborhood of some Altenburg castle); I could have my sister join us there if you wish. (So long as all summer plans are still up in the air, I do well to maintain complete silence in my family—not from joy in secrecy, but from 'knowledge of people.') My dear friend Lou, on 'friends' and on *friend Rée* in particular I will explain myself orally: I know quite well what I am saying if I call him a better friend than I am or can be. . . . After Bayreuth we shall seek another resting place for the benefit of *your health*? . . . They say I have never in my life been so cheerful as now. I trust my fate.—" He thereupon asked Ida Overbeck: "How could I fear fate, particularly when it confronts me in the wholly unexpected form of Lou? Rée and I feel the same devotion to our courageous, high-minded friend: even on this score he and I have great faith in each other, and we are not of the dumbest or youngest.—So far I have kept strict silence here about all these things. Yet this will not be feasible in the long run: indeed, my sister and Rée's mother are already in touch. I do mean to leave my mother 'out of the game,' though: she has troubles enough as is—why add to them?" And concerning Lou's impending stopover in Basel he enjoined Ida: "Speak of me with all liberty: you surely know and guess what I most need to reach my goal, but also that I am no man of action and lag dolefully far behind my best prospects. And just because of that goal I am a nasty egoist—and friend Rée in all his parts a better friend (which Lou will not believe)."

The next day, May 29, Nietzsche inquired of Rée: "What's doing with *our summer plans?*" and, after summarizing his Grunewald scheme, signed off: "I often laugh at our Pythagorean friendship. It raises me in my own esteem to be really *capable* of it. Yet it does remain laughable?—In heartfelt love, your F.N." That same day, at Lou's behest, Biedermann—though he did not enjoy seeing her in Nietzsche's orbit, much less "wholly reserved toward me on this score"[94]—formally notified Overbeck that "Miss Salomé . . . wishes to call on you tomorrow, Tuesday, at 2 PM to convey greetings to you from your friend Nietzsche." "The Overbecks received me with great warmth," Lou reported to Nietzsche.[95] The warmth was indeed so great that Lou persuaded her mother to spend a second day in Basel, then petitioned Overbeck to introduce her to his illustrious colleague Jakob Burckhardt—without success. Even so, Nietzsche was to be assured of the Overbecks' *"whole good human and friendly understanding* for my plan."[96]

Malwida was harder to please. From Basel Lou sent her a defense of the Trinity's winter plan in reply to a veritable tract on decorum in the Roman moonlight with the addendum: "I am glad you esteem Nietzsche so."[97] Malwida retorted that Nietzsche was too sick for study or Vienna. "And then this Trinity! Firmly as I am convinced of *your* neutrality, just as surely does the experience of a long lifetime tell me that it will not work without a heart's cruelly suffering in the noblest case, otherwise a friendship's being destroyed. . . . Nature will not be mocked, and before you know it the fetters are there. . . . I wish only to protect you from nearly unavoidable sorrow such as you have experienced once already."[98]

On June 4 Lou apprised Nietzsche from a sickbed in Hamburg that, between her brother's newly announced arrival in Hamburg and the Rées' impending departure for Warmbrunn, her stay in Berlin would be cut too short for a tryst. In any case, she added, "a lengthy reunion of the two of us alone is *for the moment* not possible; it is absolutely necessary first for my mother and brother to know me to be with the Rées—that is, with Mrs. Rée. After Bayreuth maybe something of the sort will work out much better. Yet it is long till then, and it would be good if we could meet in Warmbrunn. Only do believe that, if I *now* leave being alone with you out of account, this is only in the interest of our plans." And after comparing Rée with Nietzsche philosophically—"you are like two prophets, one turned to the past and one to the future, of whom the first, Rée, exposes the gods' origins, while the second extinguishes their twilight" —she concluded coquettishly: "[Your] *Flush of Dawn* is now my only companion. It entertains me in bed better than would visits, shopping, and travel dust. Could I but say: see you soon! Only remain so cheerful and healthy, everything will turn out very well. We are good hikers and find our way in the brush."[q]

Nietzsche had just then, as Lisbeth told it, "gone off somewhere or other seeking forest shade."[99] On June 7 he was back at his desk to tell Lou that he too had been ill just when she was, "which gives me a sort of bitter satisfaction: it is unbearable for me to think of you

[q] This is Lou's sole surviving letter to Nietzsche for the period from Rome to Bayreuth.

suffering alone." Triumphantly announcing "an eight-page letter from the Overbecks . . . *favorable* to our purpose," he urged silence for the rest, "even toward those closest and dearest: neither Mrs. Rée in Warmbrunn nor Miss von Meysenbug in Bayreuth nor my family need break their heads and hearts over things that *we, we, we* alone are and shall be up to, whereas they may strike others as dangerous fantasies.—For Berlin and Grunewald I was so ready that I could have left at any moment. So we shall first meet again after Bayreuth? and then only 'maybe'? Warmbrunn is no place for me; it also seems to me more advisable not to put our Trinity on display so openly this summer. . . . I too have a flush of dawn about me—and this no printed one. What I no longer thought possible—to find a friend of my *utmost joy and sorrow*—now seems so to me: as a golden possibility on the horizon of my whole future life. I have only to think of my dear Lou's brave and prescient soul and I am moved." That same day he assured Overbeck concerning Lou: "The truth is that, in the way I *here* mean to act and shall act, I am for once altogether the man of my thoughts, of my innermost thinking: this *concordance* does me such good. . . . There are lots of life secrets of mine bound up with this *new* future, and tasks remain that can be carried out only through deeds. I am moreover so fatalistic in my 'submission to God' (I call it *amor fati*) that I would run into a lion's jaws, to say nothing of— . . . I go on keeping silence here. As for my sister, I am wholly determined to leave her out: she could only confuse things (and herself to begin with)."

Evidently Lou then informed Nietzsche that Malwida was already privy to their winter plan, though probably not that Malwida disapproved of it—much less that Malwida had been urging her to team up with Lisbeth for her coming trip to Bayreuth. "Yes, my dear friend," he replied indulgently, "I do not at all fail to see at my remove which persons must *necessarily* be initiated into our purpose, but I think we should stick to the necessary ones. I love concealment in life and heartily wish to preserve you and myself from European prattle. Anyhow, I attach such high hopes to our living together that all its necessary or fortuitous side-effects now make little impression on me: and *whatever* ensues, we will bear it together and cast the whole packet into the water every evening *together*, won't we? . . . Let me know how you propose to arrange your time from Bayreuth on and what cooperation from me you are counting on. I now badly need mountains and forests: not only health but even more *The Gay Science* is driving me into solitude: I want to *finish* it.—Does it suit you if I now already set out for Salzburg (or Berchtesgaden), hence on the road to *Vienna*? . . . Finally: I am in all matters of action inexperienced and unpracticed, and for years I have *never* had to explain or justify myself to people for any sort of act. My plans I like to keep under cover; about my *facta* may all the world speak! Yet nature gave every being its own weapons of defense—and to you it gave your glorious openness of will. Pindar once said: 'Become yourself!' Faithfully and devotedly, F. N."

About this same time he wrote Rée: "I now take it *to be settled* that Miss Lou will be in Stibbe till the Bayreuth time, in any case will *remain together* with you and your mother till then? . . . I am myself thinking of setting out for Vienna in *early July*: that is to say, of trying a summer's stay in Berchtesgaden—assuming that I have *no services of any kind to perform beforehand*. All in all I beg you urgently to keep silence *toward everyone* about our winter project: one ought to keep silence about everything in the making. As soon as it is spread about prematurely *there are contradictors and counterplans*: the danger is not slight. . . . I should like to hear *as soon as possible* what I have to do and not do, so I can dispose of my summer. Naumburg is a *frightful* place for my health.—Send your next lines, dear friend, to Leipzig, *poste restante*.—Forgive this scribbling breathed over by the spirit of sickness.—In sum, we both have it quite good: who else has such a *lovely* prospect *before* him as we do?— Manuscript secretly ready: but still *uneditable. Mihi ipsi scripsi.*"

From Hamburg Lou again justified herself to Malwida, who thereupon sent her amen: "About your plan I can say no more. I fully acknowledge its ideality and grasp its attractiveness. You are choosing your fate and must fulfill it, whatever it may bring. You are making no sacrifice, though, for what you are undertaking is the fulfillment of your highest wishes under ideal conditions. From the heart I wish happiness to Nietzsche as well. May both of you but guard your health. . . . But I would like to insist *very* strongly that you not get all wrapped up in Nietzsche's work. I should have preferred your going your own way mentally, just to prove for once that, even in these highest realms of thought, a woman can stand alone and attain independent results. In so far, I am very sorry about this mental dependency. Above all, I hope Nietzsche himself steers another course than in his latest writings"—with the marginal addendum: "far away from that of good Rée, whom I cordially greet."[100] Malwida had come to treat the Trinity as in reality a twosome with Rée the odd man out.[r]

---

[r] No disaffection for Rée was implicit, for Malwida wrote him from Chiavenna on 22/27 vi 1882 about how at the sight of a beautiful house in the mountains she had mused: "Could I but live there with Paolo, only not

Possibly Lou did so too when next she wrote to Nietzsche, who, back from a dismal day in Leipzig, answered grandly: "Now, dearest friend, you always have a good word in readiness for me; it gives me great joy to please you. This frightful *renunciative* existence of mine, as harsh as ever any ascetic stranglehold, has some consolations that always make living more precious to me than nonbeing. Some large perspectives on the moral horizon are my *mightiest* source of vitality: I am so glad that our friendship is sprouting its roots and hopes in *this* very soil. No one else could so heartily rejoice over all that is being *done* and *planned* by you! Faithfully, your friend F. N."[8]

A Nietzsche folly followed. On June 15 he replied to what must have been Lou's wishes for a good trip to Berchtesgaden: "My dear friend, for half an hour I have been melancholic and for half an hour have been wondering why—and find no other reason than the communication just made through your most lovable letter that we shall *not* be seeing each other in Berlin. Now see what manner of man I am! Tomorrow morning at 11:40 I *will* be in Berlin, Anhalter Station. My address is: Charlottenburg by Berlin, *poste restante.* My ulterior motive is: 1) - - - and 2) that I may conduct you to Bayreuth in a few weeks, assuming you find no better escort. That's what's called a *sudden* decision! Your friend N.—Berchtesgaden I consider 'refuted.' For the time being I am staying in Grunewald.—Manuscript done. By the greatest ass of a writer! I am bringing along the *introduction*, which is headed 'Jest, Ruse, and Vengeance. Prologue in German Rhymes.' "[t] A Swiss tourist in Messina had commended Grunewald to him for its sylvan shade and solitude along with easy access to the big city. His devotee Bernhard Förster, a Gymnasium teacher, accompanied him the hundred miles from Naumburg—for one afternoon's walk under a pouring rain, then one morning's walk in dazzling sunlight, amidst breakfast litter and singing excursioners at that.

"So: I made a little, apparently quite foolish trip to Berlin," he notified Lou on June 18. "*Everything* went wrong; I rode back the next day somewhat more enlightened about Grunewald and myself—laughing a bit derisively, and *quite* exhausted.—But today I have fallen back again altogether into my 'submission to God' and believe

---

alone, so selfish I am not, rather with some gracious young being alongside, a select trio."

[8] Fitting this letter into the sequence here (12 or 13 VI 1882) as a second undated one to Lou between that of 7 and that of 15 VI 1882 makes a tight squeeze, but no alternative will quite do.

[t] Letter presumably addressed to Berlin, where Lou probably still was. Nietzsche may have hoped she would meet his train—yet did not stay in Charlottenburg long enough to hear from her there.

anew that everything *must* turn out for the best with me—even this Berlin trip and its quintessence (I mean the fact that I did *not* see you).—I should so much like to work and study some with you soon. I have prepared fine things—fields in which *sources* are to be discovered, assuming that *your* eyes want to discover sources just there (mine are no longer fresh enough for that!). You do know that I wish to be your *teacher*, your guide on the way to scholarly *production*? —What do you think of the time after Bayreuth? What would be most desirable, advantageous, and valuable to *you* for just *this* period? And is September to be kept in sight for the beginning of our Vienna existence?—My trip taught me again about my ineffable awkwardness as soon as I feel *new* places and people about me: I believe the blind are more reliable than the half blind. Concerning Vienna, it is now my wish to be set down like a piece of luggage in a small room of *the* house you want to occupy. Or next door, as your faithful friend and neighbor F.N." Not knowing Lou's whereabouts, he sent this note to Rée for "our very remarkable and all too *lovable* friend." He blamed "this German cloud-weather" for his Berchtesgaden blues,[u] then his Leipzig and Berlin fiascos. "For all that," he pursued, "I am full of confidence in this year with its mysterious dice game over my fate"—only to pronounce himself "no longer in any condition to undertake something *alone*." And fatefully: "I am now working it out so *my* mother too could invite Miss Lou." In a paragraph not sent he explained: "In all seriousness, it's better that way. My silence would have been impossible in the long run; it was necessary for only the very earliest period, as I had agreed with Overbeck. I myself could make this new '*demand*' on my family only after much vexation and almost a slight threat; from scratch such a venture as our Vienna plan would have bewildered them—they would have taken it for folly or infatuation." He struck out this last clause of his draft as if to deny his own suspicions about himself. And he meanwhile depicted Lou to his sister "as a human wonder"[101] in hopes of thereby making her a domestically acceptable fact.

At 6:00 AM on June 20, Ludwig Hüter, an idealistic young correspondent of Malwida's,[v] met Lou at Lou's bidding for five hours or so between train stations[w] in Berlin. "She was well rested despite

---

[u] To be exact, for his "last letter" to Rée: above, pp. 60, 64.

[v] MVM→Lou, 25 v [1882]: "Don't forget to see young Hüter in Berlin; I have had another glorious letter from him." MVM→Hüter, 24 v 1882: "Perhaps you shall soon see a young apostle of our views, Louise Salomé of Petersburg, a wonderfully gifted girl. I gave her your address to see you on her trip through Berlin. She can give you news from here." Hüter's memorandum (below, pp. 112-13): he then knew Malwida "only by letter."

[w] Between the Anhalter and Stettiner stations.

the night trip and spoke spiritedly of Rome and 'Malwida's' circle, as she offhandedly put it"—to Hüter's astonishment and envy.[102] Hüter described her at the time as "likable and engaging,"[103] adding in later years: "Impression of intellectual consequence; modest nature."[104]

Once settled at Stibbe, Lou called on Nietzsche to clarify his intentions toward her, which—with Rée's help—she now took to be secretarial use and sexual abuse.[x] Nietzsche replied on June 26 from the Thuringian village of Tautenburg, where his "good sister" had installed him for the summer in "an idyllic little nest": should "*you* have no better way to spend the month of August, and find it seemly and feasible to live with me here in the woods, my sister would conduct you here from Bayreuth and reside with you in the same house, for example at the parson's. . . . Well! And now 'rectitude unto death'! My dear friend! I am bound by nothing, and, if *you* have plans, I can alter mine most easily. And if I am *not* to be together with you, tell me this simply too. You need give me no reasons: I trust you *implicitly*, as you know.—If we are compatible otherwise, we shall be so in health as well, with some secret benefit. *Never* did I think that you should 'read aloud and write' for me, but I very much wished that I might be your *teacher*. To tell the whole truth: I am now seeking people who could be my heirs; I carry something around with me absolutely not to be read in my books—and am seeking the finest, most fertile soil for it. Observe my *self*-seeking!—Now and again I think of the dangers to your life, your health, and tenderness fills my soul: nothing else could bring me near you so rapidly. And then I am always happy to know that you have Rée as a friend and not just me: to think of you two strolling and chatting together is for me a true delight." This time, again with Rée's assistance, Lou construed Nietzsche's designs on her as indoctrination and courtship.

As for Lisbeth, Lou avowed: "I was warned against her already before I knew her."[105/y] At his next writing, on July 3, Nietzsche averred regarding Lisbeth: "She has, I find, come so far along over our long separation—is so much more grown up, deserving of all trust, and very loving toward me. Her own plans for the winter have been settled meanwhile . . . so that my concern lest they conflict with mine for Vienna is canceled. Besides, she now has her own inclinations to withdrawal and to 'uninfluencedness'[z]—so I believe, in sum,

---

[x] See below, p. 76 etc. Also D 18 VIII [1882] (addressed to Rée): "Those fancies about my sentiments which . . . exhilarated Nietzsche only a few weeks ago."

[y] By Rée, of course.

[z] "*Unbeeinflusstheit*" (in quotes in Nietzsche's text)—obviously Lou's word.

that *you* may give it a try with her and us. But now you will find that
there was no need for my whole hush-hush to begin with? I analyzed
it today and found as its basic cause: mistrust toward myself. I was
downright bowled over by the fact of having acquired a 'new person'
after overly strict seclusion and renunciation of all love and friendship. I had to keep silent, because it would have thrown me every
time to speak about you (as it did at the good Overbecks'). Now, I
tell you this for laughs. The way with me is always a human, all too
human one, and my *foolishness* grows with my wisdom." Lou did not
accept his invitation to Tautenburg without exacting in return his assurance that "as regards the winter, I have thought of Vienna *exclusively and earnestly*: my sister's winter plans are wholly independent from mine, there are *no* by-motives there."[106] This said,
Nietzsche prevailed upon his sister to arrange with Lou by letter to
room together in Bayreuth.[a] Rée's verdict was that the mad fellow
never quite knew what he wanted.

Nastiness aside, Rée was right. Since Grunewald, Nietzsche had
gone from sly and Dionysiac to extra seemly with Lou. He followed
suit *about* Lou, as when he now initiated Peter Gast point by point:
"Lou is a Russian general's daughter, twenty[-one][b] years old; she
is sharp as an eagle and brave as a lion, yet a very girlish child, who
may not live long. I owe her to Miss von Meysenbug and Rée. She is
now at the Rées'; after Bayreuth she is coming to Tautenburg, and
we are moving to Vienna together in the fall"—and then as if loudly
to himself: "Dear friend, you will surely do us both the honor of keeping the notion of an amour at a far remove from our relationship.
We are *friends*, and I shall hold this girl, and this trust in me,
sacred."[107/c] The teacher's purposes were as crossed as the friend's.
When speaking strictly, he meant "teacher" in Greek. By the terms
of his "Schopenhauer as Educator"—that "hymn to voluntary soli-

---

[a] Probably at Lou's suggestion. Lisbeth was evidently most reluctant, for
Nietzsche wrote her (from Tautenburg to Naumburg) that same 3 VII 1882:
"Here, my dear sister, is a letter of Lou's. . . . But now will you write to Lou?"
—and again some days later: "[I had] enclosed Lou's nice acceptance letter
in the letter to you. . . . But write her now and leave this letter unmentioned
and the letter itself unmentioned. Meanwhile I shall do everything to trace it.
The post here is unbearable." Thus it would seem that Lisbeth received his
earlier letter together with its enclosure (though only Lou's envelope, stamped
30 VI 1882, survives), then pretended to have heard nothing from him. And
yet she herself subsequently published these two letters from him in FN, *GB*!
As late as about 10 VII 1882 (too late) Lou asked Malwida about possibly
lodging with her: see MVM→Lou, 13 VII [1882].

[b] Lou evidently took a year off her age to impress Nietzsche that much
more once her mother was out of earshot.

[c] Similarly FN→MVM [early VII 1882], draft: "[Lou is] bound to me in firm
friendship."

tude"[108] which he gave Lou to read (and she left unread)—he can only have wanted to conduct her through his philosophy to one of her own, as he had conducted himself through the philosophy of his "one teacher and taskmaster," Schopenhauer.[109/d] To Gast he vaunted her independence—her "incredibly firm character: she knows just what she wants."[110] Yet he also stressed and overstressed his self-seeking with her. As he put it to Malwida when he thanked her for procuring him that "young, truly heroic soul": "I wish to acquire in her a pupil and, should my life not last long, someone to inherit and carry on my thinking."[111] He put it plainly enough to Lou herself at the time—and all too plainly six months later: "Back in Orta I conceived the plan of leading you step by step to the final consequence of my philosophy—*you*, as the first person I took to be fit for this.[e] Oh, you cannot suspect what resolve, what determination, this took. As teacher I have always done much for my students . . . but what I meant to do *here, now*, given my continuing physical deterioration, went beyond everything earlier. A protracted building, building up! I never thought of first asking your consent: you were barely to notice it as you entered upon this work. I trusted those higher impulses I believed to be yours. I thought of you as my heiress."[112] This subjacent plan of Nietzsche's made no provision for Lou's own problematical purpose, "free discipleship." As he afterwards declared: "I had the best intentions of remaking her into the image I had formed of her."[113] Since that image was his philosophic likeness, he was paying her a grandiose compliment with his "best intentions," however heedlessly of hers. For he set the value of what was his to impart too high for his sanity—and yet no higher than was just: tragically, he alone in his day and age knew how far above that day and age he stood.

All the same, Lou was resisting not so much an inordinate pretension as an inordinate temptation. She clung dearly to her winter plan for living under a single roof with Nietzsche[114] and envisioned learning from rather than with him there. His own project of learning with her was hardly serious, for he lumped it together with that of teaching her in the form of an inscrutable "higher goal."[f] Yet his talk of studying natural science "for a whole string of years" before writing another book[115] does at least indicate that he had no new thought in readiness. With his esoteric philosophy—with "that part

---

[d] Nietzsche knew Schopenhauer only literarily.

[e] On Lou's unique fitness see also FN→O [early XI 1882].

[f] "No one can guess it! and even I may not disclose it—but to you, and just to you, I most want to confess that it calls for a *heroic* way of thinking (and by no means a religious-resigned one)": FN→MVM [early VII 1882], draft.

of my philosophy kept almost silent so far,"[116] now to be whispered to Lou lest he not live to render it exoteric—he was bluffing all concerned, beginning with himself. In *The Gay Science* he had already closed accounts with Réealism—preparatory to closing accounts with Rée—and had already opened his next philosophical ledger, with the eternal recurrence and Zarathustra's descent from the mount duly inscribed. True, mankind's future moral mutation, recently invoked by him in Orta and Basel, was left pending. But of this prophecy he had the merest premonitions in the summer of 1882: as finally issued, it told of his experience with Lou from that summer on. Moreover, Lou was disqualified as his safe deposit for unwritten ideas by what she called "his drastically poor opinion of my health"[117] as against his own new-found hale-and-heartiness.[g] And she was over-qualified as ideational confidante inasmuch as in Orta he had found her not only *ex*piring but *in*spiring: no idea, he well knew, was ever the same for having been discussed with her. Actually his talk of transmitting mysteries to her took the place of the garrulous "hush-hush" about her[h] that "would have been impossible in the long run."[i] Less blatantly risqué, it was nevertheless naughtier in that it came down to an anal-sexual fancy of passing privy products to a daughter-bride. Subrationally it was all of a piece, with the mental creature-and-partner a vital depositary-to-be for pressing innermost secrets-to-be. Thus he cast her as mentor within her role of pupil: "Heaven protect me from foolishness! Only from now on, with *you* to advise me, I shall be well advised and need have no fear."[118]

There were extenuating circumstances surrounding his foolishness —as he indicated when, after allowing that his foolishness grew with his wisdom, he pursued: "That reminds me of my *Gay Science*. Thursday the first proofs are due, and Saturday the last part of the manuscript is to go to the printer's. I am now still occupied with very fine matters of language: the final decision on the text requires the most scrupulous 'listening' to word and sentence. Sculptors call this work of finishing '*ad unguem.*'—With this book comes to a close the series of writings that began with *Human, All Too Human*: together they were meant to set up 'a new image and ideal of the free spirit.' That this is not 'the free man of action' you will long since have guessed. Rather—but here I will sign off and laugh."[119] And his foolishness only swelled his splendid exultation of July 9: "Now the sky is clear above me! Yesterday noon was like a birthday to me:

[g] ". . . my bodily health has reemerged, I know not whence, and everyone tells me I look younger than ever" (FN→Lou [9 VII 1882]); etc.
[h] See above, p. 68.
[i] See above, p. 66.

you sent your acceptance, the loveliest gift anyone could have made me now. My sister sent cherries, Teubner sent the first three proof-sheets of *The Gay Science*—and, to top it all off, the very last part of the manuscript was just then finished and with it the work of six years (1876-1882), all my 'free thinking'! Oh what years! what tortures of every sort, what loneliness and weariness! And against all that, as it were against death *and* life, I have brewed this my physic, these my thoughts with their tiny tiny strip of *cloudless sky* above them:—oh dear friend, whenever I think of all this I am shaken and moved and do not know how it could ever have *succeeded*: self-pity and a feeling of victory fill me wholly. For it is a victory, and a complete one," and now "I want to cease being solitary and to learn to be human again. Ah, *this* lesson I must learn almost from scratch!"[120] To *this* invitation his taskmistress gave no reply.[j]

Rée for his part had long since stopped writing to Nietzsche[k] or about conscience—because Nietzsche was on his conscience, of course, but also because he was busy playing house with Lou. Lou willing, he nicknamed her "Snailie" and himself Snailie's "Housie."[l] They kept a "nestbook" on their stay in their "Stibbe nest."[121] They shared a floor there with Housie's foster sister's children, Snailie occupying a room "good and friendly, facing east, overlooking the garden, with a tall chestnut tree before the window"[122] and with the manorial horses and cows in the meadow beyond. Housie nursed her tenderly and fed her full. She rewarded him with a portrait of Gillot framed in ivy tendrils.[m] He so doted on her that he was shortly to tell her: "At times I'm awfully afraid I could one day feel nasty toward you."[123] To her delight she discovered that he was a Jew—and "the mere harmless mention of it made him faint before my eyes."[124/n] She and her new mother, rivals at heart, competed in sweetness to each other.

[j] FN→O, 18 VII 1882: "I still have no reply from Lou"; FN→Lisbeth, 17 VII 1882: "My last letter to her was certainly lost"; FN→Lou [22 VII 1882]: "Among people who trust each other, *even* letters may get lost."

[k] FN→Rée [3? IX 1882]: "From the moment Lou was in Stibbe you wrote me no more letters"—though it would appear from FN→Lisbeth, 17 VII 1882, that Nietzsche (but perhaps Lisbeth) had just heard from Rée. (Lou→Ida O [mid-VII 1882] indicates that Nietzsche wrote to Rée around 14 VII 1882.)

[l] "*Schneckli*" and "*Hüsung*" in Rée's Plattdeutsch.

[m] D 16 VIII 1882 (defaced entry). See also Rée→Lou [31 VII 1882]: after her departure, Rée stood the portrait on his desk so as to see Gillot at every pause "and study his energetic features," then set one of her before it "so that his head looked over you and away, only then it was as if he were holding you in his arms, and as I couldn't view that with a friendly eye I put you beside him": this last "made me feel terribly at home."

[n] Rée was probably the first Jew Lou knew. She grew up philo-Semitic even though in Petersburg official circles *Jew* meant *usurious gypsy* at its comeliest,

Meanwhile Lou espoused materialism with new zeal[125] and even denied idealism to Malwida after sampling Schopenhauer.[126] And she wrote an essay on women as weak, not in that they lacked strength, but in that they sought it all around them. Femininity was, she argued, a felt deficiency inclining to indiscriminate dependency, idolatry, and reverence, so that "the weaker sex is obviously more important for the genesis of religion than the stronger. And as women go, if left to themselves they would continually create out of their weakness not only 'men' but also 'gods'—the two, it might be supposed, identical: as *prodigies of strength*!"° As between Aunt Caro's alternatives confronting a woman—dependence with sex or independence without it —Lou posited the first as a norm even while personally opting for the second.

Lou set out for Bayreuth on July 21, five days before the music began. "I am happy not to *have* to be there," wrote Nietzsche, bidding her godspeed—"and yet could I be near you ghostwise, whispering this and that into your ear, even the *Parsifal* music would be bearable to me." Urging her to read his "Richard Wagner in Bayreuth" beforehand (the fourth of his *Untimely Reflections*), he added: "I have *experienced* so much in respect of this man and his art—it was a whole long *passion*: I know no other word for it. Nothing in my fate has been harder or sadder than the renunciation here required of me when I needed to find myself again. Wagner last wrote to me in a fine presentation copy of *Parsifal*: 'To my dear friend Friedrich Nietzsche. Richard Wagner, member of the High Consistory.' At the very same time my book *Human, All Too Human*, sent by me, reached him—and with that all was *clear*, but also over. How often have I, in all sorts of things, experienced just *this*: 'All clear but all over!' And how happy I am, my beloved friend Lou, that now in our case I may think: 'All just starting and yet *all* clear!' " This message reached Stibbe only after Lou's departure.

Lisbeth joined Lou en route. "Five hours after your meeting in Leipzig," wrote Nietzsche to Lisbeth, "I already had Lou's letter. I do believe that you two *are in good spirits together*."[127] They were: Lisbeth later avowed that she was "at first wholly enthused" with Lou,[128] and by the time they reached their room in Bayreuth they were calling each other *Du*. Rée, from out of his desolation, pursued

---

but her subsequent overinsistent ascription of Rée's self-hate to his Judaism suggests that perhaps *she* unconsciously hated him as a Jew—that her philo-Semitism was a reaction against unconscious hate for Jesus' crucifiers.
  ° Quoted from Nietzsche's rewrite of viii 1882, which alone survives. Lou here defined woman in effect as psychologically a castrated man: cf. below, pp. 240, 422-23, and *passim*.

Lou by mail with baby-talk about whether Snailie was her Housie's tenant or proprietor and how even out in the big world Snailie might crawl back into her Housie now and again if only she would—and fretted the while lest Snailie find, "even in Bayreuth, a better Housie than your *You*."[p] His *She* kept a diary addressed to him, which she posted serially.[q] On her insistence he kept one for her, begun after "one week asleep or mad or the devil knows what": under the motto "Frank with myself, false with others (one person excepted)," he explained how hard it was for anyone else to be honest with himself given the "moral censor," whereas "we, beloved Snailie, are, thank God, raised above good and evil and so cannot feel inclined to fool ourselves" or, by the same token, each other.

Rée also made himself an accessory to Lou's worldly cause.[r] Her best contact through him was Heinrich von Stein, young devotee of Schopenhauer and Wagner, lately Siegfried Wagner's tutor but now a lecturer at Halle. Stein saw in Rée "the shining thinker."[s] Lou at first ridiculed Stein to Rée for postulating a "pure subject of knowledge"[129] and for calling philosophy a matter of "temperamental constitution."[130] "That Stein is not to your taste delights me," replied Rée, who nonetheless urged her to show more charity, at least "toward eminent people." She did so—and was soon eagerly planning to visit Stein in Halle after her stay in Tautenburg. So Rée belittled Stein[t] and brooded.[u] Through Stein and Malwida she met Count Jukovsky,[v] Bayreuth stage designer and court painter (and fellow Petersburger): her accounts of her doings with him made Rée whimper with jealousy, "for surely he will next want to marry you. *Enfin* Lou, even then I want to remain your friend."[w] Cosima Wagner invited

[p] Rée's letters to Lou in Bayreuth and Tautenburg survive in numerous undated fragments with contents largely nonsensical.

[q] None of Lou's Bayreuth diary survives. (By Rée's report, a discriminating friend of his took it for the work of "one of our leading stylists.")

[r] Typically, he notified her about a "writers' meeting in Braunschweig on September 9-12 to which all the celebrities of Germany are coming" and again about a woman to whom he had read her Bayreuth pages and who "seems very much interested. But we are not at all close friends, I must confess."

[s] So he wrote to Rée in 1879.

[t] "Isn't it remarkable that Stein can't write a single bearable sentence?" Etc.

[u] "I've been thinking about Stein, you, and me. You need people, the world; all I can ever be for you is your faithful refuge, your Housie." Etc.

[v] Both Malwida and Stein were staying at Jukovsky's.

[w] Rée added: "I mean apart from Count Jukovsky, generally should such an unpleasant event come to pass one day. For you must at least take a husband who doesn't entirely replace me, is not an enlarged and improved edition of myself, a superior variation on the same theme."

Lisbeth *"privatissime"* with Lou,[131/x] who thereby got to exchange a greeting with the *maestro* himself. With the Overbecks Lou elaborated on a letter she had sent them about her determination to achieve triple residence in Vienna if only "slowly, through a patient surmounting of natural prejudices," thanks to her "confident courage in facing life, which has so far always led me through all obstructive difficulties, if not without struggle at all odds successfully."[132] She attended a female spiritist's séance, which left her with a repetitive hallucination of spirit thumpings[y]; Rée, shocked, insisted that "it isn't healthy for you" and argued physiology against the hallucination and "magnetism or electricity" against the original thumpings. As for *Parsifal*, on July 26 she stood through the first performance looking duly transfixed, tone-deaf though she was.[z]

Lou meanwhile suspected nothing as, in Lisbeth's words, "I gradually had to confess to myself that she was so different from what I at first thought. She knew how to construe all her doings so gloriously when really her behavior was quite ordinary; for example, she passionately enjoyed going out, but to her that was not pleasure-seeking but 'goal-striving.' I hate it when someone does something commonplace and then calls it by a fine name. Now Rée and Lou had thought of going to a university town for the winter and persuaded Fritz to come along. But as I now got to know Lou I saw right off, though I then liked her, that this talk of their living together was sheer drivel; even assuming that the girl had been quite ideally pure-minded, her habits of life were so different from ours. Fritz is so painfully orderly, exacting, and ascetically inclined . . ."[133] Even worse: by Lisbeth's account, Lou declared against Nietzsche to his Wagnerite enemies and, flaunting the Lucerne photo, "told whoever would or wouldn't listen that Nietzsche and Rée wanted to study with her and would go with her anywhere *she* wanted."[134] Except for the "whoever," this was certainly true.[a] And indignation was in order—only Lisbeth's was so shrill that Ida Overbeck, while no enthusiast of Lisbeth's

[x] Cosima's father, Franz Liszt, had visited Nietzsche in Naumburg on 25 VI (FN→Lou [26 VI 1882]).

[y] She had the hallucination at first whenever Nietzsche entered her room in Tautenburg (D 14 VIII [1882]).

[z] 1931a:102: she was "tone-deaf" (Basel manuscript: "an absolute musical dunce"), hence on that occasion "devoid of all understanding or deserving." Ironically, Lisbeth wrote Nietzsche: "I fear a deaf man would be enthused by the performance" (quoted in FN→Gast, 1 VIII 1882).

[a] On the first count: Lou's earliest Nietzschean apologists themselves (Bernoulli, Halévy, Andler, Hofmiller) all maintained that she was a passionate Wagnerite—indeed, that this was the root of the evil. On the second: how else would Lisbeth have seen the Lucerne photo then? Besides, Lou's putative boast of leading the Trinity whither she would accords neatly with FN→Lou

roommate, "took fright at her statements. She expressed a violent aversion" for Lou—so Ida testified—and, in running Lou down, "always brought herself in as superior by comparison. She had a low opinion of Miss Salomé's gifts and, given the latter's youth, wanted to keep an eye on her and send her to every imaginable school bench —at all odds away from her brother's vicinity. My impression was that she herself had nothing to match these gifts" and "was no person to assume an intelligent and sympathetic role in the relationship" between Nietzsche and Lou.[135] Ida did, however, remark to Lisbeth about having "heard that Lou's knowledge was superficial."[136] Malwida, more obliging, spoke right up against the winter plan "because she recognized the girl's bent for adventure."[137] And by August 1, Lisbeth had garnered enough strictures on Lou to return to Naumburg in triumph, leaving Lou bedridden with a cold in Bayreuth.

Nietzsche met his sister in Naumburg, whereupon he sent Lou a telegram postponing their Tautenburg idyll in view of the rain, then a letter calling off their summer and winter plans because of her conduct in Bayreuth.[b] Mournfully he told Gast on August 4: "One day a bird flew by me, and I, superstitious like all solitary people who stand at a turning of their way, believed I had seen an eagle. Now the whole world is at pains to prove to me I am mistaken—and there is urbane European prattle about it. Who is better off now—I, who as they say was 'fooled,' who spent a whole summer in a lofty world of hope on account of this bird omen, or those who are 'not to be fooled'?— And so forth. Amen. . . . —Now I am 'a bit in the wilderness' and pass many a sleepless night. But no despondency! And that demon was, like everything that now crosses by path (or seems to), *heroic-idyllic.*"[c] Meanwhile Lou, replying to Nietzsche's telegram, suggested unsuspectingly that they wait out the rain together in Jena and further that they substitute Vienna for Munich—adding thanks and regards

---

[26 VI 1882] (above, p. 66—a letter surely unknown to Lisbeth, who would otherwise have been less pugnacious thereafter lest Lou produce it) as also with Lou→FN, 2 VIII [1882]: "I believe we must give up Vienna for Munich."

[b] Neither missive survives. The telegram can be reconstructed from Lou→ FN, 2 VIII [1882]. According to Lisbeth→CG, 24 IX/2 X 1882, however, Nietzsche quarreled with Lou in "a few letters back and forth" before calling off the winter plan ("that was nonsense again, for they could live in one city well enough, that he really couldn't refuse her"), whereas D 14 VIII [1882] implies that he sent her a single "strong letter." Although Lisbeth was by and large careful to write nothing Nietzsche might contradict, Lou's version accords better with the time scheme. Nietzsche's message at all odds is in no doubt.

[c] Gast, always obliging, replied that he had been surprised in the first place at Nietzsche's prospects for Lou, as "there seemed to be too much *equity* for a woman in your way of thought."

for "your sister, who is now almost mine too."[138] Rée urged her to stay put because of her cold—the more since "the whole of August Bayreuth is a Parnassus on which the greatest minds of the time assemble," whereas in Tautenburg only letters from Stibbe and "one small wit" awaited her. But Lou was so hurt by Nietzsche's letter that Nietzsche canceled the cancellation: "I wanted to live alone. But then the dear bird Lou flew by, and I took it for an eagle. And wanted to have the eagle about me. Do come, I am suffering too much for having made you suffer: we shall bear it better together. F.N."[d]

Nietzsche sent Lisbeth ahead to meet Lou in Jena at the temporary residence of the Basel Byzantinist Heinrich Gelzer, having briefed Mrs. Gelzer beforehand on Lou and himself "to the last detail"[139] by way of precaution. Lisbeth had no opportunity to counterbrief the Gelzers, as she found other friends of Nietzsche's visiting them— *Hofrat* and *Hofrätin* Heinze of Leipzig. When Lou arrived, Lisbeth took her directly to the bedroom to arrange herself. There, as Lisbeth later related to Mrs. Gelzer, "Lou burst forth with a flood of invective against my brother: 'he's a madman who doesn't know what he wants, he's a common egoist who wanted only to exploit her mental gifts, she doesn't care a hoot for him but if now they didn't go to a city together it would mean she weren't "great," that's why Fritz doesn't want to study with her—so as to shame her. What's more, Fritz would be crazy to think she should sacrifice herself to his aims or that they had the same aims at all, she knew nothing of his aims. Besides, were they to pursue any aims together, two weeks wouldn't go by before they were sleeping together, men all wanted only that, pooh to mental friendship! and she knew first-hand what she was talking about, she had been caught *twice* already in that kind of relationship.' As I, now naturally beside myself, said that might well be the case with her Russians only she didn't know my pure-minded brother, she retorted full of scorn (word for word): 'Who first soiled our study plan with his low designs, who started up with mental friendship when he couldn't get me for something else, who first thought of concubinage—your brother!' And just as she was repeating in the most malicious tone of voice, 'Yes indeed your noble pure-minded brother first had the dirty design of a concubinage!' in you came . . ."[140] As Lou composed herself, Lisbeth got in "a few minutes alone" with Mrs. Gelzer "to explain everything as innocuously and

***

[d] This is the whole last page of Nietzsche's letter except for the close of a sentence on how hard it is to be a friend; the rest, destroyed, must have included directions for meeting Lisbeth in Jena.

ideally as I possibly could from Fritz's standpoint."[141] Lisbeth was, however, "utterly out of my element: never in my life had I heard such indecent talk (here I have reproduced it all with propriety at that). And a twenty[-one]-year-old girl was saying these things, especially about men generally and my brother in particular, and when on top of it all *she* had proposed *their living together*!! What is one to think of such a girl?! In the evening, when we were in Tautenburg and Fritz was out looking for a place for us to stay, she broke out again in a fury against Fritz and became downright grossly indecent, as when she said full of derision: 'just don't go thinking that I care beans for your brother or am in love with him, I could sleep in the same room with him without getting worked up.' Would you believe it possible? I too was altogether beside myself and shouted at her repeatedly: 'Stop this indecent talk!' 'Pooh,' she said, 'with Rée I talk a lot more indecently.' She had also told me Rée had told her that Fritz was thinking of a concubinage. So now I told her: All right, I would ask his mother, whereupon she was furious and threatened to get back at me, and she did. I was utterly miserable and didn't sleep a wink. . . . Oh what a martyrdom for my sensibility the whole story was! . . . The moment she believed she could draw no further advantage from his fame she fell upon him like a wild animal and tore his good name and reputation to bits and trampled on them. . . . The girl is not out to marry Fritz, she just wants to become famous through him. She wants to marry only a rich man because she needs lots of money and has none."[142] Again Lisbeth's account was in substance unquestionably faithful throughout.[e] It depicted a veritable hysterical outburst on Lou's part modulated by an impish impulse to make Lisbeth squirm in her straight laces. Lisbeth was indeed shocked—for life.

Lisbeth spent her sleepless night with Lou at a clergyman's,[f] Nietzsche his alone in his once idyllic peasant's hut. Lisbeth told him the sorry story in the morning—though "naturally I couldn't tell it to

[e] The tirade as reported accords grotesquely, yet only too neatly, with Nietzsche's prior letters to Lou, which Lisbeth cannot have read (cf. above, p. 74 n. *a*), and with Nietzsche's prankish, irrelevant typewritten letter to Rée from Genoa, which Rée had evidently put to insidious use. In after years Lou herself, even while officially scouting the whole vulgar incident, represented the contents of her tirade equivalently in diverse contexts; as to its form, in old age she projected the hysteria onto Lisbeth by having her vomit in shock (*Lou, in Pfeiffer, *Leben*, 313-14)—a meet conversion, as Lisbeth's own felicitous verb for Lou's two outbursts was "*ausbrechen*," which also means "vomit."

[f] His name was Stölten.

him the indecent way it was."[143] Even so, Nietzsche was aghast: among other things, the Gelzers were returning to Basel that very day, and a scandal there would threaten his tiny market as well as his pension. He had it out with Lou a first time "violently,"[g] with the result that she was asked to leave the next day—as Lisbeth hastily apprised the Gelzers. "But," Lisbeth afterwards related, "she did not *want* to leave, and made me take pity on her,"[144] until "through my foolish pity Fritz was moved to let her stay on a few days."[145] Lou explained about her reluctant host in her diary: "I *knew* that if we got together, which in the storm of emotions we at first both avoided doing, we would soon enough find each other over and beyond all petty prattle, given our deeply kindred natures."[146/h] "*One*" day of quarreling without Lisbeth and already Nietzsche was wavering.[i] "Then," as Lisbeth had it, "she pretended to be ill"[147]—or as Lou had it, she was laid up a few days with "my old coughing fever."[148] Nietzsche sent messages to her in bed, wherewith by August 13 she was well enough to spend the whole day with him—despite Lisbeth.

Nietzsche next sought to bring Lisbeth round to Lou: Voltaire was a rascal too, he told her. And Lou sought to placate her. In Lisbeth's paraphrase: " 'Heavens, she had never imagined I still had such retarded views, so what if he had intended concubinage? That would be nothing degrading surely, they were above conventionality so it couldn't degrade Fritz and she hadn't meant it to.' Then she made Fritz believe Rée had told her that about him only so as to benefit from it *himself* should she consent and so it went and Fritz swallowed it all and with her made fun of his family and me."[149] But not of Rée: Lou recorded that he laughed goodheartedly at the sight of an ivy-framed picture of Rée on her desk.[150]

Nor did Lou for an instant relinquish her notion of Nietzsche's amorous designs on her, even if she did half in earnest construe

---

[g] MVM→Lou, 18 VIII [1882]: "Why these discussions came off so violently I do not quite understand; maybe you will explain to me why once again."

[h] "Got together" renders "*verkehren würden,*" which is literally "were to have intercourse" and carries the same connotation. Lou meant that "*knew,*" for from the thick of the quarrel she wrote Rée of returning to Stibbe from Tautenburg *in September* (as emerges from one of his letters to her). On the other hand, she may then have hinted to Malwida about possibly marrying Rée (MVM→Lou, 18 VIII [1882]: "If you do not marry [Rée] . . .").

[i] D 14 VIII [1882]: "After *one* day [her fourth or fifth in Tautenburg] together in which I strove to be free, natural, and cheerful . . . he came back here again and again and in the evening took my hand and kissed it twice and began to say something that would not come out"—an account rendered, however, in the mood of the week after.

Rée's alike.[j] Rée must unsuspectingly have caught the sense of her report on "our first fight here, upon my arrival,"[k] for he commented: "Remarkably enough, Nietzsche seems to have regarded you as his fiancée as soon as you agreed to come to Tautenburg." Rée, then heading for Helgoland to wait on Lou's pleasure, did his best to sustain the lovers' quarrel by mail. He took it out especially on Nietzsche's shift of philosophical course.[l] By mid-August, however, he was reduced to taking it out on his own jealousy.[m] For through a diary installment Lou told him about having spent a radiant August 14 with Nietzsche away from Lisbeth "in the quiet, dark pine forest alone with the sunshine and squirrels," adding: "Conversing with Nietzsche is uncommonly lovely . . . but there is quite special charm in the meeting of like thoughts and like emotions; we can almost communicate with half words. . . . Only because we are so kindred could he take the difference between us, or what seemed to him such, so violently and painfully. . . . The content of a conversation of ours really consists in what is not quite spoken but emerges of its own from our tacit exchanges.[n] . . . He gave me his hand and said earnestly and with feeling: 'Never forget that it would be a calamity if you did not carve a memorial to your full innermost mind in the time left to you.' . . . But is it good for him to spend the whole day from morning to night in conversation with me, hence away from his work? When I asked him this today, he nodded and replied: 'But I do it so seldom and am enjoying it like a child.' The same evening, though, he said: 'I ought not to live long in your vicinity.' We often recollect our time together in Italy and . . .[o] he said softly: '*monte sacro*—I have you

[j] Rée invited such reconstrual by writing about then of a dress she mailed to Stibbe: "Had I not been embarrassed before myself I would have embraced the pretty waist—a pretty story!"

[k] D 14 VIII [1882]—a back reference. (Her earlier diary entries for Tautenburg, mailed to Rée at the time, were subsequently destroyed by her—and the rest purged.)

[l] "What will become of him? He cannot again devote so much enthusiasm and energy to a cause. A second love is no love. And will anything come of this one? Besides, there is subtle charm to the fact that one often does not clearly understand what he is saying and so supposes more behind it than is there. Snailie will laugh and say pure envy is speaking out of me. Perhaps—"

[m] "And I'm somewhat jealous too meanwhile, naturally—understandably. . . . Just you wait, Snailie. . . . Now that you're friends again with Nietzsche, enough! *More* you don't need, do you hear, Snailie?" Rée's mother for her part wrote on 21 VIII 1882 urging Lou to "bring extraordinary counsel from the professor [presumably concerning the winter plan], which we will then follow most exactly."

[n] Literally, "from our each approaching the other half way" ("*aus dem halben Entgegenkommen eines Jeden von uns*").

[o] Here Lou later obliterated several words, the tenor of which can be in-

to thank for the most bewitching dream of my life.' " Lou came close to perceiving a sorry truth: in nothing was she so akin to Nietzsche as in her passion for half-spoken words that denied as well as implied their unspoken half.

Nietzsche declared to Gast that same August 14: "I have an eye of my own for people; what I see exists *even* if others do not see it." The amour was on again, though again neither quite knew it.

---

ferred from Rée's outcry: "What didn't you connect up with the remarks on the *monte sacro* in the way of attitude, intonation, movement, looks!"

$\mathcal{T}$ A L K   H A D   set them asunder; talk brought them back together. Morning, noon, and night the two talked—in the pine forest,
on an inn terrace beneath lindens, along precipitous chamois paths,
in her room and in his. They talked of unholy things—of squeamish-
ness about suffering as inhibited delight in it ("we did not dare look
at each other afterwards"[151]) and, over a cognac ("Ah, how foul it
tasted!" he exclaimed[152]), of his potential for madness. More academically, he argued the original ascendancy of the "herd instinct"
over Rée's constant: egoism.[153]

Yet religion was, he later remarked, "really our sole topic."[154] They
discussed how each had relinquished his childhood faith—he all at
once and effortlessly, she with a painful struggle of mind against
heart.[p] He "discovered" her singular insight into "religious affects,"[155]
therewith adding religious psychology to her perennial curriculum,
on top of Gillot's natural history of religions and Biedermann's self-
elaboration of the idea of God. He broached some inchoate ideas of
his own on her new subject: piety as lame will to power, penitence as
the wages of impotence, salvation and damnation as weaklings'
dreams of getting overeven. They did not excite her[q]; rather Nietzsche
himself did, as an object lesson in religious genius at work—as Biedermann's "man" the god-maker in person. Together they laid plans
for his son Zarathustra.[r] "We shall yet see him the prophet of a new
religion," she noted.[156] He called their talks his "most profitable"
occupation of that summer.[157] "She is the *most intelligent of all
women*," he told Gast, adding: "Every five days we have a little
tragic scene."[158] And he told Overbeck in turn: "Our mentalities and
tastes are most deeply akin—and yet there are so many contrasts too
that we are for each other the most instructive of subjects. . . . I
should like to know whether there has ever before been such philosophical openness as between the two of us."[159] She noted correspondingly: "How alike we think and feel! . . . and how we do take

[p] D 21 VIII [1882]: "Nietzsche threw religion overboard when his heart felt
nothing more for it and, empty and weary, longed for a new all-inspiring
goal. Disbelief struck my heart lightninglike—or rather my reason, which then
compelled my heart to give up the faith to which it clung with childlike ardor."
   [q] At all odds she never adverted to them thereafter.
   [r] See Ida O, in Bernoulli, *FO und FN*, I, 338, on Lou's "direct share" in the
making of *Zarathustra*.

the thoughts and words out of each other's mouth!"[160/s] They had some new thoughts together too—which were to possess them both ever afterwards. Lisbeth complained: "To be sure, she excites him, but now he says that she inspired him and that he has her to thank for it if he has good ideas."[161] Lou remarked further: "Odd—how in our talks, without meaning to, we always wind up on the precipice; anyone listening to us would think two devils were conferring."[162] Lisbeth must have eavesdropped: "What horrid talk the two carried on together! What was a lie? Nothing! What was breach of confidence? Nothing! What was doing one's duty? Silliness. What was the most derisive talk about true friends? Right judgment. What was compassion? Contemptible. *Never* have I seen my brother together with his philosophy so mean, so paltry."[163]

Nietzsche found Lou's prose sorely wanting yet readily corrigible.[t] He set down ten compelling pointers for her on writing as perfected speaking. He also redid a few pages of her essay on woman—to uncompelling effect. After due discussion, he outlined for her a larger essay to include the additional items: "what woman conceals from herself about reality," "wherein she feels the need to affirm what she recognizes to be unreal as nonetheless true," "to what extent women treat men like children," and "pregnancy as the cardinal state which gradually, over the centuries, fixed the nature of woman." Only when Lou called woman's very frailty woman's greatness because of its religious signification did Nietzsche dissent. Otherwise he was as ready to see woman's fulfillment in her self-subordination as was Lou to see woman's vocation as biological—and this even though in his view as in hers, Lou was herself every bit woman despite her virile self-will and her mind so like his own. Rée meanwhile urged Lou to try her hand at pithy sentences in the manner of La Bruyère. She drew eight such from her talks with Nietzsche (about woman's "frightful expectations concerning sexual love," about heroism as "amenability to utter self-ruination," and the like); two escaped his rewriting.[u] She labored her diary for his scrutiny too. "I have excessive confidence in his power as teacher," she entered on August 14. By August 18, however, he has "given up on being my teacher; he says I should never have such a prop"—which on their terms meant never be a woman.

Nietzsche's encouragements, his pointers, his corrections—nothing so intensified Lou's will to authorship as his surpassing example.

---

[s] A recurrent motif of her Tautenburg diary.

[t] D 14 VIII [1882]: he said she could learn to write in *"one day."*

[u] Only the six rewrites survive (with numbered blanks for the two lucky ones).

She resolved on Nietzsche as author, in lieu of woman as such, as the subject of her first full-scale study. Even before realizing what she was about, she was devotedly taking notes on Nietzsche—juxtaposed with herself. He cleared the topic, and on August 18 she remarked: "How happy I am to have a recognized and definite piece of work before me." She had caught him at the ideal moment: in transition— or, as he preferred, transcendence. After six years of impassioned positivistic self-restraint, he was about to burst into didactics and song. With his help, she found that he would set himself a new philosophic purpose in order to deliver himself from the pain of instinctual discord whenever an old one lost its grip on him, and that he would face up to each new purpose as to "something cut off from himself and to be endured by him"—whereas she would struggle painfully toward her one (unspecified) goal[v] felt to be an innermost necessity.[164] Unlike self-critical Rée, Nietzsche tended to see himself "as he would like to appear before his god of knowledge," she maintained[165]—this time after having pronounced herself at one with him as against Rée.[166] She called Nietzsche admiratively "the egoist in the grand manner,"[167] yet saw his character as unified about its "heroic trait": the "drive toward self-sacrifice to a great end."[168] Yet again, three days later this heroism no longer lay in his bearing the pain of life for the sake of knowledge—"for then this goal of knowledge would need to have moral value"—but instead "in that power which voluntarily takes the pain of living upon itself because it ever newly feels within itself the creative strength to turn the pain into a means to an end in which it feels itself borne beyond pain . . . in that creative power for which even the hardest, toughest materials are not too hard or tough, because it is *nevertheless superior* to them, nevertheless capable of chiseling its god-figures out of them."[w] Anyhow, whatever his aims Nietzsche commanded "reverence" for his "*greatness of power*."[169]

So ended Lou's Tautenburg diary. From merely romanticizing his every sign of fondness for her, she had gone on to divinize Nietzsche in her own likeness.[x] She stood toward him then almost as she had toward her schoolmasterly god Gillot three years before[y]: as much

[v] There is some suggestion that this might be knowledge; logically, though, it cannot be, as Nietzsche supposedly changed goals without ceasing to serve his god of knowledge.

[w] Even this rhetoric yields a contradiction with the prior comment in this same passage about how pain was ever the "cause" of Nietzsche's pursuing new aims as against his "means" of attaining them: see below, p. 159.

[x] That last diary piece applies primarily to her own self-version: she had already identified herself with Nietzsche to that extent.

[y] Appropriately, on 16 VIII 1882 she went from a diary entry on Nietzsche's

in love, only this time unwillingly—the same worshipful free disciple tempted to go unfree, only this time as wary of the temptation itself as of its erotic undercurrent, hence the readier to project the erotism and demonize her idol. Her intellectual resistance was to turn on the difference she asserted between his shifting purposes and her single, steady purpose. She for her part was to stand by the positivism in which his own *Flush of Dawn* had confirmed her. In her diary finale she wrote "we freethinkers" for the whole Trinity, although she well knew that he for his part had just done with "freethinkery."[z] Meanwhile, in asserting her kinship with him as she did—more fancifully by the day—she was preparing her flight from "reverence" before him to unconscious identification with him.[a] "Strange," she noted on August 18, "the notion recently struck me with sudden force that we could someday even confront each other *as enemies.*"

With Lisbeth, matters were less conditional. "My sister has developed into a mortal enemy of Lou's," Nietzsche told Overbeck after Lou's visit; "she was full of moral indignation from start to finish."[170] Lisbeth claimed to have taken pains to surmount her "aversion" for Lou formed in Jena: "often I succeeded, but oh! toward the end of her stay Fritz so came under her yoke, began to lie and to deride his *best* friends, and was so mean and abject that I grew deeply unhappy. As far as I am concerned Lou may be however she likes, but then she ruined Fritz. . . . You can imagine with what zeal the Russian girl took up his philosophy: for her it was the finery in which her evil egoistic and immoral nature looked most passable. . . . How adroitly she now so to say uses Fritz's maxims to tie his hands is remarkably clever, but I despise her for this cleverness. . . . She is really, I cannot deny it, my brother's philosophy *personified*: that raging egoism which knocks down anything in its way and that utter want of morality." Worst of all: in the end "I had to face it, Fritz has changed, he *is* just like his books."[171/b] Fritz's infatuation was quite as Lisbeth

---

leaving her "*smilingly*" to resume his work to one on her "lonely days of struggle" under Gillot, only to wonder: "Housie, why am I telling you only the old story of the picture with the ivy tendrils?" (These fragments of the two entries alone survive.)

[z] Even before Tautenburg: see FN→Lou [3? VII 1882] and [9 VII 1882]. By "freethinkers" ("*Freidenker*") Lou consciously meant no more than "unbelievers," whereas Nietzsche's "freethinkery" ("*Freigeisterei*") went much farther—but her positivism versus his religiosity *was* her point of resistance, so "*wir Freidenker*" was appropriately inept.

[a] Cf. D 31 X 1888: had she ever met a second Gillot she "would have fled him."

[b] Cf. FN→O, 22 VIII 1882: "[*The Gay Science*] is in every respect counter

mockingly made out: "Whoever is not ravished by this Russian 'has no eye for greatness' or 'is jealous.' "[172] However, he was not *simply* infatuated. "Everything I have written you about her is nonsense," he cautioned Gast, "this probably included."[173] And to Lou he sent a message on her next-to-last day: "To bed. Most violent attack. I despise life. F.N."

Nietzsche took Lou to her train in nearby Dornburg at midday on August 26. Between them they had agreed—at his suggestion[c] (and to Malwida's contentment[d])—to change Munich to Paris in the trinitarian study plan, now set to take effect in October. Apparently Lou did not then visit Stein as had been planned in Bayreuth, but instead went directly to Berlin, and from there with Rée to Stibbe the next day. That same day Nietzsche went home to his mother in Naumburg, leaving his sister behind in Tautenburg. He subsequently assured Lou that after her departure he had spoken with Lisbeth "only a little, yet enough to send the new specter back into the nothingness whence it emerged."[174] At least Lisbeth knew better: "When Lou was gone," she averred, "I asked Fritz to leave without me, I told him I would be so aggrieved on his account and didn't want Mama to see my grief and tear-stained eyes, he need but tell Mama everything first."[175]

Whatever he told Mama, Nietzsche wrote to an acquaintance in Paris, Louise Ott, asking about a room there for him alone: "It would have to be a deathly quiet, very simple one. And not too far from you, my dear Mrs. Ott." Then in the last days of August, as he notified Lou, "the demon of music came upon me again; I have set your 'Life Prayer' to music."[176] More exactly, he turned the first stanza into a song for tenor by adapting it to a score composed by him at sixteen.[e] Some days later, in false hopes of a big choral performance,

---

to German taste and our times, and I myself am even more so. My every contact with people since leaving Genoa has taught me this."

[c] FN→Gast, 14 VIII 1882: he and Lou "meet again in the fall (in Munich?)"; FN→Gast, 16 IX 1882: "Paris . . . my suggestion."

[d] MvM→Lou, 23 VIII [1882]: "The Paris plan pleases me *much* for all three of you. The climate is decidedly better than in Vienna or Munich, life is more many-sided and *freer*, and there I can really *help* you" (socially). Malwida was due in Paris herself.

[e] Schlechta, *Mittag*, 12-14: he composed the score in 1861 and reworked it for piano on 24 IV 1873. Krug, 789, and Hofmiller, "N," 108: he turned it into a "Hymn to Friendship" for a friend's wedding in 1874. On 1 IX 1882 he sent Gast Lou's first stanza scored as a song for tenor. Gast→Hofmiller, 12 XII 1894: musically he left it at that. Although he had sent Gast Lou's poem on 1 VII 1882 (as noted by Gast on this copy), he wrote Overbeck on [14?] IX

he wheedled Lou: "That would be, then, one small path by which
the two of us would reach posterity *together*—other paths remaining
open."*ƒ*

His sister meanwhile refused to return to Naumburg as long as he
would be there.[177] "She now claims to know what's what with my philosophy," he told Overbeck. "She wrote my mother that she 'saw my
philosophy come alive in Tautenburg and took fright.' She says that
I love evil but she loves good, and that were she a Catholic she would
enter a convent to do penance for all the mischief bound to ensue."[178]/*g* He tried to coax her down from her high horse: "I hear with
distress [from Mama] that you are still suffering from the aftereffects
of those scenes which I would heartily have wished to spare you. But
just bear in mind: what came to light in the flare-up might otherwise
have long remained in the dark, which is that Lou had a *lower opinion* of me and *some distrust* toward me; and, considering the circumstances under which we became acquainted, perhaps she had a good
right to both (counting the effect of some careless remarks by friend
Rée).*h* But now she quite certainly thinks *better* of me—and that's
the main thing, isn't it, my dear sister? In view of the future, moreover, it would be hard for me to have to assume that you did not feel
as I do about Lou. Our aptitudes and views are so similar that our
names cannot fail to be linked at some time or other, and every defamation directed against her will strike me first. . . . Two things my
philosophy forbids me unconditionally: 1. regret, 2. moral indignation. Do be sweet again, dear Llama!"[179] Llama stayed sour, and
Nietzsche shortly reported to Overbeck: "I have the Naumburg virtue against me, there is a real break between us—and even my mother
so forgot herself with one remark that I packed my things and
left for Leipzig in the morning."[180]/*i* He was to specify thereafter:
"My mother called me a disgrace to my father's grave."[181]/*j* From

---

1882: "She left me a gripping poem, 'Gebet an das Leben,' behind," and
Lisbeth was often to relate that Lou had produced the poem in Tautenburg,
causing her and her brother to weep with emotion.

ƒ FN→Lou [16? IX 1882]. FN→Lou [26? IX 1882]: he had altered the text
(*further*—but this time only slightly) to meet choral requirements, and he
appealed for a title other than " 'Lebensgebet'—an impossible word!"

g Lisbeth forgot that she had repudiated Nietzsche's philosophy before
Nietzsche knew Lou (above, p. 57 and n. 90); the novelty was her repudiating
him along with it.

h This obviously refers to Rée's use of the Genoa letter: (cf. above, p. 77
n. *e*).

i He left on or about 8 IX 1882.

j According to Lisbeth→CG, 24 IX/2 X 1882: "[Mama] finally says one day,
'Why doesn't Lizzie come home or write? I'm sure the poor child is fretting

Tautenburg his sister quoted *The Gay Science* to him: " 'Thus began Zarathustra's descent.' In fact," he assured Overbeck, "it is the *beginning* of the *start*."[182]

Nietzsche meanwhile sent Lou "the old deep heartfelt request: *become yourself*! One must break free of one's chains to begin with, but of this *breaking free* itself in the end!" He signed off: "In you too I love *my hopes*."[183] At the same time he resumed his correspondence with Rée by vindicating Rée for having let it lapse on Lou's account: "There is no *writing* about Lou," he owned. ". . . Let us see whether we can ever bring it to *speaking* about her!—I have behaved in this whole affair as befits *my private morality*; and, as I do not hold others to this, I have no call at all today for praise or blame—a further reason to write no letters." And far more darkly: "Is *The Gay Science* in your hands, the most *personal* of all my books? Considering that everything very *personal* is really wholly *comical*, I am in fact expecting a 'gay' effect. Read 'Sanctus Januarius' once in context! There stands my entire private morality as the sum of *my* requirements for existence: they prescribe only an *ought*, in case I do not *want* to *myself*."[184] Lou at all odds read "Sanctus Januarius"—and blithely took the passage exhorting an estranged friend to be one with candor and good grace for a message to Rée.[k]

Rée looked just a bit contemptible to Lou after Tautenburg—and felt rather more so. On a note of apology, he promised Nietzsche a frank talk in Leipzig.[185] Under the same cover he announced that Lou had won him over to Nietzsche's view that egoism had been celebrated before coming to be reviled[l]: he was back at playing second fiddle, only now under Lou's baton. "Decidedly," he remarked, "Lou grew a few inches taller in Tautenburg."[186] Lou on her side reported herself "all buried in books and works"[187] now that Tauten-

---

over this person who has been hanging onto your coattails.' Thereupon Fritz declares he will leave and never forgive Mama this remark. He rode to Leipzig . . ." That may be what Franziska Nietzsche told her daughter she had said—but the "or write" is a patent misstatement.

[k] FN, *Science*, 279 ("stellar friendship": our earthly ways have parted, but let us trust that, though we may yet become earthly enemies, our celestial orbits will cross again sometime); 1890a:142n. Nietzsche unquestionably had Wagner on his mind when penning this passage (though Hofmiller, "N," 111, without dissenting, located the germ of it in FN→o, 14 xi 1881)—but Rée may have already been at the back of his mind then and certainly was in ix 1882.

[l] FN→Lisbeth [6?] ix 1882: "She has converted Rée to one of my main ideas, which *altogether* alters the fundament of his book." According to Rée, *Entstehung*, 23: the oldest signification of "good" was distinguished, powerful, rich, and of "bad" lowly, weak, poor: this was Rée's one new Nietzschean thesis since his *Ursprung*.

burg had given her "a goal."[188] Nietzsche answered her from Leipzig with no hint of his family feud: "It now looks to me as if my *return* 'to men' were to result in my *losing* the few I still in any sense possessed."[189] With that, Rée was ready to crawl contritely out of the Trinity. On September 11 Lou berated him for slovenliness, and the next day he pleaded irremediably guilty in a farewell note concluding: "So—let us go our separate ways to our graves."[m] But Lou's separate way would have led straight back to Petersburg. "No," she subjoined to his note, "certainly not! Let us live and strive together until you have *revoked* this!" Next Rée received from Leipzig a handsome photo of Nietzsche with a letter to match: "My dear friend, it is my opinion that the two and the three of us are wise enough to be and stay good to one another. In this life, in which people like *us* so easily turn into frightening phantoms, let us be pleased and *pleasant with one another*, and be inventive in this—I for my part have much to catch up on here, lone monster that I was." And he told of his sister's new-found loathing for him without citing its cause beyond a greeting for "our dear Lou, *my* sister (as I have lost my natural sister, a preternatural one is due me)."[190] Rée thereupon returned to the fold. "My dear, dear friend!" he replied. ". . . Just now and for all time *nothing* can part us, as we are bound in a third party to whom we bow down—not unlike medieval knights, only with better cause."[191] And to Lou he sent a writ of retraction. "This much I know," it read in part: "you were for me the greatest loss *that I ever in my life* suffered or can suffer. That is just why I, a pessimist, believe you will not long remain with me." That part Lou annotated: "Now you are *mine*."[n]

Rée's access of self-contempt had turned his philosophy inside out before Lou's eyes. All at once she saw that in calling men worthless egoists he was boosting as well as blasting his own ego, and that in explaining away morals and conscience he was parrying his own morbid self-reproaches—as against Nietzsche, whose value-creating, a counterpart to his personal dignity, was his way of filling his dead god's place. Hot from her moment of truth, she wrote Nietzsche suggesting "the reduction of philosophical systems to personal dossiers on their authors."[192/o] It took genius to suggest such reduction; it took

[m] Note misdated 12 VIII by Lou—in memory of her Tautenburg quarrels.

[n] She pasted the page of Rée's writ bearing this old annotation into her 1900-1903 diary, presumably just after his death.

[o] Lou conceivably took her cue from Spinoza: "We neither strive for, wish, seek, nor desire anything because we think it to be good, but, on the contrary, we adjudge a thing to be good because we strive for, wish, seek, or desire it" (*Ethics*, III:9, translated by H. Hale White).

Nietzsche to perform it—in due course. For a start, he hailed the suggestion as "truly a thought from the 'sister brain' " but mistook it to mean giving the authors of superseded philosophies their just due.[193]

At Stibbe all September Lou lived for Nietzsche. She read his fresh, racy *Human, All Too Human*, which became her lifelong favorite. She drafted a sketch of his character, which he *pre*judged "true, as you say," and apposite to his poetical plea in *The Gay Science* for a closer look at himself than just a friend's.[194/p] And she filled half a notebook with aphorisms mostly based on their Tautenburg talks. She invited Rée's contributions—but not his corrections. Indeed, Rée had penned the first entry: "Every joy dies of itself"—and she the second: "Every joy survives itself." By late September her eyes were as sore as they had been some three years before, but this time from overwork for Nietzsche—and from imitation of him.[195/q] Myopic, Nietzsche prescribed swimming in a Leipzig ladies' pool.[196]

"Latest news: Lou comes here October 2," Nietzsche informed Gast on September 16, with no thought for Rée; "we leave a few weeks later—for Paris, and stay there, maybe years." While awaiting Lou, he took up with some old friends, mostly musical and philosophical, the former to promote an opera by Gast, yet all to oblige Lou—and perhaps also to disoblige his mother and especially his sister, who fretted: "Now he wrote that he wants to take his revenge on us (!) and have Lou come to Leipzig and go visiting with her. . . . Lou forever boasted of her evil nature (evil being a greater source of strength than good), so now poor Fritz is making himself as evil as possible."[197] Left behind in Tautenburg, Lisbeth sat sulking for a whole month "in the greatest solitude." As she explained: "I have lost my ideal and cannot console myself." Thereupon "Mama came to Tautenburg and found me consumed with woe, my eyes inflamed from so much crying. . . . Naturally I told Mama everything and wrote Fritz also I would now tell the pure truth about Lou whenever the subject arose. . . . I said farewell to Fritz for as long as he stands under the Russian girl's influence."[198] Back in Naumburg, Lisbeth sent off fourteen big pages of "pure truth about Lou" to Clara Gelzer on October 2. Clara having already told the Overbecks about Jena, Lisbeth now implored her to tell them *all* about it—or preferably

---

p That he was not *judging* Lou's draft characterization (*"Ihre 'Charakteristik meiner Selbst,' welche wahr ist, wie Sie schreiben"*), first shown to him in x 1882: see 1890a:4. His poetic plea (titled "Bitte") is the twenty-fifth in the prologue to FN, *Science*.

q Further imitating Nietzsche, she adopted his splendid capital N after trying handwriting variants on the front and back of her aphorism notebook.

read them all about it.[r] For the rest: "*Please* for heaven's sake tell no one anything." This was half in earnest: Lisbeth did wish to spare her brother a scandal in Basel—and while she was at it, to win the Overbecks' help in bringing him back to himself, meaning herself, even though "Oh! the Overbecks to be sure can do nothing either!"[199] But she also wanted revenge on Lou for the Jena calumny—or on Nietzsche in case it was no calumny. Here she compromised at first by repaying Lou in kind within Nietzsche's inner circle. Nietzsche was the angrier with her since at heart he felt quite as she did about Jena—except that he wished it could be undone, while she was intent on keeping it actual. His estrangement from Naumburg only swelled his grudge against Lou. The first surface effect was the opposite, however: a sense of release, even rebirth. "All lies new before me," he exulted to Overbeck.[200]

Lou arrived in Leipzig on schedule and set up with Rée in adjacent rooms. The first night Nietzsche took the newcomers to a séance, having prepared to expose it to Lou as fakery; it exposed itself.[201] Five busy weeks about town followed. Georg Rée joined the party at one point. Romundt, due to leave Leipzig, stayed specially to meet Lou—and then on and on. Gast came before long and duly deemed Lou "heroic" and "a genius" upon their first meeting—yet politely declined a second.[202] Stein, summoned by Lou "in the name of our Trinity,"[203] showed up one day only to find no one home; a note of regret from Nietzsche started the two corresponding.

Between times, Lou was again Nietzsche's self-willed schoolgirl. They discussed her plans for a study of religious history[204] as well as her draft sketch of his life and works.[s] The Trinity viewed *Nathan the Wise*, whereupon she composed for him her first piece of theatrical criticism. It anticipated her later mastery of the genre to the limited extent of her predilection for staged ideas. She quarreled with Lessing for having made his Jewish sage as "*pedagogical*" as himself: Nathan, for all his wisdom, gave the truth only its "*aptest*" and not its "*highest*" expression, she complained. And she judged that those characters came off best who could "dispense with pathos."

But Nietzsche troubled most about Lou's aphorisms, by then a Nietzsche-style opus in preparation. He struck out some and queried others; he rewrote sparingly but tellingly for brevity and point; he picked his favorites, arranging and rearranging them under diverse

---

[r] Lisbeth professed a by-motive too: "I know in advance Lou will cause trouble, now at least it should not be said she was spoiled by Fritz's philosophy. So I mean to relate how she *already* spoke and acted."

[s] 1890a:4—which also, however, falsely implies that Nietzsche approved the first and most middle portions of 1890a.

heads. He even contributed a few, and Lou in turn added some more. In his marginalia he named himself "Nico" and Lou "Märchen" ("Story"). And perhaps she took their sessions over her notebook for story hours with Saint Nick, for she never applied his literary lessons. Nor did she follow his Tautenburg advice and learn for herself; for years to come she remained as loyal to the manner of her copy as to the matter. Characteristically she wrote of metaphysics that "it divinizes our deficiencies of understanding as religion does our deficiencies of power." Nico commented: "Obscure." The line could fit right into a work by her dated thirty years later,[t] obscurity and all. In another sentence she spelled out the spirit of the optimism professed by her ever after: "The optimistic nature finds joy in the very feeling for life; the pessimistic nature finds a feeling for life only in joy." Nietzsche cut this one down to size: "Some get a feeling for life only from joy, others get joy from a feeling for life."[u] More felicitous all around was her allegation that "what does not engage our feelings does not long engage our thoughts either," which Nietzsche could not vivify[v]; she recurred to it in so many words twenty years after.[w]

But Lou's aphorisms registered her momentary even more than her abiding preoccupations.[x] They diagnosed each member of the Trinity in turn: "woman does not die of love, but wastes away for want of it," "the greatest pain is self-hate," and "Nietsche's [sic] weakness: supersubtlety." As for the Trinity itself: "Two friends are most easily separated by a third." With a view to Rée she remarked: "Friendship between the sexes is a noble artificial plant, but one that requires gardening talent." With Rée still in view she adopted Nietzsche's aphorism: "A woman may well enough form a friendship with a man, but to sustain it she needs the help of a little physical antipathy"[205/v]—adding "or great mental sympathy" to accommodate Nietzsche. She fast qualified this, however, when discussing love. "The closer two people stand to each other inwardly," she affirmed, "the more readily they become for each other the condition under which alone their two beings find expression." Again, if what sounds

---

[t] 1909a.

[u] Nietzsche's German even eliminated Lou's ugly "*Lebensgefühl,*" as my English does not: "*Dieser empfindet das Leben erst im Glück und jener das Glück schon im Leben.*"

[v] His try: "What neither pleases nor pains us gets little welcome in our heads."

[w] 1899a:234.

[x] And this no doubt still more in the many pages subsequently torn out and destroyed (thick with marginalia by Nietzsche, as the remaining edges show).

[y] That she meant Rée: 1931a:257. That she could not have meant Nietzsche: above, pp. 52-53.

in one person's breast resounds in another's, this is either the cause or the result of their falling in love, and when two people "forget themselves in a common interest," they are like lovers forgetting themselves in a common desire. Such a "great, life-filling common interest" alone preserves affection in the long run. By the same token, "one must love, as the Christians said, 'in God.'" Love on high is heady, though: "No path leads from sensual passion to mental sympathy, but one does lead the other way." Worse, "mental closeness between two people calls for physical expression, but the physical expression devours the mental closeness." Accordingly, "*all* love is designed for tragedy."

Nietzsche's annotations were in some cases revealing beyond his intent, as when he affixed two questions marks to "Greatness lies not in purpose, but in strength of purpose," which pertained to him,[206] or when he termed "unmarried living together" an "impossible expression." In other cases his intent was to reveal Lou's own unsuspected meaning. Beside "Sentimentality is not feeling too much, but valuing feeling" he specified: "On Nico." Concerning how someday the "'great thought'" will betray the "'little thinker,'" he noted quizzically: "At the Jena catastrophe."[z] And he boiled down a big one to "Friendship rests on knowledge, love on faith," then densely designated it "Märchen's love-recognition at Nico-end."[a] No doubt such comments annoyed Lou, who had been ill aware of her immediate subject. To top them off, Nietzsche inscribed on her notebook cover: "Sister—brother. Father—child." Seen from her angle, these were the two short legs of the triangle into which the Trinity had long since turned.

In Leipzig, the three-way tensions mounted beneath the surface. In the first place, Nietzsche was under the weather. To Naumburg he reported concerning his birthday: "With the fifteenth of October, winter began,"[207] and to Overbeck at the start of November: "Perhaps I have never endured such melancholic hours as in this Leipzig autumn—even though I have reason enough *about me* to be of good cheer." Gast related that "he mostly came to me *before* going to Lou and Dr. Rée" and that then he "seemed not to be all there," for "the thought of Lou inspired him with great enthusiasm."[208] For all this

---

[z] He also—for whatever reasons—wrote "Jena" beside: "There is more greatness in admiring than in being admired," "The greater the intimacy between two people, the firmer bounds it requires," and "Lack of magnanimity may well be lack of strength. The weakness that seldom knows victory feeds on others' defeats. Magnanimity is the expression of great conquering power."

[a] "*Märchen Liebeserkenntnis am Nicoschluss.*" "Nico-end" designated the last aphorism of the series selected by him, as his numbering indicates.

enthusiasm, however, Jena was preying on his mind increasingly. Perhaps from the Heinzes, whose library he used, he heard that talk was spreading in Basel. He was still stalwartly above blaming Lou; yet day by day he hoped to find her sorry about the outburst, or at least about its outcome. She could hardly have obliged, for she took the break with his family to be good riddance for him, and Jena to be more than ever valid. He did "bring it to *speaking*" with Rée about her misbehavior beginning with Bayreuth; to his harshest charges Rée replied: "You're *perfectly* right, but that changes nothing in my relationship to her."[209] As concerned his own relationship to her, Nietzsche gathered that Rée resented it as an encroachment. By then each realized that their respective claims on Lou were exclusive. And Lou was by then as coarse about Rée as she was sure of him: "In Leipzig she never called him anything but 'slob'—which revolted me," Nietzsche afterwards affirmed.[210] Rée could take worse from her—and *this*, construed broadly, was his advantage in the unavowed rivalry: he was reliable. Perhaps her choice between them was a foregone conclusion; if so, however, she was then still critically far from knowing it.

The emotional disarray that was Lou's in Leipzig is graphic in her piece on Lessing, in which her ordinarily exemplary handwriting was vacillating and gaudy[b] as it was nowhere else outside of her school notebook of seven years earlier. And like her hand, so her whole body. "Lou's health is lamentable," lamented Nietzsche. "I now give her much less time than even last spring."[211] With Rée's assistance, she projected onto Nietzsche—disparagingly—the affectivity disturbing her on Nietzsche's account. Thus a diary page of hers: "Leipzig, October. Just as Christian (like every) mysticism passes into crude religious sensuality right at its highest ecstasy, so can the most ideal love become sensual again in its ideality just because of the great tensing of feeling. An unlikable point, this revenge of the human element—I do not like feelings where they reconverge in their circulation, for that is the point of *false pathos*, at which truth and integrity of feeling are lost. Is this what is estranging me from Nietzsche?" She left a loophole of ambiguity as to whose love was turning sensual—large enough for one of her aphorisms to show through: "The sensual moment is for women the last word in love, for men the first."

Even at that the trouble remained subjacent. As of late September, Rée's mother was expected to set up in Paris for the winter with the

---

[b] This was not true of her last aphorisms, evidently penned by her earlier in x 1882.

Trinity—to Malwida's relief.[212] By mid-October, Lou and Rée were arranging instead to spend "some time" with Mrs. Rée in Berlin[213] and then proceed to Paris without her. Early in November, Lou engaged Nietzsche to petition Petersburg in favor of the Paris sojourn and thus against any use of "*law* and *compulsion*"[214] to repatriate her. About then he inscribed her copy of *Human, All Too Human* with eight waggish, frolicsome, exquisite verses "to my dear Lou":

> Darling—quoth Columbus—never
> Trust another Genoese!
> For he stares offshore forever,
> Drawn beyond all seven seas.
> If he loves, he lures afar
> In space and time too eagerly:
> Above us star shines unto star,
> Around us roars eternity.[c]

Lou tacitly took the inscription for a half invitation, which indeed it was.[d] But it was first and foremost the presage of a new Genoese departure the precondition for which was that it be imagined as a double departure. "The last I saw her," Nietzsche related afterwards, "she told me she had something further to say to me. I was full of hope."[215] On November 5[216] she rode off to Berlin with Rée, leaving that something unsaid. Nietzsche assured Overbeck anyhow: "For me personally, Lou is a real *lucky find*; she has fulfilled all of my ex-

[c]
> *Freundin—sprach Kolumbus—traue*
> *Keinem Genuesen mehr!*
> *Immer starrt er in das Blaue,*
> *Fernstes zieht ihn allzusehr!*
> *Wen er liebt, den lockt er gerne*
> *Weit hinaus in Raum und Zeit—*
> *Über uns glänzt Stern bei Sterne,*
> *Um uns braust die Ewigkeit.*

"Der neue Kolumbus"—as, with a new second stanza, it came to be called—was almost certainly composed in XI 1882, the date of the draft line to Lisbeth quoted below, p. 98, which bears on the back a first version of the Columbus poem's twin, "Nach neuen Meeren" (below, p. 130 n. *v*), under the heading "To L." and with the ending (later replaced) "Courage! steer the ship yourself/ Loveliest Victoria!" ("*Mut! Stehst du doch selbst am Steuer,/ Lieblichste Victoria!*"): Bernoulli, "Erlebnis," 24n., quoting a letter from August Harneffer. The Columbus theme in Nietzsche's poetry goes back to his "Colombo" of 1858 (FN, *HKG:W*, III, 443), one of his many youthful poems about sailing the high seas—but the only actual sailing he ever did was that to and from Sicily in 1882.

[d] Though perhaps it was also a mark of derision, given FN→o [27? VIII 1883]: "Even writing letters to my sister is no longer advisable—except for those of the most innocuous sort (I sent her another letter full of merry verses lately)."

pectations—it would not easily be possible for two people to be more akin than we are." And he told Romundt: "Lou, fully absorbed in religious-historical studies, is a little genius; to look on a little now and then and to help along is a joy to me." He applied to Paris for "a furnished apartment with several rooms,"[217/e] though he also advised Overbeck that "*nothing* is decided yet. . . . Paris is still in the foreground, but . . . I somewhat dread the noise and would like to know whether the sky is *serene* enough."

Then on November 8 he opened hostilities—but with such restraint and regret that there was no telling for sure what he was about. "Dear Lou, five words—my eyes hurt.—I attended to your Petersburg letter. And I wrote your mother two days ago (indeed, at some length).—I also sent off two letters of inquiry to Paris. How melancholic!—Until this year I did not know how very mistrustful I am. Toward myself, I mean. Associating with people has spoiled me for associating with myself.—You had something further to say to me? —I like your voice best when you are requesting. But this is not heard often enough.—I shall be studious—Ah, this melancholy! I am writing nonsense. How *shallow* people are to me today! Where is there a sea left in which one can still really *drown*? I mean a person. My dear Lou, I am your faithful F.N." Lou's retort presumably reached Nietzsche only after her mother's admonishment: "*Law* and *compulsion* have never been brought to bear against my daughter." Whatever Lou may have retorted, Nietzsche next announced to Rée[218] his departure for Genoa via Basel, where he stayed three days beginning November 15—Overbeck's birthday. From the Overbecks he heard with horror that his sister was busy setting the Jena record straight. He spoke warmly of Rée[f]—but added, without explanation, that all was over with the Trinity. Ida Overbeck later recollected: "He still expected letters and pinned hopes on them, asked whether none had come, even feared I might be keeping something from him. He was painfully affected." And: "I did not grasp the whole horrid pain of it as he said to me in parting: 'So I am really going into utter solitude.' He kept on hoping till the last minute."[219] Then he moved on to Columbus's city, from which he had originally sailed to meet Lou—in the wrong direction. He had come full circle. Some days later he set up in nearby Santa Marguerita for the winter. "Cold. Sick. I am suffering," he apprised Gast—citing no clearer reason than "the nightmare this year brought."[220]

e To one Dr. Sulger.

f FN→Rée [23? XI 1882]: "I praised you so in Basel that Mrs. Overbeck said: 'But you are describing Daniel de Ronda [*sic*]!' Who is Daniel de Ronda?"

Rée evidently took this second false departure as much amiss as the first,[221] for Nietzsche next wrote to him: "But dear, dear friend, I thought you would feel *the other way round* and rejoice in silence to be *rid* of me for a while! A hundred times this year since Orta I have felt that you were 'paying rather too steeply' for my friendship. I have already come in for much too much of *your* Roman find (I mean Lou), and it always seemed to me, particularly in Leipzig, that you had a right to become a little sullen with me.—Think as well as you can of me, dear friend, and ask Lou from me to do the same. I belong to both of you with my warmest feelings—as I mean to have proven through my departure more than through my *nearness*. All nearness makes one so insatiable—and in the last resort I am an insatiable fellow on the whole.—From time to time we *will* see one another again, won't we? Do not forget that *from this year on* I have suddenly become poor in love, hence much in need of it.—Write me something *really* accurate about what now most concerns us—what 'stands between us,' as you put it. All my love, your F.N." On second thought Nietzsche enclosed this letter with one to Lou: "*You* read it, it shall be up to you alone whether Rée is to read it too. Take *this* as a sign of confidence, of my *purest will* to confidence between us! And now, Lou, dear heart, clear the sky! I want nothing but pure, clear sky, in every last corner of it. Otherwise I shall scrape through, hard as this may prove—but, being so lonesome, I suffer frightfully from any suspicion about the few people I love, especially when that suspicion concerns a suspicion against my whole being. Why has all serenity been wanting in our association so far? Because I had to do myself too much violence: the cloud on *our* horizon lay upon me! You perhaps know *how* unbearable all wanting to shame, all accusing and having to defend oneself, is to me. One does *much* wrong, inevitably—but one has also the glorious *counter*power of doing good, of creating peace and joy. I feel every stirring of the *higher* soul in you—and love nothing about you but such stirring. I am glad to renounce all intimacy and nearness if only I may be sure that where we feel *at one* is just where common souls do not attain. Am I speaking darkly? Should I have the confidence, you will learn that I have the *words* too. So far I have *always* had to keep silent." And breaking a cognate philosophical silence: "Mind? What is mind to me! What is knowledge to me! I esteem nothing but *impulses*—and I would swear we have something in common here. Do look *through* this phase in which I have lived a few years—look behind it! Don't *you* be fooled about me: *you* surely don't believe that 'the free mind' is my ideal?! I am—Excuse me! Dearest Lou, be what you *must* be. F.N." Lou of course passed both letters on to Rée. Of herself she understood that the "suspicion" suspected by Nietzsche was hers voiced in Jena. Rée added that what Nietzsche wanted from her was an apology for Jena. She must have sent back a reaffirmation of Jena instead, for from his autumnal dismay Nietzsche descended into a winter of despair.

Muffling his sentiments about Lou was painful enough: "This compulsory muteness sometimes chokes me—especially as I love you both," ran a letter draft of late November. Venting his sentiments thereafter was agonizing. In the process he noted: "Affects are devouring me. Dreadful pity, dreadful disillusion, dreadful feeling of wounded pride—how can I stand it any longer? Isn't pity a feeling out of hell? What should I do? Every morning I despair of lasting the day. I no longer sleep—what good does eight hours' walking do! Where do I get these violent affects from! Oh some ice! But where is there ice left *for me*? This evening I'll take opium till I lose my mind. Where is there a person left whom one could *respect*! But I know you all through and through!" He verged on suicide[g] as his exchanges with Lou deteriorated throughout December.[h] "How stunted your humanity looks alongside of friend Rée's!" he railed at her. "How poor you are in respect, in gratitude, in piety, in courtesy, in admiration, shame—not to speak of higher things." Worse, she was "giving free rein to everything contemptible" in herself, thereby perverting her impulse to "sacred self-seeking" into "its opposite: the predatory pleasure-lust of a cat." In the margins of his letter drafts he commented: "Monstrosity! . . . 'A brain with only a rudiment of soul.' A cat's character: that of a beast of prey posing as a domestic ani-

---

[g] FN→Rée and Lou [XII 1882]: "Should I . . . perchance take my life, that would not be all too regrettable either."

[h] Before the year was out, Nietzsche had sent three or four letters to Lou, probably two to Rée, and one to both. In all, only a fragment of the last-mentioned letter survives—but so do Nietzsche's drafts (and side jottings). The drafts to Lou were patently so many replies. It follows that Lou received and indeed answered the corresponding letters short of the final one—which, however, the lifelong sequel shows her to have received in its turn. Gast, who knew Nietzsche's literary habits as did no one else, thought it "unlikely" that the letters corresponded closely to the drafts (Gast→Hofmiller, 10 XI 1896). Gast, however, was even then a party to Lisbeth's forgeries (below, p. 166), and his judgment may well have been affected by the Nietzsche Archiv version of Nietzsche as gentleman (below, p. 167). More, the single fragment preserved by Lou (the first page of Nietzsche's "opium letter") reduplicates the final draft almost word for word. So for present purposes I shall treat the final drafts as equivalent to letters actually sent. As for Rée's and Lou's replies, no trace of them remains except in Nietzsche's drafts.

mal. Nobleness as reminiscence about association with noble people; strong will, but with no great object; without diligence or cleanliness, without civil probity; cruelly misplaced sensuality." Then looking backward: "Backward children? a sequel to sexual stunting and retarding." And forward again: "Capable of enthusiasm for people without love for them, yet love for God: need for effusion; shrewd and fully self-controlled in respect of men's sensuality; heartless and incapable of loving; emotionally always sickly and close to madness" —and so on.[i] Back out of his margins, he resumed: "These are all things that one has in order to surmount them, to surmount *oneself*." And she was uniquely endowed for surmounting—"only some basic mishap in your upbringing and development has temporarily *crippled* your good will for this. Just think: that cat-egoism unable to love any longer, that professing nothing together with a feeling for life . . . and then knowledge as a pleasure among pleasures. And if I understand you at all: these are all voluntary and self-imposed tendencies with you—for as much as they are not symptoms (about which I have a heap of painful hindthoughts)." He was "more offended by attributes than by acts." Correspondingly, "whether I have suffered much— that is all nothing to me as against the question of whether you find yourself again, dear Lou, or not." In her loss of herself she was that strongest offense to him: "the caricature of my ideal."[j] Yet he took her to task as noisomely for particular acts. That she had made light of him with Wagnerians in Bayreuth came in for a single mention—to Rée. Not so the aftermath of Bayreuth: "You have done damage, you have given *pain*—not only to me but to all who loved me: this sword hangs over you."

His sister—who, according to a draft to Malwida, "regards Lou as a poisonous reptile to be destroyed at all costs"—reported after due field work that, like all Basel, all Leipzig in turn was saying dirty things about him, and he brooded over his blackening name.[k] But his own fit of Naumburg virtue at Lou's expense did not endear Lisbeth to him. Quite the contrary, he broke off correspondence with her late in November, specifying: "Souls such as yours, my dear sister, I do not like: and I like them least when they are morally bloated." Now in December he conceded to Lou: "I have long known

[i] Gast→Hofmiller, 10 xi 1896, affords the usual verdict on Nietzsche's depiction of Lou's "cat egoism": "What Nietzsche in excitement and under the influence of old wives' tales wrote about her is not quite true." In fact it is the truth and nothing but—if far from the whole truth, as Nietzsche himself repeatedly remarked in the same context.

[j] A phrase that Nietzsche crossed out.

[k] Gast, misled by the Overbecks, had misled Nietzsche in turn into believing that Lisbeth had brought the gossip to Basel: cf. below, p. 104 n. *w*.

that people of my mother's and sister's kind must be my enemies: there is nothing to change in this, it lies in the very nature of things."

He smarted no less under "this summer's incredible outcome: Lou, after making me suspect to my family and in Basel, now treats me like a low-minded fellow, and one who deals furtively to boot." This was "incredible" coming from the intended recipient of his philosophical legacy: "I believed no greater gift could be made to anyone," he told her, so that "the thought of recompense in any sense," being an insult to him as teacher in *any* case, was in *her* case outright brazen. Or was she just acting her age? "My dear Lou, I must write you a nasty little note. For heaven's sake, what *do* these little girls of twenty[-one] think who have pleasant feelings of love and nothing to do but be sick now and again and lie in bed? Ought one perhaps to run after these little girls to chase away the boredom and the flies?" And more solemnly: "Formerly I was inclined to take you for a vision, for the earthly apparition of my ideal. Observe: *I have poor eyes.* . . . Had I created you, I would have given you better health, to be sure, but first of all some things that matter *far more*—plus maybe a little more love for me (although that is just what matters least)." When Rée or Lou charged him at one writing with "delusions of grandeur" and "wounded vanity" in consideration of his Orta dream and his rudeness on awakening, he replied: "What are my vagaries to you two! (Even my truths have been nothing to you as yet.) Consider well with each other that I am sick in the head, a semilunatic, wholly dazed by long solitude. To this insight—which I think *sensible*—as to how matters stand I come after having taken an enormous dose of opium in desperation."

Considered well, Nietzsche's Orta project was a delusion of grandeur only by ordinary standards and only if resisted; ordinarily, though, Lou was no ordinary girl and her will to compliance no figment. His vagaries came to a singleminded insistence upon out-of-the-ordinary realities: that he was at his best a great philosophical innovator and she at her best a willing and able successor-to-be. His ideal Lou was no optical illusion—and no prefashioned vision, as he next suspected she was[l]—but a very real figure cut in Orta and Lucerne, then undercut in Bayreuth and Jena. He had seen her straight and now saw straight through her—but not through himself with his fine talk about fashioning her. He was, like her, the more religious for being godless and was, like her, godless for having once identified himself with a god. His, though, was an earlier, firmer identification, so that he came away from it with a temptation to worship himself the

---

[l] See below, p. 543.

match for hers to worship a god-figure like him—and with a deep dream of wedding his own creature[m] the match for hers of wedding her own maker. Twins spiritually, they were sexually the titillating reverse. Only the same taboo on both sides brought their mating to a stalemate as its sexual motive loomed lurid to them both—that is, to each of them in the other's case.

Nietzsche besought Rée to help Lou apologize. As instead she only recriminated,[n] he asked Rée: "How can you stand being near such a creature?"[o] Rée called her his "fate"[222]—to which Nietzsche commented after some months' delay: *"Quel goût!"*[223] Meanwhile, he broke with Naumburg altogether on Christmas Eve by returning a letter from his mother unopened. And on Christmas Day he wrote to Overbeck of his winter: "This last *morsel of life* was the toughest chewed by me to date, and I may quite possibly *choke* on it yet. I have been suffering from the abusive and tormenting memories of this summer as from madness. . . . At bottom it is a conflict of contrary affects to which I am not equal. I tense all my fibers for self-mastery—but I have lived in solitude and fed on 'my own fat' too long, so again I am the more readily racked by my affects. Could I but sleep! . . . If I do not hit on an alchemical trick for turning even this —dung into *gold* I am lost. Here is my *very loveliest* chance of proving that for me 'all experience is useful, all days holy, and all mortals godlike'!!!! All mortals godlike—. . . My relations with Lou are now in their last, most painful throes: at least I think so today. Later, if there is a later, I mean to say a word about even that." He thought better of saying the one in his draft to Overbeck: "Today something occurred to me in passing that made me laugh hard: she actually treated me like a twenty-year-old student—a quite permissible approach for a girl of twenty[-one]—like a student who had fallen in love with her. But sages like me love only ghosts. Woe if ever I love a human being—I would soon go to ruin. Man is too imperfect a thing." To another correspondent, Erwin Rohde, went the succinct variant: "Heavens! how lonely I am!"

Those last throes were indeed most painful: "But Lou, what letters you write! Little vengeful schoolgirls write *that* way: what use have I for such paltry stuff? Do understand: I want you to *raise* yourself

[m] This Pygmalion motive went back to his romance with his baby sister following his father's death.

[n] ". . . which brings to mind Lou's defense. Strange! whenever someone defends himself to me, it turns out that I am supposed to be in the wrong": thus Nietzsche's "opium letter," which Lou preserved only down to the word "defense."

[o] See Appendix B, i, pp. 543-44, for some of Nietzsche's fragmentary letter drafts to Rée of xii 1882.

before me, not lower yourself still further. How can I forgive you if I do not first rediscover in you the being *for whose sake* alone there can be any forgiving! . . . My heart is wide open to differences among people, only it will not bear respecting someone for qualities the reverse of his real ones. . . . Shall we work up steam together? do we want to raise a rumpus? I not at all: I wanted clear sky between us. But you are a little gallows-bird! And once I took you for sprightly virtue and decency. . . . Today I blame you only for not having been candid with me in good time. In Lucerne I gave you my piece on Schopenhauer: I told you that my basic views were in it and that I believed they would be yours too. You should have read it and said no *then*: much would have been spared me. . . . I expressly wrote requesting Mrs. Overbeck to inform you about my character on certain counts precisely indicated by me, so that you would not expect from me what I cannot do for you. . . . Say nothing, dear Lou, in your favor: I have already adduced more in your favor than you could—before myself and before others. . . . No one can think better of you, but no one worse either. . . . What would you reply if I asked you: are you honest? are you incapable of duplicity? . . . In your mouth, such a poem as 'To Pain' is a deep untruth. In such matters I hate all *superficiality*. . . . Only a *high purpose* can make people of your sort *bearable* to others. . . . In me you have the best advocate but also the most inexorable judge! I *will* you to condemn yourself and determine your own punishment. . . . If, my dear Lou, my whole soul's torment proves the means of eliciting this feeling and this letter from you, I shall have suffered gladly. . . . My dear Lou, take care! If now I reject you, it will mean a frightful *censure* of your whole being! You have had to do with one of the most forbearing and well-meaning of men: but note well that I need no further argument against all little self-seekers and pleasure-seekers than disgust. Think twice, think of yourself!" The final message was downright ghastly: "No, my dear Lou, we are nowhere near 'forgiving.' I cannot shake forgiveness out of my sleeve after the offense has had four months in which to burrow into me. . . . Adieu, my dear Lou, I shall not see you again. Preserve your soul from such doings and make good with others, in particular my friend Rée, what you can no longer make good with me. I did not create the world and Lou: I wish I had— then I could bear the guilt alone for its having come to *this* between us. Adieu, dear Lou, I did not read your letter through, but I read too much already."

Out of the agony of telling Lou off, Nietzsche reported to an old friend: "I am a hermit once again, and more than ever; and am—

consequently—thinking out something new. It seems to me that only the state of *pregnancy* binds us to life ever anew."[224] Fast upon his "adieu" to Lou, and just nine months after meeting her, he delivered the first book of *So Spoke Zarathustra*, written in a trance, as if from inner dictation, in ten "absolutely serene and fresh January days."[225/p] His son by Lou owed to her, beyond his begetting, only a sermon on woman—with a misogynic twist in her dishonor at that. For the rest, Zarathustra revealed what Nietzsche had meant to demonstrate after completing those projected scientific studies: that man was the way to the overman.[q] In Nietzsche's latent conception, Zarathustra with his eagle and snake perhaps signified the Trinity duly reconstituted. Certainly there was a breath of Genoese winter to all Zarathustra's dicta—in favor of "free death," against "despisers of the body," on chastity as "for some almost a vice,"[r] on "the bestowing virtue" as against "sickly self-seeking." And with its gospel of self-surmounting, the book perpetuated Nietzsche's quarrel with Lou. It also blazed his break with Réealism. Yet his fantasy union with Lou, generative of Zarathustra, was at bottom one with Rée, now tacitly sanctioned by Zarathustra's message of moral transcendence—though again, that fantasy union with Lou was also a self-distancing from Rée by the very same means of a woman interposed between them. Nietzsche herein recapitulated his break with Wagner, from which he had come to positivism and to Rée in the first place. Already with Cosima he had countered a homosexual inclination to the unconscious effect of indulging it. And his tacit apologia for it then had been *Human, All Too Human*, which had blazed his break with Wagnerism—the break with Wagner following automatically. Now on February 13, 1883, his first *Zarathustra* was ready for the printer— "in just the holy hour in which Richard Wagner died," he later specified.[226] The break with Rée was thenceforth a mere formality. Later in the month Rée—with Lou's foreknowledge, though while visiting Stibbe without her[s]—wrote confessing "guilt feelings" toward him[227]

[p] FN, *Ecce*: "Also Sprach Zarathustra, I," reckoned his Zarathustra pregnancy at eighteen months (and called this a hint, "at least to Buddhists, that I am at bottom a female elephant")—counting, however, from his first "thought of the eternal recurrence" (VIII 1881) to the last editorial stroke of his pen (13 II 1883). The first conception of *Zarathustra* dates, though, from his encounter with Lou. On Lou as his "inspiration" for *Zarathustra*: Gast→ Hofmiller, 10 XI 1896; cf. Bernoulli, *FO und FN*, I, 352.

[q] The mode of revelation was doubly ironic in that Zarathustra spoke not only without Nietzsche's full endorsement but frequently with tongue in cheek.

[r] Especially: "And how adroitly the bitch sensuality knows how to beg for a morsel of mind when a morsel of body is denied her."

[s] Rée→Lou [late II or early III 1883] (Stibbe to Berlin): "I have written Nietzsche; I am hoping for a letter tomorrow."

and proposing to dedicate the history of conscience to him. Nietzsche declined—"and," he epilogued, "therewith put an end to a relationship from which much ruinous confusion has resulted."[228]

After delivering *Zarathustra*, Nietzsche relapsed. "It is again night about me," he moaned to Overbeck. "I think I shall inevitably go to ruin unless something happens, I have no idea *what*. . . . I have such a *mani*fold burden of torturesome and hideous memories to bear. Thus for example it has not left my mind for one hour that my mother called me a shame on my father's grave. Other examples I shall keep to myself—but a pistol barrel is to me now a source of relatively pleasant thoughts."[229] Wagner's death brought momentary relief: "It was hard having to be for six years the adversary of him whom I most admired," he explained.[230] But by February 22: "I am *very* ill. . . . No! *this* life! And I am the advocate of life!! . . . Nothing helps me: I must help myself or I am done for."[231] Instead of helping himself, he caught influenza.[232] On recovering he told Gast: "I shall not survive another winter like this one"[233]—and Overbeck: "At the very base, immovable black melancholy. . . . I no longer see any *point* at all to living even another half year, everything is dull, painful, *dégoûtant*. I forego and suffer too much. . . . I shall do nothing good any more, so why do anything!"[234]

For all that, Lou began falling back into proper focus in Genoa right after the first *Zarathustra*. To Gast, who had evidently been humoring him, Nietzsche remarked: "I had to laugh hard at your words on Lou. Do you suppose my 'taste' differs from yours in *that*? But in this case it was *damned* little a matter of 'attractive or not,' but one of whether or not a greatly endowed person goes to ruin."[235/t] And to Overbeck: "Lou is by far the *cleverest* person I have met. *But* etc. etc."[236] Then similarly to Overbeck again: "My severance from my family is beginning to appear to me as a true blessing; oh, if you knew all I have had to overcome on this score (since my birth)! I do not like my mother, and hearing my sister's voice upsets me; I have *always* fallen ill when together with them."[237] Already on March 17 Overbeck wrote to Gast: "You know *how* pleased I am that the matter is done with."

Then, after the earliest compliments on *Zarathustra*, Nietzsche began looking up. "I am leaving for the mountains as soon as I can," he announced to Malwida; "*this* year I wish to speak to nobody."[238] And soon he was chuckling to Malwida: "Last year in Germany I

---

[t] Since Leipzig, Gast had been convinced first by Lisbeth that "Lou is an adventuress" (Gast→o, 20 XII 1882), then in I 1883 by the Overbecks in Basel that Lisbeth was "raving" worse than her brother (o→Gast, 17 III 1883).

found superficiality matured to a point of inanity such that I was confused with Rée. With Rée!!! I think *you* know what *that* means—!!"[239] With spring, serenity set in, whereupon the second book of *Zarathustra* emerged. Lou cast only a fleeting shadow over this one: "Once I yearned for lucky bird omens: you then led an owl-monster across my path, an unpropitious one. Ah, whither flew my tender yearning then?"[u] Ida admonished the hapless seer "not to forget that he had expected too much of his sister, as he himself knew,"[240/v] so when his sister sent him a "most conciliatory" note[241] while visiting Malwida late in April, he replied that after his "hardest and sickest" winter he was again in control of himself, reconciled with life, and ready to "put my human relations, somewhat jumbled just now, back in order—beginning with you. . . . As for the typewriter, it is on the blink like everything weak men take in hand for a while, be it machines or problems or Lous."[242] His next word to Basel was: "To give you some idea of how my humanity (let us say: 'geniality') is waxing along with my health, I report that Thursday [May 3] I shall go to Rome for purposes of conciliation (a stupid trip in all other respects) and that I have even written my mother."[243]

To all appearances, Lisbeth too had recovered from Lou after a hard winter's rectifying of Basel rumors by mail and worrying lest "Fritz . . . were secretly sitting together with Miss Salomé."[w] She "behaved perfectly" on a visit to Gast in Venice late in March,[x] Gast having beforehand "explicitly requested that no word touch on Lou."[244] Nietzsche followed Gast's example[y] to nearly the same effect, and after six weeks in Rome he took his Llama on a sentimental journey along the Italian lakes before repairing to Sils late in June. He was subsequently to complain: "Perhaps my reconciliation

[u] From the "gravesong"—identified in Gast→Hofmiller, 10 xi 1896, as a follow-up to FN→Gast, 4 viii 1882 (above, p. 75).

[v] Ida later commented: "This did him good and built a bridge toward conciliation." Overbeck himself was warier of conciliation (o→Gast, 17 iii 1883).

[w] Lisbeth→Ida O [25? i 1883]. Ida on about 27 i 1883 directly accused Lisbeth of harming her brother by spreading tales about Lou out of jealousy. Lisbeth replied on 29 i 1883 that she wanted on the contrary only to set the tales straight where, through Nietzsche's own fault, they had already spread and that she was ready to come to Basel in person "to check the gossip." Overbeck himself on reinvestigation had to admit that, for all Lisbeth's obstreperous faults, "we really did her a wrong on one point. That Professor Gelzer (the channel for Basel) was drawn into the matter in question by Nietzsche himself in Jena I did not suspect" (o→Gast, 17 iii 1883).

[x] Gelzer escorted her.

[y] FN→Ida O, 29 vii 1883, draft: "In Rome I did not want any talking about all that"; FN→Georg Rée [early viii 1883], draft: "In Rome this year I always insisted that last year's ugly happenings not be discussed in my presence."

with her was the fateful step in this whole business: I *now* see that *it* led her to suppose she had acquired a right to her revenge on Miss Salomé."[245] For July brought him a copy of a letter by her to Rée's mother[z]—"a female masterpiece," he commented, and one that gave him "new lights and new tortures."[246] He notified Overbeck: "Things are moving again. My sister wants her revenge on this Russian—well and good, only so far I have been the victim of her every initiative. She does not even notice bloodshed and the most brutal possibilities hardly an inch off."[247]

On rejecting Lou he had told the Overbecks: "You are about the last foot-breadth of sure ground left to me."[248] Now he preferred wobbly ground. When Ida urged him not to revert to his old weakness out of false brotherliness, he raged: "Do not imagine 'weakness' and such like: *if* I go to ruin in this business, it will be just because I do not wish to give in to the human heart's quite natural impulse to 'vengeance,' hence because of strength. Do not talk of a relapse either: unfortunately it is a *pro*lapse: I have gone through hellish days and nights on account of something first learned by me three weeks ago. And do not worry about my false footing with my sister; the truth is that all my footings so far *with everyone* have been false: she was at least as much affronted as I was, with good right too, and if now she means to work it out for Lou to be sent back to Russia, she will be doing more good if she succeeds than I with my asceticism. She was too considerate of me last year, so that the most incriminating facts of this matter, which she kept back from me in Tautenburg, became known to me only three weeks ago. . . . Of a sudden Dr. Rée steps into the foreground: to have to *relearn* about someone with whom I shared love and trust for years is frightful."[249] He ranted to Malwida in turn: "Last year's evil tale falls upon me again; I have had to hear so *much*. . . . From all that I have *now* learned—oh *far too late*!— these two persons, Rée and Lou, are not worthy of licking the soles of my shoes. Excuse the all too human metaphor! It is a vast misfortune that this Rée, a liar and crawling backbiter through and through, ever crossed my path. And what patience and pity I have long shown him! . . . Schopenhauer-style 'pitying' has so far always done the *top damage* in my life—whence I have every reason to fancy *such* morals as still include a few other impulses under morality instead of tending to reduce all our human prowess to 'pity.' This is actually not only flabbiness such as every high-minded Hellene would have laughed at—but a serious practical danger. One should *enforce one's human ideal*, compel and subdue one's fellows with it just like one-

[z] FN→Ida O, 29 VII 1883: he had received it "three weeks ago."

105

self: and so work creatively! Only *that* entails keeping one's pity well in hand and also treating whatever *counters* our ideal (such rabble as Lou and Rée, for instance) as *enemies*. You hear *what I* 'make of morals': but coming to this 'bit of wisdom' almost cost me my life."[250]

Alarmed on his account, the Overbecks implored Nietzsche none too hopefully to sever relations with his sister again.[a] Instead he wrote poison pen letters at his sister's bidding. The first was an elegant one to Lou's mother: she alone, it ran, had gainsaid his fair image of Lou, and this only too rightly. "I will not say *what* pains I took to sustain even the last vestige of that image and *how* much I have had to forget and forgive in this. Still less do I mean to tell you, her mother, what an image was *left* with me in the end." The second, inelegant, was for Rée: it detailed Nietzsche's unprecedented disgust "at the thought that such a furtive, underhanded double-dealer can have passed for my friend all these years"—a foul offense to him and to friendship both. "*Pfui, mein Herr*! . . . So the defamation of my character stems from *you*, and Miss Salomé was only the mouthpiece, the very unclean mouthpiece for *your* thoughts about me? You it was who, behind my back of course, spoke of me as a common low egoist always out to use others? You it was who maintained that I pursued the dirtiest of designs in regard to Miss Salomé beneath the mask of ideality? You it was who dared assert that I am mad and don't know what I want? *Now* I understand this whole performance, which came near to costing me my life and estranging me from my closest and worthiest relations: no one could understand how I could stand by my worst enemies, who have probably been playing me dirty everywhere for years already. I would delight in giving you a lesson

[a] O→Gast, 31 VII 1883: "Morally he is in a bad way just now, screaming like a Philoctetes and doing everything to sharpen his pain beyond endurance. Above all he has been irresponsible enough toward himself to let that business which fell out so badly last year be revived in letters from his sister even beyond what life it unfortunately is bound to have for him in any case. Now he takes in stories about atrocities of every description of which he professedly had no inkling whatever till now, joins his sister in schemes for vengeance, and torments himself over the retrospective lights now cast on the whole affair by his imagination, so wild to begin with but now perpetually prodded. You can guess how his solitude is now shaping up, with what demons it is now peopling itself: it were a thousand times better he quit it. For the time being we have urgently begged him to put a veto on all further communications from his sister. I fear it will be too late and, after all that seems to be set going again in this matter, futile. Happy as we were to know Nietzsche to be—by his sister's own accounts in the spring—now removed from immediate involvement in this business, we were not a little affrighted as this removal suddenly turned out to be illusory. Now it is as if one were witnessing a self-immolation. About suicide—a thought that every lengthy letter from Nietzsche in over half a year has expressed—I feel quite as you do: nothing can make it acceptable except desperation."

in practical morality with a few bullets: maybe in the best case I could manage to deter you once and for all from *dealing in morality,* which calls for *clean hands*, Dr. Rée, not clammy fingers!" In the end Nietzsche, clammy-fingered, despatched in lieu of this revilement of Rée a still more scurrilous one addressed to Rée's brother and containing just an incidental word on "that scraggy dirty smelly she-monkey with her false breasts." In drafting it, he wrote at one point: "The whole abominable calumny inflicted on me by"—then struck out the "by" and resumed: "and my sister . . ."

Again thwarted affection had erupted out of Nietzsche as wrath, but this time the eruption was simply grotesque. Invective apart, the charges against Rée were as valid as the precedent ones against Lou except that, by the time Nietzsche pressed them, Lou's delinquency rated forgiving, and Rée's forgetting. In December, however, besides swelling the charges against Lou, Nietzsche had brought only the single, disputable one against Rée of having built her up to him instead of running her down.[b] He now treated it as a dire revelation that Rée was behind Lou's Jena tirade—after having treated it as a laughing matter in Tautenburg. His belated, angry denunciation of Rée as the underhanded double-dealer behind Lou's imputation of dirty concealed designs on her went to show that his dirty concealed designs on her concealed others on Rée against which his inner defenses had been working overtime. These doubly concealed designs on Rée became conscious only at Lisbeth's provocation and then only in the guise of Rée's abominable double-dealing with him. Unrecognizable to him in this guise, they were yet so unspeakable that he could only complain to Overbeck in the first instance about unspecified outrages "five times more than sufficient to drive a normal person to suicide."[251/c] *They* were the ground for the pity and revenge he took on himself indirectly, through Lou and Rée—and eventually repudiated in turn.

His vengeance deserved repudiating. Nobly as he had borne himself toward Lou and Rée in the sequel to Jena, he bore himself that ignobly a year later. And he of all people knew it. Having sent off his missive to Georg Rée, he told Lisbeth: "Your brother is really quite unhappy. No, I am not made for enmity and hate: and since this matter has gone too far for a reconciliation with those two to be possible any more, I no longer know how to live; it is on my mind continually. Enmity is incompatible with my whole philosophy and way of thinking: to have entered the lists of the hostile (and against such

[b] Below, p. 544. He reiterated this grievance in the letter to Georg Rée.

[c] Also: these outrages "could have turned one into a Timon of Athens overnight."

poor folk) drags down my every aspiration. Never before did I hate anyone—not even Wagner, whose perfidy went well beyond Lou's. For the first time I feel humbled." The threat of a libel suit from Georg Rée fast exalted him: "I threatened him *with something else in return*," he blustered to Basel.[252]

Ida having admonished him to leave off his false pathos and true nastiness, he now bade her show due regard for the "deepest pain" and *"sublimest"* deeds of his life. His draft letter to her is revealing through the passages finally rejected: "*Since* my sister is acting in this matter (I had implored her to leave it to me), I am obliged to act *with* my sister. . . . My experience last year has led me to a singular realization: long a stranger to practical life, I act 49 times out of 50 on a motive no one seeing me thinks of, so that I almost always arouse misunderstanding and wind up my own victim. But now I think that what counts in victimization, disappointment, pain, and the like is just to endure them: then they are life's mightiest furtherances and sources. . . . Such pain (it was as if a knife had been put to all my sore spots at once!) is a high distinction. You perhaps know that I am proud of being among those who have the most experience in *physical torment*. My body and soul are so constituted that I can suffer frightfully in both: and as for my soul, I was last year like someone who for many, many years running had experienced nothing: whence my soul was without any skin or natural protective device. . . . [Revenge] is my sister's good right: the trouble is that all these hostile measures are aimed at persons whom I have loved and perhaps still love: at least I am ready at a moment's notice to cast aside the whole lot of past insults and injuries to me if I knew I could really help them. . . . It may speak for what is distinctive about Rée that for years Malwida von Meysenbug honored him as the best expression of human *goodness*."

Nietzsche did see his way clear to sending Ida "one word more on Miss Salomé. Quite apart from the idealistic light in which she had been presented to me (as a martyr to knowledge almost from infancy on, and even more heroine than martyr), she is and remains for me a being of the first rank, about whom it is a pity forever. Given her energy of will and originality of mind, she was headed for something great; given her practical morality, though, she may well belong rather in a penitentiary or madhouse. I *miss* her, for all her bad qualities: we were disparate enough for something useful to have been always sure to come out of our talks; I have found no one so unprejudiced, so clever, so well prepared for my sort of problems. I have felt *ever since* as if condemned to silence or humane hypocrisy *in my dealings with everyone.*"

To Overbeck he then declared that, except for his *"goal"* of turning the dross of his sorry lot into *"gold,"* he would long since have taken his life. As for breaking with Naumburg again, "I am not hard enough for that. But every contemptuous word written against Rée or Miss Salomé makes my heart bleed; it seems I am not made for enmity (whereas my sister just wrote me again: be of good cheer, it's a 'gay, fresh, holy war'). . . . Do think about finding something *absolutely distracting*! I believe the most drastic means are now needed— you cannot imagine *how* this madness rages in me day and night. . . . As best I can reckon, I still *need next year*—help me to *last* another fifteen months." Thereupon Overbeck, on returning with his wife from the Tyrol, took a detour alone to meet Nietzsche in Schuls-Tarasp (Lower Engadin) on August 26.[d] "I found him knocking about with thoughts of duelling Rée and half mad with fury against Miss Salomé," Overbeck later related.[253] A single day together so calmed and even cheered Nietzsche that he wrote Overbeck on the morrow: "The separation from you threw me back into the deepest melancholy, and the whole return trip I was lost to evil black sentiments, including true hate for my sister, who for one year now has deprived me of all self-control with ill-timed silence and ill-timed talk: so that I have wound up a prey to pitiless vengefulness, whereas my innermost way of thinking precisely rejects all avenging and punishing:—*this* conflict in me is driving me step by step to *madness.*"[254] He nonetheless left for Naumburg a few days later—and there, in a month of being tirelessly chided and taunted, the crisis passed. Lisbeth had found "something *absolutely distracting*": anti-Semitism, the highest lesson she had drawn from the Trinity fiasco. That month Naumburg celebrated her engagement to Bernhard Förster, who was laying plans for an Aryan colony in Paraguay.

After three days' convalescing at the Overbecks', Nietzsche again went south for the winter. As Lisbeth next took to defaming him[e] along with Jews and Lou, he began to see his falling out with Lou as all Lisbeth's fault. In February he told his mother: "Whatever may be said against the girl—and surely much more than my sister says— the fact remains that I have found no more gifted, more reflective

---

[d] Overbeck had been proposing a reunion there since VII (o→Gast, 31 VII 1883).

[e] FN→o [1? IV 1883]: "a letter from her in January full of the most poisonous incriminations of my character—a nice companion piece to the one to Mrs. Rée—has now enlightened me sufficiently."

creature. And though we never agreed (any more than did Rée and
I), after every half hour together we were both happy over the lot we
had learned. And I did not score my highest achievement these past
twelve months without cause. We were warned about each other
amply: and little as we loved each other, just as little did we need to
give up a relationship in the highest sense useful to us and the world.
. . . That the two behaved vilely toward me is true, but I had forgiven
them, as I had forgiven my sister worse."[255] He had remembered the
warning and the forgiveness only at the cost of all agreement and all
love.

By April he had broken with Lisbeth again—this time "radically,"
for "between a vengeful anti-Semitic goose and me, conciliation
is *impossible*."[f] He did think wistfully of conciliation with Lou
(and parenthetically with Rée, now in the background again).[g] And,
mindful of Lisbeth's libel of him, he penned his best post-mortem on
his Lou romance, which ought to have been his last: "I now understand only too well . . . *how easily* my own life and fate could come
into the very same disrepute as hers—deservedly *and* undeservedly,
as is ever wont to be the case with such natures."[h] Lisbeth on her side

[f] FN→MVM [early V 1884], copy. Cf. FN→O, 2 IV 1884: "Accursed anti-
Semitism is the cause of a *radical* break between my sister and me."

[g] FN→O [7 IV 1884] projected a literati colony in Nice to include "maybe
even Dr. Rée and Miss Salomé, to whom I should like to make good a little
of what my sister [!] made bad." Lou thereinafter came in for some special
attention, and she was practically the sole issue in FN→MVM [early V 1884],
copy (see next note), after an apology for his "*inhumane* letter" of the preceding summer to Malwida—which, however, had primarily concerned Rée!

[h] FN→MVM [early V 1884], copy—which is worth quoting at some length:
"I am chafing over that *inhumane* letter I sent you last summer; I had been
made downright sick by unspeakably repulsive goading. Since then the situation has changed inasmuch as I have broken with my sister *radically*: for
heaven's sake do not think of mediating and conciliating: between a vengeful
anti-Semitic goose and me, conciliation is *impossible*. Moreover, I exert for-
bearance in full measure because I know *what* can be said to excuse her and
what is behind her conduct, ignominious and unworthy as it is to me: love.
She absolutely must sail for Paraguay as soon as possible. Later, much later,
she will come to see by herself how much she harmed me with her continual
dirty insinuations against my character those two years—in the most decisive
epoch of my life. Now there remains for me the very touchy task of making
good in some measure with Dr. Rée and Miss Salomé what my sister [!] has
made ill. . . . My sister reduces such a rich and original creature [as Lou] to
'lies and sensuality,' sees no more in Dr. Rée and her than 'two duds.' *Against
this* my sense of justice now revolts, though I may have good ground for considering myself to have been insulted by both. It was most instructive of my
sister to have cast suspicion on *me* of late just as blindly as on Miss Salomé:
I *then* first realized that everything bad believed by me about Miss Salomé
goes back to that squabble that preceded our closer acquaintance: *how much*
my sister may have heard wrong or imagined! She lacks any and all knowledge of people; heaven preserve her from one of Dr. Förster's enemies ever

insisted that his intellectual and personal nastiness was alone to blame for the new falling-out between them—not her "so gentle, good-natured anti-Semitism," which she had been overstating of late just to bear out his *"fable convenue,"* and still less that "dull old Rée-Salomé story. Fritz," she told Gast, "decked out a not exactly pleasant yet most ordinary experience as a true horror. It kept on acquiring new color and new life whenever it was happily thought to be dead. Finally my patience snapped, and the whole business came to an end."[256] She too was cured of Lou—until further notice.

Nietzsche was to come around to his sister more than once—superficially. But fundamentally, he was estranged from Naumburg for good and all upon his recovery from the Trinity fiasco. Naumburg was the final loss (if loss it was) he suffered from his promising encounter with Lou—on top of his friendship with Rée and his last earnest hopes for a return among men, for a philosophic succession, and for a woman's love. Despite all this forfeiture, and for all his show of anguish and fury, he surmounted the sentimental casualty of 1882 more rapidly, more fully, and more healthily than either of his two erstwhile consorts. He wound up, moreover, one endurance the richer—his hardest ever—and all set to turn the dross of it into purest gold. Nor was Lou lost to him even then: off his mind, she was not out of it but inside it, where their exhilarating dialogue was yet to resume as a monologue.

---

getting eloquent about him before her! . . . Extraordinary people like Miss Salomé deserve, especially when so young, all consideration and sympathy. And even if *I*, for various reasons, am in no position yet to *hope* for a new contact between us, I do mean to disregard all personal considerations on my side should her situation shape up ill and grow desperate. I now understand only too well, from *manifold* experience, *how easily*" etc. (He of course had tormented himself over nothing imaginary.)

L O U A N D Rée meanwhile did not go to Paris. Instead, Rée's mother consenting, they set up a chaste ménage in a Berlin boarding house suite consisting of two bedrooms separated by a parlor.[i] Lou sought to turn this parlor into a philosophical salon—copying Malwida to the extent of calling herself Louise *von* Salomé.[j] Among her first callers was Malwida's idealistic correspondent Ludwig Hüter, then studying under the eclectic philosopher Friedrich Paulsen. "Big fight over Paulsen," Hüter later recollected. "Dr. Rée offhandedly dubs him a 'brother believer' . . . hence a materialist, since he calls himself one *de pur sang*. Astonished, I modestly object. . . . Lengthy exchange. Rée of course my superior in logic, yet his dogmatic arguments strike me as sophistical. Pressed, I finally venture (again with all the modesty of a twenty-year-old toward a professional philosopher so much older): if Paulsen must be labeled, then I consider him a 'monistic sensorialist.' Superior smile from Rée, to which unfortunately Miss Salomé seems to subscribe. Finally, Rée: 'Well, we'll see, won't we, Miss Salomé? We are hoping to have Paulsen here one evening soon. We have invited him.' Later I once told this all to Paulsen himself; about his only reply was his placid-superior smile. At one point in the other conversation Miss Salomé, vividly recalling Friedrich Nietzsche, speaks of his 'beautiful mouth.' Rée pricks up his ears, somewhat piqued, and says with the usual faint irony: 'But Miss Salomé, how *would* you know? His mouth is overcast by a formidable moustache.' Miss Salomé, smiling equably: 'Yes, but when he opens his mouth (and how often I did speak with him!) I see his lips perfectly.' I, after all an alert youngster, reflect secretly: Rée—somewhat jealous (understandably, for Louise Salomé is beautiful and emotionally bewitching); she—well, *if* she can flirt, she does so almost unconsciously, but here she is after all playing a little with serious older men and—does not say what she thinks (unreservedly) without danger. With such remarks (perhaps primarily meant as aesthetic, but grazing naïve sensuality) she can pit off two—rivals against each other. Even intellectually, doubtless chiefly so in the first instance,

---

[i] In Hedemannstrasse (Deussen, 220-21), at matronly Mrs. Wilkie's (Lou→ Rée [early] 1883).

[j] Perhaps progressively: her Celerina hotel registration of VIII 1883 reads Louison (!) Salomé, that of 1885 Louise von Salomé.

harmlessly recollecting the impressive absentee as a help—*against* the potent mind of the one beside her, lest he triumph too conspicuously. . . . The two disputants even appealed to me. She: 'Isn't that simple and natural, Mr. Hüter?' He: 'Do you go along with Miss Salomé?' "[257/k] Hüter mediated with a jest and withdrew—permanently. In his report to Malwida he called Lou "too odd a girl to be easily made out . . . a likable, winning, truly feminine being who renounces all womanly resources in the struggle for existence and instead takes up men's weapons with a certain harsh exclusiveness. Sharp judging and, as it turns out, condemning of everything; no trace of mercy, so dear to woman; clear resoluteness in every word, yet her character only appears the more onesided for being so resolute in its one direction; music, art, poetry are discussed, to be sure, but gauged by a strange standard: not pure joy over their beauty, pleasure in their form, comprehension of their substance, poetic enjoyment with heart and soul, no—only a cold, too often negative, corrosive philosophizing about them. Behind her stands Dr. Rée . . . somewhat Mephisthophelean, grasping everything, dissolving everything. I had to stick my neck out three quarters of an hour for *Wallenstein*. . . . Then came music: *Fidelio* was 'not bad'—to cite one small example. In brief, I really got mad, and not much came of a debate between two parties so deeply at odds that they may not have understood each other at all; I dislike that skepticism which picks holes in everything and yet can offer nothing positive.—And yet I cannot believe that Miss Salomé will lose herself completely in this criticalism. She is not what is called disputatious: with her wonderful clarity of mind she aims only at truth, like all good people. . . . A reaction must set in sooner or later; then her awakening femininity will assert itself, and something superb will come of this richly gifted girl."[258] To Malwida's specific queries—"Was Rée's mother there too? And who were the men that gathered there?"[259]—Hüter gave no reply.

The first men to gather there regularly were Romundt, Stein, and the great adept of Schopenhauer and exponent of Indian philosophy Paul Deussen,[l] who with their host and hostess formed "a philosophic circle."[260] Deussen was, like Romundt, an old friend of Nietzsche's, and Stein a new enthusiast—the one sort being then about as rare as the other. The "impressive absentee" haunted Lou's and Rée's whole entourage in Berlin from the first, even as ostensibly the pair was doing fine without him. "He stood as if in veiled outline, in invisible

---

[k] There is a faint trace of this quarrel in 1890a:11 (above, p. 52): Nietzsche's moustache "almost" concealed his mouth.

[l] FN, *Genealogy*, III: 17, called Deussen "Europe's first real *expert* in Indian philosophy."

form, in our midst," Lou later recollected.[261/m] His occult sway over "our friends"[262] brought home to her his superiority as nothing else could—to the detriment of her chosen alternative to him.

Yet she countered his traumatic refusal of her apology (such as it was) with the pretense that he had never so much as existed for her. Right after receiving his "adieu," she inaugurated 1883 with a diary piece addressed to Rée that depicted the old year—"which was so good to you and me"—as a dual progression from Rome via Orta "with its *monte sacro*" over pale landscapes bathed in sunlight to Lucerne and points north till "the day we left Stibbe hand in hand like two good comrades and entered the 'big world' confident that we could not be misunderstood." In this goody-goody extravaganza, her parting from her mother was "my life won back," her "peculiar friend-liaison" with Rée one "such as perhaps has not its like in this intimacy and this reserve," their ménage one "proven viable *before ourselves* and *among men*." Despite some disapprobation "from afar, indeed from friendly quarters . . . we met with only cordiality and warmth among people who were *close* to us." Ignoring prejudice, they won "respect and love" on all sides "through a full living out of the personality." Finally, "our friendship, like a carefully sheltered and tended artificial plant, has done honor to our gardening talents." The only silhouette to stand out sharply from this white-on-white tableau was the one erased from it.[n] In the same vein, Lou was soon playing Rée's child-bride on paper: writing him babyishly from bed in February 1883, she treated a brief trip of his alone to Stibbe like the breach of a honeymoon in a nursery.[o]

No less "naïve-sensual" in the drawing room, she engaged the hearts there along with the wits, as if involuntarily. Early in 1883 she commenced collecting precipitate marriage proposals with one

[m] Lou's ostensible point here (1931a:110-11) was the complex, elusive one that "Nietzsche's distinctive genius" lay in "the very power *of his capacity* to express" the "joys and sorrows" attendant on the "heroic" truth-seeking then current with its "ever purer and stricter separating out of subjective admixtures from what was scientifically called 'true,'" even unto "introspective self-humiliation" before "'truth,'" whereas "our friends . . . belonged together in one point: in valuing their objectivity—in striving to keep their excitations distinct from their will to knowledge, to remove them as far as possible from the scientific task to hand, to discharge them privately." Thus nominally the invisible presence was *impersonal*—was an unscholarly orientation contrasting with that of "our friends." Yet that orientation was called unobjective for the very reason that it was all too *personal*. Furthermore, the characterization of "our friends" applied to Rée alone.

[n] Here was a pure instance of Lou's first step toward autobiographic invention: eliminating unpleasant realities from her past—or clearing the way. She was increasingly to superadd even while eliminating.

[o] Here sole surviving letter of 1883 to Rée.

from the experimental psychologist Hermann Ebbinghaus—her object being, vanity apart, to supply Nietzsche's omission in the long run by the logic of one more, one less. Rée, naggingly jealous, complained once when absent from Berlin: "My thoughts are two-pronged: either I imagine you alone and one prong stings, or—and the other does." And he asked fearfully another time: "Whatever will it be like if one of us marries someday?"—meaning her. He cut a sorry figure procuring fresh minds for her continually and belittling them to her continually. In one respect only, though, did she find him a trying social partner: if a new acquaintance turned out a Jew, "he would make scenes that for ridiculousness and dreadfulness baffle all description."[263] The Danish cultural historian Georg Brandes, later Nietzsche's first notable publicist, evidently escaped detection.[p]

In the spring of 1883 Lou and Rée urged a friend of Brandes', the brilliant young sociologist and ardent Nietzschean of the first hour[q] Ferdinand Tönnies, "with friendly-violent insistence"[264] to join them on a trip to the Engadin. "Maybe I shall meet Nietzsche there too," wrote Tönnies to Paulsen, his ex-teacher and good friend.[265] Paulsen himself would not join the party—"though I by no means like leaving you alone to the Rées and Nietzsches," he told Tönnies; "I much enjoy conversing with Rée but do not expect I could live close to them. There is something morbid there . . ."[266]

Late in June, on her way south, Lou paid Biedermann a surprise visit. Six months earlier Biedermann had sent her a stern reminder of her prior assurances "that with all her studies she did not mean to overstep natural feminine bounds"; it had gone unacknowledged. Now, even as he "remonstrated with her" about her exclusively literary ambitions, she gave him "the same old heartwinning impression of a being pure to the innermost core of her."[267/r]

Early in July, Tönnies joined Lou and Rée in "Flims with its placid lake,"[268] where Lou was learning from Rée to love natural beauty as distinct from Nature. The three took a whole floor to themselves in a rooming house.[269] "We are living here as a most debonair trio," Tönnies shortly told Paulsen. "Miss Salomé runs the household

[p] Brandes→FN, 17 XII 1887, lauded Lou's "genuine gifts" and called Rée "a quiet man, distinguished in his bearing but of somewhat dry, narrow intellect." Brandes also quoted Rée about living with Lou "as brother and sister"—yet he did not know the two well enough to consider that Nietzsche might need no telling who they were.

[q] See Tönnies, *Kultus*; also Tönnies→Lisbeth, 1 IX 1900 ("I believe Georg Brandes also first heard his name from me, in the winter of 1879/80 at Friedrich Paulsen's house").

[r] So Biedermann told Lou's mother in a most flattering letter presumably prompted by Lou to counter the threat from Lisbeth, who had just written to Rée's mother.

with a superior assurance and tactful finesse positively admirable. She is really an altogether extraordinary being: so much cleverness in a twenty-one[sic]-year-old girl would almost make your flesh creep were it not for her truly tender disposition and utter demureness. She is a phenomenon that must be seen from close up to be believed. And a single look suffices to annihilate any thought of a 'woman of loose ways,' as the preacher says: cut off both my hands if I am mistaken! Her grasp of religion and of the moral content of nationality is deep and strong, her power of expression significantly rich. She is a genius." As for Rée, "his congeniality, humor, and intelligence always thoroughly delight me"[270]: *this* judgment Tönnies was to stand by.[271]

Rée was revising his manuscript, which he had been unable to finish up since Nietzsche's refusal of the dedication. "He is very diligent," Tönnies affirmed; "it will be a sociological-inductive book full of quotations. He is an astoundingly careful, conscientious worker, who studies from the sources and with the best techniques."[272/s] For all his sources and techniques, Rée was still deriving conscience from vengefulness by way of public sanctions and writing it off as a corrigible mistake—only now, lest the point conceded to Nietzsche ten months earlier subvert his utilitarian thesis, he argued bizarrely that, even if the *men* first called "bad" were the *lowly* ones, the *acts* first called "bad" were the *harmful* ones.[273] Similarly, Tönnies now convinced Rée that "something like conscience has existed from the very start"[274]: Rée inserted a concessionary clause,[275] yet went on calling his work *The Emergence of Conscience* and meaning it. Tönnies preferred discussing Nietzsche, and Rée told him tantalizingly that Nietzsche was at his best in conversation and his next best in correspondence.[276]

In mid-July, the threesome moved on up the Swiss Alps to Churwalden, where a Gymnasium teacher named Halbfass joined them briefly. "There we had it even better," Tönnies reported: "a whole cheap little *pension* to ourselves."[277] The company engaged in group readings and discussions, with Lou darning socks and pouring coffee for her "big children."[278/t] On July 26 Tönnies struck the first sour note by complaining of senility as he turned twenty-eight.[279]

When August came, the trio proceeded further uphill to Schuls, in the Lower Engadin—and there the mood changed. "I feel all alone and averse to new acquaintances, quite unhappy," declared Tönnies.[280] For one thing, he was courting Lou: enough said. For another, it emerged that the three were not to ascend the Inn valley and go

---

s But Tönnies, "Rée," treats Rée on the contrary as strictly aprioristic.

t Lou was evidently following the example of Malwida in Sorrento (see above, p. 43 n. *a*).

visiting in Sils-Maria together. Quite the contrary, news of Nietzsche's two vengeful letters then reached Schuls,[u] whereupon Lou slowly coaxed Tönnies into a lone mission of peace. On August 19, with Tönnies established in Sils at last, Lou signed herself and Rée into the Misani hotel in Celerina a few miles below. In Tönnies' words: "I encountered the hermit frequently and felt the piercing gaze of his feeble eyes upon me. I believe he knew of me but am not sure."[281] Nonetheless, Tönnies—"out of a strange mixture of motives"[282]— could not bring himself to break the silence between them. "An alien fate deterred me" (*"da trat ein fremdes Geschick hemmend dazwischen"*), he epilogued.[283] On August 26, when Nietzsche left to meet Overbeck in Schuls, Tönnies reported his failure to Lou and Rée,[v] who by then had heard about Georg Rée's threat of a lawsuit and Nietzsche's of a duel. Lou, furious, packed off with Rée, and Tönnies lamented to Paulsen: "Things have gone ill indeed with me . . . only do exempt me from explaining."[284]

By early September Tönnies, having wended a forlorn way to Bellinzona, succeeded in arranging by mail to rejoin Rée and Lou in Innsbruck.[285] There Lou forgave him only *pro forma* and would not see him alone, much less let him call her *"dear* Loulou" as of old.[286] Soon she left with Rée for Munich, whither Tönnies followed on September 24, having implored her *poste restante* for a tête-à-tête— "preferably outdoors"—at which he might tell her "much that will be decisive" and then learn *"how* it will be."[w] It was in fact to be cosier

[u] Lisbeth's letter to Rée's mother went out in the first days of VII 1883 (cf. above, p. 115 n. *r*), Nietzsche's letters to Lou's mother and to Georg Rée at the very start of VIII or possibly the end of VII 1883.

[v] Tönnies→Paulsen, 3 x 1883: he "met fleetingly" with Lou and Rée in late VIII.

[w] This dark petition reads in full: "Innsbruck, 23 September 1883. Honored and dear Miss! Grant me too a hearing once, that I may speak to you more fully and truthfully than I was so far able. My heart's need will loosen my tongue. And yet you need not fear my making a nuisance of myself again. What is on my mind is so convulsing me that only knowing everything can give me peace again. Sooner would I never see you again than pass these . . . *months* in trembling uncertainty as to *how* it will be. On this score I must tell you in confidence much that will be decisive. When and how can I see you *alone*? away somewhere, outdoors preferably. The English Garden in Munich, which you go to by carriage? Please, please, do not deny me this favor! If you have truly forgiven me for what out of a strange mixture of motives I failed to do, then I may speak to you again out of the simplest and clearest motive, as you earlier permitted me. Therefore let me say once again: *dear* Loulou! I shall arrive in Munich on Monday evening [24 ix], am thus at your orders from Tuesday morning on and shall await a reply *poste restante*, Munich. I am your faithful servant, Tönnies. If I find *no* reply Tuesday, I shall first assume that this letter was not picked up, find out where you live and send you the message: 'There is a letter *poste restante*.' "

than was to his liking, for upon his arrival Rée charged him with looking after Lou while he himself returned a few weeks to Stibbe (where Lou was now *persona non grata*—by the two Nietzsches' doing). "To be sure," Tönnies told Paulsen, "my role is restricted to my having taken a room in her vicinity"—in fact he had taken one for her in his vicinity, at her peremptory bidding[x]—"and my going to her afternoons for a few hours to read, etc. That I find it a pleasant role I cannot quite say."[287] He bought Lou a copy of *Zarathustra* I and read to her from it. She was not a pleased father. He later recollected: "Its pathos and unctuousness struck us somewhat funny. We thought the more authentic Nietzsche to be in those earlier writings dedicated to Voltaire's memory and created under Rée's influence."[288/y] By November Lou was sorely ailing, and as Rée arrived to take her south for the winter, Tönnies bade them both a hasty farewell.

Lou thereupon spent the better part of a year with Rée in the southern Tyrol—first near Bolzano, where there was a "dusty . . . woolly" air and nowhere to walk, then delightedly in a vegetarian establishment outside of Meran[z] run by "a former actor, now farmer and doctor, who . . . gave us meat at our request."[289] Nietzsche's midsummer fury had left Lou doubly apprehensive of forcible repatriation,[a] so she cloistered herself on her sun-baked balcony[290] and urgently applied herself to authoring. The point was to acquire a profession in any case and maybe even a livelihood just in case. The yield was an essay on "religious affects," the subject "discovered in her" by Nietzsche,[291/b] and a great labor of love: *Im Kampf um Gott* (In Struggle for God).[c]

[x] Lou→Tönnies [29 IX 1883]: "*Please* come here tomorrow Saturday at 11 AM; I must leave the apartment *at once* and hence look for a room or hotel as fast as possible. Would there maybe be one at your inn? Loulou."

[y] Tönnies specified that he saw the proofs of *Zarathustra* I in the Sils post office, then brought Lou "the brand new book." He can only have seen the proofs of *Zarathustra* II—but bought *Zarathustra* I. Lou and Tönnies were not the only ones disappointed: cf. e.g. Gast→o, 14 XI 1883 ("I think illness hampers his writing").

[z] The Martinsbrunn—today a large sanatorium.

[a] Her defensive measures (staying outside Prussia eighteen months and establishing herself professionally) were valid against Rée's family only, though she feared only hers. Half a century later she still insisted: "They were trying to drag me home"—but added incongruously that her family then agreed to her plan of publishing a book so as to obtain a "permit for [residence] abroad" (1931a:108).

[b] This essay, evidently the one begun just after Tautenburg, no longer exists —but see below, pp. 147, 222.

[c] Probably begun earlier also, since Lou→Caro [1 I 1884] mentions it in the way of a familiar topic after apologies for a long silence.

Im Kampf um Gott, a *roman à double clef*, recounted Lou's Nietzsche experience not only disguised, but modified in accordance with her attendant hopes and fears. Her narrator-hero was Kuno (read: Nico), a preacher's son who, having lost the paternal faith in his youth, seeks to override the resultant "inner conflict"[292] by setting himself successive intellectual tasks contrary to his inclinations.[d] He feels toward truth as toward a "higher power" which his thought subserves[293]—and this even when he ceases pursuing "exact knowledge of life in its sober coldness"[294] and commences exalting enthusiasm instead.[e] As a full-time, impassioned thinker, he is a "bacchant" and an "ascetic" in one, simultaneously reveling and renouncing.[295/f]

Lou herself came in three self-editions, one each for her three encounters with Nietzsche. And the three came in reverse order[g] beginning with the Lou of Leipzig and after, beauteous Margharita. A student with Kuno, Margharita loves the ascetic in him and lusts after the bacchant. He dismisses her as the merest flirt until his young friend and condisciple, the Count, tells him: "I do all I can to interest her, but she seems to be waiting only for you to begin with."[296] Kuno obligingly divests her of her "untouched purity,"[297] then casts her cruelly aside with an aphorism (out of Lou's notebook) about how woman's two charms are purity or coquetry. Margharita, having adored Kuno even in lust, feels godforsaken and infinitely lonely.

Kuno's use and abuse of Margharita went back to Lou's wishing and dreading about her winter plan (accommodated to Nietzsche's passion for chastity and whores). But the seduction was also sentimental fact as of Leipzig, and Nietzsche's subsequent rejection of his fallen angel of Orta (hard upon his warning: "take care! If now I reject you . . .") had left her a fallen woman such as Margharita felt herself to be.[298] Perhaps the kept woman ensued: Lou's allowance from home may have been cut in 1883 (in any case Rée paid most of

[d] That this was Lou's version of Nietzsche: see below, p. 148. Kuno's identity is obvious enough for commentators to have regularly denied it. Nietzscheans in particular miss the point, which is not whether Kuno matches their conception of Nietzsche, but whether he matches Lou's. This he does in fact positively all the way—whereas the Count, for instance, represents Rée primarily by contrasting traits.

[e] To this new exaltation Kuno joins the exhortation: "Let us fight for dying gods" (*ibid.*, 205)—meaning not Zoroaster but the Catholic Christ, for according to 1890a:49 Nietzsche had spoken to Lou about winding up his self-renewals a Catholic.

[f] For "*Bacchant*" Lou repeatedly wrote "*Bachant*," which means *itinerant scholar*.

[g] As far as the three erotic high points go, that is: see further below, pp. 123-24 and n. *b*.

their way). And sure enough, when Margharita turns up next she has made herself into a classy courtesan, with as it were a wink at Kuno from afar—one by Lou at Nietzsche. Her perennial protector is the Count, who would really rather marry her. He is a suave, worldly, artistic, life-loving Rée: a Rée suited for the role into which Lou cast him after the dire "adieu." With him, she has been putting up a brilliant show of mundane, refined pleasure-seeking—with secret sadness, though, having wished to do more with her life than just enjoy it. Kuno sojourns briefly in the same university town and forms a second, Platonic friendship with her. Before leaving, he considerately proposes. She declines in kind, pretending to have become unmarriageable through being "the slave of my own unrestraint."[299] He departs relieved. She histrionically follows through by taking poison—and dies weeping.

Their twilight reunion was the Leipzig one, with the Columbus lyric behind Kuno's proposal. It was also a hope for the future: thus Lou prefaced it with her "Life Prayer" in Nietzsche's adaptation,[300]/[h] which had preceded Leipzig and had presaged their approaching posterity together. Through Margharita's inner misgivings over her cat-egoism, Lou was retracting her final, self-justificatory letters to Nietzsche; through Margharita's noble shamming of depravity, Lou was roundly refuting Nietzsche's final indictment of her; through Margharita's suicide, Lou was living up to a remark of Nietzsche's, proudly noted by her, about how a nature as "*concentrated*" as hers really ought to issue in "a *deed*."[301] And throughout she was accusing Nietzsche in return—besides poking some fun at herself for her heroic posturing.

The Lou of Tautenburg and its aftermath is pious Jane. Nietzsche and Lou having relived their religious childhoods in Tautenburg, Kuno and Jane live theirs together as playmates and sweethearts. Kuno's, however, is not Nietzsche's as Lou knew it, but Lou's own. Little Kuno fashions a personal god unknowingly out of an idealized parental image and loves it with morbid intensity until one day late in his youth it vanishes, its credibility having worn off. Yet his heart clings to the faith "with childlike ardor" (to quote Lou's Tautenburg text about hers)[i] as he convicts himself of criminality, of satanism, of theocide, before settling into a brooding homesickness for God over the months and years. Before leaving for the university he even clashes loudly with his father over his loss of faith—thus endorsing

---

[h] Yet not exactly as later published by Nietzsche, who perhaps touched up his version even after Leipzig.

[i] See above, p. 81 n. *p.*

Lou's version of her clash with her mother. But he drew nothing further from Lou except for a share of his residual religiosity. In particular, his freethinker's fascination with Jesus was more hers than Nietzsche's: thus after defiling Margharita he returns to his solitude to ponder "the great Nazarene, who called religion a child's love for its father."[302] The complement to Lou's attributing her childhood to Kuno rather than Jane was Jane's playing along with Kuno's god only so as to be like Kuno. When Kuno avows that his faith is spent, Jane promptly and painlessly discards hers—and takes to devising ideals for substitutive worship. In later life Kuno tells her (just after she has spoken gushingly of woman's creativity in love): "You *are* my father's child!"[303]

By then Jane has married the man of her late father's choice[j] after having lived with him for a while at his family's estate—a nameless[k] nay-sayer without faith or ideals who claims to be exposing prejudice while merely picking away at anything and everything lofty or profound.[l] He improves on Rée only in letting Jane in her loneliness draw as close to Kuno as she pleases. But he cautions her beforehand: "Friendship between the sexes is a noble artificial blossom requiring efficient gardening talents. I once read that it even calls for a little physical antipathy."[304] She retorts: "Or great mental sympathy!"[305] —words she will soon eat. She appoints herself Kuno's "guardian angel,"[306] bears him comradely and motherly love, becomes for him "in the deepest sense a home for a weary warrior"[307]—following up Nietzsche's "I thought an angel was being sent to me . . ."[m] The two are "one with each other" in that he is her "work of art" and she his "creator," given her sympathetic grasp of his innermost being[308]— meaning Lou's character sketch of Nietzsche as a reply to his poetic "Plea."[n] The Count turns up to assure Kuno that Jane is "appeasement for your raging conflict, heaven and peace for your struggling unrest"[309]—Rée's commendation of Lou to Nietzsche, poetized.[o]

Jane and Kuno first talk Tautenburg when he calls women's tendency to devotion their "weakness" and she calls it their "greatness."[310] She defines love as seeing into another's depths thanks to "deepest affinity."[311] As he eclipses her self-given ideals, she kneels to him in

[j] Read: of *Nietzsche's* choice—an allusion to Nietzsche's urging Rée in Rome to propose to Lou (above, p. 53).

[k] Rée signed his letters to Lou "Your You" or "Your Nameless One" before settling on "Housie."

[l] Jane's husband loses her dowry through speculation—an allusion to Rée's gambling (see above, p. 49; cf. pp. 119-20).

[m] See below, p. 543.

[n] See above, p. 89.

[o] See above, p. 51, and below, p. 543.

"loving reverence,"[312] feeling most artistically creative and calling the capacity to worship one's creatures "woman's religion."[313] He sees "religion, highest morality, ardent faith"[314] in her love for him as it impels her to total, exclusive devotion. This "all-for-my-sake"[315] inspires him with a wondrous sense of his own great capabilities. It also enflames him emotionally—and here Lou's aphorism notebook took over from her Tautenburg diary.[p] "No path leads from sensual passion to mental sympathy, but many lead the other way."[316/q] So Kuno purposes to decamp—but he tarries, for "the lowliest love, the sensual, rates its force highest."[317] The Count, by then "almost" in love with Jane, decamps instead.[318] In his case, Jane has not healed an acknowledged inner rift but bared an "unsuspected" one.[319] Pronouncing her "the most glorious madonna-image," he tells her: "Before your radiance I grow only too keenly aware of my own limitations. I must flee you . . . so as to recover my self-confidence"[320]—this being Rée's post-Tautenburg resolve rendered courtly but also efficacious. Kuno moves to follow the Count's example; only "in leave-taking we love most,"[321] and Jane, feeling compassion for him in his passion, seduces him[r]—which was Leipzig righted. They part afterwards, he feeling like a "desecrator," she like a "fallen angel." She bears him a daughter, then dies of shame, whereupon her husband, who had forgiven her infidelity in advance, succumbs to grief.

Jane's daughter by Kuno is the Lou of Rome and its aftermath: fabulous "Märchen," as Kuno nicknames her[322] upon finding her in a solitary dream-world at puberty. Märchen is Lou's prototypical image of herself as a child or as childlike: all fantasy and candor both, as pure and warm as sunshine, inexhaustibly exuberant, elementally ravishing. Märchen has passed from some dreadful foster parents (read: Lou's parents) to a superstitious old housekeeper (read: Lou's Russian nurse) in a mountain village, where she fables away to herself day in, day out, seated upon a dusty staircase or kneeling before her reflection in a brook. Kuno, withholding his identity, asks her straight off whether she will love him; she promptly answers *yes.* When he tries educating her, however, she stubbornly resists before finally yielding. As then she hugs his knees while learning her lessons and tells him her fantasies in between, he thinks wistfully what a lovely wife she would have made him. Nietzsche had fused with his predecessor, Gillot.

---

[p] For the Kuno-Jane love sequence I count twenty-odd units from Lou's aphorism notebook (using fractions for fragments)—more than for the whole rest of the novel.

[q] See above, p. 92.   [r] *"I did not seduce Jane—she seduced me."*

Likewise Rudolf, Kuno's brother some twenty years junior, was Rée in the approximate position of Gillot's son.[s] During Rudolf's visits, which interrupt Märchen's studies, the two are like brother and sister together, the great figure of Kuno towering above them. A free-thinking theology student,[t] Rudolf is a melancholic misanthrope with a heart of gold. "Every joy dies of itself," he tells Märchen glumly, to which she replies: "Every joy outlives itself."[323/u] She once draws his portrait, which turns out "a grim, gnarling Moor's head looking into the world with infinitely dear, guileless sky-blue eyes."[324/v] Rudolf, who does not suspect Kuno's secret, is smitten with Märchen. And the Count, visiting briefly, is bewitched by Märchen, who imagines him her father. Kuno is saving the happy surprise for her seventeenth birthday.

Months before then, Märchen tells him she wants nothing so much from the whole big world as to make him happy forever; Rudolf turns green, and the housekeeper admonishes Kuno: "The child's only god *is you yourself*."[325] Kuno for his part expresses this fatal love through a poem summoning Märchen to caress him as he lies cold upon his bier.[326/w] Preparatory to breaking the news, he asks her whether she wishes to call him by "the dearest name" upon his return from a brief trip[327]—therewith emending Nietzsche's "I should consider myself duty-bound . . ."[x] and especially his "I absolutely must speak with Miss Salomé again,"[y] but also Gillot's " 'transition.' "[z] Märchen's "I do" sounds "like a prayer,"[328] and that evening she tells the housekeeper that she will wed Kuno. The old lady, having divined the truth, cries: "Child! Lord Jesus, punishment!"[329/a] and drops dead. Kuno, back for the burial, declares his paternity at last. Märchen faints away; a few days later she drowns herself, thereby returning "home to nature."[330] Uncle Rudolf, who had survived "having to give up Märchen to another man,"[331] cannot survive her death: fever and delirium consume him in a year's time. Kuno lives on as a hermit—but also as a "victor," for he has "outlived life."[332] His loyal friend, the Count, survives to bury him, having "outlived himself."[333]

In *Im Kampf um Gott* Lou did not so much reverse the amorous

---

[s] Cf. 1893g. [t] Cf. 1895f. [u] See above, p. 89.

[v] Cf. D 21 VIII [1882]: "You [Rée] are like a dark beauty with blue eyes."

[w] 1931a:37-38 contains a more pointed, superbly macabre version presented as a childhood original.

[x] See above, p. 53. [y] See above, p. 55. [z] See above, p. 50.

[a] Lou probably did not draw this divine curse upon incest from Attic tragedy, which she seems never to have read—or even from Racine's *Phèdre*, which she must have read.

sequence from Rome to Leipzig[b] as indulge increasingly deep attendant wishes: from Nietzsche's seducing her, to her seducing him, to his
turning out to be her father. The death penalty took novelistic effect
in a matter of years, of months, and of days respectively. At the same
time, the curse upon her romance with Nietzsche emerged progressively in that, when loving Kuno, Margharita is a virtual stranger to
him, Jane a virtual sibling, and Märchen a virtual daughter who turns
actual. In this last case, Lou's inner erotic impediment showed as
an outer one, with the advantage that she could then romance with
Nietzsche in all innocence—up to a point. That point was the one
at which, aboriginally, shame had cut short her romance with her
father. In memory of this infantile romance, Lou not only mothered
herself through Jane's mothering Märchen, but fathered herself too
in that Jane is the dominant partner in Märchen's begetting—and that
in any case Lou identified herself with Märchen's father to the extent
of attributing to him, beyond her religious childhood, her novel itself, which she styled as his memoirs.

But this self-identification was first and foremost the one with
Nietzsche—underway since Tautenburg and urgent since his "adieu."
Its mood was suicidal despondency: witness the gloom and woe per-
vading her narrative. Thus she turned upon herself the full negative force of her ambivalence toward Nietzsche,[c] with the result that
Kuno, even in acting out—with Margharita—her worst suspicions
about Nietzsche,[d] then reenacting Nietzsche's "adieu" with a vengeance, was purely heroic. Indeed, he was a "victor"—and she vicariously his treble victim. Beside her, Rée was fictionally a mere steady
loser, forever stepping aside for Nietzsche—and graciously at that. Fittingly, Rée followed two Lous to the grave in grief, surviving the
third, Margharita, only by dint of being well off stage when she played
her "great role"[334]—and this, one suspects, just so as to be available
for bearing the old hermit's pall.

Lou of course knew just what was autobiography disguised in this
well-documented reverie, but there is no telling how clearly she saw
her wishes and fears behind the rest of it for what they were. While
she was composing it in Meran, Gillot evidently fronted for Nietzsche

[b] That is, the erotic encounters proceed from Margharita's to Jane's to
Märchen's; however, Margharita follows Jane into the novel and out of it.

[c] The precedent was her mourning for her father, which began just after
she turned seventeen: Märchen drowned herself at that very same age. Lou
did herself more physical than moral violence on losing Gillot, and now
fictional violence alone on losing Nietzsche. (All three patterns were to recur.)

[d] But not her second worst, which thus proved unessential: Kuno does not
exploit Margharita intellectually (though he does take her more lightly than
she likes).

in her consciousness even unto arrogating Rée's place beside her: "At every turn I catch myself in thoughts of him," she told Caro, "and lately I was so deep in them that as Rée chanced to open the door and walk up to me, I confused him with Gillot in a sort of madness and, trembling in every limb, nearly fainted away."[335] She then felt the need to see Gillot again "at all costs"[336] and implored him for a reunion. He entered into Kuno not only as Nietzsche's original but in his own right: Margharita is eighteen when seduced by Kuno, Jane calls Kuno her substitute for a lost god, and Märchen is Kuno's fantasy-ridden pupil. Lou even signed her novel "Henri [=Hendrik] Lou." With its completion, moreover, all of her bodily symptoms, the precipitate of her encounter with Gillot, vanished,[e] with only the insomnia and the heart trouble ever to return.

Through the central concern of *Im Kampf um Gott*, that of drawing earnest ethical consequences from loss of faith, Lou did Nietzschean penance for her frivolity toward Nietzsche. By then she was semiskilled at having it both ways literarily about God's existence: because no man is quite himself except in God's sight, she argued, men make their own gods, God willing, so that human life is "a wandering from god to god."[337/f] The larger theme of wishful illusions crumbling was to persist for some time in her fiction over and beyond the specific case of religion. It entailed an ironical admission of fantasy's hold on her mind, for the hard realities disclosed to her characters were invariably wish fantasies of hers—such as having lost her virtue with Nietzsche, or that Nietzsche was her father. And one character of *Im Kampf um Gott* was to persist even longer, becoming a stereotype in the end: charming Märchen.

For all its juvenility, *Im Kampf um Gott* is a grand morality play.[g] There is something stupendous and elemental about it such that even its most awkward contrivances of plot (misunderstandings, overhearings, implausibilities galore) have a naïve authenticity to them. And it is none the poorer for its angelic sinners' pursuing its thematic purposes so singlemindedly. It possesses one quality in unique measure: originality. *No* literary influence on it is perceptible; conception and idiom were Lou's very own.[h] Its big failing is one of form: a poor synthesis of fabulous with didactic matter, each looking more exces-

---

[e] Lou→Tönnies, 5 XI [1886]: in Meran she "recovered extraordinarily well and was durably strengthened—really took away a body totally changed." (Cf. above, p. 124 n. *c*.)

[f] Kuno's last words.

[g] Bäumer, *Gestalt*, 498-99, compared it finely to the old Faust puppet show (what with all its devils yearning for God).

[h] Or maybe there is a touch of *Madame Bovary* to the Jane sequence.

sive than need be. The pattern is five or ten pages of action followed by ten or twenty of moralizing, as if the former had been penned "dreamingly"[338] by moonlight and the latter thinkingly by sunlight. Lou's tendency was thenceforth not so much to blend nonfiction with fiction more artfully as to sort them out into separate works. She was also to psychologize increasingly in her stories insofar as they did remain didactic; however, her characters, ill apprised of the change, were to act each on some one principle or other no less insistently, exclusively, incredibly—allegorically. Again, what her fiction was to gain in sophistication it was to lose in scope: *Im Kampf um Gott* is vast. It was a great promise—renewed once or twice but never kept.

More immediately it was a secret message to Nietzsche (like "Märchen's love-recognition at Nico-end"[i]): the declaration of a love that could never be. In the spring of 1884 the hapless lovers communicated indirectly, probably through Romundt. Nietzsche learned that he had "*actually* done her much harm" the preceding summer[339] as also that she was in Meran with Rée and about to publish "something on 'religious affects.'"[340] She on her side heard that Nietzsche was ready to resume relations. Perhaps Stein was answerable to her when he answered an invitation to Sils late in May: "I cannot dispose of any time before August, and then not wholly independently."[341/j] At any event, she was in Celerina again at midsummer, this time without Rée,[k] and was in Munich afterwards with Stein, whom she engaged to plead before Nietzsche for a reconcilement—and mention her novel to him. Then Stein visited Sils for three enchanting days beginning August 26. He not only mentioned the novel,[l] but also, Nietz-

[i] See above, p. 92.

[j] No further exchanges between Stein and Nietzsche are available until FN→ Stein [20 VIII 1884].

[k] A diary fragment addressed by Lou to Rée, absent on the North Sea coast, refers to walks and talks in the first person plural under the heading "Celerina, July 29, July 31," whereas Lou signed into the Misani in August of both 1883 and 1885; there was another hotel in Celerina then, but its old registration book no longer exists. According to Lou→Frieda [late 1901], Lou regularly spent her summers with Rée in Celerina; hence Rée may have joined her there in 1884. Lou cannot have traveled to the Upper Engadin, then almost untouched by tourists (the Misani averaged a dozen registrations a year), without purposing to encounter Nietzsche—who, as Stein knew, was due there in mid-VII 1884. In D III 1918 Lou reminisced about a brief stay with Rée in and around Schmargendorf before the two joined Gillot in Bavaria during the late summer of 1884 (a first sampling of the Berlin "countryside" with its "unspeakable dusty dryness, sober horridness," which they promptly fled—as Nietzsche in VI 1882 had fled its damp horridness); however, this stay took place, if ever, not in 1884 but before their departure for the Engadin in 1883 (with Gillot later fronting for Nietzsche in her memory).

[l] FN→O, 14 IX 1884: "*Der Kampf um Gott*, novel by H. Lou (Stuttgart:

sche told his mother, "spoke with *the highest regard* of Dr. Rée's character and of his love for me—which did me *much* good." As for the plea, it went unheard, having perhaps been inaudible.[m] And when three months later Stein, then back in Berlin with Lou and Rée, wrote urging Nietzsche to join him by mail in weekly discussions with "two friends,"[342] Nietzsche did not penetrate Stein's "dark letter,"[343] which merely estranged him from Stein for some months.[n]

Lou and Rée spent the late summer of 1884 at Sankt Quirin, a village on the Tegernsee in Bavaria. The four Gillots took a house nearby. Rée received their initial visit only "after having groomed himself five hours before a lopsided mirror," Lou told Emma, adding: "Naturally the first collision between the two powers was a somewhat painful one, the more since Rée had gone bounding about just beforehand but run into the cow stalls by error in the first fright and then needed a little time to air himself out . . ."[344] And later: "I take a peculiar pleasure in seeing the two men together. Past and present then curiously intertwine in my imagination, and I feel glad. Theirs is a most cordial bearing toward each other, and it is a lovely sight when Gillot in his warm way throws his arm about Rée's shoulders— his face with its vigorous mold and his placid, sarcastic mouth [beside] Rée's sharply cut, most candid dark features. . . . But I should also be *able to get to know* Gillot like anyone else, and this I can no more do today than ever. He remains for me what my emotions make of him."[345]

Lou was back in Berlin by December, when her novel appeared.[346/o] It brought Henri Lou, besides rave reviews, a satchel-

---

Auerbach)—Stein spoke of it to me." (But Wilhelm Friedrich of Leipzig published it.)

[m] Lou's version in 1931a:106—that to Stein's plea Nietzsche replied, "What I have done cannot be forgiven"—would hardly be acceptable even if anything else in that work were: see e.g. FN→o [7 IV 1884] (above, p. 110 n. *g*). Nietzsche did not know that Stein had seen Lou in Munich (FN→Gast, 27 VI 1887: Stein came to Sils "straight from Bayreuth").

[n] Inept as well as obscure, Stein indicated that the weekly talks bore on Wagner. Perhaps he did not quite realize that Nietzsche had broken with Bayreuth (though Lisbeth imagined mysterious pressures on Stein from Bayreuth: *FNsGB*, III, No. 12, note)—or perhaps, smitten with Lou, he bungled his commission out of jealousy: his invitation was phrased almost discouragingly. Nietzsche drafted a rough reply, then sent a moderate one in early 1885 about how he was not inclined to join in celebrating Wagner (Stein, though, had not said the discussion was necessarily pro-Wagner). That Nietzsche was then still well disposed to a reconciliation with Lou and Rée follows from FN→ Lisbeth, III 1885: "You compelled me [!] to give up the last people with whom I could talk without masks about what interests me. What they thought of me did not matter to me at all. [!] . . . Now I am alone and bored."

[o] But it bore the publication date 1885. (In 1886 it appeared in Dutch with no translator's name.)

load of fan mail. One enthusiast declared: "I and a whole circle of kindred spirits to whom I took your confession wish to express our warm and sincere gratitude"—only to confess his own soul's ills in return for eight pages, concluding with a plea for just two lines sometime about whether "when one is weary he too may one day sleep at last—and long, long......" On the sober side, the Norwegian literary couple Arne and Hulda Garborg sought out the maiden authoress's acquaintance. Deussen afterwards recollected having been "among the first to whom she gave the book," and "I must confess that as I read it my love for Lou blazed up in bright flames. With its various suicides, adulteries, and the like, it is diversely judged. My friend Ebbinghaus called it 'nun's fantasies.' But I found much spirit in it and fell in love with the spirit."[347] Lou regained some esteem from Ida Overbeck through what Ida described to Nietzsche as Lou's "sort of memoirs and seminovel."[348] Late in 1885 Overbeck himself judged it "the most astonishing book I have read this year."[349] He subsequently sent it to Nietzsche's old friend the classical philologist Erwin Rohde, who "read it with much interest. For all its great faults (its bodilessness, ghostly spirituality, etc.), it is enticing by virtue of the pure ardor and genuine sentiment bursting forth throughout. Yet every page exudes a frightful melancholy unmitigated by a free-floating will to life: really something such as stirs in Nietzsche's late writings, ghastlier than blackest pessimism, a suppressed crying alongside mock courageousness shammed as an antidote. . . . Health, with its brutal but vital *trascuranza*, is utterly lacking—and yet we have nothing better."[350] Ages later Nietzsche's biographer Charles Andler found comparably that "there is a little too much dying of sorrow in this tale," but that "Nietzsche could not have put it better" than did Jane in calling religion an innate propensity to divinize what one most loves, or than did Kuno in calling his "religious atheism" a Buddhism rendered active as befits Europeans.[351]

As for Nietzsche himself, in May he considered that, given the fine tidings of Lou's book, "I ought to like it heartily: she has finally fulfilled the hopes placed in her by me in Tautenburg. For the rest, the devil take her!"[352] In October—"by a neat twist of fate," as he put it[353]—his copy arrived from his bookseller's along with *Die Entstehung des Gewissens*, off Rée's conscience at last. The Réealist work he called "splendidly pellucid" but "pathetically, incomprehensibly 'senile.' "[354] And again: "How empty, how dull, how false! . . . Pity there is no more 'contents' in such a garment!"[355/p] Its companion

---

p Similarly, Paulsen→Tönnies, 1 III 1885, pronounced Rée's book too

piece, however, "struck me quite the other way round. What a contrast between the girlish, tame manner and the matter strong in will and wisdom! There is loftiness in it, and if the eternal feminine is not likely what is drawing this pseudogirl aloft, perhaps the eternal masculine is.—A hundred reminders of our Tautenburg talks too!"[356]

Nietzsche thereupon did some reminding of his own in *Beyond Good and Evil*, then in the making. After first observing that "behind all personal vanity, women have impersonal contempt for—'woman,' "[357] he rewrote his Tautenburg rewrite of Lou's essay on woman as a diatribe on Lou from start to finish—from "Woman would become independent, so she is beginning to enlighten men about 'woman as such': *that* is one of the worst steps forward in the general *uglification of* Europe" to "I think him a true friend of women who calls out to them today: *mulier taceat de muliere* [women should keep quiet about woman]!"[358/q] He drew on his Tautenburg outline for her further researches,[r] his Tautenburg instructions to her on style,[s] even her Tautenburg aphorisms as rewritten by him.[t] He epilogued on Tautenburg and after: "the same affects differ in tempo from man to woman, so that man and woman do not leave off misunderstanding each other"[359]; "when a woman has scholarly leanings, usually something is out of order with her sexually"[360]; "a soul that knows itself to be loved but does not love back shows its dregs: what is bottommost in it comes topmost"[361]; "a person of genius is insufferable who lacks at least two things more: gratitude and cleanliness"[362]; "the thought of suicide is a strong means of consolation: it pulls one through many a bad night"[363]; "who has not once, for his reputation's sake, sacrificed—himself?"[364] He wrote "eternal masculine" over Goethe's

---

simplistic and rationalistic (take man-the-egoist, add institutional punishment, and conscience results), but "for the rest, the purity of thought and language is a pleasure." Tönnies→Paulsen, 6 III 1885, called it a most serious but "inadequate treatment of such problems"—and subjoined an ample but still less adequate countertreatment centering in the point that moral approbation has latterly tended to denote a will favorable to the party expressing it.

[q] His whole section on woman (*Beyond*, 232-39) is replete with Louisms twisted against Lou well beyond her deserts (which, however, did include being echoed mockingly on women as properly childbearers rather than men's competitors): it was by all odds the worst intellectual aftereffect of their encounter.

[r] *Ibid.*, 148: "To seduce the next fellow into a high opinion of them and then implicitly trust the next fellow's opinion of them: who can pull this trick off like women?"

[s] *Ibid.*, 128: "The more abstract the truth you would teach, the more you must seduce the senses with it."

[t] *Ibid.*, 114: "A woman's colossal expectations from sexual love and her shame over them spoil all her prospects from the first."

"eternal feminine"—this time as what draws "every nobler woman" aloft.[365]

And he sort of semitook Ida Overbeck's hint about Lou's "sort of memoirs and seminovel"; that is, he made Lou's post-Tautenburg proposal for a "reduction of philosophical systems to personal dossiers on their authors"[u] his own—fatefully for the future course of European thought. "Gradually I have come to realize what every philosophy has been to date," he asserted: "its author's confession and a sort of unintentional and unrecognized memoirs."[366] So to his intellectualized memoirs and ideational mementos of Lou he joined his first "reductions." These he performed on Europe's philosophizing in lieu of Lou's romancing. In instance upon instance he showed up the former to have been so much self-defense against deeper insight—brilliantly, but all too triumphantly, as if such reduction spelled refutation (the very reverse of what he had taken the "thought from the 'sister brain' " to mean on claiming priority for it three years before). He concluded *Beyond Good and Evil* appropriately with a *poème à clef* about how at high noon "one turned into two" and, as light wedded darkness, "friend Zarathustra came."[v]

---

[u] See above, p. 88.

[v] Nietzsche on 31 x 1886 sent to Gast for a copy of his "Idyllen aus Messina" (a set of verses completed in Messina iv 1882 and published shortly afterwards) so as to rework them for appendage to a second edition of his *Science* (prefaced in "Ruta by Genoa, fall 1886"); he thereupon renamed them "Lieder des Prinzen Vogelfrei" (which means "songs of the outlaw prince"—but also literally "songs of the prince free of a bird," whereby, punster that he was, he signaled the final lifting of the shadow cast upon him by his eagle and gallows bird, Lou) and added one (entitled "Sils-Maria") that rendered the verses concluding *Beyond* less enigmatical:

> *Hier sass ich wartend, wartend—doch auf nichts,*
> *Jenseits von Gut und Böse, bald des Lichts*
> *Geniessend, bald des Schattens, ganz nur Spiel,*
> *Ganz See, ganz Mittag, ganz Zeit ohne Ziel.*
> > *Da plötzlich, Freundin, wurde eins zu zwei—*
> > *—Und Zarathustra ging an mir vorbei . . .*

> Here I sat waiting, waiting—yet for nought,
> Beyond good and evil, taking now the light
> And now the shade, nothing but a game,
> Nothing but sea, and noon, and time without aim.
> > Then one turned two, sweet friend, to my surprise—
> > —And Zarathustra passed before my eyes . . .

("sweet" being more than Nietzsche said but the best I can do in English to feminize his appellative for Lou, "*Freundin*"). Nietzsche too now had a fantasy memory of 1882, for Zarathustra as distinct from *Zarathustra* had preceded Nietzsche's mythic fission into shadow and Lou. Nietzsche also added "Nach neuen Meeren" ("Toward New Seas") out of the same mold as the Columbus poem (above, p. 94 n. *c*). It was, if possible, even more exquisite:

Paul Deussen's flame for Lou, fanned by her spirited nun's tales, "was soon sorely dampened," he recollected, "as in our philosophical circle I noticed that Lou was giving her preference to Heinrich von Stein's somewhat turbid views over mine. Our friendship survived nonetheless, though only as such."[367] Deussen may have slipped out of the circle by the spring of 1885, when Gersdorff, visiting Berlin, noted with amusement that Romundt, newly settled there, was participating with Rée "in a *philosophicum* in which Heinrich von Stein, the Russian girl, and one Mr. Haller discuss a new philosophy."[368/w] Ludwig Haller, once a public prosecutor and state councilor, had retired young so as to seek the great All. He found "the great nothing" instead[369]—whereupon, by Lou's delightful account, he "came down from the Black Forest out of long silence and diligence with a manuscript under his arm and, in ultraprivate lectures, let us in on his metaphysical triumphs and tribulations; in middle age, after seeing this work (*All in All: Metalogic, Metaphysics, Metapsychics*) into print, he dove to his death for expressly mystical reasons while sailing to Scandinavia one day."[370/x] Rée once cautioned Lou: "Beware *of Haller* too,"[371] maybe meaning intellectually.

That winter Lou and Rée left their circle temporarily to visit Jenia, still a medical intern in Vienna. Then in the summer of 1885 they were off with an enflamed reader of Lou's, a Berlin lawyer named Max Heinemann, on travels ending in Celerina. There, on August 3, Lou signed the "trio" into the Misani.[y] Again Nietzsche was close

---

> *Dorthin—will ich; und ich traue*
> *Mir fortan und meinem Griff.*
> *Offen liegt das Meer, ins Blaue*
> *Treibt mein Genueser Schiff.*
>
> *Alles glänzt mir neu und neuer,*
> *Mittag schläft auf Raum und Zeit—:*
> *Nur dein Auge—ungeheuer*
> *Blickt michs an, Unendlichkeit!*

(Word for word: "Thither will I [go]: and I trust / Myself from now on and my touch; / Open lies the sea, into the blue / Heaves my Genoese bark. / All glistens to me new and newer, / Noon slumbers upon space and time—: / Only thine eye—frightfully / It stares at me, infinitude!") Again he was embarking as Columbus under the sign of infinitude—this time affrighted without his captive darling, yet steering a steady course away from her.

[w] Lou and Rée probably knew Haller as early as 1883.

[x] Hartmann, 142-43: Haller's was "an ingenious but wholly disorganized mind," and his system was "abstract monism . . . a new variant of the irrational dialectic," relativistic and mysticistic. (I could not obtain Haller's *Alles in Allem*.)

[y] Six days later a medical student named P. Heinemann registered with a

by,[z] as the duo well knew.[a] Indeed, he was just then exceptionally well disposed to let bygones be bygones[b]—only fate would have none of it.

In early October 1885 Nietzsche, traveling near Naumburg, ran into Stein, who told him about Lou and Rée. Afterwards Stein wrote Nietzsche urging a reunion. Nietzsche replied: "I . . . am *hiding out* in my 'cave,'" whereupon he damned Rée's book on conscience ("one should talk only about what one knows firsthand") and praised the "seminovel of his *soeur inséparable Salomé*."[372] By mid-November, when Nietzsche went south again, it was clear that even Stein could not, or would not, patch up the Trinity.[c] Rée then separated after all from his *soeur inséparable*: 1886 found them living, as Lou then put it, "at opposite ends" of Berlin "like children mad at each other."[373/d] The thrill but not the guilt had gone out of their make-believe ménage. Besides, Rée had had enough of chaperoning Lou, and Lou enough of his chaperoning. The previous fall Rée had again failed his examination for a university lectureship, this time in Strasbourg, whereupon he had commenced studying the natural sciences with a view to grounding his moral philosophy in them[374]—the old Trinitarian "winter plan." Midway through 1886, after publishing a pamphlet on "the illusion of free will," he perforce moved to Munich to study medicine, leaving his old life behind with Lou, private papers[e] and all.

Lou continued to see Romundt and Stein philosophically. Otherwise her consorts were elder suitors such as Baron Carl von Schulz, who wrote her with baronial flourish beneath flamboyant insignia on the morrow of his undeceiving: "The blow took me too much unawares. No wonder if I spoke out of conflicting emotions like a madman. . . . I kiss your two hands mentally and bless them for the

---

doctor named Haring. Ages later Lou reminisced about how she and Rée once lodged with millers in Celerina till the first snowfalls, then slowly descended to Meran by mailcoach (1931a:107)—the grain of truth here being perhaps the length of her stay in 1885.

[z] Till mid-ix 1885.

[a] At all odds from Stein, who was then bidding Nietzsche to come north (FN→Stein, 30 VIII 1885).

[b] See e.g. FN→Paul Widemann [mid-summer? 1885] on sharp-witted Rée.

[c] Nietzsche's letter of 15 x 1885 is the last one known to have passed between them, but Stein did not likely leave it unanswered. Pfeiffer, *Leben*, 328, quotes from a letter of 12 XII 1885 by Stein to Lou indicative of meetings as usual in Berlin.

[d] Lou's address was then Potsdamerstrasse 92, Second Floor, c/o Hanna Krügel. Rée seems to have moved out on Lou early that winter, whether from this or another address.

[e] Including her own letters to him (most of which she eventually destroyed).

kindness and love that I have *deeply* felt and that remain no mere memories but are tucked away for the cold end of my life. . . . Please destroy these lines at once. . . . P. S. I meant to be strong but cannot. I must see you again: *please, please* do not refuse me this."[375] She despatched him with some candid doggerel on a calling card:

> That thou wouldst set me on a throne
> > To rule thy heart has caused my love to flee,
> For we belong to him alone
> > To whom, at his behest, we bend the knee.[f]

She sent Tönnies a bid to resume relations now that she and Rée had separated; it came to nothing.[376] She spent the high summer of 1886 in Lübeck, where one J. Gildemeister penned dozens of verses for her, beginning: "You have taught me how to pray again / Before the ideal."[377] "A love poem from Gildemeister!!!!!" she noted on the back. A common friend thereupon gave her a letter to himself from Gildemeister about being too modest to propose but unable to face a life without Lou.[378] Lou helped Gildemeister over his modesty, left him in high hopes, then wrote darkly that she could never see him again —and added his forlorn appeal[379] to her collection. Next an acquaintance from her earliest days in Rome, one Professor Schuhmann, took her to the Berlin zoo,[g] and "Just think! in these hot dusty days Schuhmann proposed to me. Yet I was so frightfully unlovable," she protested to Emma, with a copy for her own files.[380] The day after the zoo she sent for the despatched baron, who replied tardily and oddly: "Upon receipt of your so kindly lines I wanted to scurry right over to you, only I have a headache. . . . I have now earnestly resolved to change: to give up furthering myself and instead to strive, without any selfish willing or demanding, for a love that does not further you."[381] Finally, after returning from a few weeks in Bavaria spent principally with Jenia, Lou received a proposal from Fred Charles Andreas, a prodigious philologist; the engagement followed secretly on November 1, 1886.[h]

Born in Batavia on April 14, 1846, Andreas was half German, half Malayan on his mother's side and princely Armenian on his father's.[i]

---

[f] *Dass Du mich gar so überzeugt*
Zur Herrin wolltest, liess die Liebe fliehen.
Wir sind nur Dessen, der uns beugt,
Und unser Liebstes ist, wovor wir knieen.

[g] On 24 VIII 1886.

[h] D 1 XI 1893: "Our seventh engagement anniversary."

[i] My sources for Andreas's early life were virtually all secondary (chiefly Selle, Lentz, and Lou).

Part II: Youth

At six he went to Hamburg for schooling, then at fourteen to a Geneva lyceum, where he excelled at music and languages. Afterwards he studied medicine, zoology, and mineralogy at Halle and Göttingen, and at twenty-two he took a doctorate in oriental philology at Erlangen. Two carefree years in Copenhagen followed during which Georg Brandes initiated him into Eddas and runes. Next he fought in the Franco-Prussian war,[j] then spent four years in Kiel studying Old Persian. In January 1875 he was attached to an official Prussian "astronomical expedition" to Persia as epigrapher and archaeologist. What with six months' preparation in England, then cholera plus side research on the Parsees in Bombay, he first reached Persia in January 1876. There he early befriended the governor of Fars, a mighty prince[k] who accorded him every facility. However, Berlin deemed his reports irrelevant and recalled him. He fulminated, backed up by his colleagues, with the result that the whole expedition was recalled. He remained. For over five years he worked at odd jobs, from private tutoring to the postmaster generalship of Persia, becoming indigenous to all walks of Persian life and meanwhile evolving a theory according to which two dialects ("southwest" and "north") had originally branched off from Middle Persian. Only when he injured his eyes deciphering inscriptions in bright sunlight did he return to Europe—as courier to his royal patron, himself en route to Wiesbaden for eye treatment.

On reaching Berlin in January 1882, Andreas collapsed; he was one year convalescing. Afterwards he gave private language lessons, taught Turkish officers in a military school during the winter of 1883-1884, and as of November 1886 was slated for appointment in 1887 as Professor of Persian at the Seminar for Oriental Languages, a school for diplomats and businessmen due to open in Berlin. This prospect was an academic joke, for by then he had mastered Greek, Latin, Pahlavi, Sanskrit, Old Norse, Aramaic, and Hebrew, in addition to Javanese, Dutch, German, French, the Scandinavian tongues, English, Hindi, Arabic, Turkish, Armenian, and just about every dialect of Persian, from Afghan to Baluchi (including Dravidian Brahvi) to Ossetic to Kurdish. Furthermore, in each case he had an expert's knowledge of the corresponding literature, religion, and folklore, as also of the history, geography, and archaeology. He deciphered inscriptions with surpassing ease, memorizing even as he deciphered. His special province was Persia since antiquity, notably Zarathustra's legacy. His special concern was how dead languages

---

[j] He fought at Le Mans (10-12 I 1871).
[k] Sultan Iḥtišam-ed-daule (or Ihtišām el doulet), cousin to the Shah.

sounded, particularly how sound relates to writing and how dialects emerge, then vary; he intended to do a great book on all this once he was settled professionally. He entered into his materials with boundless passion and patience both, averse to all speculating about them[l] but also to all inductive inquiry concerning them. To his mind, a scholar could gain intimate knowledge of his subject only if he delighted in it for its own sake like a lover; it would disclose its secrets to no mere pryer. With this unhurried intuitive approach went an eclectic, godless, Oriental-style faith. His mode of living was distinctively his: he would work by night and sleep by day, wear starkly simple clothing, eat no meat, drink terrifyingly black coffee, take hot and cold baths by quick turns, and walk barefoot through brush. He adored animals—who reciprocated: strange cats would climb him as he ambled along.[382] Photos show him on the short side, with a thick, black beard and huge, wonder-filled eyes.

Lou was to depict him as the ultimate in demonic violence and instinctual disarray, domineering and weak-willed by fits and starts, his hybrid blood running alternately hot and cold like his baths; others saw him rather as manly and gentle in the long stretch, though with some temper and much caprice.[m] Whereas he called himself Charles, Lou called him Fred (in writing, mostly "F."), and soon after their engagement he Germanized his given names to Friedrich Carl. This hints at Nietzsche. So do his age and profession, his interest in Zarathustra, even his eye trouble—and a friendship with Erwin Rohde.[383] But Lou's love for him was a repetition primarily in that it "began with an inner dictate" in reaction against which she suffered "torment" searching out his failings.[384] Nietzsche had supplanted Rée by proxy.

"To me too Miss Salomé announced her engagement," Nietzsche wrote Malwida in May 1887; "but I did not answer her either, sincerely as I wish her happiness and prosperity. This sort of person who lacks reverence must be avoided."[385] Done with Lou as far as he knew, Nietzsche turned against Rée in July 1887 with *The Genealogy of Morals*, subtitled "a polemical piece." In the preface he declared his arguments of 1876-1886 against Rée's moral theory to have been just that, pretending, however, to have drawn them from an age-old theory of his own about to be expounded in full for the first time—

[l] Yet not to all speculating: Hegelian lore from his library survives with cross-referenced marginalia by him on such points as whether or not Being relates to Nothingness in the twofold mode of identity and distinction.

[m] According to oral tradition among Göttingen philologists, he came into a fair-sized inheritance while in Copenhagen only to blow it all whoring and resume his studies in a matter of days: this, then, passed in his mature years for having been just like him.

whereupon he presented them newly consolidated, sharpened, recti-fied,[n] amplified, supplemented, and cleansed of Darwin's and Bage-hot's traces.[o] By predating this theory before his acquaintance with Rée,[p] he was extirpating Rée from his past. He was also repudiating Rée the positivist par excellence when now he represented the sci-entific ideal as a derivative of Christian asceticism, Europe's mortal malady,[q] and repudiating Rée the rationalist par excellence when now he treated thinking as instinctual like everything else in life, only surreptitiously so.[r] Thus confuted, Rée became for him "congenial Dr. Rée" again.[s] And then, while in *Ecce Homo* he claimed to have meant himself by his *Human, All Too Human* tribute to "one of my friends, excellent Dr. Rée—fortunately too fine an animal to . . . ,"[386/t] he also supposed that a subsidy remitted to him by Deussen from " 'unknown' Berlin admirers" came out of Deussen's own pocket and, he told his mother, Rée's.[387/u]

[n] In particular, he set his old thesis of master morality versus slave morality philologically straight: the masters first called themselves "good" and the slaves "bad," whereas the slaves later called whatever was masterful "evil" and whatever was slavish "good."

[o] Still quite perceptible in *Beyond*, especially Bagehot's (e.g. *ibid.*, 201). *Genealogy* does retain Bagehot's distinctive frame of reference—nature's huge enterprise of making the human animal law-abiding—but no hint at a natural selection of those primitive tribes having the hardest cakes of custom. As for Darwinism, the old "herd instinct" gave way to the slavish principle of strength in numbers.

[p] See above, p 44 and n. *c.* FN, *Genealogy*, Preface: 3, even cites an imaginary first essay designating God the father of evil: cf. FN, *HKG:W*, I, 1-32, especially 31 ("my first notebook").

[q] Lou is dealt with separately in FN, *Genealogy*, III: 23 (on rabble playing at the pursuit of knowledge for want of a great ideal or love while dispirited beneath sham continence).

[r] Considered tentatively as "will to power" in *Beyond*, now in *Genealogy* as a derivative of thwarted aggression (and as originally an establishing of equivalences among pains for purposes of requital—hence as essentially valuat-ing or moralizing). On Rée as Nietzsche's model rationalist, see e.g. FN→Rée [late VI 1877]: "I ever more admire how solid your exposition is on the logical side. Yes, I can do nothing like that, at most sing or sigh a little—but *prove*! for the *good of the head*! That you can do, and that is of a hundred times more consequence."

[s] FN→Brandes, 10 IV 1888. Nietzsche was not just aiming to look congenial to Brandes (who was then preparing to lecture on him), for FN→Gast, 6 I 1888, maintained—too generously on Rée's account—that Brandes had cor-responded "about Dr. Rée and even Miss Salomé, with great honor to both" (cf. above, p. 115 n. *p*).

[t] See above, p. 46. Nietzsche's dots, presumably meaning: "have taken the tribute seriously." Nietzsche might likewise have put himself retroactively on the receiving end of FN→Rée [VII 1879]: "Long live *conscience*, since now it is to have a history and my friend has become a historian!"

[u] This was undoubtedly mere wishful thinking concerning Rée but not necessarily Deussen, who was perhaps responsive to a tribute to him in FN, *Genealogy*, III: 17 (above, p. 113 n. *l*).

Once again he had assailed Rée only after having assailed Lou—this time taking off from his bookseller's "joke" of October 1885.[388/v] But whereas he had earlier assailed Lou with her own thesis on woman, he now assailed Rée with Lou's reductionism, which he applied in *The Genealogy of Morals* not to a handful of thinkers and believers as in *Beyond Good and Evil*, but transpersonally to the regnant morality of Europe, disclosing its secret purport.[w] Thus in the depths he had identified Lou with himself even in dissociating Rée from himself—and made his peace with both. Closer to consciousness, however, the quarrel still raged—gigantically. For the big news in *The Genealogy of Morals*,[x] crucial to its whole argument, is the world-historical role of the Jews, a sly priestly folk with a genius for rancor, who, subjugated by Rome, incite the slaves of the Empire to moral revolt against their masters, thereby determining a unique historic reversal of values with modern nihilism as its final consequence—pending a transvaluation of values. Even in applying Lou's dictum on philosophy as personal confession, Nietzsche had complied with it, for this news was a subtle parable of the Trinity drama of 1882. The villain of the piece was Rée, the "priestly" Jew, an ex-master[y] who had instigated the "unclean" slave (disciple) to convict the "distinguished" master of evil purposes beneath his grand egoism and to infect him with compassion and vengefulness[z] such that his only deliverance lay in a prodigious stunt of self-surmounting. Lou was —subsidiarily—Jesus presented to Rome by Paul as "a martyr from earliest infancy" crucified by his people and hence received by Rome as a godsend: the "bait" swallowed by "'the whole world.'"[389/a] Yet that bait had been "temptation in its most sinister and irresistible form,"[390] so that Nietzsche, tempted, was also subsidiarily Jesus.[b]

[v] See above, p. 128. *Genealogy*, over-concealing its "origin," mentioned only Rée's *Ursprung* but meant rather Rée's *Entstehung*, alone purportedly a derivation of conscience. Nietzsche's new preface to *Science* (cf. above, p. 130 n. v) had faintly foreshadowed the intellectual assault on Rée: "In a single case I did everything to encourage an inclination and gift for this sort of [moral] history—in vain, as it seems to me today."

[w] FN, *Genealogy*, I: 14 (on "how ideals are fabricated"), is the epitome of historic reductionism.

[x] Clearly anticipated, though, in FN, *Beyond*, especially 195.

[y] The priests in *Genealogy* frequently seem, however, to have been mere adjunct masters.

[z] As also with the auxiliary slavish sentiments (such as moral indignation).

[a] But Lou was also Israël, for "Rome viewed the Jew as something against nature, an antipodal monstrosity so to say" (*Genealogy*, I: 16).

[b] Similarly, "the mystery on an unimaginable extremest cruelty and self-crucifixion of God *for man's sake*" (*ibid.*, I: 8) echoes Nietzsche's "Whether I

It went with his parable that Nietzsche no longer held compassion and vengefulness to be natural to the human heart, as when he was struggling to dominate them in 1883[c]; instead, the masters now had to learn both—compassion *for* the slaves and vengefulness *from* them.[d] Through his parable Nietzsche further associated Lou with himself inasmuch as privately he saw his person as heir to both the master and slave moralities in their most acute form—to the ethic of obduracy and to that of fellow-suffering, of vitality and decadence, of egoism and the bad conscience.[e] Almost consciously he was nonetheless still sniping at Lou in *The Genealogy of Morals*, as in the dictum that the idealism of marriageable girls derives from their inhibited sensuality[391/f]—though in such contexts she was by then more of a datum than a target. Most consciously, meanwhile, he had dismissed her as "this sort of person who lacks reverence" when he learned of her engagement. In Tautenburg terms, though, "reverence" was feminine love, and that he meant love for himself is clear from *Ecce Homo*: "Females . . . all love me—an old story: except for *abortive* females, the 'emancipated' ones, who lack what it takes to make children."[392/g] Explicitly he had only fairest courtesies for Lou too after *The Genealogy of Morals*: in *Ecce Homo* he called Lou's "Prayer to Life" "an astonishing inspiration" and his music for it a splendid symptom of his "tragic pathos" of 1882. "At some future time it will be sung in my memory," he added hopefully.[393/h] *The Genealogy of*

---

have suffered much—that is all nothing to me as against the question of whether you find yourself again, dear Lou" (above, p. 98); etc.

[c] See e.g. FN→Ida O, 29 VII 1883, draft.

[d] Here Nietzsche's primary sources were his notations of XII 1882 on compassion devouring him and on Lou's "vengeful schoolgirl" letter (Lisbeth's vengefulness having come six months later as a mere complement to that meanwhile acquired by him).

[e] The discrepancy between this his conscious thesis about his "decadence" and his unconscious contention that he first acquired the slavish virtues through his Lou fiasco carries over into his genealogical theory in that the masters come by their bad conscience all at once as against the long ages required by the slaves.

[f] Also: "Ordinarily a woman will botch the defense of 'woman as such'" (FN, *Genealogy*, III: 11); "the sick woman in particular: no one outdoes her in wily devices to rule, oppress, tyrranize" (*ibid.*, III: 14); etc.

[g] See also below, p. 240 n. *r*.

[h] See further FN→Carl Fuchs, 14 XII 1887 and draft (on top of FN, *Genealogy*, II: 7: "For my part I doubt not that, measured against a single night's pain of a single hysterical bluestocking, all the sufferings of all the animals interrogated to date with the scientist's knife are as nothing"). Nietzsche was making good an omission by Gast, who in 1887 published the "Prayer to Life" with music under Nietzsche's name alone. (Gast had added the second stanza, changed the key signature, and turned Nietzsche's song for tenor into a song for mixed choir and orchestra. He also brought out a piano arrangement

Morals was the moral drawn from his "bitterest experience": he had turned that dross into "purest gold"—unawares.[i] Yet his memoir writ large as history was indeed history, for he was a paradigmatic *Kulturmensch.* The supreme exponent of our conflictual moral heritage was also its supreme victim: this much of his memoir was not "unintentional" or "unrecognized." The rest was efficacious to the extent that neither of his two former partners in the Trinity, though they had possessed his mind maddeningly in their time, so much as figured on his premonitory mailing list when, at the close of 1888, madness did set in.

Rée broke with Lou altogether upon her engagement.[j] That winter Gersdorff, as he afterwards put it to Nietzsche, met Rée in Berlin "sunk in thought: I now know what an abyss divides you."[394] Rée took his medical degree in 1890, then set up in Tütz as a medical saint. Living alone in a hut on the family estate, he tended the community free of charge for ten years without a break. He would carry bread and wine to poor patients beneath his priestly mantle and readily finance trips to the distant clinics.[395/k] He came to hate Lou,[396] and he dismissed Nietzsche as all "morbid vanity" and "raving" in "clever" and "beautiful" phraseology.[397/l] He was preparing a supreme opus, *Philosophie,* and sought to buy up its forerunners,[398] which he called "immature works of youth."[399] Yet his thinking was no more mature now, only more set. He was still deriving transcendental concepts such as "justice" from selfishness progressively rationalized—still writing history a priori, only now without

---

in 1894.) As *Ecce* was not published until 1908, Lou may well have held Gast's omission against Nietzsche. (In reference to Brandes, "AR," which gave the "Prayer" as Nietzsche's, Andreas on 17 v 1890 sent the *Deutsche Rundschau* a Louish letter of rectification containing such unnecessary detail as Nietzsche's words about that "one small path by which the two of us would reach posterity *together.*")

[i] He did, though, boast outright of having recovered: "To be incapable of taking one's enemies, one's mishaps, even one's *misdeeds* seriously for long— that is the sign of strong, rich temperaments with surplus powers of resiliency, of recuperation, also of oblivion" (*Genealogy,* I: 10). He even exposed his "alchemical trick" for recovering (above, p. 100) as the anal one it was: "A strong and well-bred person digests his experiences (deeds, misdeeds inclusive) as he does his meals, even when he has tough morsels to swallow" (*Genealogy,* III: 16).

[j] To my knowledge, the last record of a link between them is Schulz→Lou, 2 IX 1886: "You probably mean to spend tomorrow with Dr. Rée."

[k] He would also rise between three and four to walk or write before his consultations began.

[l] (He was returning Nietzsche's compliment with a vengeance.) In this same context he averred that the first he ever read of Nietzsche's works was a few quotations in XI 1897—an outright falsehood (see Rée→FN, 30 XII 1877, [early v 1878], [22 III 1879], etc.).

wasting labor on corroborative research.[m] His philosophy, once daring, was now dated: like his counterpart the Count, he had outlived himself—and not only philosophically. Early in August 1900 Stibbe was sold over his head, whereupon he left promptly by night for the Misani in Celerina.[400] There he spent the next fourteen months[n] taking long walks alone, practicing medicine benevolently on the sly, and laying out his manuscript for the printer. At high noon on October 28, 1901, he fell to his death in the Inn gully from a steep, icy ridge beside it.[o]

As for Malwida, Hüter recollected that, when he asked her about Lou once in 1892, she "replied—gruff, embittered, deprecatory (not at all like herself)—'I was deceived in her. She let me down,' something like 'unworthy.' I said no more . . ."[401]

[m] "Justice" was still Rée's chief concern—especially the problem of how the idea of punishment came to be linked with that of transgression. But his *Philosophie*, a collection of sundry essays, contains some minor novelties, notably that love for one's mother underlies unselfishness. (On *Philosophie* as repetition rather than renovation, cf. Tönnies, "Rée," 668.)

[n] Or perhaps (despite Kolle, etc.) not all fourteen of them, for he signed in on 13 VIII 1900, then again in early VI 1901 and on 25 VII 1901—this third time with his sister, brother-in-law (Professor Sellin), and niece.

[o] The police at first suspected mischief but finally pronounced the death probably accidental. In V 1962 the elderly proprietress of the Misani confirmed the police verdict to me in vivid reminiscence, specifying that, while Rée was depressed at the time by his niece's recent suicide, he was also suffering from diarrhea and was evidently emptying his bowels when he slipped—though again, the worthy lady also recollected Rée, Lou, and Nietzsche drinking beer evenings together by the hearth.

"IT GRIEVES me that you should think me so gullible," wrote Louise Salomé late in May 1887 to her daughter, who, on top of earlier dark words about how "experiences and circumstances render it desirable for me to live alone," and again about "conflicts that make me suffer and impede an early marriage," had specified reluctance to play the fiancée as her "sole reason" for insisting on yet a seventh month of secrecy about her betrothal—which was no secret in any case, her mother added, as a most upsetting anonymous letter about it had been received from Berlin, and as a cousin of Lou's had heard "that you were engaged to a rich Persian who would buy you a villa outside Berlin and move there with you. Now what do you say to all this?"[402/p] Whatever Lou said, she was just then summoning Gillot to wed her in the church in which he had confirmed her. As he said *no* and again *no*, she threatened him with a full-dress affair in Petersburg at which, "because of the confirmation," he would be "officially" bound to officiate.[403] He capitulated by telegram.[404] The civil ceremony took place in Berlin on Monday, June 20,[405] the religious one between trains the following Sunday before the astonished Sandpoort parishioners. By making Andreas kneel with her before Gillot in Sandpoort, Lou meant to demote Andreas from an untouchable father-god. She succeeded only in antagonizing Gillot.

With Fred she proved frigid: the marriage could not be consummated.[q] Brooding through the first long months, she traced her trouble to a fixation "on the recent past: . . . detaching myself from it appeared to me on Rée's account as misconduct, infidelity—not toward him, but toward myself."[r] Waking and sleeping, she pined after Rée, nostalgic for the "childlikeness" of their association. She suffered the more for feeling that marriage entailed "the task of being happy" and for realizing that it was "no fate come upon us, but one chosen by us," and "not something we *have*, but something we *make*."

---

[p] Thus Lou must have sent announcements to Nietzsche and Malwida (above, p. 135) even while enjoining her mother to keep the secret.

[q] That this was the case (even if she did approximately say so herself: below, p. 472) follows from all the evidence—except one line in 1909a: "Even the most 'reasonably contracted' marriage is based on sexual relations."

[r] This and the unidentified quotations immediately following derive from the few diary fragments of circa 1888 that Lou preserved.

She ruled out divorce because of "the *bond*, the *word* . . .—they retain their sting: he is still alive, he is, exists, and you have abandoned your freely chosen task!" Yet she declined that task in the flesh, noting with revulsion: "One does not really know a person before having seen him gesticulate voluptuously in his sleep." At length[s] she told herself that loving, as against mere lusting or liking, was "a being bound" *in* something—in "as it were a common height to which we would both attain." To be sure, Gillot had been that height in person for her, only that was in "early youth"; later in life "a god-man is no longer wanted. . . . No longer one person kneeling before another, but two kneeling together." And as against lordly Gillot, the very man for such conjugal kneeling was "F. through and through— in his dedication to what he deems worthy or great, in his simplicity, his feeling, his deep hate for dishonesty, sham, pretense, and in his will to know." From the first "my bond with my husband . . . did indeed take me back to my earliest youth and even specifically to the period of my relations with Gillot—but exclusively to the threshold of the little Sandpoort church in which Gillot at that time" came apart from God.

In sum, she denied intending F. as godly-fatherly lover—in the vain hope of undoing the dire taboo.[t] She nonetheless nicknamed him Oldster (*Alterchen*); he reciprocated with Little Daughter (*Töchterchen*). And she wrote for his scrutiny those first years as formerly for Gillot's and Nietzsche's. She meanwhile copied him in that she learned to love animals,[u] to walk barefoot in forests, to eat and dress ultraplainly. Her letters told of her sitting up nights working or talking with him[406] and again of her doing all her reading with him[407]; according to her diary, however, "marriage seals one's lips . . . even when they 'must' cry out." As for hapless F., he was dismissed from the Oriental Seminar after his second year there—doubtless through "all sorts of intrigues,"[v] though his trouble with Lou must have hurt him on the job. He resumed tutoring; the great book was postponed indefinitely.

[s] Fragment dated 31 x 1888—the eve of her second engagement anniversary.

[t] Her later imagery for lovers corresponded to that of 31 x 1888 for her marriage (e.g. 1931a:44 and below, p. 208 n. *k*). One latent sense of her aspiration to converge with F. in something over and beyond themselves was the desire to have a child by him.

[u] To the extent that, as per Lou→Freud, 3 v 1930, "the animal soul . . . is, unfortunately, closer to me than the human one."

[v] Lentz, 5; cf. 1931a:240, 261-62 (he was too scholarly for the seminar's purposes). Among his colleagues had been the future foreign secretary Dr Friedrich Rosen; his prize student had been the future colonial secretary Wilhelm Solf.

The couple lived first in Tempelhof just south of Berlin—in Andreas's bachelor apartment to begin with, and then in a dilapidated mansion.[w] For two years they saw virtually no one except the Garborgs and Andreas's friends the Stolzes.[x] "Yet even out of a retiring life one can keep up with intellectual movements and interests in Berlin," Lou told a Petersburg cousin early in 1890, when already that retiring life was no more: "this year we were able to follow much, especially by reading and also as members of the Freie Bühne,[y] which on Sunday afternoons, with the best of actors from all troupes, performs dramas here that the official theater must decline for reasons of outer scruple."[408]

The Freie Bühne, directed by Otto Brahm, was the showplace of Naturalism in Germany beginning on September 29, 1889, when it opened with a performance of Ibsen's *Ghosts*. Throughout most of Europe, Realism had already yielded to Naturalism on stage and in letters a decade or two earlier. That is, the inescapable banalities of social life had yielded to its inextricable problems, the pointless norm to the pointed extreme, occurrences and recurrences to situations, data to theses. Flaubert having shown that adultery was as dull as marriage, Ibsen and Strindberg were now showing that marriage was anything but dull given its inherent perils, including adultery—and dullness. In Germany, though, where Realism had been best known in translation, Naturalism was naturalized belatedly—on the stage for the most part, and with a strong admixture of dialect, reverie, and rhyme. Just so it created a scandal: on October 20, 1889, the Freie Bühne's first domestic offering, *Vor Sonnenaufgang* by the unknown Silesian dramatist Gerhart Hauptmann, drew riotous cheers and jeers for blending didactics, lyricism, and crudity. January 1890 saw the emergence of Naturalism's press organ in Germany, *Die Freie Bühne*, a literary and social review published by four entrepreneurs in modernity: Wilhelm Bölsche, a novelist and popularizer of science; Bruno Wille, a Socialist novelist and educator; and the brothers Heinrich and Julius Hart, both poets and critics. All four were convivial hosts in Friedrichshagen, near Tempelhof.

Lou met Bölsche in September 1889, and through him their avantgardist neighbors: Otto Brahm, whose rehearsals she soon attended; the playwrights Richard Dehmel, Max Halbe, and Arno Holz; Wille and the Harts; the Scandinavophile literary couple Ola Hansson and

[w] Albrechtstrasse 2.

[x] Franz Stolze, the astronomical expedition's photographer, had remained a while in Persia with Andreas after its recall. (Lou also wrote Tönnies on 5 IV 1889, again seeking to renew relations.)

[y] "Free Stage": later called Deutsches Theater.

Laura Marholm; the painter Walter Leistikow; the novelist John Henry Mackay; and in October 1889 Gerhart and Marie Hauptmann, with whom the Andreases became most neighborly.[z] Quitting her seclusion, Lou moved into the front ranks of the Naturalist movement in Germany not only socially but literarily, as a leading contributor to *Die Freie Bühne* and other journals animated by the spirit of renewal, no thoughts barred. Only that spirit was hers in the first place, and hers refused to turn programmatic. She believed in individuals alone as against movements or schools. And she disallowed Naturalism specifically on its home ground, the stage, as defeating its purpose the way an actor would in performing without make-up.[a]

It was in *Die Freie Bühne* of September 1890 that Lou broke a six-year literary silence with an apotheosis of Hedvig, heroine of Ibsen's *The Wild Duck*; it reappeared the following year in her *Henrik Ibsens Frauen-Gestalten*. She showed herself unsuspectingly self-conscious about Ibsen's female characters beginning with Hedvig, who, "being still a child, . . . can become aware of her little self only in credulously cuddling up to her father, in sacrificial love for him."[409] By Lou's retelling, Hedvig's love flourishes within a fantasy world centering about a captive wild duck, so that when of a sudden her father doubts his paternity and turns against her, she, uncomprehending, resolves to sacrifice her duck for his love's sake, only to take her own life instead upon overhearing him gainsay her honesty and loyalty. Lou contrived to see in Hedvig's fatal bent for make-believe a deeper sincerity ("sham and lies are intimately alien to her"[410]), in her Jesus-like self-sacrifice the proof that she was her father's "bodily child"[411]/[b]

[z] (Also with the Carl Hauptmanns, Gerhart's brother and Marie's sister.) Gerhart Hauptmann, who had known Bölsche since 1888 in Zurich, moved to Charlottenburg on 15 ix 1889, then in v 1891 to Schreiberau, whence he frequently visited Berlin. Lou may have had some sentimental interest in him circa 1890, given the parallel between her later nastiness toward him over his love for a young girl (below, pp. 283-84) and toward Gillot and Beer-Hofmann for the same reason (below, pp. 310, 445). But Hauptmann himself never betrayed more than cordial respect for Lou in letters or diaries. Lou was not likely the chief model for the cerebral *femme fatale* Anna Mahr in his *Einsame Menschen* of 1891 (cf. Peters, 188-89): the characterization hardly suits Lou, the plot contains nothing overtly autobiographical, the dedication to "those who have lived" the drama does not imply himself—and in any case Lou's comments on the play (1891a:670-73, 696-701) betray no suspicion that it might have been about her.

[a] 1907a:251-52 argues that Maeterlinck came closer to reality than the Naturalists. Similarly 1891a:697: Johannes's bodily frailty in *Einsame Menschen* was merely a distracting "concession to Naturalism."

[b] Again: "she is obviously Hjalmar's child" (1889a:69). Hedvig's unhappy surprise was Märchen's in reverse, so that Lou's tacit logic seems to have been: inasmuch as Hedvig did not rejoice, her father must have been mistaken. One might add: like Ibsen himself.

after all (though "not his mind's child"[412]), and in her death a liberation from a constricting human milieu.[413] Lou's sympathy went to Nora (*A Doll's House*) and Ellida (*The Woman of the Sea*) as well as Hedvig—to Ibsen's three "thwarted dreamers."[414] Lou was even soft on Rebecca (*Rosmersholm*), who, out of fierce and tender craving for her late father,[415] incites Pastor Rosmer's wife to suicide so as to take her place.

By contrast, Lou was hard as nails on that general's daughter and professor's wife Hedda Gabler. Ibsen, in calling Hedda's play by Hedda's maiden name, underscored "the fact that she was her father's daughter rather than her husband's wife."[c] He also managed to give Hedda Lou's physique by and large and her age as of late 1890, when the play appeared. Lou hammered away at Hedda as a "childish,"[416] de-intellectualized pleasure-seeker,[417] aimless and nugatory,[418] self-confined within a pregiven decorous mode of life[419] while dreaming of bold and wicked deeds,[420] basically still actuated by an envy and vanity blatant in her earliest life,[421/d] when "in her father's house"[422] she had adjusted to the world only detachedly, ironically, reserving an inner freedom[423/e] that duly issued into outer "unfreedom to the end of untruth."[424] This mighty animus against Hedda was meant to dissociate Lou from the Lou-like monster-wife who would destroy a great work of scholarship in which her husband was involved.[f] Lou on her side produced a work instead—and with help from her husband, who translated *Hedda Gabler* for her orally and later looked over her manuscript. At the same time she harked back to Nietzsche by way of a symbolical prologue representing her six Ibsenite women as so many birds in an attic,[g] and especially in that her work as a whole was a thematic follow-up of her old essay on woman. As such it reechoed Caro, for to Lou's mind the toughest choice faced by Ibsen's women was that between self-assertion and

[c] Michael Meyer, in Ibsen, *Hedda Gabler and Three Other Plays* (New York, 1961), 262. Furthermore, Ibsen noted: "The daemon in Hedda is that she wants to influence another human being, but once that has happened she despises him" (quoted *ibid.*, 266). Conceivably Ibsen had heard about Lou to this effect from Brandes—but without getting her name straight (below, p. 146 n. *i*). (More likely, though, Hedda's—and possibly in some measure Frau Lou's—original was the heroine of Strindberg's "Corinna.")

[d] Respecting her hair in particular.

[e] Cf. 1893g:38—above, p. 9.

[f] Not a work of his own, to be sure, though it does virtually become one. While deriding Hedda as no more able to destroy than to create (1889a:161), Lou correspondingly overvalued Hedda's husband.

[g] FN, *Beyond*, 237: "Women have hitherto been treated like birds by men"; etc. On Lou as bird, see above, pp. 75, 76, 101, 104, 130 n. *v*, etc. (The attic in the prologue was in effect Hedvig's playroom enlarged.)

self-subjection in a man's world. She advocated the emancipation of women, but with the proviso that new, self-given obligations and interdictions should replace the old, man-given ones. She dealt with wives' problems most pronouncedly from the standpoint of modern, enlightened womanhood, upholding the ideal of a "true marriage," meaning a marriage based on perfect good faith and on a freedom achieved within the frame of conjugal duties—the ideal measure of how false *her* marriage was. In fact she signed the book Lou Andreas-Salomé, refusing to be fully a wife even in pen name. Yet she was wishfully Ibsen's Ellida, whose marriage went from "false" to "true" when her husband (a doctor) got her to realize the nullity of her yearnings after an unearthly girlhood lover, "the Stranger": thus Lou as Ellida daydreamed about becoming a "true" wife to Andreas as Gillot.[h]

Though Lou's Ibsen book was extravagantly acclaimed in its time,[i] its big talk about ideals—about self-liberation versus self-alienation through ideals, and about self-sacrifice for ideals or for want of them—rings false in ours.[j] It was overwritten besides, with an excess of metaphor. And résumés make up far too much of it—though they do incidentally show to how great an extent "the on-stage Ibsen drama constitutes as it were only a last act, sums up a long development,"[425/k] which was one ground of Lou's affinity for Ibsen: she too considered even the most spontaneous-seeming conduct to have its complicated prehistory. Finally, she discussed neither Ibsen's plays nor even his characterizations, but his characters themselves, quite as if they were real people: her original sin. She returned to theatrical criticism proper—the field of her last literary exercise for Nietzsche—only by way of a lengthy book report of mid-1891 for *Die Freie Bühne* on "a Dutch judgment of modern German dramas"[l]; a brief study of a novelist,[m] then one of a poetess[n] followed in 1892.

Lou could develop no farther as authoress, feminist, or female except as Nietzsche's ex-disciple. In "Der Realismus in der Religion" of late 1891, she implicitly declared herself loyal to Nietzsche's some-

[h] Lou treated Ellida as a madder fantast than did Ibsen (see 1889a:115-24, 130-38, 140-45, 152).

[i] Ibsen himself saluted it affably in a letter of 5 II 1891 to the author—headed "Dear Sir"! Hulda Garborg translated it into Norwegian for publication in 1893 with a foreword by Arne Garborg.

[j] But even forty years afterwards Meyer-Benfey, "L A-S," 306, called it "doubtless the most wonderful book ever written on Ibsen."

[k] Only in this line from a footnote and on the title page is Ibsen named in the book.

[l] 1891a—which contains practically no commentary of Lou's own.

[m] Ossip Schubin (= Lola Kirschner): not available to me.

[n] Emil Marriot (= Emilie Mataja): not available to me.

time Réealism.[o] Her professed purpose was to pin down "the religious affect,"[426/p] as Nietzsche had prompted her to—and she did identify its two edifying components quite nicely: a feeling of deepest personal insufficiency and the very opposite.[427/q] Her final purpose was what she took Nietzsche's to have been: religious prophecy. She contended that the "science of religion"[428] must henceforth attend to the religious affect, presumably an all-human affect given a huge recent crop of books arguing from man's "inner need" for religion to its "pragmatic value."[429/r] And she went on to present worship as the supreme manifestation of man, which rises with him from crude wishing through god-making to a longing for holy communion. She saw nothing to hamper piety in the recognition that gods are man-made; on the contrary, she declared that the only true gods were those knowingly devised by a worshipper to suit himself. Her hints at how gods are devised were strictly rhetorical: once the religious affect is self-avowed, "human strength and majesty . . . create a god owing to no inconsequence of thought, but to the religious productivity of the entire self aspiring aloft"[430]; religious mystification will soonest cease "if modern man gains the force not only to turn away from whatever his reason exposes as deception, but also to turn toward whatever conduces to his uninhibited inner development"[431]; to become religiously productive as of old despite the new "frightful unbridgeable gap"[432] between "thinking and believing,"[433] we must face up to "our need and loneliness in our god-abandonment"[434] and not "try to fool ourselves with any philosophical sham-god"[435]; the "one thing needful" is the courage to look within ourselves to where "the saving god has every time emerged."[436] These prescriptions resemble nothing so much as Lou's Tautenburg formula for Nietzsche's idealizing, the more since now as then she treated ideals as equivalent to gods for devotional purposes.[437/s] Thus she set up as Nietzschean god-maker—while tacitly asserting that she had created her childhood god knowingly and that he had been true nonetheless.

Following Nietzsche's breakdown, Lou filled in her old sketch of him and brought it up-to-date as she pored over his life's work. The

[o] She ranged herself among the "religious realists" (1891b:1005).
[p] Cf. above, p. 118.
[q] Cf. 1890a:230-31 on this as Nietzsche's religious affect.
[r] Lou's essay was nominally a commentary on one such work, an anonymous confession (*Die Religion der kommenden Zeit*) of a lifetime of prayer to an orthodox god, to nothingness, and to the world process by turns.
[s] Similarly in *Kampf* between times she represented ideals as home-made like gods (withholding the recipe)—but, confusingly, spoke of Kuno (also of Nietzsche in 1890a) as having fashioned an ideal when he only adopted a pregiven value (e.g. truth) as absolute.

result was the first significant treatment of him in print[t]: ten precursory articles of 1891-1893, elaborated into *Friedrich Nietzsche
in seinen Werken* of 1894.[u] This final product was intended as a case
study of a freethinker religiously creating and miscreating ideals and
as an object lesson in reducing a philosophy to a personal dossier on
its author.[v] Nietzsche's writings emerged as symptomatic expressions
of a self-induced nervous derangement at distinct stages of its development toward insanity. This thesis, startling for its time, was damning
for Nietzsche in effect and in aftereffect, confused as were Lou's intent
and argument respectively.

According to *Friedrich Nietzsche in seinen Werken*, Nietzsche's
life was dominated successively by his boyhood religious faith, his
philological studies, his devotion to Schopenhauer and Wagner, his
positivism, and finally a prophetic-mystical exaltation of the will.[w]
The transitions, abrupt, were marked by acute pathological crises.
Each was a deliberate "*falling ill through thoughts and getting well
through thoughts.*"[438] For "whenever he began to feel at ease within
one outlook"[439] he would repudiate it, unloosing instinctual turmoil
within himself; then he would engage in a new intellectual enterprise
entailing a new instinctual harmony. This "psychic process . . . is his
ever-recurrent typical experience,[x] through which he ever again
straightened himself out, raised himself up over himself—and finally
fell head over heels to his ruin."[440] He took his power of recovery for
a sign of health; just as surely as he ever cured himself, however,
"just as necessarily did he, after long convalescence, require suffering
and struggle, fever and wounds" again.[441] "Over every goal reached,
every convalescence completed, stand the same words: 'He who attains his ideal thereby goes beyond it.' "[442]

[t] Brandes, "AR," 59, proclaimed itself "the first study of whatever length"
concerning Nietzsche: it consists of thirty-seven superficial pages. Other
Nietzscheana prior to Lou's were crackpot adulation or defamation.

[u] Lou's articles (six appeared in 1891, three in 1892, one in 1893) reappeared
in sequence with few changes early in her book, which she was correcting in
proof by 25 XI 1893 and until 20 II 1894.

[v] Lou declared this latter purpose—to depict "Nietzsche's thought-experience
in its signification for his psychic person, the self-confession in his philosophy"
—at the very outset (1890a:6), after quoting Nietzsche's letter about the
"thought from the 'sister brain' " (in facsimile) and his restatement of that
thought in *Beyond*.

[w] This fivefold distinction is somehow subordinated in the first instance
(1890a:9-11) to a threefold one between successive decades as student,
philosopher, and hermit respectively; of the five periods, moreover, the last
three are soon alone at issue—as "Nietzsche's three periods" or simply
"Nietzsche's periods."

[x] This follows up a quotation from FN, *Beyond*, 70: "If one has character,
one has an ever-recurrent typical experience."

This pattern was possible because of what Nietzsche himself called his "decadent" emotional constitution. Even just before a crisis, when he was at his healthiest, his drives were at variance, only directed to a common goal—as if vying for honors in the same heroic campaign.[443] And yet even then his drive to knowledge actually lorded it over the others, since it was as knower that he set his drives their new goal of knowledge in the first place, then watched them rally. The "power of knowledge" was in fact so "divisive" as to "make it *look*" as though the goal lay "*outside*" of the drives, which consequently only pressed the harder toward it "as if to elude themselves and their conflict."[444] Nietzsche could draw bliss "from such a transparent self-deception"[445] through all his suffering because his religious affect, stirred by this sacrifice of one part of himself to another, fixed upon his own person for want of a more credible object—wherewith the "cleavage" turned into a "dividuum."[446/*y*]

Indeed, his mental peregrinations began when in his boyhood he forsook the paternal faith, dear as it was to his heart, because "his mind needed emotional battles, pains, and convulsions so as to attain to itself in potent development."[447] Thereafter he "longed for the lost paradise, while his mental development compelled him to depart from it in a straight line,"[448] so that he sought God "*in the most diverse forms of self-divinization*: that is the story of his mind, his works, his illness."[449] In his positivist period, he exalted rationality over against affectivity as if to spite himself. The result was "that religiously motivated *self-split* required by Nietzsche by dint of which the knower can look down upon his own being with its stirrings and drives as upon a *second* being"[450]; thereby "he so to say sacrificed himself to the truth as to an ideal power"[451] in "an attempt to intoxicate himself through this self-coercion,"[452] even while regarding his new ideal as cool balm for his overheated soul. Even at that the new unity set in, whereupon he sang and sighed again with his whole heart.[453] Only the next time round did he (with "secret ruse"[454]) "finally solve the tragic conflict of his life—the conflict of needing God and yet having to deny him. First, drunk with longing, he fashioned the mystical overman-ideal in dreams and raptures, seer-like; then, to escape from

---

y Choice rhetoric follows: "Health was attained, to be sure, but by means of illness; real worship, but by means of self-deception; real self-affirmation and self-elevation, but by means of self-injury. Whence in the potent religious affect, from which alone in Nietzsche's case all knowledge proceeds, lie inextricably intertwined: self-sacrifice and self-apotheosis, cruel self-destruction and voluptuous self-divinization, woeful languishing and triumphant convalescing, glowing ecstasy and cool self-awareness," each "ceaselessly" conditioning its opposite (1890a:35)—"a chaos that would, that *must* bear a god" (*ibid.*, 36).

himself, he strove to identify himself with his creature by a frightful leap. Thus at the last he turned into a double personage: half sick, suffering man and half redeemed, laughing overman."[455] This was madness already—and through his mind's "highest sacrifice, the sacrifice of itself,"[456] he had come full circle, "like a weary child returning to its first home."[457]

In point of fact Nietzsche's insanity was due to a brain ailment of physical origin, hence was not mentally self-induced,[z] and there is no correlation whatever between the onsets of his malady, his intellectual self-renewals,[a] and his alternations between felt instinctual harmony and felt instinctual chaos. He does seem to have induced and relished many a crisis, only not knowingly. Lou, however, lacked a conception of unconscious purpose,[b] for all her strong sense of it: thus she was attempting a psychoanalysis without the theoretic means. Nietzsche did somehow, from childhood on, prepare for a psychic split "into sacrificial god and sacrificial animal."[458] Lou, though, despite her reductive intent, respected his own intellectualizations of his instinctual trouble—beginning with the "religious affect" and the "knowledge-drive." Besides, if his knowledge-drive did set the direction for all his other drives, there was no "inner cleavage."[c] And anyhow,

[z] That his symptoms were all psychogenic is the sense of her whole thesis (see especially *ibid.*, 87-88, 248-55), which, however, she supplemented once by treating his madness as a publicity stunt on behalf of *Zarathustra*: "The madness was meant to attest to the strength of the life-truth at whose brilliance men go blind" (*ibid.*, 252) by virtue of his own view of "states of madness as proofs of special election" (*ibid.*, 246, drawing on FN, *Dawn*, 14, which accounts madness a prime qualification for prophesying new values in that it breaks the bond with the old).

[a] He suffered continually from 1873 on, but not at all during the first two of the four transitions at issue. His worst long crisis before the last commenced in 1879, in the very midst of his positivist period; FN→Brandes, 10 IV 1888, gave the crucial explanation: "My father died quite young, in the very year of life in which I was myself closest to death" (imitating his father exactly would have meant his falling ill in VIII 1878 and dying in VII 1879). According to D 21 VIII 1882, the pain from which Nietzsche found (without seeking) release upon dedicating himself to new philosophic aims was strictly mental, and his physical suffering was only an oddly parallel instance of "the passiveness of his sorrow." 1890a, while consistently designating the physical crises that attended his transitions as his worst, once curiously treated such crises in general as mere sequels to stretches of robust mental activity (1890a:87-88)—hence as neither self-induced nor contingent on a change of philosophical course.

[b] Cf. below, p. 153 n. *n*. Earlier she had written most promisingly of Nora's entangling herself in a net of lies with the unconscious purpose of being detected, and this "in unconscious protest against father and husband" (1889a:25) —and more such was underway. Meanwhile, her notion of a repressed religious affect avenging itself was nicely proto-Freudian.

[c] If "in consequence of this self-deception all powers press enthusiastically toward knowledge" (1890a:33), then it was no self-deception; etc. The logical

this whole problematical scheme loosely adapted from Nietzsche cannot accommodate his transition of 1882 from exalting the dispassionate quest for knowledge to denigrating it on the instincts' behalf.[d] As to the why of his successive self-renewals, her referring them back to an original repudiation of Christianity merely displaced the question. What "drove him" from his "warm 'home' " in the first place (along that straight[459] circular[460] course)? A "dark instinct."[461]

Were his new departures so very abrupt? The one treated as prototypical—his abandonment of Christianity—appears to have been gradual, and Lou's own detailed account gradualized those to and away from positivism.[e] Again, were they so very radical? Possibly he said so in Tautenburg. But later he boasted lifelong philosophic constancy for all his Wagnerite and positivist posturing—and, at the other extreme, perpetual philosophic experimentation.[f] There was certainly more continuity, even fixity, to his constructions and valuations than Lou's thesis allowed.[g] His self-imposed orientations remain: philologic scholarship, discipleship to Schopenhauer and Wagner, positivism. But after 1882 did he not simply come into his own?

---

trouble came down to her treating drive and goal as equivalent in the case of knowledge. Indeed, throughout 1891d (below, p. 160) she wrote correspondingly of having deified her own *drive to* knowledge as a surrogate for her own lost god—thus situating the surrogate within.

[d] 1890a:169-70 conceded this implicitly in maintaining that Nietzsche the postpositivist forcibly subordinated his knowledge-drive to his affectivity and obtained the same old religious uplift. The relationship of knowledge-drive to chaotic instincts cannot be simply inverted, however, for then instinctual chaos would set the psychic pace and direction, with the religious affect on the side of the squelched knowledge-drive—and with Nietzsche mistaking his instincts for no part of himself.

[e] As against Nietzsche himself, who dated his positivism from 1876 (FN→ Lou [9 VII 1882]; reproduced 1890a:92-95) and from *Human* (FN→Lou [3? VII 1882]; passage not quoted in 1890a), Lou dated it from 1878 (1890a:10), but also represented *Human* as a transitional work (*ibid.*, 97-98) even while terming his transitions "abrupt" (*ibid.*, 98)—and as transitional because written without full *inner* conviction, though her point was precisely that he changed his mind fast and his heart slowly. At the other end, *Science* "so to say already belongs to the following mental period" (*ibid.*, 123), is in fact "the work that inaugurates it" (*ibid.*, 144), while *Dawn* (1881) was ideationally the most clearly transitional of all his books (*ibid.*, 131), and the shadow of "The Wanderer and His Shadow" (part two of *Human*: 1880) was one cast by a setting sun (*ibid.*, 124)—all of which leaves nothing in between.

[f] This is the gist of *Beyond*, prefigured by many an earlier utterance (e.g. *Human*, I, 483: "Convictions are more dangerous enemies of truth than are lies").

[g] When speaking summarily, Lou let nothing philosophical survive Nietzsche's self-renewals beyond his philosophical personality itself. She might consistently have let many concepts, some constructs, and even a few values get by—and in fact did repeatedly note specific instances of continuity on all three counts.

And was his output all of a piece from the visionary *Zarathustra* through the reflective, argumentative *Beyond Good and Evil* and *The Genealogy of Morals* to the frantic Nietzscheana of 1888? Her characterization of his final personality split, lurid as it may be, is quite apposite to these last[h] (except for the laughing[i]) and premonitorily to *Zarathustra*—only in that case he took his "frightful leap" right over those two sturdy, searching works in between.[j]

Actually Lou had more than she could do to schematize Nietzsche's last six years' work, let alone schematize it under the sign of self-imposition, especially as she rightly denied that it came to any "system."[k] On one of her pages Nietzsche, dreading a final solution to his beloved problems, "plunges definitively into the eternal riddles of mysticism"[462]—which just won't do. On another he is a "Columbus in reverse" in that, striking out from positivism, he alights unknowingly on his prepositivist shores of "metaphysics"[463]—only these same old shores turn antipodal when the late as against the early "metaphysics" is called an affirmation as against a negation of life: "sansara" as against "nirvana."[464/l] Into her extensive definition of "Nietzsche's final philosophy"[465] went a "repudiation of his former purely logical ideal of knowledge" together with a "displacement of the foundation for truth into the world of emotional impulses, source for a new appraisal of all things,"[466] a "mystical philosophy of the will"[467] informed by a conception of "everything highest" as "a kind of atavism,"[468] a preoccupation with dreams and madness, a "glorification of artistry"[469] as alone imparting final meaning to existence, and, overriding even this last, a cult of genius amounting to "the mystery

[h] Especially to his megalomaniacal *Ecce* and his final death sentence on Christianity, *The Antichrist*—the more wonder since neither had yet been published when she wrote.

[i] Which ended with *Zarathustra* IV.

[j] Evidently she took his *Zarathustra* IV (first published in 1891) for his "last work," written "on the threshold of madness" (1890a:38), only to learn belatedly that it was actually completed in 1885—and to say so in her conclusion (*ibid.*, 261) without altering the earlier passage or her notion of a "frightful leap" presumably from *Twilight* to *Zarathustra* IV.

[k] She maintained, however, that he had meant it to come to one (1890a:154-55), which is questionable. If he did toward the last, his starting point was to have been the "will to power," which she avoided discussing.

[l] (Actually Nietzsche never advocated nirvana.) Between these two extremes: once his reversion becomes "a sort of regression" confined to aestheticism and the cult of genius (*ibid.*, 153-54—though a fundamental difference concerning aesthetics crops up: *ibid.*, 216-21), once "the thought-contents of the new theory turn out to be an ingenious union of the two [preceding] philosophical phases" (*ibid.*, 158), twice this ingenious union becomes a mere semiunion (*ibid.*, 168ff. and 181-82), and once the likeness between his prepositivism and his postpositivism comes down to the underlying feeling (*ibid.*, 241-42).

of a prodigious self-apotheosis"[470] and issuing in "a religious mysticism in which God, world, and man fuse into a single prodigious superbeing."[471]

Lou's aptest point was of no real use to her argument: that then as before, only more so, Nietzsche "generalized his soul into a world soul"[472] and voiced his "inner inspiration" as "a commandment for all mankind."[473] Accordingly, his own instincts being anarchic, he called all mankind decadent, and hailed the overman for the sake of his own self-redemption. Only she added that his late hypotheses—and "most particularly" those about Jesus as "bait"[474]—were consequently not to be taken seriously "on their scientific side,"[475] for "exact scientific inquiry now played no further role with him"[476/m]: that he was merely "out to elicit from and project into human history something the significance of which lay for him within a hidden emotional problem. . . . The basic question for him was not what the emotional history of mankind had been, but how to construe his own emotional history as that of all mankind."[477] This is inexact and unjust enough for Lou to have "most particularly" *sensed* what "hidden emotional problem" he was construing. For, properly stated, his purpose was to study his own *moral pre*history introspectively while knowing the external facts of it. And the resultant hypotheses were scientific inasmuch as they cut straight through a whole mass of historical data, cutting out none. Hypotheses drawn from introspection are, if anything, less liable to be vitiated by unwitting projection than others. The "slave nature," Lou contended, was Nietzsche's own ego, the "master nature" his self-ideal, "whence his conception of the historical battle between the two is in its entire import nothing but a coarsened illustration of what goes on in the highest human individual."[478/n] But of course! Except for that sly "entire," Lou's reduction was here no less valid than Nietzsche's introspection—only to reduce is still not to refute. At the same time, it was her good right —and better—to reject his oracular valuation of historic values. For whereas it took introspective genius to date the human soul from when bullied weaklings first made a virtue of bullying themselves in retaliation, and even granted that self-bullying is self-defeating in the long run, Nietzsche's prescription for speeding delivery of the overman (through intensifying humanity's nihilistic birthpangs[o]) was

---

[m] Cf. above, p. 56 n. *i*.

[n] Lou treated even such projection by Nietzsche not as unconscious but only as "naïve" (1890a:23), "paradoxical" (*ibid.*, 143), and the like, though here she *required* a psychology of the unconscious.

[o] Lou's version of how Nietzsche meant this (*ibid.*, 205: that the cure for mankind's vices was their overindulgence) was adapted from one of Rée's con-

no more binding on others than were his incessant dictates concerning good taste. Yet again, through nothing did he show up our ethic as ascetical and other-worldly (hence superannuated) so neatly as through the demonic question of whether, if we knew that we should be bound to relive our lives *ad infinitum*, we would not live them differently. Lou, however, saw in this "eternal repetition of that which is of itself senseless"[479] only a fearsome *idée fixe* of his late period from which he looked to himself as philosopher-savior for deliverance.

Lou's animus against Nietzsche's postpositivism is plain—and was plainly affectionate at the source, for the sense of it is that Nietzsche had taken a bad turn in quitting the Trinity.[p] Yet she was also insisting that, as his disinherited daughter-bride, she had missed out on only desultory ravings. Through her thesis about his self-induced transitional crises, meanwhile, she was declaring herself the merest innocent occasion for his pain and fury after Leipzig. Representing his ailments as psychogenic, she was returning the compliment of his last letters to her. Representing his madness as psychogenic,[q] she was denying the hereditary factor[r]—anxiously, given her felt kinship with him. For all that, she did not vent her spleen on post-Leipzig Nietzsche alone. His religious genius, which had enticed her in Tautenburg, was morbific in her book. Further, her drift was that his philosophizing was false from the first inasmuch as it was from the first directed and redirected according to his neuropathic needs, with his impulse to know straining over against his other impulses as he investigated these[s] on the wild assumption that his was the European psyche. She refuted him piecemeal here and there besides, begging off for the rest on the ground that what mattered to him was not whether his ideas were right or wrong, but only what it felt like to have them.[t] And not even *his* ideas at that, for, she affirmed, he took up others' continually.[480/u] He was fertilized intellectually the way women were physi-

---

tributions to her aphorism book—and later ascribed by her to Dostoevsky (1919e:382)! Nietzsche's tacit moral absolute was evolutionary progress—as was the case for all of his nineteenth-century prophetical compatriots from Hegel to Haeckel.

[p] Similarly, Nietzsche as a "Columbus in reverse" (above, p. 152) would have left Leipzig only to find his pre-Leipzig Lou again.

[q] See above, p. 150 n. *z*.

[r] 1890a:8: "If Nietzsche's own, oral remarks are to be credited, this ailment was of a hereditary nature, and his father succumbed to the same one."

[s] Lou saw a double trouble here: the thought destroyed the immediacy of the instinctual activity observed, which in turn "loosened" the thought (*ibid.*, 34).

[t] *Ibid.*, 5, 127, 157 (in "extremest exaggeration"), etc.

[u] (The dominant ideas of his three periods plus many others.) Lou overstated this: Nietzsche did have big ideas all his own, he rarely appropriated ideas with-

cally, she added[481]: thus she claimed masculinity for herself.[v] The "original form" of his positivism, she maintained in particular, was Réealism.[482/w] He made a passionate experience out of Rée's radical segregation of thought from sentiment, she pursued[483]; over all their years of "constant association and intellectual exchange"[484] Rée, "the sharper mind,"[485] had the theoretic initiative, while Nietzsche "drew the practical consequences from the theories and sought out their inner significance for culture and life"[486]; Rée, "acutely onesided,"[487] despised himself as a sentient being, his cold head taking no hint from his warm heart, so that Nietzsche, being prone to the opposite excess, "valued and overvalued in Rée what came hardest to him himself"[488]; and so on—from one plausible misrepresentation to the next.[x]

But Lou's anti-Nietzschean drift was stemmed all along the surface of her book. What with his "genial manysidedness," ran her text on his Réealism, Nietzsche filled in the gaps left by Rée's logic and made Rée's very mistakes exciting, so that Rée "saw with astonishment how his tight and clean-spun threads of thought were transformed into living, fresh-blooming tendrils at Nietzsche's magic hands."[489] Again, that Nietzsche "trimmed others' theories"[490] was "a fact absolutely immaterial to Nietzsche's true significance,"[491] which lay not in

---

out improving them, and he did care whether his ideas could be "substantiated or refuted by argument" (*ibid.*, 5). He seems to have "hit on" others' ideas unsuspectingly after forgetting that he had read or heard them—like all full-time thinkers. Lou's "thought from the 'sister brain' " was an especially simple case in point in that he knew her personally; more complex was his almost word-for-word appropriation of Paul Bourget's concept of literary decadence (Hofmiller, "N," 75, 122) or especially his excogitating the "eternal recurrence" after having regretfully rejected it as Pythagorean superstition in *Untimely* (above, p. 48 n. *s*) and though it was then a current notion in Europe (half subscribed by Flaubert and George Sand). Such unwittingly recollected ideas struck him with uncanny convincingness just because they were full-blown, indeed often ready-worded.

[v] Cf. above, p. 148 n. *v*.

[w] Again, Nietzsche's positivism "took its point of departure in a personal relationship" (1890a:98); etc.

[x] Nietzsche in fact came to positivism independently of Rée, helped Rée along theoretically in Sorrento, had no intellectual and little other traffic with him thereafter till 1882, and overrated him out of fondness (FN→Lisbeth, 20 v 1885, blamed his earlier overpraise of Rée on "fits of loneliness . . . I have been *laughably* happy whenever I have found, or thought I have found, any old speck or corner in common with anyone"—an accurate overstatement)—somewhat facetiously (e.g. FN→Rée: "Basel, 19 November 1877, in this year of disgrace in which the origin of moral sentiments was discovered"—not even saying by whom). But Lou's account is false primarily by reason of the huge prominence implicitly accorded Rée in Nietzsche's life: as Rée alone of Nietzsche's associates enters into her discussion of Nietzsche's positivist period, he comes to look like Nietzsche's solitary associate of that period.

any "theoretic originality, not in what can be substantiated or refuted by argument, but in the intimate power with which a personality here speaks to the personality."[492] A supreme master of language,[493] "he so to say created a *new style* in philosophy," one "which expresses the thought not only as such, but along with the entire tonal wealth of its emotive resonance and with all its subtle, secret connotations," and which exceeds the confines of language "in enunciating through the mood what otherwise remains mute in the word. But in no other mind could mere thinking turn so completely into true experiencing, for no other life was ever so completely devoted to turning the whole inner man to account in thinking. His thoughts did not arise out of real life and its happenings [!] as thoughts ordinarily do; rather, they *constituted* the only real happening of that solitary life."[494] Here was mere considerate compensation. There was also discrepancy, however, as again and again Lou lauded Nietzsche's strict, methodical thinking along with its ever so novel and significant results.[y] But even short of such discrepancy, ambivalence sounded through every tribute that rang true in that depreciative context. And Lou conveyed true admiration through her words on "his talent for subtleties, his genius in the handling of finest things,"[495] and the like—indeed, true awe through her depiction of his self-renewals themselves as a "heroism of readiness to sacrifice convictions."[496] As in Tautenburg, she still deemed him most heroic in his "apotheosis of life," since it only intensified his misery[497]; once she called "this emotional struggle" in its turn "the true [!] source of his whole final philosophy" and final ruination[498]—perhaps, though, only as pretext for an apocryphal anecdote about his interrupting musical labors on her "Hymn to Life" in Tautenburg to pen the message: "I despise life."[499/z] No one has more movingly evoked his need for masks (masks of formality and of foolishness, of cruelty and of godly laughter)[500] or the impress of suffering and solitude on his works. Her descriptions of his person,[501/a] finally, were loving and lovely both, as well as scrupulously exact—which last entitled her to fable about her relations with him.

Nearly all of Lou's fables in *Friedrich Nietzsche in seinen Werken* come under a double head: heiress pose and Nietzsche romance. She later claimed to have authored the work "exclusively" out of "a sort of obligation toward Nietzsche" to set his philosophic purposes

---

[y] See especially 1890a:130ff., on his having discerned the emotional source of even the most rational thinking.

[z] Cf. FN→Lou [3? IX 1882]—above, p. 85.

[a] See above, pp. 52-53.

straight.[502/b] It does manifest a will to expound along with the will to reduce, refute, reject. For the bulk of it she sorted out Nietzschean thematic threads and tied them together expertly—authoritatively. At the very start she claimed special investiture in that she quoted his letter hailing both her "thought from the 'sister brain'" and her prospective sketch of his character. Similarly, she told of his initiating her into the "eternal recurrence" as if into a holy mystery,[503] citing an imaginary "series of letters on the subject" for good measure.[504/c] By sleight of hand, meanwhile, she contrived to imply a lifelong intimacy about which she was seemingly being discreet for reasons easy to supply. She told of his youth as if from direct personal acquaintance,[505/d] then drew on his old letters to Rée as if they were to herself.[e] From his actual letters to herself she quite gratuitously quoted insinuative-tender passages followed up by suggestive suspension dots........ which in fact suspended only innocuous matter.[f] In contrast to her fanciful retrospect of New Year's Day 1883,[g] she now pre-

[b] She added: "In truth it is as Nietzsche-glorifying as I could at all honestly make it."

[c] On the subject of Nietzsche's would-be scientific grounding of the hypothesis, to be exact, though neither the hypothesis nor *a fortiori* its grounding ever came into their correspondence.

[d] Romundt was probably her informant.

[e] On quoting from his letters to Rée, that is, she would sometimes specify that they were addressed to Rée or else to a "friend" (masculine), but also again and again would specify only when they were written and not to whom, deftly implying, however, that they were written to her. Thus she introduced a few successive excerpts (1890a:88-89): "On May 12, 1878, he wrote from Basel . . . But then followed, on December 14, 1878 . . . Finally, in a tone of peaceful resignation, a letter of May 15, 1879 from Geneva . . . Soon afterwards . . . he called himself a 'sick man who . . .' (letter to Rée)"—very much as if all but the last had been letters not to Rée, but to someone else whose identity went without saying. This implication was irresistible in the long run and in the context of all her quoting from letters patently directed to her (likewise often without identifying the addressee) and of all her collateral illusionist devices (e.g. *ibid.*, 136, after quoting from *Dawn*: "Then, one year after its publication, Nietzsche came to write about new philosophical hopes and plans for the first time again: 'Now, sweetest friend, you always have a good word in readiness for me . . .'"—wherewith in not naming the "*liebste Freundin*," whose identity did go without saying, Lou in effect assimilated her to the unnamed recipient of the earlier letters about hopes and plans excerpted beforehand).

[f] To be precise, suspension dashes— — — —except in facsimiled letters. These latter numbered three. From FN→Lou [16? IX 1882] (about the "sister brain") she deleted a line and a half following: "Can you guess, my dear Lou, what I am asking for?" and from FN→Lou [22 VII 1882] (about her soon coming to Tautenburg) two and a half lines following "and the 'goodest' of these things was your letter of acceptance!" The deleted matter was no less relevant to her subject than much that was quoted—only in a third case she deleted a whole patently irrelevant paragraph without using suspension dots, as the context was not a suggestive one.

[g] See above, p. 114.

sented her trip northward from Rome as an idyll with Nietzsche alone. Or rather, she did this only by deftest intimation: ". . . as he visited the Tribschen estate near Lucerne with me during a trip together from Italy . . ."[506] Indeed, she registered all her encounters with Nietzsche only incidentally and as if ever so sparingly, on the order of ". . . while he was staying with me in Thuringia, near Dornburg, in the summer of 1882."[507] She reduced the Trinitarian study plan to a lone resolve of Nietzsche's to which she was privy[508/h]— one abandoned because of "his headache,"[509] or again for "inner and outer reasons."[510] This last was her closest allusion to the aftermath of Leipzig. For the rest her Nietzsche, on closing accounts with positivism, took his leave of Rée[511] through "the beautiful words" in *The Gay Science* about friends whose ways part[i]—his relations with *her* persisting uncontradicted.[j] Beyond the material particulars, the mood of these relations was transformed: what had been tempestuous emerged as serene. It was probably during this emergence that she removed all traces of his nastiness toward her from the papers in her possession.[k] Her first large-scale autobiographic hoax[l] was, then, an approximation to that great coveted but forbidden spiritual and carnal union between them, rendered celestial and eternal by being depicted only dimly and solemnly and without temporal beginning or end.

Lou romanced the more intensely with Nietzsche throughout in that she was concurrently identifying him with herself following the precedent of her novel. Her explanation for his going mad—that he had created a deity, then taken its place—was doubly autobiographic.

[h] Having dissociated Rée from Nietzsche in this, she reassociated him remotely and belatedly in respect of his medical studies: "Somewhat later than Nietzsche, Rée too felt the need to come to terms with the natural sciences . . ." (1890a:141).

[i] See above, p. 87 and n. *k*.

[j] The reader has no reason to expect her relations with Nietzsche to have changed along with Rée's, she having at no point connected herself with Rée. Besides, in contexts in which it would clearly have been in order to indicate any such change, she indicated none (e.g. 1890a:10, about her continuing her literary work on Nietzsche over the years after he approved her first pages in Leipzig). Thus she did not need to strain much to maintain the illusion without actually lying. She nonetheless repeatedly contrived to recreate it with phrases on the order of one about *Zarathustra* IV as written in 1885 already "but first made generally accessible in 1891" (*ibid.*, 261—as if it had been accessible to her in particular before then)—a phrase which, however, also rectified her running error as to when it had been written (cf. above, p. 152 n. *j*).

[k] Then or later, besides purging his letters to herself and Rée (below, pp. 476-77), she obliterated many of his notations in her aphorism book and tore out many of its pages annotated by him.

[l] The first small-scale public one, "Gottesschöpfung" (below, p. 160), appeared after her first articles on Nietzsche.

In the first place, she had once done just that herself. Indeed, his "tragic conflict" commenced, by her account, with his mind's declaration of war upon a beloved childhood god—a traditional god, to be sure, but one to whom, she insisted, his divine creature of the final hour threw back. Thus his starting point was identified with hers, as it had been in *Im Kampf um Gott.*[m] Only what in her case had been a progression toward sanity came out the reverse in his: evidently *she* was homesick for Kuno's childhood god.[n] According to her Tautenburg diary, moreover, *she* had driven her childhood faith from her heart on her mind's account, whereas Nietzsche's heart had felt nothing more for his childhood faith one day and his mind had followed suit; now according to her Nietzsche book, Nietzsche (as he "again and again emphasized," she having "discussed the matter with him in especial detail"[512]) did just as, by the earlier account, she had done in pointed contrast to him. "With Nietzsche," she had noted further in Tautenburg, "pain has always been the *cause* of a new development; with me it was always a calculated *means* to grasp at my new goal looming higher"—as now it became for Nietzsche instead.[o] Again, she had taken Nietzsche at his word in Tautenburg that his goals were external as hers were not, whereas now she exposed the difference as a fatal self-deception on his part. And again, her Tautenburg Nietzsche had felt himself to be passively bearing up under his goals, whereas the Nietzsche of her Nietzsche book felt his goals to be invigorating as he robustly struggled toward them— just like her Tautenburg Lou.[p] Thus her self-version as of Tautenburg supplied the mental mechanism now ascribed to Nietzsche to

[m] Which is why she was loath to pry into that "dark instinct" (above, p. 151).

[n] In a revealing *non sequitur* she wrote (1890a:35) that Nietzsche, being a religious freethinker, had to worship himself. Her full meaning was that he *had* to make his own god, which *could not but* be a glorified self-image, and that he *did* identify with this last. By the "*had*" clause she meant no more than that he had to worship something: such was the sense she then gave to the word "religious." The "*could not but*" clause held as a general rule with her all her life, even though in later years she also maintained alternatively that gods are glorified parental images. This later-life discrepancy is clarified by the "*did*" clause in its autobiographic purport, for her own father-god had become her glorified self-image—a sequence reversed by her in Nietzsche's case, like the sequence from sickness to health and for the same reason: "homesickness for God."

[o] On this point there are a few slight variants in both diary and book, but they do not blunt the contrast.

[p] Again, such is Lou's dominant meaning, but both texts contain inconsistencies—doubtless hers, as she had a hawk's eye for his. (That Lou used this Tautenburg material along with the unconscious side of her childhood history by way of identifying Nietzsche with herself suggests that by then it too was unconscious, hence that she did not know she was abusing her yesteryear's truths.)

explain away his post-Leipzig crisis. Besides, Tautenburg apart, whose psyche was she probing when she discovered a regressive aspiration toward God at the pit of his? And if now she called him "the philosopher of our times" because he suffered "in his flesh the whole frightful fire and fury of a religiously inclined freethinker,"[513/q] just what was she calling herself? But her chronicle of his folly was autobiographic in the second place in that she had identified herself unawares with an exalted Nietzsche by fits and starts beginning in 1882, then in late 1891 through a leap back to her childhood religion, the ground for her parallel identification of Nietzsche with herself—through her "Gottesschöpfung" (God-Creation), which, published along with her first articles on Nietzsche,[r] told of how already in earliest childhood she on her side had divinized herself unawares[514/s] in a prototypical "fusion and confusion of what is most intimate, most personal, with what is highest."[515] By her telling, her "fusion and confusion" was of course so neat and naïve and wholesome[516] that it put any more rationalized religious construction to shame.[517] But the payoff was that, blissfully unsophisticated, it had yielded altogether to her very first rational doubt, with no struggle of mind against heart[t]—and accordingly "no secret hope of reconstructing along the path of knowledge what has been lost to religious ardor."[518] This "no secret hope" was illicit gain from the pious exchange with Nietzsche. She overcompensated the loser: in "Gottesschöpfung" she designated the earliest religious experiences the healthiest[u] upon

[q] Or if she now called him most heroic for his sufferer's yea to life: above, p. 156.

[r] On Nietzsche, I and II 1891; "Gottesschöpfung," II 1892; on Nietzsche again, III 1892 etc.

[s] Her very term was "unconscious self-divinization."

[t] Cf. above, p. 81 n. *p.* There was a fictional precedent to this reversal of her Tautenburg account: *Kampf,* in which Kuno loses his faith the hard way, whereupon Jane follows suit promptly and without inner conflict. The fictional reversal in turn goes back to her Tautenburg diary phrases on her basic similitude with Nietzsche (as against their superficial differences, meaning their recent spat). "Gottesschöpfung" allowed at least that she suffered long and much over her sudden loss; the recollected suffering was, however, to contract over the years to her "hour without God" (her "*Stunde ohne Gott*": 1919d) and abate to mere remorse quickly supplanted by a compensatory healthful reverence toward this world. Even the instantaneous mind-heart conflict consented in "Gottesschöpfung" was to go, her god simply vanishing before she was old enough for a doubt about him to have crossed her mind (1913c:462: ". . . a decease, an abandonment, not any doubting of his existence or disloyalty on my part")—leaving her *ne plus ultra* godlessly openminded and morally robust.

[u] Her full argument was historical (*à la* Biedermann) in the first instance. A primitive deity, she held, is ever indistinct, so that believers each breathe their own soul into it, therewith "sublimating their ego" (1891d:171); the individual believer will only "unconsciously or half consciously" (*ibid.*) dis-

backdating her loss of faith,[v] whereupon she issued Nietzsche a tacit bill of health in her Nietzsche book by backdating his correspondingly.[w] Moreover, if her reduction of his high mental purposes was perhaps only retaliatory, she was surely identifying herself with him when, at the very start of her book, she reclaimed the "thought from the 'sister brain' " only to adopt the thought from the brother brain

---

tinguish the divine attributes piously supplied by him from those that are progressively standardized by the community in accordance with the prevalent moral viewpoint until, having become dogma, they supersede the first; as meanwhile reason graduates from subserving dogma to subverting it, men first cling to the faith with "morbid exaltation" or "fanaticism" (*ibid.*, 170), then deny it together with their religious need—only to seek substitutes unwittingly. The modern child relives this whole history sooner or later—only the later, the more its primitive phase is telescoped, and vice versa.

[v] To the inception of rationality, apparently set at puberty. Afterwards, she maintained, she had deified knowledge (like her Nietzsche), retaining only "a final remnant of mourning and melancholy over what had been lost" (*ibid.*, 177), and this only until her catechism began. (She also claimed to have forgotten her entire religious experience between the time it supposedly ended and her confirmation, when it did end.) The backdating was to progress with the years: at the extreme, 1920b:365 set her loss of faith implicitly at age seven (hence way back in the dusk of her childhood: see next note). "Gottesschöpfung" was no more valid on its other autobiographic counts. By its terms, Lou's god was the result of a self-idealization (1891d:173); his invisibility disturbed her "astonishingly little" (*ibid.*, 170); she was robbed of him by her nascent reason (*ibid.*, 171); in her dismay, she divinized knowledge in his stead (*ibid.*, 177), compulsively (*ibid.*, 174), burning the midnight oil; at odds with her whole milieu, she yet felt free because she was acting out of inner necessity (*ibid.*, 176); she realized all this joyously in a revolt against the catechism that left her break with the church a mere formality (*ibid.*, 177). A lyrical finale found her incongruously being confirmed after all—in Holland, by "a friend, the only one I had" (*ibid.*, 178), to the tune of a prayer to life and her invisible god both at once (*ibid.*, 179).

[w] 1890a:47 set his "way back in the dusk of his childhood or at all odds of his boyhood," whereas *Kampf* had set it—correctly, as would seem—just before his departure for the university, stressing its lateness to boot. In Tautenburg, on comparing her own loss of faith with his, Lou had dated neither. Other portions of her Tautenburg diary and other documents of 1882 (e.g. Rée→Lou, 12 IX 1882) indicate, however, that she had not begun backdating hers at the time (unless, as some marginalia to her Zurich lecture notes suggest, she clung to a residue of faith even after her confirmation—pending her encounter with Rée), and in *Kampf* Jane was even a bit older when she shed her faith than Kuno had been on relinquishing his. The backdating in her own case was independent of her Nietzsche complex: see below, p. 471. Its textual point of departure was the "childlike" of her heart's "childlike ardor" for the faith (D [late VIII 1882]: insofar, she was aligning Nietzsche's case on hers as of Tautenburg after all), and Märchen set the fictional precedent. There was no textual point of departure or fictional precedent in Nietzsche's case: his age of reason simply fell with hers, the sufficient cause being the biographic exchanges with him then underway. (She could not very well exchange ages of reason with him, these having been about the same, but neither could she very well lower hers without lowering his while in the process of interchanging respective religious histories as contrasted in Tautenburg.)

in turn and insist that, though his philosophy could be refuted, he could not[519/x]—or when she asserted in the same context that his three philosophical periods, which he had delineated for her in 1882 as of that date, "were distinguished and distinctly characterized for the first time" in one of her articles.[520/y] There was room in her book for no further self-identification with him than this. And there was need for none: after her "Gottesschöpfung" leap of 1891, her need was rather for her diabolization of him to catch up, proceeding as it did haltingly from article to article to book.[z] It proceeded autonomously too: at the time of her book she was still devoted to him in her uppermost as well as her innermost thoughts—in rating him as well as in romancing and identifying with him—despite her reductive thesis in between. Her readers were bound to notice the conflict at the surface and sense the one in the depths. And of Nietzsche's intimates, one at all odds, galled by her thesis, was bound to attack her on it *ad mulierem*, exposing the romance as fraud while dismissing the eulogies as deceit. This she expected[a]: it was the built-in penalty.

The book was grandly launched by Lou's literary set,[b] which took her to have surmounted Nietzsche's influence by refuting his philosophy after having been his confidante and disciple until his breakdown.[521] Most neutral reviewers "were quick to hail it as a psychological masterpiece," noted one big exception, Josef Hofmiller.[522/c] Within Nietzsche's old circle Erwin Rohde, after deeming Lou's first articles on Nietzsche incomparably fine and deep,[523] now told Overbeck that she was "above all a literary parasite who would just like

[x] Cf. above. p. 148 n. *v.*

[y] Even so FN→Lou [9 VII 1882], which clearly drew the distinction (as far as it went), was reproduced in facsimile farther along (1890a:92-95). Actually Nietzsche's transitions to and from positivism were patent to all who followed his work in its time, including even Lisbeth (e.g. Lisbeth→CG, 24 IX/2 X 1882: "My dear Clara, do not read my brother's books, they are terrible for us. . . . Oh! and take no pains and do not torture yourself to harmonize them with the earlier ones, it is not possible").

[z] In the book, a handsome photograph of Nietzsche and a hideous one, placed before and after the title page respectively, render this diabolization graphic.

[a] Though she may have told herself that Lisbeth would not dare attack lest the presumably intimate passages elided from Nietzsche's letters—or, worse, other passages damning for Lisbeth personally—be published.

[b] Her articles had already been publicized in 1893 in the *Mercure de France* by a frequent visitor to Bölsche *et al.*, Henri Albert. Bölsche hailed the book as "first-rate"—lengthily though imprecisely—in the *Neue Deutsche Rundschau* (*Die Freie Bühne*, renamed). Brandes summarized it in a five-page postscript of 1894 to a reedition of his earlier essay on Nietzsche (*M und W.* 204-09), asserting that Lou had been close to Nietzsche all through his decisive years (Brandes did not know Nietzsche personally).

[c] Hofmiller's review evidently appeared in *Die Gesellschaft* of IV 1894 (not available to me).

to live off Nietzsche a while as off a suitable substratum while also putting her own person to advantage, and this not so tactfully or nicely."[524/d] Overbeck in 1894 called Lou's "the best and most qualified word ever publicly sounded on Nietzsche"[525/e]; subsequently, though, he shook his head at her fakery[526] and pronounced her "reflexions and constructions" about Nietzsche's illness "sufficient in themselves to rule out any really intimate association or communication."[527/f] In July 1893 Peter Gast, in his introduction to a reedition of Nietzsche's *Human, All Too Human*, upbraided Lou for her latest articles: he threw back her charge against Nietzsche of mystical madness,[528/g] refuted her on point after point beginning with Nietzsche's having come to positivism through Rée,[529] and denounced her trickery about how long she knew Nietzsche[530/h]—all this too late, however, to affect her book. In July 1894 Gast discerned in the book itself "only rejection: Nietzsche rejected by the ink-stained hand of a Russian general's daughter: so long as there are such spectacles, life is a heartening thing."[531] Two months later Gast nonetheless considered that "Lou's culture is simply too extraordinary; she may even be 'right' about much, as abnormal high tension in feeling and thinking is nothing for the masses, who dismiss it as 'pathological,' 'crazy,' and the like, then go about their business. It was clever of Lou to prove the point with great psychological to-do and win the assent of all the 'healthy.' Yet for all that, her book remains an astonishing achievement. I know of no woman's work that could come near hers (for intellectual schooling)."[532/i] Gast eventually wrote off these con-

---

[d] Rohde pursued: "Clever and subtle enough she is, and unfortunately the final catastrophe was certainly announced well in advance in Nietzsche's writings and theories and meanderings: he was long since unhealthy at the core. Yet in his wrestling for serenity and self-assurance and strength and total sincerity there is something not only painfully moving but also conducive to deep reverence, and this the lady seems not to have properly sensed. A Laocoon striving with all his might to break loose from the dreadful serpent . . ."

[e] Lisbeth's first volume had just appeared.

[f] Overbeck nonetheless deemed—mistakenly, I trust—that Lou's "first word on Nietzsche's inner relation to Rée will likely also stand as the last" (Bernoulli, *FO und FN*, I, 214).

[g] And called *her* melancholic (Gast, Introduction, ix).

[h] To be exact, about how long after 1882—the only half of that hoax yet in print.

[i] Again, Gast→Hofmiller, 10 XI 1896: "Lou is not quite the most miserable person. . . . Of human warmth there can be little question, to be sure, but her brain, her mind, her understanding, is of the sort seen in a woman only five or six times a century. To have lived some while close to Nietzsche and, instead of being enflamed, have been only a cold observer and scholarly recording machine—that's something too!" (To have misunderstood Lou so—that too is "something too"!)

cessions to Lou on "my animosity toward Mrs. Förster at the time."[533/j]

Mr. and Mrs. Förster had founded their colony—"New Germania" —in Paraguay early in 1886. In 1889, facing financial ruin, Bernhard took his life; Lisbeth carried on alone, slowly retrieving the deficit. She returned to Germany in the fall of 1890 for eighteen months to boost subscriptions, then definitively in September 1893 to cash in on her brother's growing fame. She wrested his literary estate from Gast's hands, then from her mother's proprietorship. In February 1894 she founded the Nietzsche Archiv in Naumburg with Gast's help—only to turn Gast out that very spring. For she intended using the Archiv to represent Nietzsche's life and thought in the way of her neo-Germanic propaganda, anti-Semitism and all. Her very own first project was known in Archiv parlance as "the biography."

Lou's quasi-biography incensed her for every reason beginning with its success—and perhaps most for its allusion, however skeptical, to the paternal brain ailment.[k] Of her old motives for rancor toward Lou, one was more valid than ever: Lou was the cause of her latterly warped relations with her brother, which she now had to smooth out for the record. The scholar's fee for the use of Archiv material was set at a poke or two at Lou in a preface.[l] Following Gast's leads, Fritz Kögel, his successor at the Archiv, reprobated Lou in February 1895 in the big literary journal *Das Magazin für Literatur*[m] for her hocuspocus with Nietzsche's letters to Rée, for misstatements about Nietzsche's life and misconstruals of his writings, but especially for having directed "the art and artifice of a neurotic female psychology"[534] "against Nietzsche"[535] in a "fantasy"[536] "the more dangerous for ostensibly honoring him and purporting not to harm but to explain."[537] Gersdorff jubilated to Lisbeth: "Kögel has lifted the evil Amazon out of the saddle! I have not read her book and do not mean to

---

[j] Gast did so with some uncertainty, however—and in fact Gast→Hofmiller, 13 VII 1894, was still merciless to Lou (ten months after Gast's quarrels with Lisbeth began).

[k] See above, p. 154 n. *r*.

[l] E.g. Steiner, Preface, 34-35 (signed IV 1895): "My picture of the overman has shaped up as the exact opposite of the caricature traced by Mrs. Lou Andreas-Salomé in what is just now the best-circulating book on Nietzsche. Nothing could be brought forth more contrary to the Nietzschean spirit than the mystical monstrosity made out of the overman by Mrs. Salomé. . . . Such a mediocre mind as Paul Rée's could make no significant impression on Nietzsche's. I would not even broach these matters had not Mrs. Salomé's book done so much to spread downright offensive views of Nietzsche . . ."

[m] Gast→Hofmiller, 10 IV 1895: "Dr. Kögel's essay is on the whole a clever paraphrase of my objections against Lou": it was.

either."[538] Romundt alone spoke out loud for Lou[n]—encouraged by Overbeck[539] and counseled by Lou herself.[o] Gallant, Romundt rebutted all Kögel's charges, founded as well as unfounded. Nothing, he maintained, justified casting aspersions or suspicions on Lou or on her book; in no wise hostile to Nietzsche, she had sought and found in his works their significance as thought-experience and self-disclosure, as was only fitting. Her half year's acquaintance with him had helped her in this task, and while she would be the last to deny that a longer one would have helped her more, to say that she had tried to make hers seem longer was "wholly baseless calumny"[540]; besides, what counts in such a relationship is its intensity more than its length. Lou's long researches were assisted moreover by friends of Nietzsche's including notably Rée, who *was* important for Nietzsche's development even though he only touched off what was impending and even if Nietzsche's Réealism never was pure or wholehearted. In any event, the chief value of Lou's work lay elsewhere, in its distinction of his three philosophical periods. She could consult only his published works, of course, but these were sufficient for her purpose. If Kögel could fill out Lou's picture of Nietzsche's literary personality in any way, might he do so—and Romundt himself led off by quoting some lines addressed to him by Nietzsche about "ever uplifting oneself and others, with the idea of purity before one's eyes as an *excelsior.*"[541]

Kögel took the hint about intensity from Lou's "delightful Sancho Panza" as a cue for compiling "an 'inside' story of this friendship written *only* by Nietzsche."[542] In December 1895 Hofmiller, this time at the Archiv's prompting,[p] went out of his way to attack Lou in a laudatory review of Lisbeth's first volume, which, he held, proved Nietzsche's youth to have been one long, serene, harmonious development implicating his entire philosophy-to-be. "The legend is destroyed!" Hofmiller concluded, meaning Lou's.[543] Hofmiller then proposed to look into Nietzsche's Lou affair. "Lou will not oblige you,"

[n] Bernoulli, *FO und FN*, II, 389, says Andreas did so too, but I could not discover where or when.

[o] Romundt→o, IV, 1895: he wondered whether his essay's "objectively requisite form, which Frau Lou also wanted, will not affect [Lisbeth] even more sorely" than would a polemic. Again, 20 v 1895: "I recently received several letters from Mrs. Andreas [in Vienna]. . . . She is especially pleased that I omitted any attack against Mrs. Förster, who will presumably feel the point well enough. . . . She charged me with cordial greetings to you." Already a year earlier Romundt had protested to the Archiv for its aggression against Lou (Kögel→ Hofmiller, 29 IV 1894; Romundt→o, 10 II 1895).

[p] Insofar, that is, as I was able to decipher Kögel→Hofmiller, 3 XI 1895.

Kögel warned him; "she is, and will remain, mute. She has her reasons not to enter the controversy *herself*"—the same reasons for which, he added, he had demolished "her excellent book on account of a few miserable surface errors."[544] Some months later Kögel read to Hofmiller from Nietzsche's draft letters to Lou of late 1882. Gast told Hofmiller afterwards: "I would have esteemed silence more"—and besides, "Dr. Kögel did not read you Nietzsche's draft letters to his mother and sister. . . . But I have nothing further to do with that dirty linen."[545] So Kögel soon took a new look: "Through no one, not even Lou, did Nietzsche *suffer* so *much* as through his sister," he owned[546]—whereupon he began secretly excerpting everything to do with the Lou affair from Nietzsche's notebooks, being "convinced that here Mrs. Förster would one day do the most retouching," in fact "falsifying."[547] In 1899 Gast returned to the Archiv, by then in Weimar, to underwrite the falsifying. Later Hofmiller, who went the opposite way,[548] reminded Gast of his verdict on Lou of the middle 1890's; Gast replied coyly, "I have learned much since then."[549/q]

In 1900 the Archiv began publishing Nietzsche's letters: forged ones to Lisbeth reviling Lou and Jews plugged untoward gaps. A year later *The Will to Power* appeared, a concatenation of Nietzsche scraps presented as Nietzsche's supreme work—as if to render Lou's study obsolete. Lisbeth meanwhile more than once called Lou a liar in print—notably in 1899 concerning Lou's pretended conversations and correspondence with Nietzsche about the eternal recurrence.[550/r] In 1904 the volume of the Archiv biography covering 1882 appeared.[551] By this account, Lou approached Nietzsche as a would-be disciple, but fast showed herself to be intellectually unfit and only out for an amour, so Nietzsche, who really just wanted a secretary anyhow, sent her packing. Lou's book, "utterly false and untrue,"[552] contained "conversations never held, excerpts from imaginary letters, and events that never took place."[553] It was "an act of revenge upon sick Nietzsche due to wounded feminine vanity"[554]—and was "perhaps meant to win back Paul Rée's alienated affections" to boot.[555]

---

[q] Gast added: ". . . and also taken a good look at the relevant source material. And now I should like to say: it was a good thing Lou and Rée pulled out of Nietzsche's life."

[r] Nietzsche had tried a few words on the subject with Lou but had found her too uncomprehending, Lisbeth maintained—in the course of introducing her translation of a French work on Nietzsche that characterized Lou's book as a "very curious and quite captivating psychological and literary study which, however, must be consulted with much caution" (Lichtenberger, 185). In those years Lou was defended no better than by Naumann, I, 9: Lisbeth, in glossing over Nietzsche's enmity toward herself, "fabricates even much more unscrupulously than Mrs. Andreas-Salomé and yet much worse!"

This time the publicist Maximilian Harden protested in his review *Die Zukunft*: Lou, his collaborator since 1898, was, as he knew her, incapable of deliberate falsification.[s] Lisbeth sent Harden a rebuttal for insertion: "Everything she publishes is untrue—legend, to put it mildly."[556] Reiterating her old charges, Lisbeth specified that "the few letters [Lou] possesses from Nietzsche, barely five or six, . . . were in truth directed not to herself but to the ideal image of a disciple drawn by Malwida von Meysenbug and Dr. Paul Rée. The passages printed in the text come from Nietzsche's letters to Rée."[557] Genius, she added, was in fact not pathological, but was rather the culmination of generations of family virtue and strength.[558] For in the official view, Nietzsche's illness never affected his intellect before extinguishing it. Indeed, to have explained away his fond letters to Lou (or foul ones to his sister, or philo-Semitic sentences) as aberrant would have legitimated Lou's approach. So, laboring his own point, Lisbeth represented him as having consorted and corresponded with an ideal image on all counts contrary to the real Lou. He came off only the madder, the more since Lisbeth had him belittle the real Lou between times in those forged letters to herself—which time and again contradicted unforged ones to others, so that the mad double-dealer turned liar besides.

Unfortunately for Lou, the mud slung at her was made up of pure grains of truth—or rather, fortunately for her, the pure grains of truth were all mudded over. So, speciously wondering that anyone could regard her book as directed against Nietzsche, she dismissed the Archival slander as beneath her dignity to read, let alone refute[559]; she went so far as to leave the pages about herself uncut in her copy of "the" biography and read them elsewhere.[560] Harden himself found her book "unpretty,"[561] yet appealed to her through a friend, Frieda von Bülow, to refute the Archiv's charge of fraud, if only over Frieda's signature. Lou of course could not oblige, as the Archiv well knew.[t] However, stung to the quick by Lisbeth's having called her book "a spurned woman's act of vengeance,"[562/u] which among other things it was, she committed another such spurned woman's act of vengeance, which was likewise other things as well. Her ethe-

---

[s] Repeated in Harden, 170: I was unable to locate the original, there cited incorrectly. Lou→Harden, 24 i 1898, had established contact (on Fritz Mauthner's commendation), and Lou's contributions to *Die Zukunft* had begun with 1898d.

[t] That is, she could not produce her authentic Nietzsche letters (well over "five or six") without establishing by default that she had quoted from letters to Rée as if they were to herself—and without exposing her sly use of suspension dots.

[u] (Lou's rephrasing.)

real, ageless romance with Nietzsche having been refuted, she made him over into a nasty suitor—indeed, a vengeful spurned man. "If I do reply," she told Frieda, "then I must clear up the issue once and for all. But my relationship to Nietzsche involves most personal matters such as marriage proposal, brush-off, and *very* unlovely reaction of his jealous rage against Rée, which sullied us as utterly as could be."[v] Harden did not go along: he stayed loyal to Lou in *Die Zukunft*, but mutual feelings chilled.[w]

Others did go along, though, as Lou elaborated and reelaborated the tale. The crux of it was that Nietzsche had—through Rée in Lucerne—asked her to marry him if she would not have him otherwise, then refused to take no for an answer until his final fit of fury.[x] Another friend,[y] Ellen Key, spread it for her among Nietzsche scholars wary of Lisbeth's handouts. The first, Daniel Halévy, passed it on noncommittally.[563/z] In Basel, rallying point of the opposition to Weimar, Carl Albrecht Bernoulli was more credulous: reporting it along with the Kögel excerpts to an assemblage of philosophers in 1910, he declared Mrs. Förster foiled.[564/a] The third, Charles Andler,

[v] Lou→Frieda [late I 1905]. This first nonfictional version of the proposal fable was characteristically ambiguous: "such as marriage proposal . . ." faithfully renders the elliptical original.

[w] See below, pp. 318-19.

[x] Note that Lou enunciated these fantasies autobiographically only after Rée's death. The proposal fantasy goes back through *Kampf* to Nietzsche's "Löwengarten" letter from Lucerne, the proposition fantasy through *Kampf* to Lou's Jena outburst; as for Nietzsche's jealousy (superadded to his post-Leipzig rage), it was Rée's own, wishfully-meanly transferred. (The sole indication that Nietzsche could even have seemed jealous of Rée to anyone except Lou if only from a distance is a supposed quotation in Lou→Frieda [late I 1905] from a letter by Malwida: "Nietzsche is just airing his jealousy.")

[y] Frieda had died meanwhile.

[z] Ellen Key learned the tale from Lou in Paris in V 1909, transmitted it to Halévy in VI 1909, checked back with Lou in Kassel later that month, then corresponded about it with Halévy until his book was ready. Evidently Lou's terms were that Halévy tell *her* tale exclusively, that he not commit her, and that he avoid all polemics even should Lisbeth retaliate (EK→Lou, 5 VII 1909) —and when Ellen sent Lou a news clipping on the first adverse reactions in Weimar, Lou typically replied [23? III 1910]: "I want to know and hear nothing of the whole business!" Halévy's account is made up of misstatements of every description: just which were his own, which Ellen's (whose German was a joke), and which Lou's is impossible to say. The gist of it was that Nietzsche, after being rejected by proxy in Lucerne, pressed his suit in person, vainly; that in Tautenburg "he insisted on absolute assent to every one of his thoughts" (Halévy, 255); that in Leipzig he suspected Lou and Rée of secretly conducting a love affair and laughing at him, whereupon he vilified Rée to Lou—who, angered by this and (decisively) by a letter from Lisbeth, broke with him.

[a] Kögel had died in 1904; his widow made the excerpts available in Basel. Overbeck, who died in 1905, had built up a small Nietzsche archive there to offset the one in Weimar. In 1908 Bernoulli in a two-volume work on Nietzsche

mulled it over for years, then drew the final consequences: Nietzsche's final attitude toward Lou was "iniquitous,"[565] his "injustice" to her "immeasurable."[566/b] Such was the latest unhappy ending to that tortuous love story. By way of protest, Lisbeth's writings on Lou grew downright scurrilous.[c] Yet Lisbeth was most to blame in spite of herself if the picture of Nietzsche as a jealous unwanted suitor won credence over the whole documentary record, until it was a wonder *Lou* had not told *him* off. Or had she?[d] In this contest between fabler and forger, the one sure loser was Nietzsche himself.[e]

---

and Overbeck, had appealed to Lou to break her silence (*FO und FN*, I, 346). His provisional account of the affair had relied heavily on one specially prepared by Ida Overbeck, who thought the big difficulty to have been that Nietzsche was unreasonably presumptuous toward Lou philosophically and in love with her without knowing it, whereas "Miss Salomé was not of a mind to dissolve into Nietzsche" (quoted *ibid.*, 343: in fact the trouble was that Miss Salomé was of half a mind to do so), and who stigmatized Lisbeth first and foremost for the whole pathetic burlesque that followed Leipzig. According to Bernoulli's supposed revelations of 1910 ("Erlebnis," 30-34), Nietzsche had commissioned Rée to propose for him in Lucerne, since a concubinage was probably not to be hoped for; Lou had refused because she had sworn off love for ever, she preferred Rée anyhow, and she moreover suspected that Nietzsche was only transferring a fantasy ideal onto her; the Bayreuth incidents had concerned her unconcealed disagreement with Nietzsche over Wagner; in Jena she had merely laughed in protest at Lisbeth's calling her brother a saint; etc.

[b] Andler's account (Andler, 280-306) is a string of errors of every magnitude: Lou was "of Finnish origin" (*ibid.*, 281); she came to Malwida as a "Wagnerite" (*ibid.*); her mother let her travel freely because "no feminine brain was less subject to dizziness" (*ibid.*, 282); she merely "consented" to be initiated into Nietzsche's philosophy (*ibid.*, 283); Nietzsche was astonished at her "Jewish vivacity" (*ibid.*, 284); in Lucerne he bade Rée propose for him, adding with a smile that "there is surely no point in thinking of a concubinage" (*ibid.*, 285), whereupon she and Rée decided, by way of sparing his feelings, to pretend that Rée had not found a chance to do his bidding (*ibid.*, 285-86); then, coyly silent over the marriage proposal, he visited Tribschen with the enticing Wagnerite, who restrained herself so as to avoid a showdown (*ibid.*, 287); furious at her in Tautenburg for having denied him to Wagner, he was won back by "To Pain," only to be again worked up against her by Lisbeth, who venomously built up a chuckle of Lou's that in Jena had followed the mention of his saintliness; his ill will vanished upon his reunion with Lou and Rée in Leipzig, only to revive over a spiritist session compromising for a friend of his or else because Lou then rejected his suit definitively; etc. Andler indicated that Lou "was herself perhaps not without foreknowledge" of his "long talk" with Ellen Key (*ibid.*, 281). His version of the Lucerne proposal was likely Lou's very own of the time, for it so to say blamed her fantasy on Rée, as was indeed halfway justified.

[c] See e.g. E F-N, *Der einsame*, passim (50-odd pages).

[d] This was the Halévy version, superseded by the Kögel excerpts.

[e] In this contest, Lisbeth's demerits doubtless exceeded Lou's in that Lisbeth falsified documents, whereas Lou only mutilated and misattributed documents, and that while Lisbeth's forgeries were spiteful toward Lou, Lou's fables hardly affected Lisbeth. Certain current conclusions against Lisbeth are nonetheless

Due largely to the Archiv forgeries, Nietzsche's memory grew offensive to Lou over the years—although she was always pleased to be known socially as his sometime girl friend. For the rest, her diverse motives toward him persisted. She paid him occasional huge tributes, more often than not in a negative context. She decried his late philosophizing in new terms: in 1900 she noted that "sick Nietzsche fashioned the vision of a super-Nietzsche only so as to make the lack of a healthy, normal Nietzsche bearable to himself,"[567/f] and again in 1911 that "he foundered on a certain philosophic-theoretical shallowness" when instead of inverting his positivist maxim, "Even the thought-drive is a life-drive," he exalted its second term at the expense of the first.[568] She romanced with him with the full latent force of her pseudoreminiscences about propositions and proposals. She heaped scorn upon her "sort of memoirs and seminovel," *Im Kampf um Gott*. Indeed, only insofar as her Nietzsche experience was repetitive did it show on the surface of her later fiction—though one reader caught it anyway in the recurrent theme of a young girl's free discipleship to a self-willed master turning of a sudden into a frenzied temptation to mental and erotic thralldom defended against "with a sure instinct."[569]

Meanwhile Nietzsche grew on her. She contracted personal habits of his, such as alternately working long weeks or months in solitude, then living socially awhile. She took up physical attitudes of his once lovingly noted by her, such as his cautious, pensive gait and his air of "hearkening to all things"[570]; likewise, her voice softened to a hush, and stopped for any but intimate company, even as her youthful forwardness gave way to a discretion and reserve far too marked to have been a mere matter of age or marriage.[g] She also drew a dispensation from "second-rank scruples," meaning all scruples, from Nietzsche's "sacred self-seeking, or instinctive obedience to what is highest"[571]—to which Nietzsche had denied her title.[h] But what she

---

false. She did not nearly drive her brother to suicide over the Lou affair, for she neither invented the Bayreuth and Jena data that upset him nor set the gossip going in Jena, Basel, Leipzig, or anywhere else—and besides, he went along with her campaign of vengeance only when and insofar as he chose. Her vocation for falsification and forgery may well have come of her Jena shock, for the two served to mend her love-image of her brother, shockingly rent by Lou.

[f] This repudiation of Nietzsche on the new basis of his "incapacity to come to terms with everyday life" because of "sickliness first, and then . . . the approach of a mental illness" foreshadowed her repudiation of Rilke then pending (below, p. 299, 499). The "first, and then" hints that Lou inwardly recognized Nietzsche's mental illness as physical in origin.

[g] The Archiv scandal may also have helped.

[h] See above, p. 97.

took from Nietzsche was chiefly intellectual, from pet expressions (such as going out "among men" and returning "to myself") to historical theses (about justice,[i] Christianity,[j] and the like), by way of his new psychological approach according to which the psyche is an archive, culture denotes inhibition, memory is weaker than forgetfulness, perception works to prevent seeing too much and intellection to prevent understanding too much, a manifest virtue is the obverse of a latent vice, and one's sexuality informs the highest reaches of one's mind. She was to work through many a Tautenburg topic on these terms to his own conclusions and beyond—including notably woman as such—even as in her expository prose the sentence gradually yielded to the paragraph, didactics to imagery and incantation: Lou as positivist to Lou as Nietzsche. And in her case in turn, the ideal of cold-blooded cognition yielded to awe before the instincts. In fact she filled her own bill for Nietzsche's late thought in due course—all the way from a "repudiation of [her] former purely logical ideal of knowledge" to "a religious mysticism in which God, world, and man fuse into a single prodigious superbeing."[k] Thus she took up his succession after all—which shows that she had never really said no to it in her heart. Just so, she now denied the postpositivist Nietzsche in terms pointedly (and poorly) calculated to dissociate her own postpositivist course from his.[l] All in all, this self-identification with Nietzsche went much farther than the one with Gillot; indeed, it opened the way for her to wind up her unfinished business with Gillot's memory.

In one vital respect Lou's postpositivism did differ from Nietzsche's —the one to be expected from her having had not only an enforced asceticism of the spirit to surmount, but also an inveterate asceticism of the flesh.

[i] Once, above the words "as I have always believed," she wrote that "originally guilt was a breach in the objective world order to be expiated no matter how or through whom . . . the deed not being identified with the doer," that "with *deepened* guilt, guilt psychologically grasped, goes a concomitant *weakening* of the notion that it entails punishment in the way of a natural catastrophe, as an *objective occurrence*," and that the two conceptions later conjoin in the religious one of redemption through suffering (D VII 1917)—all of which would pass as notes on Nietzsche's *Genealogy*.

[j] That Christianity made sin dirty by making it washable (1914a:257), etc.

[k] See above, pp. 152-53.

[l] D 13 VIII 1900: *she* had come to terms with "everyday life." D [summer?] 1911: *she* affirmed the mentalization of instincts as itself instinctual.

PART THREE · WOMANHOOD

JN 1892 Lou Andreas, thirty-one-year-old virginal wife, and Georg Ledebour, a Marxist journalist and lecturer eleven years her senior, fell in love. Lou enjoined Ledebour to be patient until her husband was over a worrisome illness. Ledebour complied until on October 18 the three met unexpectedly at the Bölsches' and a robust Andreas glowered at Ledebour demonstratively a whole evening through. *That* was the worrisome illness, Lou told Ledebour: it would pass. Ledebour, calling her marriage madness, demanded to confer with Andreas. "He did not know *how* impossible it would be," Lou lamented, "and that Fred spoke only with knives and tears."[1] She insisted on working things out her own way. For months thereafter she lied to the two overwrought rivals by turns until she no longer heard what they growled or hissed back at her. She grew numb and skeletal. Once she reflected: "To fall ill, ill unto *unconsciousness*—that *too* is beautiful. Only conscious life is hard, is frightful. And don't children and sick people get whatever they want?"[2]/[a]

Ledebour went to jail in May 1893 for a political offense. Lou thereupon resolved ot give him no sign of life for a year, but then to separate from Andreas lest he and she "die of each other."[3] She later wrote concerning Ledebour: "It was my way of thanking and of loving him"; and concerning Andreas: "It was my final gift to him, my final proof of love."[4] Andreas saw it otherwise—to her feigned surprise. And the summer's end found her again meeting Ledebour at workers' clubs where he taught. Now he was curt with her: he would talk to her divorced or else to Andreas alone. She last saw him on February 23, 1894. Four days later she left for Paris with a poodle for company. There she compounded a journal of the affair out of memoranda painstakingly composed and recomposed: it reads like a cheap *feuilleton*, what with its serial, episodic train of events, its narrative voice alternately moralistic and pathetic, and its stilted dialogue backed by extravagant posturing and gesturing—including Ledebour's "literally"[5] gnashing his teeth and clenching his fists and Andreas's rolling his eyes and snorting.[b] Lou was the hapless heroine caught between two total claims upon her, intent on doing her best

[a] Lou actually added: "Isn't it my turn to ask and get instead of struggling and renouncing? I would get *Him* in my bed."

[b] Andreas as cutthroat crybaby is particularly lurid, while the histrionic Ledebour-Lou love-and-hate scenes and the moody episodes (particularly one

by both, wherewith the worst ensued. Even so, the dilemma did emerge here and there as one of the heroine's own contriving. Thus the first sequence concluded: "Meanwhile dinner was served, and I thought incessantly of the *knives beside the plates*. But . . . neither the horrors that could result if Fred lost all control as at home nor even our being already so frightfully compromised seemed to me the worst of it. The worst *for me* was Ledebour's irremediably altered conception of our marriage—the impossibility of my ever again making him see it with *my* eyes, think of it with *my* judgment. Therewith the power of determining him this year in accordance with my plan and will slipped from my hands." And the last: "In the conversation to come I must mollify him by new devices. And so forth. A pretty task!" Unmollified, Ledebour married one of his pupils in 1895—one of approximately Lou's own age and social standing whom he had known, like Lou, since 1892. She made him a tender companion through a stormy career and—following Hitler's advent— a long exile. A political associate was to say of him that, fearless himself, he could not abide "the evil fruits of fear: cowardice, insincerity, duplicity."[6] Had he been fearless this way before knowing Lou?

Lou's Ledebour affair paralleled her Nietzsche hoax as her sorriest off-paper attempt since girlhood to impress fantasy upon reality. Even so, it was her farthest advance toward womanhood to date—a roundabout advance as if to a second adolescence, this one compelling. Her first documented amour since her marriage, it was also her last with an older man: thereafter, while remaining a child-wife at home, she resumed her maidenly coquetterie abroad with new earnestness. For all that, Ledebour personally left little behind with her—not even an idea or idiosyncrasy as souvenir. And in fact, whereas her memoir of the affair argued her intensest full-time involvement in it, Ledebour came into her calendar notations, which superseded her other running chronicles in November 1893, only inconspicuously.[c]

---

in which, arms outstretched in the moonlight, she cries "Only forgive me!" with boundless longing to embrace an unidentified "him") are too ridiculous to be ridiculed. She was not working out her Ledebour experience literarily, but using it for literary effect. Indeed, successive versions survive of a passage containing a parenthesis on how she had *only just noticed* ("strange! . . .") that she had been writing "*Du*" in the dialogues between Ledebour and herself for what had in reality been "*Sie*" on both sides ("the '*Sie*' is so utterly felt by me as a '*Du*' that it comes out of my pen in no other way").

[c] For four meetings in no wise singularized. In the calendars she also reported herself jolly more often than glum during this period and treated Andreas— "Oldster" as against the journal's "Fred"—to fond words unthinkable in the journal.

Meanwhile the Andreases left their old Tempelhof mansion—despondently[d]—in October 1892 for nearby Schmargendorf. There they soon quit their first apartment for a second, "comically tiny" one[7/e] consisting of a bedroom above a grassy courtyard, a study overlooking a tree-lined street, and in between a parlor and balcony opening southwards onto a meadow as if they were "embedded in nature."[8/f] The couple's friendliest new neighbors were the Fritz Mauthners: Mauthner, famed for his parodies and parables, was co-founder of *Die Freie Bühne*. Lou also made acquaintances fleetingly with August Strindberg, tenuously with the lesser playwright Otto Hartleben, and abidingly with the Danish translator Therese Krüger.[g] And early in 1892 she met Frieda von Bülow, soon her closest friend. Frieda was manly in manner and morose in spirit. In 1887, aged thirty, she had gone to Zanzibar on behalf of a national woman's league[h] to help the colonist and *Weltpolitiker* Carl Peters organize medical assistance to natives; she returned after one month with a transient jungle disease and a lingering addiction to Peters and sadism-masochism. She lusted for erotic "crucifixion"[9]—and looked to Lou, "majestic and holy," to wean her from her "poison,"[10] alias Peters. A most possessive friend,[i] she nonetheless had mixed, unstable feelings toward Lou, who was unfailingly devoted to her.[j] She produced novels about East Africa, whither she re-embarked in June of 1893.

[d] D 15 x 1892 (fragment) represents Fred bursting into bitter tears on leaving the house and Lou shielding him from passers-by while thinking: "He must not suffer! I *will* not be guilty." Only ten years later could she bring herself to return to Tempelhof. She then found it "urbanized" (D 2 III 1903). As for the house, "I stood long by the hedge" while—in different ink—"a nightingale sang" (*ibid.*).

[e] By XI 1893 at the latest.

[f] But D 1 x 1897—"in Oldster's bedroom the first night" (with Rilke presumably in hers)—suggests rather a repetition of her domestic set-up with Rée: two bedrooms separated by a parlor.

[g] Who translated the first part of Lou's Nietzsche book for *Samtiden* (Bergen) in late 1899.

[h] Deutsch-Nationaler Frauenbund, founded by Carl Peters.

[i] She took offense when once Lou wrote her into an indiscriminate "my friends" (Lou→Frieda [late I 1905]).

[j] Lou→Frieda [1905?] deals with Frieda's contention that they "could no longer be anything" to each other: "For many long years now this idea has been popping up on your side at the slightest provocation with the uttermost rapidity and even at regular intervals. You also ascribe the most frightful attributes to me with the greatest equanimity from time to time without my quite knowing why. All this I have swallowed as part of our friendship, telling myself it comes of your entire disposition and nervous irritability as also of your not really knowing me—whether because you are so very different or because, as I think, you are simply no especially good connoisseur of people.

And all this time Lou wrote. Her articles included another two on religion, the first of which[k] took off from a best-selling latitudinarian history of Christian dogma[l] to show how Christianity was—like any institutional religion—a continual invention progressively dogmatized at the expense of the ardor behind it. Latter-day laxity about dogma within Christianity was nonetheless self-defeating, she added, for it led the faithful to sense that heaven was open to innovation.[11/m] She implied that heaven was concocted half knowingly in the first instance inasmuch as she contrasted the molten holy image or fluid holy writ hot out of "the heart's innermost need" with that confronting its author "a short time afterwards" as if petrified.[12/n] She concluded with her loudest repudiation of the faith, which was also her last profession of positivism. Religion, it ran, is an illusion due to human frailty, a fictional "correction and completion" of the real world[13]: we must extinguish the last lights of heaven if we would see any of the earth below with full clarity—"maybe just enough to stand on, yet enough to live and die on without God and heaven."[14] But she could not stand out the paragraph on her godforsaken clod without calling a *deus ex machina* to the rescue. The best religions, she pursued, have simply enabled men to face life and love life, so that to transcend religion is to fulfill it by embracing "the naked truth," a god more jealous than even its Semitic forebear in that "it blesses only those who come to it at the price of being damned by it"[15/o]— and she wound up quoting a Catholic poetess against the saints' intercession: "For rather Thou shouldst damn me / Than another save me."[16] Her next votive offering, "Von der Bestie bis zum Gott" (From Beast to God),[p] was a delectable scholarly study of how deities, on losing their following, turn satanic and how, conversely, frightful beasts work their way up through totemism to fusion with tribal fathers, then withdraw to the wilderness as divinity sets in.[q]

Thus I decidedly reject your assertion that I have no capacity for friendship"— rightly. (Incidentally, Frieda's handwriting was heinously angular.)

[k] 1892b.

[l] Adolf von Harnack's *Grundriss der Dogmengeschichte.*

[m] Lou here—in tacit self-criticism for "Realismus"—rebutted the anti-dogmatists who urged men to reject outer props to their faith and heed only their hearts' needs: how, she asked, could one's *needs* edify one?

[n] In fact she did not state unequivocally that its author was the party thus confronted; indeed, in one passage the first, creative moment of Christianity was centuries long. Besides, she often called pious invention "unknowing" ("*unbewusst*"). The implication to the contrary is clearest in her distinction between the "then" of invention and the "now" of implicit assent (1892b:1220).

[o] Cf. FN, *Genealogy*, III: 27; etc.

[p] Certainly completed by XI 1893 because not on her calendars.

[q] The finale is subtly autobiographic: "The piety and love enjoyed by the

For *Die Freie Bühne* of January 1893, Lou covered some local guest performances by Eleonora Duse: the Duse, she found, was all too intent on putting her personality across and ceased being stagey only when her native dolefulness broke through. Thence Lou passed to play reviews, beginning with a triple one—of Sudermann's *Heimat*, which, she noted, employed social types to argue individualism; of Ibsen's *The Master Builder*, which employed hyperindividualized characters to argue that "there is no psychic health at all . . . in the freedom and self-determination of the individual . . . separated from God"[17]; and of a triad by Strindberg, "poet" and "shocker-psychologist,"[18] whose men trembled not before God like master builders, but before everyday women "satanized."[19]

Her next few reviews show some relevance to her Ledebour affair, then underway. First the heroine of Hartleben's *Hanna Jagert*, like the child in Ludwig Fulda's dramatization of "The Emperor's Clothes," stripped that most imaginatively adorned of monarchs, love, of all moral and aesthetic finery even unto the cloak of fidelity.[20/r] But on reconsideration even Hanna proved guilty of minding appearances to her own detriment in that she spoiled liaison after liaison in her eagerness not to seem self-seeking.[21] The truth behind Max Halbe's drama of young love, *Jugend*, was for Lou that so-called "free love" is an unequal exchange, the woman being perforce more deeply and lastingly affected, especially the first time[22]: "a truly free development," she decreed, ". . . surmounts asceticism . . . but may not fall *beneath* it" into license without and chaos within.[23] She took the message of Hartleben's comic satire *Die Erziehung zur Ehe* to be "the right and duty of the truly live personality" to represent his life falsely.[24] Hers was represented to her truly on November 14, 1893, when she previewed Hauptmann's *Hanneles Himmelfahrt*, a poetical tragicomedy about an introversive little girl who, driven to suicide by a cruel father, envisions a whole gala assumption for herself with her

---

tribal father certainly contained the most intimate religious sentiment of which man was capable, and even the most highly cultivated religion could not go beyond the father-child relationship. But fear, need, and horror first unloosed human fantasy; in the struggle with the beast of the wilderness, the uncanny and preternatural exerted its effect and opened up new conceptions, new vital possibilities; piety toward the tribal father slowly fused with awe before the incomprehensible power of nature so as to *bear a god*" (1893f:402). According to Houben, 1894a (not available to me) concerns "the contradiction posed by heathen old-Arabism to the religion and culture of Mohammedanism."

[r] Nominally Lou was here reviewing Fulda's adaptation from Andersen, performed in place of *Hanna Jagert*, which was delayed by the censor but already in print. Coincidentally, Hanna's first infidelity was to a jailed Socialist militant; Hanna, though, had militated along.

beloved teacher as Savior. Lou grasped her own case as Hannele's,[s] beginning with Hannele's having been starved for her father's love. Hauptmann, she insisted, must have been recollecting a personal experience to have expressed naïve religiosity so gloriously as—like creative fancy generally—a wishful, dreamlike correction and completion of real life.[25] She called the play Hauptmann's supreme achievement in drawing drama from simplicity. His intent, she held, was the reverse of sentimental: Hannele is brought on stage already dying, just so that her inner beauty might be enjoyed tearlessly and that the joke of how humans would rise by the gods they devise might draw a "good, earnest, liberating laugh."[26] A half century later Hauptmann noted about Lou: "The first reviews to show full understanding came from her."[27]

Just before writing on *Hannele*, Lou began a novel suggested by it, *Ruth*, which she afterwards completed in three months[t] of fairly steady, "wildly happy" labor.[28] *Ruth* was all about Lou's Gillot affair, with Lou as Ruth, an orphan since age six or so (when Lou had virtually lost her own parents), and with Gillot as Erik (after Hendrik), a schoolteacher (after *Hannele*[u]). Ruth lives in a fantasy world, and Erik strives to draw her out of it in Gillot's fashion.[v] Except that there is no religious motif in *Ruth*[w] and that Ruth does not know she loves Erik, the corrections of past reality were piddling[x]—up to a point. Fatefully, late in January 1894, just as Lou was approaching the denouement of *Ruth*, Gillot's wife died.[y] Lou must have dimly envisioned this death in 1878-1879, with herself then filling the vacancy. So instead in *Ruth* Erik's invalid wife, Klare-Bel, discerns Erik's love for Ruth and nobly steps aside, therewith recovering her health as reward and her faith as consolation. Ruth, who has been studying abroad, is then carrying on with a young man in Lou's own naïve-risqué manner. Ruth's foster mother writes Erik uneasily.[z]

[s] Perhaps rightly: Hauptmann could hardly *not* have heard from Lou about her childhood, which is as if crudified by *Hannele* (cf. below, pp. 284-85).

[t] Begun 18 XI 1893; completed 17 II 1894 (according to Lou's calendars—as against a notation by her on the manuscript quoted by Pfeiffer, *Leben*, 291); published late 1895 (last printer's correction 2 IX 1895).

[u] Also like Ledebour: see below, p. 181 n. *d*.

[v] *Ruth* is herein astonishingly like a psychoanalytical case history strong on transference and countertransference, but unfortunately blank on the sessions themselves.

[w] This omission was the fictional complement to her nonfictional backdating of her loss of faith (above, pp. 160-61 and n. *v*)—which indeed began fictionally (above, p. 161 n. *w*).

[x] For instance, Ruth's little schoolmates all listen eagerly to her wild tales.

[y] D 28 I 1894: "Sunday. *Ruth* V [last chapter] begun. Gillot's wife †."

[z] From Heidelberg (= Zurich)—but here the name of Ruth's foster parents

Ruth writes in turn to explain herself, telling overingenuously of walks arm in arm and of a kiss in bed[a]—not meaning to arouse Erik's jealousy, to be sure. Erik's reply strikes her as mistrustful, unlike him,[29/b] so she takes the night train back to Petersburg. Erik proposes. Offended, Ruth departs with the ideal Erik in her heart, leaving the real one behind on his knees. This final option for unreality shows Ruth to have been imperfectly cured—and herein the story was true to life again.

Erik's proposal derived from Gillot's letter to Lou in Rome about his having meant her independence as a "transition"—and derived by way of a similarly ambiguous clause of her diary asserting that she had taken leave of Gillot through her confirmation "even though I *could* have stayed with him."[30/c] Her fantasy proposal from Gillot, now fully conscious for the first time, was conscious as just that: she well knew that she had not left Rome for Petersburg even by day. Blending this fantasy with the corresponding facts, she was validating it—and, through it, that fond suspicion she had earlier required in order to reject the real Gillot and introject the ideal one. This is Ruth's own project from the very outset, when she tells Erik that she would rather be the gardener than the gardener's tree ("though maybe it's just about the same"[31]). Ruth's pupilage repeated Märchen's of that Italy-based, Gillot-inspired final sequence of Lou's fictional romance with Nietzsche. Even Rudolf reappeared—as Erik's son, whose sole function was to court Ruth fraternally and in vain. It was, then, on the ground of her prior fictional alignment of her Nietzsche on her Gillot experience that Lou first fictionally reconstrued the latter, with Kuno's nonproposal accepted passing over into Erik's proposal nonaccepted—itself a precedent for Nietzsche's in her pseudoreminiscences. At the same time, her self-gratifying novelistic embellishment of her frustration over Gillot helped her up from her Ledebour let-down.[d]

---

comes into prominence: *Römer* (= Romans). Erik has been writing affectionate letters to Ruth all along but destroying instead of sending them.

[a] And of a proposal from Jurii (= Rée Russified), "but" of one delivered in Russian (= Rée's *Plattdeutsch*) (1893g:273).

[b] No text for Erik's reply is given. (The sequence of Lou's 1882 exchange with Gillot was reversed.)

[c] This phrase tends, however, to suggest a fantasy proposal before her confirmation: cf. below, pp. 281, 469-70. For a neatly equivalent misleading phrase see below, p. 268 ("did not remain in the family circle").

[d] D [27 XII 1912]: ". . . narcissism ('where we are one with our longings'): how all life-renewals, . . . even in creative work, ever again derive thence"; etc. Moreover, *Ruth* was indirectly about Lou's Ledebour affair, for in "Paradies" (below, p. 184) Ledebour's counterpart strives *à la* Gillot to

Lou's last blatant semimemoir, *Ruth* was also about her worst piece of prose through all its three hundred saccharine-stained pages full of masterful big Erik and darling little Ruth. Yet the press acclaimed it, deeming the prose fresh and nuancée, the plot intriguing, the technique "wholly objective,"[32] the psychology subtle, the heroine a creature of pure poetry. It ran several editions while the controversy raged as to whether Ruth was to blame for tempting Erik half knowingly or Erik for acting like a child.[33] It gave Romundt pause, however, and oddly so after his defense of Lou's Nietzsche book: "too much psychological spinning for my taste," he told Overbeck,[34] and again "the air in it is not pure and healthful enough."[35] A few years later a critic reappraising it considered that, despite its wealth of art and science, "it is by no means all true and beautiful," and pronounced it on the balance "a novelistic curiosity."[36] So be it.

It was just after completing *Ruth* that Lou left for Paris. She rode with Fritz Mauthner, was met by Therese Krüger, and soon[e] struck a staggering pace of social life within—strangely, for she knew French—foreigners' Paris. Her principal escort was Paul Goldmann, a Viennese would-be belletrist then serving with bad grace as the *Frankfurter Zeitung*'s Paris correspondent: he was the image of Paul Rée. Goldmann's seconds were Hartleben and the publisher Albert Langen to begin with, then one Countess Nemethy, novelist and cosmopolitan hostess. Lou met, among others, the Danish novelist Hermann Bang[f] and the Norwegian physical and literary giant Knut Hamsun.[g] In May, Frieda von Bülow, returning from Africa, and Frieda's sister, Sophie, spent two weeks with her. Her brother Jenia turned up in June. The only natives on her lists were the Germanist Henri Albert (whom she knew from Berlin) and an Alsatian flower vendor for whom she substituted one day with Sophie's assistance.

She read Huysmans, Barrès, and Verlaine the first weeks. She also frequented museums, galleries, and cafés, and attended debates in the Chamber and Senate with Goldmann, rehearsals of German and Scandinavian imports at the Théâtre Antoine, and the evening *cirque d'été*. At the Countess's on the eve of Bastille Day she met Frank

---

draw Lou's out of her fantasy paradise: Lou thus assimilated her duplicity vis-à-vis Ledebour to her daydreaming vis-à-vis Gillot. Klare-Bel's illness due to vanish by enchantment was moreover Fred's out of Lou's tall tale to Ledebour, physicalized and displaced—with the noble stepping aside also wishfully Fred's.

[e] After a first week in bed with a swollen ankle—possibly a memento of Ledebour: see below, p. 185 n. *w.*

[f] (Through Therese Krüger, his translator.)

[g] (Through Albert Langen, his publisher.)

Wedekind, whose drama of sex among the adolescents, *Frühlings Erwachen*, had shocked all Germany three years before: the pair went off slumming together at Les Halles, whereupon Lou, agreeing to coffee in Wedekind's room, misled him into taking the follow-up for granted.[h] "Adventure!!!!!" she told her calendar. After this misadventure, she frequently went strolling with Wedekind or else joined him in visiting the poet Georg Herwegh's aged, destitute widow. "He is already reared," she noted the fourth week[37/i]—whereas he decried her in his private correspondence, especially for the "pure humbug" behind her Nietzsche and Wagner tales.[38/j]

In late August she journeyed to Zurich with a gigantic Russian doctor and anarchist in exile named Ssavely.[k] Goldmann promptly joined her (coming from Frankfurt)—and promptly left again, evidently on account of Ssavely. A chaste pastoral idyll with Ssavely followed: the two coauthored a drama, romping barefoot between times.[l] The drama does not survive[m]; neither does a "sketch," "Die Stadt der Toten" (The City of the Dead), penned by Lou earlier in Paris.[39] In that live city she was bleakly dispirited time and again for all her social rounds, outings, and escapades—and more so than ever when, two weeks after she had reclaimed her poodle from Goldmann's manservant upon her return from Switzerland, Goldmann visited her at her request, only to "swap letters" and "part with a handshake!!"[40] She thereupon returned suddenly to Charlottenburg. Her third day back—September 30, 1894—she noted in retrospect: "Everything like a dream."

There followed "a month begun in hope and ended in despair"[41]—for literary reasons. After laboring away "with torment" at an essay on Jesus,[42/n] she began one short story ("Verjährt")[43] and then another ("Knechtgestalt").[44] Come mid-November she noted: "Still innocuously idiotic, unfit for mental work. Obtuse. Pleasure in prac-

[h] Cf. below, p. 212 (that she misled him guilelessly is where the fiction began).

[i] (*"Er ist schon erzogen."*) According to her calendars, she was with him on fourteen different dates after their misadventure, generally alone and for hours on end.

[j] Wedekind's naming his fictional "sex demon" *Lulu* may well have been "his subtle revenge" on Lou, as Peters, 194-95, suggests (the more since Lou did style herself Lulu on occasion)—and may also have been perverted wishful thinking.

[k] Ssavely (so named in 1931a:128-29) appears on her calendars for Paris as "the Russian" and for this excursion as "K."

[l] Bölsche and others visited them from Zurich, and once they met with Jenia in Lucerne.

[m] Lou read it to her Russian circle in Paris on her return and reworked it in Charlottenburg on 7 x 1894.

[n] Begun 10 x 1894.

tical chores. Big cooking feasts."[45] Next she was laid up with severe headaches. Three shiftless weeks thereafter and she was off to the Black Forest for the holidays.[o] She meanwhile read Bourget and Maupassant, whose psychological and narrative art respectively marked some of her tales to come. She also visited with Therese Krüger, Frieda, and Frieda's friend Johanna Niemann, a novelist; with the Mauthners and Hartlebens; and with Gerhart Hauptmann, who just then took a Grunewald apartment without Marie. She even ran into Baron von Schulz one day. In January 1895 she returned from the Black Forest with refreshed wits[p] to complete a new short story and some verse in hiding at Frieda's. After having been "located" by Andreas, she went home to an unsociable February of "uninterrupted work . . . but at length overwork,"[46/q] from which emerged a brief study of Ricarda Huch's first novel, a further short story, and a draft of the Jesus essay.[r]

The verse came to a dozen undistinguished lines addressed to you-through-whom-it-was-given-me-to-see-God-and-bury-him[s] and two dozen charming ones on some oak leaves that cling to the bough through the winter only to drop away in the spring.[t] Ricarda Huch's historical romance *Ludolf Ursleu* was explicated enchantedly. Before Lou published the explication she sent it together with a letter and a photo of herself to the great romanticist schoolmistress in Zurich, who remarked in return: "I am not suited for correspondence with famous contemporaries. That is simply because I am lazy and so dreadfully realistic."[47/u] The first story completed was "Das Paradies" (Paradise), in which a girl dreams of taunting her elderly bridegroom (a friend of her father's) by flying from his side on great grey wings. It turns out that she has recently fled her marital paradise in terror. Her divorce counsel (a cousin) is enamored of her fantasticality, yet strives to draw her out of this dreamier paradise. She resists till one day she discovers a baby starving in a garret overhead. And so Ledebour's[v] social conscience overcame Lou's selfish mendacity for a happy ending. In the second story she finished, "Vor dem

---

[o] Just beyond Stuttgart, to friends unidentifiable from her XII 1894 calendar (I 1895 is missing).

[p] D 28 II 1895: "*Erfrischung durch die Reise.*"

[q] She visited only Frieda.

[r] D 23 II 1895: "completed"—but revised VIII 1895.

[s] "Durch Dich."

[t] "Winterlaub."

[u] These lines, read aloud to me (see below, pp. 557ff.), are all I could learn of this correspondence except that it evidently lapsed after a couple of further, brief exchanges.

[v] Siemsen, 17: Ledebour aspired to be a lawyer.

Erwachen" (Before Awakening), Lou depicted herself as the virginal child-wife of an aged uncle. Between trains in Lübeck she is blissfully half seduced by an artist friend while half asleep. She resolves "to take herself to task" as she rides away, but instead "sleeps tight and sweet, and dreams about a wide glistening white snow bank upon which a sled with jingling bells is gliding down,— — —down—"[48] And so Lou slept off Ledebour on the train to Paris.[w] The somnolent rapture in Lübeck was a direct derivative of the fantasy-work accompanying her childhood autoerotism.[x] In her fiction from "Vor dem Erwachen" on, she could enjoy sex with a father surrogate only while dozing (only behind her own back, as it were)—just as she conceived the "highest creativity" in religion or ethics or art to be of necessity self-concealed and self-forgetful. More generally, her fiction henceforth conveyed rather—to use her own words—a "wish-text" than its "formal mastering."[49] Autoerotism, the life of "Vor dem Erwachen," was also the death of it in that the narrator's swooning over the heroine spoiled it as even its nonsensicality did not. What came off best in it was Lübeck by lamplight.

According to "Jesus der Jude" (Jesus the Jew)—Lou's only essay ever to mean much to her[y]—the modern, rational scholar, in treating the old two-way relationship between God and man as one-way, has been missing the crucial point, which is "the countereffect of a deity, however he may have originated, on those who believe in him."[50] The historian should consider how a long-established, oft-refashioned godhead mediated by great religious leaders can itself become creative, acting through a whole people bound in its service. Within any given faith, specifically religious motives commingle diversely from man to man and from age to age with the profane motives—fear, need, hope—that induce men to fashion and refashion gods. The more intensely a faith affects the faithful, the more personal is each experience of it and hence the less accessible to scholarship. Only once in an epoch does a religious genius find adequate expression for a distinctively personal yet universally appealing vision of a received

---

[w] Ledebour sketched. He also had a stiff leg—displaced onto Andreas in the tale.

[x] Its proximate antecedent was the Wedekind incident, the sense of "before awakening" ("*vor dem* Frühlings *Erwachen*") being: before I woke up to what he was about. Wedekind's forerunners here were those supposed would-be seducers Gillot and Nietzsche—and more specifically Andreas, who had, before Wedekind, taken her for granted carnally, with perhaps even an attempt to seduce her in her sleep (see below, pp. 472-73 and n. *e*).

[y] Intrinsically, that is ("'Anal'" meant much to her extrinsically). "Jesus" was her only published essay of which she preserved the manuscript or to which she referred back in later years.

faith. Such a genius was Jesus, whose conception of God as a loving father, and of inward nearness to him as the one thing needful, not only gave "highest religiousness" its "classic expression" "for all time,"[51] but "for the first time resolved the emotional contradiction implicit in man's kneeling before a man-made god."[52] Like all other great founders of religions, Jesus did not fashion a new godhead: he changed the way of experiencing an old one, correcting the distortions due to its human origin and therewith *revealing* it in its divine purity: he turned a remote Lord of Might into an intimate God of Love. But his pure vision rectified one discrepancy only to intensify another in the long run: that between religious vision and rational experience. The attempt to rationalize Jesus' vision was one day to cost it its purity all over again. This, though, was no concern of Jesus', whose sole purpose was to depict his god in inner verity even if in outer folly.

Others may have felt their god as truly, Lou pursued; it took a Jew to depict a heartfelt god so graphically. Traditionally "the Jew did not rack his brain over his god, but suffered and lived and felt him."[53] Earthy at even his most soulful, he demanded with stout, simple faith that divine promises be fulfilled here and now: the hereafter was not his native soil (he first trod it late and in exile), just as "contractual-mindedness" came to him only with religious senility.[54] But every man-God relationship is at bottom contractual, and a religion's vitality depends on how well it succeeds in making the parallel lines of divine promise and worldly experience appear to converge at the vanishing point. Judaism, keyed to immanent convergence, racially exclusive besides, was winning few converts in Jesus' time what with the universal cry for an afterworld, a "cry of distress from weary, declining cultures."[55] Worse, life and faith were coming apart within Israel: witness Job's anguish or even the Pharisees' "frantic last call for divine righteousness."[56] Messiahs were wanted to heal the breach. Jesus' appeal lay less in his message, which was by no means unique, than simply in his assurance of having God's love, like the prophets of old. His joyous peace of soul *suspended* doubt; to *obliterate* it, however, a most tangible blessing was wanted, as he well knew. So he sought to establish the Messianic Kingdom politically, never imagining that his Father would let him down. In his martyrdom, as in all else, he was no transcender of Judaism, but its supreme expression: having put God to the crucial test of keeping faith with his people, he died vainly looking upwards. He agonized only as all other believers do unknowingly, so that religion personified bled to death at Golgotha in all its truth and folly. Perhaps he forgave his god in the final hour: "Eli, Eli," with its despair and shame, may have been put into his mouth by disenchanted disciples. Either way the finale was tragical for Judaism, which, admitting defeat, languished inwardly. Meanwhile, reports of the resurrection revived the disciples' old mood, whereupon Judaism in its decline mysteriously "gave life to a new universal religion."[57] Judaism furnished the historic tradition, paganism the heavenly sequel, with the resurrection in between, fulfilling the one, prefiguring the other. In contrast to that "highest emotional process by which an individual religious genius receives and announces his revelation of God,"[58] inner tension and outer frustration drove the pagan world to convert Jesus into a new god of Heaven. Again need had led to god-creation. The need was met as, "with paradoxical boldness,"[59] "the fatal contradiction between suffering and righteousness"[60] was resolved through the image of God on the cross —a symbolical reminder that only the rarest of individuals ever experiences religion in "its true bliss and full tragedy," which "the masses below never learn. His tragic end, his tragic realization, remain as singular and mysterious as were his beatitude and his union with God," so that for all we know his cry of abandonment— "religion's last word"—may yet prove a "cry of triumph."[61]

The tacit argument of "Jesus der Jude" was that even a man-made god who produces effects is *ipso facto* real. Lou helped it along by repeatedly writing for short about Jesus' god rather than about his conception of one. It was for her own benefit that her Jesus, who never questioned *his* god's credentials, "resolved the emotional contradiction implicit in man's kneeling before a man-made god." And at that the contradiction was not emotional, but logical; its resolution, though, was nothing if not emotional. The pseudologic was that to call a god loving is to revoke the "man-made," as men do not make gods for love, and that accordingly Jesus was not projecting a loving Father onto a blustering old Lord, but reacting in kind to an acting upon him. By the same token, while Lou used all of her science to show that Jesus was immanently refuted, she used all of her art to intimate that he was transcendently vindicated. She let religion bleed to death with him only that its Christian rebirth ("wonderful and mysterious"[62]) might read like a rhetorical warrant for his own resurrection. More explicitly: "We deny the resurrection for logical, not historical, reasons, as we do not know what then took place; we can but infer the cause from the gigantic effect by which Christianity stands or falls"[63]—the very same argument as her tacit one for God's

187

existence. And most explicitly: paganism "seized on the new fact that a man had risen from the dead."[64/z] So Jesus' god came through after all—"as surely as that the man on the cross and the man who rose are one."[65]

Lou's singular fondness for her Jesus essay was matched by its singular unoriginality among her essays. To treat the idea of God as no mere fancy, given its effects, was Biedermann's first lesson to her.[a] Her pious abuse of this treatment derived from Biedermann as well. So did much of her scriptural exegesis.[b] With her main point, meanwhile, she was rebutting Nietzsche's conception of Christianity as "the final Jewish consequence"[66/c]—and this from Gillot's pulpit as well as Biedermann's chair, for Gillot too gave Jesus to be a "final flowering" of Judaism posthumously misconstrued as a guide to heaven.[d] And yet her Jesus took after her Nietzsche. He too was a solitary religious genius who demonstratively chose this world over against the other on the strength of an inner truth that was outer folly. There was also something of the "frightful leap" to his relocating his remote god in his own heart.[e] Of course her Nietzsche had taken after her Jesus in the first place. And in the very first, the resemblance between the two was Platonic, for it derived from their resemblance to a common archetype: herself. Before her Jesus, she herself had transformed a remote traditional god into a proximate loving father: hers was that refashioning called revealing, motivated by that love pseudologically denied. She it was who, while still sure of her god's love, had demanded a sign for worldly reasons. And hers was the god who, having let her down terrestrially, would yet lift her up celestially—hers the cry of abandonment due to turn into a cry of triumph.

The crucifixion as prelude to a love feast: here one source of her

---

[z] "*Dass ein Mensch auferstanden war*"—not even *wäre*.

[a] Incidentally, this first lesson of Biedermann's went from Lou to Georg Simmel, who objected to it in "Jesus" (probably in Simmel→Lou, 10 v 1896, which was withheld from me) only to write it into the closing pages of his *Die Religion* ten years later—as Lou (D [1912?]) slyly noted by way of displacement in remarking apropos of *another* idea in the same "somewhat flat booklet" (that men refashion themselves in the image of their gods): "How well we would have agreed, whereas at the time of my 'Jesus der Jude' essay, which Simmel disputed, such thinking remained foreign to him."

[b] That "son of God" meant *earthly King* to the prophets (1894b:349); etc.

[c] Unlike Nietzsche's, Lou's Jesus was neither rancorous toward Rome nor his rancorous people's bait; rather, Rome put him to otherworldly uses all its own —for which he was nonetheless fit. Herein lay also Lou's covert reply to Nietzsche's covert Genealogical thesis (above, p. 137).

[d] See above, p. 14 (Gillot having been closer than Nietzsche to Nietzsche's original, Heine, who in *Zur Geschichte der Religion und Philosophie in Deutschland* II treated Jesus as Jewry's "finest blossom").

[e] To his "union with God" (1894b:351).

affinity for Jesus, her masochism, was in evidence. Another, her castration complex, showed in her insistence that Jesus was a Jew—meaning circumcised—until the resurrection. Philo-Semitic to a fault,[f] she always wrote about the Jews, too, autobiographically: about how, after their long, agonizing struggle to compose life's ideal with its practical requirements, they resigned themselves to that tragic duality, adopting the world's ways with surpassing facility "while yet maintaining their ideal final goal, which really stands radically opposed to all that"; how their courage was at best negative, was an unreadiness to die, "as if death were in secret their race's problem"; how they were individuals by dint of their individual ways of facing up to death.[67] For only one other people did she ever feel affinity, and this again extreme: for the Russians, by reason of their supposed childlike piety.[g] And sure enough she saw no end of likeness between Russian and Jew, beginning with a common "depth of feeling, inwardness, broader and mightier than Westerners'."[68/h]

Lou revisited none-too-Russian Petersburg for seven weeks beginning early in March 1895. She stayed with her mother and Jenia, then living on each other's nerves. To explain why he did not move away from his mother, Jenia would say: "She needs to fret over me"—insincerely, Lou told Caro, "for he bitterly believed that on the contrary she had *little* need for him and would get over him quickly."[69] Between domestic scenes and family gatherings, Lou saw Gillot at his home and in his chapel, her demon having told her at his wife's death that he was free at last: they took grandiloquent leave of each other for life.[i] She also read a little Tolstoi in Russian and attended a "gloriously beautiful"[70] production of *Hannele* "with naïvely stylized Byzantine heaven and savior."[71] Frieda joined her the second week to

[f] But see above, p. 71 n. *n.*

[g] 1919e:381 expressly asserted the Russians' singular kinship with the Nazarene in his sufferings—besides the primitive wish-fulfilling character of Russian religiosity (*ibid.*, 380-81), its "principle of a direct God-incarnation" even when most rationalized (*ibid.*, 385), its "positively pious" erotism even in castration orgies (*ibid.*), etc. It also depicted the Russian's "nature" as "heedlessly living out its drives" (*ibid.*, 384) and as one that "senses its worst linked to its best, the sole truly divine grace revealing itself therein" (*ibid.*, 382)—in effect, as Lou's own would-be Nietzschean instinctuality beyond good and evil. (On Lou and the Russian's "nature" see also below, pp. 215, 260, etc. —and 441 n. *l.*)

[h] The preceding, opening line of this diary entry reads: "I should like to write a psychology of the Jews, a parallel between them and the Russians"; the sequel was destroyed. Cf. 1897d.

[i] D 21 IV 1895: "At Gillot's sermon. Text: 'On old paths.' Closing words: 'I thank thee.'" 1895e ensued: sixteen dreadful verses to you-of-mournful-mind-and-visage, "gardener of my roses," to whom I-of-high-spirits merely return what is yours as I beam at you lovingly.

shiver and sniffle a while,[72] then gallivant with her and the family.[j] Afterwards Frieda accompanied her via Warsaw to Vienna—and left her there to her own devices after receiving a first local caller with her on April 29: Arthur Schnitzler.

A year earlier Lou had read two unpublished one-act plays of Schnitzler's[k] provided by his friend Goldmann, then had written him prettily that, while he modeled weighty substance with an "incomparably light and tender touch," his men came off so badly as against his women in the process "that one is tempted to see it as just a bit calumniatory."[73/l] Her second day in Vienna she sent asking him, "Can I meet you personally?"[74] He called to find her nursing a cold with Frieda's help. She proposed a new meeting, promising to be "better company."[75] Evidently she kept her promise, for she thereupon took a place of honor in his circle of convivial literati, joining them daily for outings to the theater or excursions to the Vienna Woods, for gondola rides at the Venedig or snacks at the Wurstl- prater or supper at the Impérial, followed ever and again by "white stearin" at the Griensteidl café, their usual starting place.

Having found Vienna enchanting at first sight,[76] Lou now found it doubly so. Schnitzler was then, on turning thirty-three, a physician who dabbled in letters; only later that year did his drama *Liebelei* invert the formula overnight. Nor were his cronies yet celebrities: Richard Beer-Hofmann, going on twenty-nine, author of two short stories; Felix Salten, twenty-five, theater critic; Hugo von Hofmanns- thal alias Loris, twenty-one, poet-dramatist—the one non-Jew of the four.[m] Lou saw the least of Loris, then serving with the hussars. She saw the most of Beer-Hofmann, who at their first encounter recited poems by Loris and Schnitzler "so finely."[77] Ages afterwards she called this performance "a mere beginning thousands of verses ago."[78]

Beer-Hofmann's way of "blithely sauntering" through life cheered her.[79/n] His single sorrow was literally a farfetched one: his mother's death five days after his birth. For the rest, his family, well-to-do, had covered him benignly even when, after taking a law degree to no pur- pose, he entered upon a precious aesthetical retreat. He came out of it halfway in 1891 with the story "Camelias," in which, however, the

[j] Frieda stayed at a hotel. 1931a:131: "Eugene very deeply befriended her."

[k] "Halb Zwei" and "Eine überspannte Person."

[l] She specified in this letter that it was written on Goldmann's insistence (despite D 14 v 1894: "Letter from Arthur Schnitzler [to Goldmann?]. Read both his manuscripts"). Cf. 1893a:168: "Thus far Strindberg's dramas have all been . . . a slander on the male."

[m] He was, however, of one-fourth Jewish descent.

[n] Cf. below, p. 192 n. *q*—and 1897a:85.

effeminate, decadent bachelor finally lets the budding girl go lest she disrupt his set existence. He came all the way out of it in 1893 with "Das Kind,"*ᵒ* in which his self-styled hero, Paul, drops his mistress, a simple girl beneath his station, with a yawn and a shrug soon after they have given their child away. Then by and by Paul learns of the child's death in poverty and, remorseful, seeks its grave in vain, only to recover his innocence and enter upon a "springtime of glory" by way of a vision of things as all indefeasibly conjoined: "They no longer stood alien *beside* one another—a thought cast a bond around them."[80]

The moral edge to this vision was that nature knows nothing of evil, which men invent to give point to their lives—that nature is rather a system of interlinked fates (animal, vegetable, and mineral), with the child's death serving to teach Paul this very lesson. As a solvent of guilt feelings, the vision was cosmically egocentric. Yet it proved a solvent of egoism as well, indeed almost of the ego, as it filled Paul full of fresh, ecstatic, indiscriminate joy in things. Of a sudden he felt consanguineous with them all, part and parcel of them, as if after a lifetime of severance. In this feeling lay an antidote to the fear of death—inconspicuously in "Das Kind," conspicuously in a novel begun by Beer-Hofmann in 1894 about an equivalent Paul whose close experience of a friend's death draws him out of dreamy detachment from the world by way of the selfsame cosmic vision with the selfsame moral edge to it (though this time the instructive decease was none of Paul's doing).

With Beer-Hofmann as with Lou, the dread of death was thus a guilty one. Lou was the more readily taken with the new elixir of life brewing from Paul to Paul. But she was taken first with the alchemist —that scrupulous artist and gracious person with so much of his working title about him, *Der Götterliebling* (The Darling of the Gods). Once Schnitzler noted after dining with the two: "Lou is turning a bit female"[81]/*ᵖ*; and again after a night at the theater with them: "Peculiarly vexed mood of Lou's toward Richard, out of the need to be desired."[82] Richard for his part reported to Loris toward the end of Lou's stay: "Frau Lou is still in Vienna and with us several hours a day. It looks as if she were quite fond of us (that is, Arthur and you, me); I believe we signify something private to her or are symbols for something or other we cannot know. She is getting to like much in Vienna just because of us—and then again sees much in us that is

ᵒ Published with "Camelias" in 1893 as *Novellen*—but with "Die Verlassene. Erzählung von Richard Beer-Hofmann" (and a forlorn-looking lady) on the cover.

ᵖ Cf. below, p. 202.

really only Vienna. She calls us 'happy people' because, among other reasons, we love the city we live in, it is the city we were born in, and we have one another. Her eyes and smile are so young that we only recently discovered how much younger we now find her than at first. I lent her . . . the d'Annunzio series and a few poems of yours. She likes and respects Gerhart Hauptmann and his *Hannele*—but finds us 'richer.' "[83/q]

Lou quit the magic circle just long enough to befriend the poetess Emilie Mataja and the grand old lady of German letters Marie von Ebner-Eschenbach. Of historic Vienna she saw only the Stefansdom beside her hotel.[84] After four "wonderful weeks" during which, as she put it, everything worked out and the sun shone,[85] she returned home, having laid plans beforehand with the two civilian "happy people" for a late-summer beach party near Copenhagen.

There followed for Lou a month of "vain attempts to work,"[86] with attendant "melancholia"[87] and "desperation"[88] punctuated by housework, reading, and visits—mostly to Frieda or Mauthner and including one from her brother Roba. For June 26 she noted: "Work-frenzy comes at last!" With it came the bulk of a novel, *Aus fremder Seele[r]* (Out of an Alien Soul), about a woman who compensates for her own loss of faith by sustaining the morale of a disbelieving pastor over the years. Lou's pastor was first of all an unpretty Rée—a coward who, suspicious of himself because of a Jewish mother,[s] compensates through strained benevolence. With this jeer at Rée went, however, a wish: that he should have needed her beside him while doctoring the poor in Stibbe. The pastor was next Gillot in that he originally takes God's place for the youthful heroine,[t] who then

---

[q] Cf. Schnitzler's diary, 19 v 1895: "Lou recently said we three—Hugo, Richard, and I—are really the happiest people she ever met: first, we are not ambitious; second, we lived in Vienna, a city we like; third, we had found one another.—Today she said: Richard the happiest, sleek, nothing quite touches him—I the unhappiest, pensive, yet [she] would best like to be 'me.' " *Ibid.*, 23 v 1895: "Lou: Richard is cooler than you. Men, trees, things—all one and equivalent, whereas you depict everything from the vantage of the human soul. That is why Goldmann, who really always craves and dreads life, does Richard such good." *Ibid.*, 24 v 1895: "Lou leaves today.—She told Richard she is 'grateful' to us. It is gratifying that, evidently quite apart from our doings, we signify something positive or even beautiful to her. Richard: she seems to ascribe to [us] much that is Vienna and vice versa."

[r] At this stage: "Der Himmelspastor" (Pastor of Heaven).

[s] Cf. above, p. 49 and n. *t*. Lou on 10 iii 1894 noted Rée's mother's death (the pastor's mother has died a year before the novel opens). Perhaps she sent Rée condolences and received no acknowledgment, whence her novelistic ill will toward him.

[t] She was a staunch believer until this encounter—in overcompensation for "Gottesschöpfung" (but cf. above, p. 180 n. *w*).

promptly seeks to take *his* place—sitting at his desk on the sly, reading his impious books, stealing his wicked thoughts. In time she comes to run his whole life, growing mannish thereby. By her grace he earns the nickname "pastor of heaven"—wherewith he passes over into Jesus in that he tells wondrous parables, and back into Rée in that Jesus healed men's bodies too. And Lou accumulated these identities vicariously in that the pastor lives out of the heroine's soul —until, that is, her hold over him is broken by young Lou as young Nietzsche: the pastor's loving son.[u] Actually the story begins where Lou's Nietzsche story began: as the son loses his faith. Having divinized the truth in the process, the son avows his apostasy to the pastor[v] in fear and trembling. The pastor merely smiles, and gradually the son learns why. He is aghast. The pastor, hoping to make amends, confesses his imposture from the pulpit, but the boy meanwhile has shot himself. The pastor goes mad, whereupon his successor more or less restores the congregation's peace of soul by explaining that the confession was pure raving already.

Besides the full gloom of *Im Kampf um Gott*, *Aus fremder Seele* has much the same grandeur. Artistically it is finer wrought: pointed, dramatic, all of a piece. The characterizations are superb—especially one Uncle Justus, a comical Paul Rée in love with the heroine, who could steal a scene by Dickens, and except only the son, whose attributes (notably his sex) could be altered unnoticed one and all save his "incorruptible truthfulness."[89] A perfect Ibsenite effect is achieved as the past intrudes bit by bit upon the present, disrupting it at last. There is even a shade of *Ghosts* upon the unholy household—and a quack of *The Wild Duck* to the moral of the tale: better illusion than disillusion. But then, there was a touch of Ibsen to young Lou.

In August 1895, Lou left her novel in abeyance to begin two short stories,[w] then set those aside to do two book reviews[x] and revise her essay on Jesus. Paul's elixir from the graveyard may have assisted in her Jesus' resurrection,[y] for she had just then finished arranging with

---

[u] Actually his adoptive son, who, however, calls him father.

[v] After Kuno's example.

[w] Called "Gegen den Strom" and "Totentanz" on her calendars.

[x] The first—on Erwin Rohde's *Psyche, Seelenkult und Unsterblichkeitsglaube der Griechen*—I could not locate. According to Houben, the second—1895g— is a critique of the Dutch pastor W. Brandt's *Evangelische Geschichte und der Ursprung des Christentums*, itself basically "a critique of the testimony concerning Jesus' agony and resurrection."

[y] Cf. below, p. 262 (Lou on Beer-Hofmann's death and resurrection). Conceivably Lou already knew that the second Paul was to feel at one with historic Jewry primarily. The Brandt book (see preceding note), which occupied her on 6, 9, and 10 VIII 1895, must have prompted the "Jesus" revisions of 11 and 12 VIII 1895.

Beer-Hofmann to join him as well as Schnitzler, Salten, and others in Salzburg prior to the projected bathing near Copenhagen. In July he had sent her some photos including one inscribed with what she pleasedly took to be a "pledge of reunion."[90] In reply she had compared his stories to Schnitzler's to the effect that whereas Schnitzler would concentrate on some one human soul, showing "how it fares among lesser things called 'the things of life' " casually strewn about it, Beer-Hofmann would painstakingly order the matter and manner of his tales so as to fit "man in all his ways and deeds, his entire psychic constitution, into the whole outer scheme of the world round about him." She had added: "I always think of you all with so much joy and gratitude"—and singularly: "You happy man!"[91]

After some arranging with Schnitzler in turn, then five days with Andreas at the Ammersee near Munich, Lou arrived in Salzburg late on August 20. The next morning she toured the town with Schnitzler and Salten. Others soon joined the party beginning with Beer-Hofmann,[z] who came that afternoon[a] from nearby Ischl for two or three days' outings. And Loris in his Balkan barracks was "heartily glad" to know Schnitzler in Frau Dr. Salomé's company, "in which one's intimation of the youth of the soul becomes credible."[92] At daybreak on August 24, while Lou took the train back to the Ammersee, Schnitzler "bicycled off"[93] into the Alps with Salten. Five days later he was in Munich with Paul Goldmann, "who," he told Loris, "is looking good but is little content with his lot and his prospects."[94] Beer-Hofmann joined the two there at the month's end. Lou came on September 3 for three days with the threesome in forests and cafés. Then Schnitzler left for Vienna and early *Liebelei* rehearsals. For the following day Lou noted: ". . . Copenhagen plans fall through . . ." and for the next two days: ". . . Evening all dined in garden; our departure, Goldmann's brother-in-law along to the station. Moonlit landscape, the Russian. At 1:30 AM in Innsbruck, Hôtel de l'Europe. The next morning two-hour carriage ride to Schönberg im Stubaithal and back. Returned afternoon with luggage. Glorious up there. The first night in the farmhouse on the slope, arrival in the dark over the meadows." Then for September 10: "Moved into the garden house, a most charming little hermitage [beside the inn]; walk to the enchanted forest. Evening on the veranda by candlelight. Night in the garden house by moonlight. Fear of thieves. Wodan."

Lou's diary-shy consort was Beer-Hofmann, who wrote Schnitzler

[z] Also Tomaselli, Sratick, Sudermann, Feldmann (D 21-23 VIII 1895).
[a] Schnitzler had vainly telegraphed him on 19 VIII 1895 at 3:30 PM: "Do come tomorrow evening so we can all be together at least all Wednesday."

that same September 10: "Dear Arthur, I am not in Copenhagen: the evening before, I discovered I just did not want to go and simply begged off. Only it wasn't all that easy. I had to—or rather, I let myself be talked into a compromise by the terms of which I shall be alone not straight off, but in 3-4 days. Frau Lou has come with me temporarily but leaves at the end of the week. *Officially, she has been hindered from going to Copenhagen before early October.* I beg you to endorse that. Even with her. . . . So, I wish to be alone. But—that's better gone into orally. It is simply glorious here: the village is 1,000 meters up, 2¼ hours' drive from Innsbruck. Absolute quiet, a small inn arranged for transients not at all like a hotel. I spent last night in a farmhouse because my room will first be free today. But Frau Lou is just now coming to table. Adieu." For September 11 Lou noted: "In the garden house after breakfast; splendid morning, then storm in prospect. Singers at the inn. Thunderstorm. Rainy night in the garden house . . ." Then for September 12: "Rainy day, bitter cold. In bed. Toward 1 AM feeble moonshine. Wotan, the moral dog." And for September 13: "Cold; rare flashes of sunshine. Up late, to the post office together. Quarrel." Through that day's post passed a letter from Schnitzler to Beer-Hofmann with most cordial regards to Lou,[95] then the reply: ". . . Frau Lou returns greetings, etc. Beginning tomorrow morning I am alone! . . . I inform you that it is best to travel *alone*. The two of us (you and I!) and Hugo excepted." On the morrow's agenda, however, stood: "Walk to the post office. Cold. The cigarettes. Late to bed."[96] Only the day after was Lou off: "Down to Patsch together in the morning. From there Innsbruck-Munich . . ."[97] To Schnitzler's enquiry "Tell me, how did Lou take having to go alone?"[98] Beer-Hofmann replied: "Too hard to put into words. Just this much now: she is not going to Copenhagen—she says. But that is not official."[99]

In fact she went back to Munich for ten days of visiting and writing,[b] then home for eight weeks[c] culminating in "work fever"[100/d] —whereupon she returned to Vienna with Frieda. Arriving late November 21, she wrote to Beer-Hofmann the next day: "I must read [Loris's] 'Robespierre'! As you did not send it to Berlin, I came to Vienna . . ." and to Schnitzler: "Probably I shall call on you tomorrow (Saturday) at your consultation hour. I have been commissioned to send a copy of *Liebelei* to Copenhagen as early as possible." Schnitzler dropped in on her the next morning and took her and

---

[b] D 19-24 IX 1895: "work" (unspecified).

[c] Or possibly to Copenhagen between times (D X 1895 missing).

[d] She completed "Gegen den Strom" (above, p. 193 and n. *w*) and wrote "Eine fixe Idee."

Frieda to coffee that afternoon, then to *Hannele* that evening, then to the Griensteidl, "where Beer-Hofmann was waiting"[101]—and where others joined them. She and Frieda spent the following evening "at Schnitzler's *Liebelei*. With him, Beer-Hofmann, and Loris in a box. Then in the Griensteidl."[102] Schnitzler sent her the text of *Liebelei*, which she pronounced "most beautiful" as against the performance, adding: "Of the three of you—you three happy friends—it is you the happiest."[103/e] Another day and Frieda fell ill: Lou sent for Dr. Schnitzler, "who then sat with me through the evening."[104] Next came an "appointment with Schnitzler at Beer-Hofmann's in the evening," followed by the theater and the Griensteidl.[105/f] Then: "In bed till noon. Frieda goes shopping, meets Beer-Hofmann, who sends a book."[106] And then: "Beer-Hofmann's cancellation, evening with Schnitzler and Salten at the Volkstheater, afterwards in the Griensteidl."[107] Lou thereupon came down with a cold; she rose the fourth day—Tuesday, December 3—when she was "taken to Griensteidl by Schnitzler and wife. Frieda also there from Burgtheater; Loris, Beer-Hofmann, etc. Home with Loris and Beer-Hofmann."[108/g] For December 4 she noted: "Morning, long walk: sunshine and thaw. Evening with Schnitzler and Salten in the Griensteidl. Slack mood." In that mood she had posted a note to Beer-Hofmann: "Please do send me the letter in your possession as you promised yesterday; I waited for it all day today.—I take it that after our exchange of words yesterday we shall meet again as good friends whenever you have the time and inclination to get together with the others and me as of old." This closing of sentimental accounts reached Beer-Hofmann the following day.[h]

Of that December 5, 1895, Beer-Hofmann recollected half a century later: "In the morning, after a sleepless night, I resolve to have told Papa by December 31 at the very latest that I can no longer bear the life I have been leading—that I must leave home for a year or two, travel round the world, to utterly foreign countries, among utterly foreign people . . ."[109] He sulked at home all afternoon, then rushed out impulsively to a *Konditorei* just before closing time to order French candied fruit for someone—presumably Lou.[110/i] "At

---

[e] Cf. above, pp. 192 n. *q*, 194.

[f] Schnitzler's diary, 27 XI 1895, explicitly includes Frieda in this outing.

[g] Lou→Schnitzler [1 XII 1895] had requested an escort.

[h] Postmarked in his neighborhood 7-8 AM, 5 XII 1895.

[i] On 6 XII—St. Nicholas' Day—Austrians give goodies to children of all ages. The *Konditorei* at issue was the Victor Schmidt branch at the Stefansplatz down the street from his flat—and beside Lou's hotel. On Lou, Beer-Hofmann, and candied fruit, see further 1896c:53 and Lou→B-H, 11 IV 1913 (below, p. 445).

his first glimpse of the girl who did up the package he was smitten conclusively—having been alerted by the sound of her name: Paula. To that name answered "a slender, overgrown girl" with "fine silken hair standing out from her forehead, parted, in light brown waves outglistened by airy blonde ones . . . and hands that already appear familiar to me."[111] In her physique, carriage, facial structure, and childlike mien, Paula was of the very same stamp as Lou. "How alike they looked! How come he lent the one the other's features? Was what was beginning in this way love?" asked Beer-Hofmann in his second Paul's case.[112/j] As against "the other," however, Paula was sixteen and simple, like the girls in Beer-Hofmann's two earlier tales.[k] Poor Lou was only his way to Paula: she never stood a chance herself.

That same day Frieda left—but Lou stayed ten weeks longer. For several days around Christmas, Beer-Hofmann did meet her again "as of old"—by Schnitzler's arranging in the first instance[l]—until once he took her home from Griensteidl alone[m] (after sending her a roomful of flowers for Christmas). She then closed their material accounts: "Dear *Herr Dr.*, would you now be able to send me the things left behind by me in the spring? Please do not forget to add the child's picture from the Tyrol. I am returning the two d'Annunzio volumes with many thanks. Cordially, Lou AS."[113] She withdrew from Schnitzler's entourage except that Salten entertained her a few times during New Year's week[n] and a new recruit, the future satirist Peter Altenberg, visited her once.[o] She also dropped all her older acquaintances in Vienna[p] save Marie von Ebner-Eschenbach, whom she saw once thereafter.[q] With Schnitzler himself, however, she kept in touch—if

[j] "The one" was in this second case a woman "seen in the clouds."

[k] Through his moving, half-century-long romance with Paula he rectified "Camelias" and expiated "Das Kind."

[l] Through Schnitzler→B-H [16 XII 1895]—in anticipation of a visit from Max Halbe, whom Lou had recently frequented in Munich. Schnitzler's diary, 16 XII 1895: "Lou here. Talk about love. . . . Richard in love." Lou had excused herself to Schnitzler from the Griensteidl after 6 XII 1895 but saw him during his consultation hour on 9 and now 16 XII 1895.

[m] D 28 XII 1895: "Home with B.-H. The manuscript"—which followed Lou→B-H [27 XII 1895]: "If the snow sticks, perhaps [Schnitzler and I] shall be riding out to the fens in the coming days. If you find it possible and wish to do me this pleasure, do come along."

[n] The last was 5 I 1896.

[o] On 9 I 1896, Lou having first met Altenberg (Richard Engländer) on 17 XII 1895.

[p] Already D 14 XII 1895: "Very much bored at Müllner's"; D 15 XII 1895: "Marriot [Emilie Mataja] here: also boring." (She last saw Marriot on 8 I 1896.)

[q] On 7 I 1896.

sparingly—for the duration of her stay.[r] In this she proved a point to herself: that her basic relationship throughout had been the one with Schnitzler. She therewith topped off a repetition of her Nietzsche affair as exact as she could make it what with her three encounters with Beer-Hofmann in spring, summer, and fall respectively, her letter comparing his writings to Schnitzler's, the idyll in a woodsy village—in lieu of a beach party and preceded by a rebuff from him. She even brought Beer-Hofmann in his turn close to fleeing her to the antipodes. Only instead of fleeing her, he supplanted her. Whether she then knew it or not, she felt it.

Her reaction was duly unprecedented: she took a lover. He was a Galician Jew nearly eight years younger than herself: Friedrich Pineles, called Zemek. A junior medical colleague of Schnitzler's, Zemek was an internalist specializing in nerves and glands[s] who was then serving an internship at Vienna's public hospital and taking Freud's seminar on neuroses.[114] In appearance Zemek was Beer-Hofmann's virtual twin.[t] Lou met his sister, a painter named Broncia, the second day of her yuletide reunions with Beer-Hofmann and "the others."[u] She met Zemek himself four days later at lunch with Broncia, for whom she was posing. On Christmas Eve he took her "to the insane asylum" for a "ceremony there," then to friends in the country for a "charming idyll," finally "to the Griensteidl at 1:00 AM."[115] He brought her mistletoe the day after Christmas, and they met the two afternoons following her last evening with Beer-Hofmann. On New Year's Eve he took her out together with Salten, and she spent New Year's Day at his family's in Oberwaltersdorf, south of Vienna. Another week—an insomnious one—and she had for-

---

[r] Lou→Schnitzler [9 I 1896]: "I am too weary for the Griensteidl: I sleep so very little and must often get an early start." Schnitzler's diary, 10 I 1896: "Read *Ruth* by Salomé" en route to Frankfurt. Lou→Schnitzler [19 I 1896]: "I was dreadfully sorry to have missed your call this morning. . . . I can no longer quite bring myself to go to the Griensteidl, but maybe we shall get together once again in the theater or elsewhere?" D 20 I 1896: "At Schnitzler's consultation hour." Schnitzler's diary, 25 I 1896: "Supped with Lou and others." Lou→Schnitzler [27 I 1896]: "Thank you for the visit! I was so sound asleep I did not even hear you knock. You will be in Berlin before me: . . . I shall look you up as soon as I arrive—*if* I arrive." D 31 I 1896: "Letter from Schnitzler in Berlin." She did not see him in Berlin—and for some ten years had no further direct dealings with him beyond a thank-you note for a book.

[s] He published works on sensory nerves (1891), on hemiplegia (1896), on the endocrine gland (1899), and on the cerebellum (1899).

[t] *Miss Naëmah Beer-Hofmann pronounced his photo in Peters, 160-61, mistakable for one of her father; Mrs. Miriam Beer-Hofmann Lens agreed, if hesitantly.

[u] At a party apparently held for Halbe en route from Beer-Hofmann's to the Griensteidl (D 18 XII 1895).

saken her former existence in Vienna for one running from Broncia's studio and the public hospital out to Oberwaltersdorf and back to Zemek's rooms in the Piaristengasse by way of a whole string of new haunts and a whole host of new friends. As her train left Vienna the "quiet, glorious, starry night" of February 11, 1896, she "did not sleep, but lay and looked outside and mused, with much gratitude and joy."[116]

Three months later she was back in Vienna after having put the somber finishing touches to *Aus fremder Seele* and produced an essay on the Scandinavian authors of the day beginning with Knut Hamsun and Peter Nansen, judged to have been gaining and losing authenticity respectively.[v] Three days in and around the public hospital and she was at Oberwaltersdorf for a "*wunderschön*" Sunday,[117] whereupon Zemek took her for a week's sporting about Hallein with Broncia and husband, newly wed, then four days' hiking with rucksacks in the mountains above Ischl: they bathed in lakes and romped barefoot in meadows between times, traveled by train, coach, boat, and mule, and slept twice in an Alpine dairy, then once at an inn: "Dinner upstairs. Moonlight. Nighttime."[118] Another evening in Hallein and the two separated, Zemek returning to Vienna and Lou proceeding to Munich, where the portraitist Simon Glücklich entertained her the first full day[119]—and here the record of Lou's life breaks off for four months, during which she quite possibly underwent an abortion arranged by her brother Jenia.[w]

That Zemek was a stand-in for Beer-Hofmann in Lou's amorous experience down to her first pregnancy inclusive emerges graphically from her subsequent fiction, beginning with five short stories evidently all written within some two years of the real-life outcome.[x] Three take off from her excursion to Schönberg im Stubaithal: "Mädchenreigen" (Row of Girls), "Inkognito," and "Jutta." In the first, Lou is Hans,

[v] 1896b. She was probably in Petersburg between times (calendars missing for III–IV 1896).

[w] No direct documentary indication of her activity VI–IX 1896 is known to me except that as per D 6 v 1896 she was arranging the apartment for "Mama's stay." On the presumable pregnancy and abortion see also below, pp. 201, 204 n. *u*, 209 and n. *p*, 221 n. *e*, 226 n. *p*, 229 n. *u*, etc. (*Ellen Delp, Franz Schoenberner: Lou often spoke of an accidentally interrupted pregnancy in the springtime of her "engagement" to Zemek—but cf. below, p. 305.)

[x] I can identify only one on Lou's calendars: "Inkognito," written in VIII and XII 1897. "Abteilung 'Innere Männer' " was first published in II 1898; it reappeared in Lou's *Menschenkinder*, assembled early in 1898, followed by "Mädchenreigen," "Unterwegs," and "Inkognito"—quite likely by order of composition. "Jutta," never published, unquestionably belongs to the same productive period (below, p. 483, notwithstanding): Lou must have set it aside as too embarrassingly autobiographic.

a boyish feminist and pre-law student literarily inclined, who flirts with girls "like a lady-killer."[120] "What girls need they best get from their own kind," she declares.[121] She intrigues artistic young Alex, one of three friends reunited at her hotel—the other two being Goldmann and Schnitzler in almost all but name.[y] Alex invites himself along when she leaves for the mountains.[z] There he courts her tenderly. She falls in love, turning girlish all at once—whereupon he shows himself uncertain about his own feelings and especially hers, fearing that she loves in him some mysterious unidentifiable ideal.[a] She wonders anxiously: "*Is* it then you that I love?"[122/b] And "of a sudden he felt incontrovertibly that upon Hans too, all his love and concern notwithstanding, lifelong solitude would lie"[123]—an ending incontrovertibly nonfictional except for the implication that the love and concern would be lifelong too.

In "Inkognito" Lou was Anjuta, esteemed young coeditor of a cosmopolitan feminist review, who lives and works exclusively with men—and especially with gaunt coeditor Wiranoff (Goldmann disguised) and voluble literary editor Ludin (Schnitzler caricatured). She has three elder brothers and is still mourning a fourth, the eldest, whom she has succeeded professionally. One day, weary of her mode of existence, Anjuta makes off for Schöneberg im Stubaithal, seeking solitude. She finds it in the "garden house," a hut[c] beside the village inn, only to share it soon with an artistic young architect staying at the inn, Erwin von Stein. Because he denigrates intellectualism in women, she conceals her identity. They fall in love—he, though, with a woman that is not. He discovers the truth as some luggage he is fetching for her in Innsbruck[d] is recognized by Ludin out searching for her. All day she vainly awaits his return; at nightfall Ludin arrives instead. Erwin follows pensively in the morning; she observes him unseen while catching—or, rather, missing—an early train back to her old "existence of toil and proficiency—home to life."[124]

[y] In point of fact Beer-Hofmann had joined Schnitzler at the Continental, whereas Lou had stayed at the Marienbad with Goldmann.

[z] For the Isar valley (above Innsbruck): "I want to go up the Isar valley. Luggage for a couple of weeks can follow" (1897a:101).

[a] Cf. above, p. 191 (". . . I believe we [read: I] signify something private to her or are symbols for something or other we cannot know . . .").

[b] Lou of course loved—through Beer-Hofmann—Nietzsche: cf. below, p. 201.

[c] Which reminds her of her childhood playhouse on the family estate in Russia (1897h:254).

[d] By the terms of D 9 ix 1895, Lou conceivably went up to Schönberg from Innsbruck alone the first time, then returned to fetch her luggage and Beer-Hofmann.

In "Jutta" Lou was guileless Jutta, who announces herself averse to intellectualism or professionalism in women and eager to marry well and raise a large family. "If *I* finished college," she remarks, "that was probably out of unconscious imitation of my three brothers." Her eldest brother, a law student, invites her on a holiday; six student comrades of his show up in his stead, declaring that he has been detained by a foot injury. All six compete in gallantry toward Jutta, especially three close friends among them, one of whom, Florian, speaks of leaving because he cannot bear to share her: she does not understand. The others have chosen Florian to test her virtue[e]: they see the pair off to the mountains with knowing glances.[f] The first night he asks whether she prefers one room or two; she replies that one will suffice for her.[g] And so forth—until her naïveté lapses, and she gets pregnant. Her set idea is then to go home to her brothers. The eldest reprimands her by mail, but the youngest promises her to fix things up. Though Florian implores her to stay,[h] she persuades herself that she is going by his will as well as her own. He bites her back bloody by way of saying good-bye—a hint at what she is going to. Repeatedly she reflects that a first lover is really a second.[i] Once she dreams of Florian's original but cannot make out who he is—and no wonder, for Florian's original as Lou's first lover was himself an erotic proxy for the man through whom she had relived her great *amour manqué* of 1882.

Lou's three successive Schönberg heroes, while all distinctly modeled after Beer-Hofmann, yet increasingly represent Zemek as well: Alex holds a medical degree,[j] Erwin stands outside the editorial circle, and Florian attains the status of lover.[k] Lou's heroines meanwhile, though blatantly herself, take after Beer-Hofmann increasingly: Hans is a pre-law student[l]; Anjuta lives within a continental

---

[e] Whether or not Jutta's eldest brother, who never shows up, is party to this ruse is unclear. No doubt the ruse was originally a hopeful sneaking suspicion of Lou's in Munich.

[f] The literary effect of such passages is incongruous in that naïve Jutta is herself the narrator.

[g] This *must* approximate a true exchange reported to Schnitzler by Beer-Hofmann, for Schnitzler (who cannot have read it in "Jutta") burlesqued it along with the entire Schönberg episode (plus Lou's rhetorical kneeling to her men, her retrospective romancing with Nietzsche, etc.) in scene 8 of *Reigen* (*La Ronde*).

[h] Why marriage never occurs to either lover is not clarified in the story.

[i] "*Der Erste ist doch immer der Zweite.*"

[j] This, though, primarily by displacement from Schnitzler.

[k] But Erwin presumably leaves from Anjuta's bed to fetch her luggage before she wakes.

[l] In return, Alex is from the Baltic.

literary group as one of its three mainstays, is weary of her existence to date, wants to be alone in the mountains, is loved for what she is not; Jutta, maneuvered by Florian up to Schönberg, breaks off the idyll against his will. This dual fictional progression was Lou's own toward getting over Beer-Hofmann. What he meant to her is yet inscribed in all three stories equally: their three heroines, alone in Lou's fiction, *turn* feminine.[m] To begin with, Hans is as boyish as a girl can be, Anjuta has been living as a peer among men, and Jutta fraternizes with her brother's cronies as if sex did not exist. To be sure, Jutta declares for marriage and motherhood at the outset, which sounds feminine enough—but which turns out to have been Anjuta's imposture all over again. For Jutta too was playing up to Beer-Hofmann, who did not relish cerebral women, as he may well have apprised Lou[n] and as at all odds Lou must have gathered from tidings of her successful rival. Her vain day's wait for Beer-Hofmann while he was building up to Paula showed through the vain day's wait in "Inkognito" (after a possibly vain one at the hazy end of "Mädchenreigen"). When, replying to Anjuta, Ludin remarked that Erwin "seemed to be in no hurry at all" to come along,[125] he was doubtless echoing Schnitzler on Beer-Hofmann's not coming along to the Griensteidl that dismal evening.[o] Again, Anjuta's observing the next day that "no haste showed in his bearing" during her silent non-encounter with Erwin at the station[126] denied Beer-Hofmann's precipitance to meet Paula after his "exchange of words" with Lou: this was an ending the happier for Anjuta's symbolically snuggling under a sunbeam instead of catching her train. As Anjuta, Lou showed Beer-Hofmann how she could have played sweet and dumb. Through the juvenile version of herself vis-à-vis Beer-Hofmann that followed,[p] Lou impersonated Paula: Jutta's pregnancy was subsidiarily Paula's of 1897. Yet for all her fictive flirting with him alone, Beer-Hofmann partook of a continuum with Zemek in Lou's fancy. In actuality, Beer-Hofmann had been the stimulus, Zemek the fulfillment; in the fictional

[m] "Before the first man she loved, she was ashamed of everything not of woman about as deeply as a girl is ashamed for her lost chastity" (1897h:265): this suggestive line suits all three tales equally. Cf. Schnitzler's notation above, p. 191.

[n] See 1931a:132 on the cult of "the *merely* sweet girl" in the Vienna circle (with the accent displaced onto Schnitzler).

[o] Perhaps also on his coming to Salzburg tardily the previous August (see above, p. 194 n. *a*)—with a built-in reminder that he had dragged his feet on the way to Schönberg.

[p] Lou's first juvenile act did not fool Alex: in Hans's absence Alex, who sketches continually as did Beer-Hofmann (see Lou→B-H, 17 vii 1895: "Your high drawing art"; etc.), draws her as old and pronouncedly manlike.

sequence as in the back of the authoress's mind, the two men merged, Beer-Hofmann predominating. This merger mended the rift of December 1895 by adjoining Ischl to Schönberg.

In "Abteilung 'Innere Männer' " ('Internal Men' Ward), written before the Schönberg series,[q] that rift was wide open. Here Lou was a hospital nurse who, overwrought by a doctor's overlong courtship, allows herself to be half seduced in half sleep by a deaf-and-dumb laborer confined to a ward dubbed "internal men" (men with internal diseases): the courtship ceases when the doctor catches the two in the act, whereupon the nurse kills the patient half intentionally and lives on to an overripe young age as a tormented angel of mercy. The doctor is blatantly Zemek—which would make no sense except that Lou appears also as the nurse's beloved spirited sister, who rides off in high hopes one day with a young writer, returns alone, and yet keeps smiling. In Lou's self-reproachful fantasy, the patient was for Zemek the proxy that in reality Zemek was for Beer-Hofmann. Beer-Hofmann's displacement was, then, displaced—and displaced so that a value judgment was implied: Zemek is to Beer-Hofmann as a sick deaf-and-dumb laborer is to Zemek. Indeed, with the nurse out of his life, the doctor turns Philistine.[r] In a death note to him she incidentally sets forth the psychodynamics of a substitution of persons in no uncertain terms: "You cannot imagine how exclusively you occupied my thoughts throughout this entire period. You alone did I care about, you alone did I love! . . . I know only that I was aware of no infidelity toward you—that in fact the very same intense passion aroused by you made me helpless before him, the sick laborer. I felt weak in my arms and knees when I was with him, and I wept for you in my dreams when I slept. Could one but penetrate the nocturnal dreams of a human soul, perhaps one would often understand it in its contradictions and secret fears. In my dreams, both figures commingled so inextricably that I believed I was seeing a single loved one, and that one was you. It was to you I lent his body, and it was you I implored to tell me about your love, to give me assurance and support, to cast off that outward regard which made you so reserved and formal with me—and it was you who could not talk to me because he was deaf and dumb."[127] Lou's literary intent was a Maupassant-like retrospect on two lives spoiled through a circumstantial misunderstanding. In point of autobiography, that misunderstanding

[q] Under the Nietzschean title "Unzeitgemäss": above, p. 199 n. *x*.
[r] He begins by taking a wife—who is Paula in reverse ("he chose excellently: the most solid wares"). Apropos of Zemek as mute: judging by Markus in 1904a, Zemek was not very articulate—but on the physical representation of mental qualities in Lou's fiction see further below, pp. 417ff., 500ff.

was a reversal of cause and effect—of her rejection by Beer-Hofmann and his replacement by Zemek.[s] And yet Lou was half ready to murder Zemek half intentionally in return.

"Unterwegs" (En Route) recapitulates the Ischl excursion, with the roving couple contemplating suicide because unable to wed. He, though, is an artist. More, an old peasant woman in the Alpine dairy, nonplussed at seeing him sneak off to the hay garret after she has surrendered her room to the pair for the night, dozes off in the kitchen reminiscing about how once, ages since, she put up a princely manner of wanderer[t] without finding alternative accommodations for herself: how ". . . toward morning—half dreaming, half waking—she felt herself embedded in his arms, felt his strength and warmth enfold her like intoxicating violence, and—half dreaming, half waking—she sank into this violence."[128] This was Lou's first night in Schönberg recollected half in sleep. It was also the dairy maid's last with Prince Charming, though on leaving at dawn he told her to expect him back by evening: a vain day's wait ensued, for she did not suspect "that he was only timid about saying farewell."[129] Repairing Beer-Hofmann's bigger omission, Lou had traded the conjoint sleeping accommodations of the dairy near Ischl for the separate ones of the Schönberg farmhouse.[u] In all this, the novelty was not that a "second" took over from a "first" in her experience but that a "first" took over from a "second" in her reverie. And this that first did most grossly in "Unterwegs"—under cover of a mood so thick and dark that no plot shows through.

After the summer of 1896 Lou was to maintain her liaison with Zemek but concurrently to work out an amorous routine involving an "almost rhythmic turnover" of lovers young enough to have been her sons[130/v] (offset in time by juvenile girl friends called "daugh-

---

[s] There was, though, an unreversed biographic antecedent in Goldmann's break with Lou of VIII 1894 over her Russian he-man. For the nurse compromises herself just as the nurse's beloved sister is losing her man *in Paris*— a reminder that Beer-Hofmann was himself a Goldmann surrogate of sorts.

[t] Beer-Hofmann was known for his princely personal style. On Beer-Hofmann as wanderer, cf. 1897a:85 and D [late XII 1912] (above, p. 190).

[u] But I confess to a minute irreducible doubt about that first night in Schönberg—as also about whether Lou's first night with Zemek was not perhaps the one spent at the inn near Ischl. Concerning this inn: "Unterwegs" ends abortively as the couple detains a peasant boy who leads them there from the dairy with the result that on his way home after dark he stumbles to his death (cf. D 27 V 1896: "the valet and the boy").

[v] Discussing her typical experience (cf. above, p. 148 and n. *x*), she maintained that, just as she had twisted Gillot's (after God's) image to her own uses and had preferred parting with Gillot (after God) to letting the tables turn on her, "so I also certainly 'abused' Z. and the others (who, likewise

ters"). Her sons-and-lovers, anxiety-ridden beginners in life, were father figures by way of contrast. In time the turnover approximated the pregnancy cycle,[w] so that the severance signified parturition. By the very succession of lovers she assured herself that she meant it personally with none of them.[x] She did see each in his veriest particularity and bring out the unsuspected best in him—magically, but also through unremitting exactions both imperious and tender, like a mother-goddess grooming a beloved mortal for immortality: like a god-*woman*. But then as suddenly as she had come and summoned him, she would dismiss him and go, leaving him shattered. "Only my *small* misdeeds grieve me," she would boast to herself,[131] or else she would apprise herself of our need to economize our goodness "lest bitterness ensue."[132] Once she ascribed her "obstreperously good conscience over brutal rupturing of relations etc." to her voluptuous ideal of "being compelled to do service be it in the hardest, most painful way (as, say, God compels man)"—adding, however: "This thought would ease my black egoist's soul!"[133] That final, most compulsive moment of her rites of incest with a god in disguise corresponded to the hysterical recoil climaxing her former flirtations with her father-gods. By the same token she now inverted the old pattern of rejection *by* her father-gods, above all by Nietzsche—and not alone preventively or vengefully, as she thereby also resumed her full father-identity on returning "home to myself," meaning from boudoir to writing table. Through that "brutal rupturing of relations etc." she was also reenacting a mythic castration[y] which, deep in the fantasy work to which she withdrew, she was still denying—and this may be why, brutally as she would rupture them with any son-and-lover, she would bid to resume them amicably at some later date.

Between encounters she would write about her lovers as her in-

---

unconsciously, followed the given signals); nonetheless it came to turnover, almost rhythmic turnover, because my strong subjectivity ever and again won freedom for solitude, for 'fructified peace.' "

[w] In the two cases in which it exceeded this term (those of Zemek and Rainer) there was a lengthy separation after the ninth month.

[x] As a repeated cheating on Andreas, this succession also avenged her punishment by her father for cheating at school: in 1900b:291-92, Mascha (Lou having an affair) cries out unexplainedly on hearing that Assja (Lou at school) has copied a composition.

[y] Besides taking the sperm home to nurture it within because she unconsciously equated it with a penis (1899a:229: female nature rests in what it has once internalized, growing with it organically): thence her repeated conceptions. Her sperm complex embraced the equivalence of sperm with the germ of an idea, whence she appropriated germinal ideas from her god-men—including this one of literary pregnancy adapted from Nietzsche's teachings and example (see 1890a:43-44).

struments of self-gratification, thanking them rhetorically.[z] In due course she maintained that, on either side of the act of love, male and female conjoined "procreatively"[134] in a harmonious hermaphroditic self. "A mere exciting occasion is the love-object," she then declared.[135] Love, "in one of those paradoxes such as only the creative rule of all things can devise, joins two persons, man and woman, in a superpersonal unity precisely by setting each of them apart in his deepest independence within himself, his all-eternal selfhood"[136]; love "brings out in each of them that duality creatively implanted in all becoming, that it may grow beyond itself,"[137] even while there hovers about love "something like a primal dream: in which one's own self, one's beloved, and the child of both can yet be one"[138]; and so forth. A man loves in a woman "the mother eternal, the child eternal,"[139] deemed Lou as man of Lou as woman. Her own perpetual child, she took to signing herself familiarly "the Lou child" (*"das Loukind"*). Once, outdoing herself, she called maternity the outlet for homosexuality in women even when they remain childless.[140/a] Her phantom internal love partner signified her father just as did alternatively that faceless stranger outside—that "diaphane with human contour"[141/b] bearing "the dearest name."[c] She affirmed that she never loved a man except in his creatureliness—as an instance of the vital "all" and medium for life eternal—and that, his love service done, she would restore him to "the totality whence he came,"[142/d] where he would stand amongst his brethren "placid and solid and at one with Being itself."[143/e] Therewith "a new sort of sympathy and love arose: to be sure, less for the everyday person, let alone due to private relations with him, yet by no means solely contemplative, but enthused with his individuality: as if we were to set his soul before his god, in whose sight he is creative, 'god-made,' and asking none of our (quite unimportant) love for himself—just as, for our authentication, we need none of his."[144/f]

[z] Lou's thanking—"*danken*"—strongly suggests "*abdanken*," to dismiss ("thank off"). Its deeper source was the anal complex (gift=turd/penis/child) even as regards Lou→RMR, 24 II 1922: "This inner thanking is like the single valid proof of God's existence, presence. . . . Only the thanking in a creator's bestowing gesture . . . wholly designates God."

[a] ". . . *Mutterschaft* . . . *auch wo diese sich nicht physisch betätigt*": here she indeed meant child*bearing* as well as -rearing by "maternity," for she called it "creative" as well as "protective, nutritive, directive, yea regal" (1914c:651). Short of herself, her "daughters" were implicated.

[b] See below, p. 555.

[c] See above, p. 123.

[d] As per 1913a:163, this restoring went back to her rediscovering her fictitious Petersburgers in the flowerbeds of Peterhof.

[e] On lovers as proxies see further 1913e:11-12 (below, p. 555).

[f] (The weird syntax is Lou's.)

By Lou's testimony, a memory and an anticipation of coalescence with the cosmos met in orgasm as a sensation of absorbing while also being absorbed—the very sensation also called by her "the religious affect." Such testimony would readily pass over into an exultant confession of reverence for "whatever is" (unto the very "cosmic dust") and profession of indefeasible involvement with it all.[145] This intellectualized affect was also an idea erotized: Beer-Hofmann's idea of a cosmic bond, which was to dominate her late work. It was, then, through self-identification with Beer-Hofmann that she conceptualized her sex life, which began as a vicarious fulfillment of her love for him. At the same time her old yearning for her father came full symbolical circle with the shift from "ideals" and the like to the plenitude of reality. And the father-words of her youth therewith turned a little quaint in her vocabulary, though she might yet pronounce love to be aiming over and beyond its object at merely everything high[146] or ideal[147] or divine.[148] If it was contradictory of her to construe her phantom lover as inside and yet all around her—well, "woman is always contradiction itself in as much as, in her creative doings, life itself is at work within her."[149] As basically her commentaries on her sexual practice were intended for her father just as was that practice itself, she systematically concealed her lovers' identities from her very diary while also advertising their multiple existence—inconsiderately of Andreas, who himself turned to amorism for solace. She moreover flattered herself that among humans "the natural love-life . . . is grounded in the principle of infidelity," the domesticated love-life in a vestigial vegetative instinct.[150]/[g] Nietzsche before her had pronounced love of one person uncouth, "for it is practiced at the expense of all others"—only he had added: "Including love of God."[151]

Whenever she represented love-making as hermaphroditic self-gratification or procreative self-confrontation or cosmic communion, Lou was making shorter shrift of the love partner than her own experience warranted. Her theory was not a departure from practice, but a demand laid upon practice in advance: already in her maidenhood she wrote of "the most noble and spiritual love" as at one with the crassest lust in bypassing its ostensible object[152] and again of the thanks due from a woman to her lover for opening up "her way into herself."[153]/[h] In practice she was all too wrapped up in her lovers, as she also admitted on occasion. She was furthermore too self-conscious to confront herself and too lucid for even parochial, let alone cosmic, ecstasy: by her own avowal, she gave her body but kept her

[g] Alternatively, she called infidelity a masculine trait (1913e:8)!
[h] (As if announcing a fantastic stunt of autoerotic acrobatics.)

head.[154] And generally: "Alone, we enjoy the love extract pure in dreamy visions. Only it is lethal: if taken in reality, it would fast wear us down, kill us off: all life is a diluting and polluting of essences."[155/i] This discrepancy between her practical deficiency and ideal sufficiency in love fell in with her alternation between daughterly-hysterical extroversion among men (incidental mannishness notwithstanding) and fatherly-narcissistic introversion at home (incidental girlishness notwithstanding),[j] a scheme rendered graphic after 1900 in her diaries with their tight-packed, telegraphic-style day-by-day notations on forays among men between stretches of essaylets treating of things *sub specie aeternitatis*—and one which was, all in all, sanest prophylaxis for a personality split.

Another erotic image carried over by Lou from maidenhood to womanhood was the one—in 1888 adhibited to her marriage—of lovers aspiring together to a common goal beyond themselves as if confraternally.[k] Often she called her lovers *brothers*, and not alone as a median term between *fathers* and *sons*: after all, her earliest this-worldly father surrogates were her real brothers, who were also her fantasy sons. Her lovers took after Jenia in particular, from that intern in Vienna at the first to a series of literarily and neurotically inclined doctors at the last.[l] It was her first lovers, though, who cut the most brotherly figures in her life on a par with her last prelovers. Her turning from ascetical coquetterie to ritual amorism actually began with her trip to Paris in 1894 and lasted for some years afterwards. Beer-Hofmann and Zemek were hardly father-gods to her, yet

[i] She added: "If ever *everything goes right*, each party providing just what the other dreamed of for himself, one often feels like cutting it *short, short*, for it means dying. We live on *un*fulfillment, for our longings disclose great forces at work within us, life-creating and life-destroying, of which psychology has yet to take stock and which likely cannot balance off except through the trivialities and accidents of existence. If ever someone had breadth and potency enough to dispense with these latter, life would of a sudden turn into something all new and wonderful, the expression of human omnipotence" (with a postscript on "God" as originally not only a cry of distress but also an announcement of this mighty potentiality). She also conceded the discrepancy between her theory and practice (darkly) in 1931a:45. It is confirmed by Peters, 272, quoting Bjerre on how "she always talked about ['merging into her partner'] but she could not do it," except that she never talked about "merging into her partner"—even when she talked about "that radical one-and-the-sameness of self and beloved: as if we were being generated by it and therewith generating it out of ourselves at the same time" (1936b).

[j] 1913c:465: her "loss of God" in adolescence was likewise already a "returning home to myself."

[k] D [30 XI 1912]: "Only in bilateral interplay between masculine and feminine are two [lovers] *more* than one, no longer being directed each to the other (like two halves that must stick together to make a whole) but both together to a common goal outside."

[l] Indeed, Rilke coalesced with Jenia in 1900d, as did Tausk in 1919g.

neither were they as children beside her. "Jutta" quite literally represented them both as big-brother substitutes along with her other
Viennese consorts; both partook of a sequence having Goldmann and
Wedekind as its first terms. The sequential brethren had some near
precursors, notably Paul Rée—even if he was on the senior side, prefiguring Andreas in her first mock ménage. Indeed, her encounter
with Tönnies was arrestingly like a later ritual one in many externals
through to her subsequent bids for amicable renewal.[m]

Lou's choice image for hallowing carnal practice was that of the
madonna—the madonna "with her full force, even extraerotic, consecrated to the end of conceiving" and for whom "sensuality and
chastity . . . converge[n]: in woman's every highest hour, the man is
but Mary's carpenter beside a god."[156/o] In Lou's books, though,
Mary the love-servant of a god regularly passed over into, not the
holy mother and child, but the *pietà*, on the theory that a mother
truly becomes such only upon giving her child away "to the world
and to death"[157/p]—or else into a prostitute, characterized alike by
"dedication without choice, even without voluptuousness, to a nonerotic end."[158] Here was no mere paradox or profanation: Lou conducted her own love service in the spirit of that spiritual ancestress
of Mary's, the temple prostitute, for whom sanctity and sex were
one.[159/q] Lou's maidenly forebodings of the temple spirit were awful,
from the death in Margharita's heart to Erik's nightmare in which
a grotesque of Ruth "as a prudish hysterical old maid, with unful-
filled longing in her worn gaze," suddenly turns into another of her
as a "naked beauty . . . shamelessly giving herself to strange men . . .
kissing and laughing."[160/r] That spirit's inception was yet worse: a

[m] The data on other precursors and prelovers are too scant for precise gen-
eralization. Lou seems, though, to have moved more or less steadily toward
the ritual after Ledebour. Her first out-and-out filial lover was Rilke, who,
however, outlasted the ritual cycle. Nor can I say just when the ritual took
over, for whereas general testimony on it abounds, specific data are wanting
for the years after 1900 except for 1911-1914, when it was in full swing. Or
did it only then—during Lou's last fling—attain its normative form?

[n] Cf. fn, *Genealogy*, iii: 2: "between chastity and sensuality there is no
inherent contradiction: every good marriage, every true love affair, has overcome this conflict."

[o] Lou's "man" was thus wishfully Andreas—the virgin bride's Joseph of
"Vor dem Erwachen" and "Paradies."

[p] Behind this theory was evidently (short of Lou's anal complex) an abortion: see below, p. 250 and n. *k.*

[q] Cf. 1927b:29 (before being a spouse, woman was "a shimmering midway
thing between whore and madonna"), 1929a:65 ("prayer and sex . . . forever
dependent on each other"), etc.

[r] "Giving herself" renders *preisgegeben*, which connotes religious sacrifice
and prostitution both.

Part III: Womanhood

Lou heroine of late 1896[8] is surprised as her young heart goes out to a *grisette* in a Paris bistro,[t] but then winds up envisioning herself with loathing as a *grisette* among *grisettes* in the same bistro, having between times indulged a first love which, upon reconsideration, strikes her as lust—and no wonder, for she argues at the very outset that it is virtual prostitution for a woman to give herself in the man's way, with less than her whole soul full-time. Lou's supreme depiction of sex as physically and morally humiliating for a woman dates from when she was already promiscuous,[u] and she went on blaming and shaming herself in dreams long after she had literarily turned sex from an abomination into a mystery. Similarly, her wariness of sexual love as entailing the woman's drastic surrender of identity found its fullest expression on paper only after many months of her experience to the contrary,[v] and in her fiction thereafter it yielded only gradually and imperfectly to her nonfictional celebration of sexual love as a vehicle for a woman's coddling and mothering herself.[w]

In some verse of early 1896, Lou called (a bit shrilly) for drawing strength from the loss of a "vital ideal."[161] This was her epitaph on her asceticism. From then on, she mourned her maidenhood even as she rejoiced in her womanhood. Calling the ascetical the "true" life, she tried redefining it as a continual communion with God and oneself through all one's dealings with men[162]—which would have made

[8] 1896d: see below, pp. 212-13.

[t] Cf. D 15 III 1894: "Lovely episode with a *grisette*." Also 1931a:126 on prostitution in Paris as delightfully aboveboard.

[u] 1897j: below, p. 220.

[v] Ditto.

[w] Thus the regression implicit in this exchange of a hysterical for a narcissistic love model took effect intellectually rather than imaginatively in the first instance—a breach in the law of psychic gravity. Conceivably the exchange turned on Lou's experience of—to quote D [mid-II 1913]—"the great difference between such lovers as only excite each other and such as find peace with each other. Sexuality threatens the independent ego . . . only in the first, one-sided case." According to Brausewetter, 9, published in 1898, what was "typically feminine" by the terms of Lou's fiction was for a woman not only to lose her head when in love but to mother herself voluptuously through her lover, so that every erotic relationship was doomed or, at best, salvageable in a companionable marriage (in fact the few abiding love relationships in Lou's fiction as of 1898 are not notably companionable, but are notably those of parental figures—the exception that explained the rule): evidently Brausewetter wrote only after speaking with Lou, whose theory was just then changing. Even after the second model won ascendancy, the first still recurred in her fiction—subordinately in 1904a (in which the mother [Lou] has surmounted her impulse to subjugate herself to her husband [Andreas], calling it "original sin": *ibid.*, 264), dominantly as late as 1916a. Indeed, a friend wrote for Lou's seventieth birthday that all her life Lou was torn between being a "woman," which meant "devoting herself," and being a "person," which meant "asserting herself": Stöcker, "L A-S" (1931), 393.

her a Kuno-like ascetical reveler. Then, reverting to the old accepta-
tion, she inveighed against the "modern frailty" of "crossing oneself
before the word 'asceticism,' " considering that without the fact of
asceticism there was no getting beyond oneself.[163] Meanwhile her
feminism turned about-face as she threw up to emancipated woman
the old-style feminine virtues of discipline and dedication. On learning about endocrine glands from Zemek, she wondered "whether
chastity (in the full, pure sense, with no playing around or fantasy
indulgence) is not a treasure house for the strength which, even *sexually* active and constructive, pervades the body and nervous system.
Chastity may likewise help heighten all of man's nonsexual powers
even in the intellectual sphere, in hard mental labor . . ."[164]/*x* And
was not her autoerotic construction on the act of love a first word in
reclaiming her virginity? Her sexual coming of age, finally, reactivated
the heart ailment due in the first instance to her espousing asceticism
in lieu of Gillot.*y*

Yet pictures from the late 1890's show the sometime ascetic looking plumply radiant for all her subjacent remorse—and the self-
styled hermaphrodite looking every inch a woman.

x (This was a Schopenhauer-Nietzsche theme.) Cf. D 1 I 1907: "It is to
be regretted if, through the movement toward free love, the middle-class girl
shakes off a habit that, as I think, centuries-long servitude rendered almost a
matter of course; such a heritage is lost in few generations, though just now
it could have borne a blossom reminiscent of Jeanne d'Arc's words: 'There is
nothing so strenuous on earth that a pure maid could not accomplish it.' An
intimate inquiry (were one possible) among those who live chastely even in
fantasy would yield strange results . . ."

y The "Unterwegs" heroine expects to die shortly of Lou's malady—the first
token of it since Meran. Zemek treated her for it subsequently: this in fact
became the official reason for their meetings beginning in 1901.

"**W**OKE UP in Vienna," reads Lou's calendar for October 1, 1896; then after a week in Zemek's entourage, ". . . in the hospital with Zemek. The summons to the dying man. Night in the hospital. Departure at 5 AM . . . for Hallein," alone. That night was the one in Lou's touching story "Eine Nacht,"[z] in which a young intern, Berthold, while receiving his fiancée's clandestine visit from out of town one night in his room at the hospital, is called to attend a dying man. He goes reluctantly and returns hours later, aghast and distraught, to rail against death, which has just claimed a humble young husband and father. As at length he dozes off, exhausted, his fiancée steals away to the station, feeling closer to him for having sensed the dread beneath his indignation. The theme of death entered Lou's writings, then, through Zemek. Only again Beer-Hofmann is discernible behind Zemek, for *Bertho*ld's indignation conveyed that of *Beer-Ho*fmann, Lou's stand-by thereafter for the Jews' secret fear of death —and her source for an antidote to her own.

Lou spent a few days in Hallein with Broncia, now an expectant mother, then a few weeks in Munich, where Glücklich again entertained and now also painted her. Between sittings she met Helene von Klot-Heydenfeldt, a Livonian some four years younger than herself, who "had written a good book, *Eine Frau*, after reading Tolstoi's *Kreutzer Sonata*."[165] Helene fast became her best friend after Frieda. Unlike Frieda, Helene was of ever-warm, ever-steady affection—and, to judge by her letters, utterly charming. Lou loved her very own fortitudinous self in "Helene with her wonderful blend of two rare qualities: fortitude in dreaming and fortitude in living."[166/a]

Home for the winter,[b] Lou busily fictionalized her past—and not alone the Beer-Hofmann complex (presumably "Abteilung 'Innere Männer,'" "Eine Nacht," and "Mädchenreigen"), for in "Fenitschka" she turned her Parisian misadventure with Wedekind into a comedy of errors in which her counterpart had never met an "improper" man and Wedekind's never a guileless girl before.[167] The

[z] Written late XII 1896 (unless the "*Spitalnovelle*" on her calendars designates "Abteilung").

[a] Lou's choice of lady friends was invariably narcissistic.

[b] By 22 XI 1896, when she congratulated Broncia: "You must feel as if you had returned from a long journey full of marvelous adventures with the little miracle as booty in your arms" (Peters, 257).

ink was barely dry on her draft when she ran into Wedekind at the theater.[168] The upshot was a sequel in which the hero encounters the heroine in Petersburg a year later and strikes up a proper friendship, only to learn that she has a lover and thus to feel like a two-time fool. She reassures him: the lover, her first, is a first love come lately. Her beloved lover proposes, whereupon she, fearing domestic servitude in marriage,[c] runs a fever, then sends him packing—"out of an intolerable conflict that she had fallen into with herself. But she thanked him,"[169]/[d] observes the hero, whom she has posted at the keyhole.[e] She was too kind: he had killed the comedy.

The spring of 1897 found Lou in Petersburg[f] consorting chiefly with Akim L'vovich Volinsky, a Russian cultural historian and critic about two years younger than herself, who aroused in her a passion for his subject. She traveled back to Berlin in mid-April with the Freie Bühne troupe, which had just brought Hauptmann's latest play to Russia: all stopped off for an Easter party in the Balkans. Home again, she read in Russian, corresponded with Volinsky, and quarrelsomely annotated a bad review of *Aus fremder Seele.*[g] Then late in April she went to Munich, where Frieda joined her in a pension and where her social rounds, vertiginous, passed primarily from Helene to Glücklich, to the local dramatists and actors, to a circle around a learned, eccentric Jugendstil architect and aesthete in his middle twenties named August Endell and a boyish girl photographer nicknamed Puck, and thence to a lettered set including notably Jakob Wassermann, just turned twenty-four.

At Wassermann's for tea on May 12, Lou was confronted with a veteran poet of twenty-one who, with huge soulful eyes, "narrow shoulders, thin neck," "receding chin and almost no back to his head," looked to her like a "sickly aristocrat."[170] He was visibly awestruck

---

[c] 1897j gave this same fictional reason for Lou's having declined Zemek's fictional proposal.

[d] There is some ambiguity as to whether the heroine has not fallen back into her lover's arms rather than "thanked him off."

[e] How guilty Lou felt before Wedekind—who perhaps, like his fictional counterpart, had dropped an innuendo at their chance reunion—is implicit in the fact stressed by Bab, 65, that the whole tale is seen through the hero's eyes.

[f] D IV 1897 begins in Petersburg (D I-III 1897 missing), but Lou was in Schmargendorf at least as late as 6 II 1897, when she wrote Tönnies acknowledging his *Der Nietzsche Kultus*: "I wish I could meet you again personally in the course of time and discuss much that you touched on in your book."

[g] One by Ernst Heilborn, editor of the feminist *Die Frau*, in which—not without some courtesies to Lou—he (wrongly) called the plot "artificially constructed" (Heilborn, "Schaffen," 390) and the basic conception too "intellectual" and "abstract" (*ibid.*, 391). (D 20 IV 1897: "Essay for Heilborn, dissatisfied"—but no essay by her appeared that year in *Die Frau*.)

in her presence. "The Viennese," she noted on her calendar. In fact he was from Prague and, as a message the next day apprised her, signed himself René Maria Rilke. "Yesterday was not my first twilight hour spent with you," it began. The preceding winter he had exulted to find the visionary stuff of his inchoate "Christus-Visionen" set forth in her Jesus essay "with the gigantic impetus of holy persuasion": his dream come true. "Do you comprehend how I yearned for yesterday afternoon?" But tea-time was no time to give thanks for such a "consecration": might he read her one of his "visions" sometime? Meanwhile, he added, maybe he would see her at the theater the next evening. And he adjoined a volume of his poetry inscribed with some verse about Christ's wounds: it was as remote from her Jesus essay as were his "visions" themselves.

Lou did see him at the theater the next evening—with Endell and others. As for his "visions," she could find time for them only between engagements three days later and only tentatively at that. But he could not wait: he was expecting to be conscripted any time. He searched town for her the second day with a bunch of roses till they wilted, then searched with a lady of her acquaintance instead. "That way I could at least talk about you with someone," he wrote her in the morning amidst lyrics about longing and prose about leaving. "I greatly dread it," ran the prose, ". . . and clutch with both hands at every second that you are meanwhile willing to bestow upon your *RenéMaria.* You will yet let me know about this afternoon?" That afternoon she heard three of his "visions" and found them as girlish and gushy as his letters. She was far from suspecting his genius. And no wonder, for he was then in his artistic incunabula, which were all sensibility, sentiment, and fancy, in rich effusion.

Humanly, though, he was winsome, and by the end of the month—between engagements—she became his mistress and taskmistress. In the latter capacity she incited him (ever so gently at first, through nuances of reprobation or approbation as—to put it his way—she smiled down into his soul[171]) to restrain his lyricism and train his intellect, to acquire a sense of craft and a stock of ideas. In the former capacity she spent a night with him once in Wolfratshausen, in the mountains south of Munich, followed by breakfast at 3:30 AM, gathering of wild flowers, and sailing on the Starnbergersee: a "storybook morning," he afterwards called it, likening it to an island in time.[172] Two days later, on June 3, he left for Prague and the army, a copy of *Ruth* in his briefcase; another two and he was back in Munich, exempted. The love and learning resumed. So did the letters: "My clear fount, through you will I see the world: for then I see, not the world, but ever only you, you, you! You are my feast day, and when I go to you in dreams I always wear flowers in my hair. . . . I have never seen you otherwise but that I wanted to pray to you . . ."[173] And again: "I want to know nothing of the time that came before you in my days or of the people who live in those days. . . . I now want to be you. And my heart burns before your grace like the eternal lamp before the image of the Virgin Mary. You, . . . what makes me be—is you. I shall often, often tell you so, ever more plainly and simply. And when one day I tell it to you altogether simply, you will understand it simply. That will be our summer, extending over all the days of your *René*. Are you coming today!?"[174] At least his handwriting firmed, though along the lines of her own. And by mid-June, when she moved to a cottage in Wolfratshausen with Frieda, she had changed his first name for him to the Germanic, manlier *Rainer*.

Rainer went along to Wolfratshausen—followed by Volinsky, who, long awaited by Lou, had finally arrived in Munich on June 10 and had at once taken precedence on her calendars over everyone else. For the second day in Wolfratshausen she noted: "Afternoon Volinsky's arrival; Rainer moves to Dorfen,"[175] a neighboring village. A month of strange relations ensued, with Rainer repeatedly changing lodgings and Lou repeatedly "in Volinsky's room," and further with Volinsky feeding Lou raw material on Russia, Lou working it up into essays, and Rainer doing the copy-work. Only one such essay—a study of Nicolai Leskov—cited Volinsky as its source.[h] Another[i] argued that if the Russians, given their religiosity, are ever to develop an autochthonous philosophy, they must do so not by denying God but, like the Jews of old, by learning to grasp him abstractly as against pictorially. The conclusion was that Jews should be admitted to professorships of philosophy in Russia—a plug for Volinsky. Another[j] characterized the Russian people exhaustively (as childlike, forthright, simple, big-hearted, sensitive, lyrical, devout, lawless yet good,[k] torpid unless frenzied, disposed to change but also to quietude, and unfathomably melancholic) in the course of discussing the mutual attraction between Russian authors, wide-eyed before experience, and Western authors, weary of it, the *mélange* of authenticity and

[h] 1897c (of late vi 1897), not available to me, which—according to Houben—concerns "Nicolai Leskov, after five essays by A. L. Volinsky," this having perhaps been Lou's subtitle. Cf. 1931a:350; on Lou's Leskov also 1919e:381, etc.

[i] 1897d.

[j] 1897b.

[k] Her specific point here about the Russians' construing criminality as a misfortune (*ibid.*, 574)—and this "not out of mere softheartedness" (1919c: 382)—was prefigured by FN, *Genealogy*, ii: 15.

artlessness in Russian letters, and the Russian literary giants one by one up to Tolstoi, who, himself morbid in the Russian way (hypersensitive, depressive, obsessed with death), was incensed with Russian morbidity. The lesser Russian authors were left to a sequel, which notably disparaged the entire breed of Russian critics down to A. L. Volinsky exclusive.[1] What Lou took from Volinsky she assimilated on the spot: these engaging essays read like conceptions all her own. So it was only right that they should have established her as an authority on Russian culture.

Between sessions over Pushkin and Garshin, there was outdoor frisk and frolic. There was also pageantry: a linen pennant, inscribed "Loufried" at Rainer's suggestion, was hoisted atop the cottage. Helene and Puck joined the party successively. Then Endell came to stay: a group photo taken at the cottage bower shows him squatting in the entrance, gnomish and sullen, staring askew; Frieda seated on a bench out front, massive and freakish, staring askance at the camera; Lou draped in an ornate Russian peasant costume, leaning forward through a lattice window lined with ivy, smiling graciously down to the camera; and Rainer within, perched upon something invisible, gazing wistfully up at Lou.

Rainer was misbehaving meanwhile with his Lou mother, throwing fits off and on. Or, rather, half of him was, for he would then "split up into two beings too alien to each other even to suffer over each other."[176] Later Lou once recalled to him "what you and I called the 'other' in you, who would be by turns depressed and then excited, all too fearful and then all too frenzied." And she redrew the "clinical picture": "Lame will along with abrupt, nervous outbreaks of willfulness tearing through your entire organism, obedient to any and every suggestion! . . . wavering uncertainty along with shrill tones, strong words, asseverations compulsively meant to be merely mad, never true!"[177/m] Only to Lou did Rilke ever attest this split in himself. Perhaps she first attested it to him, for it eventually shaped up like Nietzsche's in her books even while at her fondest she fancied herself healing it through personal magic. Yet there was an antecedent to it on Rainer's side in that his real, daft mother raised him as a girl (Sophie) and a boy by turns. Besides, his personalized

[1] 1897f—written only after Volinsky's departure and forthrightly dubbed "Volinsky essay" on her calendar. It committed the one big *gaffe* of predicting a meager future for Chekhov as dramatist. (Lou's calendars cite two additional essays written with Volinsky in vi and vii 1897 respectively: below, p. 569.)

[m] This confirms by omission D [vii 1913] to the effect that Rilke's hysteria underwent little physical conversion in these early years.

"hell" took after Nietzsche's in multifarious externals, beginning with his calling it that. But of the "many fears"[178] then in him, the biggest doubtless went back to an un-Nietzschean girlish fright at his phallus, as Lou held in after years.[179/n] He, however, would coyly follow his fears only a few years back—to a military boarding school—and Lou was soon to throw it up to him that he would not "plunge down into the plenitude of the past so as to assimilate, digest, develop all over again—healthily."[180/o] He looked to art instead for deliverance: could he but perfect his cries of anguish and longing, he believed, they would turn into psalms of joy. But just as imperfect release brought imperfect relief, no release brought no relief.[p] So there was the devil to pay straightaway, for only if he first stopped crying could he learn to sing.

Frieda left on July 13. Volinsky went on July 16 by way of three days in the resort town of Kufstein with Lou after a "quarrel"[181] and "reconciliation."[182] It was there that Lou, for whatever circumstantial reason, began "Unterwegs."[q] Rainer meanwhile besought her: "Do come back again soon; it was so sad when no reply came to my 'Good night.' "[183] She had him escort her back—first to Munich for a night, then with Endell to the upper story of a barn in Wolfratshausen: "Loufried II." The next day came a telegram followed by Andreas the day after. Endell and Rainer decamped in between to the local inn. They came calling in due course, the first times with Wassermann. By August "Loufried II" was sleeping four, who once lined up on the veranda for a photo: Lou on the one side, a Mona Lisa in profile, gazing over her men's heads and away; Andreas on the other, a princely visitor from the Thousand and One Nights, glancing forward as if from afar out of deepest, blackest eyes, the conjugal poodle in his arms; between them Endell, this time looking for all the world like a chubby old lady napping upright, and Rainer, lifting tired, tormented eyes from an open book and wearing junior whiskers to match Andreas's.

Most of August the four read art history, entertained, hiked in various combinations. The men also went off to Munich singly— Endell for days on end, Andreas for hours at a time, and Rainer once,

---

[n] The phallic anxiety-fantasy that closes the waiting-room sequence of Rilke's *Malte* was anticipated by RMR→Lou, 30 VI 1903, on his age-old "dread as before something too big, hard, and close." Lou privately related that a nonhysterical anatomical difficulty with his genitalia made erections agonizing for him.

[o] After Zemek's Freudian prescription: below, p. 218.

[p] According to D [early X 1913], Rilke found some alternative release and relief in one-way conversation.

[q] That is, if "Unterwegs" is the "Amor" of her calendars.

to ward off his father come to haul him home to Prague. And throughout, Lou worked as hard as in Schmargendorf: she finished the Volinsky essays and the Kufstein tale, then began "Inkognito" and "Ein Wiedersehen" (A Reunion). This last concerns her revisit to Gillot after his wife's death: Gillot is a sometime Russian reformer who has renounced young Lou on his wife's account years before,[r] then gone West, and Lou has since become a doctor in eastern Russia. On a holiday abroad, she seeks him out in a hotel—on the Stefansplatz. "How come you are a doctor? No, if you had any ability then, it was for creative writing or some such thing. A person who construes life for himself to suit his poetic fancy . . ."[184] She finds that he has turned Philistine. He proposes, of course. She departs without notice. Gillot revisited was, then, that Philistine that Beer-Hofmann in "Abteilung 'Innere Männer' " had become some twenty years after *his* failure to woo her conclusively.[s]

Wolfratshausen was at length abandoned—first by Andreas, next by Endell, then by Lou when on September 3 she left for Broncia's in Hallein, where Zemek soon joined her. "All sorts of overlapping walks and talks," she noted for her time with Zemek. They discussed Rainer: Zemek, fearing the worst, bound her to draw out the suffering youngster about his earliest childhood in Freud's manner and to deter him from assuming personal obligations in the meantime.[185] Rainer on his side would not leave Wolfratshausen until he had bidden a sad adieu to everything there to which some memory of Lou clung. "That will take three or four [more] days," he wrote her on her second day away. And sure enough, three days later he took leave of the last birds and squirrels on his sentimental itinerary: "Your soul alone was beside me in that gentle hour . . ." The next afternoon he was in Munich: "Stay not a second longer than for whatever reason need be; I know, I must be patient in any case for days, days . . ." For six days —after which she moved into his pension for the rest of the month. Together they mostly read about painting and visited galleries. Then she took him home to Berlin.

There he found a room within easy reach of her and spent much of the fall and winter at her side. Andreas did not mind; on the contrary, he felt solicitude for the growing poet. Together the lovers walked and talked, viewed paintings and plays. Once they went with the Georg Simmels to hear Stefan George recite some of his still

---

[r] This rectified *Ruth* with its proposal.

[s] This equivalence suggests that, Gillot having failed because he was married, Beer-Hofmann may have failed because *she* was. (Gillot's tardy proposal in "Wiedersehen" was a repetition of Kuno's to Margharita: cf. above, p. 181.)

lyrics: these "underwent overwhelming, victorious transformation," Lou remarked, "as if floral corpses from a herbarium, finely laid out, were reviving of a sudden into a flourishing garden of life."[186] As George afterwards chatted with the happy few, his patroness observed Lou listening "quite devoutly"—but also found Rainer a "most harmoniously balanced young man."[t] Rainer was in fact to shudder at the memory of his symptoms in those "Berlin winter days" of fearful self-mistrust.[u] Lou meanwhile did not suffer a moment's dejection. Frieda being away, she saw much of only the Mauthners and Therese Krüger socially—with Rainer as often as not. For the rest, she worked steadily[v] and in top form, thanks no doubt to stimulus from Rainer but also to her new den upstairs, "the blue room."

Lou's output that season[w] included three pieces of fiction one of which she had discussed with Rainer in September[187]: "Ein Todesfall" (A Decease). It concerns the death in despondency of a successful artist's only son, who was gifted with a double dose of his father's talent but none of his father's poise. He had won no real understanding or recognition from his benignly patronizing father, let alone his animally loving mother or a foster-sister for whose veneration he had pleaded and yearned. His death opens his father's eyes to his true greatness[x] with edifying effect: a superb bust results in which the son is resurrected. Latently, Rainer was the son, while Lou was the father, mother, and sister all at once; the decease was Zemek's gloomy prognosis, the bust "Ein Todesfall" itself. At least unconsciously, then, Lou discerned Rainer's superior endowment even while playing the Lord to his Jesus. In "Ein Todesfall" she also implicitly conceded that he had inspired her to surpass herself with this work. And a grand work it is, in which for once everything—characterizations included—conjoins to tell a lovely story. For once too Lou is not recognizable from close up—not even as the sister, who was superficially Broncia: a dark Judaic beauty, maternally inclined, and . . . lacking all artistic discernment![y]

[t] Lepsius, 17-18 (where the soirée is dated 15 as against 14 XI 1897 on Lou's calendar).

[u] RMR, *Tagebücher*, 136; Lou→RMR [26 II 1901] checks by implication.

[v] Noting only nine "vain attempts to work" in five productive months.

[w] Besides producing those works discussed below, Lou then finished "Inkognito" and "Wiedersehen," wrote a couple of more pieces for Volinsky (see below, p. 569), and "worked on" two further essays (ditto).

[x] To be exact, his letters to his foster sister do so when she shows them to his father afterwards.

[y] The son's craft, though, was Broncia's (by displacement)—as also that of the masters whose lives and works Lou had been studying with Rainer.

Part III: Womanhood

In the novella "Eine Ausschweifung" (A Dissipation), however, Lou was blatantly herself as the heroine unbalanced between the conflicting claims of independence and love: between her will to vie with men and her thrill at mortification by a man. Sex has menaced her ever since earliest childhood, when, as she recollects, she saw a wetnurse being lashed bloody by a valet and smiling up in ravishment at him: the masochist's "primal scene." A psychiatrist cousin courts her until the impassioned anticipation of being smashed "to a thousand bits"[188] has worn her young nerves away. She then sets up abroad as an artist—successful, loveless, contented. Years later she revisits her ex-suitor, whereupon the fearful, alluring prospect revives, more compelling than ever: "It was just as if he were coming upon me with a gigantic cudgel to lay me out."[189/z] Instead he falls to his knees before her, only to turn contemptible in her sight. In order to squelch temptation utterly, she calumniates herself to him—and therewith feels the old wicked thrill. With this perverse climax, Gillot came under reprobation for his share in having "made me incapable of serious and full love"[190/a]—his figure overcast by that of Zemek as Beer-Hofmann in "Abteilung 'Innere Männer.'" Lou designed "Eine Ausschweifung" for publication with "Fenitschka" in a single volume, which one reviewer found all too ostentatiously brainy[191/b] and another—the brilliant feminist Helene Stöcker—a "mine of psychological discoveries" and a "small feast for the select circle of those able to enjoy her art."[192] The earlier tale deserved the blame, the later one the praise. Strict in form and classic in style, "Eine Ausschweifung" is moreover a remarkable psychoanalytical portrait of a lady[c] short of its overt pretension of dealing in normal feminine psychology.

By comparison "Zurück ans All" (Back to the All), bizarre literarily, is psychologically naïve, though no less revealing about Lou's psyche. In it Lou divided herself between warm Ella, whose whole soul is in her secret betrothal, and Ella's cold cousin Irene, who runs a profligate old uncle's homestead. The cousins meet and clash—

[z] In this sequence, Lou also appears as a nineteen-year-old cripple madly in love with the psychiatrist, who has restored her mental health—a most candid unconscious confession.

[a] The self-calumniation was originally Lou's of her letter to Gillot from Rome, which in *Ruth* on the contrary prompts the marriage proposal; it was also Margharita's of *Kampf* (cf. above, p. 218 n. s), which, however, issues in suicide rather than "slave bliss" ("Sklavenglück" was Lou's working title for 1897j).

[b] Though with praise for the "admirable" style.

[c] Its talk about infantile instinctual life and about unconscious remembrance was obviously informed.

primarily over sex, which, sacred for Ella, is dirty for Irene.[d] Ella is revolted that her uncle originally wanted to marry Irene, aged as he was; Irene replies, "His age was the one thing about it that didn't revolt me."[193] And Irene explains to Ella, who is horrified at her pitiless dismissal of a milkmaid found pregnant: "I simply can't stomach this—this—Even murder is more to my taste than this—this damned smutty life-making."[194/e] Yet Irene loves plant and animal life—pistils, eggs, and all. Thus she constitutes her inheritance rights to the farm as a dowry for Ella (poor Andreas!) and makes off mysteriously to rejoin the elements. This last was Lou's retreat to her "blue room" to write about rejoining the elements. The cosmic yearning involved was the affective dowry afterwards brought by Lou to Beer-Hofmann's philosophic estate.[f] Cosmically endowed, Irene departs for the "all" with a funereal demeanor reminiscent of Märchen's damp return "home to nature." Before long, though, Lou was to intone Irene's adieu to identity like a bridal hymn.

Meanwhile nonfictionally in "Aus der Geschichte Gottes" (From God's History) Lou held that the beatific moment when the ego, expanding boundlessly, yet contracts to the vanishing point before a divinity of its own making (the old "religious affect"[g]) marks the debut of every historic religion. A shared inspiration at first, it is fast individualized. Lest it disintegrate, orthodoxy would bind men's thoughts to their god. Next, asceticism would bind their wills to their god in denial of the wishful thinking behind their faith. Mysticism would then bind their feelings to their god; however, sterile in its ecstatic snobbery toward everyday life, mysticism also virtually confuses "God and me,"[195] thereby threatening the faith while exposing its secret. So rationalism sets in, instituting new divinities—all abstractions from the old one—even in unsuspecting believers' hearts. Thus Christianity has been rationalized or allegorized away, Jesus alone having come in for enough reverence as moralist to prevent

[d] Nonfictionally, meanwhile, Lou insisted on the root synonymity of *sacred* and *dirty* (1893f:401).

[e] For "murder"—literally "a murderer"—read "abortion"?

[f] As an eager prospective housewife who despises professionalism in women, Ella was (like Jutta, only more so) a flirtation with Beer-Hofmann. Ella's fiancé was Zemek—though what prompted Lou to make her home over into a homestead was (apart from the greater proximity to the elements) the setup in "Loufried II." Heilborn, "L A-S," 27–28, contended that in this tale especially Lou's art dissolved into pure intellection (offset by sensual motherliness toward her characters).

[g] Cf. "Realismus" above, p. 147. Only now she added that one might well fall out of cosmic presumption not onto his knees but, Lucifer-like, back into mere everyday life—and therewith showed which moment of the religious affect came easier to her.

panic over his Father's demise.[h] But rationalism is religious self-denial par excellence; hence it in turn is offset by increasingly frequent mystic moments. As these of themselves do not " 'save,' " and as science is hard on them, the "modern man" of Christendom is left watching scientifically "whether his own needs and longings can bestow another savior upon him—or not."[196] That "modern man" was Lou.

According to her similar "Religion und Cultur," religion is creative just like sex or art, and God is "a symbol for whatever in human life is too intimate, intense, or precious to go by a human name."[197/i] The pressure of cultural development upon piety gradually turns established religion from a natural vehicle for intimate, immediate, all-embracing relationships with God into a system of mediation between a remote spiritual overlord and his unworthy suppliants as also of accommodation between holy and unholy experience. Hell gains on heaven as men blame and deny themselves in their God-forsaken-ness, until at last true prayer becomes once again churchless and unintentional. Hence perhaps man's dream of salvation "has come true only at the two end-points of human development: down in its darkest beginnings, where man first came into his own as he imagined himself descended from a god, and up on the splendid highest peak of culture, where man imagines himself truly a man at last as he bears a god."[198]

This same prophecy sounded through "Vom religiösen Affekt" less cryptically,[j] though oddly "the religious affect" was here for once neither cosmic nor mystic—nor even, for that matter, an affect. Modern men, Lou now argued, see the same earthly reality only in its banality; as somehow grand or enchanted they see it each in his own, incommunicable way. Such creative visions are the very substance of religion. Their incommunicability is a cultural achievement: they were tribal of old even as men were less individual and their banal perspective more rudimentary. Religious dualism developed along with this banal perspective distinct from the spiritual one. At the same time, individual transfiguring visions departed from the dogmatic norm, until today each man creates his own godhead, though he call it by an orthodox name or no holy name at all. And just as in our age men have a common empirical language, so will they again speak to

---

[h] 1897k in fact begins as a critique of Wolfgang Kirchbach's *Das Buch Jesu*, a popular exaltation of Jesus the moralist against which Lou contended that there was no worldly point whatever to Jesus' injunctions.

[i] Cf. 1897k:1215: God is merely an empty space into which "everything dear to us" is projected.

[j] Cf. above, p. 118 and n. *b*.

one another from the heights of their religious experience in another age—itself due to pass away in its turn, "a mere symbol of our highest dream."[199]

For all that, Lou was still writing as an unbeliever—in fact less equivocally so than in "Jesus the Jew" because with no suggestion that a departure from orthodoxy might be revelational rather than simply "creative" and with no equivocation about responsiveness to a pregiven divine image. Now, though, she almost outright called herself religious. To be sure, she now presented religion as simply an alternative way to the positivist's of experiencing the selfsame world —as an "inner truth" *without* "outer folly." However, God stirred in that world as a connotation of "religious." Besides, her tacit pseudologic ran: religion views only what science views, but sees it differently; seeing it differently, religion may well see God too; therefore God exists. The sense of the religious renaissance she prophesied was that she would recover her lost god. The prophecy did not commit her to share him with others; rather, it put others to ratifying her "highest dream" about him. That her highest dream made no sense in the interim she now blamed on the growth of individuality.[k] Under this head she was soon to indict, over and beyond men's growing apart, their growing away from a primal, confident intimacy with the world at large. Not to disavow a lifetime of self-affirmation and self-cultivation, however, she was to point her nostalgia forwards and upwards: toward a surmounting of individuality.

Over some days in February 1898, Lou drew on these and earlier studies of hers for the draft of a "book on God" to be built around "Jesus the Jew." She would have been better advised to plan a book on art instead, for between her disguised devotions she had turned out a most compelling, clear-cut statement of what art is about, "Grundformen der Kunst" (Basic Forms of Art). By its terms, even a true-to-life painter, insofar as he is an artist, conveys not intelligence of his subject matter, but an inner vision released as his sensations before his subject link up with current fancies and old sensate memories. Most nonartists discharge equivalent stimulation promptly and practically, though they too all live out of an "emotional underground"[200] more or less resembling the artist's and which only art can reveal. The pleasure taken in an artist's works derives from this resemblance alone and not from either his subject or his technique—even though technique is what makes such revealing more or less successful. This re-

[k] That is, on the individuation of religious experience, which, however, no longer varied with its intensity as in "Jesus" but instead progressed with individuation at large.

lationship of subject and technique to emotional underground holds for lyric poetry no less than for landscape painting. To be sure, the lyric poet's subject is itself emotions—indeed, his own emotions—and not fields of corn; yet even so it is fully distinguishable from his subjacent response to it, which constitutes the true contents of his poetry. His technique likewise serves solely to mediate this response, which has no more artistic value on its own than does technique itself. Great deeds too originate in that "most secret emotional center,"[201] just like great works of art, and they too are elicited by outer occasions, even if they generally spring forth full blown like the conception of a work of art preceding its material execution. Everyday things become "symbolical" in the artist's use of them to actualize an inner configuration: we thence call them " 'beautiful' " and their effect on us " 'aesthetic.' "[202] Artistic expression and aesthetic pleasure have always been of this nature, however much the artist's utilization and understanding of his medium have varied historically with prevailing trends and theories, themselves precipitates of the thinking and feeling of their time. For, Lou concluded, artistry is but one way of humanity, and "even the most intimate, secret artistic content is itself but a form in which something deeper-lying and decisive finds expression—and all art ultimately but one of the hidden paths from the sanctity of humankind up to its hallelujah and hymn of praise."[203]

Before folding her hands Lou had deftly applied this theory to the technical and sentimental refinements of the French decadents, to unnamed gentle, solitary young lyricists in Germany seeking new forms, and to that "inimitable phenomenon"[204] Stefan George, who consummately fused poetical form and content both with his own fabulous personality.[l] She ignored musical composition, which, however, to fit the formula would require only an auditory stimulus equivalent to the painter's visual one. To this effect she concluded in due course that so-called nonobjective painting has objective as well as true content, "only the object has become invisible, being abstractly concealed behind that which, in the shapes and colors, is at once entirely extrinsic and entirely subjective."[205/m] For she continually

[l] The rich six-page essay also contains a number of neat minor theses, such as that artistic formalism develops steadily in a culture (and often in an individual) along with the still, level gaze over all life until the repressed energies of art burst forth in crude new forms progressively refined in their turn (see further D 24 III 1904).

[m] This was her best but not her last word on the subject. D I 1918 treated of abstractionism as a new religious art—a learning to see things anew according to "saving inspiration"; for D [III?] 1918 she experimented with abstracting progressively in her mind's eye from natural colors and lines round about

elaborated her "Grundformen" theory,[n] of which Jane and the Count had inklings already. The doctrine of art as objective even when seemingly most subjective and vice versa[206] fell in with her coming insistence on an original felt unity between self and world, and psychoanalysis was only to add some particulars about those primal visions pressing for representation.[o]

Lou's last work of that winter was a critique of a volume of essays by the Swedish feminist Ellen Key. Against stock feminism Ellen Key argued that women could not help being feminine in their highest as well as their lowest functions, but also that in emulating men they risked impairing their femininity: Lou noted the inconsistency. For Ellen Key, woman's natural vocation was maternal, while for the other big dissenting feminist of the day, Laura Marholm, it was erotic. Lou objected to both their conceptions for connoting passivity: erotically the female is not subordinate to the male, she retorted, just as in reproduction the female is no mere passive vessel but a progenitress in her own right, who rears the embryo to boot. Similarly, both tended wrongly to "displace woman's center of gravity outside of herself, be it onto the man or the child."[207] And both were too schematic: real women put all theoretical feminity to shame. So may women, once emancipated, just blossom freely awhile, each in her own way, the botanical classification being left for the future, Lou concluded. The implicit advice was to fall on no ears deafer than her own.

On March 1, 1898, Lou departed for Petersburg, her brother Jenia having been stricken with tuberculosis: he died on May 4. By then she had despatched Rainer on a tour of the art centers of Italy—despite Andreas's urging that he take his putative university studies seriously instead, and despite "Ein Todesfall," in which he had taken that same southern route to his grave. Lou made him keep a diary addressed to her and due to be submitted to her. He was as much at a loss with it at first as Paul Rée had been. "You do not expect a travel

---

her: she found that deepness, jaggedness, and the like did not register so well beyond the point at which the object ceased being recognizable and that this point was farthest removed for human subjects; and so forth. That all art should have objective content was no requirement of her main "Grundformen" thesis, which merely denied the aesthetic significance of such content. To fill her bill, incidentally, the objective content of a work of fiction (or for that matter of a landscape painted from imagination) would have to be its unsuspected referents in the artist's recent outer experience—an implication she might profitably have drawn (see below, pp. 386-87).

[n] And departed from it momentarily too (e.g. D [III?] 1918: to those receptive to an objective painting, it presents objects divinely in their "independence and particularity").

[o] That psychoanalysis altered nothing: see D 23 I 1904, then D [17-20 VIII 1913].

log from me, complete, continuous, and chronological, do you?"[208]
And again: "Every day I have had the good will to keep up my journal; but today . . ."[209] By this entry he was decorously marking time in Viareggio with a genteel substitute for Lou—Elena, twenty-seven-year-old daughter of a Petersburg scientist—while eagerly expecting Lou to join him. But from Zoppot beach outside Danzig Lou summoned him on May 26 (after a stay at Johanna Niemann's nearby) to meet her in Berlin early in June and escort her back to Zoppot, there eventually to wait out a further sojourn of hers in Petersburg. Evidently she had not attended her brother's funeral. There are strong grounds for suspecting that she then underwent an abortion, thus perhaps her second.[p] In any case her summons left

[p] I was shown no chronicles of Lou's for II-V 1898 (some certainly exist for V 1898: see Pfeiffer, *Briefwechsel*, 33n. and 516-17). Lou→Caro [2? VI 1898] (draft?) implies that Lou (though conceivably only Caro) was "weeks at Eugene's sickbed." Likely she was headed there when as of D 27 II 1898 she "packed with Rainer" and as of D 28 II 1898 spent a "last evening in the blue room" (D 19 II 1898: "wrote Mama, Roba, bad news from Jenia"; D 25 II 1898: "Sasha's letter about Jenia"; D 26 II 1898: "wrote Mama"), and evidently she was back early enough to have seen Rilke again before his trip south (he reached Florence by 15 IV 1898 after visiting his father in Prague and his mother in Arco). She was already in Zoppot on 14 V 1898, when she wrote Rilke from there a first time (see Pfeiffer, *Briefwechsel*, 33n. and 516-17), so that her subsequent change of plans for meeting Rilke was apparently not due to Jenia's death. As per Lou→Caro [2? VI 1898] (draft?) and [6? VI 1898] (draft?), Lou quite clearly had not seen Caro since Jenia's death; for Caro's lone deathwatch, see also below, p. 433. Butler, 22ff., judged from Rilke's diary (and conceivably some confidential material in the Rilke Archiv) that Lou was then pregnant. The evidence in Lou's own writings is more compelling, the biggest single pieces of it being in 1904a, where the fictional Lou finds herself pregnant just after the fictional Rainer leaves for Italy (she having packed with him beforehand), and in 1919g, where the fictional Jenia dies (in fact kills himself) because to his horror his sister revisits a shady doctor known to her through him and later arrested for unspecified sexual malpractice. This second, suggestive sequence roughly recapitulates one in 1900d, in which the little heroine twice visits a poet-criminal, the first time as her brother (Jenia-Rainer) waits anxiously downstairs, the second time behind his back; the heroine is thought to be seeking a midwife on her first arrival (an intrigue on her second) and winds up waxing sentimental over a pregnant maid at home. The pregnancy theme was sounded for 1919g in turn when in 1933, for no good literary reason, Lou joined it to "Jutta" as a two-part (draft) novella. Insofar as the "Jutta" finale is autobiographic, it refers of necessity to a pregnancy before Jenia's fatal illness (for as much as the obliging youngest brother was Jenia and not Jutta's alter ego as in 1919g, on which "Jutta" was superficially aligned in 1933). Rilke was associated with about all aspects and elements of Lou's writings of 1898 and after that bear on pregnancy or hint at abortion, beginning with her overtrumping his Florence diary passages on woman's maternal vocation in her essays from I 1899 on (below, p. 229 etc.) but most distinctly in her tales thereafter: in 1900b pregnancy is dark and evil (as also in Rilke's writings sub-

Rainer "shaken and affrighted. . . . I was so looking forward to the summer and felt it like a clear bright promise over everything. Only now doubts and worries come, and all paths get crossed. . . . All at once it is so dark around me. I feel only that I must ride among strangers one day and then another and a third to be finally beside you—maybe so as to: take leave."[210] He took courage on the morrow: "There is no fear left in me today, darling, only the clear joy of having you again in six to seven days. . . . What fear have I of a desolate beach in East Prussia!"[211]

From Schmargendorf early in June Lou wrote to Caro, Jenia's sole confidant at the last, that were she in Petersburg she would fight the urge to relive her brother through Caro's reminiscences, "for Mama, my poor dear Mushka, . . . would sense something and be mortally vexed. She suffered so dreadfully, more than I can say, from Jenia's mounting disaffection for her—for years, and of course most of all now"[212]: Lou's own disaffection for her had permanently subsided. Four days later she sent Caro a moving memoir on Jenia ("I almost

---

sequent to the Florence diary), threatening a narrow-hipped landlady and victimizing the little Lou-sisters' mother, then their canary, then (presumably) the elder one of themselves, all to the tune of a macabre lyric by Rilke, who appears as the hapless sister's guilty lover; in 1899f, an apotheosis of motherhood, the Lou-mother, in her desolation on parting with her second child (called Sophie—as was René when mothered as a little girl), has no one to lean on but an aspirant poet whom she knows through that child and who, returning from a visit to his family abroad, has first stirrings of true artistry and manliness on seeing her in her renunciative victory (an allusion to Rilke in the summer of 1898); in 1900c the hero, who takes a Volga boat ride with the heroine recalling Rilke's with Lou, sees pregnancy as the frightful finish to a maiden's "dreaming and drowsing" (1900c:398); 1901a, which abounds in miscarriages, stillbirths, and infant mortality, ends as the hero, by then Rilke, departs confusedly, leaving his wife behind pregnant (which would conjoin 1898 with 1903, when Rilke ran out on his wife and child); in 1904a the mother feels that she has truly become a mother only through having lost two children (before her final pregnancy, which was Lou's of 1901); etc. On 10 VIII 1903, concerning the artist's need for "much standing aside, much solitude," Lou told Rilke: "Yes, even I could say of myself that I denied myself motherhood out of such austerity and modesty." With Rilke as with Zemek, Lou—exceptionally—remained intimate well beyond the ninth month (when, however, she dispatched Rilke to Italy). Again, Lou→Emma [undated] (draft): ". . . The first time it happens *to* us, so to say, comes upon us, like a mystery, without our participation or comprehension; the second time we feel it as our own colossally important and serious doing that we should be bringing a person into the world . . ." Finally, according to *Franz Schoenberner, Lou fell into a fearful rage in the 1920's because she believed a pregnancy of hers by Rilke was being bruited about by Ellen Delp, whereas *Ellen Delp dismissed the hypothesis of such a pregnancy as wild (cf. below, pp. 443-44 and n. *w*).

wrote 'your Jenia'") "through Roba, lest Mama needlessly notice my writing you again."[213/q]

On June 8 Lou met Ellen Key, then passing through Berlin, for a two-hour chat in a little *Konditorei* with all too much unprivacy.[214] Ellen took to Lou right away: as she wrote Lou the next day, she loved "odd people." Lou responded uncertainly at first: she promised Ellen a novella by mail, a new review of the essays on woman, even a visit to Sweden—then went about her business. Ellen, though, prodded her into corresponding and in due course won her heart. Where Lou was by character both age-old and childlike, Ellen, eleven years her senior, was strictly youthful: big-hearted and openhearted, full of humor and *sans-gêne*, with an ungovernable penchant for friendship and sunshine such that she was most in her element when sun-bathing nude in good company. Herself on the odd side, she closed an early letter to Lou: "I stroke your lovely hair and am your devoted EK." Their written exchanges—in which, great travelers though they both were, their relationship mostly consisted—evidence an attraction of opposites, for Ellen rambled and scrawled in a German too outrageous not to have been intentionally so.

Rainer reached Berlin by June 8 and accompanied Lou back to Zoppot, where he submitted to her his Italian diary bursting with notes on paintings and people and with pronouncements on art and humankind. A final entry dated July 6, 1898, after she had proceeded to Petersburg, tells of its fateful reception: it enchanted her despite her low morale, only hardly was she done reading it when already she was mentally bettering the best of it for her own purposes. "I traveled a broad road through Italy to the summit that this book signifies; you overflew it in a few short hours and, before I was even done climbing, stood upon its clearest peak."[215] In thus reaffirming her easy intellectual ascendancy, he pursued, she had shamed him,[r] the worse since she was so infuriatingly nice to him about it—and especially as by then the fortitude and cheer he had originally put on for her sake had worn off, laying his desperate self open to her motherly solace as of old. He was bluffing himself about the diary so as to feel better about feeling bad. Nothing in it was ideational news to Lou, as he must have known only too well. For the most part it repeated her own teachings supersententiously: "What Napoleon was toward the outside, the artist is toward the inside"[216] and "Know that the artist creates for himself alone"[217]; "God is the oldest work of art"[218] and "Everyone

---

[q] With these two letters to Caro from Berlin, Lou was obviously avoiding any indication of her stays in Danzig.

[r] "All inside me was shame, shame" (RMR, *Tagebücher*, 135).

comes in mourning from the deathbed of his childhood god"[219]; and so forth. One of its messages was also Lou's-to-be: that "woman fulfills herself in the child."[220/s] Here, then, was "its clearest peak." To be sure, Lou had said as much once—to Nietzsche—but had said it derisively and hardly repeated it.[t] Ellen Key had just said it hymnically, and Lou took up the refrain from its chorister Rainer in souvenir of their "mutual sorrow."[221] Unwilling to practice maternity[u] —for fear of everything from social awkwardness to hereditary insanity[222] and death in delivery[223]—Lou thus came around to preaching it.

Meanwhile Rainer in his dismay hated her "as something *too big*"[224] and felt like crawling off "into a deep nowhere."[225] He spoke at length of pulling out of her too gracious orbit. "What will you do?" she asked at bed-time. And through her "estranged voice" he heard Destiny addressing him.[226] After a sleepless night of anguish he made his submission, considering that his highest calling was to trail after her intellectually forever.[v] So he told her in his diary, which, true to his word, he thereupon wound up with the self-consoling reflection that anyhow all artists are merely heralds of the overman, who will sum them all up—the conclusion of Lou's second "Russische Dichtung und Kultur" of Wolfratshausen, itself an echo of her Nietzsche book's late Nietzsche. If he sounded his submission jubilantly at the time,[w] he later claimed that the Zoppot fiasco had lamed him artistically for life.[227] In fact it was an artistic boon in that it put an end to his poetically sterile straining to outthink Lou. In Zoppot meanwhile,

[s] Also *ibid.*, 119: "woman's way always leads to the child, before motherhood and after," etc.—and "a woman artist must cease producing on becoming a mother," which may well have been meant for Lou but which no less paraphrases "Ausschweifung." To some other themes of Rainer's diary Lou did give *fuller* and *finer* expression after VII 1898 (especially in 1899b). The diary shows young Rilke to have aligned himself with Lou not only ideationally but in his very way of construing himself on his tour of Italy as constituting a "storehouse" of memories to be drawn upon afterwards (RMR, *Tagebücher*, 21). Indeed, it bespeaks thralldom to her for all his nascent pride in his own powers: he typically credited her with the room in his soul for Italian art (*ibid.*, 117), and when once he impressed someone conversationally he felt like rushing home to her, "for I know something in myself you do not yet know" (*ibid.*, 114).

[t] Except halfheartedly through Ella (1898a) and Jutta (1898f).

[u] "I never had the nerve to bring a human being into the world" (1931a:41).

[v] Literally, to *ascend* after her—a case of the eternal *masculine* drawing him aloft given his girlish hate for Lou as phallic mother (as that "something *too big*").

[w] Some fifteen months later he even rhymed it:

Ich geh doch immer auf Dich zu mit meinem ganzen Gehn,
Denn wer bin ich und wer bist Du wenn wir uns nicht verstehn?

—to Lou's unending delight (1931a:187).

the one diary closed, he opened another likewise addressed to Lou which, however, was not necessarily meant for her sight: this far he did go toward doing without her.

By July 23, 1898, Lou was back in the Danzig area touching up some poems of Rainer's with him[228] after a few weeks during which, she told Ellen, "I spent nearly every hour with my mother and family."[229/x] She returned with him to Berlin the last day in July, then left again in August for some "lovely summer and autumn weeks"[230] first in Munich,[231] then in Hallein with Broncia and Zemek,[y] and finally in Biebrich am Rhein (near Wiesbaden) with Rainer.[z] From there she sent Caro a glorious defense of her mother, whom Caro blamed for Jenia's final wretchedness: there was a Jenia whom Caro never knew, it ran, and whose mother needed "the uttermost goodness and devotedness" to put up with him over the years.[232/a] (The tables had turned on Caro in twenty years!) The last day of September found Lou home in Schmargendorf "amid chests and trunks . . . healthy and happy . . . looking forward to my quiet winter's work, which consists of all sorts of essays and stories."[233]

No stories emerged. In the end she assembled her old ones not yet between hard covers to make up *Menschenkinder* (Children of Man),[b] which reviewers praised more as psychology than as literature. What did emerge was, first, a fine study of Tolstoi as heir to the conflict rending Russian literati since Peter the Great and Pushkin the great, its two terms being superrefinement in the Western manner and adulation of the simple Russian folk: "What makes him so great, what makes him unique, is the violence with which his genius strives to resolve it, as if worlds should burst asunder and worlds be born that a man may find peace for his soul."[234] By now she spoke unfalteringly about ikons and izbas and Leskov's forgetful but ever com-

---

[x] This was an excuse for not having written sooner—phrased to suggest that she had been in Petersburg her whole time away from Berlin.

[y] To be inferred from Lou→Broncia, XI 1898 (Peters, 257), according to which she had seen Broncia's recently born second child, and from the material on endocrine glands in 1899a, which, like the psychoanalytical material on hysteria in 1899b, certainly came from talks with Zemek (who just afterwards published a monograph, *Blutdrüsenerkrankungen*, and whom Lou→EK [VIII 1901] cited as her source on the subject).

[z] Rilke may have been with her in Munich too and, to go by 1899f, called for her in Hallein.

[a] Lou added concerning 1895 that she "saw in Mama then as never before a weak, suffering, infinitely touching being." Perhaps—but her first surviving expressions of tenderness for any mother date from after Jenia's death.

[b] D 7 II 1899: "contract"; D 27 II 1899: "proofs." Literally "children of humans," "*Menschenkinder*" in ordinary usage amounts to just "people," with a faint suggestion of "poor mortals"; Lou, though, who overused the word, generally managed to make it sound like a plural for "son of Man."

passionate god. She spoke best, though, about art, rebutting Tolstoi
—and refining Rainer. Tolstoi was wrong as only he could be in saying that artists create so as to communicate: they create simply because such is their "way of living life . . . but what is wrong as regards
the *motivation* is right as regards the *distinguishing mark* of all
art."[235] Yet to rebut Tolstoi is not to be done with him, she added, for
his argument is really a sentiment, and one out of which came his
glorious "Master and Servant." It is a sentiment out of the popular
Russian side of his soul, moreover, and he is preaching it to the other
side. So ran Lou's reduction; as for her reconstruction, it left Tolstoi
like Rainer "a poet of God's grace even when he would be a thinker
—a priest of the unnamed god we all serve."[236]

From the unnamed god Lou passed to love life in nature as she
lengthily reviewed a volume on the subject by Bölsche.[c] Bölsche's
treatment of human copulation and parturition as mere refinements
of infusorial ingestion and excretion ravished her. His account of the
increasing complication, differentiation, and specialization of organic
functions through evolutionary time prompted her to surmise that
maybe mental functions follow suit with a huge lag most evident in
the erotic realm. The human sexual function, while physically highly
specialized and localized, she reflected, amounts mentally to a downright infusorial yearning for reunification of all our faculties and
utter fusion with our loved one, though by and large "love's frenzy
only temporarily stultifies and lames" our nonsexual faculties.[237]
Surely this comical backwardness will be outgrown in time so that love
will cease encroaching upon man's whole psyche. "New, superior
human types, with new capacities and riches, will emerge"[238]—perhaps, though, with the same sort of loss as when new cultures supersede old ones, for perhaps much of our deepest inner life "proceeds
from just that persisting disparity between the stages of development
of 'body' and 'mind.' " As against the evolutionary novelties forever
emerging from the darkness of time, "what keeps on receding—the
old—might well turn out in one instance or another to have also been
the beautiful when time is at an end."[239] She did not say how psychic
erotism, so obstinately archaic to date, could be expected to go modern all at once. Nor did it occur to her to doubt that more evolved
meant more complex. Yet already, thanks to her regressive nostalgia,
she saw through the value judgment latent in the phrase "higher
forms of life"—even while realizing that human "depth" and
"beauty," once bygone, would not be missed until the end of time.

That fall Lou produced a few briefer reviews as well—of a col-

[c] *Das Liebesleben in der Natur,* I.

lection of aphorisms[240] and a set of notes on madhouse life,[241] which she judged respectively not often merely witty and too often merely realistic; of a trisexual love story, which, replete with "phantoms and Nietzsche phrases," made her long for mere realism again[242]; of some speeches by Prince Sergei Volkonsky on Russian intellectual life, which she found just grand[243]; and of a novel about the brazen serpent of fate, in which the author himself seemed to her to have lost interest midway.[244]

Meanwhile she noted ruefully on October 31: "Religion book cast to the winds again." She retrieved the leaves and sewed together a few, some old[d] and some new, for a symposium on egoism—"hastily," she afterwards told Ellen,[245/e] and grudgingly, for, as she straight off remarked in her "Der Egoismus in der Religion" itself, we see religion only the less clearly by fixing on the egoism in it. Seemingly— she went on—egoism recedes within any developing religion as men charitably blame themselves for God's failings, and yet it is most in evidence on religious summits. There are two opposite kinds of egoism in religion: the Semitic, which, blood-bound, aims at worldly self-fulfillment through godliness; and the Aryan, which, breath-bound, aims to triumph over worldliness through grace. The Jews, in demanding that righteousness be rewarded here and now, pushed the first to its tragic limit. Buddhism, in teaching quietude beyond all doing or feeling (nirvana), carried the second to its comical extreme: Buddhist life eternal is this life bled white.[f] Christianity superimposed an Aryan otherworldly settlement of earthly accounts upon a Semitic fundament which, together with the church establishment, has kept the faithful from ever being carried away by celestial *élan*. Like all good religions, Christianity engendered a new culture which took over from it in due course, secularized and specialized. The science, the ethics, the art born of Christianity have grown away from it and apart from each other, remaining Christian siblings nonetheless. Similarly the Christian individual, bereft of the implicit, integral faith of yesteryear, has been splitting up psychologically into diverse faculties and appetencies. He has gained knowledge of his own and the world's oneness at the cost of his immediate sense of it, which he can retrieve only through self-dedication to something above his own person and universe. At the height of his exploits in art or science,

---

[d] These mainly from "Jesus."

[e] Further: "I hope you will never read [my] little article . . ."

[f] Nirvana—the absorption of individual life within the great life-stream of the universe—was in fact roughly Lou's own idea of salvation, true as she remained to the earth. (As already with mysticism, so now with nirvana: she attacked it in defense of her originality.)

love or war, hence at his most triumphantly egoistic, he feels himself to be serving some higher purpose just as intangible with respect to his mind as his mind is over against sensory reality. This distinctively religious persuasion is itself a cultural derivative in even the most deviate cases. In Christendom today the individual lives out of it as once his culture did. He may yet even see it for what it is: " 'God' is perhaps the last word of human egoism as it was the first."[246]

Already Lou had come to regard differentiation within mental life as a strictly cultural phenomenon obtaining where piety did not, regrettably but remediably. This too was provisional: she was working her way toward a new, more advised construal of Bölsche's material, yet tending to represent woman in effect as no mere woman but a man as well, indeed as a whole unitary, harmonious, self-sufficient erotic world unto herself. The theme of womanhood—*her* womanhood—had preoccupied her at least since the preceding summer, when she had written Ellen: "My own thoughts on this matter elude theoretical formulation—perhaps only till I have found it, perhaps also because I instinctively seek artistic expression for something I rather feel than think. But I may come to it again presently . . ."[247]

This she did through a public reply to a public protest by Frieda against women's writings being called feminine disparagingly, for— Frieda asked—what else should they be? Frieda was confusing self-exposure with art, Lou rejoined. Men's art does not document masculinity. The true artist forgets himself for his work in progress, which uses him to its own ends; it does not convey his personality except indirectly, by the "artistic detour"[248] of gripping others in turn after completion. Women, however, cannot get outside of themselves given their biologically grounded "lesser capacity for differentiation"[249]— their grand virtue, which yet disqualifies them literarily beyond "self-reduplication on paper."[250] The finest works of woman are ever cherished for their intimations of a still finer person behind them— like those of Marie von Ebner-Eschenbach, which drop like autumn leaves from the great tree that is herself. All this is no reason for women not to write, but is one for them not to take their writing "so frightfully seriously."[251] May they just open their hearts from time to time in print, Lou concluded, and mind their woman's business in the meantime.

In all, her sole point against Frieda was that good art does not disclose the artist's sex. Her calling women incapable of such art read like a gratuitous point against herself, with her talk of women's psychic concentratedness as meager self-consolation. However, her portrait of the artist belabored by his works was a self-portrait; likewise, a word in passing on literary ambition as unwomanly unsexed her. And with that "lesser capacity for differentiation" now ascribed to women as against men went saving grace already and—with reference back to the Bölsche review—beauty under the aspect of eternity. What else went with it went into a beguiling elaboration of the thesis, begun just before she took Frieda to task,[g] tellingly titled "Zwei als Eins" (Two in One) at first, then definitively "Der Mensch als Weib" (The Human as Woman).

Bölsche's account of how sex first came to be, Lou began, reads "like a tale out of an early, early childhood of our own."[252] One-celled parents divide asymmetrically, and their smaller progeny, harder put to it to link up again, are perforce more enterprising than those nearer parent size to begin with: only when wooed by a swarm of mobile "male cells" does the sluggish "egg cell" open up and suck one in. Thus from the very first the feminine element is the less developed, the more undifferentiated—and as such achieves its prime purpose. Already as a cell the male is the predestined agent of progress, forever dissatisfied, forever taking on new tasks and pushing on to new goals out in the alien open realm of possibility, developing by dint of his drive and need, whereas the female remains within her native sphere "as if she were more immediately in touch with the boundless plenitude round about her, hence more lazily attached to her native ground."[253] Thus already on the cellular level the feminine is the more intact harmony, the greater roundness and completeness, as opposed to the male principle of a restless, uncertain seeking, with ever greater dispersion of forces and specialization of activity. Again, feminine is to masculine as the bluest-blooded aristocracy entrenched in its castle is to the most enterprising upstart who, venturing farther and farther afield, sees his ideal of fulfillment, like the horizon, recede indefinitely.

Male and female are two modes of life, Lou continued, and no mere correlatives or halves of a whole, as calling them respectively active and passive implies. Coactive reproductively, male and female mammals both discharge fertile cells, which unite in pairs—hers bigger, his more mobile. Hers, though, is direct heiress to that aboriginal carrier of sexless generation. As mammal mothers moreover nurture the embryo inside them, they virtually reproduce themselves. The cellular contrast is one of vital deficiency to vegetative near-sufficiency, it psychic counterpart man's "selfless devotion to a goal" as against woman's "fond lolling within herself."[254] But even before being relatively deficient the male element is the more differentiated, for

[g] Mostly, it would seem, in the form of notes on Rudolf Virchow, Johannes Ranke, Ernst Haeckel, and Carl Claus.

its whole history is one of "dividing and altering its primal substance and differentiating its functions ever further" as against "that satiety in creative self-reproduction, in holding all one's forces together generatively within oneself."[255] More: the higher the animal functions a cell performs, the less fertile the cell, so that the female's lesser capacity for differentiation is at the same time her greater power of creation. Her organism remains the home base for every masculine departure. She is an entity in her own right tending to concentration as against specialization—and these together make reproduction possible. The male, though more aggressive sexually, participates in procreation only "momentarily and fragmentarily,"[256] directing his impulse outward in a single, particularized act; the female, her doing a mode of being, joins organically with what she has once internalized and lives at one with what she creates until it is all ripe and ready.[h]

More physical by nature, woman discloses the more clearly "that the whole of mental life is itself ultimately only a most finely transmuted blossom from out of the great, sexually conditioned root of all being—sublimated sexuality so to say."[257] Yet just because it is suffused throughout woman's whole being, sexuality does not "penetrate her consciousness"[258] in the localized, specialized way it does man's. Hence the seeming paradox that the sexier sex is also the less crudely sensual: less apt to feel mere lust, woman at all odds cannot gratify it without her whole person's becoming involved—whence in turn her erotism's "deeper beauty."[259] Woman is always either virginal or maternal—or *both*, the connection between the two being "emotionally a much deeper one than the passage from virgin to mother can alone disclose."[260/i] For woman, these "powers of being, between which she lives,"[261] vitalize every "transitional interlude [!], even if it happens not to issue in physical motherhood,"[262] and render it ever and again "all new, originally childlike and innocent as on the first day."[263] On the other end, "man's love is at bottom contained in the reverence with which he feels a woman to be enclosed by these two mysterious worlds which he can only divine, not coexperience."[264]

As against man's sexuality with its urgent, outward manifestation,

[h] The female's creating, given her concentrated nature, culminates *not in a deed*, Lou specified, but in an outpouring of new life (1899a:229)—a neat little instance of her repudiating Nietzsche (he having told her that her nature, so concentrated, ought normally to issue in a *deed*: above, p. 120) but especially of her riding a theoretic war horse (here the one that woman's doing is her being, which had quite a career with her thereafter) against a first position of her own, however briefly held (for she had subscribed Nietzsche's formulation delightedly in its time).

[i] Cf. RMR, *Tagebücher*, 73, on "motherly virgins" as against "virginal mothers."

woman's, which works inwardly, has been illumined only "recently and scantily," through the study of women's physical and mental illnesses.[265/j] It would have been better illumined by authentic contemporary female artists had there been any. As is, it is best illumined by male artists, obtuse as they may be about it. For the male artist at work is extraordinarily womanly: less pointedly conscious, objective, active than otherwise, more unitary, organic, fused with what he is creating, in closer touch with its deep source behind all thought and will. He is even effeminate when in travail: moodier than otherwise, more sensitive and impulsive, less in control of his ability. But what holds for him only in his productive capacity—when the emergent work possesses him—holds for woman's whole unitary self, which, being its own highest purpose, issues in no such discrete, extrinsic works. Everything live in woman seems to circulate internally as if, like blood, it could emerge only through a wound; or again, woman is like a tree expending its sap and vitality within, living for itself and not for such fruit as may fall from it in season. Woman cannot give herself utterly to works of the mind as men do, but only halfway at most—by straining, and with resultant psychic dislocation and inner conflict. Hence her best works will never compare with men's, and her emulating men in intellectual endeavor as of late is "pure devilry," the more since it awakens ambition in her, which is fatal to "her natural greatness: her solid assurance that she need bring no proof of herself in order to feel within herself the highest self-justification."[266]

And on it went, with many a lilting turn of phrase and crafty turn of argument, plus metaphors galore to bridge the gap between biology and psychology, through numberless variations on a single theme: woman the internalizer, man the externalizer; woman spherical, man distended; woman unitary, man divisive; organic, analytic; instinctual, rational; cohesive, disjunctive; generic, individual; primal, progressive; abiding, transitional; refuge, refugee; rest, unrest; sufficiency, need; acceptance, defiance; woman the plenitude of life in its intact harmony, to man "a symbol of what he tore loose from in becoming a man and cannot yet reach again in a new, higher phase"[267]; woman's life moving in concentric circles, man's in straight lines; woman luxuriating within herself, man expending himself in self-surpassing; woman curling or kneeling before her god, man standing tense and erect before his fate; death man's tragic limit and contradiction, wom-

---

j Here Lou learnedly discussed endocrine glands (thanks to Zemek) and cited systematically collected "experiences with the emotional cohesion of sexuality" (meaning Freud's).

an's natural goal and fulfillment; woman moreover beauty, goodness, wisdom, joy, health, reverence for life, eternal mother and eternal child, the womb and its fruit in one, house and home, species preserve, nutriment, refreshment, paradise, plant—until she dies like a droplet of water that falls into the ocean, losing its shape but returning to its element, a whole rejoining the whole, wherewith the dream underlying her entire existence comes true, "a dream out of deep, grey ages when she was still everything within everything, everything with everything, and nothing alone (because nothing was outside of her)."[268] And throughout, Lou's woman was no complement to man but a positive value in her own right, requiring only to discover herself as such in order to unfold along her own lines, broad and powerful, yielding to neither of the equally unfeminine alternatives lately confronting her of partial, outward development through professional activity or of subserving a man as mere appendage to him and means to his self-realization. Lou predicted with assurance that woman would come back to herself from her frenzy of job-hunting and man-hunting only the richer and riper[k]—yet added: "Which will prove stronger, woman or the unwomanly demands she is making on herself, time will have to tell."[269]

"Der Mensch als Weib" drew plaudits long sustained. It was cited whenever the call went out for a volume of Lou's essays. Georg Simmel for one was sold on it at first. In time, though, Simmel came to wonder whether what disabled woman intellectually was not her culture rather than her organism—and Lou dismissed Simmel's wondering as "a mere philosophical compliment" to woman, whose self-expression in motherhood *"is just plain nature* and not logic."[270] Meanwhile, her essay on woman brought Lou herself a philosophical compliment from Martin Buber: "Every subject, it seems to me, possesses, if at any time then in ours, a single human mind that is there to present it and express its essence. In my eyes, such a relation obtains between this subject and you."[271]

The aptest commentary came from a contradictor, however: lushly sarcastic Hedwig Dohm, a senior feminist of Lou's acquaintance,[l] who, writing some months after her, denounced a "reaction within the women's movement" against the principle of parity between the sexes, the chief reagents being Laura Marholm, for whom woman's

[k] Woman ran no more risk of losing her feminine vocation than a snail of losing its house-shell from wandering too far afield (1899a:236)—which shows who she thought the man was and who the woman in Snailie's ménage with Housie.

[l] Lou noted visits to Hedwig Dohm in Berlin on 6 and 14 vi 1895.

highest end was the man; Ellen Key, for whom it was the child; and now Lou especially (*"Et tu, Brute!"*[272]), for whom it was woman herself "as such."[273] Dohm found that Lou's manner was as devious as her message was dubious: "On soft soles she glides, almost soaring aloft, over slippery ground, as with sounds of harp and lute she elegantly grazes the most ticklish motifs in sex life. She envelops the starkly nude in shimmering haze. She moves round and round, chanting and swaying. She looks out as if from under long lashes, sidewise. There is also something mystically seerlike about her, only unlike the spiritist she does not materialize spirits but spiritizes crude matter. Her psyche, rising high above reality, easily soars out of sight."[274] Again, her metaphors "sound like elfin rondos or anything else poetically dreamy" as "she leads us into a fairyland of pure minds and hearts, where . . . all women glow, dew-hazy, resplendently youthful and beauteous," devoid of all physical or psychic hunger: "in this El Dorado, woman has it so good, so good in and by herself. . . . Ah yes, I too should like 'to be at home in my own castle like a bit of age-old, bluest-blooded aristocracy' . . . I too should like to unfold like a flower, exhaling fragrance afar, to roll up soulfully with languorous smile, in intact harmony, like a shimmering droplet of water. Only ordinarily things do not work out that way at all. Frau Lou's magical melodies half allured me; I half swooned. Then I reread her piece, and the spell was broken." For no one model will do for all women: apart from Lou's woman, there are "women like storm and fire. There are Amazons and sacrificial lambs, Hypatias and simple housewives—all wanting to act out their own inclinations, and right in this, a thousand times right. This time round I found in Frau Lou's feminine ideal a subtle, sublimated touch of the harem (minus the sultan, to be sure), of self-infatuation and obesity of soul: her starry-eyed sluggards resemble Narcissus in their sentimental satiety. Her ideal hits up all too hard against reality. To actualize it would call for altering all extant social relations first, so as to assure woman of a state pension sufficient for her to round out soulfully in her castle unimpeded, in age-oldest, bluest-blooded femininity. And even then: would not man be something of a woman's slave, waiting by the sweat of his brow for the girth of the glorious shade-dispensing tree of femininity to grow to intact harmony? Frau Lou takes her own to be man's feminine ideal as well: 'The manly man,' she says, 'shudders alike at the man-mad as at the emancipation-mad woman.'[m] I am not so very sure about that first shudder,"[275] and as for the second: "A shudder for *unpleasant* women—yes. But there are such under all

[m] Cf. below, p. 242 n. *u.*

latitudes geographical and intellectual, among the most professional and most professionless."[276/n]

So much for what was special to Lou's feminist reaction; for the rest, pursued Hedwig Dohm, Lou agreed with her two predecessors first of all that woman's brain-work was expendable, calling it "autumnal fruit": "Autumnal fruit indeed! Autumnal fruit Frau Lou's works too? If I thought so I would never lay hand to them, but I always do. And these ladies' ideas of woman's goal: autumnal fruit? Should they not, in the interests of one of the biggest social questions, have abstained from shedding it?"[277] "By God, if these dear gifted authoresses are so down on careers for women and on their competing with men, then why do they turn out autumnal fruit and suchlike stuff?"[278] "Woman ambitionless! What madonnas, Ephebian virgins, or Arcadian shepherdesses have these ladies frequented?"[279] But they would, like Achilles' lance, heal the wounds they inflict: thus Lou, denying woman the power of differentiation, calls the lack of it woman's specific genius.[280] "Even Lou" has only youngish women in mind, as when she writes of man's descending from the heights of productivity into everyday life, there to see "eternity itself in the form of a young being kneeling"[o]: "And what if he were to see a shriveled old housewife or a bespectacled grandmother kneeling?"[281] But the worst treble failing was want of straightforwardness: "Why the artistic drapery, the mystic tripod, the proud buskin? There are so many more suitable subjects for poetical outpourings than the woman question!"[282] Lou's sole excuse was the very frivolity of her purpose: "Indeed, Frau Lou simply aims to produce a gilded, scented picture of woman as, seerlike, she has seen woman in her soul."[283]

Did you read it?! cried Ellen from Sweden.[284] "I read *nothing* of that sort," replied Lou, "because I find it so very disturbing"[285/p]— an avowal that she did read *something* of the sort, it being easy to guess what. Perhaps most "disturbing" was the charge of "reaction," since for all the "confidence in human longings" liberally urged and felt by her[286] she was indeed beckoning backwards through evolutionary time, counter to her Bölsche review; or perhaps it was the echo of Nietzsche's stricture on her for treating of woman "as

[n] Lou's woman was most unprofessional to please Beer-Hofmann—after Anjuta in "Inkognito."

[o] ". . . *whether so as to be closer to earth or more tractable to heaven*: both are at one in her expression just as if it incorporated something of what sounds forth exultantly like a symbol of all mankind from the old Biblical words: 'All is yours! but you are God's!' ": the finale of "Mensch."

[p] Lou added that she would mind criticism were she writing "for people with whom and with whose country" she felt "wholly in unison"—meaning for Russians!

such,"[287] or the reduplication of her own critique of Ellen for doing just that. Another of her points against Ellen was now valid against herself: she could not very well maintain that women were naturally inclined to behave like predifferentiated lumps of protofeminine protoplasm if emancipated women were all misbehaving. And why should women be held to their natural inclinations anyhow?

Lou really inferred women's inclinations from the human genital anatomy and not the oversized cell. Inferentially this was no improvement: women hardly act more like their wombs than like their earliest evolutionary ancestresses. Nor did Lou's talk of a distinct way of life complete in itself ring any truer in consequence: genitally, the circle is complementary to the straight line. And her designating woman's way "sufficiency" was strictly wishful. The "sufficient" female was a fantasy female: a female with a secret penis, this being variously her womb (for it too discharges fertile cells) and her womb's child (which is virtually all hers), an appropriation from the male (for she joins organically with whatever she internalizes[q]) and the male entire (bound to her like Antaeus to the earth). By this genital fantasy Lou would have healed the protoplasmic rift between the sexes—that is, between herself and her father as in her oldest nativity myth. Arguing as she did from genital to emotional sufficiency, she countermanded her pre-Tautenburg thesis of femininity as felt deficiency—yet did so in the Tautenburg sense of "pregnancy as woman's cardinal state, which gradually, through the centuries, fixed her nature. Relation thereto of all feminine ways of thinking and acting."[r]

Lou's scheme of female genitocentric sexual and emotional self-enclosure rendered woman's unitary proclivity plausible; but, habituation apart, there is nothing in woman's psychology to bear it out. By psychological "differentiation" ("or differentiatedness" or occasionally "dissociation"), Lou apparently meant not only the faculty of having an exclusively erotic or social or aesthetic or intellectual experience but at the same time the ability to divide one's attention or interest continually. That such a climactic dissociation of mind from body as asceticism was a masculine prerogative followed—as did Lou despite her own ascetical bent. That pure rationality was beyond woman's reach followed too, and there was subtle self-flattery to

[q] The male is correspondingly "deficient."

[r] Cf. Nietzsche's old fury against Lou as it sounded its last in FN, *Ecce* (then still unpublished), "Why I write such good books," 5: "Woman needs children, man is ever but a means: so spoke Zarathustra.—'Woman's emancipation': the instinctive hatred of the sickly woman (that is, the woman incapable of bearing children) for the healthy one."

Lou's according her sex this handicap. There was also subtle insincerity to it: proceeding as she did ratiocinatively, if she made her point it was therewith refuted. One might call differentiatedness masculine as against feminine (everyone being a little of each) and thus elude the difficulty—if at some cost to the essay's bearing on the woman question. But just this Lou could not do, for the very reason that she was in fact working from the genital and not the cellular model: her subject was not femininity but womankind, despite the surface sense of her title—and even though she tended to imply woman-pure-of-masculinity, and to mean woman-possessed-of-masculinity. Her subject notwithstanding, the male term of the antithesis differentiated/concentrated had the initiative in her mind, where the biological datum of the many sperm for a single egg joined up with her age-old self-assurance that through all his occupations her father loved her continually.[8] Similarly, "dissociation" associated the datum of ejaculation with her deep wish to appropriate a penis. Nominally her thesis was that *all* biological development goes the way of greater differentiation except that phylogenetically the males lead the way; her woman as such would have none of this tagging after men, however, and resolutely entrenched herself in primal psychosexual integrity, evolution be damned. The biographic terms of this discrepancy were Lou's progressive self-identification with her father on top of her persistent denial of original separation from him. Her psychological delineation of woman, the extension of a biological wish fantasy, was itself fantastic: that woman felt no need to assert or prove herself (her fantasy woman had no call for penis-envy) blatantly reversed the truth about herself, to look no farther. In fact whenever Lou specified man's work it turned out to be her own work.

In insisting that woman is in no sense passive or even merely reactive vis-à-vis man, Lou was again arguing from the genital, not the cellular, model—to the effect of denying her same old felt deficiency. In her Freudian period she was to allow that, psychologically understood, masculine/feminine meant active/passive (in a bisexual universe)—but only to insist then that femininity was, even if passive, "positive." She was also to repudiate the whole basic approach of "Der Mensch als Weib," calling the attempt to construe psychic and somatic phenomena in the same terms unscientific: when we make it, she psychoanalytically declared, "we speak as it were with a bad conscience, uncertainly and ambiguously."[288] Yet "Der Mensch als Weib" was about the most Freudian of all her pre-Freudian works, given its

---

[8] 1913e:8 pointedly denied that the disjunction of tenderness from erotism was due to the incest taboo rather than simply to developmental need.

radical grounding of psychology on sexuality and its radical principle of a phylogenetic conservation of instincts. Beyond this, it contained its full share of psychic insights drawn from the special cases of lovers, dreamers, artists, madmen, and children (many probably at least suggested by her indirect knowledge of Freud's work)—but, oddly, no hint at any human sexuality short of the genital kind or at any mental system short of the conscious one, closer to the visceral source of rhyme and reason.[t]

Lou's nonfictional female of the species was the very antithesis of her stock fictional heroine of the preceding few years, who, just because she is emancipated (whether militantly or thoroughly), is torn between her human need for self-development, which makes her into the man's rival, and her feminine erotic need, which would make her into the man's slave: "Der Mensch als Weib" denounced both well-nigh vituperatively as false needs and morbid signs of the times.[u] In repudiating both the imitator and the idolatress of men as equally unladylike, Lou was repudiating her own youth by way of surmounting it. Her image of woman as such was her new ideal self-image —the "super-Lou" (to adapt her word on the overman as Nietzsche's "super-Nietzsche")—most lovingly drawn, as was only fitting, and posited prophetically à la Nietzsche (evolution, unctuousness, and all) for the great noonday when, following Nietzsche's advice to Lou herself, woman shall have broken free of her breaking free. But Psyche looks back even as she looks ahead: when Lou voluptuously depicted her woman's death as a curling up in soft round nudity so as to be enfolded by the power of life,[289] she was figuratively caressing that

---

[t] Lou's talk of motives penetrating into consciousness can be misleading: it meant only their going from visceral to mental. Elsewhere (e.g. 1899b) she did evince awareness that there was an unconscious mental system, though, and here she did give Nietzsche's term "sublimation" its full Freudian force. Beyond 1899a:231, 1899b in particular (below, p. 243) makes transparent reference to Freud's work, even drawing on the substance of his and Breuer's *Studies in Hysteria*. She seems not to have read these studies herself, however. Similarly, her notations of and on dreams after 1900 suggest indirect, but only indirect, knowledge of Freud's dream book.

[u] That Lou meant the dilemma to hold for all enlightened women: Stöcker, "Frauentypen," 633. As per "Mensch," however, woman's shrill cry to man, in whom she would forget herself deliriously as if possessed with a god, maiming all her faculties if only he will let her live off him parasitically, as also woman's drive to professional activity for the sake of distracting, engrossing, publicizing herself—both break her golden circle, externalize her center of gravity, unbalance her, aberrate her, reduce her to idolatry. "Manly" men shudder at both, wanting woman to affirm herself in her own realm and not lose herself on a man or a profession (1899a:242), and "the woman having the most to offer . . . because she gives out of wealth and fullness will linger far away from all that, in great collectedness of soul" (*ibid.*, 241). On Lou's fictional countermotif see above, p. 210 n. *w*.

cherished child of her fancy as her father's child in Kingdom come. Swooning over her super-Lou was decidedly masculine of her, which is another, ironic reason why the mythic creature had to be gyneomorphic and not, like femininity at large, amorphous. In fact Lou's swooning was supermasculine, for her woman as such was of the very same mold as men's divinest old spiritual-carnal dream girls such as Isis and Ishtar. Yet Lou's dream girl managed to be Mary to boot—even "between" her eternal virginity and eternal maternity "as on the first day."[290/v] Anyhow, holy or no, Lou's enchanting if unconvincing sheman would be eminently mistakable for a woman did she exist. How much more can be said for any Woman?

From the creative moment in religion, then in sex, Lou turned to that in art with her charming "Vom Kunstaffekt" (On the Artistic Affect), which followed up a clause of her rebuttal of Frieda. What is unique about artistic experience, wrote Lou, is the concentration of all one's energies whether one is producing or consuming—in tension and relaxation respectively, tending to frenzy and reverie. As a rule the producer is an ungracious consumer, though, for in the intervals between creative spells, instead of relaxing, he feels shame, impotence, despondency, listlessness, then at length "a whole inferno of self-contempt, helplessness, wounded pride, dire ennui, even desperation"[291]; he thinks of changing professions, wonders why suicide is so infrequent, sickens of everything including his future projects, which he feels no more qualified to discuss "than a valet his master's secret intentions."[292] In even his most nearly normal state he functions improperly: instead of responding to stimuli straight off, he stores his responses, which then dully press for artistic expression. He perpetually faces the same danger as do those suffering from hysteria, who can find relief from their pathogenic "undigested emotional residues of life . . . of which they have no conscious inkling"[293] only temporarily, thanks to "fortunate circumstances or a successful hypnotic treatment."[294] The artist, though, is superhealthy: he cures himself. "His seeming suffering from life is only the obverse of his power over all of life's depths"[295]: what makes him appear neurotic is the same law of extremes by virtue of which the frenzied creative mood in art and the siestalike recreative mood (the cause and the effect of purest art) meet, as both alike reunite the vital energies split up by wide-awake everyday particularized thinking, feeling, and acting. Restlessness, irritability, dejection, wistfulness on the idle artist's part signify that the worst of his waiting is past—as when a convalescent

v This last implicitly affirmed the virgin birth between the two eternities even with Joseph doing service for the Holy Ghost.

child starts misbehaving. He is not yet producing, but " 'it' " stands ready "beneath the threshold of consciousness."²⁹⁶ If even an iota of patience be left to him, this final hour of expectancy proves blissful "almost beyond compare."²⁹⁷ Radiant love and joy encircle him, illumining no object in particular at first, then one or another as if at random. He feels how kindred is all creativity—how all life would be a work of art, and all art would be life immediate and entire. And when at last he does focus on a single point of existence, it is as if he were forsaking "the great creative all-unity for a point at which to make it all come true and alive in his work.—Now he produces the work, a sum of all life in miniature, an organic whole independent of him: at bottom he produces it for himself, that it may speak to him as a remembrance of his fervid consecration. That is why all criticism of it is in such a bad way and forever runs the risk of criticizing itself. For the work can speak only to him who is correspondingly disposed toward it and in whom it arouses like remembrances."²⁹⁸ Wisdom itself cannot override an inner resistance to it, yet even a fool may postcreate it. Its value lies solely in its being "alive,"²⁹⁹ which is why, like people, it can make new friends or enemies at any time, and why it eludes all final judgment. Artistic creation and postcreation compound the mystery of life: the artist says "Live!" to lifeless matter, which then comes alive for responsive minds while remaining for others so much "paper, wood, iron, color."³⁰⁰/ʷ Here is man's "highest, ultimate doing."³⁰¹ Biologically he can engender only "inchoate, arbitrary possibilities" above which he will ever stand in his maturity, whereas his work of art is a "golden roof" atop him from first to last; "it alone is wholly life of his life, it alone the lump of clay vitalized by him and hence sacrosanct. To those of little understanding who would take it apart and dispose of it, it remains the lump of clay; only through contact with its own sort is it born to life ever anew."³⁰² And just as in Italy, between holy services, beggars nap and children play in the churches without profaning them, so this "symbol of all life waits silently from passion to passion, from prayer to prayer—and lives."³⁰³

Lou's big fault in "Vom Kunstaffekt" was to make a norm of an extreme. Authoring as frenzied gestating after agonized waiting and blissful conceiving, indeed *pre*conceiving at an annunciation of an incarnation due to surpass the feat of the Fifth Day: perhaps Lou was alone at that extreme. Many have approached it, though. Of Lou's entourage Nietzsche did especially: in Tautenburg she noted how they

---

ʷ Lou forgot sound.

were both alike "*possessed*" by their work.[304]/[x] Rainer did not as yet:
he was then still unlearning facility in Lou's school of superhealth.
He was also still learning from Lou who their spiritual as distinct
from their vocational kinsmen were: in Italy he had drawn a thick
horizontal line between artists above and mere people below. Lou
now drew thick vertical lines instead—or rather *re*drew them, for she
had called art esoterical in this sense before. She had also called it
holy even earlier, on the ground that it was produced in the same
manner as gods. She may nevertheless have been following Rainer in
now calling it both esoterical and holy at once. However, in calling
it a "highest, ultimate doing" in contradistinction to parenthood, she
was speaking quite for herself. Even Nietzsche had not exceeded "that
fearful egoism of the artist, which . . . knows itself to be justified from
and to all eternity in the 'work' just like a mother in her child."[305]
Lou as authoress never lorded it over mere mothers again, but she did
insist to the last that an artist feels his work to have been *re*ceived as
well as *con*ceived by him (in the way of her own childhood tales twice
told), to have been accomplished as much *through* as *by* him—in
brief, to have been mothered.[y] Hers was, incidentally, the trancelike mode of parturition in the case of essays and stories alike—that
is, whether she was writing thinkingly or dreamingly, and even though
once when in the throes of most exacting disquisition she noted that
she felt herself to be "traveling in a wholly different country and season (—but, I hope, only as a vacationer due to return to more home-
like fabling)."[306] And she insisted in particular (self-confessionally)
that the best "self-confessional writing," whether fictional or nonfictional, issues straight out of "the emotional-embryological act"
for the very reason that the worst merely recapitulates outer
experience.[307]

After the religious affect, the artistic affect in turn had now canceled inner personal differentiatedness, meanwhile radically diminished for women. The erotic affect was to follow, eventually betoken-
ing an end of all outer, bodily separateness in the bargain—well
beyond the mere fusion by twos that Lou, in reviewing Bölsche,

---

[x] (Also how they regarded every side emotion "as a sort of infidelity"—
which nicely qualified the possession.) Though after 1899a and 1899c Lou
styled her own writings "autumn leaves," her calendars and diaries betray
her "artistic affect" continually (see below, pp. 293ff.; also D 30 V 1906, D
15 VI 1906, etc.).
[y] 1936a—which plays on the German "*empfangen*" (receive/conceive) from
her tales twice told on up to art, but which for once distinguishes between
motherly artists ("*Empfänger*" or "*Empfangende*") and "mere masters."

had called it archaic for enjoining. Add the concordance of psychic and sexual constitution posited by "Der Mensch als Weib" and Lou had countermanded her Bölsche review straight down the line. An impulse out of earliest infancy had prevailed against the unconscious sense of her first reading of Bölsche—against her acceptance of having grown away from her father. Already that same impulse had burst forth joyously in "Erleben" (Experience), which began argumentatively by countering eudaemonism and utilitarianism on the Nietzschean ground that, as against commodious, expedient living, only intensest endeavor after one's greatest deed obviates degeneration and despair[z]—on the ground, that is, of a tacit redefinition of happiness and utility. Action and reaction, self-assertion and dedication, joy and pain—so Lou pursued—are all elementally one within such self-forgetful striving. Artistic creation typifies it, being a delayed reactive mastering of stimuli. Religion exemplifies it historically as man's progressively enlarging his sphere of confidence world-wide. Whenever men experience life most deeply, they piously give of themselves till harmony with it ensues. Thus, to that aboriginal subjective harmony recovered through intensest esperience, Lou adjoined a harmony of self and nonself due to be called likewise aboriginal on being erotized the next time round—a second mythic aboriginal embrace reduplicating the first. "Even 'God' is but a final accent on this experience," Lou concluded.[308]

Socially meanwhile Lou's winter season of 1898-1899 was uneventful, indeed eventfully so on at least October 14 with its "clear east-wind weather. Morning walk. Odds and ends. Romundt." Late in 1896 Lou's "delightful Sancho Panza"[a] (and sole informant on Rée[b]) had written her from Freiburg about some new Nietzsche business; he was apprised in return that "it lay too far from her now."[309] A year later, "after I sent her my *Eine Gesellschaft auf dem Lande*, which does her no wrong, she behaved quite strangely," Romundt complained, "and spoke mysteriously about wanting to enjoy life, which I do not think I prevented her from doing."[310] The volume was one of imaginary urbane chats on Kantian aesthetics by personae not much personalized—not even voluble Dr. Paul, "*Dr. med. et phil.*,"[311] and least of all Frau Louise, "cunning lady-friend" to all.[312] Lou sent Romundt a "farewell letter"[313]; undaunted, Romundt called on her that October day when visiting Berlin, only to learn through Andreas that "she was not to be spoken to."[314]

---

[z] "Greatest deed," which conveys Lou's meaning perfectly, is from FN, *Genealogy*, III: 7.

[a] See above, p. 165.

[b] Romundt's dear friend to the last: see Romundt→o, 8 XI 1901.

Incommunicada or no, Lou was again living almost daily with Rainer—even during his Christmas visit to Bremen and the nearby art colony of Worpswede,[c] but except for a late-winter jaunt of his to his mother in Arco, then to his father in Prague, and then to "the Vienna of Schnitzler and Loris."[315] (Through "Der Mensch als Weib," begun just after he left for Arco, Lou assured herself that, far afield as he might venture, he would come home to his mother earth "to stay alive."[316]) Frieda visited the pair in February, by which time they were already "eagerly looking forward" to a summer stay with her in Meiningen, her current residence.[317] And before the old year was out they were also planning an Easter trip to Russia with Andreas.[318] "It is now settled," wrote Rainer to his junior Lou, Elena, early in March,[319] and on April 22 to Frieda: "I have equipped myself with a string of introductions. . . . Maybe we shall even get to see Leo Tolstoi."[320]

Three days later Lou was off for Moscow with her two men and her poodle. Arriving the afternoon of April 27, they put up beside the Kremlin and that same evening visited the outdoor market and climbed the great bell tower. The next morning, while Lou "rummaged and wrote," while Andreas was "scalded steam-bathing," and while the poodle committed some "misdeed," Rainer presented himself to Leonid Pasternak, professor of painting at the Moscow Art School[321]—and sure enough, thanks to Pasternak, who was Tolstoi's portraitist, that very evening he and the Andreases were at Tolstoi's winter house. Evidently Lou carried the conversation; Rainer, unable to follow, made up for it in his letters afterwards with panegyrics on Tolstoi, "the 'eternal Russian.'"[322] Then came Easter: the three tourists spent much of the morning in the Kremlin church, much of the afternoon with Pasternak and the sculptor Prince Troubetzkoy, then half the night in the Kremlin again—the occasion for many a later commemorative exchange of the Russian hosanna "Christ is risen" between Rainer and Lou. The next three days, while Lou nursed a cold and then packed, her husband and lover together took in the local monasteries, churches, pastry shops, and points between; she was up to only the Alexander garden, the Tretyakov gallery, the Romanov house, the Church of the Savior, and again the Kremlin. At 1:00 AM on May 3 the party left for Petersburg in a crowded train beneath a rainbow.

There they were met in falling snow by a column of Lou's relatives, her mother (then seventy-six) foremost—"Mushka!" she wrote sim-

---

[c] The artist Heinrich Vogeler, whom Rilke had met in Florence, was his host. RMR, *Tagebücher*, 235, mentions the Worpswede "music room. You know it . . ."

ply. The Andreases lodged with Mushka, Rainer at a pension. "Rainer at Elena's," Lou noted repeatedly beginning on the morrow. Rainer would see Elena in her rooms—"again at our hour, between 8 and 9"[323]—to talk "endlessly" of Russian culture and his literary projects,[324] writing to her between times. Soon he grew tender and talked instead of his hell within—after a whole year's manly, worldly stance toward her on paper. "We have gone through it again, dear Elena," he wrote on May 10. "Already I was fearful lest my complaining dampen our holiday, but your dear, friendly letter makes it clear that the sense of these holy days of ours is now first fulfilled: in your giving and my dark neediness." To top it off he was sorely under the weather, the days having turned hot while the nights remained freezing.[325] Whatever Elena's first impulse, she evidently lacked true feeling for "this new form of our beauty," as Rainer called it: she just was not Lou. "Elena's cancellation, Rainer here," noted Lou for May 12. Thereafter he joined the Andreases more and more frequently as they saw sights and Salomés. He replaced his visits to Elena with fond poetic letters to her in which he pretended not to notice their estrangement. On May 18 he told her that he was unexpectedly obliged to be back in Berlin by June. Lou noted a last "Rainer at Elena's" for May 23: Elena thereupon left for Finland. Rainer kept up the correspondence until the following September, when he sent finest good wishes to her on her betrothal.[326/d] He meanwhile celebrated his homecoming to Lou by three days alone with her in Moscow[e] in and around the Kremlin—especially listening to its bells, which pealed to the two straight from mother Russia's soul. "In these days I feel that Russian things will give me names for those most frighted pieties of mine which ever since childhood have been yearning to enter into my art," Rainer wrote Frieda,[327] and Lou was to tell Ellen after returning to Germany: "This time I brought away deep impressions drawing me back to Russia. There one finds worlds of feeling and thought having little of Western culture about them, perhaps destined to complete it someday deeply and humanly."[328] Nonetheless, back in Petersburg the two turned cultured and cosmopolitan again as they toured the galleries and museums, meeting Westward-looking artists and writers between times.[f] Lou also spent much time alone with her family—especially with Caro, who accom-

[d] In 1925 Rilke had a reunion (just one) with Elena, then an émigrée in Paris.

[e] 26-28 v 1899 (they took the night train both ways).

[f] Before their Moscow jaunt they had already met the Naturalist painter Ilya Repin (18 v 1899), then the translator Friedrich Fiedler (23 v 1899)—their go-between for Drojjin in 1900.

panied her on a sentimental journey to Peterhof one whole day. Without Lou, her two men haunted the Hermitage together except for one excursion "to the islands."[329] On June 17 the trio left for Danzig, arriving the next morning for four days of outings with Johanna Niemann; then the Andreases returned to Schmargendorf with the poodle, leaving Rainer behind for a few days at Johanna's.

Lou's days without Rainer all went in vain attempts at working, except for a couple of visits from Endell (in from Munich), some reading, and a brief review of a medley of essays by Ellen Key, which she pronounced a poor second to their authoress in person.[g] Ellen later pleaded mistranslation,[330] and Lou rejoined that she had of late lost the knack of reviewing[331]—a falsehood. Rainer arrived on June 28, and the next day a strict double regimen of Russian studies commenced, with Lou as Rainer's Volinsky. A respite was called when on July 27 Lou joined Frieda, already installed for the summer "in an old Gothic house with an old park in the country atop a mountain"[332]—Bibersberg near Meiningen. Lou's "disciple," as Frieda styled Rilke,[333] followed in two days, and the regimen resumed on a bucolic basis: "much milk and eggs,"[334] barefoot walking, berry-picking, reading on the meads and "in lovely spots."[335] "Barefoot. Rainer and I living only each other too much," Lou noted once at the start of August,[336/h] and once at the end: "Work and oats. The days too short for us!"[337] Frieda later concurred bitterly: "I had precious little of Lou and Rainer those six weeks together. After their lengthy Russian trip (with Mr. Lou) in the spring, they had pledged themselves body and soul to Russian studies, so all day long with phenomenal zeal they conned language, literature, art history, world history, cultural history of Russia,[i] as if they had to prepare for some frightful exam. Then when we met for meals they would be too exhausted for any stimulating talk."[338] Lou sang another song to Frieda years afterwards: "The tragedy of your life has been nervous affliction, the joy of my life simply health, with the rest, whatever its substance, mere words to the melody. I remember Bibersberg: there you often became unrecognizable to me, physically like someone else, *without* my changing toward you at heart in the slightest: only had I been estranged over just that would I have changed. You were not yourself. The cause lay in health—in a nervous pressure transforming you. In such cases please *always believe me*; I too can be disgustingly selfish and cold, but then I don't hide it; that you did not believe me

[g] 1899e. (Lou found Ellen's psychological analyses—especially that of Maeterlinck—best, her preaching individualism to the masses worst.)
[h] The line looks post-added, though: cf. below, p. 301.
[i] Frieda's enumeration checks perfectly against Lou's calendars.

shakes me so."[339] The nervous pressure on Frieda had grown since 1896, when the Reichstag began its stormy disciplinary proceedings against Carl Peters for cruelty to African indigenes: Peters, now an irate self-exile in England except when appealing the verdict against him or prospecting for King Solomon's mines, was giving Frieda more call to suffer for him—and less opportunity to resist. And Lou did take time out in Bibersberg to read Loris and Ricarda Huch, Ruskin and Conrad Ferdinand Meyer. On September 11 she even began work on a new novel—and was at it again "diligently" on the morrow when word came from Andreas that the poodle was deathly ill. "Howls. Packing. Excitement."[340] She traveled back home with Rainer that night, arriving at 7:00 AM to find the poodle "better."[341] She spent two days beside it, working on her novel; then after a restless night it died, and "toward ten in the evening the three of us buried her with her things in her little basket in her woods by moonlight."[342] Well before she had finished mourning she was again busily writing, and by late October she was able to tell Ellen that a novella "linking up with a subject we discussed orally—a mother who grows beyond love of husband and child into what is religiously highest—is almost finished."[343] It was finished early in January and called *Ma*.

Ma is a long-widowed mother who, after her two daughters have grown away from her, refuses a marriage proposal for fear of a final estrangement from them. Lou later gave the didactic sense of the story to within a crucial nuance when she declared that woman's "one cultural act" is "the child" and that "though she bears the child as a part of herself, then tenderly identifies herself with it as long as possible, . . . she is really drawn out of herself for the first time as this warm egoism grows into a confrontation with a second person, an other, a world outside herself, which she has given forth from out of her deepest depths."[344] Ma, though, will not relinquish her children[j] in this second, moral sense: passing up the chance for a happiness of her own, she clings to her identity as a mother whose children have grown away from her. Ma in her glory is precisely *not* that "highest image of woman . . . the mother at the cross: she who sacrifices what she bore, who gives her son away to his work—to the world and to death."[345] Ma is rather Lou herself, Ma's children "those I might have had" (to quote Lou out of context)[346/k]—only in this wish fantasy Lou did have the children physically, besides holding on to them morally forever. (While writing *Ma* Lou appropriately asked Ellen:

[j] Particularly not her *second* child.
[k] Cf. below, p. 496; also above, p. 226 n. *p* (especially the last quotation) in conjunction with p. 250 n. *j*.

"Don't you too sometimes have the feeling that we really do not mean books at all when we write them?"[347]) Ma's daughters were Lou roughly as she had been at just over and under twenty respectively—a somewhat mannish feminist in Berlin and a somewhat sickly prospective student in Switzerland. Both love their mother well enough, but just do not want her around their necks. Ma is correspondingly Lou's real mother in turn: Lou made up to saintly Ma for her sins of youth against Mushka. Superficially, Ma was perhaps one Emma Olga von Mohl as well, for years later Lou maintained that "the story . . . arose out of an amorous conversation with Madame von Mohl in which I thought of myself as a man (Tomasow): the whole point was to make Ma into this lovable object, and the deadliest critique of the book would be one proving Ma unlovable: she was meant to entice."[348] The conversation was probably apocryphal,[l] but Ma's patient suitor Tomasow was indeed Lou as man, his principal function being to adore Lou as woman down the years. Succeeding Ma's dead husband,[m] he was also the virtually superfluous male of "Der Mensch als Weib": he counsels her on occasion. And Dr. Tomasow was Zemek: when Ma seeks to explain herself on a walk with him ("you are ever and ever my best, only, dearest friend—")[349] he wryly turns her over to an acquaintance of her younger daughter Sophie's chancing by, the aspirant poet Hugo Lanz, who then rises to poet in the making[n] upon beholding the sacrificial mother triumphant—from the heights of the Kremlin, to the sound of Christmas bells.[o] For Ma, a Russian of German stock widowed in Italy, has raised her girls in Moscow. And the time of the narrative is Christmas—by the Russian calendar, with atmosphere and accessories to match, all exquisitely rendered. The characterizations, perforce less Russian, likewise come off singularly well, the subsidiary ones included—notably Lou's cousin Emma as Ma's sister and foil Ottilie, who, despite her romantic bent in youth, has turned out to be an insufferably level-headed wife and mother. With *Ma*, as befitted the psychological sense of it, Lou began turning back toward her youth and childhood for overt fictional materials. Except for the foolishness that was its *raison d'être*—except

[l] Lou said it took place "in long Schmargendorf walks in the woods" (D VI 1917), whereas she had visited Emma von Mohl in Petersburg, once alone and once with Rilke. (*Ma* was dedicated to Emma von Mohl.)

[m] The husband, an artist, is identifiable as Heinrich Vogeler through an etching by him in Ma's possession (which was one by Vogeler in Lou's possession) and through his sojourn in Italy, etc.; I have no clue, though, as to why Lou saw herself as Vogeler's wife.

[n] (Also child and man in the making.)

[o] Lou may well have seen Zemek shortly before or even after her Russian trip (on which she bought shoes for Broncia: D 29 IV 1899).

that Ma was adorable beyond all adorability, or that her human transcendence was humanly defeating—*Ma* might well have been great; for by sheer story-telling, without overt didactics, it fathoms a nearly universal womanly experience nearly universally neglected by novelists, that of motherhood with its renunciative issue (Lou being perhaps the sole exception to *both* near-universals). It was hardly more praised than blamed in its time, with Ma herself most maligned.[p]

At work on *Ma*, Lou declared herself "as ever very happy in the total stillness and solitude," adding: "I do not go into town at all."[350] That stillness and solitude included Rainer, absent only for a brief Christmas visit to Prague. He was painlessly productive for a change[351]—mostly of "monk's songs" (the first part of his *Book of Hours*), which Lou greeted discriminatively one by one; but also, one stormy night, of the martial *Cornet*, which registered his Nietzsche-style fantasy of noble descent; and all along of a whole diary-load of notations for poems, plays, and stories, with personal bits in between. One of these reads in full: "So without suspecting it I came around to your feeling in this. And what I might have written here I now told you, as I much prefer doing."[352] And another: "If God gave a law, it runs: be solitary from time to time. For He can come only to one" (did he pause here?) "or to two whom He can no longer tell apart."[353/q] Meanwhile he attended courses dutifully, and early in December he noted: "These past days I devoted wholly to my Russian, long enough neglected already."[354] New Year's Day he even helped with the Andreases' heating and cooking: "We had a good laugh," noted Lou.[355/r] Out of these happiest days with Rainer came Lou's grand and grisly "Gedanken über das Liebesproblem" (Thoughts on the Problem of Love). In her fiction she had often told in a low key of why girls in love are in for sorrow; now on a note of thanksgiving she argued that true love between the sexes can hardly last—and that in fact there is little betweenness about it in the first place.

By Lou's account, everyone—be he hard or soft, selfish or selfless —displays both of the two contrasting tendencies to amass and to

---

[p] Platzhoff, "Ma," called it "a new disappointment" from Lou, yet lauded all the characterizations except that of Ma; Eloesser (1901) took it out ironically on the closing pages, "where the aureole over the portrait of this *mater dolorosa* glows resplendently, to be sure, but somewhat gainsays our earthliness." Ma and *Ma* both fared better among later surveyors of contemporary letters (e.g. Heuss, Soergel) before being forgotten.

[q] Was this Lou's cue for 1900a:1021-22 (below, p. 256)?

[r] D X-XII 1899 are missing.

bestow goods, in effect to assert and to surrender himself. Indeed, neither tendency could have its way altogether, for to acquire certain things one must open oneself to them, and to go on giving one needs reserves. The two may even "interact at bottom somewhere, somehow, as if yet another secret longing underlay both: . . . the individual's longing to attain to the whole of life around him—to enter into it, become filled with it,"[356] so that egoist and Samaritan, expropriator and participator, the domineering and the submissive alike "stammer the same prayer to the same god" for whom "self-love and self-forgetfulness mix indistinguishably. For 'I want to have everything' and 'I want to be everything' is . . . the same passionate demand,"[357] no more to be satisfied the one way than the other.

A third affective relationship, erotic love, "seems to have its roots way down below, just where the other two come apart—where man first emerges from darkest primal longing to confront the world"[358]; in it the other two mix in wondrous contradiction as the lover feels that he is coming into full possession of himself but also passing beyond himself into all of life. In sexual love, exact opposites most naturally come together—genetic opposites in the sex act and ambivalent feelings on either side of it. Likewise, love's passion thrives on unfamiliarity and lapses as its object ceases to signify "alien possibilities"[359]; a "long period of fervent sympathy"[360] may follow, but that is something else, and then precisely what once charmed the lovers about their heterogeneity will vex them instead. A lover's total claim on his beloved, a passionate self-seeking, conjoins with equally impassioned well-wishing and "overprizing"[361]; lovers' egos do not conjoin in kinship but rather concentrate, through climactic awareness of mutual differences, to the point of overflowing onto each other in "productive release"[362]; satisfied lovers feel like world-conquerors for having mated with the quintessence of otherness, just as biologically each sex most affirms itself in conjoining with the other. Thus the supremely individualistic and the supremely social impulse flow "undifferentiated in the deep dark basic form of erotism,"[363] whence each of these two so different "emotional worlds"[364] originally derives.

Another running adult distinction of ours to be dissolved erotically is the one between mind and body. Ordinarily we pay our bodily processes small heed beyond acknowledging that they underlie our mental ones. The erotic affect, however, even while filling our soul with ideal illusions, makes us "brutally, ineluctably"[365] aware of their bodily source. And yet such is the force of this distinction between body and mind that we instinctively strive to subsume the whole phenomenon love under the one head or the other. Here even the ex-

tremes—rhapsodical and cynical—both command assent for all the
rough contrast between them, which is the rougher since the physiological incentive, as specialized and localized as any, yet excites the
whole physical and psychic apparatus as no other can. Shame over
sex may arise not only from inexperience or out of early moral instruction but spontaneously as, from a total personal involvement,
love passes over into a specialized bodily performance, as if body
were of a sudden intruding as "a third party."[366] For erotic stimulus is
indivisibly psychic *and* corporeal; before two bodies and two minds
conjoin, each lover's mind, rather aloof from his body otherwise,
joins it in its every innervation in a reunion of "sudden, elemental
might."[367] Such body-soul embrace is "the true manifestation"[368] of
love's bliss; it reinvigorates the lover like "a divine miracle-bath"[369];
it is what makes even hapless love happy. The joy of requital is really
a "joy of reduplication, as over an echo—astonished delight as what
is out there returns our cry of jubilation."[370] Ever more "inventive"[371]
in sending out our soul's tender secrets and receiving them back,
overpraising our beloved yet understating our own love, we believe
ourselves to be all wrapped up in him when we are really all wrapped
up in ourselves within "a thousandfold aloneness"[372] that contains
him only as a dream contains a sound or scent that sets it off. Our
mind turns inward like a seer's as our lips discourse unwontedly
through a smile of childlike surprise; or else it looks out naïvely and
trustingly upon a fresh, genuine, "improbably glorious world."[373]

Mental creation requires just such intense reunifying of all our
faculties and drives, just such renewed vital contact with "the darkest,
most secret springs of our being"[374] as derives from the erotic affect
alone (in contrast to mere bodily lust, however refined). New lovers
falsify their everyday selves without affectation or vanity, even with
some embarrassment, as out of love's inherent need each strives to
conform to the other's fanciful image of him. For love must be admitted decorously through its very own ornate portal and lived out
in its own stylized manner for its rich poetic contents to be absorbed—
for the lovers to charm each other into creative self-concentration
and self-release in all walks of life, even while meeting psychically
only the way they fuse physically: at a single "deep stimulation point
that releases everything in them productively."[375] Similarly, only select
aspects of things strike an artist's lyric or pictorial fancy, but then
those aspects become for him in his "grateful, surging overvalua-
tion"[376] everything that has ever stirred him; they seem to enter into
him or he into them, "which is the same psychic process"[377]; they are
but the occasions for his creative act, though their sovereignty is

"most potently clear"[378] to him just when he would make most personal use of them.[s]

Art is at bottom the same imperious, joyous, creative impulse as love. Both are transient yet experienced as if timeless, like "all such mighty outbursts of ourselves."[379] Between times, artists and lovers resume the fragmentary relations and partial activities of normal, sensible life, using their capacities for art or love, if at all, without inner necessity, hence without that "consummate homecoming to themselves."[380/t] They would do better to wait—even though, hellish as such waiting may prove, no act of the will or understanding can foreshorten it. Because of a misunderstanding, lovers suffer even more over such transiency than need be: whereas the painter does not take his version of his subject to be a mere documentary replica of it, the lover does just that—with his subject's complicity. After the inevitable let-down, his passion must accommodate itself to the ordinary demands of life if it is to survive at all. Life and love, henceforth separate, make distressing concessions to each other: love relinquishes its festive garment and stance in return for some extra honeymoon time. In truth, though, "the beloved, even when his impassioned lover lent him such sweet names and seemed to be dreaming of him alone, was not, as he liked to fancy, the content, the goal, the center of that erotic state, but only its stimulus,"[381] peripheral to his lover's "center of being"[382] from the first, "condemned to indirect effect."[383] Nor can it ever be otherwise—and indeed, such self-absorption and self-unfolding is precisely the "greatest blessing"[384] of erotic love, which leaves it to other, paler sentiments "to curtail one self for another's sake."[385] Love will retain its rightful glory only so long as the beloved is used as fire-kindler and not hearth—or better, is used as the lover's point of juncture with "the otherwise unreachable 'outside,'" as the "medium through which life speaks to him with sudden wondrous eloquence, as if with angels' tongues."[386] "Love means knowing of someone whose hue things must take on if they are not to impress us as strange and frightful, or cold and hollow."[387/u] Many a love song celebrates the beloved as the whole of Being—fluttering leaf and glistening beam of light, "transformer of all things transformed into all things."[388] Nothing threatens love more than a straining to live up to such fond fancies so as to be more substantially at one with love's fool: in the long run, one can be lovable only by re-

[s] For the parallel case of the lover, Lou meant to write "the sovereignty of the beloved object is most mightily clear to us," but actually wrote "the sovereignty of the beloved resistance . . ." (*"Widerstand"* for *"Gegenstand"*).

[t] Literally: "to ourselves."

[u] Perhaps the loveliest definition of love ever given.

maining "wholly oneself,"[389] not by engaging in "anxious bilateral adjustment and attrition"[390] or embarking upon "that whole course of endless reciprocal concession."[391]

Such mutual tolerance of mutual parasitism is the more nefarious the more developed are the parties to it: not infrequently when one "half"[392] dies the other will emerge astonished from blackest mourning into "a wonderful late second blossoming" of his or especially her "repressed, almost forgotten real nature."[393] For even perfectly adapted "halves,"[394] existence is always "narrow and bad on both sides."[395] "They say 'we' instead of 'I,' "[396] but soon the "we" does not carry much more weight than either "I"; they have lovers' memories and desires, but all the charming novelties of their love have lapsed into "deathly trivialities"[397]; after having feasted on each other, they consume each other—"with much shyly hushed hunger."[398] They know each other too well for passion: passion rules out any perceptive " 'getting acquainted' "[399] in favor of evasion and illusion. Fundamentally frivolous, true lovers cherish each other through the years as congenial mysteries, and this only gradually "with an air of expertness"[400]—even into old age, when their erotic frenzy lives on as an intimate "memory companion" in their love's abode, whose first chamber it had occupied. Around this chamber "high walls and snug work-corners and broad balconies"[401] were gradually built; now aged and faded, it still contains sundry wonderful odds and ends from way back "at the sight of which old people smile so distinctly. 'Do you remember?' they say to each other at the sight of them, then sit down to muse over them. Soon the remembrance is like one out of childhood—as distant already and just as innocent, just as immeasurably deep."[402] The mystery of such love, which seasons rather than spoils, is that "two are at one only when they remain two."[403]

Amour-passion, with its threat of personal impoverishment, has gone out of fashion in recent times, as if in evidence that men of old were "more sure of their less complicated inner life and, especially, less aware of its nervous complications"[404]—and even though, following the increasing differentiation of individual life, people meet far more easily nowadays, with quieter signs of recognition and softer greetings. On the other hand, less was required of each experience within the bonds of traditional fidelity than is today, when lovers know that they never " 'possess' "[405] each other but only win or lose each other at every moment. Hence passionate love has become more difficult to demarcate from mere amorousness, even though there is less indifference than ever about *whom* one loves and *how*: whereas formerly even the most sterile relationship could draw lifelong sustenance from its supposed divine sanction, nowadays a relatively rich and deep one that is recognized as not providing all that love can provide may be given up sooner than was a typical old-style liaison. Such recognition, while cruel, also comes of "seriousness about life,"[406] for, wherever love would be more than a "sensual or sentimental pastime," each lover will tend to "experience everything through the medium of the other" and to become the other's "beloved, spouse, sibling, parent, friend, comrade, playmate, stern judge, compassionate angel" all at once.[407] While we are pleased not to fuse physically *in toto* and then fall apart into children the way amoebae do, we are emotionally and morally partial to the "amoeba standpoint"[408] in love, as if psychic evolution had lagged far behind organic; otherwise we would want no more from love mentally and physically than to become fruitful through contact, the way an artist does without losing his identity in that which sets his fantasy going. But just as artistic fantasy work remains merely that, for all its pretension to encompass the whole of existence, so does the erotic process remain such, whatever vital forces it may activate.

Erotism can be as much falsified by physiologizing as it can by moralizing or aestheticizing: its unique function is to heal the breach between bodily and mental impetus. Sovereign, it harbors contradictions: thus one may feel erotic attraction together with personal disinclination, or even the full fertilizing, vivifying effect of love at loggerheads with one's better judgment. "We speak of a struggle between love and scorn and, oddly, expect any decent fellow to surmount his passion without further ado—though no one, not even he, may suspect what gods are fighting for his heart and which way lies the heavier renunciation, the graver curtailment."[409] For by and large we are all less compatible with those with whom we fall in love than with those to whom we otherwise incline—as we readily perceive in the case of others. Thus after someone's physique (his gait, bearing, smile, voice) has aroused a passion, his psyche may turn out to speak "quite another language,"[410] as if it were someone else's. The physique, the "more conservative power,"[411] may be a heritage "from ages back"[412] or the relic of a childhood "inwardly buried,"[413] bespeaking a person no longer there. Since all true passion fixes on the outer as a token for the inner person, the result is a conflict as tragic as that between love and scorn. In our instinctive erotic wisdom we rightly see the body as the unmistakable be-all-and-end-all, on which "no line is writ in vain,"[414] so that without sensual crudity we may be forever ravished by a neckline or discomfited by a vocal timbre. But the body may, like light from a dead star, betoken a reality wholly transcended, so that we love what both is and is not. Typically, a little of this tragicality inheres in all erotic love with its bondage to the body. If only because erotic love attaches exclusively to "what has as it were acquired bodily symbols,"[415] lovers can meet at best only most indirectly, on the ground of such physical disclosures, out of which for each of them "a shiny image of the other shapes up productively"[416]: thus it is easier to go on loving someone who suffers disfigurement than to fall in love with someone already disfigured. Love clings to the body as a symbol for the whole person, and to that symbol the lover's whole person responds. Accordingly, even the most fortunate lover's lot is deepest solitude within deepest intimacy. And only as such a secret tragedy can love exert its potent, fertile effect. The lover cannot live directly out of that subsoil of life where opposites all avail unsundered without feeling both joy and torment in "their mysterious unison, for what befalls him there lies not only beyond all onesidedness, all rifts between selfish and selfless, sensual and spiritual, but likewise beyond all painstakingly secured contentment. . . . Only the man who creates knows that joy and anguish are one and the same in all the intensest experiences of life. But long before him a man in love stretched out his hands in prayer to a star without considering whether he prayed for joy or for sorrow."[417]

"Gedanken über das Liebesproblem" must be read to be believed —in Lou's original, with its rich, beguiling texture of intricate logic. In intellectual intensity amidst lyrical extensity, it is a match for any prose from either sex, "Der Mensch als Weib" notwithstanding—and even though here again the argument was not worth the argumentation. The big trouble with it was just like that with her theory of worship: who can *knowingly* love a phantasm? That love images were phantasmal she knew from Nietzsche's conflict between love for the Lou of Orta and scorn for the Lou of Jena: her essay reversed his option. She had fictionalized the point already with Hans and with Erwin, who each loved someone who was not—a reversal of Beer-Hofmann's contention that she was idealizing him.[v] Her experience was otherwise, with Nietzsche and Beer-Hofmann inclusive: she saw strikingly straight even while swooning. Although she declared midway that her essay was no "exhortation to ever-deepening isolation for all who would do well by love,"[418] it is just that. In time she extended the exhortation to cover "being friends," which she said meant "sharing reciprocal solitude *in order* to deepen it. . . . *Friend* means, then, pro-

[v] "Liebesproblem" implicitly condemns Alex for denouncing Hans's illusion as well as Anjuta for playing along with Erwin's. (For the biographical referent in the second case as against the first, see below, pp. 434-35 n. *q*.)

tector against ever losing solitude in anything whatever—*himself in-cluded.*[419] Given her Bibersberg complaint that she and Rainer were "living each other too much," it follows that she was exhorting *her-self* in the first instance[w]: "Gedanken über das Liebesproblem" ex-pounded an ideal to be realized thereafter. Exhorting herself, she re-peated herself over the years, notably in aligning lover and artist as both sensually excited by their mind's creation unto fusion with "all-unity" in a so-called rehearsal of dying.[420/x] Her opposition to the "amoeba standpoint" vis-à-vis the beloved[421] was her single abiding point of fidelity to her Bölsche review. On that point she committed a fault of reasoning: because physical and mental love are "the two sides of one and the same process," she wrote, it is unnatural for lov-ers to desire more mental intercourse than matches the local physical fact—even though they do.[422] She did uphold the "amoeba stand-point" meanwhile for the *inner* process of love, despite a fine dis-cussion of inhibited love[423] sufficient to refute it. She had corre-spondingly reversed her conjugal ideal in the ten years since her Ibsen book, when its first principle had been reciprocal disclosure and rec-ognition, its highest reward intimacy. And yet her model for the dura-ble erotic relationship, now grounded in reciprocal espousal of il-lusions and refusal of concessions, was again her own ménage, again wishfully reconstructed as regards its central fact—formerly "marital duties," now love's "first chamber." Nonwishfully, just as the mutual seclusion attendant on love was virtually physical as well as moral in her text, so was the payoff: "Two are at one only when they stay two." The promise of consummation implicit in her old (Ibsenite) formula was implicitly kept by her new one—in tacit recognition that it would never be kept otherwise. She no less avoided the word *mar-riage* in her essay on love so as not to change the subject.

According to "Gedanken über das Liebesproblem" as against the Bölsche review, erotism induced momentary functional unity instead of momentarily stunting the nonerotic faculties. With this change of heart, Lou was beginning to shift allegiance from rationality to in-stinct, with due rationalization. She continued to reprove psychic fusion by twos as retrograde, only to urge a self-absorption instead that meant self-surrender to an innermost craving for coalescence with the cosmos. This program was yet more regressive in that its instinctual end was the narcissism anterior to object-love: years

[w] Correspondingly, her lovers' "homecoming to themselves" (above, p. 255) was their love-making—the very reverse of her usage in her own case.

[x] She even averred that artists die easier than nonartists for that very rea-son (D 16 I 1904). Further, D 29 VI 1906 and 1909b:25 echo "Liebesproblem" on how what at first delected her in a lover irritated her at last; etc.

ahead of Freud, she expounded its two terms of give and take, undifferentiated at the source—its "double direction," as she later put it[424]—with nearly as much science as art. In her view, the narcissist standard was set by the plant, which draws its nutriment from the common subsoil while blossoming out to the universe at large until at length it outgrows its individuality. Rilke took up the standard in turn, imagery inclusive—he who, more than even Lou herself, was resolutely rootless to the last. Lou's premise was young Nietzsche's: the conflict within us between the "*principium individuationis*" and "our innermost being and common substratum."[425] Her narcissist view was nonetheless her very own on the psychological inside—and Beer-Hofmann's on the cosmological outside.

In 1898 Beer-Hofmann's exquisite lullaby "Schlaflied für Mirjam" had appeared; it sang of his daughter's blood bond with the Jews—whereupon Lou, already an authority on Volinsky's Russia, began discovering her spiritual bond with the Russians.[y] Late in 1899 Rainer picked up an advance printing of the conclusion to Beer-Hofmann's *Der Tod Georgs* (Georg's Death) alias *Der Götterliebling*, "and," he noted, "I hardly like to set it down. I hold on to it as to a letter."[426] Perhaps Lou acquired one of her own; in any event the book itself was soon in her hands. When early in March the author sent her a copy—a first gesture since their falling out—she replied: "I have read from it daily since its appearance, all filled with a great joy. Never did I believe there was anything so beautiful!"[427] She was to reread it year after year: "It is as if this book becomes the more beautiful the longer one possesses it," she once noted.[428] She later recast its message in the idiom of her essay on love: "Beer-Hofmann imparts not only the sensations of a soul's sucking up and containing everything, but also the deeper experience of its realization that it in turn is entwined with everything, belongs to everything."[429/z] Then again: through Georg's death Paul "matures unto feeling that 'to live' is not to arrogate all things to oneself for pleasurable use, but rather to enter into their being, give oneself to them, linking what has been with what is to be."[430] For by then Lou was playing off the one term of that innermost drive against the other: like Zarathustra, she was preaching the "bestowing virtue" against "sickly egoism"[431]—like Zarathustra, against *herself.*[a] She was to carry this option forward

---

[y] Lou→EK, 29 X 1899, contains her earliest hint at this discovery; she was then writing *Ma*, which quotes the "Schlaflied" to render Ma's sorrow at the moral loss of her daughters (1899f:179). As of Lou→EK, 22 IV 1900, she felt "far more at home" with Russians than Germans; etc. On Jew=Russian for Lou, see above, p. 189 n. *h.*

[z] She was here comparing him with d'Annunzio.

[a] See above, p. 102.

into psychoanalysis in favor of a selfless "protonarcissism" distinguished from selfish narcissism proper.[b]

Beer-Hofmann's cosmic idea meanwhile gave intellectual licence to the cosmic pathos already hers. His idea was that of an ineluctable running involvement of all things, selves included; her pathos was an exultant pseudorecollection and pseudoanticipation of coalescence with the cosmos through reciprocal absorption. Beer-Hofmann's Paul also brought intense feeling to that idea in that he thought it for dear life—this, however, as if his thinking himself to be utterly involved in all things would obviate his becoming any further involved in them after death. For Lou too the involvement was of this life—indeed, exhilaratingly—but not accessible to consciousness except in instants of ecstasy: hence death was a release.[c] Paul acquired a continuing sense of participation in a continuum; Lou, however, felt acute tension between self and nonself except where the two overlapped (where, say, in starvation "my stomach" becomes all "I," or in dieting "my hunger" becomes all "it") and except when they of a sudden enfolded each other voluptuously—auspiciously. Out of intellectual scruple, she spoke of her afterlife tryst only with subtle equivocation. Beer-Hofmann for his part used fine irony to keep his own distances from Paul's resurrection: just as "*a* thought cast a bond around" things in "Das Kind," so in *Der Tod Georgs* that thought brought Paul "peace and comfort. As if a sturdy hand lay appeasingly on his right hand, guiding him; as if he felt its strong pulse beat. But what he felt was only his own blood throbbing."[432/d]

Emotively as Lou intoned Beer-Hofmann's idea, she abstracted from his sensorial imagery. So did his authoritative interpreter, Erich Kahler, who maintained that, through Georg's death, Paul attains to "recognition of man's boundless involvement with everything surrounding him, everything from which he derives and into which he issues, unintentional, inescapable involvement through the laws of an all-embracing fate"[433/e]—which reads uncannily like Lou's own late prose on the order of her words ascribing to her experience of God(!) "the most positive thing known to my life: a decisive basic sensation of boundless community of fate with everything that is."[434] Incidentally, much as that community meant to Beer-Hofmann and

[b] To be sure, the protonarcissism was selfish too by dint of the law of undifferentiated opposites, its supreme statute—only each time Lou said so she managed to make the selfishness selfless and not vice versa. (See below, pp. 340ff.)

[c] And not a "dispatch" as for Beer-Hofmann: below, p. 263.

[d] Cf. 1913e:13: below, p. 556.

[e] Kahler sees this as Beer-Hofmann's chief literary theme.

Lou, it meant little otherwise. According to this little, the universe, material and spiritual, was a closed metabolic system in which all identities except its own were . . . well, *transient* is the word, and both did say it, but somehow they always made it sound like a synonym for *abiding*. Either way, it remains that intimations are no evidence of how the universe works.

Lou clearly saw the cosmic bond as an antidote to the fear of death —in Beer-Hofmann's case. " 'Death,' " the "intimate life circumstance" for all Jews, was such for Beer-Hofmann par excellence, she wrote in 1910. A mere kill-joy in "Das Kind," she pursued, "it firms spiritually in *Der Tod Georgs* as first in a dream he tastes the whole hard fact of it, and as then the hard fact expands to take in the reality of dreaming—as Being and Nonbeing merge. In *Der Graf von Charolais* [1904] the initial significance of the blood bond reemerges (after the lullaby): the eternal, the consoling—only by now, an all-encompassing ring, it has come to encircle even mental life. The leitmotiv of all his work: 'Not to die, Romont, not to die!'[f] turns into rebirth in the All-Being, deeper than for the non-Jew because more consciously experienced. Death is already behind him, suffered through: he is resurrected!"[435] As if this were not self-identification enough with Beer-Hofmann as Jesus, Lou later likened his creation of *Jaákobs Traum* with God's own Creation as per all scriptures.[436] More, she repaid him for his idea, which she introjected, with her motives, which she projected: she saw guilt behind his fear of death[437] and surmised incest behind the guilt.[438] Or rather, she detected his guilt, for it was an extreme equivalent to hers: it was guilt over prenatal incest, with his mother's death on bearing him construed as a penalty.[g] For no apparent reason, Paul feels the same responsibility for his friend Georg's death in the novel as for his child's in the short story. In fact he experiences Georg's death dreamingly as that of a strange yet familiar woman: the author's mother. Disculpating providence, Paul disculpates himself: ". . . what seemed injustice was only

---

[f] From the close of *Charolais* ("*Ich geh*' . . . *nicht sterben, Romont, nicht sterben*").

[g] In *Charolais* the father is smitten with his daughter, aptly named Désirée, even before her birth—this romance being a transposition of Beer-Hofmann's with his mother. Désirée's father arranges a match for her with Charolais. She commits adultery. Charolais torments her—and as he does so, "hotter than for her body is his craving 'to flee from myself into her' almost as into a maternal haven when 'the fear born with all creatures' comes upon him" (1905a:288): thus Charolais was Beer-Hofmann as bereaved infant. Charolais delivers Désirée up to the guilty father to be condemned to death: Beer-Hofmann's birth. Beer-Hofmann's substitution of daughter for mother had well withstood Lou's charms; Lou, however, declared Désirée's fate to be woman's generally (*ibid.*, 289).

the knot into which just fates, life-weaving, had tied themselves."[439] His self-reassurance is measureless: "No wrong could befall him, pains were no rejection, death did not sever him from things. For, necessarily and indispensably wedded to everything, deeds were perhaps offices, suffering dignities, and death a dispatch."[440] Then he identifies with his ancestral people: ". . . and he too was of their blood."[441] This blood bond meant shared guilt, which is less guilt, even as the cosmic bond meant exoneration from all guilt—and annulled the penalty in any case. Lou was shy about calling the cosmic law one of justice[h]; but since Beer-Hofmann had done so, she did not need to. The cosmos was, then, Beer-Hofmann's mother-goddess before becoming Lou's father-god, so that in neither case was "the individual's longing to attain to the whole of life around him"[442] the root motive she took it to be: it was rather a florid rationalization.

The thematic sequel to *Ma* was one to "Gedanken über das Liebesproblem" as well: in order for a woman to reemerge socially from erotic self-enclosure by love's own way, she must bear and raise children, then relinquish them. That sequel lay years ahead. Meanwhile, even while hallowing Eros in "Gedanken über das Liebesproblem," Lou shuddered at him in "Die Schwester" (The Sister). The sister is both Mascha, seventeen, and Dascha, sixteen. Motherless, the two live only in each other's love—as far as Dascha knows—during a prolonged absence of their father's. One day Mascha drowns, and a strange young man appears, looking distraught. The suggestion is that Mascha has taken her life because she found herself pregnant. The guilty lover fits Rainer's description—kid gloves, walking stick, and all.[443/i] Through the tale runs a weird refrain by Rilke that ends:

> You have sung my fate too soon
> So that as I bloom and bloom
> I may no longer live it.[444/j]

But the stranger is also, dream style, one with the missing father, so that the fatal transgression was drowned Märchen's again—and so that fictive Lou, being both sisters ("at his lute's first sound," runs the keynote verse, "something in me split in two"[445]), again only half committed it. Dascha's verdict points deepest: "Mascha loved a man!

---

[h] Rather, she declared her faith in the cosmic bond *proof against* morality (1931a:27).

[i] Except that his complexion is dark—due perhaps to an 1898 Italian sunburn, or else a 1900 diabolization.

[j] "*Mein Schicksal sangst du viel zu früh / So dass ich, wie ich blüh' und blüh'— / Es nie mehr leben kann—*"

That's why Mascha's now dead!"[446/k] Inasmuch as suicide remained unspecified, Lou was moreover rewriting "Das Kind," the moral of which she misread to be that nature punished "youth's enjoyment" with death.[447/l] "Die Schwester" maintained the same physical distance from death as did "Das Kind" with Paul failing to locate his child's grave. For death, the invisible side of life in Lou's philosophy, was only a behind-the-scenes vanishing in her fiction from "Eine Nacht" and "Ein Todesfall" until after Rainer himself had died a thousand deaths laying out the grandfather's and father's corpses full length in *The Notebooks of Malte Laurids Brigge*.[m]

That winter of 1899-1900 Lou also did a brief review of some chatty Bölsche essays on science[448] and read heaps of books about painting and Russia. With Rainer she received Endell and visited Helene, now married to an architect, Otto Klingenberg, and living in Berlin.[n] She and Rainer also assiduously projected a great dual pilgrimage "to southern Russia, to the Black Sea, to Kiev etc."[449] Together the two entertained Sofia Schill,[o] a lettered social revolutionary ordinarily engaged in dispensing instruction and enlightenment to workers and peasants of the Moscow area: "this fine good little soul that recently spoke words as bloody as if she were herself capable of throwing a bomb," Lou once noted.[450] For future convenience, Lou and Rainer represented themselves to her as cousins. Schill later sent Rainer some new Russian books for possible translation. He was taken with one by a peasant poet, Spiridon Drojjin, and requested three more by Drojjin named on the jacket.[451] Soon he was pressing her to fit Drojjin into his and Lou's itinerary. Schill wrote immediately to Drojjin, whom she barely knew: ". . . I hope that these dear, good, simple persons will not burden you and that you will find suitable accommodations for them should they wish to stay the night. They would so passionately love to see a Russian village and get to know real peasant life."[452] As for city life, Rainer told her: "Please do not look for an apartment for us; we shall take our old rooms. . . . We would not believe ourselves in Moscow without the little silver Iverskaya chapel before our windows again."[453] He also assured Pasternak

---

[k] Eerily, Dascha at first thinks that maybe Mascha has died in order to escape the nosing about her due to her death (1900b:330-31).

[l] With the child's death rather than the expectant young mother's, to be sure, but to the same effect—namely, "fright at youth's enjoyment, the little child's death painful in the sight of all-fertilizing nature as it seems to be punishing enjoyment."

[m] Lou solemnly brought a corpse on stage in 1908a, then coolly described a deathwatch in 1919g.

[n] "Afternoon with Rainer at Helene Klingenberg's: fight over baptism."

[o] Pen name: Sergei Orlovsky.

in advance that he had mastered enough Russian and art "to linger in your circle longer this time, as a knowledgeable insider."[454] In April Lou told Ellen, then about to tour England, France, and Italy: "While you are enjoying Western culture I want to forget it a bit in the still, green steppes of Russia, on the Volga's shores and in its cloisters and forests, and amidst a people with whom I feel far more at home[p] than here in Germany. We [Andreases] are finding it increasingly uncongenial here: to stay fond of what is right about Germanity one must first back far away from what goes by the name of German *today*"[455]: this lent a Nietzschean rationale to her self-Russification.

In February the big departure was set for early April,[456] in March for late April.[457] Early May found Rainer moving to Schmargendorf and Lou taking long daily walks in the woods with him, with Andreas, and with a new poodle, in diverse combinations. Finally Lou noted for May 7: "Forest walk, hair wash, last lunch, final packing, by carriage at 5:30 to Charlottenburg station. Departure 6:50 in empty car, good night till the border at 1:00"—and then bizarrely: "Slept well from Alexandrovo with the Jew till Warsaw."[q] The pilgrims' land was next.

p ". . . *dem ich viel mehr Heimatliches fühle* . . ."
q "*Von Alexandrowo mit dem Juden bis Warschau gut geschlafen.*"

$\mathcal{A}$ R R I V I N G in Moscow on May 9, 1900, Lou and Rainer took their "old rooms." For the first night Lou noted: "Bedbugs!" For May 14: "Bugs in the tea!" and for May 15: "Moved." The two visitors consorted mostly with Sofia Schill, attending a "people's lecture" or two given by her and even meeting workingmen.[458] As Rainer told his mother on May 21: "Every day brings surprises and occurrences that penetrate deep into experience."[459] They saw Pasternak once,[460] then other artists. Again they frequented galleries, churches, and the Kremlin.

As they were about to board the train for Kiev at noon on May 31, they spotted Pasternak inside. His impressionable son, Boris, aged ten, recollected half a lifetime later: "Someone in a black Tyrolean cape appeared in the window. A tall woman was with him. Probably she would be his mother or elder sister. The two of them and my father discussed a subject to which they were all warmly devoted, but the woman exchanged occasional words with my mother in Russian, while the stranger spoke German only. Although I knew the language thoroughly, I had never heard it spoken as he spoke it. And for this reason, there on a platform thronged with people, between two bells, this stranger struck me as a silhouette in the midst of bodies, a fiction in the mass of reality."[461] The subject discussed was Tolstoi, whom the odd couple was minded to revisit.[r] Pasternak obligingly produced a copassenger[s] who, claiming intimacy with the Tolstoi household, declared that the count was just then at Pirogovo or else at his estate of Yasnaya Polyana and who wired en route requesting the countess to advise the two further at Tula. So the two got off at Tula—and, wrote Boris, "they waved their handkerchiefs in farewell. We waved back. We could just see how the coachman with his long red sleeves helped them up, how he gave the lady a dust apron and raised himself a little to adjust his belt and gather in the long tails of his coat."[462] Lou noted that evening: "Walk to the post office. Early to bed, all eagerness."

---

[r] While in Moscow they had evidently sought a new approach to Tolstoi (RMR→Schill, 2 VI 1900, treats their revisit as a familiar topic). Perhaps Lou had even written him in vain: her calendar features anxious, frustrating visits to the post office.

[s] Named Bulansche (RMR→Schill, 2 VI 1900) or Boulanger (D 31 V 1900).

In the morning, with no word from the countess, the celebrity hounds rode to the station nearest Pirogovo, there to learn that the count had left for Yasnaya the day before. They took a freight train in his wake, then a carriage to the manorial portal. After some vain waiting at a glass door in the rear, they rounded up a servant to take in their cards. Another unwelcome wait and Tolstoi was of a sudden discernible within. The door opened to admit Lou, then slammed in Rainer's face. Nor was Tolstoi in a mood to recognize Lou: Rainer let himself in just in time to hear the reluctant host snap out a few words and see him stalk off—"violent, offensive, almost inaccessible."[463] His eldest son, who witnessed the rude reception, made feeble amends by showing the callers some ancestral portraits, serving them coffee, and conducting them through the park. Left to themselves again, the two might well have beaten a proper retreat. Instead they construed a curt, garbled utterance of Tolstoi's about not caring to see them now as an invitation to come back later. So they loitered about the grounds till noon, then returned to the inhospitable hallway. It was fraught with sounds of a prodigious domestic quarrel. Even they were about to quit when the countess chanced to enter. She checked her hysterics to inquire their business and, hearing it, icily declared the count ill. Lou rejoined that they had seen him once already, whereupon the countess muttered an apology, shuffled some books to regain poise, and withdrew. The quarrel resumed, gravitating gradually to the middle of the house, with doors slamming, feet scurrying, the countess wailing, and the count roaring. Then a horrendous silence broke out—interrupted of an instant as the count tore in, distraught and trembling. Hardly recognizing the pair from the morning, he asked Lou something deafly, then shot Rainer the question: "What is your work?" Rainer—to the best of his later recollection—replied: "I have written a little . . ."[464] Tolstoi again withdrew; whispers and sobs, scolding and assuaging, emerged from within, followed by Tolstoi anew, cane in hand. Ironic and impatient, he asked whether his guests preferred lunching with the others (a mandatory gesture in rural Russia) or walking with him. They chose the walking: it proved a rushing alongside him out into the birch- and meadowland, his bushy grey locks, beard, and brows fluttering as he monologued about Russia, nature, and death—majestically, elementally, and just about inaudibly. His gaze, blurred in the hallway, sharpened fearsomely, and to punctuate his discourse he would pluck up forget-me-nots, sniff them, and flip them to the winds, absentmindedly: a prophet possessed.

Part III: Womanhood

Lou's calendar notation for that day reads: "Toward 8 AM to Latsarevo station; there otherwise advised, with freight train back to Kenpi, where Yasnaya Polyana. Thence by foot toward 3 to Kozlovika, where roamed about till evening. Back at 8; station buffet, early to bed." The unmentioned fiasco would not be put out of mind, however; it pressed to be set aright retrospectively—without patent misrepresentations in the first instance. So the next day in Tula Lou began a Russian travelog: her first diary since the Ledebour melodrama. The key entry opened: "On May 19 Russian-style we were in Yasnaya Polyana," only to shift at once to the weather that "whole day long" and to the local landscape and foliage. Next Tolstoi's son cut in with a word on birches "as he escorted us through the garden a first time. Then, as we took the walk for the second time with Tolstoi himself, we no longer looked about us, but at him absorbing this landscape, bending down from time to time to pluck . . . forget-me-nots with a quick motion of his cupped hand . . . as if to snatch up the odor too from the stem; he would then hold them close to his face and breathe them intensively, consume them as it were, and then let them fall to the ground. From the very beginning—already as he appeared behind the glass door of the hallway and we had only just entered through the portico with its comical parapet on which dolls, roosters, and horses are carved out—he this time made so singularly spiritualized, so touchingly moving an impression, like someone no longer belonging to the earth." And next, after some fine lines on the mighty figure cut by the little man: "In the house he stands in solitude —driven into utter solitude amidst an alien, *utterly* alien world, and I dare say even in the great long dining room with the ancestral portraits and two of his busts (Troubetzkoy and Günzburg) in the corners he never sat at his place at table like one belonging there—and *not* only because he ate oats instead of roast with us. What he said I can note only gradually, as it dawns on me. We put such peace as we could around the impression won through him, did not remain in the family circle, strolled long hours about Yasnaya, and today celebrate another half day here, on our table the forget-me-nots gathered by us there."

Lou had lent the dross a semblance of gold—lent a fiasco the semblance of a serene encounter backed up by a substantial, timeless acquaintanceship only discreetly evoked. Unpleasantness was eliminated, whence the ghostliness of her narrative. The morning's rebuffs went, the callers' grudge against Tolstoi's family alone remaining, bereft of its original occasion and as if unilateral. But the family quarrel went too except for that single abstraction from it, Tolstoi's estrangement from his family, which thus supplied the missing occasion for the grudge, as if in mute testimony to the callers' deep personal rapport with him. Pleasantness was superadded, notably that roast "with us" (a marginal insert)—which was arguably 'the roast Tolstoi told us *we* might eat with the others though *he* would not, and this not only because he was on a diet of oats but also because he was estranged from his family.' Primarily, though, the few tolerable bits of truth were bloated to fill the void—especially Tolstoi's nervous abuse of forget-me-nots, which Lou turned into a veritable event. "An event" is in fact just what she called it thirteen years later when, reviewing a volume of Tolstoi's letters, she evoked "the last minutes in which I saw Leo Tolstoi."[465] Contrasting the so-called event with his "pamphletlike" talk,[466] which had since dawned on her, she expanded capaciously on it in comparison with her diary account. She also topped it off with a peasant pilgrim greeting him quasi-liturgically from afar, though in Tula the first time round, as she searched the Yasnaya horizon in her mind's eye, that pilgrim was nowhere visible among the forget-me-nots.

Nor did Rainer find him that same time round for his huge report to Sofia Schill, according to which Lou and he "lightly trod the quiet forest street like pilgrims" up to that glass door, soon to perceive behind it, "in the dusky hallway, the figure of the count. His eldest son opens the glass door, and we stand opposite the count, that venerable man to whom one ever comes as a son even if one wishes not to remain under the power of his fatherliness. He seems to have grown smaller, more stooped, whiter, and his shadowlessly clear eye, as if independent of his old body, awaits the strangers, looks them over, instinctively blesses them with some ineffable blessing. He at once recognizes Frau Lou and greets her very cordially. He excuses himself and promises to be with us from two o'clock on. We have made it . . ." They stroll two hours with the son; the countess is rude to them afterwards; the count is heard to console a crying girl within, then "comes in to us, asks us a few questions distractedly and excitedly, and again leaves us." The two are just wondering whether their timing was opportune when "the count reenters, this time all attention to us, encompassing us with his great gaze. Just think, Sofia Nikolayevna: he proposes a walk with us through the park. Instead of eating together, which we had dreaded without any higher hopes, he gives us a chance to be alone with him in the fair countryside through which he bore the heavy thoughts of his great life. He does not partake of the meals because, ill again the last two days, he consumes almost nothing but coffee with milk, hence this is the hour he can easily take away from the others, to bestow it on us like an unexpected gift. We stroll slowly down the close-grown long paths in rich conversation, warmed and livened by the count as formerly. He speaks Russian, and unless the wind conceals the words from me I understand every syllable. . . . From time to time he bends down to pluck a flower with a motion as if to grasp the odor along with it, and he drinks the aroma out of his cupped hand, then negligently while talking lets the empty flower fall into the superabundance of the wild spring, which is none the poorer for it . . ."

Now, there is nothing tricky, ghostly, out of focus about *this* hoax. Its author was chronicling the facts straight in his mind while rectifying the nasty ones on paper. The rectifications were unequivocal—forthright, as it were. And the sense of them was winningly modest: Lou is promptly recognized; the great man graciously shares his spare hour; "I understand every syllable." No slap in the face, but no run of the house either. By reason of this modesty, a good deal more of the real happening came through: the countess's rudeness, the crying inside, the count's momentary distraction. For the rest, Rainer followed Lou in implicitly blaming the countess for the count's offenses and in opportunely concentrating on the count's physique[t] and especially on the forget-me-nots routine. Indeed, he followed Lou in falsifying: never on his own was he coy about his discomfitures. *She* "put such peace as we could" around the Yasnaya tableau that afternoon on the back roads of Tula; *he* dragged his feet. Three months later he copied a message from her into his diary: "Tolstoi has fallen gravely ill in Yasnaya Polyana," adding in her own spirit: "Perhaps we have taken leave of him after all." But then he pursued: "How exactly I see every instant of that day before me!" and began relating the visit again in the way of his Tula letter, only with new material details—and with the disobliging truth breaking through first sparsely as the glass door shuts in his face,[u] then irrepressibly as commotion sounds within the house. The count questions his tremulous callers "with cold courtesy," and—the entry breaks off.[467]

That day's doings stayed fresh in Rilke's mind for the rest of his life: a quarter century afterwards in Paris he gave an irresistible oral account of them embellished by nothing but his sense of humor, his narrative art, and Lou's choicest judgments of Tolstoi.[468/v] For all his

[t] For brevity's sake, I have omitted these similar passages from both accounts.

[u] But Tolstoi is then greeting Lou.

[v] This Paris account *fits over* Rilke's two prior accounts perfectly: even where all is disparity from one to the next, the same original facts are obviously at issue in the same sequence. And on most points of disparity the first and sec-

reminiscent levity, what kept the memory fresh was the pain bound up with it: first and least with the Yasnaya humiliation itself, next and more with his having falsified under Lou's sway,[w] last and most with the realization, inescapable in Tula, that while he was fooling only Sofia Schill, Lou was fooling *herself*. This realization was no easier to face for being inescapable: the result was a psychic relapse during the following weeks, aggravated by another on Lou's side. For beginning with Yasnaya, where she made herself at home as of time out of mind, Lou discovered her immemorial Russian homeland as if fast upon her adolescence, wide-eyed yet quite by herself. Her traveling companion entered her journal only as the invisible member of an occasional "we."

"Samovar and forget-me-nots," Lou noted for June 2; "joy over the month's start yesterday at Tolstoi's. . . . Glorious weather. Departure." And for June 3: "Ride to Kiev in heat with dreadful people"—who, she soon discovered, "were simply Kievers: people as obtrusive, unpleasant, silly as the great Russians are simple, candid, kindly. . . . Up there we were amazed at how true giants passed unnoticed; here we no longer much notice the crippled dwarfs all around. There one could go about as one pleased; here inquisitive glances, tactlessness are the rule. Nothing distinctive anywhere; everything banal, mediocre imitation. The common people contrast much more sharply with this human average than in Moscow: here the local costume signifies 'uncultivated.' It is colorful and glorious: more ornamental and less clean than in Moscow. Often the ribbons and beads dangle on the women with their thin little figures as on dolls: the 'cultivated' women gaudily overdo Western dress. The places frequented by the 'people' are likewise distinguished from those of the 'good' public: they do not as in Moscow adorn their citadel with their prayers and their simplicity."[469] Scenically, however, Kiev was "ravishing"—especially when viewed by moonlight from its acajou-decked heights. So on their third day, quitting the cosmopolitan district, the two tourists moved up beside the imperial gardens, where they heard gypsy orchestras and along which "one

---

ond appear as wishful distortions of a reality essentially congruent with the third (despite Betz, 154: "I twice heard him tell of this meeting, each time with different details"). The reverse is by and large inconceivable: why, for example, would Rilke, who otherwise gave Lou the benefit of every doubt, have alleged falsely that Tolstoi could not quite place her? Moreover, Lou's literary abreaction of the event argues independently for Rilke's version most disobliging to her.

[w] He falsified to please Lou, including the "Lou in him" (to paraphrase Nietzsche)—whence his diary entry just mentioned above, p. 270.

sees almost only common people passing . . . above all pilgrims—
people from the most diverse provinces, in the most diverse attire, on
their way to the Petchersk. . . . They appear as *the* people of Kiev,
for whose sake the city stands with its cloisters and churches beside
the thoroughfares. In Petchersk itself they fill the church courts and
the caves, bringing their smell of sweat and poverty, their infirmities
and sorrows, into an atmosphere already glutted with incense and
mustiness. The physical disgust imbued in me by this was strengthened by what here over and again struck me as revolting about the
priestly deportment: I understand the struggle of the most enlightened
Moscowers against the clergy and against superstition. When one sees
how this people that has starved its way here must buy red candlelight
for a full 10 kopecks from monks who even quarreled (on our account!) over whether Berlin is a 'famous English' city or is located in
France and who yet would remain this people's only instructors, the
adversaries of all worldly schooling—when one sees this people seeking consolation and sanctification in dirty fountains and kissed stuffed
saints, one comprehends all at once: this whole clerical establishment
is not simply a traditional symbol that day by day sustains the people's sense of higher things, but above all a living institution, one
directed and maintained by men, which diverts a lot of financial and
spiritual force from truer sources of nutriment. To take this away
from the people may be dangerous, but to leave it to them can be far
more so. It is all a matter of humanity: put wise and good men in
priests' mantles and you will be putting angels on earth though they
espouse the crudest superstitions a thousand times over. In itself
superstition is but a vessel and can be filled with precious contents;
when in the grip of predatory greed, however, it serves to drain all
spirituality dry (whereas science preserves its objective contents whoever dispenses it). The end term of such development would be a
people negligently tilling its fields not to still its hunger but to fill
Petchersk, glut the priests there, and deposit its last kopecks on up-
holstered saints' breasts."[470] The enraged Russian reformer in Lou
was haranguing the pilgrim in her—and the pilgrim beside her, who,
by then an out-and-out Slavomaniac straining to find his Slavic
brethren all holy, had waited in the pilgrims' line in outlandish garb
all his own and with spookiest spirituality all his own, his fist clenched
on the sly, to kiss a stuffed saint. They had visited the Petchersk caves
their first day out; the rest was strolls, Dnieper bathing, and church
upon church after church, except for three rainy days of reading,
writing, and poring over maps indoors beginning June 10: Pentecost.
That day Lou learned of Gillot's engagement—to an adolescent

girl! Thenceforth in her heart she traveled with Gillot as of twenty years before.

On June 17, after buying a saltshaker and an ikon at the Sunday market, Lou and Rainer sailed from Kiev down the Dnieper with "a mass of pilgrims," the women sitting and sewing, the men squatting and singing. The next morning Lou watched as most of them disembarked and filed away over broad, damp fields toward a dismal factory village. That afternoon, "after landing in Kremenchug, we rode out some way in a wagon, astonished at the bleak landscape and characterless houses. To singularize the place, there is only the sand lying all about, dunelike, in broad waves; everything is coated with thin white dust."[471] They took the next train to Poltava, arriving for a midnight ride from the station "through a gorgeous moonlit landscape into a town itself resembling a landscape in that it passes over on all sides into gigantic wild parklike clusters of trees and the rusticity of poor huts."[472] Not unlike Kiev in layout, Poltava was yet to Lou "infinitely more Russian, most likable, with charming, pleasant people"[473]; Rainer, though, later recollected only its "huts so pale and lonely in the nearness of night."[474] They left it at noon the third day for a forty-eight-hour ride eastward to the Volga during which the "weather and landscape hardly changed at all." Between trains they spent five hours in Kozlov "with its endless grassy squares, hedges, poor houses. . . . The people all without special apparel. Straight off, a well-dressed pope with glasses and long blond hair begged 5 kopecks from us. Before us walked a strange, somber, greyish man in cloak and cape with a solitary gait, as if out of another world."[475] In Saratov on the Volga their cab horse collapsed and they missed their steamer, whereupon they explored the town by foot as far as a Cossack suburb.

The following evening, Rainer having taken in the Pushkin museum while Lou rested, they boarded the *Alexander Nevsky* to glide upstream through starlight and sunlight, then drizzle and haze, ripples shimmering below them and gulls fluttering overhead, the steppe with its clusters of huts around churches on the one bank, bluffs topped with white clover or shaggy woods on the other. Their copassengers were "most disturbing" to Lou because they belonged to that class apart, officialdom, with its "Western presumption, prying, and snobbery"; the people encountered in ports of call were again thoroughly Russian, though, in their "mixture of temperament and spontaneous simple warmth, with an enthusiastic openmindedness as if dutifully excluding all sentimentality, hence in effect *broad as all things in themselves*. And," Lou added, "through this human type so many childhood memories revive in me! as in so much homecoming!"[476] The *Nevsky* docked briefly in Samara at noon the second day, then sailed "the most glorious stretch" till night fell at Stavropol.[477] The next morning's landing beneath Simbirsk was to Lou "like a homecoming into quiet loveliness once dreamed by me. . . . *Here would I remain forever.*"[478] She sailed on nonetheless: "like pain the landscape's slipping by, the quick deep greeting to each shore like a continual leave-taking."[479] And just then the sound that was Russia for Rainer began turning into song; the lyrics struck him as unduly solemn, however, so they ceased.[480] The next day came the end of the line for the *Nevsky*: Kazan. "The Tatar city," Lou noted, "was a big disappointment to us" in its ugliness, yet in its "deep stillness" was indicative of Asia, where "one would perhaps not discern the inner life of men with such individual distinctness, but the general type would, as I increasingly believe, bring us cultured peoples closer to our human origins of yesterday . . . of which we hasty homunculi take cognizance almost only in death. And against that Asia, which I long to know at any stretch of its border, lies Russia as a living synthesis of it with us, as a living home, yes my dear, dear home through and through!"[481]

Late that night the Volga voyagers reembarked aboard a swifter, less lulling ship, along a shoreline henceforth less majestic, more like the Petersburg hinterland what with its "fir forests, dear little villages, nasty factories in between."[482] Nijni Novgorod along the way proved "a likable, lovely old Russian city quite unexpectedly rich in glorious churches" as also in "greenery and breadth."[483] On the sixth day they landed at Yaroslavl, which was "splendid. Full of antique churches —and so remarkably distinguished too, almost elegant with its wide avenues and green squares. Every last person likable!" Their third day there a cab driver whom they befriended took them to a nearby farming and factory village, Kresta, where a peasant family put them up in an empty hut, fitting it out first with one sack of straw, then with a second on demand, and at length with a wooden vat, a samovar, and a table. For four days they fought off flies, swallowed dreadful porridge, virtually cohabited with poultry and cattle, listened to their landlady's village sagas, and gathered armfuls of flowers, the Volga rippling in their ears all the while: they were heartbroken to leave.[*] During this Volga trip Lou was gripped as never before or after by the world round about her[484]—minus Rainer. Midway she even stopped taking notes—with no detriment to her later descriptions. It

[*] Lou's diary passage on Kresta is precise and earthy—the reverse of that on Yasnaya Polyana.

was for her a "fulfillment beside which all turns peaceful in the soul, as if now all were well,"[485] "a world of holy fulfillments,"[486] "the prodigious consolation of a fulfillment forever"[487]—so that she felt no call to renew it in later years.[y]

This held for her new old homeland in its entirety beginning with "glorious Moscow," where she arrived with Rainer from Yaroslavl early on July 6 "as in a homecoming."[488/z] They took a round room across from the Kremlin, atop "the loveliest, homiest hotel anywhere." The first days Lou listened to Kremlin bells and watched Kremlin processions through the window, feeling "rather ill at ease in the wide, comfortable bed after the Kresta straw sack" and "quite as if a dusty pilgrim's staff were standing in some corner." She reflected that having been drawn out of herself brought her closer to childhood, "for then we are not yet so pointedly subjective—are far more interwoven with everything, are still uncomprehended, undelineated possibilities to ourselves."[489] She read about Russian churches, visited galleries with Rainer, began translating Gorky. Rainer wrote four lines of poetry in memory of Kresta.[490] "We made no new acquaintances," he reported to their go-between, Sofia Schill, then in the Crimea.

To the village poet Drojjin, who had left her first plea unanswered, Sofia had recently sent a second: "Your translator, the German poet Rainer Osipovitch Rilke, and the well-known German authoress Lou Andreas-Salomé, who is accompanying him . . . would like to spend a week in your village. Frau Andreas is a very gifted novelist. She studied in Zurich and was a friend of the philosopher Nietzsche. I hope, honored Spiridon Dmitriyevitch, that you will accept my dear friends. *They so passionately love Russia and everything Russian* that we are in duty bound to give them the very friendliest impressions of our homeland." On Sunday, July 15, Rainer Osipovitch and Lou Gustavovna themselves wrote from Moscow: "Most honored Spiridon Dmitriyevitch, we would very much like to visit and meet you; we arrive at your place Tuesday; we hope to be able to find accommodations in the village for a few days. Excuse us for knowing Russian so badly." A card from them followed: "We arrive Wednesday, July 18, at Savidovo station. We could not get away from Moscow yesterday. We greet you!" Still Drojjin did not reply, nor did he leave a message at the station—yet at the first news of the prospective visit he had mentioned it to his friend and landlord, Nikolai Tolstoi, a distant relation of Leo's and occasional poet and artist, who had

[y] But see below, pp. 286-87 and n. *a*.
[z] A homecoming to "mother Moscow" and "holy Moscow" at that (D 7 VII 1900).

thereupon helped him to install a new log cabin with "suitable accommodations."[491]

In Nizovka on the Volga, northwest of Moscow, toward 2:00 PM on July 18, "sleigh-bells sounded in the village street," Drojjin later recollected. "As I stepped out of my door, a mail coach with three husky horses was already pulling up to my house. First Rainer Maria Rilke leaped out of the wagon. He wore an English knitted jacket and low shoes with long black stockings and held a walking stick in his hand. After we had exchanged greetings, I led my dear guests into my log cabin prepared for them and fitted out with the requisite furniture; it was divided into two rooms, and its four windows overlooked my little garden of raspberry, gooseberry, and red-currant bushes. After we dismissed the postilion, who had brought in the luggage, we sat down to the samovar and drank tea. Soon the conversation was underway. Rilke, unlike his companion, Lou Andreas-Salomé, spoke no very correct Russian, but he could be easily understood. He handed me a clipping from a Prague review of April 1900 with two poems translated by him from my *Songs of a Peasant*."[492] Next, by his own dry account, Drojjin showed his guests his library, some fresh-sown fields, and the Volga shores, where all gathered wild flowers. The party then viewed a chapel, a forest, and a cranberry swamp. After dinner Drojjin read from his poetry on request, and "the next morning—the sun had just risen, the shepherd had driven the flock onto the meadow, and I was still asleep—my guests were already up, had drunk fresh milk prepared for them by my wife, and gone barefoot to the shore meadow to run about in the dew-damp grass. As they later explained to me, they believed that to be very healthful . . ."[493/a] The following morning Drojjin joined them: he wore boots. With him, they picked more flowers and made a sport of hunting mushrooms, rare that year. At one point he asked Lou how she liked his native region; she replied, "It is so beautiful that I should wish to settle in your village forever were that possible."[494] To the second or third evening belongs Lou's most distinctive impression of Nizovka, noted by her there: a neighing colt nimbly rejoining its herd after a day's labor, trailed by another with "a block of wood tied to one of its legs to keep it from leaping wildly into the grain."[495] The fourth day, July 21, Drojjin took his guests to Novinky, Nikolai Tolstoi's country seat. "Here the whole family gave us a most cordial reception," Drojjin recollected, "and we passed the time very pleasantly in friendly talks, strolling in the great garden and the age-old fir forest. At the urgent entreaties of Nikolai Alexeyevitch

---

[a] Drojjin's ellipsis.

and of his mother, Nadesha Alexandrovna, we stayed the night"[496]—
and the morning after. A day later the visitors left Nizovka: Lou,
inscribing Drojjin's guest book after Rilke, "wrote almost literally
what she had told me on that walk: 'I have here made acquaintances
with the Russian village and should like to be able to stay forever.' "[497]
They drove off to the station "grateful and contented," waving their
handkerchiefs until the two-horse chaise provided by Nikolai Tolstoi
had vanished from sight.[498] Earlier Rainer had written to Sofia Schill:
"We are at dear Spiridon Dmitriyevitch's and feel very well in his
great hospitality. How grateful we are for your good offices! With
these days we are completing a great step toward the heart of Russia
after long listening to its beat with the feeling that it gave the right
measure for our own lives as well." Thereupon Sofia thanked Drojjin
exultantly for his goodly reception of the two "fine, likable people
. . . a little inclined to idealize our Russian reality."[499]

Goodly as was the reception, Rainer and Lou had cut the intended
week's stay by two days, and Drojjin no more answered Rilke's letters afterwards than before—the first of which, he noted, bore "yellow wax and a singular signet."[500/b] Some of the reason why is discernible from Lou's diary account of the visit. A first installment,
drawn up the fourth day, begins right in the log cabin, wasting no
words on the self-invitation. It is a high-flung tribute to the Russian
peasantry, with the Nizovka villagers—Drojjins foremost—as mere
cases in point. And already in this perspective Spiridon came off a
bit badly—"this poet, himself but a peasant. His wife is yet more of
one: the life of a *mujika* is not sung in his songs exactly as it is heard
from her lips in simple recapitulation of experience. He still takes joy
in flowers—in haying, since it stirs his appetite; she works from the
night into the night, in her overexhaustion no longer eats, drinks
swamp water in her raging thirst while at work and retches as she
inhales the motes of dry hay. Charming and moving are these people
in their simplicity and strength . . ."[501] One passage neatly supplements her remarks to Drojjin: "Everything here is so endearing that
one would like to stay forever, yet I never could without homesickness for the *great* Volga . . ."[502] And another leads ironically into a
sequel: the stillness in which Russian villagers live "is one reason why
they are profound and seem not to require culture: whoever speaks
with them is always straightaway at the bottom of things, close to
the big problems, to the thought of God, death, spring . . ."[503]

Lou penned that sequel the evening of July 26 on the train to

---

[b] In 1913 Drojjin finally did send Rilke "a long letter, which was returned,"
then another through Rilke's publisher (Droshshin, 232).

Petersburg from Novgorod, "bygone beauty and power," which she
and Rainer had spent one day reaching from Nizovka and two admiring. Headed "Novinky," it began: "The first visit to the nearby Tolstoi estate very soon led to a second, and the second to sleeping there
and remaining there" until an eventual departure "from Novinky
through a priceless Russian night" toward Novgorod!*c* Meanwhile,
"if the great, rich gifts at our journey's end in Drojjin's village came
as a surprise, this look into a delectable type of Russian manorial
life unexpectedly enhanced our whole trip. Drojjin himself lost thereby. It was quite remarkable: at the very start, at his place, he struck
us as the ideal peasant and a mighty personality uniting in himself
the prose and poetry of daily life. Then, as his wife came into prominence, it turned a little pathetic, though to the detriment only of his
poetry, which appeared no longer as a total expression, rather as a
poetical miscoloring of Russian peasant existence. With the finely
cultured, original, stupendously coherent Tolstois beside the peasant
poet, this faint tone of poetical deviation from the truth, delicate and
pleasing when it first came through to us, turns almost shrill, unpleasant, almost ridiculous. Drojjin is insecure, delights in being
teased, often becomes nearly vain and silly. And we cannot see it
without pain, for we heartily respect him. What triumphs over him
is not wealth and culture alone, but primarily the true superiority of
people who have grown up strong. They too grew up within confines—those of their political and religious conservatism, their belief
in miracles and their patriarchalism; only these are firm universal
stages of mankind, which give security to those passing squarely
through them, whereas Drojjin, despite his return to the village, for
all his sincere deep joy in the village, left the village inwardly insofar
as he was intent on making himself into a poet and even a thinker
(*into an exception*). The secure originality of these three Tolstois—
Babushka, Nikolai, and Maya—beside their children made an un-

---

c Drojjin's schedule for Lou's and Rilke's stay as reported above, evidently
based on precise notes, checks with Lou's calendar at least as regards the return
to Drojjin's from Novinky, further documented by Lou's dating ("July 10,
1900"—July 23 Western-style) of her entry in Drojjin's guest book (subsequently donated by him to the Tver state museum). Even so, Lou was
equivocating: the "first visit" was the first time *indoors* at Novinky (before
the long walk with the Tolstois, or perhaps before a nighttime ride to the
village and back: see RMR, *Tagebücher*, 412), "and remaining there" was
routine bluff, and the departure "from Novinky" toward Novgorod was a play
on the genteel Russian practice of designating a village by the name of the
landlord's estate. In prolonging her stay at Novinky by tricks of style, Lou
could not imagine that Drojjin would later publish a record of it (as a
memorial to Rilke!)—just as she could not have imagined that Rilke would tell
the Leo Tolstoi story straight. (She did not later revise her diary in either
case, though.)

forgettable impression on me, the strongest I could have after observing Moscow's selfless liberal 'people's educators.' Long shall I
think about it, enjoying the fullness of the experience and enriching
myself. For the pious yet individually strong *barin*-lord is something
else from the pious peasant, who needs to develop less. Such a *barin*
as Kolya is perhaps a whole drama in himself, while the peasant is
only a peaceful hymn. Not the usual drama of someone revolting
against tradition, nor even of someone defending it as a reactionary
against the floodtides (like, say, Germany's liberals and her nobility), but as one who voluntarily conforms to it because he sees how
fruitful elements are destroyed through criticism and how the individual has to join with the peasant in bowing beneath what is highest.
Thus his noble pride is humility, and his individual strength struggling
for development is only an accent on the requirements of tradition."
This snobbery of Lou's, however dramatized, strikes a refreshing
note after all her hymnic slumming.

That memorandum on the Nikolai Tolstois was the merest prelude: Lou's single unsolicited welcome in her whole vast homeland
had a colossal course of postelaboration to run. It pressed to get
started, hence for Lou's inner retreat without outer distraction—
meaning without Rainer, in whom by then she "saw the old clinical
picture"[504] with new horror. After a single day in Petersburg she left
Rainer alone in a rooming house with his trepidations and joined her
family at Sasha's summer place in Rongas, there to pen a volumi-
nous "supplement" to her Russian log. It related Kolya's outer and
inner history since boyhood[d]—one of familial piety, benevolent traditionalism, and genteel humility, with no violence knowingly done
to his strong individual talents and inclinations, so that his "tragedy"
was now only "slumbering within him." It also depicted Babushka in
the full range and depth of her fabulous personality—Babushka who,
perpetually relating holy miracles, manipulated her entourage from
within her gloomy chambers by means of shrewdness and will power
but through the medium of prayer, quasimagically. The overnight
visit itself came in for only a subtle ". . . on the next-to-last day . . ."

This Novinky extravaganza plus two charming poems—the one a
prayer to "My land that I so long neglected," the other an assevera-
tion to the Volga that "Far off as you are I look on you still"—and
Lou's record of her rediscovery was complete. "My land dreamed

---

[d] Beginning matter-of-factly: "As a boy he . . ." In the same vein: "Looking
at Kolya, I often thought: 'What good fortune kept you' " (*dich*) " 'from
playing the tragic role you' " (*du*) " 'were meant for' " (a rhetorical *Duzen*
readily mistakable for the real one).

by me in childhood"—as one verse of hers ran—was really the land learned by her from Volinsky, only it had now been most particularly relearned: henceforth it was hers in ever richer remembrance. She had earned the privilege of calling herself un-German[505] upon returning to Germany for good.

Meanwhile she dallied in Rongas with its old familiar beach and woods, rounding out her journal locally. Her first new entry was "a verselet from out of a bright Rongas night of many years ago, come back to me at the seaside amidst stones and firs, from wherever it lay hidden the while in moss and seaweed through dim nights and bright": her lovely prayer to be shown the way home from men to her self and her god—which was doubtless the lovelier for the seasoning.[e] Some new verse followed concerning her sudden recognition of a stormy seascape out of her childhood. Next she considered how only in self-forgetful attention to what is most foreign to oneself does one ever disclose one's distinctive, determinative, innermost self whether in philosophy or art, in love or great deeds, or "most unconditionally" and "to the utmost" in religion: between her lines, " 'God' " sneaked into existence as the believer's subject matter analogous to the thinker's or the artist's[f] and again as what is disclosed to the believer even in his self-disclosure.[g] Then in a sparkling Nietzschean paragraph she argued that moral greatness is not a matter of deeds or motives, but one of room in the soul even for "dangerous things," even for "great joys." She was finer still on *the* "sin of culture: its using matters of the eternal life of all as means to its ends, be these ever so noble, as in marrying and procreating for ulterior purposes, whether money, status, or anything but love, killing or maiming for cultural reasons, slighting the body, violating the sanctity of meals, of rest, of animals, out of onesided obsession with cultural ends"—finer, that is, until she called religion "at bottom nothing but" the way a man's day-to-day purposes and achievements relate to that "dimmest composite substance of all his days" which, she specified, was God's sole concern. Next she was plausibly paradoxical: the vitality and perenniality of culture both depend on youth's irreverence toward it, and "one must rise very high above everyday life to live it properly as a chain of pearls, a sequence of golden minutes"—and in this glistening context she denounced Nietz-

---

[e] Cf. above, p. 18 and n. *l*; below, p. 470.

[f] " 'God' ever sustains, redeems, fully expresses us only because he is that to which we give ourselves most unreservedly, in which we absorb ourselves most utterly."

[g] Like the totemists of old, "we still find a god today wherever we dare to say *yes* to that which is frightful . . ."

sche's "incapacity to come to terms with everyday life."[h] Then came
a remembrance of her father, who had "so much Russian simplicity
and Russian greatness" in him ("when he embraced and kissed me,
then some warmth or other passed over me, half understood. . . .
—Now—now I would have become his child altogether")—followed
by a remembrance of Gillot, who "at a single stroke removed me
from dream into life" and so "saved me from later succumbing to
vagaries." This Gillot did, she maintained, simply by being her fantasies made flesh, whereas by training her intellect he only aroused
in her "a dreadful struggle of fear and spite," so that "henceforth he
could never again become what he later longed to: a person near me,
loved and loving, within human, civic bonds. . . . All this I always
knew. What I know only now—only since, say, Kiev—is" that she
had to escape being bound to Occidental rationality personified just
so as to pass beyond it one day, "to the inner home of simplicity and
humility and serenity and that nestling confidence for which the Russian landscape is like an image." In fact what she hoped to know
"since, say, Kiev" was that Gillot's recent betrothal had clarified his
"transition" letter of 1882—and she now declined him transitionally
(transrationally) *ex post facto*. But "much more often than about
all this," she concluded, "I think yet farther back. . . . In the end, the
very end, I see myself as a tiny girl evenings in bed . . . telling the
Good Lord the loveliest tales in lieu of saying prayers."

To Rainer too meanwhile, after two weeks' separation and, as he
put it, "that ugly letter" out of his "unaccustomed, unbearable aloneness," Lou wrote at last—purportedly out of a great chorus of "holy
voices and silences" round about her[i] in which, he gathered, the
sound of his woe was unwelcome: "I can hardly bear it. . . . What
ought I to do?"[506] His letters reminded her of those from Wolfratshausen to Hallein three years earlier—and of Zemek's glum prognosis. As he saw it, though, the whole trouble was "that I yearn for
you and that it was indescribably fearful to live through these days
with no news at all after that unexpected and quick parting, amidst
the almost hostile impressions of this ponderous city. . . . Come back
soon. . . . For two weeks I have been thinking everything only with
the proviso: when you come."[507] She came eleven days later—just in
time for him to escort her home,[j] then proceed to Worpswede, where
some illustrations for a book by him were waiting. He returned thence

[h] Cf. above, p. 170 and n. *f* ("everyday life," now in favor with Lou, had
begun with her as Luciferian three years earlier: above, p. 221 n. *g*).

[i] This last was Rilke's presumable paraphrase of Lou ("here your words are
echoed").

[j] Traveling via Danzig, they arrived 26 VIII 1900.

to a "new nest" in Schmargendorf on October 5,[508] having completed his old diary spiritedly among the artists, with ever fewer, less personal *you*'s, and having begun a new one with none.[k]

Lou, off traveling somewhere then,[509] was back by November 18, when Gerhart Hauptmann noted, of all things: "How thoughtless many otherwise thoughtful people are with regard to life, e.g. Lou. She says the memory of the dead is painful to her. But how congenial it is for someone alive to think that he is thought of with love. Etc. etc."[510] And typically that was all the notice that egocentric diarist gave his first reunion with Lou in six years.[l] In town for the rehearsals of his *Michael Kramer*, he had left a new son behind in a hideaway in Silesia but brought along the mother, ravishing little actress Margarete Marschalk. The evening of Monday, November 26, Lou visited the couple after some time with Helene discussing Helene's sister Alma—evidently together with Rainer, who that day noted: "Today L. remarked following Helene's visit, during which Alma's fate was also discussed—she very finely remarked: that is what God is needed for, to witness events and fates seen by no one because in no sense spectacles . . ."[511] Three days later, though, Lou inaugurated a new series of regular diaries with an entry on "Alma's fate" making that same Nietzschean point[m] in roughly the same words, yet commencing: "Monday Helene was alone at my place, upstairs in my blue room." Poor Rainer!

Hauptmann, to be sure, came off hardly the richer on the balance for four most personalized pages: "Monday from six on at Gerhart Hauptmann's. Many a memory was revived of the time when, young and blond, almost modest yet full of fermenting creative force, he still stood in the circle of the 'pioneer realists.' Around him his family: his clever, charming wife and their children—Ivo then already a young man playing in *Hannele*. It was marvelous to think of him as the three children's father, as suddenly great, famous. How simply and contentedly he still ate awful pancakes with us evenings then. . . . In our tête-à-tête it was hard drawing out what lay hidden within him, almost none of which was clearly conscious moreover, and he spoke badly, groping for words. But he recited gloriously and smiled with exceeding loveliness. In our last talk, after *Hannele*, he was al-

---

[k] His Worpswede diary entries were exacting accounts of day-by-day experience—in abreaction of his Tula trauma.

[l] Lou had last seen Hauptmann on 27-28 XI 1894, his brother Carl in XII 1896.

[m] FN, *Genealogy*, II: 7: "In order that hidden, undiscovered, unwitnessed suffering might be removed from the world and honorably negated, men were then almost obliged to invent gods."

ready in the grip of unrest: 'First one must get out front—then maybe one can even move on from plays to epics.' His proudest plans culminated in epics and lyrics, slighting the theater. But before he could even begin to tap these depths of his originality, he fell prey to the two powers that were to age him drastically: ambition, which like a fearful whip impelled him to produce overhastily, artificially, after he had been wont to produce altogether naturally, as a bird sings. And erotic passion: as I see it, likewise only a too tardy amour, taken too tenderly by him just because he is by nature so solemn and chaste, and that had no business destroying his domestic happiness and conjuring up forever an inner conflict, since it could never replace and supersede what once was. Even now Grete still strikes me that same way in Hauptmann's rooms: amidst this Gothic gravity with its simple grandeur like a dash of spice, soubrette-style, in a hypermodish fashion show.[n] And his look and demeanor clearly bespeak indulgence, delectation as if with an ornament, a condiment, an amusement become dear to him—instead of the stylistic harmony of a unitary conjugal life. His wife remains, as it would seem to me, in all eternity his wife, who endured all his struggles, shared all his concerns, and bore his children[o]; Grete, come to him when his fame was at its height and life easy for him, is not housewife, not mother, not companion to him—only amorous recreation. But Hauptmann has surmounted this love episode as well as his consuming ambition. And beyond them both he has come back to himself, to the homogeneousness of his own life and work. And there now is the great beauty about him: it was like an event for me Monday! He and his rooms and his words are all one, all simple, likable, distinctive—ripe. Intellectually too he has decidedly attained clarity. How candidly he spoke about this as we sat out the music alone in the library. He now creates without outgoing ambition and wants only peace from life. The natural consequence is that he will leave Berlin and is building himself a house in the mountains of his native Silesia. From this tree that—a rarity in our time!—will be rooted sturdily and broadly and peacefully in its own soil, his works will then fall to us as ripened fruit from autumn branches. Whether those will still be Gerhart's great, his most significant works—who can tell? He himself is aware of having paid dearly, perhaps too dearly, for the time between. He has aged; here and there a trait of senility shows in his colossally consolidated features. Perhaps something of his full force was drained for good in that ceaseless struggle with outer impressions such as threaten all of us,

[n] The metaphoric splurge is Lou's.

[o] Despite the dissymmetrical lack of a third "all," Lou evidently did not yet know about Grete's son.

in his case fame and love. . . . When now of a quiet evening he sits beside the splendid fireplace, a few wax candles burning behind him
and his favorite strains of Bach sounding softly from Grete's violin,
perhaps then he thinks of his family with melancholy—while his
violinist suspects not whom she serves." On Hauptmann's account
alone did Lou ever do such violence to her theory of love, for she
made of his former status of conjugal "half" a paradise lost and of
his taking erotic passion seriously the original sin—or to her theory
of sex, according to which *virile* meant ambitious, alert to outer impressions, and possessed rather than treelike when producing. In fact
she identified Hauptmann throughout with her fantasy self as the forlorn half of a primal incestuous[p] whole—a half that, for all its nostalgia, has attained to emotional self-sufficiency by way of amorous
digression.[q] At the same time she saw Hauptmann as a superfather:
a father from the first,[r] become great and famous, now even a bit
senile. Only in consideration of her readiness to identify this superfather with herself does the sequel begin to make sense.

Rilke met Hauptmann at Lou's on December 1.[s] "It was a fine
evening," Rilke recorded: "we spoke of the death of animals." And
he characterized Hauptmann in terms resembling Lou's.[512] Lou subsequently obliterated her account of this soirée, leaving ". . . Rainer
dreaming, Grete in back of him with her violin, in her coquettishly
charming overslenderness . . . demonic music . . . enspirited stillness
. . ." just barely decipherable. Hauptmann next invited Lou and
Rilke to a semifinal rehearsal of *Michael Kramer* on December 19—
as sole spectators.[t] *Kramer*, it turned out, was Lou's own "Ein Todes-

---

[p] This because she called his first wife by implication *his* "mother" (above,
p. 283) and because that wife was Carl Hauptmann's wife's sister.

[q] The "by way of" is perhaps clearest in a passage elided for brevity's sake
on Hauptmann's having become "the perfected picture of himself" with Grete.
Lou's identification of him with herself is further evident in another elided
passage: "Never did I see rooms in which I felt so strongly: here you could
live right on without changing anything at all—so much are they not stylish
Gothic rooms but *Gerhart's* rooms . . ."—but also in her thinking his secret
thoughts for him, etc. And in *her* having graduated from worldly to higher
ambition: she wrote to Schnitzler on 9 i 1896 in quite another vein that
"Hauptmann's flop has utterly depressed me in recent days; he himself is quite
broken, to judge by Berlin letters [a Louism meaning letters not from, only
about, him]. And just now he so needed a big success."

[r] In fact a father of three sons, like her own father.

[s] Heinrich Vogeler was there too.

[t] RMR, *Tagebücher*, 421: "I sat all alone with Lou in the dark theater . . ."
In a note to Lou that was withheld from me (cf. below, p. 559) Hauptmann
presumably invited Andreas rather than Rilke, though this perhaps to the full
dress rehearsal on 21 xii 1900.

fall"[u] in all essentials except that the father's grand death mask of his genius son, begun during the lad's lifetime, fittingly figured a crucifixion instead of a resurrection. As to details, Hauptmann had artfully theatricalized and Naturalized Lou's original. Thus he turned the son from a merely weak into a degenerate replica of the father, with deformity replacing sickliness and with neurotic violence replacing hypersensitivity. Thus too he wrote a public suicide over the solitary expiring. Similarly, he broke the Jewish foster sister up into a real sister and a sluttish waitress, converting her last respects into a bouquet of flowers sent by the waitress with poignant gaucherie. The dumbly doting mother he carried over intact. Not so, though, Lou's ready-made Naturalistic curtain-ringer: a sometime hapless sculptor himself, Hauptmann substituted a painting in process behind a veil for her lordly bust in the foreground. He also devised some new, distracting characters and episodes, and he made up for the overall coarsening with some terminal bombast about Life and Death—whereas Lou's original had spoken so well of ineffables without help from the characters or narrator.

Evidently Hauptmann was unaware of having drawn on Lou's story for *Kramer*.[v] But there was no chance of his two privileged spectators' not noticing[w]: the result was two experiences one stranger than the other. Six nights earlier Rainer had groaned to his diary from out of a godforsaken "midway land" between life and death all in "dampness and rot . . . hopelessness, soul's gasping . . . lone consciousness . . . ruination . . . disgust . . . fear, fear of every event and nonevent . . . confusion and madness . . . deluge and malediction, over and over again. . . . This had to be written as a sign to myself. Help me, God"[513]: apparently Lou had been mistreating him. The next evening he had noted, as if to outdo Lou: "Often I recall exactly things and times that never were. I see every gesture of people who never lived and hear every intonation of their unuttered words. A smile never smiled glows. The unborn die, and the living lie with folded hands, copied in fine stone, on long smooth sarcophagi in the half light of churches built by no one. Bells never having rung, of metal still unformed and unfound in mountains, ring. Will ring: for the never-was is the coming, the coming upon us, the future, the new.

[u] A first version of *Kramer* entitled *Marcus Hänel* is dated *mid*-1890's by Behl and Voigt, but I could discover no reason why.

[v] As perhaps he had drawn on her life for *Hannele*: see above, p. 180 and n. *s*.

[w] Rilke had known Lou's tale from its very conception (see above, p. 219), in which he may even have shared.

And perhaps I recall distant futures, when what never was in me stands up and speaks."[514] And so he did: the bells rung toward the close of *Kramer* signaled his own resurrection out of his living death, for he was the prototype of the deceased and transfigured son. And his very next, huge diary entry, all about that "day of conception, painful and joyous"[515] and that "high point in the development of the modern theater,"[516] was nonetheless one long celebration of death as a disclosure and dignification of life. He was to commemorate the anniversary of the *Kramer* rehearsal with an acknowledgment to Hauptmann: ". . . everything simple and beautiful that I have experienced since then has been related to *Michael Kramer*, everything that I was deeply glad about or really suffered over, and everything through which I have grown: everything important in my life went back to it and told of it."[517] The Kramer diary entry was his last ever: its big "Amen"[518] struck a note of deliverance from Lou as well as from his "midway land." Even so, Lou's suggestive influence prevented his noticing that he had noticed Hauptmann's appropriation: instead he indicatively omitted from his recapitulation of the *Kramer* climax every distinctive, significant dramatic invention of Hauptmann's, from the suicide in a beer hall to the very ringing of the bells,[x] besides using the word "*Todesfall*" in his commentary with the full force of Lou's use of it in her tale.[519/y] For Lou would not suffer any extrinsic noticing of her own, let alone of Rainer's, to intrude on her intimate, holy joy of recognition. Her one uninhibited sentiment was gratitude toward Hauptmann—gratitude such as she otherwise professed only toward her lovers for confronting her with herself.[z] For now a story once told by her was told back to her from on high, out of the clear blue: her childhood dream come true. She received Hauptmann's brain child by her as "the fruit of the whole tree 'man' " served up to "the soul in its every connection with life's dark, ultimate depths."[520]

She meant to publicize at once her "thanks for Gerhart Hauptmann's having become the author of a *Michael Kramer*,"[521] but overnight the surge of gratitude touched off a prepotent creative *élan*. Prior inchoate conceptions matured faster than she could deliver them. The first was "Wolga," her fictional realization of a new, down-

---

[x] He did, however, insist on that final moment: "Never have I seen such a happening on the stage, never suspected such a return of monologue, such force, simplicity, beauty in words, which surpasses everything said and sung, is in fact pure gesture and image" (RMR, *Tagebücher*, 427-28).

[y] The son's was, he specified, no mere decease—in effect no decease all, but an illumination, a revelation, a magnification.

[z] Except later correspondingly vis-à-vis Freud's work: below, pp. 362-63.

stream Volga voyage projected in Moscow but called off "in tears" for want of funds.[522/a] She now sailed in imagination as a young girl who turns adult as her suffuse, selfless absorption in her natural environment passes over into a pointed, self-conscious absorption in a mature and manly doctor, dedicated yet disabused, who boards the ship midstream before Kazan. This was the therapist Gillot of her Finnish diary entry, removing her from dream into life at a single stroke—from a Russian landscape dream, however, so that her progression beyond Gillot, lately rationalized as her highest destiny, was wishfully reversed.[b] Her imaginary trip was also her real one as she had made it in her heart: thus Rainer took it with her among those "most disturbing" copassengers—as an importunate simpleton under his mother's thumb.

At Christmas Lou left the *Alexander Nevsky* temporarily somewhere north of Samara for a "midway land" of her own situated at the antipodes from Rainer's: she wrote "Im Zwischenland," which found her back in Petersburg at the awkward age between childhood and adulthood, reveling in it and even enjoying a merry Christmas *en famille* (minus her mother, to be sure[c]). Actually Lou's midway Lou, little Musja, came out neither betwixt nor between, but all too babyish and sophisticated both: a Märchen overdrawn. And Musja's experience was Märchen's corrected, for at a single stroke, without guidance and without tragedy, Musja unlearns fabling about life. That stroke follows upon a double visit she pays to a Russian poet, idol of her brother Boris, to inquire how Boris might school himself to be a great Russian poet too. Her first audience so enchants her that she bungles her practical errand. She returns, only to be outraged as her sometime enchanter curses, spits, drinks from the bottle, accuses her of prying, sneers enviously at her family's wonted luxuries, even makes a pass at her, then calls himself a wretch upon finally letting her go. Thenceforth she can no longer believe with Boris that an empty notebook contains his collected works: such foolery, she assures him, spells madness in the grown-ups' world. So Boris too renounces make-believe. He renounces his poetical ambition as well, after some kicking and screaming, at news of his idol's arrest for forgery. And Musja warms to his grief over that dream poet who "in

---

[a] The project was probably a side effect of Drojjin's uninvitingness (above, p. 275).

[b] Doctor Valdevenen was, by the same token, successor to the Gillot of "Wiedersehen," who had inspired the corresponding Lou heroine to practice medicine in central Russia—which Valdevenen did, moreover, in Paul Rée's own near-cynical, near-saintly fashion.

[c] Literally, at her widowed grandfather's with her youngest brother.

reality never was," because for that one moment it is as if the great man "had truly and palpably existed after all, just the way he had in their fantasy."[523]

That moment vindicated Lou's first diary entry on Drojjin. For Musja's disillusionment was Lou's over Drojjin, its occasion the return from Novinky to Nizovka censored out of Lou's diary (and out of Drojjin's memoir[d]), the forgery Drojjin's inauthentic village poetry. And maybe Rainer did throw a fit of disappointment in Drojjin. At all odds, that blank notebook was Rainer's in Russia: ironically, the first fact of life Lou faced up to as disenchanted Musja was that Rainer was no poet. There is no telling how much of the delightful business between Musja and Boris Lou drew from Rainer's antipodal "midway land," where she may well have chuckled at his attempted Russian poems of the previous few days,[e] or made light of his poetical pretensions in general,[f] or even convicted *him* of self-hallucination, hinting at potential insanity.[g] In her "midway land," meanwhile, Rainer's self-dupery over Yasnaya Polyana was one with her own until she undid it: for Musja's second, straight look at the poet also figures a second, straight look at the Leo Tolstoi visit such as Rainer had tried to take in his diary[h]—and Boris's fit over the poet *dis*figures Rainer's over Lou, his literary idol exposed as a literary fraud hard upon that second visit to Tolstoi. Thus illusion won out in Lou's "midway land," her dash of self-criticism on this count notwithstanding. It won out again inasmuch as Musja was Lou espousing veracity in adolescence for good and all. And it triumphed through the moral of the tale, which was that children are all fantasts such as Lou herself had been, and simply outgrow their fantasticality —with Musja even a bit precocious in this. Herein Lou went one better on her "Wolga," which, following her Finnish diary piece, dis-

---

[d] Except for the leave-taking, which he represented as cordial.

[e] See RMR, *Tagebücher*, 408-09, 412-15 (29 XI to 7 XII 1900; the "midway land" entry, which followed the poems on 13 XII 1900, concerns "the last few days").

[f] See 1890d:81: "I can't figure you out today," exclaims Boris. "Never before did you doubt my greatness."

[g] See especially *ibid.*, 83-84 (Boris: "If one makes believe who knows what, though it isn't so. . . . You know, we do that sometimes, only that's—that was just a game. . . . Just think, otherwise we'd really have been crazy all along. Yes really, in the asylum long since." Musja: "We did believe it. Really and truly did") and 50 (poets go mad "most easily")—in conjunction with Rilke's "midway land" diary entry (above, p. 285) expressing a dread of insanity quite new to him, with his entry on seeing things that never were (above, pp. 285-86), and with Lou→RMR [26 II 1901] (below, p. 299).

[h] See above, p. 270. The two may well have discussed the first, crooked look (perhaps on 13 XII 1900: above, p. 285), especially if Rilke showed Lou his diary—and evidently she saw the Russian poems in it.

missed Gillot's lessons as therapeutically superfluous: she dismissed Gillot himself as therapeutically superfluous.[i] For besides romancing with Gillot unconsciously ever since Kiev, she had been half consciously rejecting him (over and beyond the rational orientation he had impressed upon her) with womanly wrath—or, on the surface, benevolent detachment. She was settling with him as earlier with Nietzsche, who had died during her trip back from Russia seemingly without her noticing.[j]

Between visits to Drojjin in her "midway land," Lou was fictionally at home in Petersburg—but by implication at Novinky as well. And sure enough, she had only just drafted that disgraceful, delightful post-mortem on Drojjin's hospitality when, as she sat chatting with her two men after their New Year's dinner, "the Nikolai Tolstoi material surged up in my soul irresistibly for the first time as a compelling whole."[524] That material was the tragedy latent in the Kolya of her two diary pieces on Novinky combined[k]—plus the wishful thinking so prominent in the second. The compelling whole was a prospective work of fiction planned roughly as follows. Witalii (Kolya) was to live a time at Margot's (familiarly: Musja's) during her Petersburg childhood as virtually one of her brothers. Throughout his youth he was to rebel against Russian traditionalism generally and his mother specifically, with inner misgivings, until hearing the song of his homeland in the Petchersk caves of Kiev along with a love song for Margot, then about to leave for the West. Thereafter he was to serve Babuschka and man with enlightened ancestral humility, but also with a growing sense of unfulfillment eventually issuing in "personal ruination"[l] under the very eyes of Margot, come from Germany to spend a full summer on his familial estate of Ródinka, diary in hand. He was to have a brother besides, one under their mother's thumb: Dimitrii, a religious poet—who was to be a virtual brother to Musja as well, and her first admirer.[m]

[i] Except to the extent that the disillusioning revisit recalls "Wiedersehen" and that Musja vis-à-vis Boris recapitulates Gillot vis-à-vis Lou.

[j] Nietzsche died on 25 VIII 1900, while Lou was between Danzig and Berlin.

[k] Above, pp. 278-79. The relevant lines of the "Finnish supplement" were: "This man would become an independent in the West, developing at the expense of all family tradition; here he becomes a continuer of what Babushka wanted for her *babushka*. It is imaginable that this thought might come to him one day and the tragedy slumbering in him become conscious: a conscious renunciation would ensue having the same significance as personal ruination."

[l] See preceding note.

[m] Here and throughout, I am distinguishing "Witalii" from *Ródinka* (which it later became) according to the indications furnished by Bab (123ff.), who was able to study Lou's 1904 manuscript (except the last sixth, which does not survive)—but am also distinguishing as far as possible the several moments

Part III: Womanhood

But Lou had to clear the way for Witalii beforehand. She polished "Im Zwischenland" and then, as she noted for January 5, "laboriously worked back into the Volga novella." On January 7 she was hoping to finish "Wolga" by the morrow "so as to be able to review *Michael Kramer*." On the morrow it was still "not quite done, because the great New Year's Evening material is fermenting in me—irrecusably, irresistibly . . . just as if someone else instead of me were already writing it in me on the sly."[525] So early the next morning, feeling "like an exposed nerve—yet how lovely it was!— . . . I started quite as if I had neither the short story nor *Michael Kramer* around my neck: grandly I wrote the title and beginning—pages long. Rainer came too in the morning sunshine at the very outset; the softest frost full of sun held sway outdoors; I ran into the woods, then in the dark of evening into the street again. Now I shall sleep—with a bad conscience and as yet unstilled longing . . ."[526/n] Not long after she next woke, the worldly-wise doctor told the wide-eyed maiden as the morning mist was lifting from Samara on the Volga: "Look! If on your return trip it's as it is now at this spot, we'll be together again . . . and then stay together"[527]—whereupon he disembarked, blending (by the logic of reverie) with her father waiting at the end of the line. "Wolga" was off Lou's neck. Alongside her lines about how "Witalii" interfered with it, she later jotted in her diary: "That's what made it flop." Frieda, however, deemed it Lou's "artistic virtuoso performance,"[528] and this it was: the love story is told principally through a gradual narrowing and sharpening of the narrative focus, which, after the beloved's departure, reopens onto the Volga panorama and beyond. The infinite parentheses around the amorous encounter were Beer-Hofmann's; so was the technique Beer-Hofmann's as Lou had characterized it when in 1895 she commented to him on the "concentration" in his stories, "every last detail" of the "world picture" round about the hero being "related to him, imbued with him."[529/o] This side of the horizon, "Wolga" enlists a shipload of highly singularized characters and accessories in the heroine's purposes. A stylistic tour de force, it is a thoroughly lovely short story too: indeed, Lou's very finest.

---

of "Witalii" in the making. Lou must have had this first complete conception of "Witalii" by mid-I 1901 (cf. below, p. 293)—though the Kiev romance may have been invented rather than only intensified in II 1901 (below, pp. 296-97 and n. *i*).

n The elided passages concern her "wicked gang" of characters, who were evidently more distinct at this stage than the plot.

o In D 29 XI 1900, just before conceiving "Wolga," Lou remarked comparably on B-H, *Tod*, which she had apparently just reread (ditto in D 24 III 1904—at greatest length).

Kramer's turn came that same evening—after she had run into Hauptmann and Grete that afternoon while strolling with Rainer in the Grunewald.[530/p] Two days later she was at Hauptmann's: he read to her from his *Hirtenlied*, which she found, like *Kramer* and *Hannele*, "truth become poetry. Something of this has now brushed off on him personally. And yet, as I shortly before stepped into his sad, empty bedroom, from which he often flees into a still emptier court room to find peace at night—perhaps peace from his dreams of longing for 'my homeland, land of my youth,' as the *Hirtenlied* runs—it depressed me. He must continually pay . . ."[531] The next day she did her "most substantial work" on her review: "I was so deep in it that, without my having touched a morsel, I thought breakfast over and done."[532] Another morning and "Ein Dank an einen Dichter. Zur Würdigung des *Michael Kramer* von Gerhart Hauptmann" (My Thanks to an Author. Toward an Appreciation of Gerhart Hauptmann's *Michael Kramer*) was at long last ready, with her thanks to the playwright obtruding sufficiently on her appreciation of his play to overrule any suspicion on her part that she might have been reluctant to express them. Obtrusion apart, Lou—unlike Rilke—singled out for appreciation what was distinctively of Hauptmann's own devising, such as the sensational tavern tragedy. Yet she did so by way of comparing *Kramer* point by point with Hauptmann's like but lesser *Friedensfest*, so as to show that what made the big artistic difference was *Kramer*'s crass externalization of "the true ugliness and brutality of life"[533] as a foil for its "beauty and nobility"[534]—which, to be sure, made the big artistic difference between *Kramer* and "Ein Todesfall."[q] And the points were well chosen in this latter respect, beginning with the one that the *Kramer* son cut a less ideal figure in contrast to his family circle than did the *Friedensfest* son.[535] More, Lou closed her "thanks" by redressing Hauptmann's balance between crucifixion and resurrection in accordance with hers of "Ein Todesfall": she drowned the *Kramer* crucifixion motif in the sound of those church bells, which she blended rhetorically with "the bell thunder of resurrection" heard by her once from the Kremlin towers at Easter.[536/r] In fact she led off by calling *Kramer* the ripest fruit from the Hauptmann tree and quoting " 'by their fruit shall ye know

[p] Five days after D 5 I 1901: "Early this morning Gerhart Hauptmann came home from Dresden, unfortunately missed me."

[q] At one point Lou even called those Hauptmann touches of crudity "distortions" (1901b:74).

[r] And this after having remarked that "at any point of emotional life [it is] a matter of blind chance whether we are crucified or resurrected" (*ibid.*, 76).

them.' "[537/8] Her insistent designation of Hauptmann's works as fruit of the tree contrasts too pointedly with her recurrent diary notations of those days about being possessed by her own incipient works not to suggest that she was putting herself in Hauptmann's place as author pursuant to her theory of woman's as against man's authoring.[t] And in "appreciating" Hauptmann's *Michael Kramer* as Michael Kramer appreciates his son, was she not setting up as the play's father? In any event she was one with father Kramer two days later in a brilliant diary essaylet headed "resonances out of my piece on *Kramer*" which concerned the "poets of death," who, unlike him, gaze on cooling corpses merely "aesthetically."[u] On the rolls of these postdecadents she perforce inscribed "even Beer-Hofmann,"[v] though with the saving clause: "short of that darkly concealed vital undercurrent to his glorious book which designates him poet of death, to be sure, but man of life."[538] With Beer-Hofmann thus saved again, Lou had disposed of her last inner distraction from her "New Year's gift."[539]

The big outer distraction remained: Rainer. On New Year's Eve she had penned a postscript to her Russian journal denoting Rainer recognizably at last: "Just about all I want from the coming year, all I need, is quiet—more solitude, such as I had until four years ago. For the rest," she had added, "I look back today only on *the* experience of 1900 for me, on Russia. And all individual recollections run together into One Feeling as of something broad, silvery, as of loftiness with no dismal gravity, as of confidence without narrowness, about like the little huts cuddled along the Volga somewhere amidst boundlessness": with a retrospective squint she had dissolved Rainer into the Russian all.[w] She could then simply have told him to go away—the more since Andreas was at last beginning to find the relationship morbid[x]—but her feelings were mixed. Every other day or so after registering that New Year's wish she blithely recorded some excursion with Rainer "to our 'Volga,' "[540] or Russian Christmas cele-

---

[s] Incidentally, some years later Lou again considered *Hannele* Hauptmann's "sweetest and deepest work" (1917a:785).

[t] However, she had called his production arboreal before the *Kramer* rehearsal: above, p. 354.

[u] "What to Kramer is the most painful experience of his life comes naturally to their placid aesthetical gaze. . . . This is not exactly the poetry of decadence; . . . it follows the poetry of decadence as death does sickness. . . . It can bear nothing live, not even anything sickly" (D 16 I 1901).

[v] Along with Loris, d'Annunzio, Maeterlinck, "and others."

[w] This postscript may well have been penned some weeks afterwards and backdated (below, p. 301)—especially since it strikingly recalls her New Year's retrospect on 1882-without-Nietzsche, which followed Nietzsche's break with her.

[x] This much is fairly clear from 1904a.

bration with him beside her lighted tree, or "pilgrimage" together to Frieda's for Russian New Year's,[541] or look at Russian picture books together, or plain German stroll together hours long. Then "on the seventeenth—with a 'finally!'—splendid two-hour walk in the woods *alone* between noonday sun and evening mist; the whole day devoted for the first time to the great, the one task; till late evening yesterday too, already indisposed . . . [whence] the whole room full of festivity, with all my characters parading before me like holiday guests."[542] Again on January 20: "Celebrated gloriously yesterday and today. Everything fixed by and large toward evening today with huge strokes, the way a painter notes intended colors with a few dabs. Later it must all run back together in the original thousandfold hues and nuances—unless it dies: in which case the dabs upon dabs come out as a dead mosaic. But woe unto him who now would kill it." And on January 21: "Days and hours when the thing already contains all in readiness, seen in minutest detail, animated through and through, and the one thing now needful is quick action to get the child out fast and whole before it chokes. Likely such dreadful excitation *must* go with every creative impulse. For who could save, could bear— and then calmly give shape afterwards! That will not do for a child or a work: they depend on the act of delivery, which can mar what is ready. Where it is otherwise, where—as Richard Beer-Hofmann once said of himself—one deliberately prolongs it over the years so as to enjoy it longer, one is not creating out of live matter any more, one has achieved artistic craftsmanship and must pay through a less blissful pregnancy. But it could almost be felt as perverse, as unnatural, that child and work stand in need of this act of birth—that one must first create what one *has* created and often lose it through some silly accident. It is among those things that could easily drive one to the grave in desperation except that all, all are alike up against it." On the morrow, though, she read Dostoevsky and Russian art history with Rainer. The next day they talked Russian letters and painting, and again the next—Lou noting remarks of his with approbation. And the next they waited in vain for Frieda and Sophie, took "a long walk in the woods" barefoot, then read some more Russian art history. By that time Musja's grandfather, seeing Musja sick unto death over having to leave Russia, had arranged a brief prior holiday for her in Kiev with Witalii[y]—and off she was.

[y] Musja's grandfather stood for Lou's father (as in "Zwischenland," of which the mood and the matter carried over to the start of "Witalii"). Musja, however, has a father too, a professor just appointed to Freiburg, who accompanies her to Kiev—an undeveloped character probably contrived in late 1903 (below, pp. 312-13), after Andreas's appointment to Göttingen, as a device for

Part III: Womanhood

Rainer thereupon resolved Lou's dilemma for her. She cannot have seemed quite lovable even to him in those days. After one spell of delivering, she herself remarked: "I must often have been odious at home" and "I am a monster."[543] Anyhow, the young Worpswede sculptress Clara Westhoff visited Rainer; Rainer spoke to Lou of maybe marrying; and Lou told him to leave her in peace for good and all—unless in some "direst hour."[544/ᶻ] They agreed to destroy each other's letters: Lou kept her nicest ones.[a] And he left his newly composed "monk's songs" in her hands.

Rilke left Lou resolutely—for a lifetime of remote dependency. She had not mothered him long enough for his purposes, though all too long for hers. The first thrill of infidelity past, he found sex without her miserable. He was to advance devotionally toward her Spinozistic god who "does not love back but to love whom is sufficient joy"[545/b]—toward her herself apotheosized. In ideas he never moved much farther away from her than to contrariety[c]: he surmounted her intellectual dominion only by surmounting intellection in some most meaningful late poetry the prose for which he himself did not know. In art his defiance of her was at first as pronounced as in love. In

---

making Musja's emigration to Germany reluctant. Musja's dearly beloved mother died when Musja was the same age as Lou was when her own father died, and a year or so before a second sojourn by Witalii in Musja's family circle—all of which points to Gillot. (Cf. 1901a:23: "Witalii reentered our life for the first time . . ."!) Musja's going to Kiev straight from her grandfather's is, to speak like Lou, a "resonance" out of Lou's Russian journal entry on Yasnaya Polyana.

ᶻ The parting date is uncertain (Lou later destroyed her diary pages from 26 I 1901 to 21 III 1901). It probably followed Lou→Harden, 9 II 1901 ("hearty thanks for the friendly greeting conveyed to me by Mr. Rilke"), but definitely preceded RMR→Paula Becker [17 II 1901] (". . . So much lies before me. You will soon hear [from Clara] what"), and cannot have come many days later than 26 I 1901 if, as seems likely, Dimitrii was already engaged as of the very first draft of the Kiev chapter in "Witalii": hence about 10 II 1901.

ᵃ Cf. below, p. 400 (Bjerre). Perhaps Lou kept all Rilke's letters in the first instance, for she destroyed some in later life (below, p. 477 n. ν), and the fifteen pre-1901 survivors are not so few given the infrequency of separation between the two before 1901. But his mad letters of IX 1897 to Hallein and of VIII 1900 to Rongas as well as all his letters of 1898 from Italy are conspicuously missing.

ᵇ Cf. RMR, Malte, finale on the prodigal son (who was Rilke come home to Lou as unrequited lover). After having written Malte Rilke, chancing upon a reference to Spinoza, half recalled who had revealed that god to him (RMR →Lou, 2 XII 1913). Lou herself (Lou→RMR [5 XII 1913]) claimed no credit for the revelation; in fact in her 1911 notes on psychoanalytical readings she called Rilke typically psychoneurotic because of his "fear" of return love (ditto in 1927a:61-62).

ᶜ E.g. from considering that people should live out "the unalterable life within them" (RMR, GW [Malte], 159-60) to the Orphic injunction: "Will change" (RMR, Sonnets, II, 12).

Worpswede he had conceived of practicing the poet's craft like the sculptor's, which meant putting things into words after scrutinizing them—or rather he trusted that "everything seen truly must become poetry,"[546] as it were *of itself*, and when in Russia it did not, he only tried the harder to learn how to see. Ostensibly he had given up on putting across his inwardness through outer symbols; in Lou's words, he set out "to express things, not himself on the emotional rebound."[547] This meant holding his affectivity in check for hours on end while watching an animal or merry-go-round or flight of stairs and enunciating it. Inevitably, though, he came to feel for his subject: he was in fact working his way unawares from the opposite side—the outside—toward that same ultimate expression of himself and things together which he called "the ineffable." Meanwhile, rhyming with his eyes open went naturally with Rodin's rule of *"toujours travailler"* as against Lou's of waiting till one were "inwardly ready,"[548] her "everything is a waiting for grace and gifts,"[549] which had inhibited him poetically.[d] Sculpturing with words also relieved him nervously at first by taking him outside of himself—only to give him no end of trouble at last from checked affects or alternatively no end of existential anguish over loss of identity. He was finally to revert to waiting—ages long, for the Elegies. This reversion conduced, then, to a self-surpassing, thanks to the power of words he acquired over the whole visible world—and acquired *in spite of* Lou, even if he retained much of her diction and if, as he afterwards averred, "my whole development could not have taken the course it did . . . but for the influence of this extraordinary woman."[550/e] As for Lou's course of development, Rainer was incidental to it—and yet those years of her nurturing his poetic genius were also her literary golden age, by reason especially of her responsiveness to his responsiveness to her.

Rainer gone, Lou rejoined her party in Kiev to greet Dimitrii, who arrives unexpectedly, announcing his betrothal. Lou as Margot is merely amused at his raptures over a simple-looking girl on a photo until she suspects that his mother has guided his affection. To Witalii, who inveighs against religious obscurantism in Russia[551] after the fashion of Lou's journal entry on Kiev, Dimitrii replies with a poetical rationale of the national iconographic-hagiographic spirituality echoing some of Rilke's "monk's songs."[552] Rilke had gone over his

---

[d] As had the verbal discipline inculcated by her—that "pedantry" of his which she later called "a counterpoise to the temptation of lyrical extravagance" (D 1922).

[e] Cf. RMR→Marie Thurn und Taxis, 29 VII 1913 (his encounter with Lou had "no end of significance" for his entire life); RMR→Clara, 17 XII 1906 ("Lou was the first person to help me to . . . my work"); etc.

"monk's songs" with Lou early New Year's Evening, just before that irresistible surging within her[f]: thus Rilke was father to that obstreperous novelistic brain child[g] which she, phallic female of the species, could deliver only in his absence. Witalii spoke Margot's whole mind to Dimitrii about Russian religion, but of his own mind only the iconoclastic half that went with his pronounced individuality. For Lou actualized in Witalii the conflict at first projected by her for a Westerner with Kolya's personality who would voluntarily integrate himself into a backward traditional order out of humility and love; only on second thought, in Finland, had she represented that conflict as "slumbering" in Kolya himself, so "stupendously coherent" the first time round—so that already in Finland, as now, she was projecting onto a fictive Kolya the conflict that would have been *hers* had she, on top of her Kiev reformist tract later cribbed by Witalii, actually entered into traditional Russian life as she then rhapsodized about doing. In another recess of her consciousness Witalii was Gillot: he succeeded the doctor in "Wolga" as her authoritative guide to Russia and, farther back, that Russian-oriented reformer in "Ein Wiedersehen" who inspired the heroine in her youth, years before her reunion with him. Gillot's engagement, which had broken upon Lou in Kiev, backed up Rainer's behind Dimitrii's—which in effect topped off Witalii's courtship of Margot in Kiev, signifying Gillot's of herself. Predominantly, however, Witalii was Lou as Kolya—was her masculine and her Russian side.[h] When, therefore, Witalii embraces his "little German girl"[553] as, in sight of the pilgrims' procession to Petchersk, he magically attains to personal unison by way of a great affirmation of Russia superseding all partisan pros and cons, Lou was

[f] D 3 I 1901: ". . . the evening hours upstairs in the blue garret, beside the lighted Christmas tree: the monk's songs and other songs. After dinner downstairs the Nikolai Tolstoi material surged up. . . ."

[g] Except insofar as she could claim paternity for his "monk's songs"—and indeed, in a dream of 7-8 VI 1917 noted by her *in extenso* along with many associations, she insisted that Rilke's *Book of Hours*, in which his "monk's songs" later appeared, was her own on at least seven counts: she had mothered (hence borne) the author, she had put him up to writing it, it merely registered what he had learned from her, she had put the final (golden) touches to it, her Russian had elicited it from him, it was the very least due her in return for her long hospitality to him and her long custody of his "monk's songs," and it was dedicated to and inscribed for her in thickest letters ("Laid in Lou's hands"). This dream offset her scruples about using a letter from him in another novel (below, p. 313 n. *h*), and she shortly atoned for its presumptuousness by having him, in another dream, correct her syntax in *Ródinka* (below, p. 415 and n. *l*). Yet counts two and three of her paternity claim, alone relevant in this context, are possibly and largely true respectively.

[h] This was, incidentally, her left side, Witalii having been lamed in his right arm while fighting the Turks in his youth.

retroactively embracing herself in Kiev to the exclusion of her obtrusive traveling companion. Margot is embraced no more than that
once, not even verbally by herself as narrator. Unique among Lou's
patent self-renditions she is self-effacing, effaced. As narrator she is,
then, Lou unmanned.

Visiting Ródinka, Margot was to discover a set-up much like the
Novinky one, beginning with Babuschka's having specially reared a
young bride for Witalii at his request. And here Lou's troubles began
as well, for her Kolya had made this request in boyhood already:
"passionate love" had been one more unwitting lifelong "tragic renunciation" of his.[554] Her Kolya's tragedy would have been a belated
awareness of having sacrificed individual development his whole life
long. Witalii, however, after having been an emancipated, independent youth at odds with his own instinct of conservation and devotion,
had achieved inner harmony in Kiev, transcending rather than frustrating his individuality. For Lou had wanted Witalii to find his way
home through a love vision of Margot merged with a beatific vision
of the Russian all—even though this meant cutting the romance
short.[i] Now she was up against it: to be tragical, Witalii would have
to reassert his petty selfhood in the way of a relapse and a fall from
grace, exposing that harmonization as illusory and that transcendence
as frustration after all—or else he would have to take off from Kolya
in the other direction, upwards into some supertransindividuation.
At the Petchersk climax, Witalii merely mumbles incoherently: perhaps by this Delphic touch Lou meant to gain some margin as she
groped for something perforce as cryptic yet unmistakably grander
for him to do at Ródinka by summer's end.

While groping, she peopled Ródinka numerously and superlatively.
Drojjin was there singing while others hayed, and his wife retching
from having drunk swamp water, and the Kresta peasant landlady
discoursing enchantedly about ultimates. Towering above the whole
Ródinka assemblage, reigning over it, was demiurgical old Babuschka, passionately, primitively religious yet shrewdly manipulating the
Almighty himself, a preternatural composite of undifferentiated, undifferentiable benevolence and malevolence: Lou's greatest creation
—a portrait of the authoress as a *babushka*. Sofia Schill was missing,
having been fictively stuck back in Petersburg as a *Narodnika* who,
just as in Lou's journal, condemns nihilists for being enthused with
ideas instead of love. But the big absentee was Rainer, who as Dimitrii had forsaken his beloved wife and two children for a young

---

[i] The romance may, though, have been no part of Lou's conception of 1
1 1901 but a narcissistic consolation prize for Rilke's infidelity.

girl—as "no one could have expected," remarks narrator Margot.[555] Dimitrii's was a troubled fate: Lou had made him Witalii's brother so as to get him commodiously to the estate in the real Rainer's wake; but by the time she got there herself as Margot he had deserted the hearth, again in the real Rainer's wake. His desertion was made into the occasion for Witalii's homecoming—this being Lou's homecoming to herself. Lou put her deepest confession into Witalii's mouth: "Likely Mother would not let him return except as a penitent with his face to the ground: too mortally wounded is her love for him."[556] Lou thereupon evicted Rainer from her tale itself (his having fathered it notwithstanding) and put Hauptmann in his place. For Witalii, in discussing Dimitrii further, paraphrased Lou's diary piece about the homeland poet who had exiled himself from his own household through taking a too tardy *amourette* too tragically.[557/j] Lou was right about Hauptmann, who saw himself as Faust with the devil to pay for his Gretchen. Only she was trivializing Rainer's infidelity by the same token, since the substitution of Hauptmann for Rainer turned on the equivalence between their two amorous situations; Rainer, though, was playing not at passion, but at normalcy. Despite its Silesian original, Dimitrii's escapade came off in the Russian manner, adding a wee vista more to the almost epic scope of "Witalii," what with its coverage of Russian town and country, of Russian religion, psychology, and society.[k] What Lou had not learned in her one day at Novinky about how a rural Russian estate is run she filled in from *Anna Karenina*. Only her common folk, as usual, were just not common. And all her folk participated in an aimless succession of episodes while waiting for her to find a way up and out for Witalii. She had still found none beyond some dark hints at illegal doings of his—involving a liaison with another Lou personage, a hetaera, even though for Kolya " 'sin' would have been impossible or meant ruination"[558]—when after a month or so her creative *élan* was spent.

She took it out on Rainer—shockingly. On February 26 she sent him a message, without salutation or signature, headed "Last call." It began with some smug bluffing: "Now that everything around me stands in pure sunshine and stillness[l] and the fruit of life ["Witalii"] has rounded out ripe and sweet . . ." then came unctuously to the

---

[j] In addition, the physical description of Dimitrii as a youth matches Lou's of Hauptmann: probably she altered it in this sense in ɪɪ 1901.

[k] Surviving fragments of ᴅ 22 xɪɪ 1901 and ᴅ 12 ɪᴠ 1902 indicate that, between rounds with "Witalii," Lou was occupied with distinguishing epic from drama.

[l] Again an echo of her preposterous diary retrospect on 1882 penned after Nietzsche's break with her: cf. above, p. 292 n. *w*.

poisonous point: "a final duty devolves on me out of the memory surely still dear to both of us that in Wolfratshausen I came to you as a mother. So let me tell you like a mother of the pledge that I made to Zemek some years ago after a long talk. If you strike out freely into the great unknown, you answer for it to yourself alone; in case you bind yourself, however, you must learn why I tirelessly urged you along a quite definite way to health [recovering childhood memories]: because of Zemek's fear of a fate like, say, Garshin's": suicide. Lou thereupon rehearsed Rainer's symptoms[m] even unto a "compulsion to madness without compulsion to truth," adding: "Gradually I too grew warped, tormented, overwrought, went on beside you only automatically, mechanically, could no longer put any full warmth into it, depleted my own nervous strength! More and more often I wound up pushing you off—but if I ever and again let myself be drawn back to your side by you, it was on account of those words of Zemek's. I felt: you would recover if only you bore up! There was something more to it too, something almost like tragic guilt toward you: the fact that, despite our difference of age, I still had to grow up since Wolfratshausen, to grow on and on into what I so happily told you about at our parting—yes, strange as it sounds: into my youth! for only now am I young, only now may I be what others are at eighteen: wholly myself. Whence your person, still so clear and dear to me in Wolfratshausen, got lost to me increasingly, like single small pieces of an entire landscape—a broad Volga landscape as it were, and the little hut in it was not yours. I was unknowingly obeying the great design of life, which, smiling, already held ready for me a gift beyond all understanding and expectation. I receive it with deep humility: and now know clairvoyantly and call to you: go the same way [that pointed by Freud] toward your dark god![n] He can do with you what I no longer can—and for ages already could not with full dedication: he can bless you to sun and ripeness. Over vast, vast stretches I send out this call to you: I can do no more than that to preserve you from the 'direst hour' of which Zemek spoke. That is why I was so moved as on parting I wrote my last words on a piece

[m] See above, p. 216.

[n] Her clairvoyant prescription was already prefigured in 1889a:39 and *passim*: every true self-renewal begins as a recovery of one's "lost childhood," that wonderland of ideality. Decreasingly for the decade 1900-1910 her diaries evidence self-administered Freudianism (defectively taught her by Zemek, it would seem), including word associations carried back to childhood and especially dream elements related to current experience (D 5 IV 1902, D spring 1905, etc.); cf. 1905a on Beer-Hofmann's oneirographic techniques, and the misleading Lou→Freud, 15 III 1916: "I used to note dream fragments upon awakening—only the manifest matter, quite crudely . . ."

of your paper *because I could not speak them*: *I meant all those words*"—presumably kinder advice to cure and not marry. That prospective "direst hour" was in effect the Passion, with Lou on the heavenly end for a change. Meanwhile, her drastic "last call" was meant to expel Rilke definitively from her custody, to deliver him up "to the world and to death"—only not to a wife. The effect was the opposite: though he repudiated her tutelage to the new extent of marrying anyhow,[o] at the next alarm she loomed as his sole refuge from insanity, haven from the world, deliverance from death: her grace as his peace.

The day after her "last call," Lou acknowledged a message from Gerhart Hauptmann, who had retreated from Berlin over a month before. Not realizing how long he had been away, she assured him: "I so wanted to go to you again with my husband these past weeks . . ." Then came a faint echo of her smug bluffing of Rainer: ". . . but work on a novel pressing for completion held me forcibly back from all else . . ." As even this was too pretentious toward the great man, a mitigatory clause followed: ". . .—and you are not at all blameless here, for it was born of the warmth and joy on the *Michael Kramer* rehearsal day, out of the joyous transport during the whole period afterwards." Her virtually ascribing to Hauptmann's *Kramer*, beyond that real transport, the inspiration actually due to Rilke's "monk's songs" had the sense: *I* give credit where credit is *not* due, whereas *you* . . . But it meant chiefly replacing Rilke as her inspirer with Hauptmann, whom she had inspired. Concurrently she substituted Andreas for Rilke as her stock consort: "In the summer, before my husband and I go to Russia for two months (this time to the Ural steppes) . . ." and surmounted her antipathy for Grete to the extent of: ". . . we shall seek you out in Agnetendorf should you care to have us there a moment . . ."—with, however, the apposite reservation: ". . . but then I get act two of the *Hirtenlied*!" For the rest: "I can send you no regards from Mr. Rilke, as he is gone. Nor will he return to Schmargendorf: he had been here incessantly for far too long already, and to let that continue proved undesirable in several respects. He is a nervous, even nervously encumbered and endangered, homunculus that easily snaps between your fingers if you don't take good care. —And now a hearty greeting to you both! We too are sitting here in sunshine and snow . . ."

Three weeks later Lou reported to her diary: "A few black days because even the 'holidays' [her menstruation of some ten days prior]

---

[o] Lou whispered in later life that Clara had tricked him into marrying. (He married Clara 29 IV 1901; their daughter was born 13 XII 1901.)

did not bring back the work frenzy. Now the thing to do is at least to jot down the last few hundred pages so as to be able to resume them: as when one covers up roses in the fall lest the weather eat away at them, for one cannot hold one's hand over them week after week, lamenting. . . . And what does it matter if finally, after so much toil, the nerves rest? They must. Could one then but have them fresh for catching up on everything *else* neglected during those so very glorious times, especially the much loving one could then have done. . . . But this the very relaxation prevents. About like yesterday: when Oldster corrected the *Ma* proofs till 3:00 AM (to get them off on time) even though he was up so early from the rebuilding downstairs, then brought me coffee in the morning as I lay in bed with a sore throat. I cannot say what a whole world that is, a substitute for all work, if one simply enjoys it. I cannot put it right as I am so dumb now, but I feel it deeply: darkling, pent-up thanks."[559] It was probably not long afterwards that she subjoined to her January diary entry about being horrid at home while working: "I was bad to Rainer too but am never sorry about that"; to the one about woe to him who would kill her nascent work: "(He must go!) Outside, rain. To make Rainer go away, *altogether* away, I would be capable of brutality"; to the one about delivering quickly: "Denied myself before Rainer with lies"; and to this last one about the *Ma* proofs and coffee: "And what a monster he does that for!"[560/p]

Early in May the monster in arrears of loving enjoyed a long-week-end reunion with Zemek in Nürnberg and noted regarding the perenniality of springtime blossoming that "no less is needed for faithless people like me to be incapable of estrangement—for it to be Maytide ever again at each reunion."[561/q] She traveled to Wiesbaden in time to be "pampered by Oldster" for her next "holidays," which she spent lying in a "yellow room" listening to a rat scrape nearby and musing about the likeness between Russian and Jew.[562/r] Soon she rejoined Zemek for a month or so in the Erzgebirge.

There, in Herrnskretschen on the Elbe, poised between excursions, she composed the last and loveliest of that series of essays which critics

[p] These interpolations are all in the same ink—and were evidently overlooked when Lou later excised the pages corresponding to her break with Rilke. In addition, a penciled appendage to a passage of D 26 I 1901 about how a plastic artist must regard his work in process "strictly and coldly and exactly . . . like a judge, doctor, craftsman" reads: "This is just what Rainer has against women painters and sculptors." Some diary lines were also obliterated, likely at this same time and in this same sense.

[q] Lou was in Nürnberg 3-7 v 1901. She had not seen Zemek in two years or more: cf. above, p. 251 n. *o*.

[r] Cf. above, p. 189 and n. *h*.

repeatedly urged her to assemble between hard covers, considering how "little can compare with them for wealth of contents, depth of grasp, and breadth of view."[563] Called "Alter und Ewigkeit" (Old Age and Eternity), it presented aging as a gradual relinquishing of the capacity to respond and develop, attendant upon an unconsciously willing alteration of the self-preservative instinct and attended by a loss of immediacy. The old, it pursued, are full of richest extracts of experience such as can hardly be imparted—least of all by them, with their diminished powers of imparting. They are like trees in winter with roots dried and frozen, unable to externalize "whatever may yet live within them, secretly gushing."[564] They sever their "direct connection with life around them" and revert to an "impersonal connection with everything"[8] as if only to present "the extreme, tragic consequence" of men's inability to exchange tidings of themselves except through "most imperfect symbols."[565] "Thus old age peers out mysteriously as from one great solitude into another."[566] Its terse, noble messages from the precincts of mortality sound hollow, like the weekly sermon by the venerable evangelist John: "Children, love one another!"[567] But peace and wisdom need not come with old age, which simply discloses what has been assembled along life's way. Old age is a lifetime exposed, so that, "deep down, knowing how to live and knowing how to die go together."[568] To resist senescence is to fight life even more than death—and worse than hopelessly, for this struggle of the organism against its own inherent tendency exhausts it prematurely, turning the soul into an "analogue of fleshly decay."[569/t] The most popular modes of resistance are superrigidity, or the rock-of-the-ages stance, and superpliancy, or drifting with the times as if forever. In our modern era, aging has become extrinsically problematical as well. Men no longer work on until they feel old; instead they are prematurely exhausted or technologically outdated, while even as consumers they cannot easily keep pace with the changing material components of existence. What they help to plant perishes before their eyes, so that they must face two deaths instead of one. Only peasants still age in their own time, handing their chores down unaltered. Perhaps, though, modernity has shown old people another way "back to that great stillness with which a tree bows when its time is up and an animal lets itself die, a vestige of which still survives in the human consciousness less individually developed. For

---

[8] To an impersonal *Allzusammenhang*, that is.

[t] (More exactly, "long-surmounted atavisms" revive to turn the soul, etc.) Here Lou slipped up logically, for on her premises the "analogue of fleshly decay" ought rightly to have been serenity and not inner turmoil.

this very heightening of individual consciousness, which makes aging and dying so arduous,"[570] has empowered men to fashion their lives instead of just submitting to them—until now death too may change for men from a mere being taken away to a stepping back from their life's work in the manner of artists. Ever since the first hatchets and fires, men have been developing consciousness and so raising death as well as life from mere natural events to specifically human ones. For to men, youth now means doing the work of their time, even into old age, but age means feeling all such work to be only man's peculiar way of temporizing, even in youth—means "a positive inward experience whereby each and every moment becomes sovereign, ceasing its mere moment-service,"[571] and whereby eternity hovers over life like "unity over all diversity, dedication over all labor, quietude over all unrest," filling the soul at last as the "final outcome and experience of what made man into a man."[572]

Following Beer-Hofmann, Lou had come to grips, albeit daintily, with death, or at all odds decrepitude—so as to be resurrected in her turn. Of course she failed to talk her way out of mortality—and not altogether undeservedly, for stepping back into death to view one's life's work would be cheating,ᵘ and knowing all about death is no proper way around it. Her venture beyond the grave took off from the end term of her narcissist formula for life, noted on her return from the Volga to Moscow: "It proceeds from an unconsciously loving identification with everything to a conscious devotion to everything, a finding one's home in everything, with sexual love as principal substitute for this in between."ᵛ Another year and she was hoping for an old age as dreamy as her childhood, one that would relieve the "pressure of life"—the greater on her, she deemed, for Gillot's "purely logical training," which "is in truth only now, after some years, really falling away from me altogether."[573]/ʷ Her temptation to relapse into psychosis now revived as she closed her two outstanding emotional accounts with god-men senior and junior: those with Gillot and Rilke. It was to strengthen over the next decade, poor in surrogates of stature, her surest defense against it being Nietzsche's

ᵘ This image was adapted from one in B-H, *Tod*, later quoted in D 24 III 1904.

ᵛ D 7 VIII 1900. This essaylet on "our song of life, which is a love song," specifically prestates much of "Alter und Ewigkeit," which thus derived directly from Lou's Rilke period.

ʷ Lou added, truly: "Love can make one so astonishingly obedient that long after its total extinction everything still runs the course prescribed by it"— then self-deceptively: "And [Gillot] was right: for now this impulse to intensive experience of fantasy goes into artistic experience, whereas then it could have vitiated, instead of developing through, reality."

psychic judo stunt of engaging the rational faculties in the very service of the inner "pressure of life" upon them.[x] In brief, she looked to old age and beyond facing backwards while thinking twice about thinking.

[x] Cf. D [II] 1919: "It now looks to me as if I was cognitively motivated with such passionate dedication those many years (by Gillot's doing) *because* that was not my real domain, so I could put my whole self across in it without any fearful choosing"—which she did more nearly, however, under the later sign of trespassing.

*L*OU RETURNED to Berlin on June 16, accompanied by Zemek as far as Dresden. "Home with Oldster," reads her diary; "roses and edelweiss in the room. Late supper, then long, long, endless sleep as at the bottom of some fountain." And two days later: "No peace yet for work all yesterday, which flitted away between tries. . . . This afternoon I must enter into my work." Then on June 23: "One week now I've been back. One week without work, but full of work stirrings within. And perhaps a fresh-sown field hardly looks any different one week after."*ʸ* In fact the sowing was a month or so old —and biological. Lou called off the trip to the Urals—and that to Agnetendorf, despite Hauptmann's urgings.*ᶻ* She spent half of July 2 with Ellen, who was traveling through: she told Ellen about endocrine glands, and Ellen told her about Gammelskagen at the tip top of Denmark. There she went with Andreas in mid-July—to lodge with a fisherman's wife. In August she reported to Ellen: "We enjoy the great glorious oceanic solitude day after day with ever the same joy, take long walks and wade about like children." That she found the Danes "a bit unlikable" she saved.[574] At one point, it would seem, Andreas suspected the pregnancy—which was somehow done and over with by early September, when she returned with him to Schmargendorf, then proceeded to Vienna and Oberwaltersdorf.*ᵃ*

ʸ A line later in Lou's diary begins an excision ending with IX 1901.

ᶻ According to *Ernst Pfeiffer (cf. below, p. 559), Lou's "celebrities file" contains a letter (likely of XII 1900) from Hauptmann including the line "I despair of ever being able to tell you what you have meant to me these days," and another thanking her for her "Dank" article (hence of circa 20 IV 1901) and saluting her proposed visit (above, p. 300); a letter from Grete replying invitingly to one from Lou to "us" (which presumably answered Hauptmann's of circa 20 IV 1901), and another deploring the cancellation. According to D [late XI 1901] (mutilated), Lou saw Hauptmann in Berlin late in XI 1901, probably at the theater.

ᵃ In 1904a Anneliese (Lou), who has lost two children already, realizes that she is pregnant, as does her husband, when she faints while bathing in Gammelskagen. See Lou→EK [mid-VIII 1901]: "By September we mean to be back in Schmargendorf, which we left already in mid-July; then I am going to Vienna for a good while." According to her diary she left Berlin on 9 IX 1901 for Vienna, whence she proceeded with Zemek promptly to Oberwaltersdorf; there she remained with Zemek's family until after 22 IX 1901, when "interrupted menstruation" (again D 19 X 1901: "menstruation"). A miscarriage in Denmark seems likeliest. This pregnancy is evidently the one reported by Peters, 257ff., according to Pineles family tradition, which is generally implausible when not patently inaccurate.

Six busy, uneventful weeks with Zemek and Lou was home again—hunting for a new maid: she found a charming Swabian, Marie, who took over the household. Then, just as she had begun "to get organized" in her den,[575] news reached her of Rée's death. Her verdict was suicide on her account,[b] and she was horrified—above all at her own self-satisfaction. She spent weeks sorting out mementos of Rée, feeling that *"really too much has come my way. It humbles one."*[576/c] She labeled one well-trimmed packet: "Letters from Stibbe to Zurich and Hamburg till my arrival in Schneidemühl with Jenia," for Rée, expecting Jenia to escort her from Hamburg, had once proposed to relieve him of his charge part way, at the rail junction of Schneidemühl. But she had traveled alone in the end. She no longer remembered. Alongside her pseudomemories were memory blanks, which she filled by inexpert research into documents from which she was even then eliminating vexatious traces of the past. The big documentary casualty was the estrangement of 1885-1886 between herself and Rée,[d] which in time she displaced upwards from the heart, affirming: "We had drifted apart mentally."[577/e] At the same time, she settled into lifelong bittersweet remorse on Rée's account without overt self-reproach—not even over having teased him erotically for years only to turn promiscuous thereafter. And all the while she saw deeply into Rée. When Tönnies sent her an article underscoring Rée's philosophic blind spot for everything emotional or personal, she remarked in return that Rée's "whole life and thought" might perhaps be explained by "his morbid and immeasurable sorrow" at being a Jew.[578/f] Tönnies asked how, whereupon she laboriously composed two brilliant paragraphs on Rée as afflicted with Jewish self-hate to such an extreme that his "violent will to forget himself"

[b] Lou was shy about putting this on paper in plain words (see e.g. Lou→ Frieda [XII 1901?]: "The principal event of this late fall was for me one I was weeks in getting over, and this for rather gruesome reasons that can only be told by word of mouth"); but she spoke it uninhibitedly, and over and again hinted it heavily in writing. Her eventual thesis was that Rée had found refuge from his self-hate in her love, only to feel mortally rejected and despised when she married, hence to "let himself be carried away to hate [for me] in his helplessness. That he *did so* could not but annihilate him, for it tore open the deepest conflict he was capable of: he hated the hater in himself at the same time" (D [III?] 1918): thus hating her was his fatal mistake.

[c] Again, Lou→Frieda [XII 1901?]: "My chief impression became: too much! I have had too much! too much goodness and wealth for one human fate. It humbles one."

[d] Nothing concerning him survives in her personal records of their year apart before her betrothal.

[e] "[This] I felt even in our last years together"; cf. below, p. 469.

[f] She also affirmed that Rée was all Jewish, whereas Tönnies had said half. Otherwise she took exception in Tönnies' article only to "the 'lady of wits' I have become for you."

"brought forth" or at least "quite singularly abetted" his theorist's disregard for emotional or personal motives.[579] This analysis followed up her maiden reduction of September 1882[g] as well as Nietzsche's thesis about the scientific ideal—and it made suicide look likely. Somehow her two letters, which Tönnies passed on to Paulsen, wound up inspiring a celebrated piece of Jewish anti-Semitism, Theodor Lessing's *Jüdischer Selbsthass*,[h] a quarter century later.

That winter Lou wrote two more stories about herself as adolescent. The first, "Vaters Kind" (Father's Child), reads like a wish fantasy straight out of her childhood, with her father murderously jealous because he sees a boy kiss her as she lies dreaming.[i] Only her father murders not the boy but a pet terrier, the boy's gift, whereupon the girl's love shifts back to her mother, then way back half ironically to a half forgotten bearded god. In the second, "Eine erste Erfahrung" (A First Experience), a gallant cousin playfully names her "guardian angel" over his courtship and marriage. She shares vicariously in its bliss on both sides until one day she drops by just as his bride has caught him with the maid. "Do you hear?" the bride cries to her, "we're here only to be thrown away on the man—to be thrown to him as his booty, which he tramples—he whom we have wedded—he who is our whole life—he—he—" Dismayed, she goes back to her dolls. The dashing cousin was Hauptmann, his Gothic gravity reversed, having his fling early: the moral indignation latent in Lou's diary piece on Hauptmann's broken home was transferred from the guardian angel (Lou as author of that diary piece[j]) to the slighted wife and so was shrilly seconded by Lou's repressed wrath over Rainer's infidelity.[k]

[g] Above, p. 88. Lou→Tönnies, 1 XII 1904, implies that Lou realized all this about Rée's thought in Tönnies' time; doubtless she did in substance as of IX 1882.

[h] Lessing's book contains much material on Rée evidently obtained directly from Lou, then mangled.

[i] Putatively asleep at the time, the girl yet feels guilty afterwards: for the origin of this seduction fantasy see above, p. 185 and n. *x*; for its destination, below, pp. 472-73. The episode also makes graphic Lou's metaphoric talk to the effect of her lovers' vanishing into the all: the boy takes to his heels before her jealous and angry father. I cannot find its proximate source—which was conceivably her once having been, as she later recounted orally (*Ernst Pfeiffer), surprised by Andreas in a compromising posture with Rilke, whose departure of II 1901 would thus have been represented as a consequence.

[j] Cf. above, p. 121.

[k] Further, Emma appears as little Lou's bosom companion in daydreaming, who is also smitten with the gallant cousin, Alexander—which points beyond Hauptmann to Jenia (whom Lou made out to have been, for all his effeminacy, a lady-killer and Emma's big heartthrob) after Sasha himself (whose wedding she made the occasion in "Witalii" for Margot's return to Russia, though evidently Sasha had children as well as a wife at Rongas VII-VIII 1900).

Part III: Womanhood

To these two tales Lou adjoined "Im Zwischenland" on the one side and "Die Schwester" and "Wolga" on the other to make up a cycle advancing with the heroines through—as she had put it with respect to Ibsen's Hedvig—"those perilous years of transition" to adulthood[580]: *Im Zwischenland*. And the cycle holds to a degree: each tale centers in some eye-opening, maturing experience.[l] In the overall scheme, childhood is a world unto itself governed by playful wishful thinking. Children are (like women) beings complete in their own right, not defective adults. Adolescents, though, are betwixt and between: nostalgic for fancy but troubled by fact—chiefly by sex, which will not be toyed with. Thus they turn adult only under protest— and to this affirmation, for all the resistance it encountered,[m] Lou held fast to the end.[n] Her pubescent fantasts take heart on learning about art as an adults' game of touching things up and preserving them from transience.[o] Beyond establishing her own childhood addiction to fantasy as a generic reluctance to grow up, she was implying that since her girlhood she had put her quarrels with reality into her art alone.[p] But not only did she make the reality principle postpubertal; she also made wishful thinking presexual. Her little Lous are too goody-goody to be true—or even indicative. The first three have no sex in them; they just hit up against it. Correspondingly, it is an extrinsic, alien power over against the elder of the two sisters as, in seraphic guise, it lures her to her death, and it is a novelty to the Volga traveler as of a sudden her diffuse affections converge upon that doctor—who calls it a curse. Lou purged her girls of all lesser wickedness as well, coddling their moral along with their physical persons as she characterized them. But she eviscerated them emotionally only to overendow them intellectually, in particular as junior phenomenologists: she hit home with her own later remark, on Proust's Swann as a boy, that "a child does not confront itself so observantly: only the reminiscing author does that."[581] For the rest, she attuned the narrative voice to the heroines' sensibilities, thereby depicting their growing up without commenting on it, which was fine —except that, with one heroine after another angelically unaware of

[l] Bülow, 475, submits a (questionable) schedule of life's successive lessons to Lou's incipient adults.

[m] For example, Eloesser (1903), 268, called it "flatly false . . . an unmeaning self-deception following from the outlook of later years."

[n] In fact her very last piece of prose (1936b) vindicated the point against Anna Freud.

[o] Art as a touching up was a point in Rilke's Florence diary later quoted by Lou (1927a:84); the artist who makes it in the two last-written tales (1901d:322 and 1901e:183) thus figures Rilke.

[p] Cf. above, p. 303 n. *w*.

mischief (even when party to it!) until the denouement, the narrator continually had to hint at it without taking the hint, which was incongruous.[q] This running incongruity was in fact unintentionally autocritical: the narrative filtered the heroines' experiences for them just as Lou filtered her own for herself in first registering them autobiographically—before playing with them. The cycle as such was faulty to the extent that each heroine in turn is jolted out of childhood afresh, as if each previous jolt were unavailing after all, pending the "Wolga" one, love at sixteen—itself none too conclusive. Reviewers, though, hit out at *Im Zwischenland* almost exclusively on the score of verisimilitude[r]—whereas on this same score a child psychologist was to use it in time as a source book,[582] a psychoanalyst to deem it strictly psychoanalytical,[583] and a professor of pedagogy to feel in duty bound to thank Lou for having written it.[584] Later Lou herself, however, unguardedly declared one moral of it to be that "even the most exceptional well-meaning 'grown-ups' know nothing about the child, understand nothing."[585/s]

Lou spent the whole summer of 1902 with Zemek in Vienna and Oberwaltersdorf except for three weeks of ambling across Southern Austria with him, mostly by train, followed by a three-day jaunt to Venice on her own.[t] In October she was home again[586] for a literarily sterile winter during which she saw much of Frieda and Johanna, Helene Klingenberg and Helene Stöcker. On March 2 the Minister of Education, Eduard Schwarz, having perchance read a few articles by Andreas, offered him a specially devised professorship of Iranian and West-Asiatic languages at Göttingen to begin the following winter. Andreas managed to hesitate a few days. Another month and the couple moved for the duration to "a small villa with garden"[587] near the woods in Westend beside Berlin.[u] The first evening there Lou proclaimed in a prayer penned to "that which eternally flows within": *"My truest life goal is no longer mine, rather the reverse."*[588] On

[q] This holds for Lou's tales generally for as much as they involve nice girls in nastiness: cf. above, p. 201 and n. *f*.

[r] See e.g. Busse; Anonymous, "Notizen"; Eloesser (1903); Platzhoff, "Zwischenland"—who, however, also judged the plots and prose "trashy-sentimental" (1583) and saw no point to the girls' being German Russians (in fact until "Wolga" the one convincing touch of Russia is a night cabman who toward morning takes his successive customers to be the same mad fellow changing his mind over and over: 1901d:229-30). The exception that proved the rule was Frieda von Bülow, who found no fault with the volume except excessive artistic discipline.

[s] Her intended point was that a child is accordingly none the worse off for growing up without parental care.

[t] Excursion with Zemek 12 VIII-2 IX, Venice 2-5 IX 1902.

[u] Rüstern-Allee 36.

April 12 she left for Petersburg, where amidst family visits she "heard so much about Gillot's having 'gone to the dogs' "[589]; she ran him down in her diary afterwards for manly, ideal posturing with green girls "out of unmanly, unideal motives," which came to one: deceiving himself as to his "inferiority" by winning easy praise.[590] Back in Westend on May 1, she again tried working, only to wind up weeks later reading biographies of Goethe and Herder "so as to think about greatness. Simply incapable of anything."[591/v] In this condition, on June 23, she joined Andreas house-hunting in Göttingen: she would have none of his "last possibility" on the river by the university[592] but fixed on a fire station instead on a hillside overlooking the town,[593] then spotted *the* house up above it, which was not for sale either "and yet so clearly mine, ours! And became ours!"[594/w] She afterwards reflected: "Everything in my life has been a wonderful mixture of inner logic and outer impromptu. Just as I lack all sense of orientation and the most familiar streets hold wonder for me, I inwardly live so much by the hour that I have no notion where I am heading, yet it is always *homeward*."[595]

While in that same condition she received a request from Rilke, sent through Johanna, to visit "for a single day"—as "who knows whether in the direst hour I shall be able to come?"[596]—or else to be given Zemek's address. Come any time, Lou replied, only "let us resume by mail first."[597] So he filled her in by the ream on his wretchedness: poverty in Worpswede, then especially in Paris, where Clara was studying under Rodin; homelessness beside his wife and soon his daughter too (named Ruth after Lou); old and new agonies of flesh and spirit; poetic dismay—all eventuating in his appeal to Lou *in extremis* "because you alone know who I am."[598] Lou pointedly kept these communications from Andreas[599] quite as if they were love letters. Expiating her "last call," she offered Rilke every reassurance: she wrote off all his symptoms as aftereffects of influenza[600] and called his account of the miseries of Paris an artistic triumph over them.[601] "Never were you so near to health as now!" she concluded.[602] Privately she judged that "people who (like Rainer) do not assimilate their life's happenings . . . never attain to quietude of soul,"[603/x] and again that his seeming sympathy with the abject of Paris was really resentful self-pity, his artful evocation "selfishly" self-purgative—and yet not self-purgative or even artful after all, as "artistic sensitivity . . . in weak natures . . . yields a singular amassing of unmastered,

---

v But in fact D 3 VI 1903, on the pros and cons of squandering, is a gem.

w Herzberger Chaussée 59 (today Herzbergerlandstrasse 101).

x But her diary pages for the time of their first new exchange are gone.

unprocessed fragments of life, in lieu of which a great calm is needed for the artist . . ."[604/y] Rilke hailed her tribute to his rendition of his sufferings in Paris as "good beyond all measure" but insisted that he had been up to it "only because I am full of longing to spread myself out before you."[605] Such, then, was the motive behind *The Note-books of Malte Laurids Brigge*, already germinating in those letters.[z] Through this public sequel to his sometime diaries, Rilke was to re-cover his childhood as per Lou's old prescription—but only halfway, the other half being embellishment and evasion. Meanwhile, Lou truly rejoiced in his book on Rodin,[606] whereupon he exulted in turn, for "only now is it completed, accredited by reality, erect, and good."[607] And when she told him further: "I for my part am now sure who you are,"[608] he replied that he was nonetheless desperate for a work-aday way to self-fulfillment: "Be considerate of me if I keep you waiting."[609] Petition of distress and writ of *non constat*, declaration of dependence voided, confession and absolution on paper: the episto-lary style was set for years to come. As for a live audience, Lou meant anything-but when she told Rilke solemnly upon reading his *Rodin*: "From now on, you can rely on me."[610]

On August 10 Lou left for four weeks in the Riesengebirge under Zemek's observation.[a] There she noted: "Everything looms like big mountains, so that one goes from peak to peak like Zarathustra ever 'atop the crests.' "[611] Afterwards she was three weeks breaking away from Berlin: on October 1, after a "last Sunday with dear Helene" and a "last night with Frieda, at Wedekind's *Salomé*,"[612] she packed off to Göttingen with the maid, Marie, Andreas following on the mor-row. There, after some days at a neighboring inn, the couple gradually settled into "Loufried" for life—Lou upstairs, Andreas downstairs, both as recluses from the local community, then some 20,000 strong. Andreas held class exclusively at home and by night: he would serve Oriental refreshments of his own brew as befitted his subject each time, then digress enchantingly. His colleagues left him undisturbed, eagerly anticipating the great work on Persian philology prefigured by his twenty years of monographs. And indeed, with security, status, and leisure now his, he relaunched the project on a tight millennial schedule while incidentally analyzing some fragments of phonetic

[y] Here she was endorsing his own pessimistic verdict, which to him she contradicted.

[z] Especially in RMR→Lou, 18 VII 1903.

[a] D 6 VIII 1903: "On the 2nd, yen to go to the mountains! Telegraphed Zemek . . ."; Lou→RMR, 22 VIII 1903: "At Zemek's wish I have gone mountain-climbing for a few weeks"; and Lou→RMR [25 VIII 1903]: "Zemek wants to keep me under observation some weeks longer."

middle Persian newly discovered in Turfan and reconstructing the text of the Avesta: thus had Zarathustra spoken. He showed himself surpassingly good to his students—until they presumed to publish. His chores at Loufried included gathering firewood and weeding[613]; Lou mostly planted and harvested, while indoors Marie held sway.

Gardening apart, Lou's life in Göttingen was virtually divided between the neighboring forest and her chambers—"my own study with its glorious old desk, the peartree at the window, and from my bedroom the great view"[614] "way over the town down in the valley and over hills stretching far out."[615] She received just a few callers: the first winter her cousin Emma once from Hannover[b] and Helene Stöcker from Berlin[c] and already a juvenile girl friend from the valley.[d] Henceforth the pace of her forays among men was to quicken to a gallop in sharpest contrast to the rustic stillness of her assimilative retreats: in her diaries the compact social itinerary was to alternate with the row of meditations almost like chorea with torpor.[e] This was one sense in which Göttingen was for her the least bit of "a turning point and landmark, a new epoch of life," as she called it on arriving, adding: "I mean to die too in the little house and to live on only outwards from it."[616] Another sense was unforeseen. On moving into that epoch of life she was known to the whole German lettered public as "the very type of the modern woman in the finest sense: artist and philosopher, thinker and poetess, a strong personality yet so much a woman in every trait of her being,"[617] and above all an "artist at living."[618] *She* first and foremost had traced and projected that image through her published writings. It was to start fading as now her pen faltered.

"Began to work after mid-December, quite slowly and skeptically at first, then ever more confidently, around Christmas all in a frenzy. . . . Only through work did I really settle into Loufried as into a home."[619] She resumed "Witalii," with Margot surprisedly receiving a poem from Dimitrii about his longing to return to his true home[620]: this was latently Hauptmann's *Hirtenlied* but also Rilke's recent letters. All Ródinka was now for letting Dimitrii back except Babuschka, who said *no* inexorably, tearfully, and (like Witalii in the Petchersk caves) darkly.[621/f] Lou added to Witalii's words on Di-

---

[b] 7 xi 1903.   [c] 26-27 ii 1904.

[d] A budding poetess, Else Nonne, first mentioned in D 23 i 1904 as visiting.

[e] According to D 25 viii 1906, the needs for "living inwardly" and for "human contact" were in her case "both equally potent and passionate, but separate from each other, hence alternating," and many another would live as she did if he could.

[f] She had prayed for Dimitrii's return "as lord, father, and spouse," she

mitrii's *amourette*: "Now it's changed for him: one can't play at love indefinitely.—Only for some time now he has had a child"—which was so far Hauptmann's case too. However: "Since then the girl has been ailing and is singularly wilted. And unfortunately for her, the child did not turn out like its father: it's a comely swarthy little maiden like herself."[622] Thus Rainer was determinatively Dimitrii again—and again the inspirer of "Witalii." By then Ródinka was Loufried: "After the big house, the little one," Lou had noted on New Year's Day, arguing continuity from Russia to Loufried. And she had not yet found a satisfactory way out of Ródinka for Witalii when she conceived a whole new story centering in Loufried. A few days more and, calling it quits with Witalii *sine die*, she copied down her text such as it was in a bound volume inscribed *Ródinka* and decorated with photos of Novinky. "Completed," she told her diary[623/g]—and, making a virtue out of a fiasco, she told friends that she now wrote for herself alone (like Nietzsche, only more so).

Her new inspiration was somehow due to a letter from Rainer, now in Rome, calling himself "your somehow lost son."[624/h] Under the

---

declared, but the others had likely prayed at cross purposes with her, so that in the end Dimitrii had presumed to decide for himself what was man's way home. Hence: "Never again happy and home! Never again—my son, my child, my first-born!"

g Then, "packed away" (D 28 I 1904); "copying down begun" (D 8 II 1904).

h Rilke's letter evoked an ancient Roman mural depiction of a mature woman placidly hearkening to a youth in traveling apparel as figurative of his own eventual reunion with Lou ("my life . . . will first be when I can tell it to you, and will be as you hear it!" etc.) D 29 I 1904: "Yesterday evening 'Ehe' begun, which came to me on January 18." On this date she had received Rilke's letter, answered it with a lie about why she had not answered his last one, and commented on it in her diary irrelevantly and ingenuously to the effect that he was lucky at least to be living in our enlightened day and age so as not to feel guilty about his inner torments. Ultimately she incorporated the passage concerning the mural (nicely adapted) into the novel as one of Balduin's (Rainer's) letters from Rome to his mother, adding: "The youth poetized the live woman into a legendary one: and she maternally held silence about it, preserving it as their secret from the ridicule or astonishment of others. Now Branhardt [Andreas] even permitted her these numerous, substantial letters, and she sensed that he did so cordially, without bitterness . . ." (1904a:299). According to D VI 1917, the "emotional reason" for this adaptation was "to express indirectly (not, say, through inserting a trial creation) the fact that Balduin was creative." Her self-justification for having drawn on Rilke's letter makes little sense, as she could quite as well have invented equivalent evidence of Balduin's creativity. Her scruples over the part-plagiarism, actuated by Rilke's fast-growing glory, were offset by her wish to record who Balduin was—and also by an unconscious claim that Rilke's *Book of Hours* was after all largely hers anyhow (patent in a dream by her adduced in that same diary entry: above, p. 296 n. *g*). But the real bearing of this letter on the genesis of "Ehe" escapes me. The key phrase for Lou seems to have been "your somehow lost son," which she cited indirectly in

working title "Ehe" (Marriage) she conceived a household consisting of herself as the mother, Anneliese; Andreas as the father, Branhardt; Rainer as their son, Balduin; and herself again as their daughter, Gitta.[i] "Since the Wolfratshausen 'Loufried' I have been moving step by step toward this one," Lou had told Rilke on settling in[625]: "Ehe" relocated and updated the Wolfratshausen *ménage à trois*.

Anneliese is the exemplar of Lou's theoretical ideal of woman and of marriage: whole, round, and full, she reveres life spontaneously, avoids specially cultivating her talent for (of all things) the piano,[j] and refuses to look too close or too straight at her husband, who fondly reciprocates. Besides having had two children, she has twice lost children. She was indifferent to pregnancy the first time till "of a mild summer's night, a few months before the delivery, she all at once, by an inward miracle, came to a holiest awareness: he who is lying beside you is your lord and yet now your child too—and you, his child, are yet now his mother too. Music surged through her soul like sounds of eternity wedding her to the eternal"[626]: poor Lou!

Balduin suffers from being a poet but even more from a too tender love for his mother on account of which he makes off to Italy after arranging to write her confidentially. She has let him go for his poetic good: thus Lou joined her surface motive for packing Rainer off in 1898 to his banishment of 1901[k]—durably.

---

that she adopted another passage from the same letter—though again, her mother-son relationship with Rilke was long since plainly so-called by them (e.g. Lou→RMR [26 II 1901]: above, p. 299), and the passage adopted is too arresting, too gorgeous in itself to have been simply a substitute. Maybe the answer involves the single notable alteration of a "destiny relation" (next note) between herself and Rilke: unlike Rilke's, Balduin's letter is not an implicit plea for leave to return home to mother, as he is under no interdiction to do so.

[i] D VI 1917: the impulse behind the novel, Lou noted, was "to bring real people, . . . in strict fidelity to their psychic constitutions, into totally altered, manifoldly opposite destiny relations (also as much changed in age, etc., as possible) . . ." Thus she was as if unaware who those "real people" were (and this even though she was explicit about Balduin as Rainer: see preceding note), for she by no means "totally altered" their "destiny relations." She occasionally cited a Göttingen neighbor as the model for Anneliese, doubtless with some incidental justification: perhaps she never wrote a line about any other woman not really all about herself. In the thick of "Ehe" she maintained (D 8 III 1904) that she was combining components of real persons into imaginary ones, which was false even in the case of Markus (cf. below, p. 315 and n. *o*).

[j] Irene in "Zurück" plays the piano too (whereas Lou was utterly unmusical). Masturbation apart, the playing stood for Lou's writing (Anneliese would flow over into her "art" from time to time).

[k] The two departures were amalgamated in numerous material particulars—yet possibly Anneliese's motivation was supplied only in later years.

Gitta, newly wed, finds marriage troublesome because she prefers dreams to reality and animals to men. Her husband Markus—a Jewish doctor specializing in endocrine glands—shows her no end of tolerance, even when once she aimlessly rides away from home. Gitta was Lou as Ibsen's Ellida, restless beside her doctor-husband before being awakened by him from her reveries.[l] So in Lou's sentimental perspective Andreas, hero of her first Ellida fantasy, stood behind Zemek as Markus, hence also behind the real Zemek: Gitta's love story was for Lou a retroactive romance with Andreas, Anneliese's a perennial romance with Andreas. More, Markus was Zemek as Beer-Hofmann, for—just like Berthold in "Eine Nacht"—he comes to Gitta late one night aghast after seeing a patient die[m] and talks himself out of his fear of death by discussing his Jewish ancestors to the same effect as Beer-Hofmann.[627/n] Or rather, Gitta's rapt interest in Markus' talk about his people is what cures him. "Markus thought: she has struck death dead for me!"[628] And "Gitta, who set such great store by names and nights, later named this one her wedding night."[629] But on that omnibus night Lou also consummated her mock marriage with Rée, for of Rée's "almost unearthly goodness" she wrote in 1904: "No one knew it better than I, who sat within it like a fledgling within the maternal nest and ill requited it by flying out."[630/o]

Frieda appears as Renate, an out-of-town friend of Anneliese's: proud, brainy, mannish, but nervously degenerate and "suicidal in love."[631] When Renate comes visiting, Anneliese plays pianoforte duets with her while counseling her about her recidivous self-subjection to a lover with a stable-boy's soul. To this effect she quotes Lou's letters to Frieda, though with a permissive twist. One close quotation prompts Renate to cry: "Oh Liese, how beautiful!"[632/p]

[l] Cf. above, p. 146. The Lou-heroine of "Paradies" also flees marriage because it interferes with her dreaming—and Gitta in turn is awakened to real life by a young proxy for a virtual father-husband in that she was her father's pet just before marrying his junior colleague.

[m] An old man, however—in effect Zemek's father, of whose death Lou was advised late in IX 1903 (but not Markus' father, whom Gitta looks forward to meeting after that night).

[n] Lou reread B-H, *Tod*, during a break in her writing of "Ehe" (D 24 III 1904). Beer-Hofmann's whole thesis concerning the way out of individuation and isolation (via national self-consciousness to begin with) informs Lou's story.

[o] D 22 IX 1904, after calling Markus the "main character" of the work, remarks that, while he is (because of "one decisive trait") no " 'portrait,' " nothing about him is at bottom " 'illusion' " either—and lets it go at that.

[p] Renate has called Anneliese's indulgence for her a weed in Anneliese's moral garden, and Anneliese has replied that weeds are beneficial to the growth

The parental house holds the plotless sequences together[q] even as it binds the family as if from time immemorial in a mystic-carnal community of growth,[r] itself a mere aspect of the perpetual community of all Being. Anneliese intuits this cosmic mystery as, her children having grown up and away, she straddles the generations and triumphs over individuality, loss, and death itself[s] through a new pregnancy—first noticed in Gammelskagen. A hymnic celebration of the family, "Ehe" was, coming from Lou, even more fictional than *Ma*. Rainer had complained to Lou of feeling himself an outsider even to his own family as against her genius for house and home[633]: "Ehe" indulged his illusions. The "greater half" of it was drafted during the first weeks of 1904[634/t]; the rest dragged on for years.[u]

Tracing her new portrait of Rilke within this new tableau inspired by him, Lou grew remiss in her correspondence with him. A literary model could be used to best effect, she told herself, only if all relations, "no matter which, are altogether broken off"; for "only at a great distance and under clearest, coldest gaze . . . can new bodies arise out of old ossicles already buried. Within a human relationship everything must lie behind one already if one would, thus unnoticed, strip someone's bones of their flesh . . . the way nature does in the earth before rebuilding anew. Quite unlovely—and yet if one thinks of oneself in this as the earth, it is in the last resort again motherly and creative in respect of the ossicles."[635]

Lou's heart trouble had worsened following her break with Rilke; now by winter's end she was bedridden with it. She rose to join Zemek in Venice for most of May—and as Rilke received a postcard from her with an Italian stamp, his hopes ran a moment "high, too high . . ."[636] Before her departure he had sent her a gigantic epistle

---

of grain. In the original letter (of circa 1900), however, Lou applied this metaphor to Frieda's moral weed in Frieda's own garden, advising her to "pluck it out that your bread may bake." Indeed, this entire letter was an injunction to Frieda to squash the "Peters worm" gnawing at her, as Frieda had just taken up self-flagellation out of nostalgia for Peters pending his return from Zambezi.

[q] D VI 1917: during her work on "Ehe," Lou's " 'interior decorating compulsion' . . . grew so strong that I kept a second sheet beside the one I was writing on and discharged onto it the excess that would otherwise have swamped the tale."

[r] Branhardt tells Anneliese: "The problem of all marriage is how truly it may ever be said, 'In bygone times you were my sister or my wife' " (1904a: 102); etc.

[s] 1904a:314: "Death, where is thy sting!"

[t] Further: "300 book pages"—which, however, is the whole of the final book.

[u] See below, pp. 319, 328, 414. No essential elements of the finished product could not have been conceived in 1904.

mentioning an impending temporary separation from Clara, asking advice about university studies at, say, Göttingen, and begging leave to visit one day that summer on his way by; he sent another for her return announcing his departure for Scandinavia, where Ellen Key had arranged some summer invitations for him, and beseeching her for "just a little word perhaps" beforehand.[637] He got one putting off the advice till the time came; as for his visiting, she said only that she was due to leave for Russia any day.[638] Accordingly she corresponded with him no further during the two months she then spent in Göttingen. Instead she loafed in her garden and fretted prophetically over the Russo-Japanese war: "Modern warfare, not to be extirpated through humanitarianism, might one day founder on the very superlativeness of its methods of murder."[639] She also noted, evidently after some visits: "Meta Benfey, Amelie Meyer, Else Nonne: a few of my illegitimate children"[640]—ironically, for the next thing her diary knew, Marie was pregnant by Andreas. Or rather, her diary knew her indignation at "what ought never to have happened in this house"[641]— at the desecration, that is, rather than the transgression—followed by her leaving Oldster behind "in this grave plight"[642/v] to join Zemek for a month's tour of Scandinavia.

On the next-to-last of nine unenticing days in Copenhagen, Lou sent Rainer a card on which she merely marked her hotel with an X on the picture side. As she must have half expected, he took the first train from Borgeby gård, only to find her gone. He had just written again wistfully to Göttingen; now he left a bitterish note at her hotel, where she found it waiting two weeks and two picture post cards to him later, on her return from an exhilarating cruise with Zemek along the "grand and lovely, somber and serene, idyllic and tragic" Norwegian coast.[643] She thereupon rode alone right by him via Malmö to Stockholm, whence she sailed three days on a small Swedish vessel to Petersburg through a thick fog that lifted just before Kronstadt, disclosing the ill-fated Baltic fleet all decked out for the Czar's final blessing: "an unforgettable impression."[644] Later, her "whole heart sore" at the war news heard from the inside, she felt it "nonetheless a relief to be here, to belong to those suffering, and away from the land of those who idly criticize."[645] She found her mother, at eighty-one, "rosy and robust."[646] "The magic about her," Lou later reflected, "is that she was never a tender person and is now becoming one in old age—like a ripe fruit growing sweet. And one keeps on thinking, with fear in one's heart: before the fall."[647] The one event of her stay was her brother Roba's wedding[648/w]—except for

---

v "in diesem Schweren"   *w* Not mentioned in her diary.

her writing to Rainer the second week apologizing for her Copenhagen prank ("do not hold it against me") but declaring Loufried off limits to him still "if only because presumably (if Zemek has his way) I shall have to lie in bed two months."[649] She regained Loufried by way of Helene's and Frieda's,[*x*] then lay in bed for nearly three months and almost without a break. On Christmas she asserted that, "practically workless" as well as "ailing" throughout, she had nonetheless been "happy here—upstairs." Rainer wrote in October of having lived through the weeks before her letter from Russia "in the single thought of your nearness, in the waxing and waning expectation of meeting you. . . . Dear Lou, I have brooded nights: why did this pass me by? Otherwise things pass me by because of my irresolution, my flabby will. . . . But this time was different. For my whole resolve is upon you." And if now she was to be bedridden, "that is, as I figure, only the more reason for me to be near you."[650] She put him off by return mail—even as he put himself off in a new letter announcing an "illumination" which he had received while air-bathing "on a high wooded place" that morning in the form of an agenda full through March without her. "Then I wish to take a little trip to where you will be . . ."[651/*y*]

The Andreases went to Berlin to greet 1905. Frieda met them, "irritable and oversensitive—and I," Lou noted, "much too sick for her with this heart business. I want to see Helene, lots of her, and the *Graf von Charolais*."[652] On New Year's Day Lou went with Helene to see this drama about an incestuous father who lacks the courage of his perversion: Beer-Hofmann's first play. She thereupon wrote entreating the author to send Helene an inscribed copy; he did.[653/*z*] By then she had impulsively returned to Göttingen without Andreas: Marie was expecting any day, she told Caro, "and I did not like leaving her alone any longer, what with the distance from town especially."[654] While waiting with Marie, she did a glowing review of *Charolais*: she saw in it the moral that, God willing, sex is older than humankind,[655] and behind it the gloomy Judaic view of man as a homeless wanderer born to sin and to suffer.[656] She also saw the heroine's lover as a mere surrogate for an unpassionate beloved— just as, in her own case, Zemek had been for Beer-Hofmann. She sent the piece to Maximilian Harden for *Die Zukunft* as of old[657]; it was then that Harden invited her to rebut Mrs. Förster-Nietzsche if

---

[*x*] She arrived in Berlin 1 x 1904, in Loufried late 4 x 1904.

[*y*] Lou's letter is lost: that it crossed this one is implicit in RMR→Lou, 3 XI 1904, which suggests that it warned him against coming to study in Göttingen with ulterior motives.

[*z*] Helene acknowledged it in verse on 16 I 1905.

she could, through Frieda if she would,[658] whereupon her relations with Harden froze over.

Marie's child was a girl named after herself and nicknamed Mariechen. In "Ehe"—or rather "Das Haus," as by mid-1904 it was called—Anneliese's symbolically charged pregnancy by Branhardt at the close was collaterally Marie's taken by Lou upon herself; and Marie's figured in its own right as Anneliese, while expecting, fondly arranges to house an ailing itinerant charwoman with a motherless grandchild, Klein-Gretelein, in a spare room to be readied along with the nursery.[a] Lou was ungracious toward Mariechen for six years or so, then turned heartily fond of her with, however, some final reserve.[b] Mariechen proved alert and fantastical at once, after Lou's own heart. She played with invisible toys, which grew impressively real for her as Andreas earnestly played along. Once, hiding behind the cellar door, she wept bitterly at her own imaginary fate on hearing her mother fret over what might have become of her.[659] She loved above all else her "Uncle 'Fessor," who doted on her but who for Lou's sake never acknowledged her. Sensing her situation in girlhood already, she responded by declining any education beyond a practical one like her mother's. Her mother meanwhile took a husband in Loufried,[c] where her "benevolent dictatorship" grew such that in time Lou "barricaded herself in the upper floor, taking care of her own rooms and even preparing her own meals."[660]

Lou's illness persisted through the first half of 1905, worsened by news of Russia's humiliating defeat.[d] Ellen Key, on the road again, stopped off at Loufried in April for a "very lovely day and a half."[661/e] On the verge of departing, Ellen gave her dress for a quick brushing and sat down to breakfast in green bloomers: "Above those bloomers," Lou noted, "that kindly-soulful face: such is truly Ellen Key."[662] Ellen wrote to Beer-Hofmann afterwards: "In Göttingen at Lou Andreas-Salomé's . . . we spoke much of you!"[663] And to Rilke while

[a] The grandmother was presumably modeled on a real Göttingen charwoman. Klein-Gretelein incidentally recalls Hauptmann's Grete, represented already in 1901d as a housemaid (above, p. 307) in a situation prefiguring Marie's. Did Lou *plan* Marie's?

[b] *Lifelong acquaintances of Mariechen's attest to her horror of Lou until about age six. Thereafter Lou took to signing her letters to Andreas *"Mummele."*

[c] Marie bore her husband a daughter, Erika, who died in xii 1915: the couple may well be represented by the resident caretakers in *Haus*.

[d] D 23 iii 1905: "Sick. Still in bed, with my thoughts in Russia and Asia" and with a smile at Japan's victory through European weapons as "a joke of world history." But D 1 vi 1905 was funereal: "Fleet destroyed. All over for Russia."

[e] 15-16 iv 1905.

still at Loufried: "I have talked much about you with Lou!"[664] Rilke had seen his way clear through his agenda to beg leave—unavailingly—to "begin the Russian year in Loufried."[665] Late in April, at his bidding, Lou lent him back his "monk's songs," which he joined to other, later "prayers" to compose his *Stundenbuch* (Book of Hours). This he dedicated: "Laid in Lou's hands." The reunion with his old manuscript, he told Lou, had been like a premonitory one with her.[666] She thereupon broke down and invited him for Whitsun[667]—perhaps brought round by Ellen, but certainly touched by his premonition, for she loved his "monk's songs." He stayed eleven days[f]—just long enough to help bury the Andreases' poodle as in 1899: in this hapless context alone did Lou record his visit.[668/g] Then on July 16 she rejoined him for a jaunt to an inn in Treseburg in the Harz mountains beside the Klingenbergs' summer house. "German resort," Rilke apprised Clara the second day, ". . . I really cannot imagine how or why to stick it out here till August."[669] After one week he escorted Lou back to Göttingen and moved on.

In mid-August 1905 Lou was in Saint Jean de Luz and by early September in San Sebastian. On September 17 she met Andreas in Cologne—and fell ill. He took her to Bad Nauheim for a six-week cure; the last of October she was home for a month's reclining. Then she traveled to Berlin, where on December 6 she attended a private reading by Gerhart Hauptmann of his *Und Pippa Tanzt*. Two days afterwards she was back home in bed. Rising in mid-December, she noted: "The whole time, for months, forever fretting over Russia": she judged the Western-style agitators there unpardonable as such, and the more unpardonable since they provided excuses for reaction.

Beginning January 17, 1906, Lou spent a theatrical week in Berlin including a dress rehearsal of *Pippa* at which she encountered Wedekind; an evening with boyish, impish actress Gertrud Eysoldt[h]; a day watching *A Midsummer Night's Dream*, in which Eysoldt played Puck, then meeting the troupe and its director, Max Reinhardt; an evening at Hauptmann's; and, lastly, a première by the visiting Moscow Art Theater of Gorky's *Lower Depths* with the German czar of drama critics, Alfred Kerr, as her companion. She saw Helene Stöcker between times and spent a day with Frieda at Goslar on her way home. Reinhardt's exacting artistic command over live human materials and Stanislavsky's power of animating his whole troupe with a single artistic will had both excited her with the stage as never before. As to *Pippa*, it was for her a dance of life and death in one to

---

[f] 13-24 VI 1905.   [g] But see below, pp. 557ff.   [h] A friend since 1900.

the tune of "the great all-melody" itself: so she declared in a rave review[670]/[i] composed upon her return and submitted to Harden, Hauptmann's arch detractor, as a brazen peace offering[671] ("that a friendly voice may sound for Gerhart in enemy territory"[672]).

On February 15 she was back in Berlin for two dizzying months of theater-going and socializing. Her interest now centered in Stanislavsky's and Reinhardt's companies: she won entrée among the Russians, and she befriended Reinhardt and his star Alexander Moissi. She attended the Russian performances with escorts as enthused as herself: with Kerr or Hauptmann or else with Harden, of whom she inquired beforehand: "Did I misunderstand, or did you wish to let me look you up?"[673] Having let her,[j] Harden accepted her *Pippa* piece, whereupon she told him she would be "happiest . . . to feel myself somehow involved in something helpful or useful to you."[674] To this effect she arranged a farewell lunch for the Russians on his behalf, only to wind up attending it in his absence with Hauptmann and, she assured him, misgivings.[675] Meanwhile she went to Otto Brahm's rehearsal of a new play by Schnitzler[k] and in due course celebrated its opening with the Schnitzlers. The publisher Samuel Fischer entertained her, as did the Leistikows, the Simmels, and Gabriele Reuter. She encountered Wassermann, the Dehmels, and the Saltens, consorted with the visiting Pasternaks, and attended a banquet of a club for avant-gardists, the Sezession, with Maxim Gorky. She made acquaintances with the economist Werner Sombart, the philosopher Hermann Keyserling, and most particularly the dramatist, translator, decadent poet, and emigrant Petersburger Henry von Heiseler and his wife, Emmy, a woman of parts and means. Endell was in town, as was Frieda, hospitalized: of them, and of Helenes Klingenberg and Stöcker, Lou saw most. Except for the Rilkes: in Berlin together for one lecture by Rainer on Rodin's art and another on his own, they

---

[i] Adding that *Pippa*'s characters were conceived "less in their individual significance than at the roots of their existence—at what binds them, dead or alive, to composite being" (1906a:399), etc. Her ailment aiding, she concluded on a rare note of doubt as to whether vanishing Michel's song of salvation might not, like Michael Kramer's, have been sung in vain (*ibid.*, 404). Of all Lou's play reviews, this one is singularly projective rather than interpretive —and yet Meyer-Benfey, "L A-S," 306, cited it as choice evidence for the proposition that her reviews were "not seldom . . . more artistically effective [than the plays themselves], because she sets forth the author's true purpose more purely and perfectly."

[j] Through Harden→Lou, 7 iii 1906 (from which I was read the single line: "That there is no human understanding is a painful symptom of aging"— presumably a post-mortem on the Lisbeth incident). D 9 iii 1909: "At Harden's."

[k] *Ruf des Lebens*, on 23 ii 1906: Lou applied to Schnitzler for permission just beforehand, thereby renewing acquaintances.

stayed a month at Lou's hotel (or in fact hospice) minus a few days midway for Rainer's father's funeral. "He *avoided* leaving Berlin for Prague to see the dying man still alive," Lou afterwards recalled,[676] and still later she noted how, to a remark of hers about his seeming less rent asunder than usual, he had replied "with such a gripping expression, 'That's because now I am the other all the time.' "[677] She stopped off at Emma's in Hannover before regaining Loufried on April 13—"finally," she noted, half in earnest.

This time she stayed put, and practically idle, for over four months. Once she thought she felt the joy that heralds "work days"[678]: four pages materialized on Stanislavsky's art as *naturally* Naturalistic because it was Russian.[679] In mid-summer she petitioned all her "dearest, noblest, most serviceable friends" to find jobs for the progeny of Leopold von Sacher-Masoch, the original masochist, who were starving on account of their name[680/*l*]: to that name, then, was due her exceptional act of charity. Late in August she went to Petersburg for a month: "The people all looked out of sharp, dusky, suspicious eyes —as if they were no longer Russians."[681] Two more still months at Loufried and she was back in Berlin for one of sound and fury centering (inappropriately) in the Kammerspielhaus, which she watched Reinhardt mount: more intimate than his Deutsches Theater, it was essentially pantomimic, she judged, with words breaking the silence like "concentrated action."[682] She kept company with the Wedekinds and the Fischers, the Simmels and the Leistikows; Henry von Heiseler and Hermann Bahr, Alfred Kerr and Hermann Keyserling; the publisher Eugen Diederichs and his poetess wife, Lulu von Strauss und Torney; the lithographer of social protest Käthe Kollwitz,[*m*] the impressionist painter Dora Hitz, and the authoress Elisabeth Siewert; the Anarchist publicist Gustav Landauer and the idealistic industrialist Walther Rathenau. Harden, however, rebuffed her for having taken his magnanimity "in the *Pippa* business" for granted: but of course I did! she protested[683]—in vain. Piqued, she turned around and told Clara Rilke, now living on her own in Berlin, that if her absentee husband presumed to sacrifice his family to his poetry, the police should teach him where his duty lay.[684] She was reviving against Rainer the old Nietzschean plot against herself.[*n*] Clara

l According to D 11 VII 1894, Lou had met Sacher-Masoch at Goldmann's office in Paris.

m With whom she evidently discussed the economics of sublimation in the case of artists (D 1 I 1907).

n This fit of Naumburg virtue had been anticipated at Gerhart Hauptmann's expense: above, pp. 282-84.

balked, and the correspondence between Lou and Rainer ceased. Of her old cronies Lou saw only Helene Klingenberg, who housed her after the first week. Reinhardt and his favorite actress, Else Heims, pressed her to come along to Agnetendorf for Christmas at Hauptmann's invitation. She went home instead, there to review Reinhardt's revival of Wedekind on pubescent flowering and deflowering, *Frühlings Erwachen*: she insistently deplored the expurgations beginning with that of the girl's lusty thrashing by the boy, which alone explained her subsequent bondage to him—"her womanly fate."[685]

As of January 17 she was back in residence at Helene's for another three months spent mostly in Reinhardt's entourage but also between the Heiselers and Wedekinds and Hauptmanns, Marie Hauptmann ("how lovely being together"[686]) and Elisabeth Siewert ("scrap over Jesus"[687]), Kerr and Lulu von Strauss, Endell and Frieda and Helene Stöcker. Mornings she did gymnastics on the Wilhelmstrasse. On April 17 she accompanied Reinhardt to Bremen, where he staged *Friedensfest*: there she visited the Vogelers in Worpswede. Three days later she regained Loufried,[o] where she promptly wrote "Vier Kammerspiele" to the effect that Reinhardt's new "chamber play" technique[688] of focusing on inner rather than outer events enhanced *Ghosts*, loud with Nordic silences, *Friedensfest*, which treats a family as a universe, and Maeterlinck's *Aglavaine and Sélysette*, situated in psyche's own realm and poised between dream and reality, but turned *Frühlings Erwachen*, a tragicomedy, into a tragedy disturbed by comedy.

The next seventeen months Lou left few traces of herself.[p] A long trip somewhere ended in mid-December 1907[689]—possibly her only departure. In mid-February 1908 she brought out six pages of perceptive paradoxes on the art of acting,[q] all deriving from the circumstance that the actor uses his person as a medium; all turning about that point beyond which, the more nearly he feels at one with his role, the less able he is to act it out; all exemplified by the Duse's exhibitionism beneath the floodlights as against the subtle gesturing in Reinhardt's dim chamber; and all culminating in the proposition that he best reaches his audience who plays as players did aboriginally in the temple, before God alone. This, Lou's first and last general piece on any one of the theatrical arts, hardly fulfills the promise of all her living in stage boxes, wings, and dressing rooms. Far less do her two

o Evidently with someone other than Andreas.
p Presumably: cf. below, pp. 476 and n. *s*, 557ff.
q "Lebende Dichtung."

plays, both evidently first composed during these years of passion for the stage following upon the Beer-Hofmann première.[r] *Der Stiefvater* (The Stepfather), in free verse and high style, is a symbolical drama about a fatherless world in which sixteen-year-old Little Stepmother[s] conducts a chaste amour on her knees with her stepfather, a magician, then vainly implores him for "a sign." Little Stepmother's "grim" brother woos her as a "flower bed"; she, though, would bear sons as if by her other, gentle brother, who goes out "among men" and dies "for their sins."[t] *Die Tarnkappe* (The Magic Hood) is a surrealistic allegory about a dwarf who, headgear aiding, manages to be magician, sculptor, savior, and degenerate weakling all in one. Both are just possibly great modern mysteries—otherwise only unintriguing puzzles.

It was apparently in 1908 that Lou acquired the juvenile protégée named Lotte who addressed her a professed "pure love letter" and many another.[u] Lulu von Strauss visited Loufried in June 1908 en route to Vienna: Lou thereupon commended her to Schnitzler.[690] Ellen came early in August, due north: she and Lou agreed that Rilke's latest, supremely statuesque poems (*New Poems*) were "written, not sung."[691] Lou blamed, beyond the poet's inept technique, his making technique itself his point of departure, with the result of "very deft *writing around* an inner subject," *against* the mood and feel of it.[692/v] Later in August Lou joined Zemek for a tour of the southern Balkans.[w] Most charmed by the soulful, rueful Southern Slavs, she was most stunned by the Montenegrin landscape, a panorama of desolation ("as if all the stones in the world were here assembled to

[r] Lou→EK, 2 XI 1920, mentions two old dramas of hers (besides 1915a) then in Diederichs' hands (cf. Lou→Martersteig, 4 XI 1921 and 26 XI 1921; Lou→Schoenberner, 25 V 1933; etc.)—and there is little else to show for these years, during which she did write off and on (D 4 XI 1906, for instance, finds her working daily).

[s] Literally: Pansy (*"Stiefmütterchen"*).

[t] Lou noted a Kammerspiel cast for this play on the final manuscript, with Gertrud Eysoldt in the lead: possibly she proposed it to Reinhardt.

[u] Lotte is mentioned in Lou→Frieda [late 1908] in the way of a recent acquisition. One of Lotte's letters is dated 15 III 1911, one of her envelopes 5 VII 1911.

[v] Further: such mood as did break through here and there was "too crass, exaggerated, distilled"; in his *Requiem* he could "take off from 'emotion' again" because gripped by something "coming off at some distance from him . . . whereas what is closest in the great human experiences (wife and child, birth, whatever shakes and matures men) is now merely derivative with him." Nor did Lou quite conceal from Rilke himself her disapprobation for his postlyrical workmanlike achievements: see Lou→RMR, 17 VI 1909.

[w] Through present-day Yugoslavia, Albania, and Greece plus a corner of Hungary, from 22 VIII to X 1908 (Vienna to Vienna).

vent their grievances over being stones")—redeemed, however, by the angelic beauty of the women ("Oh to be a he!!!"). In Duino she reflected that Austria's fascination was Austria's peril: the multinational hodge-podge, all "in for a frightful blow-up." In Vienna afterwards she made notes on some portraits by Gustav Klimt, who "must have understood the soul in sex, the flower in woman." She made none on her estrangement from Zemek, which followed their return, except for the mournful postscript: "In Vienna I have my secret: often at dusk I go about in the mood that then lies upon all roofs here, seeking out the three times when 'Vienna' was an experience for me. On the Stefansplatz one spring, then one fall; then that other Vienna facing Oberwaltersdorf."[693]

Lou returned home to the news that Frieda was gravely ill. By the new year Frieda was agonizing without hope[x]: she died on March 10, 1909. All that winter long Lou argued spirit survival to her by mail—or rather release from the body ("for we *are* not bodies, but only 'have' bodies") into a "finer 'corporeality.' " "The process we call life is a death process *and vice versa too*," she asserted on the authority of "physics, chemistry, and the like," adding: "Truly as God lives, it is so."[694] In her loveliest such letter[695] she protested that, though the crest follows the pit of the wave for sure, "this does not console me for your being tormented *now, now, now*." Her death-bedside religion amounted to an amalgam of the ancient Egyptian doctrine of the somatic soul, the Socratic doctrine of the body as a prison, and Spinoza's pantheism—with some science on the side.[y] It was her esoteric faith, disguised by her as diarist and frowned upon by her as essayist.

Early in May 1909 Lou was in Paris with Ellen. By then their friendship was sizzling: "Ravishing wild Lou," wrote Ellen once, "hasn't Turkey claimed you yet for some harem? Were I sultan I should have seen to it for sure!!"[696]—and Lou: "I could kiss you deaf and blind!"[697] It was then that Lou told Ellen her Nietzsche story—not for circulation, to be sure.[z] And Ellen brought Lou and Rainer together again, maternally: years later Ellen, expecting a grandchild, remarked: "I wish I could have one from Lou and

[x] From what cause I could not determine: Lou ever afterwards treated of Frieda's fatal illness darkly, linking it with her masochist perversion (as in *Haus*: above, p. 315—a passage surely penned after Frieda's death). It followed an unsuccessful operation and resulted in her being immobilized on "water pillows" with maddening aches in every limb.

[y] In particular, Lou argued the immortality of the "life process" as if she were arguing that of the individual by the same token.

[z] See above, p. 168.

Rainer."[698/a] Lou went to Rilke in Meudon, where, as Rodin's secretary, he lodged in a "glorious refectory of the Sacré Coeur, fitted out by Rodin himself with furniture of his own," opening onto "a gigantic terrace" over a fragrant garden running to seed.[699] She met Rodin to the extent of looking "into his remarkable baby-blue eyes, which puzzle one as to how they came into that head half boar and half Zeus."[700] Rilke had only lately come back to Rodin after an estrangement due to his horror at seeing "lust grow with impotence, physical and artistic": Lou thought him ungracious in this toward his great old benefactor who had confided in him—and whom he was "presumably" only running down after having built him up too high.[701] She found Rilke moreover unbalanced from having confused "the sculptor's handiwork with the lyricist's doing": he had gotten back *to* things only to crave getting back *at* them.[702]

Lou returned home in mid-May, then in late June met Ellen and her daughter in nearby Kassel to lure them to Loufried for three days. Ellen brought Lou a dog. Lou urged Ellen to keep her off the credit pages of new Nietzsche biographies. Lou also consulted Ellen about quick, painless poison that left no traces, then sent after her asking for some. She was expecting a "horrid illness," she explained, and just because her life was "fond rapture," its "every hour a jubilation," she deserved to dispose of it with serenity when the time came. She also begged Ellen to destroy her letter.[703] "Your letter is destroyed," Ellen replied; "torn to bits and strewn to the sea: a Russian death"—and promised to send some digitalis.[704] Lou next wrote of having learned from a doctor that digitalis *"doesn't keep,"*[705] only to reproach Ellen months later with having sent none.[706] Ellen told her to buy veronal: "Any doctor will prescribe it for you—just *take double* the authorized dose."[707] At Lou's next representation[708] Ellen bade her come fetch her poison in Sweden,[709] wherewith the topic lapsed. Behind it are discernible Frieda's death[b] and the break with Zemek—only why the insistence on being supplied by Ellen? Lou was imitating her own Margharita, to whom Kuno had proposed belatedly and who had falsely rejected him, then poisoned herself. For Lou herself had just falsely rejected a belated proposal from Nietzsche having Kuno's as its precedent—that is, had just told her inside story of Nietszche's talk with her in the Löwengarten—and Ellen, the instrument of her falsehood, was the instrument of her suicide-to-be.[c] Or rather, of her suicide-not-to-be: her Margharita had not died in vain.

---

[a] Ellen's daughter died bearing that grandchild.

[b] The "horrid illness" was Frieda's: Lou was by then in fine shape again.

[c] Why *this* was so escapes me. But the association is amply grounded: Lou's request to Ellen echoed Margharita's mock life-loving and Zarathustra's doc-

With Lou's suicidal spell went work on a manuscript already "very corpulent" by late July 1909[710]: an amalgam of her old essays on religion such as she had planned a decade before. She set it aside for a trip to Berlin in August,[711/d] then in January 1910 answered a query about it from Ellen: "It is no longer my concern—as when an autumn leaf has fallen from the branch."[712] Next she undertook a volume of children's songs or poems, which busied her intermittently for two years[713]; no couplet or lyric survives, if indeed any materialized. Some "children's stories"[714] did materialize in rough form that fall, including two allegorical children's dreams involving daisies and clouds in the complexities of simultaneously being and having all. That winter a monograph followed on erotism for a series on "society" edited by Martin Buber, who had requested one from her on woman over three years before with flattering reference to her relevant back essays.[715] Substantially her monograph repeated these,[e] if with some new edge in the case of the lover who, taking his beloved for "the totality,"[716] was "unconsciously" overcompensating for "erotic self-seeking"[717/f] while also sighing back "to some lost paradise or other"[718]—or in that of the "ultimate image for all happening," now "a hymeneal fertilization and conception."[719] And now bisexuality joined the dichotomies dissolved in coital self-embrace.[720/g] The tone, incantatory and carnal-churchly, was that of a high priestess of Eros, even as the diction, in its poetic density, was just this side of sibylline sing-song. "A fundamental, pure, powerful piece of work!" cried Buber,[721] who titled it *Die Erotik.*[h]

In March 1910 Lou revisited Petersburg, stopping a few days each way at the Klingenbergs'. She found her mother, after some illness, "as robust and cheery as before."[722] Departing, she "took old letters and Grandmama's picture along."[723] She deposited her manuscript on God with her hosts in Berlin: written for Ellen in particular at first,[724] it came out addressed to Helene's children. Ellen was beside herself

---

trine of suicide, and Lou's tardy reproach to Ellen over not having sent the digitalis was formulated in the very context of a new request to be kept out of the Halévy business.

[d] And possibly to Petersburg (EK→Lou, 31 VIII 1909).

[e] And some subsequent diary entries—e.g. D 29 VI 1906 (on childbirth) and 1 I 1907 (on chastity).

[f] Possibly excepting this point, the work is less Freudian than its forerunners—even in contending that man's intellectual development entails his either sublimating or repudiating his "animal material" (1909b:57-59), for Lou here meant "sublimate" in Nietzsche's sense.

[g] As against 1912c:78.

[h] In lieu of Lou's original title, which probably involved the term "erotic affect" (Buber→Lou, 10 II 1910). Reviews were few and mixed.

that Lou could "bury a manuscript with the Klingenbergs."[725] It was then, in Berlin, that Lou must have met "this cleverest woman in the world,"[726] Lucia Dora Frost, beguiling explicator of Prussia, with whom she had begun corresponding. And she timed her trip so as to meet Buber,[727] with whom she struck up a friendship based on mutual esteem. In Buber's passive wonderment at life she admired a supreme Jewish courtesy toward God.[728] "How alike we think about 'experience,' about idealization as realization, about polarity as the point of departure for experiencing unity!" she once exclaimed.[729] She drew the line only at his construing Judaism as the religion of the Jewish people—of a tribe as such, that is, inclusively and exclusively[730/i]— and the god of the Hassidim as the Jews' mystical masterwork instead of simply their loftiest self-portrait.[731] Later Buber came to uphold the "I" in face of the divine "Thou"[j] as against Lou's clamor for their reintegration, and to deplore the profane lover's self-absorption as a sign of the times.[732] Nonetheless he followed Lou on psychology wherever she led—even into the depths.[k]

Lou was home writing poems and *Das Haus* till the late summer of 1910. Then she went bathing on the North Sea island of Föhr, where she admired the solemn styling of home life. She was probably at the Klingenbergs' in early November[733] and afterwards perhaps in Paris consorting with Russian terrorists, whose fatalistic self-dedication she assimilated to that of their peasant brethren back home, the contrast defiance-forebearance notwithstanding.[l] Between times she took a new daughter: gifted, clever, lovely Ellen Delp[m] of Leipzig, lately a child actress, who wrote her a huge self-introduction on reading *Ruth* and received a telegraphic reply.[734] March 1911 found Lou

[i] She likened his conception of his people to the "inbreeding dream of our aristocrats."

[j] This key contention of Buber's about religion, that man's basic relation to a living god is dialogical ("I–Thou"), follows Lou's perennial point about primitive or childhood religion (especially as in 1909a: chapter I: "*der auf Du und Du stehende Kinderglaube*"), which she perhaps discussed with Buber— though again, this same point figures already in Feuerbach. Buber, 88ff., rejects "God-in-self" and "self-in-God."

[k] That passion, religious or erotic, "suspends all partial activities," see Buber, 91; on the artist's relationship to his nascent work, *ibid.*, 16-17 and 51ff.; on the emergence of the ego with its "I–It" relations out of the undifferentiated "I–Thou" of primal narcissism, *ibid.*, 29ff. (cf. especially 1914b:12 on the "confluence of 'I and Thou'" in protonarcissism). D 10 III 1915 suggests that Lou wanted to teach Buber some psychoanalysis. This she doubtless did through her offprints—though by the time of his *Ich und Du* (1923), an "It" had apparently intruded upon the predifferentiated "I–Thou" of her protonarcissistic scheme (1920b).

[l] 1931a:79-80: on "my third stay in Paris, 1910."

[m] Who, however, signed herself "Ellen Schachian" at least until 1914.

just back from another, unseasonable jaunt to Föhr.[n] Buber visited her for Easter 1911. A protracted heat wave took her through to mid-August sunbathing in the nude. Then, after two days at the Klingen-bergs', she went for a month to Sweden—to a "weather box in the forest primeval"[735] and Ellen Key "naked and happy in the sun."[736/o] They sunbathed together: "a beautiful, dear time it was," Lou told her afterwards.[737]

Lou left with a distant cousin of Ellen's, the psychotherapist Poul Bjerre, who took her to a psychoanalytical congress in Weimar for three days beginning September 21. He had briefed her on the subject beforehand: evidently it sounded all new to her. Through him she made Freud's acquaintance. Afterwards she helped him prepare a re-port on the proceedings for his Swedish colleagues. And she resumed reviewing books with lush praise for one about a baby which set that "son of man" upon "a pedestal arising out of the all itself" and there-by endowed him with "the secret sense of all worlds."[738] October found her in Berlin, where she agreed with Buber on the formulae: "Magic: against causality. Mystery: against the *principium individu-ationis*."[739] At the month's end she proceeded to Petersburg—and when the time came to leave again, "my dear old Mushka . . . cuddled her dear old head up against me, and at her rare tenderness I felt with pain that we ought to have given ourselves this happiness through a long life."[740] She sailed home from Finland, reflecting on dreams as unfolding "an eternal presence, which one *lives* even unknowingly."[741/p]

Back in Loufried, she reworked her book about God reclaimed from Helene—*Der Gott*, as it was now titled. The finished product summed up a decade of her mental life in the sorry sense that there was less news in it than in even *Die Erotik,* though its themes had been with her longer. Her diary entries of that decade tell the same story: she had been rehearsing the thoughts of her own golden age increasingly,[q] but also sharpening the mystical edge to them. Now *Der Gott* repeatedly exceeded that crucial nuance between density and impenetrability. This was henceforth her running literary peril as at her worst she thought to intuit truths extralogically. To an admirer who in 1914 remarked on her "compressed (and for the average

[n] D [1911]: "Noon to Hamburg-Wyk, Friday away. Hannover. Loufried. March 1911," etc.

[o] A common friend from Kassel, Maria Breysig, accompanied Lou.

[p] And discussing this with an unnamed traveling companion—according to Wedekind, 259n., a woman.

[q] Thus, as between an early and a late restatement of 1901c (D 4 VI 1902 and D IV 1910), the latter is closer to the original.

reader all too concentrated) thoughts"[742] she replied: "I can write on abstract matters only if I consider that my essential meaning remains far, far more concentrated still, gathered into itself as into a single round point and sooner expressible as image or poem or even sigh. To loosen it even just enough to articulate in conceptually costs me inhuman trouble—no, almost more than trouble: pain. This it resists like orthopedic dislocation, whereas I would but lend it the right and straight members with which alone it wins the consideration of men."[743/r] In fact Lou seems to have worked the other way, tightening rather than loosening, for *Der Gott* is precisely old wine newly distilled. True, in dealing with religion as distinct from erotics, she strained for an ambiguity germane to her message. *Der Gott* opens with the question "whether He actually exists," only to answer it both ways at once through some 30,000 words to the effect that religion is illusion expressive of truth and that God "wanders through the ages as his own symbol"[744]: God and death wind up accordingly as "our very ultimate ways of living," with the "crumbling of our world" at death "a picture puzzle of God."[745] Her formulations of the 'nineties, transparent, had worn through—though again, *no* verbal artifice could long bind her two contrary intellectual tendencies of divinization and reduction, which goaded each other continually. Often she inclined to settle for divinizing religious creativity itself taken as irreducible, only this solution was too onesided emotionally —too masculine—to hold. Her one substantive innovation in over ten years was her affirming the transrationality of the truth about " 'God' "—or perhaps the substance here came down to a rationalization of the strain on language involved in praying against her own better judgment. Some of the obscurity in *Der Gott* also went simply to conceal the unoriginality,[8] and much was in the order of transitions to and from purple passages penned apart that did not quite fit. But if many a sentence was strictly between herself and her " 'God,' " many another yields pseudomeaning pellucidly: thus "the fullness of life consists in its everyday unfulfillments,"[746] ethical maxims "derive from a remembrance of creative aliveness itself,"[747] life is "its own

[r] Cf. D IX 1919 (on how her mind was fed by logically inexpressible thought complexes slowly arising out of deepest affectivity)—and, on "orthopedic dislocation," below, pp. 417, 422, 423, 424. She did revise her drafts in the sense of greater clarity, but not of greater length. She would generally stand by a cast of sentence throughout successive rewordings quite as if she composed with ideal words in the first instance, then supplied more and more nearly equivalent real ones. Her densest sentences make even Mallarmé sound longwinded (e.g. one in 1917a:789 on how in Symbolism mental and sensual come together and apart). But some dark passages in her latest publications were simply ill proofread.

[8] And yet *Erotik*, also quite unoriginal, is never quite obscure.

symbol,"[748] the concept of inorganic matter arises out of man's need to "dash nature to bits at some point or other" so as to feel more "complete,"[749] works of art are the "bier" on which life lies,[750] and life and death are "*one,* and for that reason twosidedly distinguished."[751] At its most tortuous, moreover, *Der Gott* was still close to Lou's late prose at its riskiest best: elliptical and intricately inflected, every noun a verb in a state of suspended animation, all bursting with vitality provided only it made sense.

Lou herself deemed *Der Gott* unfit for publication: a bound copy, complete with dedication to the Klingenbergs, joined her manuscript pile, which she deposited in a bank safe shortly afterwards with great to-do, professing to withhold her choicest output from vulgar publicity. In fact nothing withheld was quite ripe—or in her idiom, none of the babies was yet quite born. Since *Ródinka* she had been outdoing Beer-Hofmann in the slow nurturing of embryos,[t] which she now lodged where, as she said, jewels belonged.[u]

An article on Lou that appeared in October 1911 presented her admiratively as, at fifty, a "historical personality" whose career had "closed" ten years before.[752] Yet her hair had lately turned golden instead of silvery, and, queenly as was her figure by then, her face had become (by all accounts) that of a fairybook princess. And here and there throughout even the overwrought old refrains of *Der Gott* a new strain did sound—or rather an oldest one sounded with some new, unpracticed inflections: depth psychology. She now likened religious to hysterical "symptom-building,"[753] and again artistic production to excretion.[754/v] Not only did she pretty up her stock point that, as reality grows more demanding on a child, the child's natural mediators between itself and reality, its parents, come to be seconded by goblins and their ilk ("vice-mamas and -papas"), then by "the god"[755/w]: she also made the point resonant with Alfred Adler's updating of Feuerbach on God as man self-imagined without mortal frailty.[756] Most suggestively, while elaborating her own religious reminiscences out of childhood a stage further, she for once qualified them, if only *pro forma,* as of uncertain accuracy.[757]

Having set *Der Gott* aside, she noted at the close of 1911: "Psychoanalysis—with ever increasing admiration for Freud's unreservedness, rectitude, objectivity. I am getting deeper into it than through Bjerre, see where he stops short. If one avoids, surmounts that, founts gush up."

[t] See above, p. 293.

[u] See below, pp. 438-39 and n. *e*; also 1913e:1-3 (jewels as a woman's inner treasure) and below, p. 349 n. *x*. Sexual symbols apart, this showed the value she attached to her manuscripts.

[v] (Just after characterizing life as a work of art.)

[w] (Repeated in 1913c:458.)

PART FOUR · MATURITY

*Y*OU CONTINUED studying psychoanalysis at home most of 1912 with few diversions. One such was a springtime stay in Berlin during which she impressed Freud's disciple Karl Abraham with her uniquely "deep and subtle understanding of analysis."[1] Another such was an article lauding Elisabeth Siewert's writings as "nowhere debilitated by modern-day 'psychologism' with its sauntering problem-phantoms and emotional concoctions supersubtly unraveled past recognition"[2]—an odd tribute from Lou in any year.

On October 25, 1912, Lou arrived in Vienna with Ellen Delp. Following in Zemek's old footsteps, she had obtained Freud's leave beforehand to attend his university course on psychoanalysis and his private Wednesday evening seminar.[3] She had addressed herself even earlier to Alfred Adler, the first schismatic psychoanalyst, affirming that her own reservations about Freudianism were akin to his.[4] Adler's began with making light of infantile sexuality and setting its pathogenic role at naught. They culminated in his rejecting the unconscious and treating sexuality and personality both as mere "fictions" or "symbols." All life, Adler maintained, was activated by will to power, which in human culture meant first and foremost will to manliness: the "masculine protest." Mental life was compensatory for organic deficiency (primarily genital); neurosis was overcompensatory. Everything psychic, including even the emotions, was just so much "artifice," so much "arrangement," in the service of will to power. Adler's great ingenuity was bound to a petty animus against Freud: with his anti-Freudian system he was in effect calling Freud a dupe to patients' pleas that they knew not what they did or could not help themselves. If ever theory was personal confession, Adler's theory of the "inferiority complex" was. In her marginalia of 1911-1912 Lou was partial to Adler as against Freud on the balance, notably in agreeing that Freud overrated infantile experience "in every which way: as sexual, as sole groundwork for the unconscious, as emotional final cause—whereas behind it lie the biological and the 'panpsychic' factors." On meeting Adler in Vienna, Lou declared that she came to him from work in religious psychology much like his on "fiction-building."[5] There indeed lay Adler's appeal for her: he desexualized her religious childhood. She was not prepared to treat sex as purely symbolical for long, though, or psyche as strictly symptomatic even for short.[a] Besides, Adler's psychology of organisms adapting was at odds with her every notion of personal identity and inner necessitation.

Adler welcomed Lou into his own discussion group, which met Thursday evenings. Freud, perhaps suspicious, inquired on her first Wednesday evening whether she knew Adler's work; whatever she answered, she stayed away from Adler's on the morrow, then sent assuring Freud "before I go there" that Adler's was only a side show for her.[6] Freud exempted her from opting if she would engage in "an artificial psychic split, never mentioning there your form of existence here and vice versa."[7] There, it would seem, Lou protested the "masculine protest" under her breath after vainly requesting Adler to construe femininity "more positively, if you please."[8] In Freud's circle she similarly saved her say for her diary except for notes and whispers exchanged with the master, at whose elbow she sat. She contributed to his lectures by becoming his "fixation point" in the audience.[9] Her second week she sent him a belabored brief of her theoretic misgivings to date: it went from the Adlerian inferiority complex as a frustrated "coddling need" *à la* Aunt Caro to sublimation as no shift from sex to mind, but a "creative confluence" of the two.[10] "How painful it must have been for you to write out these *difficult* things so much easier to talk about," replied Freud diplomatically.[11] A few informal evening visits to Freud's on the Berggasse ensued, two of which involved psychoanalytical chatting about her childhood.[b]

Lou felt herself "in such good company" among the Freudians.[12] She caroused with them in the Café Ronacher or the Alte Elster a few steps from her hotel. She attended a new elementary course on psychoanalysis offered by one of the five young men in the Wednesday group, Viktor Tausk, and by Tausk's doing she got to try practicing psychoanalysis once at a neurological clinic.[13] Collaterally, she went to the university a few times to hear Hermann Swoboda, whose conception of a "life-germinating, growing, future-ripening" unconscious she had preferred in print to Freud's of a cumulus of psychic refuse[14]; on the podium, however, Swoboda proved too intent on being clever,[15] besides which Freud was now finding more material in the unconscious than had ever been conscious—and who knew where that might lead?[16] Before returning to Göttingen, Lou spent April

[a] She afterwards neatly observed that old-style materialists, who deduced mind from body, were "harmlessly goodhearted" alongside of Adler, who deduced it from the body's gaps and wounds, as the negation of a negation (1914a:269).

[b] 2 and 9 II 1913. As per 1913a, Lou was alone with him there only once. Cf. Lou→Freud [3 IV 1913]: don't feel you *have* to invite me before I leave.

7-9 with Ellen Delp in Budapest, where they were guests of Freud's co-worker Sandor Ferenczi: Ferenczi, who philosophized behind Freud's back, took Lou through the notebook of "his dearest thoughts" while all along calling them "his 'folly,' his 'pathological curiosity,' his 'will to omniscience.' "[17]

Lou came home an independent disciple of Freud, whom she called devotedly "my turning point."[18] The turning was one against Adler. She had overruled her Adlerian reservations about infantile sexuality to ask how come, if psyches only play games, they all play the same naughty games to begin with[19]—and to add that the libido was no mere contrivance of the ego if, as was "clear," the two are indistinguishable at the outset.[20] She was now willing to treat sex as a symbol of the ego only if she might treat the ego in return as a symbol of sex—which she managed to find all right by Freud. The same went for body and mind as representations of each other; for, following Freud's seeming lead,[21] she now declared against arguing from one to the other, invoking Spinoza to the effect that only God knows how the two come to one.[22/c] Body apart, she pursued, Adler granted each mentality its distinctive "guiding tendencies" only to talk thereafter about what *it* did with *them*.[23] In fact "under his hand the 'arranger,' the person, becomes a fiction nowhere self-sustaining, *unable to deal with himself other than as the 'as if' of his own arrangements*."[24] Besides, Adler's scheme was monistic, which of itself meant onesided,[d] whereas Freud's was becoming more dualistic by the month, with neurosis already a mutual interference of ego and libido, already virtual equals (after the libido had at least *loomed* larger). Or rather, with Adler the obstinate libidinal fiction wound up for all practical purposes as the power drive's antagonist in an unwitting dualism.[25/e] But worst of all, life itself was for Adler "a mere mirage over a void,"[26] while for Lou it was real through and through, *beginning* with the unconscious. In fact Lou rated Freud's discoveries about the unconscious well above his constructions upon them. "His

---

[c] Similarly, D [5 III 1913] in effect asserted psychology's "right" to treat even a toothache as strictly mental. The Spinozistic twain did meet, however, in D [early XII 1912], where Lou, to support her theory of sexual attraction as a "longing for ourselves," cited Wilhelm Fliess on egg and semen as maturing through the secretion of their masculine and feminine substance respectively; likewise in D [X 1913], which assimilated repression to protoplasm warding off stimuli.

[d] And Adler's single substance (will to power) was Nietzschean to boot.

[e] D [28 I 1913] and D 1912-1913, *passim*: Adler sneaked autonomous sexuality back into his scheme under cover of the ego's quest for "secondary securings" nominally over and beyond social efficacy but actually to the detriment of the "primary securing," with resultant conflict and compromise (cf. 1914a:269).

digging into it—into all these phenomena experienced by me as positive, that is—has become more telling for me than any musing over
it," she told Adler.[27] Freud for his part pointed out more prosaically
that neurosis and organ inferiority do not necessarily go together and
that children aspire to virility while still too young for cultural motivation. And he returned Adler's compliment, calling Adler a dupe of the
ego's boasts of mastery over the whole person. Freud was right—yet
he might have learned much from Adler about the ego's complicity
in the subversive enterprises against it. And though he disposed of
Adler's case against him conclusively, he did so week after week for
years.

On August 12 Lou notified Adler belatedly by mail that she had
gone all the way over to Freud's school, justifying herself at some
length.[f] His reply was so ungracious toward Freud that she called it
quits with him.[28] A year later she showed Freud their correspondence
—having first, it seems, touched up her records of her own side of it.[g]
Freud's verdict: "He is a disgusting fellow."[29] And ultimately she
interpolated bits about "scrapping like mad"[30] with Adler into her
Vienna diary.[h] She had corrected her poor choice of rationalist over
depth psychologist made thirty years before.

Carl Jung meanwhile had drawn away from Freud in the opposite
direction. For Jung, all was libido rising by phases above its crass
instinctual beginnings through evolutionary time according to an inner
perfecting principle. It was eating its own tail, quipped Lou,[31/i] adding that there was nothing crass about instincts. Jung moreover
stretched the concept "libido" too thin for words, Lou maintained:
just make his terminology consistent for any phase at issue and his
libido will come apart into ego and sex.[32] Lou's affinity for this
other philosophical monist is clear from her having charged him in
turn with her own offenses of setting theory before fact and vaporiz-
ing infantile sexuality.[33/j] Jung's innovations came to the floor of the

---

[f] Lou→Adler, 12 VIII 1913, could hardly have been sent as printed in
Pfeiffer, *Schule*, 175-78 (and Pfeiffer, *Leben*, 362-64), since Adler→Lou, 16
VIII 1913 (Pfeiffer, *Schule*, 178-80), obviously replies to a somewhat different
text; cf. n. *h* below.

[g] See n. *f* above.

[h] These bits all fall more or less ineptly at the beginning or end of regular
entries. The diary, once revised, may have been recopied (I was not shown
the document). Lou doubtless did the interpolating only after revising her
copy of Lou→Adler, 12 VIII 1913 (Pfeiffer, *Schule*, 175), which begins: "For
a long time now I have wanted to write and give you at least some hints of
what I now conceive differently from last summer, when I first wrote to you"—
words clearly incompatible with running quarrels the preceding winter.

[i] Cf. D [late X 1913]: it "turns upon itself and, so to say, eats itself alive."

[j] On the latter charge: Jung's notion of "womb nostalgia" struck her fancy

Munich psychoanalytical congress of September 7-8, 1913, as, Jung presiding, Freud declared them inimical to psychoanalysis. Lou attended after two weeks in Vienna helping Tausk with a paper on narcissism: Jung cut Tausk's delivery short. A majority reelected Jung president of the international association. A minority stood by Freud—including four non-Jews, Lou among them. Lou in fact *sat* by Freud—"and nowhere was I ever so pleased to sit," she noted.[34] Her loyalty was the prouder and firmer for covering doctrinaire differences with Freud as marked as those of the schismatics. For only superficially were her theses against Adler and Jung professions of Freudianism; fundamentally they were rather professions of personal devotion to Freud.

---

originally, except for its threat "to weaken the tabooed term 'incest'" (D [7 XI 1912]); then on second thought she approved his desexualization of infantile incest (D [early summer 1913])—before settling on the third thoughts cited above. Moreover, she consistently conceived of sublimation about like Jung, as in the long run actualizing a perfecting tendency inherent in life.

L OU'S PERSONALIZED Freudianism was a foregone conclusion in all essentials beginning with its being a personalized Freudianism. Anticipated already in her scant marginalia of 1911-1912, it was spelled out piecemeal in her diary for 1912-1913. Thereafter it was much elaborated but virtually unaltered.

The grand source for Lou was the narcissism of earliest infancy, in which ego and libido are as yet undifferentiated, self and world as yet undistinguished: "protonarcissism," as Freud called it in contradistinction to the narcissism that comes of it as the libido withdraws from objects and fixes on the emergent self. Originally there are no psychosexual specializations or localizations, no such opposites as active and passive, give and take, yes and no. In the little Narcissus, all is blissfully one. And all is love: "His loving is still his living itself, not a feeling alongside it; his innocence is so grandiose just because he does not have, but is, 'sensuality.' "[35] The reality principle intrudes upon this blessed state as the child half learns that his will is not irresistible.[k] Narcissism therewith breaks up into pairs of antithetical motivations that tend to meet—and hence revert to narcissism—at their impractical extremes, such as being and having everything.[l] Or such as pleasure principle and reality principle, which govern libido and ego respectively: the child accedes to the reality principle only in the high hope of thereby gaining mastery over the outside world so as to bend it to his pleasure. And while the libido presses continually to link the self back up with the nonself, the ego in its enterprise of objectification lops more and more off the contours of the supposed self[m]—to the same final effect.[n] Puberty is

[k] At first Lou considered alternatively that what cuts off the nascent self from the world was consciousness (below, pp. 342 n. x, 350 n. b); in fact she reverted to this notion in her last writings (e.g. 1936a: ". . . his becoming conscious . . . drove him forth . . ."), though she had meanwhile brilliantly expounded the genesis of externality out of frustration (1914a: below, pp. 349ff.). In both cases she was disguisedly blaming Gillot.

[l] E.g. 1929a:39 on "the as yet indistinguishable wanting to be and to have everything" (misprinted "distinguishable"); cf. above, pp. 252-53. Lou occasionally (farfetchedly) designated these the principles of ego and libido respectively.

[m] This phylogenetically too: see 1931a:195-96.

[n] D [8 II 1913] submitted that the ego's distancing the self from all else was already canceled at the extreme in psychoanalysis, which, "without detriment to the rational order set up by us outside, takes us home to the never-disrupted primal order of all Being."

like an infusion of protonarcissism into the postnarcissistic constitution, which in due course sorts out egoistic from sexual impulses all over again. Narcissism remains meanwhile a deepest, vital memory— or more aptly *pre*memory inaccessible to consciousness, out of which we live as out of a dark, fertile subsoil that nourishes our sexual roots and ego stems as they blossom into thoughts and deeds.[o] Narcissism also remains our "lifelong, secret" companion through being the "*creative*" goal of individual life,[36] attainable here and now only approximately at most, in an ecstatic instant, as when the artist, in the throes of creation, masters reality expressively while losing himself to the task of expressing it—or especially in erotic love, that climactic instinctual release during which ego and libido all but resume their old selfsameness even as the twoness of self and world is all but forgotten[37/p] in a bilateral hermaphroditic self-embrace.[38/q] Despite many an appearance or lapse,[r] Lou did not promote narcissistic regression[s]: the way out of human individuation and isolation, she maintained, leads *through* these into second childhood—and into death, the hallelujah chorus of "our song of life."[39/t]

Lou never expounded narcissism without celebrating it rhapsodically as the be-all and end-all of life—as, in a word, divine. In the same vein she extolled the unconscious[u] as Narcissus' legacy, excepting its malignant postnarcissistic accretions[v]: were the narcissist fun-

---

[o] This vitalistic (and anal) image, by far Lou's favorite, did *not* denote the postnarcissist's "ego-libido" (that libido ordinarily attaching to his ego and hence unavailable for object-cathexis), which to her mind was a manifestation of narcissism proper: see 1914b:6. Just what it did denote is uncertain, though, the more since Lou time and again took it literally, the "subsoil" (or "totality," etc.) becoming the earth itself, which does indeed sustain us. The image was, incidentally, adapted from FN, *Genealogy*, Preface: 2. Nonmetaphorically, Lou said only such uninstructive things as that the "living [self-world] *identity as it were pulsates on in us through each and every articulation between inner and outer*" (D [10-11 IX 1913]).

[p] Cf. D [mid-III 1913]: "Our sexuality has no more important job than that of uniting us with reality over the bridge of our bodies."

[q] Cf. above, pp. 206, 253ff., 327.

[r] E.g. D [12-14 III 1913] and D [29-30 IX 1913]: the trouble with neurotics is not that they regress but that they do not regress far enough.

[s] She even declared regression into primal narcissism impossible: see below, p. 360 n. *j*.

[t] Or, by Bab's reading of Lou's late fiction, into transindividuation *here and now*, a state of being that was evidently distinct from the mere narcissist way of life outlined below as well as from insanity or death. However, Lou hinted at immanent transindividuation only allegorically (1909c; 1915a) or darkly (1901a). Likely she did mean it as a new human possibility and as our evolutionary destiny, but could never bring it to an "Also Sprach Narziss."

[u] Meaning the libidinal unconscious only, and this by and large only in its composite tendency (as against its component tendencies).

[v] That is, she extolled "normal unconsciousness . . . wherein sexuality and

dament ever dissolved in consciousness, she held, man would turn "sterile of body and soul."[40] And she cherished the libido for its instinctual immediacy, for its "preserved affective identification with everything,"[41/w] for its ever-readiness to overwhelm the ego and restore the old unity. Her pet peeve was the ego, vehicle for "the 'original sin' of individuation"[42] what with its competitive animus and fragmenting rationality. Grudgingly she allowed that the ego breaks off from the libido only under duress and for the sake of their joint survival. She likewise acknowledged the ego's mission of leading the individual to a knowing reunion with the all—and for that reunion's sake she endorsed the historic progress of repression and sublimation away from the permanent protonarcissism of animals and savages.[43/x] Besides, to the ego's credit it betrayed its narcissistic origin—and destination—in its dedication to the "world object,"[44/y] its universal labels such as "reality,"[z] its aims of total objectivity and integral consciousness, its sense of its experience as a solvent of otherness, its very pretension to judge of what is and what ought to be. Lou saw the aftereffects of protonarcissism all around: in fantasies of noble birth[45] and convictions of immortality[46]; in the "man of destiny . . . so magically served by fate from without"[47]; in sublimation, which was a sexualization of the ego and a displacement of libido from local onto

---

ego still lie narcissistically conjoined" (D [9 XII 1912]), free of pathological repressed matter. (D [end X 1913] distinguished repressions "in the sublimation line" from "pathological" and "life-inhibiting" ones: see below, p. 343 and n. *c*.)

[w] "The libido remains for the individual like a special substitute for aboriginal all-enfolding fullness" (1914a:272).

[x] But her endorsement on principle excepted nearly every specific instance of such progress that she dealt with. The idea that animals and primitives never outgrow their naïve sense of oneness with the world around them runs through her early essays on religion—as does the contradictory notion that the savage's dread of nature as alien was the source for his propitiatory myths of common descent with his natural enemies, whence religion arose. In early 1912 she noted that to stress the savage's being at the mercy of the unmastered outside world was to overlook his "all the more intact unison with it" equivalent to the animal's and the child's. Infants, however, are specially protected by parents as grown animals and savages are not. Moreover, if incipient consciousness alone disrupts protonarcissism (see above, p. 340 n. *k*), then it will do so for savages and animals too. Incidentally, the contention that "animals are essentially in sympathetic rapport with nature" (Hegel) and that "in the brute, inner life is one with outer" (Feuerbach) runs all through German phenomenology.

[y] Likewise, 1929a:69 gave as the ego's purpose "to affirm oneself this time and not be taken away from the world again" (as at birth)!

[z] D [V-VI 1913]: our fragmenting reality, then calling each fragment "real," is "a symptomatic act" (wherewith Lou symptomatically confounded the uses of "real" as synonym of *significant* and as antonym of *imaginary*); cf. 1929a: 103.

universal objects[48/a]; in the impassioned lover's regarding his beloved as all of everything[49]; in the high value we set on love[50]; in "that huge, simple fact that there is nothing to which we are not native"[51]; in any call for "unity" and any calling things beautiful or sacred or lovable[52]; in all art, prayer, creativity, sincerity, authenticity[53]; in all neuroses even, these being bad bargains between ego and sex[54]; indeed, in just about everything psychic that succeeds protonarcissism except for its direct derivative, narcissism proper,[b] which was her own instinctual fixation point.

By Lou's provision, the ideal narcissist would be possessed of a perfectly free-flowing libido, bound to no object or instinct, which he could sublimate or not at will. He would inhibit any given drive only to indulge another—and then only regretfully, retaining it "within the conscious ego-circumference."[55/c] His love life would be a promiscuous, genital enjoyment of "the partner *inside himself.*"[56] His experience would be what he *is* rather than merely what he *undergoes.* His pleasures, while never disjoined from his pains, would constantly exceed them—or else he would go *"away from himself."*[57/d] Under no circumstances would he fail to exult in life as a graduation from selfhood into the all. With this narcissist pathos would go a narcissist world view to the effect that the universe is his greater self, and not just potentially—though in actuality, *yearning* for oneness with the universe is to *believing* in it as poetic is to prosaic madness.

Lou's prescription for the grown-up Narcissus was supposedly also a description of herself. Every element of it was well seasoned, terminology apart. Often quite beautiful, it was never quite sensible. The narcissist ethic called for fostering narcissism because narcissism was man's fate—by which line of reasoning, however, suicide would be more to the point. Saturating the ego with libido night *and* day is likewise a fatal mistake, for it imperils supply lines of sustenance and gratification. Conversely, to be sure, the more we secure, the less we enjoy, but reality would have to cooperate well beyond its means to keep a single full-time narcissistic reveler alive, let alone satisfied.

[a] By this logic Lou should have championed all-out sublimation, yet she likened unsublimated libido to "a saving raft in the deluge" swamping primal narcissism, considering that it makes orgasmic, coital self-world reunion possible (D [early summer 1913]).

[b] There are two *half* exceptions besides: the ego—and the component instincts together with the corresponding perversions (narcissistic as of D [mid-III 1913]; nonnarcissistic as of 1931a:197-98).

[c] D [end X 1913]: the "impulse to repression" (thus construed) is healthy, and the removal of all resistances would spell "illness and ruination."

[d] It is not clear whither (even if, "beyond the narrow ego bounds," an affect prevails in which pain "may be voluptuously tinged" and which, "though joy, has become nameless").

And if flaunting the reality principle is suicidal, putting the universe at one's instinctual service is unethical—or at all odds ill-mannered. Again, however primal or however perpetual narcissism may be, its message does not thereby qualify as revelation; Lou in fact took care to subscribe that message equivocally in transcribing it—like the name of the " 'Lord,' " though with a thinner margin of reserve. Besides, as transcribed by her it evanesces on close inspection. It intimates a conservation of self corresponding to the conservation of matter, in effect a universal self mortally individuated; but then our self is just that mortal individuation as against the world self's stake in us. Lou also indicated that the world soul is only an abstraction from the world body and vice versa; only then the generic term "all Being" becomes *so* abstract as, in Kierkegaard's phrase, "to have nothing, nothing to do with existence"[58]—even if she did give "all Being" to be "latent" in the "physical unarticulatedness" of "the phallus naked and dumb."[59] She owned that narcissism's affective message was illogical,[e] only to conclude against logic. However, if we are not up to grasping some truths with our logic, neither are we up to knowing which these are. Further, if the narcissistic oracle rates a question mark, "question marks are no holy mysteries"[60]—as Lou wrote in 1882. But it does not rate so much. "Round about our consolidated ego consciousness," it typically ran, "our belonging to everything, identity with everything, still holds."[61/f] Insofar as the "belonging" is compatible with the "identity," the two are synonymous, whereas the "identity" clause relies for its intelligibility on the very distinction between *us* and *everything* that it purports to deny. Lou's key narcissistic pronouncement is vulnerable the same way: that the self will enjoy its renewed oneness with the all. Such propositions assert nothing, so there is no way in which what they assert could be true. Nor is this a matter of words as against things: what signifies nothing denotes nothing that might nonetheless be real. Lou's confusion all came down to a protest against mortality, for to fuse with the immortal meant immortality: that it meant such only for the ex-self went unnoticed.[g] Frequently Lou treated death outright

---

[e] E.g. D [30 x 1913]: ". . . expressible only mystically—or, just because mystical, not expressible." 1914a:272: even the body has trouble expressing the tendency to self-world reunion, for "organ language, narrowly self-enclosed, does not quite know how to articulate these expressions beyond our isolation."

[f] In denying real otherness, Lou of course did not deny an outer reality beyond the inner one. That we cannot live long without having to distinguish the two, she argued, proves that they are not identical (D [v-vi 1913])—an argument that should convince anyone but an idealist.

[g] D [1910 or late 1909]: at our death "only that becomes extinct which

as a mere "prejudice" of faint or joyless selves.[62] The force of her narcissist theory was to open the course of life out onto eternity at both ends so that death, like birth, ceased being an event.[h] Its emotional basis was thus "at bottom none other than a fear of death . . . stilled through this prospect of being taken up into the living eternity, of the individual's complete identification with the potency and plenitude of all life": so spoke Lou of Nietzsche's supposed late-life sansara.[63/i]

Lou contended, then, that at bottom self-world unity was a fact and the reality principle a fraud. An illusion of magical cosovereignty over the all through voluptuous intimacy with its activating spirit was, however, the gist of her childhood psychosis. Indeed, her stock excuse for her childhood god was that he had sustained her infantile sense of inclusion within an otherwise forbidding world. Thus the big biographic referent for the narcissist paradise lost of her late theory was her psychosis—that dream world lost by Märchen and her breed. The fraud was, correspondingly, Gillot's therapy.[j] The all was her father alias God, with whom she was self-identified and yet craved reunion, feeling lesser inklings of it in piety and authorship, greater in love. The remote referent for her imagined self-world unity was her father romance; for its disruption, the classic rude blow to that romance—and to her childish narcissism. This blow had failed to be a rude awakening inasmuch as, stuck on her romance, she had entered upon the psychosis. And the psychosis was a throwback not to protonarcissism but to its egocentric derivative—which of course bore some protonarcissistic features, especially a presumed omnipotence of thought,[k] but which Lou was the first to insist on regarding as a radically new departure. In other words, her professed fixation on protonarcissism was a displacement backwards—one displaced still farther backwards over the years in that she treated narcissism increasingly as a psychic prolongation of the intra-uterine state.[l] And not only self and world, but all the twosomes supposedly

---

obliged us to behold Being negatively, to behold it confronting us." Cf. 1912c:58: "our bit of eternal Being"; etc.

[h] 1912c:70 is typical (on birth): ". . . earliest childhood impressions, in which past, present, and future indissolubly unite, timelessly, unto eternity."

[i] Lou's idea that the ego is really out to die went to make the thought of death bearable, as she said of Nietzsche's "eternal return," whereas her fleshly-mystical all-absorption was designed rather to cheat death.

[j] Cf. above, p. 340 n. *k*.

[k] Her arguing from the affect of protonarcissism to a corresponding phenomenal reality was a sophisticated manifestation of presumed omnipotence of thought.

[l] Lou in D [10-11 IX 1913] both denied and affirmed this on the ground that

undifferentiated at the pristine beginning stood for the same incestuous couple at the back of her mind.[m]

Pursuing her own purposes, Lou had fallen in with one millennial tradition according to which individual existence is exile, and another according to which human history is a rough progression from unknowing to knowing harmony with nature. Both throve in romanticist and postromanticist Germany, and Lou knew their local exemplars—beginning with Nietzsche, who in *The Birth of Tragedy* argued our commitment to cosmic Oneness beneath the "*principium individuationis.*"[n] Both were religious in purport[o]—nor did Lou Biblify her narcissist Pilgrim's Progress merely to prettify it. There is the same cosmogonal catch to both: why the time out from timeless bliss? is there no easier way than individuation for us to learn how good we have it in the primal lump? And Lou wound up calling "our short-term life-plunge" with embitterment "the maddest business in which ever a reasonless creature could get mixed up"![64/p] Mythic conceptions of man's lot are mismated with empirical science: Lou conceded as much in that she called the ground of her own such myth "mystical"[65] and called Freud her security against "mysticism."[66/q] Yet in Lou's case that mismating proved not only gloriously happy— it was hers with Freud the father—but fruitful to match. And its finest fruits were studies of why and how the infantile Eden is lost.

---

the embryo has no state of its own; she affirmed it in a phrase of Lou→Freud, 10 I 1915 ("in the womb, in the identity with the surrounding world"), then in a line of 1919a:359 (narcissism: "the great all-womb, in which inner and outer events occur as it were undividedly"), then insistently beginning in the late 1920's.

[m] As against Freud, she consistently conceived the libido (reservoir of the cosmic pathos) as feminine-passive.

[n] FN, *Tragedy*, I and *passim*. Also: that we find solace in art, dreams, and frenzy for our individuation (*ibid.*, I); that the conflictual dualities of human life evolve out of "the primal Oneness" (*ibid.*, IV); etc.

[o] This even though young Hegelian materialists did fasten onto the second.

[p] (She did add that the plunge "expresses its heightened vitality as *our* possibility," whatever that means, but the bitterness prevailed.)

[q] In 1897k she had contrasted her cosmic pathos with mysticism but then inadvertently called it mystical anyhow.

III · THEORIZING FOR FREUD

𝕵 NEVITABLY, Lou's apprenticeship in psychoanalysis stirred up her mighty father complex, particularly when in Vienna she lived psychoanalysis day by day. Before such a Mosaic figure as Freud, destroyer of old law and bringer of new, she perforce felt the old lure of idolatrous pupilage, even at fifty-two. In fact Freud's credentials as god-man had drawn her to Vienna: she came predisposed, notebook in hand. The weekly closed sessions with her five "big brothers"[67/r] plus Freud "at their head,"[68] all so respectful and considerate of her, took her back to her childhood[69] as it had never been. Freud's gallant bearing toward her was likewise an old wish come true. And her grieving covered secret exulting when her mother died on January 11, 1913—at nearly ninety. Her two talks with Freud touching on her childhood (held on February 2 and 9, 1913) sufficed to consolidate the transference—even though he (yes, *he*) actually accounted himself a sixth brother to her.[70/s] Her father romance was on again—subjacently. Again it strained her personality, which cohered narcissistically through her self-identification with her father-god—and which now ran the new risk that she might see through that self-identification into the complex underlying it.[t] Her ego's defensive maneuvers led into her sharpest thinking ever.

On the defensive, Lou referred all infantile erotic motives, in particular those which were pronouncedly hers, back to that original psychic system of undifferentiated ego-sex as inchoate within it and hence premoral and presexual—basically and, she implied, abidingly.[u] Freud for his part considered the localized erotic impulses to

---

[r] (She also persistently called Freud's disciples his "sons.")

[s] Cf. below, pp. 408, 410.

[t] She already felt threatened by XII 1912, when she noted that a resistance tending to protect the personality against disruption was to be expected— especially from a healthy analysand—along with resistance to the analyst's efforts to bring repressed material to consciousness (D [late XII 1912]): see below, p. 370 n. *x*.

[u] "One cannot help thinking that all affectivity is a resonance out of life's original harmony of tones that sound harsh, indeed sinful, only when disjoined —and just because disjoined—within the individual" (D I-III 1915); "only when the ego is already developed can there be any question of 'sexuality' in the stricter sense" (D [latter II 1913]); "in interpretations of 'incest' the libidinal character is often much too narrowly conceived as sexual, though 'incest' originally falls within a period in which there can hardly be any question of distinguishing between subject and object" (D [early summer 1913]); deriving

347

be distinctly felt before a distinct ego formed. Tausk provided a narcissistic prefiguration for Lou's big libidinal outlet, anal erotism, when on November 27, 1912, he reported to Freud's circle on "the relation between narcissism and anal erotism (in which we grasp a work of ours, something objectivized, as ourselves). Thence to the father complex, etc."[71/v] This formulation presupposed that in anal erotism "we" recognize an "objectivized" nonself, in which case the corresponding narcissism would be of the derivative, degenerate sort. Accordingly, Lou was quick to differentiate between our discerning where we left off and our really and truly conceding otherness. Freud deemed Tausk's conjectures "too boldly assertory"[72]; Lou deemed Freud's strictures on Tausk's filial offering unduly harsh. Lou of course singled out anal erotism for preferential presexualizing, so that three days later she balked when Freud in his course "lightly linked up 'sexually grounded anal character' with spankings in the anal region": to her mind it was sooner sex and character both that were anally grounded.[73] And she reflected that humanity as against bestiality originates with anal disgust, which in children follows upon the repression of anal delight, then rubs off onto emergent sexuality.[74/w]

Her mother's death set Lou seeking a narcissistic prototype for her old mortal hate for her native erotic rival—a prototype the harder to find since, of all objects, an object of mortal hate is par excellence objective. So Lou herself reflected[75] after the second of those two psychoanalytical pseudosessions with Freud which sealed the trans-

---

friendship from protonarcissism, Lou affirmed that the well-nigh universal denial of its sexual root was thereby borne out (1920b:371); Lou→Freud, 2 III 1922, proposed that children first get to love their bodies through physical pain plus the suggestive effect of consolation from their elders; etc. Of her own pregenital impulses, homosexuality is a special case inasmuch as in Vienna during 1912-1913 it was considered a stage of libidinal development, virtually a component impulse (D [5 III 1913]), so that she desexualized it as such (D [latter II 1913]—while also ascribing its perverse form to a fixation on the parent of the *same* sex); thereafter, however, she considered it the pendant to heterosexuality in the sense that whichever was manifest, the other was latent (1914c:650-51; Lou→Freud, II 1918; etc.)—as if her foible for girlish girls were entailed by the postnarcissistic rule of opposites. Gradually she topped off presexualizing and premoralizing with de-effectualizing: to refer particularized motives back to that composite master motive was to blunt their purpose— and yet indirectly to affirm them through her profession of protonarcissism. She correspondingly made much of the component sexual impulses' converging in genital sexuality, to which of course she likewise answered present.

v The parenthetical matter is Freud's.

w ". . . dieser erste . . . Ekel von vornherein *von der Sexualität entfernt* . . ." (whereas 1909b:18-19 had given the source of sexual shame as the discrepancy between cosmic end and trivial means). On these terms, anal delight was the more desexualized since it could be sexualized only after being repressed.

ference—indeed just after he had shown her the anal-sexual signification of her very earliest childhood memories (against her inward resistance[x]). She thereupon moved to surmount her new, quinqua-
genarian daughterly crisis by two means: winning Freud's approval
for a presexualization, even depersonalization, of Oedipus' death
wish, but then again making herself master on a plot of Freud's own
ground in his stead.

The first enterprise issued in her theorem of original, prototypical
hate: hate for the parental authority that prohibits anal licence—a
hate redirected against the anal impulse in an original, prototypical
repression,[y] then against the anal product in a unique displacement
from a component impulse, leaving the self estranged from its entire
environment, from the body and its drives on out. Such hate first
makes the world truly objective,[76] declared Lou—meaning that her
theorem first set the record straight on her matricidal hate. The repression entailed by "original hate" was bound to be that of anal
erotism, already granted priority by her in the sequence of repressions; her distinctive new point was that the party issuing the original
prohibition came in first for the hate. She associated original hate with
anal erotism even as her hate for her mother went with her love for
her father. Thus, over and beyond her thesis that revulsion attended
excretion in consequence of original hate, she tended to couch original hate itself in excremental terms conformable to a dwindle-or-die
rule laid down by her just before she met Bjerre: "We *are* only in
that we sever ourselves from ourselves continually."[77/z] Her first
notation about original hate, which followed that anally tinged reminiscing at Freud's, begins: "His 'polymorphous criminal' [for "polymorphous perverse"!] struck me as colossally exaggerated until I real-

---

[x] D [mid-II 1913] simply records the recollections discussed at that visit of
9 II 1913 (which, incidentally, figure in her diaries beginning D 19 I 1900), but
1913e:(1-)3 indicates in the subjunctive mode—that is, in skeptical paraphrase
of someone—the predominantly anal character of those same recollections.
Meanwhile by D [early summer 1913] she sought to construe her fondest
memory of the lot—one concerning the ugly little things in fairy tales that of
a sudden turn glorious—as "a symbol of symbols"; 1913e:2 first allowed those
things their anal-sexual significance; 1912c:47 (passage written late 1913) proclaimed it.

[y] Of *conscious* material, that is: the conscious system earlier exerts repressive
force on its "inner contour" against possibly troublesome stimuli (D [7-9 IV
1913]).

[z] Exclusively eliminatory, this rule nonetheless topped off a consideration of
psychic life as concurrent assimilation of new experience and elimination of
old. Lou's complete scheme, then, calls for an initial elimination of the whole
cosmic nonself, thereafter reingested and reeliminated continually—in the way
of her retroactive additions to and subtractions from her experience as recollected.

ized why an impulse analogous to hate must go with the inception of consciousness: one attains to separateness, selfhood, only by repelling something, being repelled by something. That hate or the death clause should be found in the subsoil of dreams signifies nothing but an allusion to its point of departure—to that first cooling off, estrangement, separation, without which an ego would as little come to be as would breathing through the lungs if the supply of oxygen directly through the womb did not cease."[78/a] If, however, hating is an expelling, it is not a being expelled: this false equivalence served only the analogy with birth—served, that is, to identify the object of Lou's original hate.

Just when she recognized that object theoretically is uncertain. There is no trace of this whole topic in the few neat pages she penned late in 1913 on how the besmirching of the anal function carries over to the genital because the locus and the pleasure are so similar.[79/b] Nor is there any in a piece authored just afterwards[c] which, abusing those Sunday reminiscences for Freud, ostensibly revealed the anal

[a] "Repelling" renders "*abstossen*," which is as close to excretion and revulsion as Lou could unwittingly come. The subsoil was of course anal too, as was the parturition (cf. 1914a:252 and *passim*). Further sterilizing her original hate, she added marginally: "Hate: the disappointment, on awakening out of being everything, at not being able to love everything." With the "death clause" in the "subsoil" went, then, the eternal life clause, so that besides exculpating herself as matricide Lou declared the death penalty inoperant: she was making doubly sure.

[b] Between times, D [mid-III 1913] used Hegelian-style balderdash to depersonalize and asceticize "the father conflict," which it treated as the upshot of the dialectical self-development of consciousness, without mention of original hate: the self wills conscious distance from the nonself, yet even in achieving it would restore the old unity, hence identifies with the figure most apt to symbolize the power of Being over both; the self also wills conscious distance from itself, however, so that this identification serves the self as against the nostalgia for selflessness—whence the father conflict, "point of departure for all human struggles," which all involve "ambivalent" cravings for "security and emancipation—dependency and sovereignty" (ages later 1929a:22 carried these dialectics back to a beginning: "it looks as though that which is undifferentiatedly and unconsciously all-embracing wanted, at least in this inclusion of opposites, to assert itself further by passing into consciousness"; and 1931a:204 carried them forward to a finish: man, in seeing himself as an "other," so reverses the protonarcissistic situation that all "formal thinking" becomes "ultimately a sort of 'symbolizing'" of narcissism "by way of reversal" and that reason becomes "our artifice to which the prodigious synthetics of everything existential tenders itself: openly, but—as our analytics"). To the same effect, according to 1913c:458 (summer 1913) and D [early XI 1913], the child loves the father for narcissistic reasons—as most readily credited with omniscience and omnipotence, but also as intimate to the child's own world while belonging pronouncedly to the world outside and thus bridging the two.

[c] 1913e:first half (the second, unconnected half rephrases her old theory of woman: below, pp. 555-56); Freud→Lou, 12 I 1914, acknowledges receipt of the manuscript.

source of her sexual prodigality and stinginess both. Then all at once, in the early summer of 1914, the theorem was spelled out in a little masterwork of psychoanalysis, " 'Anal' und 'Sexual.' "[d] Literally ultraneat, " 'Anal' und 'Sexual' " was scientifically so as well—not because Lou had gone back on her repudiation of reason, but because she was out for Freud's approbation. If anything, it overproves—or at all odds overweights—its point, which is that anal revelry and anal repression are both precursive.[e] For the outer truth of the point was also an inner falsehood on Lou's part: her father-love and mother-hate were no *mere* reenactments of an old auto-erotic anal fancy and an old spite against its natural adversary.[f] To more such inner effect she kept "anal" and "sexual" distinct even while linking them: she showed how virtually everything sexual was anal first[g]—and hence nonsexual. Innumerable, her anal finds were the more notable for having been made introspectively for the most part—and in a psychic stratum above the one up for investigation, which ran too deep for retrospect. For " 'Anal' und 'Sexual' " was an unintentional memoir of Lou's regression to anal erotism at the height of her Oedipus crisis. Her taking the regressive for the original experience was what lent Lou her final assurance that the Oedipal drama was a repeat performance—as indeed it had been for Oedipus. The big renunciation was hers of the erotism directed to her father; the big blow to self-world identity was the one that struck her imaginary union with her father[h]; the egocentric narcissism entered upon thereafter[i] was her psychosis. And yet the anal romance, its disruption, and the idealistic narcissistic sequel also rehearsed her romance with Gillot,

[d] D VII 1914: "A+S ended" (cf. Lou→Freud, 5 VII 1914)—probably in substance the final product already, since this was not brought into line with Freud's "Instincts and Their Vicissitudes" of mid-1915 before being shown to him (but see below, p. 353 n. *o*) and even though Lou→Freud, 7 XI 1915, does imply that it was overhauled at least once in the light of other works by him published after VII 1914. On " 'Anal' und 'Sexual' " see further below, Appendix B, II, pp. 544-48.

[e] On the overproving: e.g. Freud, *GW*, x, 409-10, remarked that the equivalence established by Lou of *penis* to *baby* to *feces*, each being a rigid body that excites a mucous membrane tube through penetration, does not hold for most children's libidinal fancies, as their sexual knowledge is inadequate.

[f] In " 'Anal,' " Lou did not say *outright* that they were: she first did so in 1914b, which further devitalized the Oedipus complex (below, p. 549).

[g] Curiosity about defecation leads to curiosity about childbirth; etc.

[h] Thus her father stood behind her mother among those toilet trainers in " 'Anal' " (a father does back up such training, and the " 'Anal' " trainee objectifies *everyone* in consequence of that first prohibition). But that the big bully in " 'Anal' " was the mother follows from its presentation of toilet-training as a throwback to the regulation of breast-feeding.

[i] The dear self being, as per " 'Anal,' " the virtual "clean self"—in Lou's case, that self divinely preelected (personified by her angelic child heroines).

its disruption, and her self-identification with him. Unconsciously, then, she was affirming that the hate that climaxed her infancy was not merely recapitulative after all, but was due the opponent of her father romance—and this in any case since she presented it as merely recapitulative of hate for the adversary of the autoerotic original of her father romance.[j] (That she did not likely receive much toilet training from her mother directly[k] is as immaterial as that her mother may never have told her outright to let *Vati* alone.) Consciously she recognized no anal overendowment in her own case, introspection or no. In fact she slanted her text so as not to see herself in it: she spared no words for the elective affinity between anal erotism and (sadism-)masochism, and she cited the traits that Freud traced back to anal naughtiness—self-will, orderliness, and thrift—only in their extreme forms of obstinacy, fastidiousness, and stinginess.[80/l]

Lou was sixteen months between first mentioning this manuscript to Freud[81] and finally—anxiously—submitting it to him in November 1915.[82] She tried its logic on him once in the interim by excusing bloodthirstiness as a derivative of the emergent ego's animus against the object world and hence " 'evil' only as judged out of later object-love"[83]; he protested benignly.[84/m] Meanwhile he came out with a theorem of his own to the effect that the first feeling toward objects was a hate for them as alien irritants that was recapitulated in all later instances of irritation—and, oddly, of frustration.[n] At first blush, this

---

[j] Perhaps a diagram will help. Lou's unconscious message to Freud was:

	Early infancy	*Late infancy*	
A	anal (auto)erotism ⟶	love for father	A'
	⋮	⋮	
H	ORIGINAL HATE ⟶	hate for mother	H'

or that H' was merely recapitulative of H, and H correlative to A; hence that H' was hardly serious—besides which it connected with A', itself merely recapitulative of A, in only the most roundabout way. Lou's retrospective source was not really her AH, however, but her A'H'; unconsciously, then, she was asserting after all that H' was correlative to A'—as she was doing in any case in that she called A' and H' merely recapitulative of AH. She was further telling Freud that the blow dealt her narcissism by her father in the second case was also merely recapitulative in that her father had backed her mother's original demand for anal renunciation.

[k] Or much nursing: cf. above, p. 351 n. *h.*

[l] Cf. Freud, VII, 203-09. Lou was self-willed and thrifty all her adult life, and her papers evidence marked orderliness from the first—though in her early youth she must have been conspicuously disorderly and even unclean about her person, Nietzsche having (after Lisbeth) made such a point of this. (Incidentally, Lou and Freud alike overlooked the trait most obviously combining anal contempt for others with revulsion for filth: snobbery.)

[m] Cf. below, p. 409.

[n] Freud, X, 228-29, 231 ("Instincts and their Vicissitudes"). Compounding

was troublesome in that it admitted hate into protonarcissism, and without the world's being objectified—a hate originally due, moreover, to irritation and otherness rather than to frustration. As against Lou's, however, Freud's original hate was too feeble and volatile to objectify things really and truly, while they had to be semiobjective anyhow before Lou's could set in.[o] Besides, Freud's theorem was plainly provisional, so that, though Lou aimed only to please, she did not trouble to overhaul hers[85/p]: instead she just hailed the "novelty" of his making hate anterior to love.[86] She departed from him besides in disclosing the genital uses of anal erotism, he having considered that there were none. This was no anal spite; it was an anal offering.

Fittingly, Freud called her manuscript "your best gift to me to date," adding: "Your incredible subtlety of understanding as well as the greatness of your bent for synthesizing what has come apart through investigation find beautiful expression in it."[87] He worked the fateful first prohibition *à la* Lou into his university lectures[88] and appended it to a reedition of his *Three Essays on Sexual Theory*.[89] Lou had treated man's moral history as one long sequel to his first revulsion[90]; Freud went one better, linking man's first revulsion to his adoption of an upright gait.[91/q] Lou's notion that culture begins with man's disgust at his own excretion was a pretty pendant to Nietzsche's that culture ends with man's holding his nose before his whole person. More, it was Nietzsche's thesis that man acquired a moral conscience as well as a soul through turning the wrath meant for his masters inward, self-debasingly—and Lou's that original hate brought a conscience or virtual "clean self" into being as well as an ego or self or

---

confusion, he defined the displeasure involved in irritation and frustration as instinctual tension—as if a *love* object did not excite instinctual tension.

[o] Cf. above, p. 348. Just possibly Lou first labeled them semiobjective within primal narcissism only after reading "Instincts and their Vicissitudes." (Her prior notes on protonarcissism presuppose semiobjectivity, but even she may have failed to notice a presupposition.)

[p] (But see preceding note.) " 'Anal' " respected Freud's earlier derivation of first, feeble awareness of the nonself from weaning (attended by nothing more hostile than a grudge against the world for not being at our instinctual beck and call); Freud fast reverted to this derivation himself. (Long afterwards 1929a:23 oddly indicted the teeth: "Oral lust still sucks in the self with the breast milk—still truly autoerotic for a moment until, with teething, more aggressive possessiveness suspects the 'other' in the background as a part of itself wrongly torn loose.") To square her original hate with Freud's as of 1915, Lou would have had to accommodate the alien irritants to the effect that things are first hated because alien, then alien because hated.

[q] But strangely, Freud supposed that the upright gait came *before* disgust and shame.

soul.[r] The perfect motto for her genealogy of conscience was in fact her favorite dictum of Nietzsche's: that moral valuation is a "sign language of the affects."[92] And speaking of genealogies: Nietzsche's phylogenetic sequence of "master" affirming the world and himself, "slave" alienated from both through a rancorous negation, and "overman" reconciled with both was the original for Lou's ontogenetic sequence of Narcissus, post-Narcissus, and transindividuated Narcissus.[s]

Freud did not remark to Lou directly on her essay's tendency to supply Oedipus with ulterior motives: her cause was won. Oedipus' guilt nagged her no less: "Whoever becomes a criminal toward men and society is killing the mother inside himself," she affirmed,[93/t] meaning conversely that she who commits matricide in her heart is a real criminal. And she was to make a world-historical issue of the Freudian fact that woman after all did not slay the tribal mother as man did the tribal father.[u] Meanwhile, Freud did cite Lou by name in a stipulation of 1923 that ran: whereas he recognized excretion and even weaning and birth as models for the fantasy of castration, he "had" nonetheless insisted that the castration complex embraced only "the stimuli and affects associated with loss [!] of the penis"[94]— a corrigendum that extended of itself to the rest of the Oedipus complex. By then, though, Lou's menopausal Oedipal crisis was past.

Lou meanwhile pursued a second line of defense against self-awareness from the very start of her psychoanalytical apprenticeship, even before the resurgence of her father complex: besides dismissing Oedipal love as nostalgia for the self-world unity of protonarcissism, she distanced protonarcissism, her pretended emotional home, in

---

[r] The child rejects its old, dirty self on behalf of its new, clean self-to-be. (Original repression requires a repressive agency antedating this ego ideal, which, Lou held with Freud, turns repressive only after the Oedipal crisis. Lou→Freud, 5 XII 1924, suggested that such a prior agency subsists as an "ego armature" behind which the ego ideal sets up the conscious system's stricter border control.)

[s] FN, *Genealogy*, I: 10: (bad) conscience went with the slave morality, which began as weaklings were obliged to inhibit their spite against "an 'outsider,' an 'other,' a 'nonself'" in lieu of lovingly affirming themselves master-style; "to emerge, slave morality always requires a counter- and outer world"; etc. However, FN, *ibid.*, II: 18, called the slave's "a soul voluntarily at odds with itself, inflicting pain upon itself out of joy in inflicting pain," whereas Lou was shortly to set up masochism as aboriginal along with sadism (below, pp. 383-84 and n. *f*)—if not prior to it, despite her rule of primal opposites (below, p. 383 n. *e*).

[t] (Referring to Dostoevsky's Raskolnikov.)

[u] See 1927b—in which Lou nominally treated of woman's not having slain the tribal *father*, matricide being, she insisted, of little account.

every which way—conceptually, phenomenologically, chronologically —from narcissistic self-infatuation, in which her own Oedipal love had in fact issued. During her term of study Freud considered that, as the diverse sexual impulses developed in infancy, autoerotism progressively took over from indiscriminate erotism, with self-affection succeeding indiscriminate affectivity as the self came to be distinguished from the world. Yet in general Freud called the second psychic regimen simply *narcissism* like the first—and therewith lumped the two in effect. For Lou, however, to single out the self as sole affective object was quite another matter from affecting at large. Nor for her did loving the self over against the world evolve by way of autoerotism out of loving the undifferentiated self-world: her theorem on "original hate" designated self-love the complement not of autoerotism, but of a first repression of autoerotism dating some time after the disruption of self-world identity.

Here was the theoretic ground upon which Lou set out to become master in Freud's stead. In a diary entry pertaining to a Wednesday evening meeting of early March 1913, she distinguished aboriginal, all-generating, indefeasible, unfathomable narcissism from ulterior "ego-vanity" as against Freud's own indiscriminate usage, then remarked: "There is no question whatever but that fights will break out on this point"—ostensibly between true and false Freudians on the point of "psychology's right" to call that substratum its own.[95/v] Whereupon she discerned, "beside the Narcissus who amorously mirrors himself" and "that *other* Narcissus, whom the name does not suit because he does not mirror himself but *becomes*, but *bears* him*self*, . . . the Narcissus turned toward himself exploratively, the self-knower"[96/w]—intending Freud, to be sure. Assisting Tausk with his paper for the Munich congress, she differed from him in turn in that she regarded narcissism as unfathomable (as a "border concept," in Freud's phrase[97/x]) both "in infantile objectlessness *and* in the vanity of libido directed to the self as its object," yet also as concurrent with life "along *all* layers of experience."[98] She was quick to specify, however, that "the truly narcissistic accompaniment to all deeper acts of life consists . . . in the *still* 'self'-forgetful identification with every-

[v] Freud considered merely that infantile narcissism could not be recollected in its *full* naïveté.

[w] This canceled D 13 VIII 1900: "He who would investigate himself would but invent instead of discovering."

[x] Freud meant that narcissism was not amenable to psychoanalytical manipulation; Lou made this nonamenability sound like inviolability (cf. 1914a: 271).

thing that is . . . in contrast to that observing, enjoying orientation to *oneself.*"[99] That same summer she confusingly extended good narcissism's sway well beyond infancy[y] even as she chalked up her childhood god to her "inborn 'everything is due to me,' "[100] which made bad narcissism aboriginal—and hers. Later that year she tied the two terms of residual narcissism still more tightly together than in "Aus der Geschichte Gottes" sixteen years before: "In that basic state which accompanies us all our life (and breaks through especially in all creative experience of things), in which we feel ourselves twice as strongly *and* yet feel as if identical with everything, it is ever as though megalomania *and* absolute dependency conjoined: and this has characterized the piety of all peoples and times."[101] Elsewhere she went on drawing a strict distinction between primal selfless devotion to things and the "splendid autoerotic isolation" of the "second Freudian phase," even putting words of Freud's own to this effect into Freud's mouth.[102] But her wedge between the two narcissisms, original hate, came looser when, hard upon completing " 'Anal' und 'Sexual,' " she discerned that murderous hate was but "injured or stifled love"[103/z]—loos*er* because already the illogic of " 'Anal' und 'Sexual' " was that, whereas discriminative object-love comes only after egocentric narcissism, original hate can be withdrawn from its maternal object only by means of concurrent original love.[a] Freud's means, self-interest, amounted on her terms to love for a nonanal self not previously hated—which would not do. Her ostensible alternative was that the anal self was hated on account of a *potential* nonanal or "clean" self made to parental prescription by reason of the voluptuousness of obedience[104]—but that beloved "clean" self was made in the parents' likeness, as she well knew.[b]

In November 1914 an offprint from Freud redefining narcissism

---

[y] See 1913c:458 (on how children wondrously make a whole world of little things); similarly 1920b:365-66 (on herself as child).

[z] (This was probably the insight joyously hailed in D 18 VIII 1914 following her first shock at the hate released by the war.)

[a] But see n. *b* immediately below.

[b] By Lou's rule of postnarcissistic opposites, moreover, the original filial hate would be ambivalent—only Lou→Freud, 15 VII 1915, made a point of breaking this rule on behalf of original hate, which she wanted original as against love. (It might seem also that the child, in hating his prohibitive elders, withdraws libido onto his anal person *as an object* known hatelessly by contradistinction. This would mean egocentric narcissism anterior to the conception of a clean self, with Lou having been blinded to it by her concern to distance egocentric narcissism from protonarcissism. However, object-choice having once been distinguished from primal libidinal cathexis, the latter covers the child's contentious solidarity with his drives.)

prompted Lou to a new effort at clarification. As Freud now had it, human life began in self-world confusion backed by undifferentiated ego-libido; in time the self was singled out as a first love object, wherewith the libido was progressively differentiated from the emergent ego while yet adhering to it, so that there was still no discernible difference between sexual and self-preservative functions, let alone conflict between them; only thereafter, as the organism came to generate libido beyond what it could itself readily absorb, did it discharge the excess outwards—subject to recall in cases of felt danger. Freud still designated the first and second of these three phases alike *narcissism* and the libido's abiding affinity for the ego *narcissistic*. In fact he differentiated the two narcissisms only to mix them back up again by writing indifferently of self-world identity or self-love, of undifferentiated ego-libido or of libido attached to the ego. And yet—as Lou vexedly perceived—his version of postinfantile, perennial narcissism harked back exclusively to the second phase with its differentiated self-world and differentiated ego-libido.[c] Worse, he called the postnarcissistic ego by turns the libido's prime object, its reservoir, and its dispenser. Evidently his own terminology was confusing him, and not only on the two narcissisms: thus he assimilated undifferentiated ego-libido to unadulterated self-love, the self-world composite notwithstanding—only to speak of the libido's finding its way *back* to objects afterwards. He as against Lou was furthermore confounding *ego* and *self*—confounding the individual's defensive system with his person as it is known to him.[d]

"I could say so much in reply to 'Narcissism,' " Lou noted; "I was already awaiting the publication impatiently; only by mail it doesn't quite come off."[105] By mail she said six days later: "Today is not the first time I am writing you since receiving the offprint . . . but it got too involved on narcissism, exceeded the scope of a letter in the end, loomed like an imposition. It will reach you in some form or other yet, because the subject has long been pursuing me; for this, as for everything, there are doubtless personal reasons, only I hope that

[c] Already noted in D [late VIII 1913], which bore down on his likening the object-lover's libido to the pseudopodia of a body of protoplasm—an image inept on most counts (especially in making it graphically impossible for the lover, who disposes of the libido, to be its object as well). Residual "ego-libido" or "narcissistic libido" necessarily harks back to egocentric narcissism alone, being fully differentiated from the ego and (in passionate love) even separable from it.

[d] Lou in " 'Anal' " implicitly let ego and sex come apart before self and world (hence within protonarcissism): thus she wrote that anal erotism, on emerging, overwhelms the ego (1914a:258).

these have not led me into error."[106] A month later it reached him as a huge letter after all. It went straight to the point after quoting him on the aboriginal ego-libido composite: "I cannot help thinking that, from the narcissism here expounded as narcissism proper, is to be set off in some measure the narcissism representing a quite definite stage of development at which the ego knowingly chooses itself as object in preference to other objects, as in self-mirroring, vanity, and the like . . ."[107] It contrasted the psychological derivatives of the two narcissisms beginning with *experiencing* versus *experiencing oneself experiencing*. "Naturally," it pursued, the two were both libidinal saturations of the ego, "but only as it were to the observer; to the subject, the ego is only in the second case what the libido is meant for, whereas in the first one can fully as well say that the ego boundlessly dissolves, ceasing to be a subject in the face of the outside world . . ."[108/e] Adler's whole error was to take "narcissism of the second sort, the libidinal hypercathexis of the ego," as his starting point, and "so long as, in the concept of narcissism, priority is granted to the ego, 'to' which the libido attaches, Adler retains his good right to assess the whole business from the ego's standpoint—as if the libido were something in the ego's grip, put to the ego's very own uses and purposes—whereas in fact for us the ego first develops out of that life of subject-object unity . . ."[109] After countering Freud's specific treatment of narcissism in love (lovers aim at reunion with the all, *not* release of tension), in illness (our sick body is experienced as "*alien*"), and in "us" generally (our physical person is as much external as internal to "us"), Lou assured him that she did not mean to refute his conception of "the reasons for the libido's entering upon object-cathexes" and would willingly say why except that "then this letter would never end."[110] And Freud's ascription of original object-love to the subject's surfeit of libido rather than the object's attractiveness really was welcome to Lou.

Freud, by way of evading Lou's objections, conceded them *en bloc* and undertook to meet them someday. "Even Adler's advantage I grant," he threw in gratuitously, only to add: "It is the advantage of a prefabricated system superimposed upon things over observation anxiously concerned to do them justice. I console myself with the thought that it is not science's job to simplify the world, at least not for a start"—as if *Lou* had supposed it were. His final retort was less than worthy: "I know that your concern with Tausk's work helped familiarize you with the subject of narcissism. But his con-

e By "fully as well" she meant "really only."

structions were totally unintelligible to me." He had made his single proper point just beforehand: "On the main issue I should like to add that my presentation of narcissism is of the kind I shall someday describe as *metapsychological*—i.e., one having no regard for the processes of consciousness, merely topically-dynamically determinate. The cases of interest to you have to do chiefly with effects on consciousness . . ."[111/f] In other words, the viewpoint dismissed by Lou as extrinsic was alone valid—and to see it as such, Freud told her, was "no less difficult than indispensable."[112] Freud was right—unimaginably right. Metapsychologically seen, narcissism is one: undifferentiated ego-libido and libido adhering to the ego are equivalent; treating the universe as one's self and making a universe of one's self come out the same.[g] In Freud's metapsychological sight, narcissism was a distribution of psychic energy such that the organism discharged its impulses in their own time without inner tension and such that, if it got along with the world in this way, its affectivity registered in consciousness as narcissism of Lou's first sort, and if not, of her second. Thus *psychologically* narcissism was two, so that Freud's treating of it in the same terms psychologically and metapsychologically spelled contradiction—and this, as good rationalists know, tells against the speller. Only Freud was precisely *not* a good rationalist. Part of his genius was the brass to perpetrate conceptual atrocities with equanimity right and left of his main line of inquiry, which was then leading to that apotheosis of the scientific ideal: discounting subjectivity as extraneous to even the inner life. Rationalistically, he went from bad to worse: thereafter he would say that in the beginning all was ego, or libido, or indistinguishably both,[h] his tacit point being that it made no metapsychological difference which.

[f] By "topically" Freud meant with respect to the systems within or between which psychic acts occurred; by "dynamically," with respect to their aim or end. (He was to add a third metapsychological determinant, the "economic," to denote the magnitude of the attendant impulse.)

[g] In integral narcissism of either sort, all tension between systems is lacking, and all impulses are discharged without inner resistance; thus, metapsychologically considered, the two models are not only equivalent but lack a topical dimension. All narcissistic regression tends to restore this model whatever the psychological symptoms, which may in fact be of both Lou's sorts at once (thus the paranoiac, even while projecting his ego's self-scrutiny and his illicit desire outside of himself, imagines that the whole world has designs upon him) —though again, psychotic symptomatology does suggest that the supposition of selflessness lies deeper than the disposition to self-aggrandizement.

[h] In chapter II of *Outline*, his last major work, Freud had the libido "stored up" in the ego from first to last, yet meanwhile differentiated from the ego and then directed to it as to an object—and all this even though, according to chapter I, there was no ego at the outset.

Part IV: Maturity

Lou acknowledged Freud's rejoinders with effusive thanks and a delay of two months,[113] during which she wrote "Psychosexualität."[i] This was her defiant first move toward a compromise with Freud that would run the two narcissisms together as a single development in two ultradistinct moments. Already in "Psychosexualität" she expounded narcissism as a continuum, nominally according to Freud but with a rigor all her own—and as comprising *two* moments of *pre*individuation. After naïve use of the world as a self, she argued, comes love of a self inclusive of the world. Then original hate, dissolving narcissism, makes love of the self as against objects possible. This discriminative self-love—"egoism"—is no more narcissistic than object-love and no less so, the two being complemental cases of mistaken identity within the competence of abiding narcissism.[j] Freud had abused Narcissus, mad as the lad was, in having him love himself *alone* and the world *as well*; Lou abused Freud, lax as his language was, in having his Narcissus love himself *as* the world. And she abused herself as to Narcissus' affective legacy, for loving one's self as the world would be not self-preservative but, like Narcissus' own infatuation, fatal. She followed Freud where he led, however, on object-love as originally a drainage of new, surplus libido,[114] and she barely cited anal self-hate (with its untimely complement of filial love) as an antecedent to egoism[k]—though for all practical purposes this last rem-

[i] Part of an unfinished work begun x 1914.

[j] Cf. d v 1916 (the lover overvalues himself absolutely to the extent that he does not overvalue his beloved absolutely); 1914b:6: ". . . original self-love—as against later, conscious egoism involving self-delineation over against others—perforce encloses all object-love, indeed the world *in toto*. In fact it takes a first trace of disappointment and displeasure even with ourselves to set us over against the object as an 'other' definitively in practice—to teach us nonlove, hate, repulsion, in short to turn our 'introjecting' (Ferenczi) into projecting, wherewith we first create an 'outside' for ourselves in the libidinal sense. If 'outside world' is still missing from the first unconscious love-totality, it is conversely most solidly 'externalized,' pushed out, set up as alien, on this border of the first experiences, beyond which we never again can expand lovingly into a totality enfolding the world unless it be in the exceptional conditions of sexually or mentally creative frenzy." Lou→Freud, 2 vii 1917, added that the ego-libido differentiation was indefeasible: though the ego be overwhelmed by the libido in anxiety, heroics, even psychosis, "it itself and its *fonction du réel* remain unimpaired." (Lou later implicitly modified this implicit vindication of her own *fonction du réel* by making notes on the impairment of the *fonction du réel*: below, p. 369.) For "Psychosexualität" see below, Appendix B, iii, pp. 548-50.

[k] The original hate in "Psychosexualität" was in fact more nearly that of Freud's "Instincts and their Vicissitudes" than of Lou's " 'Anal' "—which would go to show that she brought "Psychosexualität" more or less into line with "Instincts and their Vicissitudes" except that in the most readily revisable passage of "Psychosexualität," a discursive footnote (1914b:5-6n.), the hate comes closest to that of " 'Anal.' "

nant of her " 'Anal' " theorem alone distinguished her latest ontogenetic scheme from Freud's.[l] She depicted aboriginal erotism gor-
geously without violence to Freud or fact: that impulse to enfold and
be enfolded, fondle and be fondled (Aunt Caro's "coddling need"),
discharged along the path of least resistance.[m] As for metapsychol-
ogy, she would not touch it on her life, for it canceled the world of
difference between the narcissism claimed by her and that disclaimed
—and now even renamed.

"Psychosexualität" was part of a book-length manuscript, *Ubw.*
(Ucs.), which Lou set aside in mid-1915. By November 1915 she
had adjoined to " 'Anal' und 'Sexual' " a vindication of Freud the
empiricist against his theorizing overtrumpers Adler and Jung: Freud
dixit, it mostly ran. Digressively, she endorsed Freud on narcissism
with only the expressly sentimental reservation that for her it was not
a dead end, but a live beginning.[115/n] Even as Freud so gratifyingly
acknowledged her " 'Anal' und 'Sexual' " she took up *Ubw.* again—
and "now I notice," she noted, "that it fits into my altogether synthetic
work of former years like an inner lining to lend solidity. As I first

[l] Again, perhaps a diagram will help:

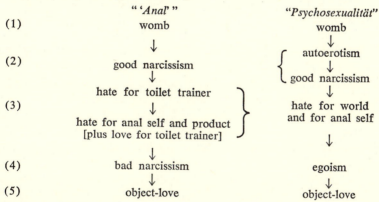

"Psychosexualität" (2) through (4) would be equivalent to Freud's scheme in
practice if the problematical suggestion of hate for the anal self were removed
from (3).

[m] At the last (in 1936b) Lou called it "our instinctive drive for contact,"
indulged by us "as if we were still seated within our object, which contained
the quintessence of everything."

[n] To be precise, narcissism was for her no mere cold stone marker beside
a psychoanalytical no man's land, but had "become to my inner experience like
a tree from which I plucked fruit to bring home to my garden." Some points
of her itemized endorsement tacitly equated narcissism with self-love (e.g.
1914a:272: that the passionate lover demands requital so as to replenish his
depleted reservoir of narcissism)—though again, many objections to Freud's
theory as of Lou→Freud, 10 I 1915, appear in this context of agreement
(1914a:271-73).

reread the old manuscript, it seemed just as if I were emerging to meet
myself from a tunnel dug through it in the meantime. My joy over
what I was bound to make of Freud's psychoanalysis is only just
becoming clear in my mind. It has been true December work: one
might say, a Christmas cake at which I have baked away these many
years. Solely concerned all along with loosening and browning the
upturned bottom of it, I completely forgot how I had once moulded
the dough. Then comes the time to flip it over—and there it stands,
its mould all its own! And yet I must say of Freud that—over the
last half dozen [*sic*] years—he has become important to me through
the addition of something new by way of substantiation: something I
would never have hit on if only because I was not moving in that
direction."[116]/[o]

Her direction at this writing was away from Freud's having provided a science to match her speculations toward his having turned up
some clinical data corroborative of *her* Ucs., then of *her* psychoanalysis. Her text was fair on the balance in that it did not overstress
the extent to which she anticipated psychoanalysis without also over-
stressing the extent to which she merely drew on psychoanalysis to
underwrite a preformulated message. But primarily it evidenced a
lordly superciliousness about evidence, Freud's in particular, beginning with that dirty bottom of things: infantile sexuality. It thereby
completed the sense of her frequent celebration of Freud's finds themselves over and above any theorizing about them.[117]/[p] It also rectified
her pronouncement on Freud as her turning point: he was rather her
terminal point—the supreme substantiation of her message about
carnal holiness hitherto sustained by Bölsche's amoebae and Zemek's
endocrine glands.[q] Unconsciously, meanwhile, from the inner lining
through that tunnel down to that loosening and browning, the anal
denigration and expulsion were graphic. But even as Lou's daughterly
defiance of Freud came to a head, so did deepest daughterly delight
at recognizing psychoanalysis as her own baby in Freud's name. It
was the *Michael Kramer* experience over again—only more so, for if
Freud had, like Hauptmann, added the naturalistic touches to the
coproduct in this case (*Ubw.*), *she* had borne it, and it was no mere

[o] ". . . *etwas, worauf ich auch der blossen Richtung nach nie gekommen
wäre.*"

[p] According to Lou→Freud, 14 vii 1929, his finds tempted her to turn
mystical but his example deterred her. In fact her small use for evidence was
the mystic's way—though again, her *first* reading notes on psychoanalysis do
abound in reflections about whether reality is as real as " 'they' " say, whether
the body is not a first hysterical conversion, and so on.

[q] These put in their last appearances in 1909b:9 and 16-18 respectively.

fiction.[r] Therefore she did not repudiate his mastery in her old maidenly way—the less since he never would assert it. Instead she sent him, like Hauptmann, rhetorical thanks in the guise of an introduction to *Ubw.* modeled on an imaginary address by her to Freud's seminar composed after her last Wednesday evening in Vienna.[118/s] As for *Ubw.* proper, she fretted to Freud over her abuse of his writings on narcissism—that is, over whether she had "understood every particular *wholly exactly.*"[119] "I cannot believe you in danger of misunderstanding anything of our conceptions," he assured her.[120] Yet she could not bring herself to submit the manuscript to him.[t] She published "Psychosexualität" in a semipopular journal rather than *Imago*: he approved her only on second thought and "especially as we may still expect the whole book."[121] Then, acknowledging the offprint, he declared: "I should only like to have your whole little book already."[122/u] In 1919 he again inquired: "Wasn't there once a little work, *Ubw.* . . . ?"[123] "After the partial publication," Lou replied, "my little *Ubw.* book no longer seemed to me good enough; there is no inhibition here, it really is so."[124] Freud was unconvinced: "Why have you suppressed or aborted *Ubw.*?" he came back a year later[125]—and there it rested.

[r] The "cake metaphor" had an epilogue in two installments. First, D [I-III] 1919: "Never shall I forget how in his course in 1913 he 'turned about' [not quite 'flipped over': '*umkehrte*' for '*umkippte*'] a 'completed' analysis, and there stood a piece of poetry of the deepest sort!" Then 1929a:14 digressed from a discussion of countertransference to tell of Freud's having once in a lecture in 1912 exposed a neurosis to its bottommost layer, then "suddenly, with a flip of the hand, the way one tilts a cake out of its tin baking-mould, lifted it to our view in its unimpaired entirety" and therewith unintentionally inspired his listeners with the astonished realization that their lives are works of art not of their own making. The phrase at the source of this pseudorecollection was doubtless one in D [16 XI 1912] on how, according to Freud, "the reconstruction of the completed analysis (from back to front) would require an artist." Incidentally, the *Kramer–Ubw.* pattern suggests that Lou's book on Nietzsche may have originated in a joy at recognizing her reductionist idea in his *Beyond*.

[s] And ". . . which I find in my written notes for that day in the following words." The wording of D [2 IV 1913] is not in fact the same, though the changes are mainly stylistic (including "two sexes" for "diverse sexes" and "brothers" for "men"). Literally, Lou's thanks therein went to psychoanalysis for having led her away from her writing desk into a scientific confraternity and to Freud himself only for having so well chaired the contentious seminar meetings.

[t] She hinted at submitting it in Lou→Freud, 11 v 1916, [21?] v 1916, and 30 VI 1916; he was more than willing (see especially Freud→Lou, 14 VII 1916 and 27 VII 1916), only not the least in the spirit of checking for accuracy or orthodoxy.

[u] He meanwhile supposed that "except for this concept [of narcissistic libido] even you would have deserted me for the system-builders, for Jung or likelier Adler" (Freud→Lou, 13 VII 1917)!

Part IV: Maturity

By then Lou had come around to the telltale use of *narcissistic* as synonymous with *self-* as against *object-loving*.[v] Another year and "Narzissmus als Doppelrichtung" (Narcissism as Double Direction) registered her final compromise with Freud on the discrimination of narcissisms.[w] Now the first narcissism passed directly over into the second, which ended as the libido overflowed. Now individuation simply befell the infant, who resented it in desolating anguish for "months"[126] before rejoicing in his new-found self. This rejoicing was fully discriminative, though beneath it "emotional identification with everything, refusion with everything" ("the libido's basic aim") persisted.[127/x] Abiding narcissism pointed equally in both narcissistic "directions," only again more equally in the one than in the other, for *maybe* even Narcissus really saw himself "as still everything": *maybe* had his mirror not been a natural one reflecting nature all about him "he would not have lingered beside it but fled."[128] Lou's lingerings apart, her compromise was roughly fifty-fifty: whereas now bad narcissism was linked to good within a developmental continuum, the link was "our original mortification,"[129] and whereas the two flowed as one thereafter, they flowed in opposite directions. The big casualty was original hate: objectification did without it.[y] Original repression was postponed, moreover, and the dear self was no longer the potential clean self. For the rest, Lou showed protonarcissism at work

[v] E.g. D v 1916, D II 1918—and here even on her way to viewing object-love as imbued with self-love ("the revered hero is oneself at the same time").

[w] 1929a:18ff. reviews her running difference with Freud over narcissism since 1912 as if this final compromise had been her position all along, even though before striking it she went so far toward repudiating Freud as to diabolize him unconsciously in 1919d and especially in 1919g (see below, p. 365 n. *a*). For a digest of "Narzissmus," see below, Appendix B, IV, pp. 550-53.

[x] On these terms, Lou could not very well call protonarcissism one "side" or "direction" of a dual tendency: it was a libidinal survival in its own right already *within* (or *beneath*) egocentric narcissism. Protonarcissism had to be postoperative within narcissism proper but could not be so without stealing the show—except on Freud's terms of equivalence. Insofar as she meant Narcissus to gaze upon "not only himself . . . but also himself as still everything" (1920b:366-67) without the first vision's yielding to the second, Lou was consecrating Freud's unhappy usage after having taken exception to it. She still implicitly denied that, once the second tendency of narcissism has emerged, it is necessarily coactive with first: thus "the psychotic . . . in relinquishing his capacity for transference, for object-cathexis, regresses to where one no longer transfers to particulars as such, hence no longer to oneself in particular either" (*ibid.*, 366). Professedly her purpose was "to turn that other side [of narcissism], recessive to ego-consciousness, face up" (*ibid.*, 363); in her developmental scheme, however, when self-world identity is manifest, self-consciousness is not latent, but nil.

[y] The implication of premature filial love was eliminated along with original hate—though somehow there are "beloved persons" before egoism sets in (*ibid.*, 364).

in love, in idealization, and in art, implicating herself continually. As in the earlier psychoanalytical essays she etherealized infantile sexuality,[z] considering it solely under the dialectical aspect of its presexual (protonarcissistic) derivation and of its genital destination. Now as before, the autobiographic referent for mournful exclusion from all-oneness was her ill-fated father romance, for lording it over the world afterwards her sacred egoism of childhood—or again her Gillot romance, then her sacred egoism of youth. And once more her big intellectual error was to equate *primal* with *prepotent* to the effect: since I loved my father as I did the world before him, he was a mere fill-in. In calling the primal prepotent, however, she was unconsciously affirming just what she was unconsciously denying, *primal* being one of her father-words. It was, then, to this double end of denial and affirmation—in this "double direction"—that she did her original work of psychoanalytical investigation and clarification, which that big intellectual error did not vitiate. For even in Lou's case the primal truth was true too.

A compromise, "Narzissmus als Doppelrichtung" was no capitulation: it could distinguish the two moments of narcissism systematically only at Freud's expense, and the more so the more it drew on Freud for authority. A compromise it was, though, meaning a compound of capitulation and recapitulation: Lou's distinctive conception of narcissism was written over. Her original work for Freud as well as that against him was done and half undone; her self-substitution for him was set back for good.[a] A personal settlement with Freud, "Narzissmus" was none of Freud's business. As against "Psychosexualität," which came into twenty letters between the two,[b] "Narzissmus," though published in *Imago*, came into none.[c] After its publication, Lou unprecedentedly took up the posture of loving, beloved daughter-wife with a joy uncontradicted from within.

[z] Even in "'Anal,'" anal erotism is only euphemistically evoked (besides being denied the name of sexuality). Here was no ladylike demureness: Lou was almost brazenly graphic about the anatomy and phenomenology of genital sexuality. She nonetheless maintained in 1931a:193-94 that psychoanalysis had taught her not to prettify infancy.

[a] The backsliding from "'Anal'" and "Psychosexualität" to "Narzissmus," paralleled within her psychoanalytical practice (below, p. 366), was somewhat offset by a new, lesser line of doctrinaire defiance concerning artistic creation (below, pp. 386-87).

[b] (Counting three that refer simply to *Ubw*.)

[c] True, Lou visited Freud in Vienna a few weeks after its publication (late 1921). Also, Freud's treatment of narcissism in *The Ego and the Id* (1923)—his most terminologically consistent—rejoins Lou's in "Narzissmus."

L O U W A S , then, pretendedly and again actually her own main subject for research into narcissism. Yet she did not lack ready alternatives, for besides theorizing about psychoanalysis she practiced it. She underwent no training analysis beyond Freud's two Sunday chats with her. After the first of these she noted that she—exceptionally—had not come to psychoanalysis to untangle "mix-ups between depths and surface."¹³⁰ In this spirit she conducted a self-analysis amounting to a reworking and especially rewording of stock reminiscences out of her childhood.ᵈ She could make out neither the wishful thinking beneath her fictionᵉ nor the human being behind her god.ᶠ In 1917 she avowed that she "did not get so far in practice" with herself as with others,¹³¹ only to declare in later years that every analyst is in duty bound to be as self-analytical as he requires his patients to be.¹³²

And yet in time she made a great analyst. After Vienna, where she had proudly donned "the white doctor's frock" in the neurological clinic,¹³³ she took on a first patient in Berlin three hours daily for one week late in October 1913.¹³⁴ In the winter she rounded up a girl to treat at Loufried,¹³⁵ in the spring a man,¹³⁶/ᵍ in the summer a lady.¹³⁷/ʰ She kept her practice from Freud until she grew submissive in this imitation of himⁱ in turn and, beginning in November 1917, sought his guidance and approbation. She did have more than her share of outlandish cases even for those times before common knowledge of neurotic syndromes had normalized them. With one case she drove Freud to doubt he could ever make simple sense of emotional life—

ᵈ 1913c:457 (on exploding bonbons and a cigarette burn) rewords 1893g:70; etc. Lou→Gebsattel, 15 ɪ 1915, draft, intimates that she was then earnest about the supposed self-analysis.

ᵉ ᴅ ɪ 1919: the "fact . . . so struck me in self-observation: how much, in the joy of artistic experience, such subjects take precedence as never had entrée to the realm of real personal wishes" (but instead derive directly from protonarcissism); etc. Her interpretive notes on her fiction (as on her dreams) are psychoanalytically inept one and all.

ᶠ See above, p. 25 n. *l*. But *Ellen Delp: in 1912-1913 Lou freely owned in conversation that her father stood behind her god, her lovers, and Freud. (Also, ᴅ ɪ 1915 represents her abiding relationship to her father, alias Nietzsche, in transparent symbols under the heading "Bird Dream.")

ᵍ Her diary implies that the man's treatment was completed within the month.

ʰ (Named Paula and possibly resident at Loufried.)

ⁱ (And—in regressive order—of Bjerre, Zemek, Rée.)

that of a girl who, after taking her father's piles for a pregnancy, thought his penis a half-born baby and his anal wind the baby's first cry, so that she grew up to be hysterically anxious lest she break off a lover's penis and lest she break wind in public.[138/j] Lou had a sharp eye for what held in her own case as well as the patient's—or, if it held all too obviously in hers, a blind spot. She triumphantly solved the "riddle" of a girl at once anxiety-ridden and orgastic when she noticed that the girl's lovers were all father substitutes by contrast,[139] but Freud had to drive it home to her that the girl's regular turnover of lovers was likewise a defense against incest.[140/k] His first, faint rebuke concerned mock confessions designed by Lou to elicit real ones from a six-year-old: he assisted her in an easy cure along those lines, then deplored the bad pedagogical example she had set.[141/l] Another time she cleared up a young man's neurosis except that an ache at the heart of it lingered on in the form of a vague afterfeeling, which baffled her until Freud suggested: "It is meant for you as transference mother."[142] She made herself into Freud's pet pupil somewhat in spite of him: he once called her a "problem-finder,"[143] and in time he told her bluntly: "Among the special advantages of the analyst's trade is this one, that in it the consultant's practice is hardly possible,"[144] whereupon she ceased reporting on cases interrogatively.

The local trade being light, Lou solicited mobile neurotics far and wide.[m] Freud sent her some beginning with an agoraphobic female, "the personification of plain, nasty lewdness,"[145] who was turning psychotic in his care—and whom she fondly cured. She would see patients at any hour and well beyond the hour: "New Year's Eve, analysis till just before midnight," she once noted.[146] She would charge as little as the traffic would bear, not excluding nothing[147] (in penitential imitation of Rée). "The fairy band that surrounded your cradle seems to have withheld from you the art of calculating,"[148] remarked Freud upon summoning her in 1923 to raise her fees as the Mark fell. She would raise them "quite without scruples or ado," she replied, except that the inflation had ruined everyone![149] Another time Freud sent her a woman with a wealthy family and an in-

---

[j] In another case a man "violently tore his hysterical wife away from me just as we were headed straight for a cure" (Lou→Freud [summer 1924]), only to report to Lou thereafter for treatment himself (Lou→Freud [late 1924]).

[k] (This he did orally in Tegel). As practitioner, Lou was especially keen on fantasies of paternal gestation and paternal violence, on infantile autoerotism and anal erotism, and on masculinity in women.

[l] Yet he had earlier urged her to drop her scruples about letting the child masturbate.

[m] See Lou→EK, 2 XI[=I] 1920 ("Send me some!"); etc.

junction to accept nothing under twenty gold Marks per hour: patient and family arrived first, and Lou took ten; Freud told the family she had thought them impoverished, so she got twenty after all. "I had to be glad you had not said five," he epilogued.[150] And again, on a later occasion: "I hope this time you did not forget your own interest altogether. I shall not ask, so as not to be vexed."[151] At least once she went as high as ten hours a day, as Freud learned "with horror"[152]; only rarely, though, could she fill out a full schedule in Loufried.[o] One slow season she took on a patient by mail. "Why not?" deemed Freud. "It's worth a try."[153] The try failed.[154/p]

In the late spring of 1920 and again of 1921 Lou practiced some weeks at a sanatorium near Munich run by an ostentatiously ethical-minded couple living communally with their patients and children.[q] The first time she went charily and returned enthused.[155] The second time she went enthusiastically, only to hear Freud called retrograde and herself a "Freud slave": she left in a high fever "which took all my hair away," she told Ferenczi, "so that I go about in a skullcap like an old matriarch."[156/r] In the fall of 1922 she set up professionally for a few months in Berlin at a polyclinic for impecunious neurotics founded by Freud's wealthy disciple Max Eitingon; her private patients followed along from Göttingen.[157] The first weeks of 1924[s] found her at a clinic in Königsberg performing training analyses on doctors and treating private patients between times.[158] The next winter and the one after she again spent at Eitingon's in Berlin.

By all the rules, Lou's regional psychoanalytical group should have been the one in Berlin. She met with it already in October 1913 and found it listless.[t] She met with it again sixteen months later at Karl Abraham's: "Superbly interesting talk by him," she commented, "but then the discussion degenerated into political twaddle."[159] The accredited Munich group having gone over to Adler, she

---

[n] (From his daughter.)

[o] *Mrs. Maria Apel: Lou averaged three or four patients at any one time in the 'twenties, two in the 'thirties.

[p] Even from letters Lou promptly saw behind the girl's recurrent fantasy of seducing a dark lady a censored old fantasy of seduction by the father (Lou→Freud, 22 II 1919 and 18 III 1919).

[q] v and early VI 1920, early IV through VII 1921: at the Marcinowskis' "Gemeinschaft der Kranken" in Bad Heilbrunn beside Tölz.

[r] According to Lou→Martersteig, 26 IV 1921, she was too busy at the Marcinowskis' even to see relatives in Munich—though here a white lie is likely.

[s] Swelled to "a ½ year" in Lou→RMR, 16 III 1924 (from just over two months).

[t] D [end X 1913]: no one spoke to the point of Eitingon's paper on non-communication from the unconscious. (She of course had held *her* tongue.)

thought of joining the sanatorium people in a rival one until they went over to Adler's rival Stekel.[160] In May 1922 she belatedly applied for membership in the international association "with the special wish of being admitted in Vienna," the central committee learned from its secretary, "as she has known most of the members here personally for some years and also has occasion to come to Vienna more often than to Berlin."[161] The committee sanctioned the "breach of geography,"[162] whereupon the group waived the initiation speech and, as Freud informed his new colleague, "was reasonable enough to congratulate you."[163] Lou called the membership in Vienna a dream come true[164]—and indeed it sealed her self-identification with Zemek. Thereafter she attended many group meetings—all in Berlin! On the eve of one of these she apprised Freud: "Tuesday H. Sachs is to tell me about Vienna."[165]

New theoretical lessons drawn from her practice filled Lou's letters to Freud and her diaries. Already in 1917 she redefined the obsessional neurosis as an intellectualized reaction formation against hysteria grounded in fantasies of violence inflicted rather than suffered.[u] In 1928 she told Freud of "notes made by me over the years on the diverse ways in which the masculinity of women hysterically and compulsively inclined finds expression."[166/v] Her most arresting jottings concern psychotic mechanisms, from everyday foolhardiness or affectation to impairment of the *fonction du réel* in dementia praecox and megalomania. Of all this empirical lore little, however, entered into her formal theorizing,[w] and what did took its place *beside* the rest, which followed up preconceptions. By 1930 she was recounting patients' sexual exploits at age one, with relish at that; officially, however, she still saw no sex to narcissism and no access to it. In fact even her most advised generalizations

---

[u] D [late] 1917: as the passive victim turns active perpetrator, his reproach against fate becomes one against himself with, however, "suppressed resentment at his having gone from victim to culprit"; cf. Lou→Freud, 27 II 1918. Freud→Lou, 24 IV 1918: "You are *wholly* right"—only not exhaustive as to *how* hysteria turns into obsession and vice versa, her derivation of obsessive doubt from irresolution over whether to yield to hysteria being furthermore "too intelligent, too rational. The inclination to doubt derives from no occasion for doubt but is an extension of the ambitendency potent in the pregenital phase." Lou thereupon noted: ". . . doubt about one's sex the ultimate basis for doubt: I should have thought of that"! She reverted to this topic frequently till D III 1918: "Came upon *Zentralblatt IV* Stekel's conception of obsessional neurosis as heightening of hysteria."

[v] (Perhaps *mental* notes, as I saw no such written ones in Göttingen.)

[w] Or even into her more formalized diary pieces. The one big exception is 1929a:50-54—a comparative discussion of hysteria and anxiety neurosis with regard to permutations of inner and outer reality.

about her psychoanalytical practice itself were preformulated.*ˣ*
Nor did her theorizing perturb her practice: she never once wrote
protonarcissism into a diagnosis.*ʸ* And, preconception or no, she
marveled ever anew at how deep every thought ran and how great
was the psychic capital tied up in any symptom. Perhaps her favorite
patient was a hysterical girl who, upon realizing that virtually since
babyhood she had imagined guilty hands to be concealed beneath the
color of clothing, took to painting hands: within weeks she was cured
—and an accomplished artist.[167] Lou felt respect tending toward
envy for every patient who dared reopen those oldest developmental
options the very closure of which he called "I,"*ᶻ* and melancholy at
every cure as at a development completed, even if for the best. And
concern: once she worked up such passion over a woman's "right" to

ˣ D [late XII 1912]: "Could we but approach the patient in his totality as
closely as we do his fragments, we would not hit up against the monotony of
a few typical basic motives in the depths of his unconscious as the analysis
draws to a close, but would, over and beyond these, penetrate the mute, solemn
miracle of a world that is also ours and that looms inexhaustible because of
this very community"; 1929a:13: to the psychoanalyst approaching a cure,
"the depths of our common humanity open up as if to his own self-comprehen-
sion" (a tacit avowal that she was reading her own mind in her patients').
Or again, 1889a:23: "the petty human fear—the fear of entering into conflict"; D [late XII 1912]: "bounds and walls jeopardize our inner vitality no
less than abysses, and petrifaction is no less a death than crumbling. . . . His
aversion for pain, his 'paltry comfort,' restrains the healthy man [from drop-
ping his resistances]. . . . Beside all resistance proceeding from the *contents*
of the material under analysis . . . there must be another, special resistance
due purely to the *form*, the overall form of the inner person. Possibly it would
be strongest in healthy persons . . ."; Lou→RMR, 16 III 1924: "I now ask
myself not only of the sick man how he fell ill but of the healthy man no less
suspiciously how he stayed well—and so there have been in the analyses
(that is, in the 'training analyses' of doctors etc., which are conducted as personally as those of patients) moments when those involved were a bit ashamed
of their cautiously, circumspectly, closely guarded health, or at least learned
new reverence"; 1929a:15-16: "there is also a variety of health . . . [attained]
in that someone settled for too little in respect of his innate possibilities. None
too rarely, for instance in 'training analyses,' as one is searching out that most
personal point from which the 'training' can take off practically, one wonders.
'Aren't you keeping too healthy?' instead of the more usual: 'What did you
fall ill of?' And then one can encounter . . . resistance that at first seems
justified."

ʸ Much less did she follow up D [late XII 1912] on a presumed limit to the
"great gain" of being able to "listen in on psychic life" directly: "that we
should at the same time have to adapt the results to our logically oriented
mentality."

ᶻ She could even show respect for neurosis itself. Thus Lou→RMR, 16 III
1924: "All neurosis is a sign of value signifying: here someone sought to
reach his limits—*thence* did he derail sooner than others; they who stayed
well took the easy way as against him; his noblest claim made him small among
them. If he becomes healthy, he towers higher than had he stayed healthy . . ."

retain custody of her children ("her lasting possession") during treatment[168] that Freud had to call her to order: "You are no legal friend or helpful aunt, but a therapist . . ."[169/a] "I am a cold old animal that takes to few people," she replied apologetically; "that is why I am so grateful to be able to boil over within psychoanalysis."[170] In old age she added: of course the patient, once cured, should not think of his analyst much, "only I can hardly conceive of the converse."[171] Doing Freud's own work after Freud's own heart, she found herself. "I am one of the happy few who day after day rejoice to be doing just what they are doing," she once told him—"what more can one ask?"[172] What more *can* one ask?

After the Munich congress of 1913, Lou and Freud consorted mainly by mail. The correspondence was studied on her side and casual on his. Though semiformal, it was highly personal, shop talk and all. Precious to both, it would yet have readily yielded to confrontation at almost any point. In late 1914 Lou told Freud that, except for the war, she would be in Vienna for more Wednesday evenings,[173/b] whereupon these "lost their value" for him, as he assured her in reply.[174] A prospect for a reunion fell through when in September 1918 the psychoanalytical congress slated for Breslau took place way off in Budapest instead. Freud reported to Lou afterwards on this *"revanche* for the Munich congress" that "everything would have been grand except that . . . *you were not there!*"[175] Lou lamented in 1919: "We shall be hobbling to each other on crutches in the end."[176] In 1920 Freud hoped to see her during the summer near Munich "before we have both grown 'stone-old and teeny-weeny' "[177]; his trip fell through. Next it was a psychoanalytical congress at The Hague: he took along his daughter Anna, "who," he notified Lou, "has long been yearning to show herself to you."[178] Lou could not afford the trip.[179] In 1921 he did vacation in Bavaria, but without knowing that Lou was there again.[180/c] He made it good that September by inviting her to Vienna the sooner the better.[181] In October he urged the fare upon her, as he was then earning hard monies, and "I would like something out of this new wealth"[182]; she

a D III 1923 is a drastic understatement: "How one stands toward the patient: with gradually a slight weakness for him. And great severity toward his neurosis for that very reason."

b Literally: except for the war she would "not [!] have been there this winter"—a token of the ambivalence then raging in her.

c He owed Lou a reply to Lou→Freud, 26 XII 1920 (which mentioned a possible summer sojourn in Austria: cf. Lou→Freud, 6 IX 1921); he presumably sent her a card (possibly coauthored by Ferenczi: cf. Lou→Ferenczi, 31 VIII 1921) from Garmisch only after her return to Göttingen.

_{rustling}

replied that her travel money was plentiful and was ~~jingling~~ with sheer impatience!"[183]

She wound up some treatments post haste and arrived in Vienna the evening of Wednesday, November 10, to be picked out of the crowd by her host's sister-in-law and his daughter. Only then did she remember: the briefest halt at the Berggasse and she was off with Anna to the meeting room, "late—but how lovely, how jolly, to show up there! Freud unchanged; half a hundred people now . . ."[184] She returned five Wednesdays running. Other evenings she saw Freud after his writing was done, usually for a midnight stroll during which, she noted, "he would often so to speak psychoanalyze Vienna: the wintry streets would stir his memories of the city's very oldest origins . . ."[185] Afternoons he would join her and Anna for his "academic minutes" between sessions and partake in their perpetual discussion of Anna's first psychoanalytical inquiry, then underway.[186] The mood was spirited and playful as the three together "turned great thoughts about" and "solved darkest problems."[187] "Only seldom did Anna and I go out," Lou remarked.[188/d] She left with the last possible train before Christmas.[e] By Freud's account, "she was a charming guest and is altogether an outstanding woman. Anna . . . enjoyed being with her very much."[189]

Anna Freud was at Loufried in the spring of 1922,[f] then again that summer,[g] and again the following spring.[h] Meanwhile the two corresponded, Lou rather the more vigorously.[i] "I cannot tell you how very glad I am at your obliging the child so fondly," declared Freud.[190] Freud worried over this youngest child of his because of her father-fixation,[191] the more since he on his side was as much stuck on her as on his cigars.[192] He looked to Lou hopefully to help him tear her loose.[193/j] Lou would not: she deemed Anna's incestuous

---

[d] This does not conflict with Freud→Ernst and Lucie Freud, 20 XII 1921— "Anna . . . visited a number of interesting people with her"—since Lou visited people with Anna several at a time: see below, pp. 445ff.

[e] D [late 1921] says Tuesday (21 XII 1921) as against Freud→Ernst and Lucie Freud, 20 XII 1921: "Frau Lou left this morning . . ."

[f] Lou→Freud [4? v 1922] and 5 VIII 1922: briefly in IV 1922.

[g] Lou→Freud, 5 VIII 1922, and Lou→Rank, 13 VII 1922 and 31 VII 1922: from 3 (?) VII to 5 (?) VIII 1922.

[h] Freud→Lou, 13 III 1923, and Lou→Freud, 31 III 1923—these being evidently Anna's travel dates to and from Loufried. A visit planned by Anna for later that spring did not come off (Lou→Freud, 10 VIII 1923).

[i] (I have seen neither side of this correspondence, which, however, figures indirectly in Lou's with Freud.)

[j] This was the expedient edge to his praise of the fine example Lou set for Anna (see e.g. Freud→Lou, 3 VII 1922).

set-up more blissful than any alternative "within normalcy."[194] Sistering and mothering his closest child for him, Lou made herself that much more of a daughter-wife to Freud. In 1925 she assured him: "I feel only too deeply how utterly utterly I am beside you, and with you, as if I were a piece of age-old Anna somehow also inseparably hanging on."[195/k] She would talk to him in her imagination—as formerly to her god. She "ever again" called him a joy-bringer[196/l] as she ever newly affirmed the "grateful indebtedness"[197] of "your ever *newly* grateful Lou."[198] And he pampered his anal daughter-wife, regularly heaping hard-won hard money upon her through the inflation years and beyond for all her assurances, exultantly given, that she neither needed nor deserved it.[m]

In the back of Freud's mind, his sublime kept woman was more nearly wife than daughter to him. She supplemented, even supplanted, his workaday spouse, whose existence he simply ignored in his letters to Lou[n]—as when he remarked about Anna: "I know she will not be stranded as long as you are alive, but she is so much younger than the two of us . . ."[199] Lou's own letters, he told her, were like beams from a hearth on a winter's day.[200] He rated her ethical ideals well above his own.[201] During the war he credited her spirits with sustaining his,[o]

---

[k] ("*Ich fühle nur zutiefst, wie ganz ganz ich bei Ihnen bin, und mit Ihnen, als sei ich ein Stück uralte Anna, das da irgendwie untrennbar mit dran hängt.*")

[l] Once she even inadvertently wrote "*Professor Freuden* [Joys]" (Lou→ Freud, 22 x 1930). (A comparable slip of her pen yielded "*Herrn Prof. F. C. Freud*" on 31 x 1917.)

[m] Regular payments of $40 to $50 monthly, which provided relative opulence in Germany then, began through Eitingon in IX 1922 and continued with few if any interruptions at least into 1925; moreover, Lou→Freud [winter 1923-1924] registers an extraordinary payment, and Lou→Freud, 24 v 1926, acknowledges a "huge rich shipment of money before which I stand thunderstruck" (adding: "Good that I need not grope for words, that you know how I feel . . ."). So far was Freud from resenting Lou's cut rates of psychoanalytical treatment that, besides subsidizing them thus indirectly, he joined Anna in a contribution to one of Lou's patients: "It seemed to us . . . that she would soon have to break off the analysis," he later explained, "whereupon you in your customary coldheartedness would have continued it without fees" (Freud→Lou, 11 VIII 1924—which incidentally mentioned that his married children were then "struggl[ing] with poverty"). The inflation did presumably deplete Andreas's stipend; what with house and garden, however, and Lou's fees such as they were, the couple was privileged even without Freud's help. Freud assumed that Lou had lately lost income from Russia (Freud→Lou, 20 x 1921) and that the Spartan bill of fare at Loufried depicted by Anna spelled "privation" (Freud→Lou, 8 IX 1922): as far as I can tell, he was wrong on both counts.

[n] (Despite Lou's own references and regards.)

[o] Freud→Lou, 31 I 1915 (you alone have preserved your creativity "in these times"), 30 VII 1915 (only you and Ferenczi are true to society), 9 XI 1915 ("you know how to give one courage and cheer. Never would I have believed, least of all in my present isolation, that psychoanalysis could mean

and long afterwards he saluted her: "My dear inexhaustible friend!"[202] He took whatever she said about herself—autobiographically or psychoanalytically—at face value,[p] with the result that he found her a being of purest "authenticity and harmony," "modesty and discretion," devoid of "all feminine, perhaps most human frailty."[203/q] His favorite reader, she acknowledged his every new work with a batch of notes of which he affirmed: "You always give more than you receive."[204] He extolled her as his psychoanalytical alter ego who put back together what he had taken apart—deepening and fortifying it, filling it in and rounding it out.[205] In 1930 he recapitulated their relations: "I call a tune, mostly quite a simple one, and you supply the higher octaves; I set things asunder, then you combine them in

---

so much to someone else . . ."); etc. Cf. Freud→Abraham, 11 XII 1914 (quoted in Jones, III, 145).

[p] Including notably her Nietzsche tale: see Freud, *GW*, XVI, 270 (also Freud→Lou, 8 V 1932, on her bearing toward the Archiv: "You are far too dignified"). Conceivably he was taken in by her indirectly in one most remarkable instance that would clear up a mystery surrounding a missing ring. According to Jones, III, 18, which confirms Freudian oral tradition, Freud gave Lou one of the rings signifying membership in his "private 'Committee.'" In fact Freud did nothing of the sort: there is no literary trace of the gift in Lou's estate, and *Mrs. Maria Apel knows nothing of the ring—either indication being practically conclusive. Freud, *GW*, XVI, 37-39 ("Die Feinheit einer Fehlhandlung"), related that, on addressing a gift card to Lou (unnamed but identified by Jones) for her seventy-fifth birthday, he wrote one word too many, then struck it out: the German preposition *bis*—which, however, he promptly identified as also Latin and French for "*a second time*," so that he straightaway interpreted the whole operation as a denial of a certain stylistically awkward repetition in his text. When, however, Anna remarked that he had already made the same gift to Lou once before—*a ring*— he concluded that his underlying motive had been reluctance to part with the second ring. His interpretation is at least defective, for denying the repetition meant *clearing* (not *barring*) the way for the duplicate gift. But again, the denial of repetition was quite possibly *correct*—that is, quite possibly he had somehow been misled by Lou through Anna into half believing that he had once made Lou the gift of a Committee ring. In this case the complete mechanism would have included, besides his writing "*bis*" and then striking it out, his taking this denial to Anna for her to contradict; the unconscious sense of the *complete* mechanism would then have been just what he said the unconscious sense of the *first part* of it was (to withhold the gift), and this would explain his having concluded as he did about it counter to his own (limited) premises; the mechanism would, moreover, have achieved its purpose, for evidently he made neither this nor any other gift to Lou in 1936 (she acknowledged none). His generosity toward Lou being above suspicion by thousands of gold Marks, what was at issue here was clearly the ring specifically—perhaps the wish that he really had given her a Committee ring earlier (or some *other* ring).

[q] But he said so in an obituary that contains the reassuring lapsus: "About her own fiction and essays she never spoke. She obviously knew where the true values are to be sought in life."

a higher unity; I presuppose our subjective limitations, you draw attention to them explicitly. All in all we have understood each other and are of the same opinion—only I tend to close out all opinions but one, you rather to close in all opinions together."[206] He was fully seventy-five when he first noticed that the voices were male and female and the duet domestic—when "something exquisitely feminine in your intellectual work first struck me. Where I, angry with the eternal ambivalences, would like to leave everything in a muddle, you straighten up, make lovely order, and show how comfortable it can be."[207] The division of labor in this figurative household was only too perfect, for, in his words, "my interest always fails me once the analysis is done."[208] Exalting Lou's womanly work, he was dismissing it. Nor did he settle for exalting: "There is no trick to synthesis once the analysis is done," he typically added.[209/r] Furthermore, his simplifications made shortest shrift of her own analytic finds and of the disputatious, revisionist crux of her syntheses—in brief, of *her*. Rarely did he repay a commentary of hers with more than a compliment. When once she gently protested his ignoring a massive critique, he taxed her with fishing for compliments—then simply paid her some when she returned to the charge.[210] Thus he slighted even the lofty hetaera after the lowly housewife.

Monological as was his share of the dialogue, Freud did, as he assured Lou, "enjoy" her rejoinders and "let them work on" him,[211] at least for as much as he could make them out: "my eyes, adapted to the dark, can bear no strong light or broad sphere of vision," he once tactfully put it.[212/s] This was plenty for Lou once she had dedicated her life to his work. The dedication took effect in the course of the year and a half that followed her stay at Freud's and the publication of "Narzissmus als Doppelrichtung" and during which his favor found such tangible expression. For some years she ceased writing for publication or even keeping a diary.[t] Not even for Freud's press or cause would she write,[u] only *to* him: wholly her father's child again, she

[r] Earlier he had called her his chosen judge of how his writings looked to the outside, only to add that he did not care how they looked to the outside (Freud→Lou, 29 VI 1914); he later called her "an understander par excellence" (Freud→Lou, 25 V 1916), only to beg her the next time round, without the least provocation from her, not to be angry at the epithet (Freud→Lou, 14 VII 1916).

[s] Again: "I should much like to understand everything you write. That I value it you know" (Freud→Lou, 17 XI 1924).

[t] D [late 1921]: "All work on books set aside for the new year." Evidently she did produce "Eros" in 1922, though (below, p. 399 and n. *q*.), besides touching up her works then being published. Her diary thinned in 1922 and broke off in V 1923.

[u] Not only Freud himself but Rank, who ran the press, besought Lou for

again rendered her accounts of the world and herself directly—by
mail. Beginning in 1922 she sent Freud a special message for every
May 6, which was his birthday[v]: thus the vital contact was secure.
When she, however, turned seventy, Freud only learned of it from a
psychoanalytical review. He called her down for excessive discretion:
"Maybe I should have liked to tell you on that very day how much
I esteem and love you."[213] She replied that she was "squarely averse to
birthdays."[214] The two meanwhile next met after Vienna when they
stayed together at the Eitingons' in Berlin for the psychoanalytical
congress on September 1922,[w] then in 1925 on the Freuds' summer
holiday in the Semmering, and a last time—after Freud had been
skipping congresses and Lou following suit—in March 1929 at a congress held in a castle at Tegel near Berlin. Here they conversed twice
—or rather, as Freud told Lou afterwards, he "left the conversation
to Anna. The reason was that, with my hearing damaged, I could
barely grasp your soft-spoken words and was obliged to notice besides that you too had trouble making out what is left of my
speech."[215] Lou replied: "I feared annoying you unintentionally
through conversation—and not merely out of modesty, but because I
well know from experience just *how* aggressive people can unsuspectingly be. One thing, though, is unpardonable: that I did not speak
loudly. I habitually do so here at home, my husband being now
quite hard of hearing, and so I take care not to anywhere else."[216/x]
As his oral cancer worsened, she shocked him in his stoicism by declaring: "One should wish to know an evil-doer behind it and rip out
his arms and legs."[217] Toward the last she greeted him: "Dear Professor Freud, dear, dear Dear,"[218] then "Dear, dear Prof. Freud—I
should soonest only repeat *this*, as if everything that fills me full were
in it."[219] Then she counted herself among "those beyond reckoning
who love, love, love you!"[220] And finally, enclosing an identification

copy (Freud→Lou, 9 ɪɪ 1919, 9 ɪɪɪ 1919, etc.). In vɪ-vɪɪ 1922 Lou half tried
editing a collection of psychoanalytical material on children, evidently at
Freud's bidding as well as Rank's, then begged off (Lou→Freud, 26 vɪ 1922,
5 vɪɪɪ 1922; Lou→Rank, 13 vɪɪ 1922).

[v] From 1923 (after Freud's mouth operation) through 1927 Andreas adjoined birthday greetings (graciously acknowledged by Freud).

[w] Evidently Freud's wife and Anna were there too. Lou stayed on alone
afterwards while working at the polyclinic, the Eitingons being absent in Sicily
(Lou→ʀᴍʀ, 18 ɪ 1923); she stayed with the Eitingons unpleasurably on her
way to or from Königsberg a year later (Freud→Lou, 10 v 1925), but then
again more congenially the two following winters.

[x] Freud wanted to invite Lou to Berchtesgaden that summer but could not
find accommodations (Freud→Lou, 28 vɪɪ 1929). Anna evidently paid a
last, brief visit to Loufried late in 1929 (Lou→Freud, 4 ɪ 1930).

photo: "If only instead I might look into your face for but ten minutes—into the father-face over my life."[221]/[y]

With Lou's swooning for her master went absolute respect for him as searching out and standing by truth however morally repugnant or intellectually awkward it proved: he was a hero of knowledge to her such as she would have had Nietzsche believe *her*.[222]/[z] Freud helped her to this view of him: "my obstinate courage for truth"[223] was a fixed self-promotional point of his[a]—quite as if Nietzsche or Ibsen or . . . Freud had never lived. Actually his vindicating ugly facts against good taste did not impress Lou so much as his vindicating hard facts against right reason. As she knew him, theory was for him strictly a synoptic transcription of phenomena and therefore had no business being plausible. He briefed her repeatedly concerning his mode of inquiry: "You know that I work with the particular until the general emerges of its own . . ."[224]/[b] And if the general emerged anomalous, he would leave it so with self-contented indifference—until further notice from his material. To the last Lou extolled his discovering above his theorizing.[225] She even came to denigrate the felt need to fit data all "under One hat"[226]/[c] as mere "attempted imitation" of protonarcissism.[227] Yet Freud actually could not interpret phenomena otherwise than schematically—could not discover without constituting his discoveries continuous with all Creation. And with age he drew the lines of continuity ever fewer, simpler, and tighter.

Given Freud's sufficiency as theorist, his biggest use for collaborators was as corroborators. Lou, realizing this straight off,[228] could only expect dogmatism of him—and in fact found, while studying under him, that "any independence in his entourage . . . harasses and injures him in his researcher's, hence noblest, egoism."[229]/[d] Amusedly she noted that even in Otto Rank, who was "wholly only a son" to

[y] These are her last surviving words to Freud.

[z] See D [17-20 VIII 1913] (below, p. 420); also 1931a:202-03 (in Freud's case the man and the investigator were "two, joined only by sacrifice"—because he would have liked the unconscious to turn out pretty and biology to take over from psychology: ditto Lou→Freud, 14 VII 1929; 1929a:5-7; D [6 IV 1913]).

[a] Cf. Freud→Lou, 29 VI 1914, 7 X 1917 ("as you know, I have in my work sacrificed whatever I could—unity, completeness, intellectual gratification—to the single criterion of certainty"), etc.—and Freud's works.

[b] Cf. Freud→Lou, 13 VII 1917 ("you noticed how I work, step by step, feeling no need for completion, ever under pressure of a problem immediately at hand, anxiously concerned to pass through proper channels. Thereby, it seems, I have won your confidence"); etc.

[c] Or to "cast a thought-schema like an untearable net over all fragmented boundlessness of the actualities impinging upon us," no less (1931a:204).

[d] Or again, that he was prone to conflict with "independent and temperamental heads" (D [27 XI 1912]).

him, Freud managed to see "menacing 'ambivalence' " toward himself of which the negative component was being worked off in research on regicide.[230] As for Freud's policy of " 'most undogmatic' freedom" within the international movement, he was being opportunistic ("even the deviators . . . must refer back to him") insofar as he was not simply seeking peace and quiet.[231/e] But then in Munich she observed that he was defending himself against Jung's pretense of saving him and his cause—only "the spear is now turned round as if *he* were incapable of any scientific tolerance, were dogmatic, etc. Who is the more dogmatic, power-loving, a single glance at the two reveals. Whereas two years ago a robust joviality, an exuberant vitality spoke out of Jung's ringing laughter, now there is pure aggressiveness, ambition, mental brutality in his earnestness. Never was Freud so close to me: not merely because of the break with his 'son' Jung, whom he loved and for whom he had virtually transferred his cause to Zurich, but just because of the manner of the break—as if *Freud* were making it out of narrow-minded rigidity."[232] Freud himself assured her: "I have never combatted diversity of opinion within the compass of psychoanalytical inquiry."[233] He spoke the truth: forever reformulating as he was, and so loosely to boot, there was nothing much for him to be dogmatic about. Lou came to see behind "the famous 'Freudian dogmatism' "[234] anything but: primarily a disapproval of controversy, at worst an unwillingness to accord the name of psychoanalysis to denials of unconscious thinking or of infantile sexuality.[f] In 1924 she joked to him about how that year in Salzburg their assembled colleagues would be quoting him chapter and verse, and this needlessly —in part because their big source went without saying and "in part because you have always held latitude to be not merely permissible but desirable."[235] And when later that same year Rank suddenly rebelled against Freud on the strength of an undisclosed new therapeutic twist, Lou howled: "What in the world has got hold of the poor devil . . .?"[236]

Lou's own was her choice case in point for Freud's brooking psychoanalytical dissent. With her absolute respect for him went no abso-

---

[e] On his nostalgia for solitude, cf. D [13 xi 1912], [13 ii 1913], [late x 1913]; and Lou→Freud, 4 v 1932.

[f] Freud→Lou, 7 vii 1914 (re Adler): "One must hold onto the unitary core; otherwise it is something else" (he never defined that unitary core dogmatically *enough*). Lou continually drew a double distinction as if after Freud: between, first, this doctrinaire core of Freudianism, to deny which was to deny Freud, and his empirical-theoretical formulations intended as perpetually subject to revision, then also between these formulations and his extrapsychoanalytical speculations meant to be taken or left by analysts as by anyone else.

lute deference to him even after the quarrel over narcissism singular or plural was buried. As she once told him: "Nothing pleases me more than to run in your leading-strings—only they must be good and long ones."[237] For one thing, she could never subscribe his life's project as expressed in his late motto: "Where id was, there shall ego be." The psyche set free from instinctuality was to her a contradiction in terms, or at all odds no more viable than a cut flower. During her study year she continually balked at Freud's "overemphasis of consciousness, as if everything infantile were pathological by reason of its immaturity": the individual, she insisted, never outgrows his "archaic" beginnings, but grows out of them continually.[238/g] She also balked at Freud's persistent countertendency to consider all repression to be against nature, "so that repression in the sublimation line succeeds as it were fatally. A clear distinction between *pathological* and *natural* repression, as between life-inhibiting and life-enhancing, would obviate theorist's pessimism such as this."[239/h] Freud wanted it both ways, she complained, or rather neither way: he gave repression to be man's taming and laming through culture but took the alternative to be "backwardness."[240/i] Culture, however, was and is on man's way, she held, and not in his way.[241] Furthermore, to sublimate an instinct was to indulge it undiminished, only to a universal rather than a local end: protonarcissistically.[242] She was outspoken enough on this topic in due course,[j] and yet not exactly *against* Freud; rather, she now and again hailed Freud's progress toward her own viewpoint, until in old age she chuckled over the bygone days when psychoanalysis, denigrating our deepest drives and their cultural debilitation alike, "aroused a pessimism like that of the forlorn neurotic it undertook to cure."[243]

Lou's illusion that Freud was reconciled with the unconscious arose out of his increased stress on its nonpathological functions.[244] As for

---

[g] (This last was also aimed at the Darwinist bias.) Cf. D [early summer 1913]: "ambivalences" are not simply primitive-morbid but express the polarity informing all life short of Spinoza's absolute.

[h] This echoes her earliest reading notes on psychoanalysis.

[i] Cf. D [26 XI 1912] (Freud's "*Kulturmensch* . . . a sadly tamed savage, and sublimation . . . basically negative in kind"), D [8 II 1913] (in Freud's course "again . . . the unreconciled antithesis nature-culture"), D [latter II 1913] (Freud as overstating the amount of repression needed to effect sublimations or reaction formations), D [early summer 1913] (sublimation is self-realization, man in culture no bondsman in torment but a "Narcissus in full efflorescence before his own likeness"). Often Lou (following Tausk: see D [early summer 1913]) wrote "*aufarbeiten*" ("work up") in lieu of "*sublimieren*" (of Nietzsche's coinage) with its connotation of "refine."

[j] But in her " 'Anal' " theorem, with which she aimed to please Freud, "original repression" follows upon a drastic cultural imposition.

sublimation, if in his usage it ceased connoting devitalization, it went on denoting an escape, however sublime, from the ego's control. Nor did he ever cease viewing culture ambivalently from the hard and fast premise that man was unfit for it. Consequently he never left off his "pessimism," though Lou would have charmed him out of it.[k] She first tried one evening in February 1913, when he complained of a "lack of euphoria"[245] just after denouncing the yen for a "definitive unity of things"[246] as unscientific and childish. "Freud admitted that ultimately this quest for unity stems from narcissism— whence, however, by his own surmise, our joy in living also comes to us."[247] Obviously, Lou concluded, he was suffering from squelched narcissism—from "*renunciation*" of philosophizing due to a confusion of " 'primitive' and 'primal,' " from "*stultification*" through scientific labor and "*a sort of repression of the self with the help of resignation.*"[248/l] Whatever she then told him,[m] he did increasingly yield to the yen thereafter—with no gain in euphoria. Assuredly it was then that, in counterpoint to his view of "my dear fellowmen" as "with individual exceptions . . . rabble,"[249] she improvised that sisterly love of her fellow men which she professed thereafter as if it had followed upon fond treatment by her big brothers in childhood and had found supreme vindication in her experience of psycho-analysis proceeding outwards from the confraternal study group around Freud.[n] Freud's rejoinder was the same down the years: that, expecting little good from men, he was never disappointed in them. "Only therein," he once told her, "do I differ from the pessimists."[250] She took the controversy from their correspondence into "Narzissmus als Doppelrichtung," where she concluded that "in the ecstasy endur-

[k] The fantasy that she had done so (like the fiction in *Haus* that she had charmed Beer-Hofmann out of the fear of death) is perceptible behind late passages of hers such as 1935a:213 (below, p. 476).

[l] This was her revenge for Freud's having somewhat analyzed *her* on two earlier visits. She, who loved Nietzsche's titles, was throwing up to Freud "*la gaya scienza*" in her own person (cf. below, pp. 385, 394). Some days later (with Tausk) she called *Weltschmerz* "a symptom" (D [mid-III 1913]), though after the Munich congress she allowed that worldly-wise resignation *à la* Freud might permit "*relative*" enjoyment of life (D [10-11 IX 1913]).

[m] Her diary account only faintly implied that she had gone as far as this diagnosis in her actual remarks to Freud.

[n] I find no trace of such professed love in her writings before 1913—or after 1913 except in patent reference to her experience of Freud's circle as a supposed repetition: cf. D [2 IV 1913]; Lou→Freud, 30 VI 1916, enclosure (*Ubw.* introduction); Freud→Lou, 14 VII 1916—and especially below, pp. 408, 410, 471 (her two additional brothers). Lou followed Freud's usage in assimilating this alleged trust in men to her "optimism"—inconsistently insofar as she derived the former from her big brothers' supposed niceness to her (but also from her cruelty to her lovers: below, p. 406) and the latter from her putative protonarcissism.

ing narcissistically behind everything, the optimist is ever in the right; in his disregard for this inner 'nonobjective' presupposition, the pessimist—libidolessly, 'lovelessly' judging—is ever in the wrong."[251] Concerning her sojourn on the Berggasse she observed: "In the farthest background he is probably the same as for years I have known him to be: rather pessimistically disposed. But in the foreground stands . . . great friendliness toward life, cheery and kindly."[252] Redressing the balance months later—after some dealings with Göttingen townsmen while awaiting a visit from Anna—she "noticed how threadbare my love for mankind has become, how the various people were purely, truly loathsome to me."[253/o]

As for theoretical narcissism, meanwhile, Freud admonished her—or more exactly, admonished the seminar after her euphoric talk with him—against "wanting to turn it into a key to every possible unsolved residue."[254] It was rather "a receptacle for unsolved residues," he specified—to which Lou, indomitable, remarked: "Just by being so defined, it becomes as it were identical with the 'unconscious' itself."[255/p] He admitted none of her ascriptions to narcissism: once, when she submitted that the superior instance smiling down at reality through humor was not the superego, as he held, but our basic conviction that we are all things and more,[256] he replied simply: "Our difference of opinion concerning humor reminded me of one problem about it I could not solve: why a sense of humor is so much rarer in women than in men."[257] He poked fun at her mania for narcissism: if she knew how much less Rank upset him than did his oral prosthesis, he told her in 1924, "maybe you would see it as proof of the intensification of narcissism in old age."[258] He shrugged at her community of being as at a losing quarrel with death: "Even the assurance to be found at its finest in Grabbe's *Hannibal*: 'Out of this world we shall not fall,' seems to me no redress for relinquishing the bounds of the self"[259]—hence still less an incentive to relinquish them. The ego's advocate, he could hardly commend the ego's abdication before a feeling, primal though it were. And anyhow, "I could not convince myself in my own person of the primal nature of such a feeling"[260/q] —though of its primal nature in Lou's person he evidently convinced himself only too well.[r]

---

o Cf. D [VIII?] 1919, on her postwar shame over her optimism, given her specially fortunate life (not to be presented as "life's true face") and her unwillingness to swap existences with almost anyone else.

p (That is, "*mit dem 'Unbewussten*,'" meaning both "the unconscious" and "the unknown.")

q Here styled the "'oceanic' feeling" after Romain Rolland.

r Freud (*Discomfort*, chapter I) noted that the feeling's advocates declare

Part IV: Maturity

In 1917 Freud, half inclined to adopt the concept of the "id" from a doctor in Baden-Baden,[s] consulted Lou.[261] She summoned him back to himself: it was not *his* concept subserving *his* research—and besides, it embraced physiological "background" data not accessible through the study of mind alone.[262/t] He ignored her objections; she boycotted the concept except to belittle it.[263] She was still harder on his late theory of a "death drive"—a tendency to master excitation and reduce tension, to disjoin and destroy—suffusing all organic matter along with a countertendency or "life drive" ("Eros"). He argued that a "repetition compulsion" took precedence over the pleasure principle itself in psychic life, and thence that all instincts aimed to restore a prior state—an original inorganic state of matter in the case of the death drive and in that of the life drive an original unity of living substance.[u] Given the vital statistics, he added, the death drive was evidently prepotent within organisms, the life drive within the germ plasm. Again, Lou declared, he was breaking his golden rule of explaining the mind on its own evidence.[264/v] He was philosophizing about it instead—only badly, for, she told him, life and death are the two sides of a single occurrence that eludes us as such.[265] She did not deny "the 'death drive' in itself"[266/w]: had she not affirmed it long before him?[x] She denied that its end was such as appeared[267/y]—and Freud, to whom its end appeared dead certain, again paid her no heed. She denied too that biology, let alone metabiology, could establish it in mental life other than alloyed on a par with its opposite forever.[268] And ever since: when she understood Freud to accord it—in all its aggressiveness—original autonomy and even present "au-

---

it rather than the "longing for a father" to be the source of religion—but he did not take his own hint.

[s] Georg Groddeck.

[t] This transgression was Adler's methodological one denounced by Freud with Lou's Spinozistic asset (see above, p. 337, and below, p. 396). Furthermore, Groddeck had followed Nietzsche's usage. (Her verdict notwithstanding, Lou admired Groddeck's work.)

[u] A unity akin to that of Lou's aboriginal "woman as such"!

[v] D [10-11 IX 1913] had already brought this objection against Ferenczi's precursive postulation (grounded in physics rather than biology) of a basic "death tendency" inherent in all life.

[w] 1929a:41 ("on the contrary . . .").

[x] See above, pp. 208 n. *i* and 302.

[y] This elusive point frequently reduced to a quarrel over words. However, one recurrent form of it (especially 1929a:41-47) runs: the concept of a death drive is supremely apt, but this just because to conceptualize is to kill—as if the intellect were to blame that death is not life. Lou added (*ibid.*, 45-46) that culture seemingly meant to the theorist of the death drive the deathly ascendency of intellect, but that this apparent neopessimism was really sobriety and objectivity such as signified loyalty to life!

tocracy" and "sovereignty,"[269/z] she likened it to Adlerian will to power.[270/a] Yet in 1920 she saluted *Beyond the Pleasure Principle*, which introduced the late theory: "You can easily imagine what a joy it was to me, as I even fretted in letters lest I not have your accord on primal 'drive-passiveness'[b]: it alone, though, makes Adler definitively refutable, as I already admonished him in Vienna. . . . You will—I feel it!—stand by this one point for good. That is everything to me!"[271/c]

What did she mean by "primal 'drive-passiveness' "? The death drive was no less aggressive for being regressive. *Femininity*, she had told Adler, was positive even if passive—even if *masochistic*—and now Freud took aggression to be self-aggression deflected onto objects so as to spare the self on Eros' account.[d] He set self-aggression in place of aggression, then, as primal,[e] whereas in Lou's view the two terms of sadomasochism, though they might appear separate after protonarcissism, were abidingly inseparable, like masculine-and-

[z] ("instead of uniting both drive directions at the root . . .")

[a] In her rebuttal, she actually disallowed evidence drawn from melancholia in that melancholia "is characterized by the fullest *unmixing* of our drives" (1929a:39).

[b] (". . . *bezüglich des primären 'Trieb-passiven'* . . .")

[c] The referent for the "it" that "alone, though, makes . . ." was literally Freud's coming round to her!

[d] Or more exactly, to have been self-aggression before its alliance with Eros—even though on his terms there never was a before.

[e] Again more exactly, he called self-aggression *perhaps* anterior to aggression and thence, confusingly, perhaps *also* primal (Freud, *GW*, XIII, 59: hitherto I conceived masochism as self-directed sadism, but now it looks like perhaps "a reversion to an earlier phase . . . a regression"; thus "masochism could also . . . be primal")—so that, without further notice from him, Lou affirmed (1920b:369): "Freud means to stand by the secondary character of masochism" (expiation for sadism: cf. below, p. 396 n. *e*). Equally confusing, however, Lou in this context cited Paul Federn against Freud's view of masochism as *also* primal, and this after having written into the margin of Lou→Freud, 26 XII 1920 (see text above and n. *c*): "P. Federn too will be happy!" In Lou→Freud, 20 VII 1920, she had urged sadism and masochism upon Freud as "identical in their contrariety" (cf. Freud, *GW*, XIII, 59: "but a turning of the drive from object onto ego is theoretically none other than its turning from ego onto object . . ."—a true Louism) and originally undifferentiable (cf. next note); here, however, far from fretting lest she not have his accord, she has just sweetly contradicted him—and, to compound the confusion, had alternatively urged masochism as "presadistic . . . primal in an identity of self and world" such that subsequently, "at pain inflicted by a beloved hand, that primal not-yet-I, still-Thou-and-I, revives like a joy." She had anticipated this inconsistency in a reading note of 1911-1912 on "the masochistic component as the whole of primal libido—with the aggressive drive to be explained as the 'interlocked' other drive (Adler) and with every consummated pleasure ever feminine"; she repeated it right down to 1936b on "our instinctive drive for contact" as conjointly active and passive, yet compositely passive toward the world (*active* and *world* having both been father-words).

feminine or life-and-death.[f] Besides, she could hardly have welcomed masochism as primal in the guise of delibidinized gangrene. So probably she most nearly meant the *regressive nature* of instincts, which did rule out Adler's thesis that they were compensatory and which her writings did all presuppose.[g] Freud on his side must have meant instincts as regressive when he wrote Lou in 1917: "Should I see my way to building the theory further, you will perhaps recognize with satisfaction much that is new as having been suspected or even announced by you. But I feel no hurry despite my age."[272/h] For no other subsequent innovation of his even half fills this bill, and he never could resist a premonition.

The theorem of instinctual regression was crucial to Freud as a link between psychology and biology—between the repetition compulsion hypothesized by him during the war years and the death drive preformulated by him before September 1913, when Lou called it "a somewhat neurotic estimate of life."[273/i] Even while later assailing this biological "bit of mythology" as just that—since it went beyond the reality principle[274]—Lou was ever coy about recalling its antiquity.[j] For Freud introduced it in 1920 quite as if it had only lately occurred to him with respect to certain mental phenomena indicative of a repetition compulsion, itself suggestive of an instinctual need to bind potent stimuli before the pleasure principle can operate.[k] However,

[f] 1913e:*passim*; also Lou→Freud, 2 III 1922 ("sadomasochism, that sham twosome"), etc.—but cf. preceding note. More generally, 1914a:272-73 argued against Adler the superficiality of the active-passive distinction as regards even the component instincts taken singly; 1914b:14-19 characterized instincts as all two-sidedly active and passive, the active side being, however, the more ego-syntonic except in the case of postpubertal girls; and 1920b:385 alleged "the as yet undivided unitariness of active and passive" (consequent on that of subject and object) in protonarcissism.

[g] These never presupposed the repetition compulsion, though: to this compulsion Freud (*GW*, XIII, 36-37) ascribed, for instance, the child's insistence that the same stories be told over and over word for word, which Lou (1920b: 385) for her part attributed to a narcissistic "need" to objectify them.

[h] I see only two other cases of possible direct influence by Lou on Freud: Lou→Freud, 20 VI 1918, on the "ego split" ("*Ichspaltung*"), is suggestive of the phenomenon so styled by Freud in his *Outline* (and aptly characterized in her diary entries about Rilke's "other"—though not in 1927a:85-86); and Lou→Freud, 18 V 1925, on a male homosexual whose "deepest disappointment in woman was that she is no boy," perhaps prompted Freud's discovery of that same disappointment behind fetishism.

[i] In old age (1929a:45) Lou displaced this verdict retroactively onto "opponents and semiopponents of psychoanalysis."

[j] Lou→Freud, 26 XII 1920, recalls that in IX 1913 with *Ferenczi* "it turned out that our opposite conceptions suddenly accorded if the words *life* and *death* were interchanged, whereupon we laughed much" (though D [10-11 IX 1913] allows of no such concessive laughter by Ferenczi).

[k] Freud in time avowed its nonempirical origins (e.g. *Discomfort*, chapter

such binding was the very pleasure principle in force in the garden of Epicurus,[l] and from even a universal almighty repetition compulsion it would not follow that instincts are regressive. Besides, far from finding support from biology, Freud had to rewrite biology as suited his purpose. He did accordingly set forth his late theory in first edition as provisional conjecture[m]—conjecture of devilish tenor on darkest matters.[n] Over the years it nonetheless "won such a hold over me that I can no longer think otherwise"[275]—and this even as his own original objections to it went unanswered, in fact as his colleagues added to them. A repetition compulsion owing to an immanent tendency of organic matter to revert to the inorganic state: this devilish intelligence about a dark process working in concealment within the organism was an anal fantasy as characteristic as Nietzsche's "eternal recurrence," and Freud used this phrase of Nietzsche's to style the outcome.[276] An *idée fixe* asserted over against his own scientific reservations of the first hour: Freud was following the bad example set by the Nietzsche of Lou's Nietzsche book.[o] His theory of a lifelong instinctual wedding between integration and disintegration was born of that clash of late February 1913 between Lou as synthesist and himself as analyst—a clash that followed upon "his horror at the 'Life Prayer,' which," Lou noted, "he must just have read as set to music by Nietzsche,"[277] and that issued in a lifelong duet.[p] Did Freud

---

iv: "Taking off from speculations about the beginnings of life and from biological parallels, I drew the conclusion . . .") but never avowed its age.

[l] Besides, such binding was not clearly involved in Freud's examples (childhood frustrations repeated in later life and the like). That Freud would not count the effect of excessive unbound energy as displeasure (see especially *Beyond*, chapter vii) was the more remarkable since he could not formulate pleasure for metapsychological purposes in the first place.

[m] See Freud, *GW*, xiii, 23: "What now follows is speculation, often far-flung speculation . . ." (but *ibid.*, 39: "We seek sober results of research or of reflections grounded in research . . .").

[n] See Freud, *Beyond, passim.* Cf. *Discomfort*, chapter vi: "We would feel it as a relief were our whole intellectual construction to prove erroneous"; etc.

[o] Cf. above, pp. 56 n. *i*, 154.

[p] See above, pp. 374-75, and cf. below, p. 394. Freud→Lou, 2 iii 1913, mentions an appointment with her for 1 iii 1913 (the first since the clash of 23 ii 1913) canceled by him on 26 ii 1913 because Ferenczi was due in from Budapest; since Ferenczi presumably then learned Freud's inchoate hypothesis of a death drive, Freud had probably devised this element of the theory in anticipation of Lou's visit of 23 ii 1913 and whispered it to her along with his " 'fantasy' " about the tribal father (below, p. 394). D [10-11 ix 1913], concerning Freud's morbid postulate of a "tendency to 'death' and 'rest' inherent in all living substance (considered to have been roused unwillingly) as its true nature," distinctly recalls D [23 ii 1913] on his dim view of life. The regressive clause of his theory incidentally covers his reversion to Em-

in 1913 emulate Lou's Nietzsche with hushed voice, bodeful tone, and all[278] as he initiated her into this main clause of a philosophy as yet unwritten—and which proved as noxious to her as Nietzsche's for the selfsame anal reason? Freud for the rest followed Nietzsche on conscience (superego) as an internalization of destructive energy,[q] only to go one better in postulating a prior externalization of destructive energy, and hence a primal masochism before that—meaning a Lou first.

In 1919 Lou styled herself "even more Freudian" than Freud in that she took fantasy to be no sickly compensation for disappointment with objects, but a healthy alternative to object-love. "The initial libido, the narcissistic," she noted, "when it stands pat for long instead of mostly dissolving into object libido, *needs fantasy* as the only means left to it of replacing object-love and of developing along its *own* line. . . . Fantasy-fed artist's libido seems to me therefore . . . only the result of normally, i.e. mentally, unfolded narcissism, which grows up alongside the ego. . . . It always issues entirely from the libido fundament, never having left it. Important as fantasy becomes, the *primal experience* is just as important, as the sole objective subsoil . . ." And she inserted parenthetically: "They don't seem to want to admit this, but I shall prove to have been right about it: already in 1912, over and against Freud's doubts, I affirmed the development of [the concept of?] narcissism itself."[279]

Lou's first unwritten purpose here was to normalize her *nonfictional* fabling: "It is indeed so characteristic of narcissism," she specified, "that in it fantasy *and* reality should attain *identical* significance . . . and something of this must stay with all narcissism—be it ever so mentalized—as hallmark."[280/r] She was contending further that, say, her Kuno romance was not in the least her Nietzsche romance or even her father romance, but again her primal cosmic romance plying these to its purpose. For the big pleasure in art, she insisted, attended "the regained objectiveness of the primal experiences, of those very ones that did not revive even indirectly with subsequent object-libido but do so only under the potent touch of fantasy."[281] Furthermore, her challenge to Freud's view of fantasies as substitutes for half abandoned claims on reality was itself a substitute for her half abandoned

---

pedocles—just as the "eternal recurrence" covers Nietzsche's recurrence to Pythagoras.

[q] FN, *Genealogy, passim*—and on the structure of conscience FN, *Human*, II, 52.

[r] Cf. D [17-20 VIII 1913] on art's "irremediable divorce from life" (which follows FN, *Genealogy*, III: 4: "a consummate artist is cut off from 'reality' in all eternity").

challenge to Freud on the discrimination of narcissisms. Thus it was a token of her semisubmission to him—and from her diary it went to him by mail[282/s] (his reply was inattentively admirative[283]), only to end up in print as the very example of her "heretical" independence within her discipleship.[t] Setting this example, she rejected his "deduction of art . . . from *repressions*: be these ever so often, perhaps always, involved as mediate occasion."[284] Meanwhile, she had openly subscribed his "main point" about artistic creation: that it is a specific against the toxic effects of repression.[285] From subscription to rejection, the constant issue between them was that of what sort of repressed material presses—or presses hardest—for release through art. Only privately, though, was it an issue at first[u]: publicly she ("even more Freudian" than Freud) at first opted in Freud's name for "the *primal experience.*" Thus in "Narzissmus als Doppelrichtung" she asserted, by way of deepening the usual "too shallow interpretation" of Freud's "main point,"[286/v] that the artist conjoins current material from inside and outside himself to register, not formerly conscious infantile designs on reality, much less actual designs suitable for consciousness, but libidinally supercharged "memory traces" partaking of primal subject-object unity and excluded from the conscious system from the time of its inception.[287/w] "No one requires the fulfillment of personal wishes less than the artist," she specified: his motive and message being prepersonal, "he is, in creating, farther removed from his private being and individual significance than ever otherwise: indeed, just this alone allows and enables him to lift repressions . . ."[288/x]

Repressions apart, this formulation of Lou's differed from that of

[s] ("Narcissistically . . . both, reality just like fantasy, . . . attain *equal* importance, [are] not at all experienced as antithetical"; etc.)

[t] See 1929a:76ff., especially 78 ("the artist as abidingly protonarcissistically disposed").

[u] And only implicitly at that for as much as she distinguished the "primal experience" from "the repressed" (D I 1919: art is "joy-giving not alone on account of the repressed" that it releases, but "perhaps *still* more on account of the regained objectiveness of the primal experiences"; Lou→Freud, 30 I 1919: "alongside of and aside from that pleasure due to the lifting of oppressive repressions . . .").

[v] Nominally the shallow interpreters were irate artists.

[w] In other words, material under repression without having ever been repressed. ("Memory traces" include some of postnarcissistic origin which, through associative affinity, join the others without first becoming conscious; Lou meant the others only.)

[x] Further, sexuality is involved in artistic creation "only in so far as it has worked itself free of private voluptuousness, so to say—as its focus has been displaced out of the personal orbit. Where this has miscarried ever so slightly, the personally coveted fantasy wish-fulfillment signifies straightaway a breakdown of creativity" (1920b:382).

the late 1890's precisely in that now the pressure for art no longer came from those "undigested emotional residues of life"[y] but rather from the "emotional underground"[z] itself, since become "that basic situation still common to us all"[289/a] with the result that the old explanation for artistic preferences was lost. Freud's own version was closer to hers of the 1890's—as was her own first psychoanalytical one, jotted down in 1913, which represented art as "a becoming manifest of repressed complexes."[290] Just about all her other psychoanalytical theses on art rejoined her prepsychoanalytical ones: witness especially her first public vehicle for her heresy in Freud's name, "Des Dichters Erleben" (The Poet's Experience) of 1919, with its poets all tremulously delivering themselves of ciphered messages from below.[b] At the end of the 1920's she told Freud: "I have learned so much new to me about how analytical solutions connect with artistic processes liberated through them"[291]—and there it ended. Her one published case study was of an artist: Strindberg, whose femininity, it turned out, gave his "genial masculinity"[292] no rest once he had learned that his mother, whom he overloved, was unwed at his begetting and vulgar besides: the result was a procession of motherly she-monsters on stage, and off stage a succession of women idolized, then traduced by him—vengefully, but also with untold relish for charging them with faithlessness, by which he meant their sexually "transmitting" him to other men.[293/c] Showing sufficient cause for Strindberg's art, she bypassed protonarcissism.[d]

And yet in art too her arguments from protonarcissism did have their supplemental validity—including the lovely one that the tragic

[y] See above, p. 243.

[z] See above, p. 223.

[a] ("Artistic appreciation can be grounded here only.")

[b] See Appendix B, v, pp. 553-54.

[c] Lou also understood that Strindberg's religious vision was one of being abused by demons as his menial mother had been abused by men—and 1917a, taking off from a recent performance of his *Ghost Sonata*, added that his was the art of a paranoid genius sufferingly enclosed within himself as within a miniature religion hostile to the world. This addendum connects back with D [VI 1912?], according to which Bjerre had interpreted Strindberg as a paranoid genius who entrenched his fantasies in reality by dint of achieving public acclaim for positing them fictionally in the mode of sober recollections of horrors: cf. below, p. 400. Lou received Strindberg's works from Ellen Key in x 1914 ("a joy after dead days"), then in D I 1915 noted his preoccupation with woman "partly as mother, partly as hated and beloved he-woman." 1919b objected to a sexological study of Strindberg that there were men behind his women.

[d] She bypassed it regressively insofar as she considered Strindberg to be out to undo his birth by projecting his own reviled femininity onto the stage (given his womb nostalgia complicated by his rejection of his mother).

hero acts out of deep-lying faith in his oneness with the world until the frightful primal undeceiving.[294] Less winsomely, she saw non-objective painting as tending toward a direct representation of subjectivity "and therewith toward fully sacred art; only its practitioners lack grandiose subjectivity reaching round to that all-enclosure of inner and outer under orders from 'God.' "[295] Its sacred tendency was a grudging concession to its practitioner Walt Laurent, against whom she had earlier contended that art without even an invisible object would signify a regression into "the objectlessness of infantility" indistinguishable from psychosis—that art never could be a religion, as Laurent called it, for the very reason that worship at its purest had no object, even invisible.[296] The original vehicle for that grudging concession was " 'Expression' " of 1917, which affirmed that art's business is to make what is unconscious conscious by means of worldly symbols, religion's to dissolve what is conscious into unconsciousness by means of otherworldly symbols—but also that the divine could turn artistic among primitives, children, and (esoterically and unoriginally) madmen, while conversely artistic expression could turn into "God-impression"[297] in Symbolist poetry, with its incantatory superallusiveness, and in nonobjective painting, with its infantile, not yet decomposed vision "in crimson sensual depths and blue premonitory distances."[298]

It holds with respect to religion even more than art that Lou found in psychoanalysis new grounds and new terms for conceptions long since hers. Her basic theses concerning religion remained that men devise gods so as to make themselves at home in an unfamiliar world and that gods as a rule outlive their usefulness to the extent of alienating men from a world become familiar, her own case being the paradigmatic exception.[e] Adler served this scheme up to a point: that of narcissism. Already in January 1913 she affirmed: "What is essential for me about religious thinking is that through it man *joined up as one* with the forces outside." And yet she supplied the sequel in Adler's tongue as, having termed primitive rites "an outburst of childlike-creative *confidence*," she added: "Only afterwards do the fictions to which they lead go on to serve insecurity and inferiority feelings as a prop, a crutch."[299] In March 1913, she nominally went along with Freud's interpretation of religious ceremonial as compulsive—as serving to prevent but also reenact the murder of the tribal father, which Freud then called his " 'fantasy' "[300] and later called prehistory—only to reinterpret it as a binding of anxiety before the unforeseeable "by means of an imitation or simulation of a sort of

---

[e] Of the old texts, 1899d:121 had put this most pithily.

system of nature uniting with the human will"[301]: in a word, as narcissistic.

That summer Lou rehearsed her own religious experience and, peripherally, mankind's for *Imago* in "Von frühem Gottesdienst" (Of Early Divine Service). By this account, the child's god grows out of the child's magic devices for regaining "paradisiac boundlessness."[302] As reason comes into its own, piety goes from naïve to fanatical—though reason itself, to which the god eventually succumbs, "also protects him so long as it needs him for every imaginable purpose alongside the religious one. . . . It puts him into one such confusing disguise after another that long after his final demise one still cannot know for sure if behind the fine front only a well-mummified god lies concealed. In religious history, this sly development is called 'spiritualization.' Mankind's childhood gods alone are not sustained by it. There they stand, still undisguised, naked unto offensiveness: bare marvels simply! Blatantly and serenely they go on exuding their full illogicality, which men cannot drag along the ways of the understanding without stumbling back at every step, for absolutely nothing about a god can be 'developed' except his contradictions. Thus nothing is so liable to mortal injury as such a divine product unless and until expediency is brought to bear on its behalf: before you realize what has happened to it, it is no longer. And perhaps this ghostly, gentle vanishing out of the fullness of reality typifies its unadulterated godlikeness no less than does the reckless, robust realism of its primitive constitution: it is, so to say, the only sort of god that comes and goes as a god and nothing else."[303] The later in childhood a first religious conception forms, she pursued, the more covert is its wishful purport, hence the more tenacious its hold on the mind. This is a pity for the mind, of course, but "also, silly as it may sound, for the god. For it defeats . . . the very point of his coming alive to men—not alone as crutch or wheelchair but" (again) "in an outburst of confidence in life satisfied with nothing less as its jubilant living symbol. . . . Hence the most divine thing about him to survive is really his repudiation"[304]: she could hardly have had it more both ways. She followed through in her diary: "In the concept 'God the Father,' self and other join back up into unbroken unity. . . . So perhaps the god did not gradually emerge from the father: *but the divine totality still shone round the father.*"[305]

"Psychosexualität" recurred to her old concept of a " 'freefloating' quantum of religiosity."[306/f] "Narzissmus als Doppelrichtung" identified "what is most inwardly operative in religion" as "confidently

f (Originally the "religious affect.") See below, p. 550.

idealizing narcissism," with "earliest parent-bound libido" caught up in "the narcissistic flow,"[307] and in 1923 her diary saw the unconscious equivalence of divine and diabolical confirmed by the fanatic's nagging doubt as to which in the world was which.[308/g] In old age she returned to the charge: "Worship is nothing other than a screen memory out of that darkness into which our primal impressions fell away before we gradually learned to make an even cleaner break between self and world."[309/h] Thus "beloved parents are seen as so gigantically mighty and kindly only because we find our way into the world as yet unsevered from them."[310/i] And thus magic, the "preform" of religion, "actualizes in rite and usage what remains with man as a presupposition: his ultimate community with the alien world confronting him in all its frightful possibilities. Religious rite and usage unite the two *de facto* . . ."[311/j]

Meanwhile, when in 1927 Freud represented religion as an obsessive illusion deriving from the father complex,[k] Lou told him: "Naturally our opinions nowhere diverge as to the contents of religious constructions: these have no other sense than do children's fairy tales." But she added that the real stuff of devotion was a native confidence in life, a deficiency of which was morbid and a profusion of which made "the good Lord" superfluous.[312] Thus she implicitly affirmed the religious illusion behind her indulgent superiority to religious illusion—and was therewith as shy about contradicting Freud as she was sly about calling him sick. Maybe he understood her, for he replied: "Do not spring to the good Lord's defense; my ire was not meant so much for him as for the benevolent providence and moral order for which he is, however, to blame. Nor am I by any means down on all illusions, but why cling to the one that slaps reason in the face?"[313] Lou was more plainspoken, if no more forthright, concern-

---

[g] Subsequently she concluded about the fanatic's doubt as to which of the two his *faith* was: "This doubt is faith itself" (1929a:58).

[h] But again: "To bridge the gap that has come about for his consciousness, man makes continual use of fantasy, which, though, may well have to adjust the pattern of its divine correctives more and more to the ever more exactly observed outer world" (1931a:10).

[i] (And to set the biological record straight: "Just as the bodily fact of birth first makes us into ourselves, so is the body our sole preserve for that primal fact out of which we lovingly attain to a 'Thou' for what is most human unto the ultimate cosmic encompassing.") Cf. 1931a:11-12 on her having enlisted her parents in the service of "a more total inclusion."

[j] Likewise: "Even before religious times, in the cult of magic, there was belief in the shaman, who, still directly embodied in the world occurrence, was less dependent on his wishes' being heard, since he himself effected events magically"; accordingly, the advent of religion proper signified that man had commenced doubting his "omnipotence and all-being" (1936b).

[k] In his *The Future of an Illusion.*

ing his *Discomfort in Civilization*, which dismissed the claim put in by a bolder correspondent of his for the " 'oceanic' feeling" (Lou's cosmic pathos) "to be regarded as the source of the need for religion."[314/l] She declared herself again "full of 'Yes!' " if again "my—how shall I put it?—mood vis-à-vis religious things remains other than yours. . . . To find it 'humiliating' for someone to go in for religious infantilism, one would have to ascribe to cultivation and cleverness a value as high as moral values, which, though, we do not hold valid either. . . ."[m] The infantile after all neighbors with, besides the retrograde (or simply backward), all the power of fantasy also astir in creativity. And when I read about your friend with the 'oceanic feeling,' who surely keeps the common man's religion at arm's length, I feel like swearing he would avow deep down: much of what 'uplifts' the common man goes into that 'oceanic.' Only rather than just go back to crude infantilism that lets itself truly work up the old parental sensations, he goes all the way back into the vague, the indistinct, and feels somehow maternally rocked. . . . What interests me so in this is why they all, from the more crudely deluded to the oceanic, tug at the same cord, for oceanics can draw but little consolation out of their 'feeling.' And here I have often told myself: where all's right with someone's outlook on life, no such 'feeling' comes in. . . . Where all's *not* right, then these 'feelings' announce themselves: not only as 'wishes' naïvely construed as fulfilled, but as a sort of dull remembrance that something else once was—whereupon the imagination helps construct something consoling."[315]

Freud's trouble was roughly the reverse: he proclaimed that his own religion derived from the infantile father complex alone and was insuperable—without, however, noticing that deep down it was *his*. Until old age he could express it no more directly than through tireless irony about "warning voices, which I always let guide me,"[316] about bodily pain as being, "if I may get personal against someone, nasty,"[317] about "the great unknown He or It behind fate,"[318] and the like. But then came "the *return of the repressed*" in the more brazen form of an attestation to the "*historical* truth" of religion—or, as he put it in a huge letter to Lou of January 1935, "my invaluable insight" to the effect that the Jews of old, after having been chosen and delivered from Egypt by Moses, a former high priest of Ikhnaton, repudiated Moses' universal father-god for an uncouth desert deity, Jahweh, who in the course of the following centuries gradually revived Moses' half-forgotten teachings in his own name (taking credit to

---

[l] Cf. above, p. 381 and n. *q*.

[m] Freud (*Discomfort*, chapter ɪɪ) had in fact found it "humiliating" for those who *knew better*.

boot for Moses' having chosen and delivered the Jews) with a "compelling force" due precisely to the mechanism of a *"return of the repressed."* Freud concluded: "What makes religion strong is not its *real*, but its *historical* truth. And now you see, Lou, in Austria today one cannot come out with this formulation, which has wholly fascinated me, without getting analysis officially forbidden by the reigning high Catholic powers. And only this Catholicism protects us against Nazism. Besides, the historical bases of the Moses story are not solid enough. . . . So I keep silence. It is sufficient for me to be able to believe in the solution of the problem myself. It has pursued me my whole life long. My apology . . ."[319]

For what—the projection? The alien orthodoxy protecting and inhibiting Freud from on high was his inner scientific one projected. For not only was his "invaluable insight" no harder on religion than any of his earlier, valuable insights, as he owned at that same writing,[n] but his new formulation was unprecedentedly lenient: taken literally, it did not deny the *"real"* truth of religion, and taken in almost any way it affirmed the historicity of, say, the Creation and the Resurrection. At the same time the new Moses, meeker than the old, scrupled over making his people "offensive in the sight of Pharaoh and his servants"[320] with an announcement of the Lord's return.[o] His people was the tribe of Abraham, to be sure, but also the tribe of analysts ("the Jew is a creation of the man Moses . . . he created the Jew"[321/p]), who, as his Moses story ran, had already begun denaturing his teachings in his lifetime and were due to finish the job after his death with all due respect—pending "the *return of the repressed.*"[q]

[n] "I said as much in *Totem and Taboo* already . . ."

[o] At the burning bush, Moses was approaching eighty (he reached eighty by Exodus 7:7), as was Freud at this time. (Freud, incidentally, published his Moses story as such in 1937 without its raising an official eyebrow, but he withheld a sequel containing his new formulation and—as preface—an elaboration of the same political self-excuse, which fell with the *Anschluss* and his exile to England.)

[p] Moses having supposedly been a non-Jew, Freud was hereby also unconsciously denying his Judaism, already denied through his Moses identification itself.

[q] There is no end of collateral evidence that this "Moses story" was Freud's prophecy concerning Freudianism after Freud (thus in his Moses letter to Lou: ". . . the analytical swarm—unfortunately much of it human material little altered by analysis . . .")—and a fairly accurate prophecy it was, to judge by the first quarter century. His Moses story was itself perhaps a *"return of the repressed"* also in the sense of his having read most of its elements in Enlightenment texts (e.g. Diderot, "Égyptiens") during his humanistic youth, only to recollect them in old age without quite realizing it and hence with "compelling force" (as he had recollected Empedocles in formulating his late theory). His Moses story was furthermore a typical "family romance" beginning with Moses' having been a princess's child.

Of that "*return*" he told Lou moreover: "This process is exemplary for religious development and was but the repetition of an earlier one,"[322] by which he meant that Ikhnaton, in conceiving monotheism, was revisited by the primeval tribal father, whose slaughter by sons jealous of his sexual prerogatives was the original sin behind bad conscience and its palliative, religion. In calling Moses' "*return*" a repetition of the tribal father's, Freud tainted it anally for all the displacement Upwards. Indeed, the process that yielded the Moses story was itself "but the repetition of an earlier one"—was an unconscious reconstrual of Nietzsche's unconscious genealogy of evil, with the turncoat master as hero now: priestly Moses, who delivered Israël from bondage, hence by implication wedded Israël in the Lord's stead. Through this reconstrual, Freud succeeded Nietzsche as Lou's master in the erotic sense insinuated by her Nietzsche book. Nietzsche's parable was likewise situated at the return of the tribal father: at his Second Coming,[r] when he sacrificed himself so as to redeem that old bad debt to him grown beyond tormented mankind's powers of redemption.[323] Already Freud had imagined the slaughter of the primeval father—his crucial supplement to Nietzsche's thesis—in order to supplant the master genealogist of morals out of jealousy over Lou, to whom he first confided his " 'fantasy' "[324] on the very evening of that contest over analysis versus synthesis touched off by "his horror at the 'Life Prayer,' which he must just have read as set to music by Nietzsche."[325/s] The patricidal-regicidal brothers were his Wednesday evening "sons" fitted out in his secret fancy with the motive of jealousy over Lou—and this same brother band later returned as the tribe of analysts behind his Moses story. His Mosaic parable displaced the erotic motive wanting for the Jews' revolt against Moses to be properly recapitulative onto Moses' revolt against Pharaoh, meaning Freud's own against Nietzsche. The tribal father's Mosaic comeback was the final installment of Freud's Lou romance, which thus comprised all his new theorizing from his encounter with Lou till his death a quarter century later. Was this sufficient cause for his confiding to Lou about Moses—or did prophet and prophetess recognize each other beneath their atheistic talk? Lou at all odds wondered that a thesis "long since so much *in your line of thought*" should "now first prove dangerous" and insisted that the truth at issue was "emotional" before becoming "historical."[326] She rejoiced, moreover, that what had

---

[r] This phrase suggests how much Judaism there is to Freudianism. (Cf. that first principle of Jewish exegetics: today's strange happening is intelligible only in the light of some age-old prefiguration of it.)

[s] Cf. above, p. 385.

emerged from age-old repression was "triumphantly fullest of life" for a change,[327] and for Freud's next birthday she mused about "how very much that Moses business had its peculiar side: in that a single towering genius should have determined everything . . ."[328]

Like art and religion, philosophy too was dreamlike in Lou's psychoanalytical view of it, its surface texts being the *"necessarily"*[329] distorted expression of a message from the depths—and this again was nothing new from her except that now she took that message to be invariable. Considering all philosophy to tend toward a single, ineffable, true confession, she repudiated the psychological reductionism of her youth in the name of the new-found means of implementing it: psychoanalysis.[330] Of the dawn of psychoanalysis she wrote late in 1912: "Never as now have we felt our *knowing* dependent on what we are and our *being* in turn released into a deep expanse behind us, inseparable from us, which becomes one with life itself,"[331] as if the facts of life were coming to her ken through a rear entrance— from Freud. Short of anality, her repudiation of reductionism reduces to a disavowal of her chief philosophical link with Nietzsche. She overcompensated for the repudiation by remarking of psychoanalysis: "You can convince no one unless he already has the right *inner* orientation."[332]/[t] She followed up the disavowal in maintaining that Freud's discovery of the nonutilitarian basis for neurotic guilt had confirmed Rée's utilitarian thesis as far as nonneurotic guilt was concerned.[333] More: as if to obviate Nietzsche's most telling confutation of it, she stated Rée's thesis as that guilt appears to be preternaturally bound up with the violation of "prohibitions the *original* utilitarian ground for which comes to be forgotten"[334]/[u]—the suggestion being that the utilitarian ground may have fallen through. She thereby only added a new problem, that of how prohibitions can outlive their usefulness if such is their sole *raison d'être*, to the old one of how this sole *raison d'être* can be forgotten.

Lou did better indeed by her own, new philosophical subjects, especially by that of our *having* as against our *being* bodies—her phenomenological forte. Having broached it brilliantly in *Die Erotik* and *Der Gott*, she proceeded to illumine it in " 'Anal' und 'Sexual' " by identifying anal disgust as the first term of the *have* clause, a clause writ the larger the more painful the anal repression. As of "Psychosexualität," the last word of the *have* clause was puberty, when the ego is overwhelmed by the body as by an "other."[335] Once after

[t] Far more sensible is 1931a:195: that mere proof of an unpleasant truth will not compel assent.
[u] (Stress added.)

Freud's jaw surgery she disserted to him on "that most distinctively human thing about a human being, that he *is* his body and yet is *not*,"[336] whereupon Freud amusedly asked her lights on a prosthesis that "wants to be ego yet cannot."[337] Regarding the cognate problematics of mental versus physical, she found no overlapping between the two but instead a "no man's land": instinct.[338/v] Each told the same story, she held, only each in its own way: she early dubbed Spinoza, whose notion this was, "the philosopher of psychoanalysis,"[339/w] after having praised Freud both for sticking to his mental side of the story and for abstaining from philosophy.[340/x] Then came her strictures on Freud's "exaggerated . . . caution" lest he philosophize,[341/y] and then those on his deathly philosophizing. In the end she chalked up his achievements to an *"original"* pugnacious refusal to depart from "purely psychoanalytical" matter and method.[342]

Lou as psychoanalyst took human bisexuality (already affirmed in *Die Erotik*) as her starting point for discussing woman and love.[z] Thus she now spoke of femininity before speaking of woman[a]: in women, femininity simply tended to prepotence and, after puberty, to predominance,[b] the more readily since girls might discharge their masculinity in motherhood by anticipation.[343] She even underwrote the equation between feminine and passive in use when she came to psychoanalysis[c]—only to insist that passivity was not inhibited activity.[344/d] To the same effect she allowed that masochism dominated the feminine complex, only to insist against Freud that masochism was no mere derivative of sadism but was "primal" too.[e] She now char-

---

[v] She was quoting Freud on instinct here (on—in her own phrasing—"what physiologists and psychologists throw back and forth, and on occasion even up, to each other").

[w] Nominally by reason of the psychoanalytical concept of overdetermination, however, which is irrelevant to parallelism because intrapsychic.

[x] (On the abstaining: D [26 x 1912] already.)

[y] Cf. above, p. 380.

[z] D [early XII 1912]: bisexuality "constitutes" all living beings; etc.—a point made *less* emphatically in her theoretical works (e.g. only *en passant* in 1912c: 74—a passage penned late 1913) than in her diaries, letters to Freud about patients, or peripheral psychoanalytical writings such as 1914c.

[a] E.g. 1913e:7: " 'Femininity' (always meant theoretically and apart from all gradations and shades of personal juncture between 'femininity' and 'masculinity') . . ."—but not so meant at bottom.

[b] 1914b:14-15 (girls' overt prepubertal masculinity is bound to clitoris sexuality, hence repressed at puberty), 18-19; cf. 1913e:7; etc.

[c] D [17-21 x 1913] (woman's "passive sexual signification"); etc. (Freud latterly cautioned against this facile equation: see *Discomfort*, chapter IV, n. 3.)

[d] Her protonarcissistic equation of active and passive nullified her concession on femininity even more explicitly: see 1913e:9; 1914b:14-15; etc.

[e] 1920b:369 (which quotes Freud: "An original masochism not . . . deriving from sadism does not seem to be forthcoming"). Cf. above, pp. 383-84 and nn. *e, f.*

acterized woman's sexuality as narcissistic,[345] nominally after Freud[f] but more in her sense of the word than his—and even in his sense of it as concerned her "woman as such" lolling within herself, who "opens out over and beyond herself" through motherhood alone.[346/g] In fact that human being as woman was unmistakable for all her new-found blatant bisexuality and concessive passivity: "regressive without neurosis"[347]; less capable of differentiation, hence sexual as well as spiritual through and through in rounded oneness, and possessed of "the placidity of the egg as against the agility of the semen."[348/h] Her second contribution to *Imago*, "Zum Typus Weib" (Toward Woman as a Type),[i] was, like her first, a rewrite.[j] And in old age she went outright regressive under the head "Was daraus folgt, dass es nicht die Frau gewesen ist, die den Vater totgeschlagen hat" (What Follows from its Not Having Been the Woman Who Slew the Father). Here, after arguing from woman's lack of original guilt to woman's lesser departure from instinctual infantility, partial exemption from the incest taboo, immunity from dread of castration, and fidelity to the old father-god, she reissued not only the super-Lou of "Der Mensch als Weib" unfolding all of a piece within her snug cosmic circle,[349] but also the conjugal twoness of "Gedanken über das Liebesproblem" as woman's natural alternative to unnaturally slaying the father out of penis-envy.[350]

Preeminently protonarcissistic, woman intends her lover preeminently as a "proxy" or "symbol" for the all whence we issue, Lou contended[351]—only to personalize the all behind that depersonalized lover by prescribing that, for a true marriage, woman "must love in the man the father's child, the child of [him in whom? that in which?[k]] she remains fixed as in the subsoil of the ultimate communion between the two, which makes spouses into siblings as well."[352] So the proxy for the universal subsoil was a proxy for the father by way of the brother—and of a brother tantamount to a son at that, for she

---

[f] Already in 1905 Freud (*Three Essays*) had declared woman's original type of sexuality to be narcissism (self-love that becomes object-love through the desire for a penis, then substitutively for a man and for a child) reenforced by a throwback of libido upon the self at puberty. Lou invoked this schema regularly.

[g] (An implicit avowal.)

[h] (A new breach of her new rule against mixing biology with psychology: see above, p. 337 and n. *c*.)

[i] Freud→Lou, 4 xi 1912, had earlier invited a *first* contribution "perhaps . . . dealing with the relation of psychoanalysis to the problems of woman's life dear to you."

[j] Largely a rewrite of rewrites as recent as *Erotik* and her prepsychoanalytical diary. For a digest of "Typus" see below, Appendix B, vi, pp. 555-56.

[k] ". . . *dessen, worein* . . ."

added: "Therewith indeed nothing were wanting for all-sided consummate 'incest'! And therewith both find their true bond and sanction in the third, the father: for the man's truest honoring, indeed divinizing, of femininity is also a case of transference—by way of the father's widow."[353/l] Here was the posthistory of Lou's father love right down to her sons-and-lovers by way of her untrue marriage.

Strange to say, this time-honored inside story of her erotic writings showed through them only the more blatantly when they went psychoanalytical. And stranger to say, of all her writings they changed the least on the outside on going psychoanalytical. The erotic encounter remained dually onesided as in "Gedanken über das Liebesproblem," with "the so-called 'battle of the sexes' "[354] internal as in *Die Erotik*. She did now call narcissism by that name in recapitulating her theory of object-love as recapitulative from the first—as a lover's making the world of an occasion.[355] Even so she argued as of old that such overvaluing, generally considered to be owing, is in fact an offense to the beloved in that it enjoins him to live up to a prodigiously false image of himself and inspires him with factitious self-assurance.[356/m] She now held abiding narcissism to account for love's encroaching upon body and mind conjunctively.[357/n] In fact she now held narcissism to account for Eros' every last deed and misdeed, including even a beloved's shame at a lover's satiety.[o] And more, she saw "infantile identifications" behind the sentimental attachments of animals,[358] and she cheered the undividedness of insects' activity and passivity as also of their aggression and affection.[359] She of course represented her own periodic use and abuse of erotic proxies as narcissistic par excellence, for "in it," she held, "the wholly selfish way of loving meets with the wholly 'unselfish' (that which 'takes no notice of the other party') as one and the same," and when Freud called it narcissistic to crave love, she charged him with confusing "narcissism with its opposite: self-doubting insecurity."[360/p] As to her turnover in

[l] (Of transference from the all, that is.)

[m] "The less personally one loves," she added, ". . . the more one gets the feel of a definite person, for, whatever his characteristics may be, they cause no disturbance. Seen *thus*, we are all, each in his own way, infinitely worthy of love. The frightful injustice of exalting a single individual through love turns into justice where the individual is grasped so deeply as to stand right beside God as 'his child,' seen individually by us in *our* limitedness."

[n] As per 1914b:1, only in the sex act do physical and mental so interact that we seem to be squinting when we view it under either aspect—but as per 1914a:261-62, the body is not felt as entirely identical with the self even in amorous frenzy.

[o] 1914b:10: the beloved is "humiliated to the very core of his belovedness" because no longer overvalued as aboriginally he overvalued himself.

[p] Cf. 1920b:375n.: "Among persons narcissistically endowed are reckoned

lovers, she gave the alternative to be a neurotic love-hate fixation.[361] Then, following up a remark of Freud's on how formerly love itself was revered as are its objects in our times,[362] she put pagan piety into her playing free and loose with lovers. In "Eros" (1922) she implicated psychoanalysis in this devotional, apologetic enterprise.[q] And, psychoanalysis notwithstanding, she solemnized as never before her rites of thanksgiving to her lovers,[363] whom she began choosing already in 1911 from among Freud the father's children.

---

too exclusively those dependent on return love (sooner the case with those consciously ego-vain or else poor in narcissism) instead of persons self-sufficient because unconsciously partaking of the all"; with these latter, "oppressed by narcissistic excess, giving can most egoistically be holier than receiving, they being more grateful for someone's power to arouse their love than for his return love, which easily may humiliate and newly oppress them."

[q] D [early XI 1913] had already called it psychoanalytical to see rejected lovers as, in all their singularity, "one with Being itself." "Eros" (after "Liebesproblem" and D *passim* to VI 1922) treated of how Christianity's slander of the body made love pathetic or alternatively banal and of how then, through becoming personal, love lost out on its "total significance" (1922a:2). Self-deception about love, "Eros" pursued, derives from the troubadours and minnesingers, who smuggled Eros the rut-god into Christendom in disguise. But psychoanalysis has shown us that glorifying a beloved is a concealed glorifying of love and that the deeper is love, the less it concerns its present object—or any object. Love's one trick is to make some poor fellow stand for the universe entire—like only God otherwise. Just as man divinizes what is earliest about himself, so can God enter into mortals only in earthly form. To depersonalize love, then, we have not to despiritualize it but to penetrate its transhuman spirit within all living creatures, our creatural distinction being only to know where we fit into Creation. And Lou concluded ineptly with a lovely quotation from Peter Jakobsen: "See me as I looked to you when you loved me most."

AT ALVASTRA in 1911 Lou seduced Poul Bjerre after having befriended his wife, an invalid, and laughed down his marital scruples: she was rectifying *Ruth*. Bjerre was then thirty-five to Lou's fifty. He had married Professor Andreas Bjerre's—his brother's—mother-in-law,[r] so that Frau Professor Andreas was taking nominal advantage of him. Lettered, he too had once written on Nietzsche as a mad genius, but expressly to eschew reductive exegetics.[364] His most recent work was a drama.[365] Pursuant to her passion, Lou learned not only psychoanalysis but Swedish.[366] By the late spring of 1912, when they last met as lovers, she had infused variants of Swedish "allness" into Bjerre's professional vocabulary but had also discounted his undersexed Freudianism against the original.[367] Whitsuntide 1913 found her contrasting him reminiscently with Rainer from head to foot as if to prove her point about her singularizing after-gaze —to which he appeared a self-concealed *arriviste*, "banal-brutal" at bottom, posing as "noblest 'helper' " even in love.[368] In Munich that September she noted having "unwittingly" missed a talk by him that went over well with the Zurichers.[369] Years later Bjerre recollected: "In Munich Lou told me that she had burned my letters and asked me to do likewise. . . . I promised to do that and I kept my promise."[370] She had fibbed—as earlier to Rainer. In January 1914, Freud told her of having received a letter from Bjerre "in which he would conceal our differences."[371] She asked to see the letter: "Should this request be utterly inadmissible, please excuse it; it then calls for no further reply."[372] It received no further reply.[s] With her essay on Strindberg a year later, Lou followed up an interpretive lead of Bjerre's noted by her in 1912.[t] About then Ellen Key ran into Bjerre, who inquired whether Lou still took Freud so seriously—and Ellen, reporting to Lou, added that Bjerre had just brought out a fine book exposing Freud's exaggeration of sex.[373] Decades later Bjerre helped the author of an exposé of "women behind the scenes" to represent Lou as so much preternatural brain and sex arousing men "to an in-

[r] He had married the sculptress Gunnhild Wennerberg Posse (daughter of the poet Gunnar Wennerberg and widow of Count Frederick Posse) on 27 II 1905, Andreas Bjerre having married Amelie Posse on 23 VI 1904.

[s] Lou→Freud, 29 VI 1914, which followed his letter containing "no further reply," enclosed her correspondence with Adler unsolicited: a mute rebuke.

[t] Likely upon Strindberg's death (14 V 1912): see above, p. 388 n. *c*.

tense inner life often neglected, buried, or denied,"[374] unscrupulously tearing them loose from all their social and moral bonds—and then, of a sudden " 'nostalgic for herself,' " returning "home to 'Villa Lou-fried' to her husband, who clings to her with boundless permissive love."[375/u]

Lou's next was Viktor Tausk, her classmate in Vienna, a Croation ex-jurist come lately to medicine and psychoanalysis. Tausk was then thirty-five and divorced, with two sons in half custody. More personally, he was a theorist of narcissism, though not enough of proto-narcissism for Lou's pleasure.[376/v] He was a Spinozist too on the sly —another "philosophical head . . . so to say cut off" on Freud's account, Lou remarked.[377] All winter long Lou took Freud to be down on Tausk just because of Tausk's brilliance and devotion.[378/w] She interceded for Tausk once in February[x]: given Tausk's "originally neurotic orientation" toward Freud, she concluded, Freud doubtless meant well, yet was perturbed by Tausk's originality all the same.[379] A month later Freud discussed "the whole Tausk question" length-ily with her: "In the end he spoke very well and tenderly," was all she told her diary afterwards.[380] Between his master's courses and his own imitative lectures, between his medical studies and his clinical practice, Tausk spent his spare hours talking psychoanalysis with Lou, especially self-analysis, and seeing movies with her,[381] or reciting *Faust* with her and Ellen,[y] or else going over an old "Spinoza dia-logue" of his with her[382] or over his translation of some South Slavic ballads with "Promethean" heroes whose "doing was felt to be Being itself" as they transgressed the world order, braced for retribution.[383]

Toward the end of her sojourn in Vienna Lou reflected that, so long as in a love affair "one" means to be faithful (and here she counted fidelity among the "noble qualities"), one shrugs off the be-loved's dislikable traits; later on, though, "it can happen that in the thick of passion, for fear of being done out of one's self, one *spies out* these little telltale emergency exits . . . till one stops fearing and

[u] Further: Bernecker, 377 ("heedless vitality and elemental directness that acknowledge no barriers"), 391 ("many, perhaps most, of the men with whom she had a liaison felt antipathy or even hate for her afterwards"), etc. Bjerre as quoted in Peters, 270-72, told the same tale, though less rancorously—whether because he told it for direct quotation or because he had mellowed.

[v] See above, p. 355.

[w] *Ellen Delp recalls that she then took Tausk for a genius of Freud's own stature bearing up loyally under Freud's jealous provocation.

[x] But to go by 1913a as against D [13 II 1913], she was one of a few guests at Freud's that evening—and silent.

[y] *Ellen Delp: Ellen read Gretchen to Tausk's Faust until Lou told her that Tausk did not really want her to—and told Tausk the converse.

tolerates velleities of disaffection amidst affection—the way we know that death will strike us sometime and our love too sometime, yet do not take our pulse or its pulse continually. On the contrary, we turn its strongest beat to fullest account."[384] At the same time she showed herself ready to thank Tausk off in that she took a remark of his about promiscuous women as a cue to distinguish in her diary between betraying a lover and returning "*home to oneself*, from there, as from outer space, to walk again sometime among men," then similarly between rude dismissal and "reverent" insertion back "into infinite contexts." Then she considered further that it is humble, not proud, for a woman shattered by love to go off and recompose herself—and that "only the renunciation of factuality, only resurrection in make-believe, permits one to say: 'Linger on!' and to say truly: 'Thou art so fair!' with a feeling beyond all vulgar fidelity: a blessing on all future loves, compensating for their mortality."[385] Back in Göttingen, she told herself that the pain felt after a conflict has been resolved the selfish way is not remorse, but hardiness.[386/z]

During her two weeks in Vienna before the Munich congress she at last discerned "Tausk's relationship to Freud in all its tragedy: . . . his 'making-himself-into-the-son' as violent as his 'hating-the-father-in-consequence.' As if by telepathy, what occupies Freud's thoughts will always occupy his; he will never take that sidewise step which would give him leeway. This seemed so very much due to their situation, but it was ultimately due to him."[387] And she depicted him dispassionately as an all too sensitive beast of prey: "The sight of it all hurts so much that one turns away, would like to go away. For"— and here she popped out of impersonality—"he is fooling himself about me, dreaming. There is no *helpful* relationship in the last resort where all reality is spectrally spun round with unabreacted primal reminiscences."[388] In Munich, when Freud split the congress, "Tausk too sat right close to him," Lou noted—"even though Freud visibly rejected him even now."[389] It was in seeing Tausk off from the Munich station that she missed Bjerre's paper.

Unsuspectingly, she then saw him off for good. A year later he was a medical officer, and in 1919, some months after the Armistice, Freud reported to her: "Poor Tausk, whom you distinguished a while with your friendship, put a thorough end to his life on July 3. He came back from the horrors of war exhausted, set out under most unfavorable circumstances to reconstruct his lost existence, made an attempt to take a new woman into his life, was due to marry one week

---

z Cf. Bernecker, 395: Lou too would "suffer awhile" afterwards, "yet always pulled through unscathed."

later—but decided otherwise. His farewell letters to his fiancée, to his first wife, and to me are all alike affectionate, attest his lucidity, blame only his inadequacy and bungled life—thus throw no light on his final deed. In the letter to me he avers steadfast fidelity to psychoanalysis, thanks me, etc. But how it might have looked behind that is not to be guessed. So he fought out his day of life with the father ghost." How it looked behind *that* to the father ghost's successor directly followed: "I confess I do not really miss him; I have long taken him to be useless, indeed a menace for the future. I had a chance to cast a few glances into the substructure of his proud sublimations— and would long since have dropped him had *you* not so boosted him in my esteem. Of course I was ready anyhow to do what I could for him, only I have been quite powerless of late given the degeneration of all relations to Vienna."[390] Lou replied: "Your notification took me altogether by surprise. Poor Tausk. I was fond of him. Believed I knew him: yet would never, never have thought of suicide (successful suicide—not attempts or threats, I mean—strikes me almost rather as a proof of health than the contrary). I do not suspect even what means he chose (poison would have been ever so easy for a doctor to obtain): if a weapon, then I could imagine this death as the ultimate in voluptuous gratification for him as aggressor *and* sufferer in one. For here lay the Tausk problem, the danger that lent him his charm (non-psychoanalytically, he might be called a berserker with a tender heart). What you write about your 'not missing him at bottom'[a] seems to me not merely understandable: I too felt him to be a certain 'threat for the future'[b] to you as also to the cause that consciously he championed with such enthusiasm and sincerity. He knew of my suspicions about him, my dread lest he insist on a university appointment in Vienna. In March he wanted to come to [me in] Munich, but I declined; I did not answer his last letter, like so many before it.[c] A year ago he wrote truthfully: 'No one will sit down at the same table with a wretch: not even you have done so.' No, not even I." And, disputing Freud the vicarious macabre honors, she pursued: "The true sufferer, as also the true beloved, is in this case his sister"—whose address she requested.[391] Freud's reply does not survive. Lou next wrote Freud nine months later for his birthday.[d]

---

[a] (Misquotation Lou's.)   [b] (Ditto.)

[c] D 1 IV 1919 (Munich): "Long letter from Tausk on paranoia as local psychosis."

[d] Freud→Lou, 9 V 1920: "Very happy to have heard from you. Whither had you vanished?" Freud had not likely described the suicide, though: according to the *Wiener Zeitung* of 4 VII 1919, Tausk shot himself in the right temple after having placed his head in a noose so that he also hanged himself in falling (cf. below, p. 419).

After Tausk came Victor Emil Gebsattel, an obsessive casuist possessed of a world of interests, as he told Lou, by way of compensation for not loving or understanding himself.[392] Lou had first met him at Georg Simmel's in Berlin early in 1906,[393] when he was a budding moral philosopher of twenty-three. By 1911, when she met him again at the Weimar congress, he was a medical doctor practicing psychoanalysis—on Clara Rilke among others—without quite believing in it.[394] At Weimar he was smitten with Lou as "beyond good and evil. You were life's unimpairedness," he afterwards recalled, "its festive innocence. . . . Were you not (so ran the refrain in Weimar) Nietzsche's 'girl friend,' his who had discovered the 'beyond'? did we not belong together in our love of this 'beyond'? I did not know then or thereafter that I was taking desire for reality in my own case, that with lyrics and arguments I was shamming guiltlessness. This inner insincerity, unavoidable, was bound to vitiate everything that passed between us."[395] Lou saw Gebsattel next at his home in Munich on her way to Tausk in August 1913. She found him critically disposed toward Freud given Freud's aptitude for ugly insights—to which she objected grandly: "As regards anything humanly great, surely it is more heartening than dampening that it should perhaps have grown great out of its infirmities."[396] Back for the congress on September 4, she moved in with Gebsattel for some weeks[e] during which he wallowed in "suddenly gushing sources of my suddenly liberated life."[397] He was with her to see Tausk off, but back in time to hear Bjerre's talk for her.[398] "He roamed amidst the congress factions ever so detachedly," she afterwards observed: "the cigarette between his lips looked like an intentional hindrance from sneering or bursting into laughter."[399] After the congress, the high point of her stay with him was a soirée featuring a supposedly scholarly "investigator of artificially induced trances" who was suddenly recognized as "a lunatic" by all present: Gebsattel, alone unfazed, steered the conversation to "this new point of interest" and won the lunatic's heart "with this (worldly?) superiority."[400/f] Even with Lou gone,

[e] Following D 4 IX 1913 as in Pfeiffer, *Briefwechsel*, 309, rather than D [7-8 IX 1913] as in Pfeiffer, *Schule*, 190-91—which was evidently meant to look decently as if Rilke too had stayed at Gebsattel's.

[f] Perhaps Gebsattel briefly revived Lou's interest in occultism (dormant since the Leipzig occultist fiasco of 1882), for D [17 IX 1913] cites a remark he had passed on the subject during her earlier stay, hence shortly before her telepathy analogy for Tausk's relationship to Freud, and a "long talk (in confidence)" with Freud in Munich "on the strange cases of telepathy, which decidedly torment him." (These cases came into later writings of Freud's, though by Lou's account of that talk Freud was, unlike herself, wary of the topic: did she draw him out telepathically?)

Gebsattel went on exulting: " 'There *is* no sin; life lies beyond good and evil'—and this very conception," he later averred, "gave sin a new hold over me by making it invisible. Only in the course of a truly unprejudiced self-analysis did I manage to grasp 'sin' again—meaning 'immediacy' infected, turned evil."[401]

Lou was his self-analytical confidante and counsellor—by mail[g] except for a reunion in Würzburg in January 1914,[402] and until another in Munich beginning July 23, 1914, to which he summoned her urgently. As he later explained: "I had to see and talk to *you*. Why is still not clear to me."[403] By her records, they scrapped off and on for days all over town. He afterwards put the issue between them interrogatively: "Were you not a symbol to me signifying that original sin was a fiction and that there are heathen, primeval, never sidetracked, paradisiac, non-guilt-laden, glorious beings, with a law of living untouched by the law of willing and acting? Did not my sacrilege consist in my not avowing this need of mine? and not wanting to heed this longing of mine? and setting such store by approaching you as a king, whereas I was a beggar? For I even sought to dupe you from whom I was expecting life—my own life. In no case was I to appear to be suffering from inner need and wretchedness; instead I simulated fullness, fullness, whilst probably green envy was secretly devouring me."[404/h]

On August 1 the European blow-up prompted Lou to return at once to Göttingen. As Gebsattel subsequently related, he took her to be fleeing him: "You did not leave me time to nurse you properly after the monster, the specter, the complex-dragon had dealt with you so ill, dear lady, so very dreadfully. You received bruises . . ."[405] —which showed only in his letters, though. "Shaken and thrown, so utterly destroyed by our encounter, you held back, and it was months before I began to recover.[i] . . . Late in August I went to Heidelberg and took over the direction of a big infirmary, ever under the dominion of that self-estrangement in which I had come away from you. Thus it ensued that I . . . finally fell ill."[406] Ill from Lou, he was by no means sick of her. "Yes, you cannot cease being reality for me, Lou. Maybe this means nothing to you. I would gladly have written you every day . . . only I let you be my dear teacher and forced nothing."[407]

On November 28 Lou learned of his breakdown.[408] At the start of

[g] As per Gebsattel→Lou, 7 I 1915 and 18 I 1915; also D II 1914 (". . . Gebsattel's 'trapdoor letter' . . ."), etc.

[h] Had Gebsattel been reading Rilke's diary for 1898?

[i] Further: "You surely recovered quickly, while I in fact lay a few months buried under the debris."

1915 she told her diary on a note of panic that before the war she had grown soft on mankind to pay for being hard on her lovers, so that with mankind now odious to her, her conscience was aching. Worse, she was incapacitated from ever again loving heedlessly. "For one would *love*, not *be* loved, at least not in the first, second, third place; one would give oneself up and away. For all his corrupting flattery, Gebsattel sometimes got at a primal truth, as when he said to me: 'Enamored you!' with regard to my trust in men and things and fate. Even when a passionate feeling recedes from me, there remains—without satiety or disappointment—gratitude and reverence in my soul, which indeed but restores the person out of [*sic*] the totality out of which he came to it. To be somehow unable to do this any longer were no clear or simple experience: everything resists it, with the result that one seeks counsel ever and again in the offenses one has inflicted, which can twist and spoil so much."[409/j] Seeking counsel, Lou sent asking Gebsattel whether he had pulled himself together.[410] His reply was a soul-searching *no* many thousand words long, which fatigue alone cut short—and this to the good, for the deeper he searched, the farther the truth receded. He had, he began, falsified their relationship by not admitting till their last night together that he had always wanted her love; only this itself was false, since in his "secret self-hate"[411/k] he really wanted to be unloved; yet again, if secretly he wanted none of her real love, he did openly want to feel and enjoy her love as if it were real; at bottom, however, he wanted to feel himself loved period, not by Lou but absolutely, "let us say: by God,"[412] but this, to be sure, only so as to be himself able to love at last; indeed, in expecting the godlike of her, he was worshipping her as a god,[l] and yet he was at times hostile toward her just because she did not accept his "state of being unloved" . . .[m]

Lou in return sent him some serene pseudorecollections out of her childhood complete with pseudo-self-analyses.[413] Before he had even read these through, a new onset of "*furor analyticus*" prompted another flood of words to Lou. And "do you know, Lou, that a letter to you as long as my last one is still lying in my desk drawer?"— whither he had cast it upon realizing that "only the old, spectral law of our relationship" underlay his wish to unload "everything deceptive, unreal, complex-ridden, sinful" upon her by mail.[414] This

---

[j] (It was to d'Annunzio's*Enamored You* that Lou compared B-H, *Tod*: above, p. 260 and n. z.)

[k] Was he claiming Rée's symptom—at Lou's suggestion? He quoted one Nietzschean diagnosis by Lou: that he was "suffering from himself."

[l] Last seven words surmised (Gebsattel's corresponding seven obliterated).

[m] Lou defaced the immediate sequel and demolished the rest.

insight was a new beginning: "Is it not obvious, dear Lou, why some-one disoriented should come to *you*—to you who, joyously at home in life with your infinitude of blissful composure, are yet able, by a miracle of sensibility, to look out to one who is estranged from life? Does he not see in your secure homelikeness a possibility of his own in effigy? Is it not easy for him to fall into the error of believing that he could, by embracing this possibility in effigy, turn into you by magic enchantment, so to say, filling himself full of your world-fed livingness? So long as he does not know himself, is there not some-thing maybe of self-seeking perfidy and of predatory cruelty about him such that he would gladly have become you while still seeking himself, would in fact have gobbled you up skin, hair, and all? And did not that 'compliancy' and 'understanding' of mine as applied to your person merely tend to the insidious atrocity of vampirishly gobbling selflessness and starved lust for life mendaciously posing as love? But then too, in the secret intention of that letter cast aside, in its will to come to you with everything I am and have, there may stir a far-flung drive to self-destruction as counterpart to that gob-bling selflessness—a wish to dissolve and go to ruin in anything at all motherly in this world, thus surrendering identity . . ."[415] And ever again: "How did you pull off that magic stunt of springing the Adamite circle of life? or that bigger one of smuggling pre-Adamite, paradisiac life into it? Are you, dear Lou, a saint, a babe in the woods, or a smuggler?"[416] And parenthetically: "Are you laughing? . . . or scowling, or shrugging? or is your concern, as I really suppose, greater than my capacity not to deserve it any longer?"[417] Lou saw Gebsat-tel on later visits to Munich[n] but wrote of him only once again: di-agnostically, as a mixed compulsive and hysteric whose "unabreacted material" emerged from the depths so ghostly as merely to haunt his consciousness without being acknowledged as his.[418]

In August 1914, her first sense of unreality past, Lou shuddered at the surge of mass hate and crude propagandizing throughout the Old World. Where there are States there will be wars, she reflected, "only one's inner outlook on essentials need not lapse."[419] As of Au-gust 8 she felt "only an immense sorrow," the greater for her sym-pathy with the peoples on both sides as against the interests at stake: "If I sat down to cry, all the tears I ever held back would pour out like blood. As if it were no longer possible to care about life."[420] Yet the very next day she railed against a pacifistic friend: "She should be able to dig down to the ground on which she is German, to feel that Germans are fighting for her. . . . To be incapable of this is sick-

[n] Beginning III 1915.

ness too."[421] Another day and she observed how men's native brutality emerged—"beneficially for them"—when their national dignitaries set the example.[422] Later that first month she wondered about the eulogists of war: "Have they no shame at all?"[423] then reflected that whereas the German's civilian vices of "pedantry and brazenness, servility and arrogance" made for soldierly virtues of "discipline, devotedness, dutifulness, etc.," there was nothing bred into a Russian to restrain him if ever he ran wild.[424] In September she considered that war seemed ultrareal to the many who in time of peace were out of conscious touch with their elemental drives; that though struggle was inevitable it did not need to be physical; that one cannot perfect anything such as war machinery without wanting to "*demonstrate*" its perfection[425]; and that mortal hate was fundamentally a fond protest against disjunction from the all.[o] October found her "almost tortured" by the chauvinistic "lies and bombast" corrupting all values: "One *bleeds* as in a battle at the spectacle of this ignoble war of minds, what with everything prized yesterday suddenly despicable and everything combatted suddenly honorable."[426/p] To a protest against debasing the enemy she nonetheless objected that "without hate and despisal the enemy would turn—human."[427]

In November she told Ellen Key: "Whatever the outcome, I do not think I shall ever be able to live as before: with the same endless, jubilant joy. No, never again just so."[428] Freud then inquired: "Do you still think all the big brothers are so good?"[429] "They have become devilish one and all," she avowed—"(but that is because States cannot be psychoanalyzed)."[430] "It is too foul," Freud returned; "and saddest of all is that men are behaving just as psychoanalysis might have led us to expect. This is why I could never join in on your jolly optimism."[431] Pressed, Lou did her protonarcissistic best short of invoking original love: "I do still think: behind individual human activities, farther back than psychoanalysis can reach, the worthiest and nastiest impulses condition each other indistinguishably, making a final verdict impossible. . . . We each live only out of such ultimate confidence, which ought then to hold for all others. It ought: it admittedly does not, not today, though it ought could one but get down deep enough beyond oneself—this alone helps me along a little."[432]

[o] D 11 IX 1914: we hate so as to objectify and thus reembrace through conscious experience—war being accordingly a way of getting better acquainted.
[p] Atop many a telling sample of newfound public Anglophobia and Turkophilia: "I read Dehmel's letter to his children, the soldierly letter, with mourning. The German simply the better man, to whom the world is due, who is now fighting for this due: why then go on speaking of the war as 'imposed upon us'?"

Freud therewith oddly lauded Lou's "truly moving optimism"[433]—
and stayed unmoved.

Lou meanwhile reflected to herself that, for war to be morally possible, not only its true objectives had to be falsified, but so did its deepest motive, thwarted cosmic love—"which is why war looks to me like madness."[434] Only some months later did she try out that deepest motive on Freud,[435] who took faint exception to the "justification of 'murder lust,' if it was meant to be one."[436/q] It was actually meant to be an apology for mankind even at the expense of protonarcissistic orthodoxy, which called for aboriginal ambivalence and original hate. It tended to cancel that "most direct effect of the war on me,"[437/r] doubtless primarily an effect of her age: remorse over her erotic past joined to anxiety over her erotic future. This effect was not heard from beyond that once when it prompted her renewal with Gebsattel: her first letter to him of that January 1915 broke off in the midst of a discussion of war as all "hate,"[438/s] and her second called hate "nothing real" despite "the war, from which I have suffered as otherwise never since childhood."[439] To Freud she reported that same January 1915: "Out of desperation over warring mankind I have just acquired a dog"[440]—a terrier. She named it Drujok (Little Friend) out of sympathy with the enemy and kept a log of its anal and sexual development. As for "this true outbreak of madness in Europe," she remarked in 1916 that, "personal mourning apart, we know it only conceptually, can no longer experience it with imagination and feeling: if we had to, it would cease—or we would."[441/t]

Lou took a long view of the war early in 1917 in a review of a book on insect life.[442] Aggressiveness develops along with erotism among insects, she observed, the solidary, untemperamental insects being by and large the more rudimentary. Men, who study insects, aspire to bridle their mutual brutality in a world community fit to restore that primal peace within which aggression and affection were one—and yet they also mean to go the limit in individual consciousness and independence. Both are possible, she submitted, if humanity is reconstrued as a brotherhood of the mind rather than of

q Cf. above, p. 352.

r Cf. D 21 x 1914 ("it has suddenly struck me what most intimately underlies my horror at the war").

s Gebsattel was baffled by the half letter, which Lou→Gebsattel, 15 i 1915, draft, half explained as due to her having changed her mind about the war midway.

t Her diary that year also included some fine pages on war psychology, concluding oddly that war drew "the three great distinctions"—man, woman, and child—together into "One Experience . . . beside men's dreams of the *suffering God*."

the flesh—a brotherhood of unlike persons doing like work. Otherwise struggle and love must come apart disruptively in the human will even while retaining the selfsame aim. For cold carnage is only a perverted embrace, she concluded, referring her readers to psychoanalysis for elucidation.

In August 1917, Lou declared concerning the revolution underway in Russia: "For the first time in three years, which have been like three thousand, I was glad to be alive, to be not yet dead. Whether or not the event takes a tragic turn for Russia changes nothing of its grandeur. And when did anything at all in Russian history *not* take a tragic turn?"[443] A month later she ascribed the soviets' "positive power" to the people's piety: "The deposed czar must signify something like: God perfecting himself in the mystery of a revolution. *Otherwise* it is *all* a big mistake. *Then* it is ruination."[444] In November she saluted the Bolshevik accession as Kingdom come—and likely to go too, "but who today with any brain or heart left can deny that it redeems direst horrors to see utopians at work amidst the power-politicians of all other peoples and lands? Thank you, Russia, little mother!"[445] At the year's end she judged "these most radical fanatics" as, "with their utopia," a menace to Russia "because more dogmatically oriented than the Social Revolutionaries, more directly accountable for the people's wishes and thoughts. Only all these differences, I do believe, are of no great account *for Russia* as they would be elsewhere, for there *one* spirit animates all deep within."[446] Then in February 1918, when Trotsky called off the peace (temporarily, as it turned out) after Lenin had called off the war: "As if one had listened for harps or trumpets and heard a street song! Not just that this damned business has already compromised the Revolution, but that it can so *parody* it: to hell with them! . . . Lay awake all night with torn heart, wailing as if silly."[447]

In May 1918 she told Freud that, given the Russian national "tragedy," her "private life" was "too painful to discuss: pen in hand, I would howl aloud."[448] Returning to the charge, Freud asked "whether you expected *that* of your six big brothers, who were all so nice to you"[449/u]: he was counting her brothers by his study group. Her first mail from Russia had come in mid-November 1914, unsealed, by way of Denmark—from Sasha, then serving at the front.[450] The following February 20 she learned of Sasha's death.[v] "*Just let me see nobody*. Sasha, dear Sasha," she wrote that day[451] —and a week later: "It now seems to me that even Mama's death was

---

u Similarly Freud→Abraham, 11 xii 1914: "She had six big brothers, all of whom were kind to her."

v (Apparently a natural death.)

not so much of a 'death' to me as Sasha's suddenly departing forever (and not alone because of Mama's age: Sasha was 'security')."[452] Evidently her nephews combatted the revolution: in October 1918 she wrote of them as all officers cut off from their families and liable to "be shot at any moment."[453] She took no written notice of the Western armistice that November. The following January, however, Drujok died, and for eighteen nights and days round about the increasingly "marblelike" corpse (while Andreas decked out a seemly grave) she wallowed in a grief of which she recorded between times how, whenever it surged up anew, she would hesitate an instant before plunging into it as if into Drujok's embrace,[454] and at last how it had all served to cover up the remembrance of Drujok's astonished, then fearful, then almost apologetic leave-taking from his loving, beloved mistress[455]—who in her formal thinking went on holding animals ignorant of their mortality. Meanwhile she marginally considered that "there is in reality only rapture or desperation for us, and . . . we call the moods in between normal only because we have had to construct our whole world by way of such fearful compromising."[456] And upon reflecting that it was just as well she had for some reason ceased letting precious milk boil over inadvertently what with Drujok no longer around to lap it up, she all at once realized what that reason was.[w] She allowed that self-indulgent grieving such as hers for Drujok might provide release for a repressed impulse unrelated to the "point of sorrow"[457]: was she mourning mankind through Drujok?

In a prophetic retrospect of mid-1919 she noted that "the most awful thing" about "the past five years" was that men had dismissed their history as oversized catastrophe—"that after experiences which ought never to have been, after every manner of infamy and atrocity on the part of all peoples involved, after senseless slaughtering and endless mutilating, we turn the single fact to advantage that it all staggers the imagination, so that we 'luckily can bear it.' We lack the courage to face the unbearable squarely, with consequent ruination and *resurrection as others*; instead we would be reasonable about the gruesome, we declaim phrases about 'reconstruction,' 'return to normal,' 'no cowardly looking back,' and so remain the same people with the same experiences ever again in store for them. Oh praise be to those were able to go mad from what was happening: *they* save our honor, in *them* are our dead most secure, our wounded most con-

---

[w] Lou→Freud, 30 ı 1919. (Lou wrote up this lapsus anew for Freud's use in a reedition of his book on the psychopathology of everyday life: see Freud→Lou, 9 ıı 1919; Lou→Freud, 22 ıı 1919; Freud→Lou, 9 ııı 1919.)

soled. That was what set hearts trembling with joy when the revolution broke out in Russia (and afterwards more briefly here): that we *wanted*, we *dared* to believe that the dreadful was dreadful enough to have turned us round about, as happens now and again at the advent of new epochs or religions or utopias, justified of a sudden for one universal moment. Instead we were only shaken so that our dregs rose disgustingly. Servitude to the phrase yielded (however garrulously) to baseness *sans phrase*."[458] Publicly she nonetheless called the revolution an enterprise of practical piety, for to "that which is of 'God's spirit' " in the Russian, the earth is the proper locus for heaven.[459] Two years later she learned that "Roba, my last brother, buried his youngest son, a war casualty in the Crimea, returned to Peterhof with his wife and daughter on a two-and-a-half month trip, lives in a few small rooms of his former country house on the estate, which meanwhile devolved upon his ostler, and goes mushroom- and berry-picking with his grandchildren to still hunger."[460] In January 1923 she concluded from a talk with a Russian refugee: "Since the Bolsheviks have been leaving off the bestiality of their methods (which stood in such dreadful contrast to their ideal social goal) . . . a younger generation is growing up there full of glow and purity, determined to reach that goal after all, hence to struggle *against* the Bolshevism of the period of concessions," and she predicted an unending contest between pragmatics and fanatics,[461] tacitly sympathizing with both. For Lou too the castrophe was history.

Lou did not, then, let the war any more than psychoanalysis change her, affecting as she deemed them both. Thus her writings ran true to form during the sixth decade of her life,[x] those about the war or psychoanalysis included.

In June 1912, she authored two letters addressed to Helene Klingenberg's boy, the first about where babies really come from and the second on how plants and animals do it ("not only the ugliest things but also the loveliest are done secretively"[462]). Late in 1913 she added a third, on adolescence as narcissism resurgent, invoking Freud. She published the three in 1917 as *Drei Briefe an einen Knaben* (Three Letters to a Boy) after appending an explication of anal disgust to the second, then altering the third to the effect that she had studied psychoanalysis only "since the time of my last letter to you."[463/y] The

---

[x] Except for the elimination of certain orthographic archaisms (affectations?) beginning with her first letter to Freud—of h's after t's ("*die That*") and, in imported words, of i's for ie's and of c's for z's ("*placiren*").

[y] (In lieu of: "in the years between my last letters.") She backdated the first letter to "Christmas 1907," the second to "summer 1911," and the third to "fall 1913" (and "Vienna"!), so as to make them look good and "*pre-*

bluff was venial inasmuch as the running initiation into the mystery of cosmic incest was all of a sacerdotal piece, psychoanalysis notwithstanding[z]—and of a piece with *Die Erotik* at that. In 1914 she published "an essay noted long since already,"[464] "Kind und Kunst" (Child and Art), which declared artists to be big children except that the how of playing is for them the whole of it. The child's play was already in "Eine erste Erfahrung"[465] and still in "Des Dichters Erleben,"[a] whereas the how clause is unexampled. The surpassing obscurity of the piece suggests that it was first "noted" along with *Der Gott* except that one darkest passage concerning a possible teen-agers' art was superadded just prior to publication.[b] Lou's undated "Der Teufel und seine Grossmutter" (The Devil and his Grandmother)[c] is a poetical mystery about the Devil, who is all intellection and individuation, God, who is life in its original inexhaustibly creative unity, and the Devil's Grandmother, mother of God, who is simply Everything: in a nurseling's vision "what never was" thrice occurs as the Devil ruses with a lover, cries out before some poets, then ups and dies; the climax is a beatific vision of the old womb herself, which turns out to be a Pietà. As the Devil amounts to God's excretory organ,[d] the basic scheme was about as old as Lou herself,[e] with neither the iambics nor the metaphysics nor even the whimsy necessarily more than some forty years newer. The grandiose heroine does look like Gebsattel's compliments on Lou's aboriginality gone to her head—but might well look less so except that a cinematographic sequence in the thick of the drama establishes it as posterior to 1912-1913, when Lou made her fond acquaintances with "the Cinderella of the arts" in Vienna,[466] and except that, by Lou's word of 1920, the manuscript then went back "years" already.[467]

---

war" (Lou→Kurt Wolff, 18 VIII 1917). On their composition see D VI 1912 ("Bubi letters"); Lou→RMR [5 XII 1913]; Lou→Freud, 3 IV 1931 (which fibs); and Lou's manuscript in the Handschriften-Sammlung der Stadtbibliothek München.

[z] (And despite the deliberate graduation from euphemistic babytalk to euphemistic pedantry.)

[a] See below, pp 553-54.

[b] Lou→Spranger, 2 VII 1914 (so as to "serve our cause in premonitory fashion": cf. below, p. 447).

[c] The title of a Grimm fairy tale but also an expression equivalent to "everyone and his brother."

[d] Bab sees the Devil's *function* as excretory, and even repressive to boot. (Bab considers *Teufel* to be, with *Ródinka*, Lou's most significant work.)

[e] 1915a:42: "Grandma! now I've caught on!— —Song without words!/ You sang of God, who, before you bore him,/ Fructified you ('twixt parentheses:/ Quite a godly trick for him to pull)."

In June 1917, Lou put a final storybook lustre upon her snug dream house of 1904, *Das Haus*, in which she felt as fantastically at home as ever.[468/f] In August she took up *Ródinka* again—"so many years removed from me, yet now as if first peeled out of me page by page. Do not know how come, just that it *had* to be there, unprinted— and that I am nevertheless almost sorry, as I should like to have it to do all over again. Probably because not I, but Russia, wrote it. In the unforgettable impressions shared by Rainer and me."[469] Anyhow, she did do much of it over—to little advantage.[g] She meant for one thing to cut out young Witalii's issueless love for Margot, and for another to carry his inner dissension concerning the traditional Russian pieties down "to ultimate depths of soul, so that only a hellish deed remains open to him"[470/h]; bits of the love story slipped by, however, and Witalii feuded on with his brother over the pilgrim folk as singlemindedly as of old. Witalii's beatific vision of the Russian all from the heights of Kiev came off the purer for the little German girl's backing out of it, but also that much tougher to top for the finale. Lou topped it: one morning Witalii, muttering senselessly, makes off from the outer edge of Ródinka, as if by fateful, awesome preappointment, *into* that Russian all, palpably *merging with it*—at all odds as seen from the horse cart in which Margot sits watching. All Ródinka divines the impending departure with hushed, acquiescent foreboding. The diarist, now depersonalized in the extreme, senses the futility of protest or even discussion. As sole witness to this final parting, she replaces Witalii's wife in particular (then expecting for a first time), of whom Witalii had taken a "brief leave barely heeded by her."[471] Add to all this the recurrent, insidious suggestion that Witalii's grand rendezvous with fatality may rather be one with a *femme fatale* hitherto frequented on the sly[i] and Witalii departing was Rainer off to Florence in 1898 supplanted by Rainer sent packing in 1901 overwritten by Rainer delivered up to his dark god. Witalii divided against himself had insofar passed over from "stupendously coherent" Nikolai Tolstoi[j] into young Rainer,[k] even

[f] Bab, 25 and *passim*, presumes (by analogy with *Ródinka* primarily) that she then accentuated Anneliese's cosmic pathos. Certainly she polished the prose, which is singularly spic and span.

[g] For the sense of this revision, evidently completed in the spring of 1919, I rely on Bab (above, p. 289 n. *m*).

[h] (Bab considered this deepening accomplished.)

[i] One due to marry shortly: in all her traits she figures both Lou and Clara Westhoff—and Witalii repeats Dimitrii's (Rilke's) desertion of house and home.

[j] See above, pp. 278, 296.

[k] (With Rée faintly perceptible behind Rainer.)

as Lou's recollection of having thrown Rainer out was passing over into one of having given him up—*through* one of having let him go: "Whoever saw it happening had to let it happen. Impotent and awe-struck."[472] (By way of self-rebuke, Lou dreamed that Rainer shook a finger at her manuscript where it read "I reached for his hands," say-ing: "*Had* reached—*had*"[473/l]: in Russia, that reaching was already *past*.) For the rest, the paternalistic *barin* had gone about his mano-rial business inwardly untorn—and the plot had gone to pot on that palimpsest once and for all, the accessory characterizations and the incidental tableaux of Russian life remaining as vestiges of a con-ception surely gorgeous back in January 1901, when Lou had been in such a dither to deliver, Rainer be damned. She reworked only one characterization: she updated the Narodnika (Sophia Schill) to a Marxist. To the tableaux she added a few of old Russia now on its way out, in particular a fine one on the Petersburg diaspora[474] and a finer one on the atmosphere in that imperial city during the winter of 1879-1880, a year before the assassination of Alexander II.[475] Did she bear these last alone in mind as she subtitled the whole pseudo-memoir: "Russian Reminiscence"?

Meanwhile Margot's original, Musja of "Im Zwischenland," re-appeared following Lou's return from Vienna in 1913 as the intro-verted little heroine of "Das Bündnis zwischen Tor und Ur" (The Covenant Between Tor and Ur),[m] Tor being a softhearted wild boy. A season's resident in Tor's town, Ur comes to play slave-and-master with him in a secret cave by a river. This inexpressibly lovely tale re-lated to the reality just in back of it in the way of a naturalistic cari-cature. Ur's playmate had been a real-life lover of Lou's, Tausk, who, having rediscovered his childhood with her, here tangibly returned to it with her. The real-life liaison contracted with intent to stay faithful became an enthrallment ceremonially sealed in blood. Freud appeared as Tor's dearly detested headmaster, executed in effigy by Tor pur-suant to the innermost truth about Tausk. This mode of distortion was not new in Lou's story-telling: the poetical faker Spiridon had turned into the poet and forger Apollon, and earlier Zemek had found himself a deaf mute for lacking Beer-Hofmann's sophistication. Its preeminence among her fictionalizing devices was new, however, and just possibly due to psychoanalysis for as much as her schooling in

[l] She had glimpsed the five manuscript words out of context at bedtime. (They wound up—modified—on 1901a:174 or conceivably 52 or 255.)

[m] Short for the Teutonic Torwald and Ursula, *Tor* also means "fool" and *Ur* "proto-" (Lou's most honorific prefix, personified by her Devil's grand-mother)—suggesting respectively the bad way and the good of being child-like.

the trade put her endocephalic editor to shifting tricks. It had also been Hauptmann's device for sneaking "Ein Todesfall" onto the stage, as Lou had obliquely noted at the time.[n] It corresponded to Tor's side of his running difference with Ur over her lush lying as opposed to his primitive intensification of the truth. The fiction of "Tor und Ur" was the covenant's dissolving of its own on both sides: Ur, besides returning Tor to the all by way of a rosebush, drops from his heart even as, following her intercession, he enters his head-master's good books. So, attachment for attachment, Ur's had been the more direct and authentic one. Behind this whole fiction about Tausk, Lou was furthermore fancying herself to have been Rée's slave from juvenile start to adolescent finish, with no servitude left over for headmaster Nietzsche: such was Lou's unconscious rejoinder to Nietzsche's unconscious genealogy of morals.[o]

In "Seelchen," which came next, little Seelchen plays at having children—more imaginatively than her parents, if all too much by the Freudian rules. Then in May 1919 Lou suddenly recollected that snow couple whose vanishing into thin air had prompted her fatal plea to her childhood god for a word of reassurance.[476] Late the fol-lowing September "Die Stunde ohne Gott" (The Hour Without God) lay written beside her[477]: it made over Seelchen's dolls and eggs more or less verbatim to Ursula, added a co-genitor, Dieter, who was a naughtier Tor, and superadded a delightful account of how her childhood god had gone diabolical, then simply gone, with a happy ending by which Ursula some weeks afterwards discovers a full equivalent for him in nature. Between the recollection and the redac-tion, Lou's current god-man had failed her following her real Dieter's suicide: her new Calvary, unavowed, carried over into that auto-biographic event, "Geschwister" (Siblings).

The siblings are pubescent Jutta[p] and her four brothers, of whom the youngest, Gottlieb, is her twin, and the eldest, Stefan, not quite an adult. Orphans, they come under the care of queenly Aunt Adele, an unwed sister of their mother's and sometime unlucky rival for their father's hand. Jutta, guileless and beguiling, is erotically bent on rev-erence. A bosom companion to crooked-chested Gottlieb, she has lately been drawn rather to effeminate Stefan and through him to his idol twenty years his senior, Klaus Trebor, who runs an orthopedic clinic and twice weekly occupies quarters upstairs from the orphans,

---

[n] See above, p. 291 and notes.

[o] Yet Tor also figures Nietzsche "*hiding out*" in his " 'cave' " (above, p. 132).

[p] The titular heroine of "Jutta" was in all likelihood so named only when "Jutta" was reworked as a sequel to "Geschwister": below, pp. 422 n. *j*, 483.

receiving young men. Jutta visits Trebor on the sly. Stefan finds out and, mincing his words, objects that she might grow dependent on the great man and suffer. "You mean: I might love him and he not me?" she puts in, only to add—too plainspokenly to be readily understood—that Stefan ought to know best "what it's about and what it's worth—and that it's worth it even then."[478] So Stefan comes stealthily round to warning her that "he knows men—she doesn't. And love and love—denotes not only that to which one looks up—"[479] then to pleading: "break it off! stop going to him!"[480] She weeps. He embraces her, feeling manly at last. From out of his arms, however, she goes straight to Trebor—"only to tell him I would not come again," she afterwards assures Gottlieb, adding tearfully that Trebor did not give her a chance: "He repelled me, repelled me from him. In such a big hurry—"[481] Stefan, having seen her heading for Trebor's, feels betrayed, whereupon he realizes that jealousy had prompted his plea to her. "Jealousy of whom—?! Of her?—of him?!"[482] Opting for the latter, he that night stabs himself. Aunt Adele's shriek in the morning tears Jutta out of Gottlieb's arms, where she has been howling for joy and pain by turns over some other news brought bright and early by Gottlieb "with the strangest smile in the world: Now just see how she has wronged Klaus Trebor with her lamentations— hadn't he told her so straightaway? If Trebor had repelled her upstairs, he hadn't done so the least bit out of wrath or antipathy or brutishness or what have you—only so as to protect her, do her good, for danger was threatening him—Klaus Trebor was taken into custody."[483] Gottlieb withheld the reason: vice. It (and "far more") comes to Jutta's ears later that day, "only given her dismay over Stefan's death, which so quickly dissipated her precedent dismay, this new information had not yet been able to find room in her waking thoughts for inner reception or assimilation" by bedtime. So she dreams of Trebor as a counterfeiter (or forger or falsifier or fraud: "*Fälscher*") brought to trial in "a maudlin magazine story" she had once read.[484]

Trebor was Freud. Orthopedics was psychoanalysis physicalized, vice being just what did pass between Freud and his students—academically. Freud's fraud was his formal insistence that, as deep-lying motives were all grisly, they redounded to no one's discredit: witness his confidential post-mortem on his hapless devotee Tausk, damned on the ground beneath those "proud sublimations."[q] Trebor the sex criminal was the substructure of Freud's own proud sublimations. Freud's post-mortem had come as a shock to Lou: the denouement

[q] See above, p. 403.

of "Geschwister" relates, indeed *constitutes*, her absorption of that shock. For Jutta was of course Lou, but so was Gottlieb. In this comical schizoid figuration, Gottlieb was Lou's mad as well as her masculine side: his chest, already twisted at his birth an hour prior to Jutta's, signified Lou's warped mind.[r] He was her intellectual side too, for he is studious and stodgy, with bloodshot eyes and stubby fingers. And he was her internalized god externalized as her diary: between escapades she returns to his arms to make her report. He dotes on her with prepossessive jealousy, feels only as she feels or might be expected to feel, cares for no one except on her account. And except for *himself*: already as a child he has nicknamed himself Liebchen (Sweetheart), the diminutive of Gottlieb—itself Lou's diminutive for the Good Lord (*"der liebe Gott"*).[s]

It is Gottlieb's office to construe harsh realities of the day for Jutta, expunging their harshness without actually lying.[t] Thus with Jutta still bewailing her repulsion by Trebor, which here stands for Lou's repulsion by Freud's post-mortem on Tausk, Gottlieb agonizes before her door seeking a way to twist the news[485/u] that Trebor has been "seized"[v] for "vice," meaning that Freud was caught as a *fraud*— for Gottlieb fails to specify the charge of vice to Jutta, who then substitutes that of fraud in her dream. "No, he could not! he would not! Oh God, if only God *were*, thought the poor twin: a god would miraculously see to it that he brought no misfortune to Jutta. And suddenly pushed open the door—"[486] to argue extenuating circumstances for *Freud*. "If Trebor had repelled her upstairs" means *if Freud had repelled Lou morally*—but also *if Freud had rejected*

---

[r] This naturalistic caricature of the mad side of herself was supported by Lou's doctrine of parallelism between body and mind, by D [mid-III 1913] on how some one physical trait can express "a being's special inner *contour*, characterizing its very own inner physiognomy—and therewith its very own limitation as well" (written in conjunction with her impending faithlessness to Tausk, this passage—which reduplicated one from "Liebesproblem," minus the nuances—was surely reread by her nostalgically along with most of her 1912-1913 diary at the news of Tausk's suicide), and by Adler's "body jargon" (D [7 XI 1912]—see further below, p. 423). The ugly little magician in *Tarnkappe* is a Gottlieb at a greater remove from the girl Lou, there prepubescent.

[s] Also for *"Gottesliebe"* (love of God)—but primarily for the Good Lord in keeping with Lou's persistent ironic usage (Lou→Gebsattel, 15 I 1915, draft: I had just been asking *"meinen lieben Gott"* about you; etc.).

[t] He stands guard at her door when information apt to upset her is headed her way.

[u] (Literally, he reflects that *he* must present the news to her lest it reach her "nonprepared, deformed.")

[v] The German verb is *"verhaften,"* meaning *take into custody* rather than simply *arrest*—an all-important nuance, as will emerge.

Tausk from on high. ". . . he hadn't done so the least bit out of wrath or antipathy or brutishness" articulates by way of denial Lou's instinctive verdict on Freud's post-mortem. Affirmatively, Jutta had brought it no farther than to denounce Trebor's "big hurry," and at that she was afterwards to exult: "It could not come off precipitously enough for him—he rushed—he rushed—did not repulse her—was saving her . . ."[487] Gottlieb's "only so as to protect her, do her good" alludes to Freud's past warnings against Tausk both as person[w] and as theorist,[x] and Gottlieb's "for danger was threatening him" echoes Freud on Tausk as "a menace for the future."[488] The notion that Trebor had done the repulsing for Jutta's sake further alludes, faintly but unmistakably, to Freud's ". . . and would long since have dropped him had not *you* so boosted him . . ."[489] This excuse for Freud in respect of poor dead Tausk kicked downstairs is downright inept, but hardly more so than Gottlieb's other considerations. And that is just the point: Gottlieb is finding any old excuse for Trebor alias Freud. Yet again, Gottlieb's excusings are *less* farfetched for Trebor than for Freud: Lou's tale was thus a contrivance in exoneration of Freud, who also benefitted vicariously from the point that, though appearances spoke to Stefan unequivocally against Jutta's last visit to Trebor, they spoke falsely nonetheless.

News of Stefan's suicide comes grimly to Gottlieb's assistance by distracting Jutta. Here the real-life sequence was inverted: reading Freud's letter, Lou perforce registered Tausk's suicide before Freud's repulsive post-mortem evidencing fraud. For Stefan's suicide was Tausk's. Lou even specified the weapon: a dagger rather than a revolver, which would have woken the house.[y] Stefan as Trebor's homosexual idolator was Tausk with the latent character of his attachment to Freud rendered manifest ("given the degeneration of all relations in Vienna"[490]). Lou, who had long since cast herself as Tausk's transference sister rather than mother, here appeared as his actual sister—or more exactly as his "residual" sister actualized, his sister-imago externalized: Stefan calls Jutta affectionately his "little old leftover."[491]

Another real-life sequence was inverted in the case of Jutta's hearing of Trebor's *seizure* first, then distractedly of his *vice*, and then assimilating this to *fraud* by way of a dream. For the text underlying Lou's association of these three terms was her diary entry of six years prior refuting Gebsattel's view of Freud as morally ugly just because

---

[w] These had come out straight in "Tor und Ur" in the headmaster's warnings against Tor as bad company for Ur.

[x] See above, pp. 358-59.

[y] Cf. above, p. 403 n. *d*.

specially fit to discover what he did discover.[492/z] In August 1919, re-reading her old Freud-Tausk diary, Lou proceeded of necessity *from* Freud's fraud in back of her mind *to* Gebsattel's Freud, who was Freud with the post-mortem tables turned on him, and *thence* to her old rejoinder to Gebsattel, which argued Freud's "simple heroism" from "the sacrifice to which he was driven with his material[a] in the midst of a throng of opponents jeering at him. Now, the heroic lies right close by the all too human . . ."[493/b] That jeering throng assembles beneath Trebor's windows after his seizure,[c] then reassembles for the forger's trial in Jutta's dream. The latent sense of that seizure was Gethsemane, since Jutta, in reverencing that healer of men in the manner of his homosexual apostles, is "as if party to all the mysteries and sacraments in the world,"[494] while Stefan's equivalent to Tausk's final estimate of Freud—"He who is more than someone all too humanly limited"[495]—alludes to Jesus even apart from Lou's rejoinder to Gebsattel. The counterpart to Tausk's final message to Freud[d] is a prayer whispered by Stefan without his realizing it outside Trebor's empty flat: "Come!"[496] The police come instead: Trebor has absconded. Hence Stefan's fatal night was also the Calvary displaced from Freud (as likewise from Lou, then reliving her "hour without God"). Jesus demonized was no less Jesus: in the back of Lou's mind, Freud had accumulated the demonic identities of fraud, then pervert, then martyred criminal. The associative transition from pervert to criminal was facilitated by her pregiven corruption of "polymorphous perverse" into "polymorphous criminal."[497/e] Jesus led the associative way, however, for of Trebor's criminality only his "seizure" comes to Jutta's full awareness, and Gottlieb contrives at that to pronounce "this dreadful word" so as to turn it "pale as can be, to take away its starkest clarity. What in the world weren't people seized for!"[498] Correspondingly, the only Freud acknowledged by Lou to herself remained the all too humanized Jesus of her rejoinder to Gebsattel; consciously she denied the pervert and knew nothing of the fraud. "Geschwister" makes just these points, in this very order, about her Freudian associative complex *fraud-pervert-Jesus*, and virtually without distortion at that—except that Jutta wails inconsolably

[z] See above, p. 404.

[a] An allusion to his having felt constrained to interpret his own rather than his patients' dreams in his dream book.

[b] See above, p. 404; cf. above, p. 377.

[c] (Hence for no good reason.)

[d] "Stefan had left no note behind" (1919g:58).

[e] See above, p. 349. Thus a pre-1919 referent for Gottlieb's protecting Jutta from intelligence of Trebor's criminal vice was Lou's glossing over the perverse sexuality in Freudianism (above, p. 365 and n. z).

when *Jesus* is signaled by the word "seized," whereas *fraud* of itself does not trouble her sleep, and except also that *fraud* rather than *vice* is given as the one of Lou's two mute charges against Freud associatively determined in Jutta's case. Lou moreover moderated the charge of fraud by indicating that sleeping Jutta owed it to some maudlin fiction.

Jutta's dream absorbed those "undigested emotional residues"[f] of her previous day's experience quite as if Stefan's death were the one harsh reality left the morning after: Trebor was forgotten. And herein lay the first function of "Geschwister" for its author: it smuggled her preconscious response to Freud's post-mortem on Tausk into her consciousness—lodged the material threatening her peace of mind, bound the attendant affects, and so disposed of the issue. Or almost disposed of it: though she never wrote another word about Tausk, she was nonetheless vindicating him when in later years she celebrated Freud's official morality in celebrating Freud.[499] "Geschwister" itself was not about Tausk for as much as Stefan's personality was Jenia's through and through according to all Lou's depictions of Jenia: effeminate, devious, self-enclosed.[500/g] She may even have *meant* Jenia, as she had meant him in "Im Zwischenland"— may have meant a whole Salomé sibling reunion, with a twin for good measure. No matter: the tale arose immediately out of Lou's muted response to Freud's post-mortem on Tausk—joined by a cluster of less urgent latent wishes and grudges and avowals and the like connected with her experience of Freud and his circle since 1912-1913 and hitherto left in abeyance.

Beyond Jutta's four elder, living brothers, two younger ones have died in childhood: herein Lou fictively validated a running bluff designed to explain away to Freud her facile, full transference to him as father-figure. She had told him that his seminar took her back to her childhood, so straight away Aunt Adele recollects how the last-born had made "a long dining table desirable," which was thereupon acquired[501]: a veritable seminar table. Freud, however, had counted himself among her seminar *brothers* to make those six. Lou actually met him halfway in that Jutta's twin may be discounted; indeed, Gottlieb accounts the others mere "half brothers,"[502] and Jutta tells him: "You don't count as a brother at all, Liebchen: aren't you a second *me*?"[503/h] The doubling (of Lou's three to Freud's six) predomi-

[f] See above, pp. 243, 387-88.

[g] See above, p. 8.

[h] Stefan too is half eliminated inasmuch as he takes over the dead father's responsibilities and as he fuses with Trebor at the end of Jutta's dream. In D [2 IV 1913] (taken up into the *Ubw.* introduction) Lou treated of Freud's

nated nonetheless: for symmetry's sake, Jutta acquired a deceased sister. Jutta's three big brothers, besides standing for Lou's own, of whom they bear some markings redistributed,[i] doubled for her three psychoanalytical lovers. Erwin, "practical" and "a protector,"[504] is Bjerre trivialized; Herbert with his " 'aristocratic tics' "[505] is Gebsattel crudely put. Furthermore, immoral Lou, who ravished Bjerre, appears as Bella Belloni, a cocotte from out of town, and premoral Lou, who ravished Gebsattel, appears as Elfrieda, an unspoiled country girl—only by way of reversal Erwin is smitten with Elfrieda and Herbert with Bella. Again, the shadowy young men around Trebor redouble Jutta's brothers in their signification as Freud's seminar students.[j]

At her first, secret visit to the orthopedist, Jutta—as she tells Gottlieb afterwards—"blurted right out that she is coming because she wants to have it just as good with 'Him' as the boys do, whereupon the Klaus doctor burst out laughing at her"[506]: and no wonder, for she meant *anatomically*. Jutta is indeed a phallic girl: she later goes to the forest for purposes of "bodily development,"[k] gathers logs for needy children, and winds up climbing a tree to the tune of an aside from Stefan to Erwin: "Jutta not only climbs trees by herself[l] but day

---

seminar as for her a "brotherhood"—with Freud at the head of the table. Freud→Lou, 7 VII 1914, indicates that in Vienna she had spoken to Freud of her new colleagues as transference brothers ("the brothers" all await her " 'Anal' und 'Sexual' "). Freud→Lou, 14 VII 1916, concerning her *Ubw.* introduction, remarked specifically on the "six big brothers, all so good and tender with their little sister" (on the "big" see further below, p. 471 and n. *u*). And when Freud→Lou, 29 V 1918, inquired (referring to mankind as Lou's transference brotherhood: cf. Freud→Lou, 14 XI 1914, etc.) "whether you expected *that* of your six big brothers, who were all so nice to you" (above, p. 410), she in her reply (Lou→Freud [8? X 1918])—grief or no—contorted syntax so as to *seem* to have more than one live brother left, hence to have had more than three to start.

[i] Sasha was for Lou, like Erwin for Jutta, "a protector" (1919g:34), and Robert's name shows in He*rbert*'s and especially Herbert's nickname, He*rr von Bert*: thus Lou, besides representing her youngest brother as Jutta's eldest, evoked her eldest and second eldest through Jutta's second and third eldest respectively.

[j] Further to this redoubling of brothers: "Jutta" as revised in 1933 to serve as a sequel to "Geschwister" (I saw no prior copy) likewise gave Jutta six original brothers of whom three remain after Stefan's suicide (the one who agrees to arrange an abortion being the youngest—hence Gottlieb, but originally Jenia). And it gave her six brother proxies (Lou's Viennese trio plus three pale ones)—this possibly in the first version already. In "Geschwister" the practice of doubling is straight off signaled in reverse in that the siblings inhabit two ground floor apartments joined together as one.

[k] "*Körperliche Ausarbeitung*" is more graphic.

[l] (Of itself symbolic of masturbation.)

by day three flights of stairs as well"[507]—that "day by day" being in actuality three times before the precipitate adieu, then impending. Jutta's account to Gottlieb of her transparent avowal of penis-envy to Trebor upstairs rectifies even as it explicates Lou's original account to her diary (her looseleaf Gottlieb) of her reply to Freud's query as to her reasons for joining his boys: the "most personal, decisive" reason was an "intimate bestowal: that radiant enlargement of one's own vital contour through feeling one's way to the roots embedding it in the all. If Freud replied laughingly, 'I do believe you regard analysis as a sort of distribution of Christmas gifts,' that may well be true, for in my case there is no question of any mix-ups between depths and surface to be set right."[508/m] This last affirmation was to be set right by Gottlieb bringing himself to break the news of Trebor's seizure: "In the midst of this hardest fight ever fought by him it yet crossed his mind that now the Klaus doctor would not be able to straighten out his crooked chest either."[509/n]

Meanwhile Trebor, having finished laughing, asks Jutta whether she has not come to him in secret, then insists that, if she will not let Aunt Adele know of her visits, she at least apprise one of her brothers —"so," relates Jutta, "I suggested Wienchen" (Erwin).[510] This was tit for tat: having turned her statement of reasons for coming to Freud inside out, Lou reversed Freud's injunction to her concerning the Adler circle, here Jutta's family circle. For in this anagrammatical text, *Ade*le plus *Er*win equals Adler; Erwin with the syllables transposed is a "Wi[e]ner" (Viennese), which Adler alone was of those with whom Lou was involved in Vienna; the diminutive *Wienchen* corresponded to Adler's diminutive stature, which "disturbed" Lou from the first.[o] Lou's tacit tale was pronouncedly Adlerian out of spite against Freud, what with all its physical equivalences to mental states, with Jutta's potent masculine protest, with Jutta's even confounding the sexes: " 'I am no girl,' Stefan repeated. And he added that Doctor Trebor would surely laugh at her for simply mixing the two."[511] Trebor's query about Jutta's visits spelled (backwards) Lou's suspicion that Freud already knew of her visits to Adler before she came clean with him: in this respect, Trebor's injunction was, *mutatis mutandis*, Lou's self-reproach for having been remiss about informing Freud of her traffic with Adler.[p]

---

[m] See above, p. 366.

[n] The word "either" makes no syntactical sense.

[o] D [28 x 1912] ("he looks like a button . . ."). "*Wienchen*," incidentally, means "little Vienna."

[p] Cf. above, p. 336 (D [28 x 1912]: "I wish to speak openly to Freud . . .").

At the same time Freud's injunction to her to treat her visits to him (and his circle) as confidential (vis-à-vis Adler) linked up with a wish of hers expressed through Jutta's confidential visits to Trebor and, further, through the narrative insinuation that there may have been more of these than the three disclosed for sure. This same wish shows through the close of her last letter to Freud before Tausk's suicide: "As you see, I am again permitting myself without further ado to visit you with pen and ink . . ."[512/q] It was the wish on which, as Gottlieb, she gave up when in receipt of Freud's reply: that she should have visited Freud for psychoanalytical treatment. As Jutta, though, she indulged it retroactive to Vienna 1912-1913, for Jutta's visits represent analytical sessions: "It was so queer how she lost all sense of time upstairs . . ."[513/r] The visits are sexy otherwise as well, so that, through Stefan's conviction of having been betrayed by Jutta, Lou was sexualizing her disloyalty of 1913 to Tausk even while insisting on the contrary, as in her diary entry of March 1913 on infidelity,[s] that she was not betraying him for another man. Through Jutta's seeming treachery, Lou arrogated responsibility to herself across the years for Tausk's suicide.

Primarily, though, "Geschwister" followed up Lou's diary entry of the late summer of 1913 and ascribed Tausk's suicide to a maddening realization that abiding infantile jealousy of his sister on his father's account, and especially vice versa, informed his adult relationships—with some due occasion wishfully thrown in. Thus "Geschwister" registered Lou's hit-and-miss attempts to visualize "how it might have looked" behind Tausk's suicide notes, which Freud said was "not to be guessed"[514] and which Lou in reply, while ostensibly agreeing with him, had already begun guessing—in unavowed competition with him as sleuth and killer both. To Freud's indictment of "the father ghost"[515] she had objected that Tausk's "true beloved" was "Jelka, his sister."[516] In "Geschwister" she shared sanguinary honors with Freud inasmuch as alphabetically Jutta and Klaus divided that "true beloved," Jelka Tausk, between them.[t] Lou took the lion's share nonetheless, even short of Stefan's option for jealousy "of him," in representing herself as that sister in person as against the mere transference father Trebor. In subordinating Tausk's father- to his sister-fixation out of rivalry with Freud, Lou reversed "Tor und Ur," just as she overly corrected "Tor und Ur" in depicting Tausk as

---

[q] This usage was frequent in her letters to Freud.

[r] Cf. 1919g:34 on Gottlieb's stake in her visits.

[s] See above, p. 402.

[t] Lou→Freud, 25 VIII 1919: Jelka's married name "has slipped my mind."

mortally desolate over her disloyalty to him when he had felt himself to be a master at last.

Lou's self-indictment for Tausk's suicide, "Geschwister" also cited her refusal of Tausk's proposed visit to Munich in the spring of 1919 —displacedly, though, through Trebor's multivalent repulsion of Jutta's farewell visit. When Jutta howled for joy at Trebor's not having repulsed her after all, Lou was howling with the hindthought that Freud after all had not repulsed *her* as he had Tausk.[u] For shame! exclaimed Stefan: but this, to be sure, at himself for having spied on Jutta "unknowingly" and for "that conversation itself" with Jutta grounded in an unknowing reciprocal rivalry with her and Trebor[517] or, displacedly, for Lou's having pried into Tausk's suicide through her hypocritical exchange with Freud grounded in an unknowing reciprocal rivalry with him and Tausk. Lou more than made it up to Tausk as, Stefan having moodily left the family table before dinner was done, Jutta took his dessert to him in his room on the fatal night: thus Lou as Jutta more than sat down at the same table with a wretch.[v] Freud's "guess" as to Tausk's motives found a remote counterpart in Erwin's prompt suspicion that Stefan killed himself because compromised with Trebor, whose seizure threatened him with scandal: here, by dint of poetic justice, the "menace for the future," as Freud called Tausk,[518/w] was Freud himself, with his rejected disciple as martyr to his cause. This suspicion—a second false appearance in "Geschwister"—spreads beyond Erwin. Therefore Erwin, as eldest surviving brother, posts Gottlieb "sentinel beside Jutta's bed" even as he puts Herbert in charge of the neighbors, who come teeming. Herbert's aristocratism "lent him a poise that did not permit the sensation upstairs, which seemed so curiously bound up with the death below, to pass the threshold"[519]: a lovely cryptogram! The threshold was that of Lou's consciousness, the sensation upstairs was the one concerning Freud and Tausk, and the death below, associatively bound up with it, was—well, in the first instance Nietzsche's of August 25, 1900.

A month before Nietzsche's death, Lou had written that gingerly diary piece on Drojjin as a faint falsifier of everyday life,[x] followed two weeks later by that gingery one on Nietzsche as, in contrast to herself, a shrill falsifier of everyday life with, however, the excuse of self-defense against the dread of impending madness.[y] This transition

---

[u] 1919g:57—"*nicht von sich stiess er sie*"—is a giveaway because the emphasis is overly displaced from the "*sie*."

[v] See above, p. 403. [w] Ditto. [x] See above, p. 277.

[y] D [mid-VIII] 1900: "the fanfaronade of the overman," including the "heroic

to the all too human falsity of Nietzsche's philosophy—the implicit thesis of her Nietzsche book—was facilitated by Rainer's having in some measure looked to Drojjin for literary guidance as formerly she had looked to Nietzsche. Four months after Nietzsche's death she wrote that "maudlin magazine story at the close of which a forger is turned over to the penitentiary"[520]: "Im Zwischenland"—and wrote it just eighteen years after Nietzsche's *repulsion* of her, concluding it on the twelfth anniversary of the mental breakdown in consequence of which he was *seized*. Now it can be seen that the poet-forger of "Im Zwischenland" was Nietzsche as well as Drojjin—in fact more so than Drojjin, if only mediately. " 'God—God, can you believe—imagine—that it's true?!' 'It is surely very unpleasant for him to have gone so wholly mad, Boris,' said Musja softly. 'He hasn't at all gone mad! Don't you understand? He's gone bad!' That was an altogether different calamity for sure, but just then the two were utterly jumbled for Musja, who could not tell them apart. 'A common, ordinary wretch they're calling him! Can you conceive of him as that?!' 'A wretch? . . . Yes, he is that for sure,' she remarked gently: indeed, he had told her so himself" (in the opium letter). "Boris turned crimson: 'Our Ignatief! Our Apollon Pavlovitch! Oh, how I loved him! Oh, how I wanted to learn from him! Our—our Ignatief—Musja!' "[521] And Boris fell to the floor kicking and screaming while Musja looked tenderly on.

Boris was acting out Lou's repressed emotion at Nietzsche's seizure twelve years before, Musja acting out Lou's concomitant unconscious self-solicitude. " 'And I wanted to ask his advice on how to make such songs! His advice all in all—his!' he cried embittered, jumping up. 'I hate him! I hate his book! I hate him!' Musja kept quiet, for she—she did not hate him."[522] Besides, she had already denounced their consulting Apollon on how Boris could become a great poet like him as no more serious than their pretending between themselves that Boris was famous.[523] She had been stunned into this sense of seriousness right after drawing on Lou's final postal exchange with Nietzsche to implore Apollon on a barely perceptible pretext: " 'Forgive me for not having been honest . . .—Yes, you are right—oh now I do feel it so, oh so strongly . . . so clearly: one must be good—upright, one may do nothing evil! Oh, you have surely never been dishonorable!' . . . She stared at him full of fear and reverence. But Apollon

---

pose" and "shrill tone," signifies "the incapacity to come to terms with everyday life—tragically determined in Nietzsche's case through sickliness first, then through the approach of a mental illness to bear the fear of which his special philosophy was necessary," etc.; cf. above, pp. 171 and n. *l*, 281-82.

did something utterly unexpected"[524]: he swore and spat. Such was Nietzsche's adieu on the receiving end.[z] Such also was the charge of untidiness reversed with a vengeance: proper Lisbeth, who first brought it against Lou while about to convey her to Fritz in Tautenburg and there supposedly to "hatch . . . little novella eggs,"[525] appears as Apollon's shady midwife of a sister who ushers Musja in. And Apollon gets sexy with the pureminded child before letting her go, thereby bearing out Lou's Jena outburst. Again, Apollon revisited was Nietzsche demonized: everything about him, formerly enchanted, becomes "nightmarish" for Musja,[526] who that night wakes up screaming as in her dreams "something wonderful"[527] turns into many ghosts, "especially two" meeting Nietzsche's and Rée's descriptions.[528] Demonized midway, Nietzsche was no less the Jesus behind this "Christmas novella,"[529] conceived on Christmas and suffused with it.

As for "Geschwister," Klaus was short for Nikolaus (Santa Claus) —Freud as distributor of Christmas gifts—which was long for Nico. More of the Nietzsche story came through "Geschwister" than through "Im Zwischenland"—and came through straighter, often disrupting the Freud story. Whereas Boris urges Musja to visit Apollon, Rée's imputations against Nietzsche emerge through "Geschwister" as Stefan's insinuations to Jutta against Trebor—which with respect to the upper inside story constitute a displacement and distortion of Freud's warnings to Lou against Tausk. Trebor, unlike Apollon, does not demonize himself; rather, he is demonized as Stefan, insinuating against him in the manner of Lou's Leipzig diary page,[a] comes full circle away from love as a looking up. Whereas Lou's Jena fancy is actualized to Musja's disgust in "Im Zwischenland," in "Geschwister" it shows only darkly, but without disconcerting Jutta: thus "when she asked how her brother could insinuate such a thing against his friend—something they ought never to think concerning the best of all men—she sounded hurt rather on Stefan's account than on her own."[530] Stefan's painful coming out with that insinuation, besides reversing the real case with Rée by dint of Jenia's circumlocutory manner, reflects Lou's own painful coming out with this admission, vicarious though it was. There is more of Lou's Rée to Stefan than to Boris; there is even more of her Rée than of her Tausk to Stefan, who vis-à-vis Trebor "had at bottom ever and alone wanted: *himself* to be the leader, sustainer, doer — — *man*."[531] Lou's three encounters with Nietzsche showed through "Geschwister" not

---

[z] (With some Nietzscheana of the summer of 1883 mixed in.) Cf. the Lou heroines of the mid-1890's who kick their kneeling lovers—a case of reversal.

[a] See above, p. 93.

only in those three flights of stairs, which were the same as in "Im Zwischenland," but more obviously in those three sure visits of Jutta's to Trebor, and more characteristically in those three intrigues with— respectively—immoral Lou, premoral Lou, and Lou as supermoral sister prone to kneel down to great men, such having been Lou's *Im Kampf um Gott* construction on her three encounters with Nietzsche (Margharita and Märchen, with Jane in between): her Nietzsche romance was, then, her manual for her affairs with Freud's three junior surrogates in turn.[b]

The hint at clandestine visits by Jutta to Trebor not otherwise registered by the narrative corresponds to Lou's running attempts to renew contact with Nietzsche after the great repulsion—attempts that had scored just such equivocal success in her Nietzsche book with its hoax of a seemingly abiding friendship seemingly more than a friendship. As for Lou's last epistolary visit to Nietzsche, Musja pays it to Apollon behind Boris's back[532/c] yet on his account, where- as Jutta pays it in seeming surreptitious defiance of Stefan, who more- over spies it out. Jutta's insistence afterwards that she had meant to break with Trebor but had been rudely beaten to it by him rings none too true as against Musja's firmly repeating to Apollon grown in- decent: "I want to go home!"[533] The false ring came of Lou's inner disaffirmation as she told herself that she had meant to call it quits with Nietzsche anyhow upon begging his pardon. The rest strongly suggests that Lou fell out with Nietzsche after Leipzig at Rée's jealous instigation—in which case Musja's revisit on Boris's account was a reversal[d]—and that she penned and posted her hapless apology when Rée was not watching.

The repulsion itself, without being vulgarized again, comes through "Geschwister" far more graphically than through "Im Zwischenland." "Im Zwischenland" explains it away indirectly in that the news of Apollon's seizure is calculated to mitigate his repellent conduct to- ward Musja in view of his imminent fear of apprehension, which emerges in retrospect. For Apollon had even shrilly accused Musja of spying on him—perhaps a charge by Lou against Rée displaced, given Stefan's self-reproach for spying on Jutta. In "Geschwister"

[b] Tausk's letters to Lou were withheld from me (see below, p. 560); that she struck a supermoral posture for the time of her Tausk cycle (that Nietz- schean pregnancy cycle) follows, though, from Freud's impression of her then (see above, p. 373).

[c] It is for this concealment (ostensibly from her grandfather) that Musja overscrupulously begs Apollon's forgiveness in the phrases elided from the quotation above.

[d] (Just as Trebor's insistence that Jutta inform the family circle of her visits reversed Freud's injunction to Lou concerning the Adler circle.)

Stefan, portending the impending seizure, pointedly reflects that Trebor has been "uneasy and distraught of late."[534] This had nothing to do with either Drojjin or Freud: Nietzsche's disquiet in the face of his impending madness was at issue, which Lou's 1900 diary entry had submitted in extenuation of his philosophical falsifying. In both tales Lou set this disquiet six years back from December 1888—by dint of Nietzsche's reference to himself in his opium letter as half crazed (on the single page that Lou preserved of all his last missives to her)—so as to extenuate his repulsion of her. Gottlieb makes this *post hoc* excuse explicit: "Danger was threatening him." Gottlieb's further explication—"only so as to protect her, do her good"—echoes Nietzsche's refrain on his noble motives toward Lou, but with the weird implication that his madness was infectious. As for Trebor's "big hurry," excused along with the repulsion, it was Nietzsche's in having bid Lou adieu without even reading her writ of apology through. Jutta's shriek of joy that "he did not repel her"[535] was Lou's old latent fable of the unbroken romance in all its purity. Jutta's concomitant shriek of pain at the seizure was Boris's fit thrown by the right party. More: it was precedently the suicide in *Aus fremder Seele*—only there the seizure for madness, being undisguisedly just that, was displaced onto the pastor representing Rée (and Gillot), with the suicide by the adoptive son representing Lou and Nietzsche presented as its *cause*.[e] Hence on the Nietzsche level the suicide in "Geschwister," besides being Rée's supposed suicide ascribed to old double jealousy,[f] was the death in Lou's heart, displaced: indeed, that false appearance of a link between the scandal upstairs and the death below signalizes the displacement. Similarly, the death below directly follows the seizure in Jutta's experience, which reverses the time scheme insofar. In the unreversed time scheme it directly follows the repulsion: thus it was also the treble death of *Im Kampf um Gott* all over again. And Jutta earlier affirming her readiness to love *even* without return was Lou affirming her love of Nietzsche despite the repulsion. The *even*, adjoined to Lou's doctrine of narcissist amorism, shows this up for what it was: sour grapes, vintage 1882, ceremonially served up to solemnify her ritual reenactments of the fearful adieu with herself in Nietzsche's place.

Correspondingly, "Geschwister" shows up those aspersions cast on Nietzsche in "Im Zwischenland" for what they were. For in "Ge-

---

[e] The undisplaced effect of the seizure is that it turns the heroine's hair white.

[f] And evoked through the misleading appearance of an accident (the upstairs signifying Sils as against Celerina)—reenforced by the general theme of misleading appearances.

schwister" Lou virtually sanctioned the sexual derangement laid to Nietzsche's charge in "Im Zwischenland," took the madness upon herself twice over (through Gottlieb's warped chest and Jutta's psychoanalytical sessions), and referred the fraud back to that "maudlin magazine story" as fictitious. This referral back was underwritten by the title "Ge*schwist*er," its stressed syllable being a phonetic anagram of the stressed syllable of "Im *Zwisch*enland"; by the ostensible subject of "Geschwister," which was the Salomé children, Jenia and Lou foremost; by its denouement especially, with a demigod seized the morning after he has repelled the little heroine—and that poignant cry as the news breaks. This cry gives the sense of Lou's self-reversal in respect of Nietzsche as between "Im Zwischenland" and "Geschwister," which went back on an original self-reversal—on her diabolization of Nietzsche. It was a cry of terror as well as love: his seizure threatened *her*, given her self-identification with him. Thence her frantic repudiation of him after his seizure, and thence her reversal of those earlier, damning charges of his against her—so as to protect her*self*, do her*self* good. For *he* had first charged *her* with sexual derangement, falsification, madness; he had even been party to that scheme of his sister's for having her *seized*.

In "Im Zwischenland," falsification took the spotlight—because of the associative link with Drojjin, to be sure, yet primarily because of Rainer's maddeningly resisted "midway land" realization that she was the dupe of her own graphic fraudulence. Musja's "playing" with Boris constitutes just such self-mystification. Only Musja rather than Boris calls a halt to it—hard upon her misadventure with Apollon. Moreover, whereas Musja's confession to Apollon of dishonorability was demonstratively wide of the mark, Apollon is himself convicted of dishonorability at the last in an ironic follow-up to Musja's "Oh, you have surely never been dishonorable!" Indeed, the latent theme of that whole jovial tale of woe was a *reversing of charges*: thus Apollon winds up in the penitentiary *or* madhouse, Nietzsche having pronounced Lou fit for the one or the other.[g]

The cue for such reversals was Nietzsche's seizure itself—or else his madness, that "frightful leap." On learning about Apollon that "the authorities have nabbed him," Musja reflects: "In any case he had gone mad." And when Boris specifies: "He forged [bills of] exchange," Musja reflects further, unmoved: "Probably one always did that if one went mad"[536]—or indeed vice versa, for beginning with *Im Kampf um Gott* Lou had exchanged religious childhoods with

[g] See above, p. 108. (The heroine of "Ausschweifung" lives a while spellbound besides a combination prison-madhouse.)

Nietzsche on paper. If Boris screams: "I would have become everything through him. I would have become a good person through him,"[537] and if Gottlieb, in the midst of his panic over editing the news for Jutta, considers "that now the Klaus doctor would not be able to straighten out his crooked chest either,"[538/h] this is because until the seizure Lou had mutely clung to the hope of Nietzsche's reversing himself and voiding the charges against her one and all, thereby redeeming her. Even afterwards that hope survived unconsciously along with the shock of its drastic refutation in early 1889 and with the unavowed pain of that repulsion six years prior, all three as actual as ever: actual, yet deactivated—through her Nietzsche book once, and once again through "Im Zwischenland," which, again rendering this unconscious material conscious in disguise, again bound the affects attending it. Consciously Lou took little direct notice of Nietzsche's death, it would seem, and divined nothing of even the Rainer-Drojjin substratum to "Im Zwischenland," let alone the Nietzsche one beneath that. In respect of her consciousness, this Nietzsche complex was her Freud complex of August 1919 upside down: she affirmed the fraud out loud and the pervert *sotto voce* while suspecting nothing of the Jesus. When in August 1919 *fraud* joined *vice* and *Jesus* in her Freud complex, the association with "Im Zwischenland" followed—that is, with the text binding all this Nietzsche material that had perturbed her consciousness in 1900. The binding came apart, releasing the material intact after nineteen years. Indeed, another text bound up with "Im Zwischenland" anthology-style came apart along with it: her Finnish diary entry pleading extenuating circumstances for Nietzsche as falsifier—for that plea registered explicitly in "Geschwister" without her having likely reread or recollected the text itself at the time. Herein lay the huge importance within Lou's mental system of her past writings: they all bound material that had perturbed her consciousness. They bound it until further notice, that is—until at the first associative opportunity the binder was torn open on the unconscious side. Then the psychic commotion would revive in its full intensity, vitality, and urgency, requiring to be contained all over again along with that due to the new, associated "unassimilated residues": a fearful task, the continual unsuspecting accomplishment of which is called culture.

As against the Freud material, the Nietzsche material associatively conjured up was this time defectively bound, as will be seen—and translucently bound, whence the mournfulness of "Geschwister." Lou probably effected the prior unbinding soon after receiving

[h] See above, p. 423 n. *n*.

Freud's letter of August 1, 1919, since she waited for August 25, the anniversary of Nietzsche's death, to reply; perhaps even, like Jutta, within a single day's mourning. Concerning Jutta's association of Trebor's seizure with the "maudlin magazine story" Lou specified: "The term 'penitentiary' mediated it"[539]—and sure enough, this term was no part of Jutta's waking experience, just as the seizure was no part of Lou's Freud complex.[i] As for Lou's association mediated by "Im Zwischenland," much eased its way. In the Freud case she was conjoining a shock with its antecedents of six and some years earlier as she had done in the Nietzsche case: almost to the day. Then too there was her sudden, unconscious diabolization of Freud,[j] which reduplicated her slow, conscious diabolization of Nietzsche following his seizure; there was the precedent of Rée's death, for which she took credit unconsciously over against Nietzsche just as she did for Tausk's over against Freud; there was her sisterly and daughterly orientation toward Tausk and Freud respectively as formerly toward her two partners in the Trinity. And in the bargain Freud had repelled her, as had Nietzsche before him, by mail.

With "Im Zwischenland" showing through it, "Geschwister" reveals much of the prehistory of Lou's 1919 Tausk- and Freud-libido. On Tausk's side the libido had passed from her own self in childhood to Jenia and, subsidiarily, her other two brothers; then to Rée, soon on Nietzsche's account; thereafter for a contrived moment to Andreas as on her 1888 diary page, given Jutta's sexy talk with Stefan about "looking up, gazing aloft, required in common"[540]; later to Rainer, with time out for Jenia at his death; briefly back to Rée at his death[k]; afterwards to her three psychoanalytical lovers, Tausk foremost; finally to Tausk at his suicide—reverting between times to herself as boyish, warped, darling diarist. Her Freud-libido for its part had come straight from Nietzsche, narcissistic interludes apart[l]—so that,

[i] Just conceivably, though, "penitentiary" was a mediate reference to the Gethsemane clause of Lou's diary piece on Gebsattel's Freud.

[j] Note, by the way, that this shortly preceded that act of semisubmission, "Narzissmus": see above, pp. 364-65 and n. *w*.

[k] Rée's death registers almost negligibly in "Geschwister" as against Jenia's— though Jenia's was in return a front for the Nietzsche story. The Tausk mourning figured disproportionately in "Geschwister," having been conscious in its time even if Jutta's for Stefan was not consciously identified with it. So in fact did the Jenia mourning, Stefan having been modeled on Jenia. Given the intensity of Lou's conscious mourning over the years for Rée as against Nietzsche and of her unconscious mourning over the years for Nietzsche as against Rée, she would seem to have mourned Nietzsche unconsciously in consciously mourning Rée.

[l] *Not* via Drojjin, who had merely fronted for Nietzsche in her identification of Rilke vis-à-vis Drojjin in 1900 with herself vis-à-vis Nietzsche in 1882.

calendar-conscious as she was, her overinsistent celebration of
Freud's birthday beginning in 1922 was a celebration of her spiritual
betrothal to Nietzsche atop the *monte sacro* on May 6, 1882. Originally some of this libido had passed with the other from herself as a
child to Jenia as substitute father: thus Stefan declares himself "somewhat responsible" toward Jutta in their dead father's stead.[541] Aboriginally it had been one with its complement as father-libido: both revert to their single point of departure at the finale of "Geschwister"
as Aunt Adele, alone beside Stefan's corpse, rhetorically addresses
her dead sister and sometime successful rival, ostensibly voicing Aunt
Caro's innermost feeling toward Jenia's mother but actually voicing
Lou's own: "I loved you, and I envied and hated you; I died with
you, yet rejoiced in your death; *for I loved him, belonged to him, for
I lived him and still live him in your living children.*"[542/m] Herein Lou
was incidentally putting Caro's deathwatch of 1898 down to jealousy
of Jenia's mother so as to assuage her bad conscience over her own
delinquency at Jenia's death—a death already treated as a virtual
suicide in her subsequent letters to Caro about his fatal attachment to
cold, damp Petersburg on his mother's account. And throughout, Lou
was day-dreaming retroactively about Caro as foster-mother during
the virtual orphanage that was her adolescence.

It is this telescoping of autobiographic substrata more than any
condensation of diverse materials within a given substratum that
made for the rich overdetermination of so many surface elements of
"Geschwister." Thus on the Caro level those secret visits of Jutta's to
Trebor were Lou's to Gillot, signalized as such by yet another reversal when, to Trebor's reversal of Freud's injunction for discretion
vis-à-vis Adler, Jutta replies that Adele is still too much of a stranger
to her to be a confidante of her visits[543]—wherewith Gillot takes his
rightful place in the sequence of Lou's transference fathers. Similarly,
behind the Gillot of the tardy proposal abroad (on the Kuno-Mar-
gharita precedent) in "Ein Wiedersehen," Nietzsche will now be
visible as himself a "cat egoist," the self-sacrificing country doctor
still following his old moral lead being Lou as Rée. And Ruth's trip
back to her loving teacher and away again, with the frustrated marriage proposal in between: did not this sequence represent, by simple
reversal, Nietzsche's trip back to Lucerne and away again, with the
frustrating nonproposal in between? Again, bad was jumbled with
mad for Musja as far as graphic fraud went, since Lou's diaries were

---

[m] (Stress added.) This reduction of Stefan- to father-libido follows one of
Trebor- to Stefan-libido, for Jutta's dream turns into a near nightmare as
Stefan and Trebor merge.

all school notebooks like that one containing her Petrischule plagiarism: fraudulent Lou had provoked Nietzsche's wrath only after her father's. And again, Stefan declaring it his responsibility as substitute head of the family to discourage Jutta from visiting Trebor was Lou's "brother Eugene, dispatched by the eldest, our father's replacer," to Hamburg in June 1882 to discourage her from visiting Rée[544]: here, what with Nietzsche as Trebor replacing Rée as bad company, Nietzsche's big hurry otherwise behind Trebor's to dispatch Jutta was replaced by Nietzsche's quick return from Charlottenburg to Naumburg—before Lou could contact him?[n]

Not even the Beer-Hofmann level was lacking beneath "Geschwister," for that big hurry had already figured in "Inkognito"—replacedly only, though, and reversedly to boot. It so figured when Anjuta's associate Ludin, having chanced upon Erwin von Stein down in Innsbruck and told him "about our weekly,[o] and," as Anjuta learns, "about Wiranoff and you—yes, especially about you, whom he naturally most wanted to hear about,"[545] answers Anjuta's urgent query, "Why then did he—did Herr von Stein not come along?" with the words: "He seemed to be in no hurry at all,"[546] which doubtless render not only Schnitzler's presumable explanation to Lou of why Beer-Hofmann had not come along to the Griensteidl after her long December day's waiting in 1895, but also Heinrich von Stein's presumable report to Lou in Berlin on his chance meeting with Nietzsche in October 1885. And it so figured again when Anjuta, as she refrains from addressing Erwin at the railroad station before her departure, observes that "no haste showed in his bearing, he stood there indecisive. . . . No, he did not look angry. Not sad either. He looked cross. Cross like someone with something painful and unpleasant in store for him, something to which he must force himself, and who stands hesitating,"[547] this being a fanciful rendition of Beer-Hofmann on his eager way to meet Paula after his "exchange of words" with Lou, but also a fair and fine likeness of Nietzsche at the Leipzig station in November 1882, when Lou, as he afterwards remarked, "told me she had something further to say to me," only to desist.[p]

Anjuta's impersonation vis-à-vis Erwin of the quintessence of noncerebral womanhood was, then, Lou's imposture vis-à-vis Nietzsche

[n] Thus if Lou *was* in Berlin at the time (see above, p. 65 and n. *t*), she may well have gone to Charlottenburg to advise Nietzsche orally that she would not be seeing him there. (Cf. above, p. 126 n. *k*, on Lou's self-confusion with Nietzsche fleeing the Grunewald.)

[o] *"Wochenschrift"* (literally, weekly writing): an allusion to Stein's "dark letter" (above, p. 127).

[p] See above, p. 94.

in reverse[q]—motivated by Anjuta's longing to emancipate herself from her emancipation conformably with Nietzsche's advice to Lou. The impersonation yielded to the imposture *non*reversed in Anjuta's self-consolation to the effect that "she could be loved for her own sake, without fretting as to whether she possessed all the virtues of a vacuous little girl. She was beloved and reverently praised to the skies on account of higher virtues,"[548] for Lou was hereby telling herself that Nietzsche's "Lou of Orta" had no call to feel bad about not being Beer-Hofmann's "*merely* sweet girl"[549]/[r]—even as this intrusion of Nietzsche's "Lou of Orta" into the Beer-Hofmann actuality denoted another imposture of Lou's toward Beer-Hofmann, whose party she had joined as Nietzsche's pretended perennial girl friend in the first flush of her notoriety due to her Nietzsche book. Her unconscious Nietzsche material fastened onto the Beer-Hofmann material processed in "Inkognito" the more readily since her Beer-Hofmann experience was a repetition of her Nietzsche experience—this last being perhaps also why *Aus fremder Seele* was written in the weeks following each of the three Beer-Hofmann episodes. And now Beer-Hofmann's special place in Lou's libidinal transference series will be evident: he straddled the father and brother lines.[s] For if Erwin all at once replaced Anjuta's brotherly peers in her affection—notably the windbag Ludin, a caricature of Heinrich von Stein, and Anjuta's editor-in-chief, Wiranoff, who, waiting and waiting through the years "for her once to hear his wish,"[550] betrayed Rée by his comic sartorial negligence over a disguise of ascetical gauntness—he likewise replaced her deceased eldest brother, who had founded and long directed the review and still inspired it, whom she had girlishly idolized with her whole heart so that she had abandoned her university studies "in order to work only for him and with him,"[551] and whom she was emulating in deepest mourning in her public and private life even unto repressing the female within her. Thus in 1919 the binding of "Inkognito" too came a little loose, and Beer-Hofmann entered

---

[q] Anjuta's remorse over having *fooled* Erwin when in fact she had only let him fool himself suggests that Lou had knowingly assisted Nietzsche to his angel of Orta illusion.

[r] See below, p. 472.

[s] Ledebour too was a straddler, though a lesser one: a brother figure in "Paradies," he was also Gillot's successor there as Lou's tutor in waking as against dreaming—indeed in truth as against falsity: a throwback to Nietzsche. And Beer-Hofmann was Gillot's successor in "Abteilung" (see above, p. 218; cf. above, p. 220), while the sharp-eyed deaf-mute of "Abteilung" as the fulfillment for Gillot was wishfully Nietzsche with his poor eyes, sharp ears, and rich talk represented in reverse.

"Geschwister" incognito through the name Erwin[t]—as also through the names of Stefan (signaling the Stefansplatz[u]) and of Herbert, nicknamed Herr von Bert (which contains not only *Beer*, but *Hov*, with an *n* to spare toward *mann*[v]). And through Herbert's elegant manner: if Gebsattel was *Freiherr von* with a manner to match, this was again superposition and not condensation.

But condensation there was in "Geschwister," even simultaneously at more than one level: thus that great repulsion was Freud's of Lou and of Tausk as well as Lou's own of Tausk, but also Nietzsche's of Lou and vice versa. Far and away the principal distorting device employed in "Geschwister" was, however, reversal or inversion. By dint of reversal, Jutta is plainspoken. Or again, the two lesser love affairs end gracefully, leaving the brothers thankful; only Stefan's with his sister turns tragical, reversing the "Tor und Ur" reversal. Advertising reversal, Bella calls her poodle "Pussy." Reversal in turn advertised the Nietzsche complex, having overwritten it in Lou's fiction since Nietzsche's seizure given her motive of reversing his charges against her.[w] Yet it was just the Nietzsche story that—in a further reversal— came through "Geschwister" more or less unreversed.[x] Inversion— the radical form of reversal—went well with the theme of homosexuality in "Geschwister." Advertising inversion, Stefan nicknames Trebor "Robert" ("the name had fallen out of those trivial letters like something meaningful out of something random"[552])—only to call Erwin "Robert" by error repeatedly, thereby setting the Salomé record straight. Stefan accidentally grounds Lou's use of inversion in admonishing Jutta that, should she mistake him for a girl, "Doctor Trebor would surely laugh at her," whereas Trebor has just laughed at her for the converse reason.[523] The ground was Lou's wish to be a boy—the deep wish suffusing this tale (as also "Im Zwischenland," with its Christmas gift climax).

Imperfect inversions—displacements, that is—abound in "Geschwister," such being, however, usual with Lou's fiction. Jenia hav-

---

[t] In "Inkognito" too, Erwin meant *Wi[e]ner* (Viennese)—and corrected for Erwin's being said to come from Graz.

[u] Beer-Hofmann lived beside the Stefansplatz, which was the only Stefan in Lou's life. ("Wiedersehen," incidentally, takes place on the Stefansplatz, I know not why.)

[v] (Plus half of *Bert*hold: see above, p. 212.)

[w] Reversal was not, however, *confined* to the Nietzsche complex in Lou's fiction before "Geschwister": see e.g. above, p. 181 n. *b*.

[x] The big repulsion as Lou's of Nietzsche (besides vice versa) was a straight rendition of a real-life reversal—as against Apollon's filthiness in "Zwischenland," etc. The notable exception was that vice squad originally intended by Nietzsche for Lou (the "Zwischenland" criminal police, uncensored): cf. above, p. 322.

ing been promoted to eldest brother, Jutta's next eldest turned out a "protector" like Sasha and "long" like Jenia. Trebor's profession (orthopedist) was a displacement from Jenia's (pediatrician). That Trebor's crime is linked to fraud by no more than casual association with a piece of maudlin fiction constitutes a displacement of emphasis with respect to Freud—and a retraction with respect to Nietzsche. Perhaps the best composite example of displacement is one connecting back with a pseudo-self-analytical passage of a letter from Lou to Gebsattel: "It is quite clear to me that . . . while in my case too an estrangement from the body set in after infantile autoerotism, the stress fell elsewhere: the body did not become suspect, 'evil,' but instead a thing only conditionally identical with me, simply that thing closest to me in the outside world. . . . Indeed, I would easily forget the fact of my 'visibility,' and much of the physical coquetry of youth was spared me in that its effects struck me as a 'being loved beside the mark'—and the more so, the prettier the girls."[554] In "Geschwister," "after infantile autoerotism"—that is, after Jutta has voluptuously slid down the tree—Stefan tells her grandiloquently that *"she should never know what it means to be loved without being loved— mistaken for one's own body—no longer distinguishable from beauty, from charm—having to struggle with shame."*[555/y] Now, ordinarily Lou cooed over comely little Lou-heroines unmindful of their own comeliness. Jutta, though, was meagerly "slender, narrow, thin— darling."[556] Where was the old prettiness? Displaced—onto Stefan, nicknamed "Fair Fanny."[z] And with it went the shame, for all strong emotions in a story are the author's own.[a] Thus Stefan is "loved without being loved" in that his beauty and charm, which are loved apart by Trebor, signify Lou's loved by Freud. One vestige of beauty remains to Jutta: her long hair. She considers cutting it off before going to Trebor; afterwards, having been called "just like a boy" in spite of it, she strokes it while reflecting that "he *must* be fond of her since he said *that*."[557/b] By way of compensation Lou made Bella Belloni beautiful twice over in name already. And she poked fun at Bella's cosmetic art, including her "improbably gold-blond hair curls,"[558] though in Lou's very own case the gold-blond was genuine and not the curls.

In brief, virtually everything out of the Freud-Tausk substratum

[y] This implies, incidentally, that all Lou's men shamed her except Nietzsche, who called her physically repellent.

[z] (Lou considered Jenia ugly.)

[a] Cf. 1914a:261 on how some feel the intrusion of corporeality on love to be shaming (and below, p. 494 and n. *e*).

[b] Gottlieb hereupon bemoans Trebor's heedlessness of *him*.

was reversed, inverted, or displaced if it was not caricatured, and often even if it was (like Freud's or Lou's rejection of Tausk)—except notably Tausk's suicide. Was this an oversight on the real Gottlieb's part—or a mad trick of his on his psychoanalytical twin sister, who might well search herself for a self-reproach should she catch on to his techniques of caricaturing and displacing? Either way, neat as is "Geschwister" on the surface, the explanation for none of its surface elements lies with any of the others. It was, then, as if dreamed up. And in this it was nothing special as fiction goes.

A tight and trim extravaganza paced by contrapuntal comings and goings, "Geschwister" was narrated in playfully overwrought sentences passing over, for the characters' close confrontations, into fragmentary indirect discourse starker than speech except for some stupendous metaphors—such as one depicting a maple leaf as freakishly jagged and battered by reason of its thousand reds, greens, and yellows fighting it out and patching it up continually.[559] Just as novel for Lou in its own way, "Die Liebende" (A Woman in Love) was middle-class realism issuing of a sudden into bass lyricism. A superior provincial housewife and mother, who has determinedly found her fulfillment, as she thinks, in marriage, narrates an afternoon spent at the house of one of her husband's colleagues, a family man with a long-standing mistress (another colleague's wife) reluctant to be set aside. The mistress turns up in person after having been characterized in just such worldly-wise, humanly stupid terms. She is winsomely gauche as the "hemmed-in poetry of her loving" betrays itself again and again, until at length the ladylike narrator's insistent self-congratulations upon having preserved herself from such unworthy man-worship are interrupted by a "trombonelike" inner voice commanding: " 'Woman, confess thy womanhood!' " Lou muffled this voice by quoting it, whether Andreas ever shook off the Dionysian woman or not.[c]

Lou declared in January 1919 concerning her literary work that "these three years past" it had grown "as important to me as in my early youth"[560]: to those years "Die Liebende" probably belongs. So does a story "about a woman unjustly calumniated for two slight (even waggish) lies"[561]: "Geschlecht" (Sex), "corrected" in July 1917,[562] then lost from sight. As of early 1919 Lou told all and sundry that she had "eight books born of fantasy"[563/d] "lying in the bank

---

[c] On "Die Liebende" see further below, p. 456 and n. *s.*

[d] Cf. Lou→RMR, 16 I 1919 ("now eight books"), and Lou→EK, 2 XI[=I] 1920 ("likely eight pieces in all, among them two dramas plus a tale with the sumptuous title 'The Devil and his Grandmother' ").

safe"[564] (now in lieu of, now in addition to, jewelry[e]) but was "reluctant to publish [them] from sheer want of ambition (a great deficiency, yet one justified in the case of women, for what use have we for ambition?), which only Mammon's very crudest down payment conquers"[565]—and as of 1920 that "mammon (though it hardly fetches much these days) is now tearing [them] from me after years of quiet hoarding."[566] Of those "eight books," only two novels (*Ródinka* and *Das Haus*), three dramas (*Der Stiefvater, Die Tarnkappe,* and *Der Teufel und seine Grossmutter*), and three or four short stories ("Jutta" and the allegorical daisies and clouds,[567] "Geschlecht" and perhaps by then "Die Liebende") were on record by early 1919, with two more tales due shortly ("Die Stunde ohne Gott" and "Geschwister"). Two others ("Tor und Ur" and "Seelchen") had already been ambitionlessly unhoarded upon a magazine five years earlier. As for nonfiction, there was only *Der Gott,* which, however, she had not brought up to par for publication, but pirated instead—in particular for *Drei Briefe an einen Knaben.*[f] She had brought out these *Drei Briefe* during the war only with some difficulty[g]: by then she was deemed *passée.* Mammon's conquest was wishful thinking. The "eight books" came to four: the two novels, the mystery play, and the children's stories (including "Tor und Ur" but not "Seelchen," pirated for "Die Stunde ohne Gott"). "Geschwister" and "Jutta" went to a magazine, which "wanted to cut the second"[568]: only the first appeared. The two unpublishable dramas Lou sent to the manager of the Leipzig municipal theater—with whom, as she reminded him, she had once picnicked in Schmargendorf "a thousand and some years ago"—asking his "advice" on how to

[e] Lou→Freud, 18 III 1919 ("to the disappointment of today's thieves"), vs. Lou→Martersteig, 4 IV 1921 ("in our bank safe, where documents and jewelry lie").

[f] Of *Der Gott* chapter V, part one (on plant psychology) went into *Drei Briefe,* chapter I (on her childhood religion) into "Gottesdienst," etc. 1911a was presented as a passage from *Der Gott* but is no part of the manuscript preserved by her. This *she* preserved even while calling it a private work for the Klingenberg children—which did not necessarily mean a work not destined for publication, given the precedent of *Drei Briefe.*

[g] Rilke, after authorizing her to append to the *Drei Briefe* some admirative words of his about them (Lou→RMR [5 XII 1913]; RMR→Lou, 9 II 1914 and 20 II 1914; Lou→RMR, 1 III 1914; RMR→Lou, 9 III [1914]; also on Rilke's admiration RMR→Lou, 20 II 1918 and 13 I 1919), evidently placed the work for her, at her oral request, with the Munich publisher Kurt Wolff in the course of the year and a half beginning VII 1914 (RMR→Lou, 26 VII 1914)—though she did bring out the first letter in a review in 1915 and did likewise sell the third separately early in 1917 with Wolff's consent (Lou→Wolff [28] V 1917: "as I am to receive only 100 Marks in advance royalties"). (The volume was taken up by the Internationaler Psychoanalytischer Verlag in 1931, the Kurt Wolff Verlag having folded.)

"place" them[569]; he found them unperformable.[570] As to crude Mammon, the inflation refined him.[h] At least the four publications went over well—especially her own big favorite, *Ródinka*[i] (which she dedicated to Anna Freud after having promised it to Helene Klingenberg: Helene forgave her again and again). Her Nietzsche and Ibsen books thereupon each ran a new edition. She was a literary actuality once more, with the added benefit of venerability, after having ceased authoring after her return from Freud's in 1921.

She stopped writing even book reviews, the literary staple of that precedent literary decade of hers. Some of her fanciest had dealt with works relating to Russia, beginning with a set of letters by Tolstoi which, as she read them, documented a lifelong, hopeless struggle to compromise belief and disbelief, to harmonize immense spirituality and sensuality, at bottom to solve the "problem of death."[571] Of a volume on Tolstoi by Karl Nötzel she wrote in turn that it had taught her to see Tolstoi newly: as suffering from an altogether normal conflict between high moral purpose and unwitting class prejudice,[j] swelled Russian-style to cosmic dimensions and resolved only in art. Lou's old Tolstoi took the curtain call, though, as "in the final hour," finding insufficient outlet in art, social action, and religious prophecy for his "overrich, infinitely whole" personality, "he lapsed —into his god"[572] (perhaps when he fled the countess). Concerning some selected Russian political essays, Lou remarked in 1918 how the Russian intelligentsia, in rallying to Bolshevism, was resolving its centennial conflict in favor of popular national as against bourgeois Western culture and, its extravagant religiosity intact, was bringing millennial Russian utopianism down to earth only that it might the sooner reascend "heavenwards"[573] (wherewith she prophesied sputnik). In 1919 the diary of Tolstoi's youth awed her just because it was so

---

[h] Lou→Kurt Wolff, 20 x 1919, already complains to this effect. (Royalties being payable once yearly, the inflation of 1920-1924 regularly devalued them even though book prices were raised by the month.)

[i] See especially Bonus; Wurmb; Christaller; Gallwitz; and Meyer-Benfey, "L A-S"—which, however, acclaimed it as proof that Lou could *still* write nonpsychoanalytically as of old.

[j] However, Lou may have meant by "Tolstoi's conflict"—called that of "man generally, of each man, even the so-called 'most normal'" (1918a:1271) —one between moral will and social realism (*ibid.*, 1274), or another attending "the fearful choice between sensual pleasure and peace of soul" (*ibid.*), or another between the individual and his milieu (*ibid.*, 1274-75—perhaps a variant of my choice), or even the late-life one between the "cultural Philistine" and the "ascetic" in Tolstoi (*ibid.*, 1273, quoting Nötzel). She in fact paraded these many conflicts only to rebuke Nötzel at the close for adding a new one (Tolstoi's "doubts about his own teaching such as made him unable to act on it": *ibid.*, 1276) to the old *one*.

undistinguished—except, that is, for the odd disclosure that rigorous self-indulgence was Tolstoi's earliest antidote for lax self-indulgence. Following Karl Nötzel, she thereupon construed Tolstoi's exuberant writings and doings of his middle years as one long, losing offensive against an early impression of social ills generative of his later pious refusal to enjoy life.[k] And she wondered: "Was not that basic impression alone really right in Tolstoi's life"—right with the rightness of "an Eros whose love surpasses the person's, whose creating excels that of art, and whose life would be world-redemptive reality?"[574] Her Witalii of *Ródinka*, then under revision, was *inter alios* this Tolstoi benevolently laboring within the old manorial system to deny an anguished social conscience which, however, at length undid "the man and the poet"[575] to inscrutable protonarcissistic effect.[576] And her Witalii as Nötzel's Tolstoi was herself, imagined by her as having striven a quarter century exultantly to live down and write off that fugitive pained impression of social injustice by means of which Ledebour had hoped to undo her fantasticality—and so imagined out of renewed sympathy for Ledebour, then awaiting trial for his life. Finally, she took issue with a work by Karl Nötzel on Russian letters for its praise of the Russian crudity of narrating man-to-man, disdaining form—and parenthetically celebrated Russian love as an elemental sensual bond with all God's children.[577/l]

Outside of Russian letters, Lou took a prisoner of war's account of his literary inhibitions during captivity as an excuse to define lyric, dramatic, and epic poetry respectively,[578/m] then compensated by nominally resting her case in "Des Dichters Erleben" on that same prisoner of war's account. Ordinarily, though, she departed from works under review only to treat of the author or, more often, authoress behind them. Her best notices, moreover, were of writers rather than writings: of Elisabeth Siewert, distinctive in Lou's view for being poetical, ethical, and humorous all at once[579]; of Agnes Henningsen, erotic realist whose sphinxlike charm Lou deemed as lovely a limita-

---

[k] Ascribing "the unmotivated sadness that often utterly overpowered him" (1918c:138) to thwarted social conscience was unpsychoanalytical.

[l] On Russian topics also: "Nadja Strassers 'Russin' " was a "joyous notice" (1149) of a work on the Russian woman in politics, from which Lou dissented only to insist that Russian passivity was not compensatory for Russian activity but somehow a thing unto itself (Lou in 1919e:381-82 half allowed that the Russian's "nature" was "passive," but then *ibid.*, 383, settled on "reactive"— therewith assimilating it to womanliness); "Die Klerisei" concerned a translation of an early novel by Nicolai Leskov judged finely pious but politically silly by Lou, who learnedly suggested other works by Leskov for the German public; "*Satiren* von Michail Saltykow Schtschedrin" welcomed this translation from "the Russian Swift."

[m] See below, Appendix A, pp. 537-42.

tion on erotic realism as any, some limitation being inescapable[580]; of Waldemar Bonsels, vagabond tale-teller, great for Lou exclusively in his digressions on wild life and men's minds.[581] And of Angela Langer, autobiographical novelist dead at thirty, who told of having painfully outgrown an intense piety and addiction to fantasy in the course of a long adolescence—but also, unlike Lou, of poverty that entailed sexual abuse by unscrupulous landlords and employers, so that she came out of it suspicious and defensive in love. Lou took the sexual atrocity stories at face value out of semimemorialist's solidarity,[n] but her felt difference with Angela Langer in love prompted her one and only try at a sociology of erotism: since at the lower extreme of society the "secure bond" tends to be sacred and libertinage to be profane, whereas "out of the other 'class consciousness' " queens beckon to favorites, maybe "natural" and "sacred" join soonest "in the broad space between."[582/o] She returned to one of her first authors as subject in reviewing a volume by Ricarda Huch nominally on Luther but actually, she maintained, on love (or rather: on "the interactions within the reciprocal super- and subordinateness of the sexes"[583]): she called Ricarda divinely deep as concerned love, but contested whether the Christian god could in his purity have created a Lucifer who, by loving himself for shunning evil, perverts the good without meaning to. She subtitled this piece "a fantasy"—by way of precaution, she explained, as the first time round Ricarda had taken her to task for missing a point.[584/p]

Ricarda Huch came into Lou's diary in the spring of 1915 for a "spat" with Rainer in Munich over nonobjective art, Ricarda maintaining, as it struck Lou, the old representationalist thesis stultified by a denial of standards for representation. She came in again four years

[n] She in fact took *all* reminiscences at face value, notably Strindberg's.

[o] Perhaps, though, there is already a touch of a sociology of erotism to "Zurück," which presents disgust with sex as in effect an upper-class malady—and, for all I can tell, a further touch to D II 1918 on the client in "interclass prostitution" who, just like the homosexual, "so underscores the opposite sex in himself that he can see the partner only in his own sex."

[p] As for the lesser notices by Lou: "Paul zu Pedro" presents *Amouresken* by Countess zu Reventlow as piquant but monotonously frivolous; "Diekmanns . . ." concerns a set of trivial witticisms on love offensive to Lou in her "love of love"; "Im Traumland" notes a collection of dreams, which Lou called it impossible for her to discuss literarily by reason of her professional bias; "Tagebuch eines halbwüchsigen Mädchens" dealt with a teen-age girl's diary, which Lou read as a lesson to parents to give their children some simple explanations; "Die Diktatur der Liebe" deemed a study of animal love too chatty; "Kranke Liebe" esteemed a confessional novel about sexual impotence too inexplicit; "Der werdende Mensch" lauded some posthumous essays by the Anarchist Gustav Landauer, recently assassinated, who, Lou remarked, had been "dear" to her.

later in Munich for the mere notation: "at Ricarda H's"[585]—completed by Lou's "daughter" Ellen Delp in a memoir on the authoress Regina Ullmann, a protégée of Rilke's, whom Ellen brought to Ricarda's together with Lou: "There is no forgetting how these three significant women then sought to establish rapport with each other, by no means an easy matter!"[586/q] Munich's medical man of letters Hans Carossa left a comparable account of a 1915 visit to Rilke at the painter Loulou Lazard's, with Loulou, Lou, and Regina in attendance: "the three women, seated rather far apart, each looked straight ahead as if leafing through her own book of memory," while Rilke went from rehearsing his ailments to reciting his old dream of becoming a country doctor.[587/r] "Rega Ullmann" was down in Lou's diary once for 1913[588] and not again before the 1919 visit to Munich—but then for encounter upon encounter,[589] with two long supplements on her as pellucidly reliving her earliest childhood within her adult relations and transposing great chunks of it into her fiction "like massive pieces of furniture raised up by her and set down intact. But not swamped with affect either; spiritual presence rather, if also *almost* psychotically estranged: thence didactic, like an old lady amongst children—and like a prophetess and schoolmistress in one when she reads aloud."[590] And there it ended. Concerning "didactic Regina," Ellen Delp quotes an exclamation of Lou's that is perhaps an explanation: "She is insufferably moral!"[591/s] As for Ellen herself, she was Lou's companion not only for that winter of 1912-1913 in Freud's entourage but repeatedly the two years following.[t] Then the contact ceased for four years[u]; midway Lou wrote that, were she to revisit Vienna, "the 'daughter' brought along would in the interim have turned into a terrier—which is, be it added, far better and more dependable."[592] Ellen meanwhile moved to Munich, where in 1919 she welcomed Lou "with flowers, eggs,[v] milk, cakes" and with Regina,[593] then occupied her stay as of old. And there it too ended: the rest of her life

---

[q] This treble encounter may be apocryphal, however: Lou's notations for her 1919 stay in Munich look too thorough for her to have omitted Ellen, Regina, and—by this same account—Gebsattel, all at Ricarda's that same afternoon.

[r] Lou noted a single meeting with Carossa on 27 XII 1921, when she passed through Munich traveling from Vienna to Göttingen.

[s] *Ellen Delp added that the two never could quite bear each other. (Lou's two diary pieces on Regina are by no means hostile, though.)

[t] Ellen was certainly with Lou at least in Budapest, Vienna, Salzburg IV 1913; Göttingen by VI 1913; Munich, Dresden, Berlin IX–X 1913; Leipzig VI 1914; Göttingen VII 1914; Leipzig IX–X 1914; Berlin III 1915.

[u] Before Lou's 1915 trip to Munich Ellen joined her (on 11 III 1915) in Berlin—then dropped from her diary.

[v] (The eggs were for Easter.)

Lou both hated and dreaded Ellen, who she thought was telling tales about her—notably that she had once been pregnant by Rilke.[w] Terrier or no, though, Lou tried new daughters continually, including one just as she acquired Drujok[x] and another just before that aspersion on Ellen[y]—both of them patients of hers. None ever quite filled the vacancy left by Ellen.

The aspersion had been addressed to Beer-Hofmann five years after a note reading: "Dear Herr Doktor, I am in Vienna for a while; can I see you again and meet your wife and children? I am not alone, though; with me is a young girl to whom it would be a great joy to meet the author of *Charolais*. Cordial greetings! Lou."[594/z] The reply was a prompt yes. Lou and Ellen together met Mirjam, already a teen-ager; Mirjam's little sister, Naëmah; the girls' baby brother, Gabriel—and the children's mother, Paula. Paula was ill throughout Lou's stay.[a] Reunions galore ensued nonetheless, notably over the big holiday week. Just before Christmas, Lou sent admonishing Beer-Hofmann: "Yesterday you kept on saying 'Madam' and worse. Out of carelessness? distantness? That runs so counter to all Christmas spirit."[595] Santa Claus brought Lou a miniature Christmas tree and a huge snakeskin purse[596]—"truly," she deemed, "as if with every glance his entire person were a meaning to bestow gifts and waiting for a joy passed up."[597] She observed that, as against the old days, "he is now settled and sad, and deep down nothing is more alien to him than what has made *me* increasingly cheerful"—meaning the rejuvenating rediscovery of childhood? or the erotic ritual?[598] Lou gave the Beer-Hofmanns to understand that her afternoons were reserved for a training analysis by Freud.[599] Between her accompanied visits they wondered what was what between her and Ellen.[600] To her delectation, Beer-Hofmann read aloud to her from his seraphic *Jaákobs Traum* then in preparation.[601] She took him to one of Freud's lectures.[602]

[w] So Lou told *Franz Schoenberner repeatedly and emphatically (as also only that Ellen had somehow made trouble with Max Reinhardt—perhaps a reference to 1915: above, p. 443 and n. *u*). Ellen certainly told no such tale, for *she found it foolish of me even to entertain the hypothesis; she did, though, enjoy denying that she was Lou's *real* daughter, let alone *by Rilke*. *She for her part recollects nothing of a break between Lou and herself.

[x] A Petersburger named Margret, who traveled to her via Sweden at the close of 1914 (D V and 1 XII 1914; Lou→EK, 2 XI 1914).

[y] Ilse Erdmann, a philosopher's daughter, who was in Göttingen in the summer of 1917 (see D VII 1917; RMR→Lou, 28 VI 1917, 14 VII 1917, 16 I 1920; Lou→RMR, 9 VII 1917).

[z] Since *Charolais*, only a "Mozart memorial speech" by Beer-Hofmann and Lou's eager acknowledgment postmarked 6 VIII 1906 had passed between them.

[a] With sleeplessness and loss of appetite (Lou→B-H, 10 XI 1912 through 7 [VI] 1913).

After a first farewell at his home,[603] Lou arranged from Budapest for a second on her way through Vienna[604]—and "wanted to say much more to you than finally came out in the Alserhof Café."[605] He gave her a memory-laden token for the train and in return received "greetings from Salzburg, where we were happy with each other 1,000 years ago. Now Ellen and I are full of candied fruit and thinking gratefully of you both."[606] And from Göttingen she asked: "Shall I soon again be able to hear you read aloud? Just as this was the merest beginning thousands of verses ago, so was my stay in Vienna, as it appears to me, the merest beginning of my coming-to-you" (did she pause?) "-both."[607] Some coming-by-mail followed; it tapered off. She did not see Beer-Hofmann in person again before her stay at Freud's in 1921—three years after saluting in *Jaákobs Traum* a second Creation surpassing the first.[608] She then called on him with Anna Freud, noting afterwards: "It was for me as it has ever been and can never cease being."[609] She met him again in Berlin the following winter. And that was that—except for her very last diary entry before her literary recess of the mid-1920's: ". . . now all of a sudden remarkably . . . Beer-Hofmann has become clear to me: formerly as a spoiled, dependent double son of two fathers, he felt all free and alive inside (as children may), but now that 'even my aunts' are dead he wants only to deceive himself about his perplexity and dread of life. And this residual infantility that he conceals from himself binds him tightest to the poor (truly gracious) woman whom he tore from *her* root-soil, from *her* traditional mainstay, and who, almost pathologically, mirrors herself in animals, knows herself to be 'so poor' too (like her mongrel puppy now dead), and even maims her love for her children. Children (the products of maturity!) play no role for either."[610] Beer-Hofmann was demonized at last and Lou's unfinished business with him finished. The trouble was that, by the terms of her obituary on Drujok, that poor woman was herself.[b]

Lou saw Schnitzler with Beer-Hofmann during her two Freudian stays in Vienna, and the Fritz Mauthners too during the first[611/c] and even Wassermann,[612] besides helping the Beer-Hofmanns entertain the actor-author Friedrich Kayssler and his wife that spring[613]; and Salten on the second[d]—and Zemek, to whom, she noted pointedly,

[b] Even the preference for dogs over babies figures in the D 2 II 1919 installment.

[c] (Lou had lately visited Mauthner's daughter in Berlin.)

[d] As against D [late 1921]: "at Beer-Hofmann's (Salten, Schnitzler)," Mrs. Katharina Wyler-Salten (Felix's daughter) recollects some "visits" by Lou evidently dating from this, Lou's last Vienna sojourn, for "she was then a real old lady with sore legs: I well know that I always brought her a second seat to rest her legs on" (letter to me, 1 x 1961).

she went "alone."[614] She met Wedekind on the train on her way to Russia in 1911,[615] besides which she attended a Vienna rehearsal of his *Pandora's Box* in 1913,[616] then in 1919 visited his wife in Munich with Ellen.[617/e] Buber went on sending her his books, and she once attended a lecture of his in Berlin.[618] According to her diary, she missed a Freud lecture in 1912 because Harden insisted on seeing her.[619] At the start of the war she found Harden's journalism alone tolerable, as it at least disdained "moral trimmings" in its bellicism.[620] In 1917, when *Die Zukunft* folded, she sent Harden her regrets,[621] and from Eitingon's late in 1922 she wrote him proposing a reunion, evidently without reply.[622] She visited Hauptmann in Berlin once in 1915,[623] then again two years later.[624] Her diary contains a lengthy discussion of his *Greek Springtime* as his "dearest work" what with its descriptions all in "extreme Gerhart faithfulness, strict and true"[625/f]—and his diary the succinct verdict on her: "Wound up with Freud. Pity."[g] She frequented Max Reinhardt's crowd again early in 1915; Else Heims later visited her at Loufried,[626] as did Gertrud Eysoldt,[h] and she saw Moissi in Berlin in 1922.[627]

As Henry von Heiseler was stuck in Russia throughout the war and revolution, his wife developed a case of nerves for which she engaged Lou's services at her estate on the Starnbergersee outside Munich for June and part of July 1919. Between sessions the splendid hostess once mediated a contact that resulted in the Musarion press for modern classics domestic and foreign, with Lou's eminently literate and, since the demobilization, available young kinsman, Franz Schoenberner, as managing editor. Schoenberner, son of Lou's mother's niece (née Louise Wilm), had introduced himself to Lou seven years earlier while a student in Berlin.[i] Lou proposed Karl Nötzel, who had twice called on her in Munich,[628] to contribute proper editions of Russian masters: in time Schoenberner was defending a lawsuit brought by this "highly intelligent but somewhat confused old gentleman" for a revaluation of royalties in keeping with the inflation.[629/j] About then Nötzel as author came in for some rare psychoanalytical

---

[e] From Wedekind, 239n., it may be surmised that Tilly Wedekind was none too fond of Lou.

[f] See also 1919c:137: "Gerhart Hauptmann's *Greek Springtime* (which I love in every season) . . ."

[g] Noted 14 II 1937.

[h] This much I gleaned from her letters to Lou otherwise withheld from me: below, p. 560.

[i] D 10 VIII 1914—"Franz's farewell letter"—is Lou's first and, until 1919, last notation on him.

[j] On the Musarion farce, see further Schoenberner, *passim* (also RMR→Lou, 16 I 1920).

consideration from Lou[k]: in urging "the deed *quand même*," she noted, Nötzel was "working out his own complexes: for in the ventured deed he opens a gate to the wild, cruel, vengeful, eruptive criminality latent in him (the subsoil to his great goodness!). Yet over and beyond everything personal, he is right . . ."[630] She returned to the Starnbergersee in February 1920 for four months minus some time "in Mrs. Heiseler's lovely farmhouse in the Rosenheim mountains"[631] and some time out at Schoenberner's, "where I am at home and enjoy being."[632] She was also at Schoenberner's the following April,[633] then again on her way to Freud's in 1921, then on her way back,[634] and thereafter whenever her itinerary permitted: he had become, in his own words, "a close friend, almost a son to her."[635]

Psychoanalysis brought Lou closer to Helene Stöcker, who joined the movement in Berlin; Helene's pacifism, however, set them asunder temporarily in 1915, with Lou contending against it oddly that peace could do "the same measure of reciprocal harm" as war.[636/l] Psychoanalysis gave her a new friend in Sandor Ferenczi, who stayed in Munich after the 1913 congress to philosophize a while with her,[m] then lost touch till 1921, when he countersigned a card from Partenkirchen with Freud[637]: he paid her a visit that October,[638] which she returned in August 1926.[639] After the 1913 congress, Gebsattel and Lou sought out the philosopher Max Scheler, who theorized for them about experience to the effect that to theorize about it was to miss the point of it.[640] Later in Göttingen, where Scheler turned up at the university, Lou judged his wartime talk of "sniveling, softhearted turning away from war wounds" itself "a sort of sniveling: *he needs it too much.*"[641/n]

On May 25, 1914, Eduard Spranger, young lecturer on pedagogy at Leipzig University, lately a teacher of girls, petitioned Lou to join him in founding an enlightening periodical for teen-agers. She replied that she meant to learn from the young, not to teach them, but invited him to correspond further. He did—with her the dominant partner, the woman of wisdom and experience, eager but cautious as, at her bidding, he opened his mind and heart to her. Within a month she was in Leipzig briefly on the pretext of having "to see one of my 'daughters.'"[642/o] "What you stirred up within me I shall keep to myself till

[k] As did otherwise only Rilke, Strindberg, and Kleist.
[l] (Discussion at Karl Abraham's.) Cf. D 1 I 1917 (Berlin): "Helene Stöcker. The 'complexes talk,' which suddenly clears up all her views for me."
[m] See D [10-11 IX 1913] (on their hard-fought differences over life and death) and Lou→Freud, 26 XII 1920 (on their laughing agreement over the same): above, pp. 382 n. *v*, 384 n. *j*.
[n] (A projective verity, since she called Scheler's needful talk "optimism.")
[o] Cf. Lou→RMR, 24 VI 1914: "was away 2½ days (to talk to someone)."

it has taken shape," he wrote her afterwards.[643] "I hope your letter was not a terminal one," she came back, inviting him to join her and Ellen in a beach party on a Baltic island in August.[644] His reply was ungallant: he preferred the mountains alone.[645/p] She actually bade him reconsider[646/q]—whereupon Gebsattel's call to her from Munich found her compliant. Spranger next hailed the war as an ultimate truth[r]; Lou called him unjust not only to the truth, but to the war too for "despoiling its fresh crudity, as if it were a war of heavenly legions."[647] She nonetheless decided to pay Ellen a surprise visit, which materialized only after a month's postponement chronicled in seven missives to Spranger, charged with her accommodations.[s] Then: "27 [September]: Evening in Leipzig. Met by Spranger, dined with him." "29: Afternoon, Spranger came with white roses!" "30-4 October: . . . get-together with Spranger explosive!!"—despite a note on October 3 advising him: "I have lots of time Sunday." "4: Sunday afternoon and evening with Spranger." "[8]: Thursday morning with Spranger in the kindergarten and ate at Auerbach's." "9: Friday evening he at my place." "[12]: Toward 10 AM fetched by Spranger with red roses, auto to station. Arrival at 2 in Göttingen"—she having sent off to Spranger in pencil, from the first train stop, her "thanks" and "hearty greetings," which spelled goodbye. This fiasco notwithstanding, Lou was in the late 1920's still up to overwhelming a Hans Blüher, proponent of "Eros as an organ," theorist of the homosexual fabric of society, poet of the migratory bird, Empedoclean exponent of Empedocles, who hailed Lou as in reality "neither a Jewess . . . nor man-mad, but a glorious woman, Finnish by blood,"[648] admirable above all for having *qua* female made the homosexual Nietzsche "momentarily ill."[649]

Of Lou's dear friends the dearest remained Helene Klingenberg, despite a "singularly rough exchange of words" during a protracted stay at Charlottenburg early in 1915[650] and, at the end of it, a "blow-up with Reinhold," addressee of the three letters on sex.[651] Maybe she followed up those letters with some practical instruction, for according to her diary the lad turned up at Loufried with a suitcase the following Christmas Eve, and the two made off discreetly to a local room where "we came to speak of all that had filled the whole month

---

[p] Lou destroyed this passage, clearly inferable from Lou→Spranger, 18 VII 1914.

[q] But meanwhile Lou→B-H, 12 VII 1914, invited the Beer-Hofmanns along.

[r] Letter destroyed (along with all later ones from Spranger); gist clear from D 7 VIII 1914 and Lou→Spranger, 8 VIII 1914.

[s] Lou→Spranger, 17 VIII 1914 (letter) and 2, 13, 13, 15, [undated], 20 IX 1914 (cards—besides which the undated one mentions telegrams).

of December for him and me, and that is not written here."[652] A year afterwards she was at the Klingenbergs' for the winter: it is a measure of her love for Helene that she reveled in Helene's and Otto's absence for a month of "the most jolly and welcome 'parental surrogation' imaginable," which largely went into reading *Faust* with the surrogate son and daughter.[653] Thereafter, with Eitingon's as Lou's new address in Berlin, Helene turned into a cherished living memory refreshed "only on my way through."[654] Others dear to Lou died, beginning in March 1916 with Marie von Ebner-Eschenbach, whom she had seen a last time in Vienna three years before.[655] "Now one of those is gone the likes of whom will not come again. I love her," Lou noted,[656] and to Freud she depicted the deceased as "a prototype of motherliness . . . the lovelier the older she grew: I was every time newly astonished at how simply and naturally she grew on—into death itself as into a final breath of life."[657] With August Endell, who ended up director of the Breslau art academy and a devotee of "material, technique, utility,"[658] Lou maintained fondest relations, which included a reunion of January 1917 in Berlin and in May 1919 an excursion from the Heiseler house in Rosenheim to a farmhouse fixed up by Endell in the nearby mountains and accommodating him, his wife, and their "seven darling children": there it was that, in an adjacent hut by herself, Lou recollected the snow couple of Peterhof. Endell was stricken in 1924 and died the following year. Lou was about to visit Ellen Key with Gebsattel[t] from Würzburg in January 1914 when a patient materialized in Göttingen.[659] She was again due to visit Ellen in August 1914 on the way to Rügen island with Gebsattel in lieu of Spranger when the war broke out.[660] November found her yearning to swim over to Ellen as soon as peace returned.[661] Three years later she still longed to be "at your lake, in your garden."[662] Her single postwar letter conveyed an apology for having passed up Ellen's seventieth birthday a month earlier: "For me you are not, will never be, seventy. . . . On no day do I forget you, you are such a sure possession."[u] Ellen, replying out of unwonted desolation, pleaded for Lou's visit,[663] which never came. She died at seventy-six.

The suffering wandering minstrel Rilke, taking year-end stock of himself for Lou at Duino castle on the Adriatic "between the two Christmases" (Western and Russian) at the close of 1911—"it is to be expected that you are at home and at peace at this time, so it always was"—remarked in passing: "*Psychoanalysis* is too thoroughgo-

---

[t] (Ellen knew Gebsattel as a friend of her son-in-law's.)

[u] Lou→EK, 2 XI[=I] 1920. (Ellen was born 11 XII 1849. Lou's XI likely came of this 11 plus the wish to have written in XI already.)

ing a help for me; it helps once and for all."[664] "You are right," he wrote again two weeks later, "I have always been this way. But you see, I am growing tired of it."[665] And then after ten days more he requested Lou's advice about his undergoing psychoanalysis with Gebsattel: "My body is in danger of becoming the caricature of my mind," he specified.[666] She advised *no* by telegram and letter, even casting doubt on Gebsattel's reliability.[v] In self-justification she noted: "It is ever and again so certain to me that he will recover anew."[667] She told him, however, in a year's time: "I think you must suffer and always will,"[668] and she incorporated into *Das Haus* a secret, trembling recognition by Anneliese that she would want her son, who had fallen ill through his poetry, to get well through his poetry alone or else perish trying. On the best construction, Lou's *no* bespoke concern for Rilke's poetry at Rilke's expense. Her private opinion of his poetry since 1901 was none too high, however.[w] Besides, in January 1912 she did not yet know enough psychoanalysis to have reversed herself advisedly since having "tirelessly urged" him into it until 1901[x]—and when she did know enough psychoanalysis, she practiced it herself on him at their every encounter[y] and throughout their correspondence.[z] To the end of her life she rationalized her hysterical about-face, arguing that psychoanalysis threatened the mature as distinct from the budding artist.[669] The vulgar truth was that she did not want Gebsattel messing around in *her* past. There was no cause for alarm: even before receiving her telegram Rilke had reverted to "that first, ever newly strongest feeling."[670] He had asked Lou's advice, then, only for the sake of asking— as was ritual with him by then. In general, he would commune with her about once a year, then go about his business—which by October 1912 included reweighing the pros and cons of an analysis. In this he did not consult her again: when a decade later he underwent treatment briefly (with Paul Federn) she never knew it.

Meanwhile, through two successive diary versions of a week spent by him at Loufried in mid-July 1913[a] she contrived to rejoice at his having by then become wholly "himself, forever Rainer, never the

---

[v] Reconstructed from RMR→Lou, 24 I 1912 (Lou's messages to Rilke of this period are all missing).

[w] See above, p. 324 and n. [v].

[x] See above, p. 299; cf. p. 217.

[y] D 1913-1919, *passim* (despite such fakery as D [10-16 x 1913]: "At this point I broke off the other dream analysis, as if what has to remain dark had already been touched on").

[z] (Much elided in consequence as published.)

[a] RMR→Marie Thurn und Taxis, 29 VII 1913: "I was a week in Göttingen at Lou Andreas-Salomé's"—likely 14-21 VII 1913.

'other' slipping away from himself,"[671] while treating it as a mere subsidiary inconvenience that by the same token "he . . . suffers well nigh utterly and must despair"[672] in that "the body itself has become the 'other' for him"[673]—meaning acutest conversion hysteria. "We spoke much about that," she affirmed[674]—in a second, improved diary version, however, which was that much farther from earth. The first begins: "During the July rains, wholly confined within them, Rainer came and stayed a while. One evening, on my return from a late walk in the woods, Marie informed me that some man had called and would call again, and as I stood waiting at the garden gate, spooning out my yogurt, Rainer approached in the half dark: our hands found each other for very long above the gate."[675] Even here the implied impromptu of the visit is suspect[b]—but so much the more so in view of the revised beginning: "One day Rainer stood at the gate in the twilight, and without our even speaking, our hands lay in each other away over the garden gate."[676] July, rains, Marie, yogurt had vanished: now Rainer was a veritable apparition, a revenant beside a garden gate itself mystically looming outside of all physical or chronological context, with hands joined away from it somewhere in the fourth dimension. The revision may well date from later years, for it issues in a reference to the Elegies, begun in Duino, as both promise and fulfillment of a supreme poetic project for expressing things without heed for comprehensibility: even granting her due prescience, the seriousness about his poetical course was too high for that season, when his glory was not yet secure.[c]

At all odds, it was nominally to discuss Rilke that Lou saw Gebsattel on her way to Vienna in August 1913[677]—while Rilke was making acquaintances with Lou's daughter Ellen, *ipso facto* his "little sister."[678] Rilke rejoined Lou in Munich for the psychoanalytical congress so as (he told a girl friend) to see Freud and meet Bjerre[679]: he met Freud through Lou, who brought him to the "Freud corner" at the time of the schism over Jung.[680/d] He stayed the month in Lou's entourage: "We read and discuss a lot together," he told a blue-blooded patroness, "and for me these hours are even here the most

---

[b] Rilke's wont was to overannounce his visits, besides which Marie knew him from 1905.

[c] Cf. Lou→RMR, 24 VII 1913, first paragraph (to which a preliminary version of the D [VII 1914] passage probably corresponded).

[d] Further, Freud→Lou, 6 XI 1913: "my youngest son . . . who is mad about" Rilke; RMR, postscript to Lou→Freud, 30 III 1915: ". . . a hearty greeting to your son"; Freud→Lou, 1 IV 1915: "please tell Mr. R. M. Rilke that I also have an 11-year-old daughter . . ." Rilke paid Freud a visit in Vienna in XII 1915, but "there was no moving him to a second" (Freud→Lou, 27 VII 1916; cf. Freud→Lou, 21 III 1916).

significant."[681] Here Lou first met Rainer's mother—a hysterical chat-
terbox in whom the genial raconteur saw just enough of himself, Lou
noted, to be dumb with horror in her presence.[682] In October, he accompanied Lou to the Riesengebirge near Dresden two weeks "for
walks in the fall weather,"[683] most of them with Ellen: there he met
his first noteworthy disciple, Franz Werfel, and Lou remarked on how
touchingly "wistful, glad, and envyless" he was before the prodigy
of freshness and intelligence, whom, however, he regretfully could
not quite recognize as a son.[684] From Dresden Lou sent apologetically
to Paris after "my dearest mortal, dear old Rainer": "It was so dreadful the last day, as if I were almost chasing you away."[685] He came to
Göttingen in July 1914 for four days at a hotel just before she traveled
to Gebsattel in Munich. He was due to join the two in Munich on
August 2, the day after the war broke up their hostilities. By then he
was sacrosanct in her books—de-diabolized. Back in Göttingen, she
noted: "He and I—that is now the same in the face of what is
happening."[686]

She was Rilke's guest in Munich for ten spring weeks in 1915[e]: on
the outs with this world, he took her visiting all manner of occultists,
who left her cold except for one clairvoyant whose visions in trance
she considered to issue straight from the "identity of all with
all" by dint of " 'emotional omniconnectedness.' "[687] Between seances
she had occasion both to delight in Gebsattel's revivification of Clara
Rilke, though "amazingly" it "made no impression on Rainer, who
so suffered (with and without guilt) from Clara's prior nature,"[688]
and to writhe as Rilke's going mistress, the flamboyant painter Loulou
Lazard, took offense at "the poison green of the English garden."[689]
In 1919, just as Lou held Drujok dying, a letter arrived from the involuntary pallbearer for two of her previous dogs: "I kissed the letter,
full of joy," she noted. "When was there an hour in which Rainer
would have been more present than this one?"[690] After nearly ten
weeks in Munich again that spring[f] involving even a socialist revolution she remarked: "If I look back at Munich I see only Rainer."[691]
Rainer had bought her a new dog, Baba. She had brought Rainer to the
nonobjective painter Walt Laurent,[g] who warranted him that, to get
over and beyond things, he need not love them.[692] As to their private
conversation, Lou afterwards called it "hardly necessary any longer:
we felt almost at one in the solemn simplicities: Rainer could be like
a boy and as he was nearly a quarter century ago."[693] She added that

[e] 19 iii to 27 v 1915.
[f] 26 iii to 1 vi 1919.
[g] She knew Laurent in Berlin as of D 5 i 1917.

he now accepted his morbid "other" as a constituent of himself,[h] with the result that his person was all " 'modesty before God' " and his writings a " 'praying before God' "; she pronounced him "great poet, genius, revealer" and deemed it "wonderful how understanding has come to me for his crotchets and peculiarities one by one (after redeeming understanding came to him too for his sexual infantility: is it not glorious to think that it is the natural residue of that which is worked up creatively?), e.g. even for his . . . singular possession with the Gotha [registry of aristocrats]. The Gotha is an appeasement because the families cited in it are therewith constituted, as if they were written; they are lifted out of contingency, are roundly and allsidedly observable, are preserved in a book, a work (probably that will be utterly misunderstood as adulation of nobility if not cringing before it). . . . Likewise determined by ultrainfantile attitudes and memories is the impulse to live in castles as if to hide in the womb of ancestral motherliness, home beyond great stretches of time."[694]/[i] Enough! She was making a mockery of her psychoanalytical bread and butter.

From Muzot castle in February 1922 came that great poet, genius, and revealer's greatest message to Lou—in two installments. First: "Dear, dear Lou, so: at this moment, this Saturday the *eleventh* of February, at 6, I lay down my pen behind the last, completed *Elegy*, the tenth. . . . Just think! I was able to hold out all this way. Through everything. Marvel. Grace.—All in a few days. It was a tempest, as earlier in Duino: whatever was tissue or fibre in me, framework, bent and cracked. There was no question of eating. And imagine, something *more*, in another context (in the Sonnets to Orpheus, twenty-five sonnets, written, suddenly, in a precursory storm . . .): I wrote, made, the horse, you know, that free happy colt with the peg on its hoof that once leaped toward us at a gallop on a Volga meadow—:

how

I made it, as if in pursuance of a vow to Orpheus!—What is time?—When is present? Across so many years it leaped toward me, its joy intact, into wide open feeling. So they went one after the other. Now I know myself again. It had been like a mutilation of my heart that the Elegies were not there. They are. They are."[695] He transcribed three of them for her on account, which she hailed as the Word recollected—especially "the 'creature' elegy[j]: oh! how it is the one of my

[h] (Another precedent for Gottlieb in "Geschwister.")
[i] (Cf. 1927a:69 on how Rilke liked aristocratic families only for the symbolism of their ancient, solid bearings.) Lou went on this same way about Rilke's pedantry and orderliness as hardly at all anal.
[j] The eighth.

most secret heart, inexpressibly the most glorious; *uttered*, raised to accessibility, the ineffable."[696] Just that elegy was the poetry to Lou's prose about deathless creaturely cosmic bondage.[k] And second: "That you are there, dear Lou! to confirm it for me so into my innermost heart! As I read your good knowing letter: how I was again overcome by that assurance on all sides that now it is there, *there*, after having emerged so long since, ever since." He had meant to copy out three more elegies for her, "but just think! in a glowing afterstorm another elegy[l] came. . . . But that did not suffice. Hardly was this elegy on paper when the Sonnets to Orpheus resumed . . ."[697] He copied a few of these for her along with "our Russian colt (how it greets you, Lou!)."[698/m] "How big as life it sprang toward me!" she returned, "and how I now see it, unbound, as *you*, the peg having been removed by the softest of all invisible hands"[699]—wherewith her softest of all invisible hands put the finishing touch to his montage of her *two* Nizovka colts.[n] The remaining poems came to Lou in due course so that they might be "beside you, dear Lou, *living* with you."[700/o] She affirmed in acknowledging them: "Never will I be able to tell you what this means to me and how I was waiting unknowingly to receive *yours* as *mine*: life's true fulfillment. I shall remain grateful to you unto the last, unto the new first beginning, dear, dear Rainer."[701/p]

Lou had by then warned Rilke of a possible "reaction" after delivery so that he should not take fright.[702] "But now I *am* affrighted, you see," he reported toward the close of 1925; "in fact for two years I have been living in the midst of fright"—and he detailed his latest ghastly somatic inventions,[703] which she interpreted for him by return mail as displaced, converted guilt over masturbation.[704] A year later he came down with leukemia—amply anticipated by his lifelong prepos-

---

[k] Perhaps suggested by an offprint of "Narzissmus" (that she gave Rilke her *Imago* offprints: see RMR→Lou [10 VI 1919]), by her diary entries on dying Drujok (presumably read by him in Munich), or at the earliest by her *Drei Briefe* (reread by him four years before: see especially RMR→Lou, 20 II 1918— never sent). For Lou's share in the Elegies and Sonnets, see also Mörchen, 11, 140, 375.

[l] The fifth.

[m] First part, Sonnet XX.

[n] Cf. above, p. 276. Rilke's Orphic colt was also, as against Lou's originals, out "to be alone at night on the meadows."

[o] In IV 1922, the Sonnets and Elegies having been published, Lou gave these manuscripts to Helene—in atonement for having just done Helene out of the promised *Ródinka* dedication: above, p. 440.

[p] Afterwards she noted concerning Rilke's letters and enclosures: "all the weeks of February burst into bloom beneath them like southerly gardens" (D VI 1922).

session with blood (blood thick and thin, blood red and blue, blood as sap and as water, and especially blood disintegrating: "it is as if a few drops of lemon juice had found their way into my blood, drawing everything together wherever they drift," he had told Lou already in 1912[705]) as also by his lifelong prayer for a death all his own. "So, you see, *that* was what I had been prepared for and warned about by my vigilant system these three years," he told Lou—who, however, afterwards asserted that "from nothing previous could it have been supposed that leukemia was threatening."[706] He added that the pain was consuming him "day and night!" and that "there is something bad blowing at this year's end, menacing."[707/q] His nurse sent this message along with one of her own: "You know his boundless faith in you—he said: Lou must know everything, maybe she knows of a consolation."[708] His doctor added: "The one thing he requested is that you be told the whole truth. I tell it gladly—trusting that you, as his true friend, will be able for all that to sustain our poor patient's will to live and his hope."[709] Lou sent many words; they conveyed neither consolation nor hope. The nurse reported to her that, "when I asked him whether to write you again, he said *no*, with a wave of his hand."[710] His faith in Lou's surpassing wisdom was at last broken,[r] tragically: what might once have meant liberation now simply intensified his agony—indeed, *perfected* it. Lou stopped writing him when she surmised that he knew the end to be near. "Now it remains only to step back from him," she told the nurse; "one should not dare raise one's voice bound to life."[711] He died between the two Christmases of 1926.

All this while, Lou's domestic existence throve on hardship. She came to dread thunderstorms during the war as the copper was removed from the lightning rods at Loufried[712] and to dread winter as coal became unobtainable after the war.[713] When the electric lights went out, however, the curfew at nightfall brought her "immense composure of soul."[714] As to that "truly blinding cold" of the winter of

[q] 1927a:112, quoting a line from this letter—"*Aber die Höllen!*" (But what hell!)—as if (but not necessarily) it were the last line before the final salutation, calls it a message from beyond human life. Challenged on this putative last word of Rilke's, Lou in a communication to the Rilke Archiv *seemingly* retracted so far as to deny that Rilke had ever written the line at all (see Bassermann, 529, quoting *Die Deutsche Zukunft* of 8 III 1936). Yet it appears in Pfeiffer, *Briefwechsel*, 505—cast just a bit differently, though ("*Aber. Die Höllen.*"), and followed by a full paragraph. Most likely the published version reproduces the original accurately, Lou having meant to retract only her abusive construal of the line—and equivocally at that.

[r] It had been shaken once, just twenty years earlier: see above, pp. 322-23.

1922-1923, "the Nordic in me rejoiced at it even freezingly."[715] Besides, in common privation seconded by age, she and her husband drew closer than ever before. Unremarkably, he traveled to her in Berlin in October 1911; remarkably, when he went to Berlin for the winter of 1916-1917 on a government commission to study Afghan war prisoners' dialects, she followed—half as if on an amorous escapade, to take "Die Liebende" at its fictive word.[8] At home the two grew ever so considerate of each other, with never a sore word between them.[716] Of Loufried she remarked in 1924 that it was "crumbling around us peacefully and without protest; the walls are fading with us, except that in their discoloration they are gradually acquiring a golden hue, we an icy grey one."[717] Andreas, ignoring his official retirement, went on conducting his seminar by night. In 1923 he came down with the shingles from fretting over the "hovering unrest" in the nation,[718] but in 1924 Lou told Rainer "about my joy at the hardiness of my dear old man,"[719] then seventy-eight. Late in May 1926 she informed Freud: "We are freezing pitifully, and my husband is complaining of the damp and the cold, which he feels in all his bones,"[720] but early the following May she reported reassuringly: "I stretch out my old bones in the sunshine, as does my husband."[721]

By that time, though, Lou was frequently ill. Hospitalized with diabetes in the fall of 1929, she would receive her patients in her sick room after 4:00—and after her husband. "As my husband spoke to me day by day at the preappointed hour from the armchair by my bedside," she related to Freud, "we two old people noticed how much we had to tell each other for which we had really never found the time."[722] On her release at the winter's end, Andreas applied his exotic salves to her,[723] which did her soul good. That summer he took her place at the hospital with cancer. For three months she kept the secret with his doctor, dreading "day and night" lest heightened pains arouse his suspicions: "as on his last night he . . . sweetly dozed off," she related to Freud again, "I felt unmixed gladness."[724] That night was October 3, 1930. Some weeks later she brought her diary up to date from 1923 in a few lines beginning: "April 14, 1926: Oldster's eightieth birthday" and added: "That he died unsuspectingly: a feeling of purest happiness, like a miracle, like a grace. It was remarkable just how far the sincere grief of those around me, his colleagues and friends, accompanied this feeling: as if nothing were dead so long as

---

[8] Reading Berlin for Paris, that is. (Incidentally, Paris as the destination of a projected semischolarly excursion by the narrator of "Die Liebende" with the professor-author after all those years is a reminder that her man-worship repressed way back was Lou's Nietzsche-worship—actualized by the enamored mistress.)

it were sustained by them all as an abiding presence. It affected me so much the more in that I had held aloof from them, antagonized them, offended against all civility, twenty-seven years long, and now suddenly stood amidst their pure tenderness and warmth. But this was so here at home too: for the devotion shown me is wholly *his* effect—so much so that clearing his rooms is not like an emptying and moving out, but like a moving in and a filling with that which is unforgotten."[725]

The big item to be removed was his scholarly papers. He had pursued his researches to the last, amassing notes that were so many new beginnings on his old questions and that consequently brought his life's work that much farther from completion. Lou maintained that this kept him young[726] but did allow that he felt bad toward the last about a life spent in preparation for a book never written.[727/t] He himself had blamed the unsettling effect of his years of professional insecurity in Berlin[728]—therewith pointing disguisedly to his matrimonial insecurity,[u] which conditioned his other insecurities. His students made honorable excuse for him after his death: that he would rather write nothing than anything merely tentative[729] and that, besides having too many interconnecting ideas ever to expound any one of them, he was assured of their inadequacy one and all by eternal standards, which alone counted with him.[730] By November Lou had sold his three rooms of reference works to the Academy of Sciences in Berlin[731]—and many of her own volumes on the side.[732] Freud meanwhile inquired how he might help; she mentioned only her want of solvent patients; he thereupon sent her 1000 Marks out of his Goethe prize money "so as to reduce a little further the wrong committed in the attribution of the award."[733] Early in the new year several crates of assorted philological notes were toted off from Loufried to the stacks of the university library in Göttingen, where to this day they rest. Andreas's associates had daily assisted the widow,[734] who now closed her neglected diary with the notation: "The astoundingly live resurrection through colleagues and students is supplemented at the turn of the year by personal recollections—objective, critical, unsentimental—which I readily accept in full so that nothing subjective shall be lost."[735]

---

[t] While in Göttingen, Andreas published—besides some monographs of lesser importance—only Zoroaster's third Gāthā in 1909 and (with a collaborator) the first, second and fifth in 1913; the complete series was published for him posthumously in 1934.

[u] He would hardly have pointed that way undisguisedly before a student —and besides, the student just cited was under Lou's strongest influence because in treatment with her. On Andreas's nonproductivity and Lou, see also below, pp. 464, 473.

PART FIVE · OLD AGE

I · REVAMPING THE PAST

*L*OU SALOMÉ'S childhood began more or less punctually with her birth, her youth upon her break with Gillot, her womanhood somewhere along the Beer-Hofmann/Zemek continuum, her maturity at Freud's elbow. Only her old age did not declare itself at any one time or through any single experience. Ascendant from the time of her essay on old age and eternity, it was already latent in her nonage insofar as it consisted in an increasing indulgence in phantasmal reminiscence, experienced as an increasing relaxation of resistance against an upsurge of old memories both pleasant and painful. She would gladly have done without decrepitude, but when, in her seventies, she thanked life for keeping an old promise and restoring the plenitude of her past to her as a present possession,[1/a] she meant it. Reaffirming her individuality by this same token, she treated Freud's work as a contribution to her existence rather than the reverse. Yet in 1926 she resumed authorship with a brief, devout observance of Freud's seventieth birthday that commenced: "It seems to me in looking back as if my whole life had been a waiting for psychoanalysis"[2] —and that plagiarized back diaries for the rest. Her essay on woman's not having slain the tribal father followed in 1927.[3]

So did a book on Rilke with a spooky foreword on how death fixes a personality so that true communication and communion with it become possible.[4] This countermanded her remark of 1901 to Hauptmann on the memory of the dead as painful to her.[b] It also expanded on a recent comment to Freud a shade less spiritistic[5]—itself foreshadowed by a diary essaylet of 1918 that was madly more so.[c] She had virtually begun mourning Rainer this way on her return from Munich in 1919, when she noted: "His spiritual being detached itself for me from all personal experience of him with a clarity and grandeur that make it almost impossible to tell whether he is still standing before me in the flesh or only in memory."[6] He was accordingly death-

[a] Cf. 1882 aphorism: "Some feel bygone happiness as a possession, others as a loss."

[b] See above, p. 282.

[c] D [III?] 1918: we live out of "primal impressions," which "nourish" our feelings, so that "as between associating with the living or with the dead there is only a tiny bit of reflexiveness, only what the reactions of the living superadd—though again, even from these we may draw only what fuses with those primal impressions"; in sum, "all are alike alive or dead."

ridden from her word go[d] as she explained his life and his work through each other while in actual mourning. By her gradualized account, the earthly god of *The Book of Hours* had receded heavenwards to the vanishing point by the time of the Elegies, the angels having taken his place for all impractical purposes.[e] Insisting that the fearful, alluring Elegiac angels were "no intercessors" with God,[7] she failed to recognize in them those quotidian intercessors with God, the Russian saints, semidemonized. She saw them instead as personality disembodied, in fact depersonalized, and took this to be a first theme of Rilke's mysterious masterpiece, with allegiance to corporeality *quand même* for a second and, for a third, continuance of individual experience through the experience of the generations unto the end of time: thus she disincarnated Rilke and reincarnated him as Beer-Hofmann. By the terms of her singular autopsy, meanwhile, Rilke, through creating out of himself those consummate beings, the angels, rendered himself "beingless"[8]—or at least got out of Being's way preparatory to plunging into the "eternally anticipated mother-womb."[9] She so hypostatized this metaphysical mishap as Rilke's tragic fate that in the end it hardly looked binding on him, as if he could as well have turned his back on it as bowed to it—and fittingly so, for it was adapted from her grandiose Nietzsche melodrama. She was likewise apocalyptic about Rilke's conviction of harboring select horrors within his soul just as she had been about Nietzsche's. Her Rilke the solitary wanderer, shuddering at his every inspiration as at a message from the underworld and trembling at his every experience as at a threat of annihilation, was her Nietzsche reedited. Her analysis of Rilke, like that of Nietzsche, was a reduction complete with grisly depth psychologizing—only it was a reduction performed in unadulterated esteem. She presented as inspired in Rilke's case what she had presented as morbid in Nietzsche's: the angels and the superman respectively, both conceived in a spirit of religious prophecy as a measure of man's inadequacy. Again, it was high seriousness on Rilke's part, after having been poor form on Nietzsche's, to bear such mythicopoetic progeny trancelike after a harrowing gestation. And again, the enterprise of speaking the unspeakable was sublime where that of transvaluing values had been self-deceptive.

[d] After her spiritistic foreword, she began: "If one looks at the works already produced by René Maria Rilke in the middle 'nineties . . . one cannot quite avoid the impression of a relationship obtaining from the first between the poet and death" (1927a:7).

[e] Ditto 1931a:156 (also 166)—but as per 1929a:83, "the angel turned into a love partner."

Biographically too, Lou's Rilke book was a positive repetition of her Nietzsche book in that it was written as if she had drawn sparingly and discreetly on a richest store of letters and memories out of an oldest, most intimate association—and this time she *had*. Along this same line, she went to the extreme of omitting all direct mention of Rilke's most formative adult experience: his Lou experience. She drew a bonus of revenge for her Nietzsche book in that this omission automatically concealed the two big breaks in her relations with Rilke (1901-1903, 1906-1909). For the rest, given that omission, she had little occasion to tamper with facts. As to that little, the second Tolstoi visit came through more cordial than the first by dint of deft suggestion,[10] and *The Book of Hours*, beloved of her, "emerged" during their "second trip of several months through Russia"[11/f] (to fill Boris's blank notebook). Reviewers called this *Rainer Maria Rilke* everything from gripping to appalling.[g]

While hospitalized during the winter of 1929-1930 Lou began composing a huge letter to Freud that was close enough to completion to be dispatched to him for his seventy-fifth birthday (May 6, 1931) in printer's copy under the title *Mein Dank an Freud* (My Thanks to Freud).[12/h] For this summation of twenty years' tireless thank-you's, she drew on earlier essays, diaries, even letters to Freud (except for one brilliant passage comparing hysteria with obsession[13/i]). At the same time she carried her stock psychoanalytical themes to their fullest development and finest expression: succeeding where once *Die Erotik* and *Der Gott* had failed, *Mein Dank an Freud* topped off a chapter in her mental life. Proposing its publication in book form, Freud called it her best work known to him—"an unintentional proof of your superiority over us all as suits the heights from which you came down to us. It is a genuine synthesis, not of our adversaries' senseless, therapeutic sort but an authentic, scientific one that can be depended upon to turn those assorted nerves, sinews, and arteries, to which the analytical knife has reduced the body, back into a live organism again. Could what you paint with such fine brush strokes be coarsened unto palpability, perhaps we should have come into possession of definitive insights."[14/j] Lou jubilated: "What more

---

[f] Cf. RMR, *Tagebücher*, 233-35 (1 IX 1900), on his having produced nothing in Russia.

[g] From the first extreme to the second: Rostosky; Gallwitz; Jancke; Essl; Meyer-Benfey, "L A-S"; Bachman; Landsberger; Hessel; Thiel.

[h] Lou→Freud, 10 VII 1931: "I know my pages to be so snug in your hands, they are so pleased to lie there and have no further ambitions whatsoever. In three spots some addenda important to me are lacking . . ."

[i] Cf. above, p. 369 and nn. *u*, *w*.

[j] Freud added: "Not everything you deal with was equally intelligible to me

could I wish?"[15/k] Freud also told her twice that "the overly personal title must go," proposing *"Psychoanalyse"* for *"Freud"*[16]; she twice said *no* because "the work is really this one word, is my experience of the man so named; what it would have been like as mere objective knowledge without this human experience I simply cannot imagine. (Am after all a woman too.)"[17] The title remained.[l] One young psychoanalyst, observing that *Mein Dank an Freud* "reads like a holy *disputatio* on ultimates," likened it to Diotima's colloquy with Socrates.[18] He also remarked on the "manifold counterpoint in every sentence, echoing things already said or anticipating those to be said later," the effect of which was that "to understand any section fully, one must first understand the whole."[19] Both comments are apposite to Lou's psychoanalytical works in general: they help explain why, despite her prestige among professional Freudians, her influence among them was confined to Freud himself.

Her open letter to Freud done, Lou composed a memoir on Andreas in consultation with some of his colleagues and students. This most engaging characterization conveyed the tacit argument that even without marital trouble he would have been eternally incapable of completing his opus one. "The way of rational proof," she averred, "seemed to him endless—interminable, as it were—as against the inner evidence that his subjects of investigation possessed for him straight off."[20] Again, she maintained that his strictures on publishing as perforce premature were a defense against recognition of the basic conflict within him between "overthoroughness" and the "gift for overall divining and combining," between his "Occidentalism" and "Orientalism"—a conflict by virtue of which he was, on the plus side, a preordained professor.[21] Similarly, she insisted upon his insisting upon tackling problems in their full, hence overfull, context.[22] And so on—with so many truths in lieu of one.[m]

To this memoir Lou added others during the next two years under

---

or seems to me equally worth knowing. But I am—all phrases notwithstanding—after all no artist; I should never have known how to paint light-and-color effects, only hard contour lines."

[k] Cf. above, p. 371.

[l] Even so, Lou later pretended that the birthday letter had been published "without her wishing it": Bäumer, "L A-S," 308.

[m] Lou's truths check out against Selle's and Lentz's, besides which she cited a corroborative unpublished study of Andreas by another student of his, Herman Lommel (1931a:243 and Pfeiffer, *Leben*, 369-70)—though again, these students took most of their biographical data and explanations from her in the first place.

the general title *Grundriss einiger Lebenserinnerungen.*[n] These so-called recollections of her life in outline were no mere reminiscent reveries: she penned them open-eyed with her old, trimmed documents beside her, then belabored them tirelessly.[o] Throughout, she sought to apply a concept developed by her over the years[p]—that of "experience" (*"Erlebnis"*)—to selected, improved remembrances of a life lived with autobiographic self-consciousness in the first place. By an "experience" she meant, roughly, a lifelong running response to something or someone, whether actual or bygone. In a diary essaylet of 1912 she preformulated the corresponding *"literary* technique (—this old dream of mine!—)," intended as a corrective for the "rationalization" and hence "falsification" inherent in the *"chronological depiction"* and *"psychological unraveling"* in use with other autobiographers.[23] Theoretically, then, her memoirs were meant to exclude any and every fact of her life extrinsic to her chief constitutive "experiences." Since she did live by patterned responses—by Nietzschean typical experiences—the procedure was in order. She did not follow it, however. Instead she scorned patterns for quintessences verging on the cosmic pathos and passing over into it again and again. And this was only when she proceeded systematically; for the rest, she repeatedly lapsed into chronology and psychology. The results squarely reversed her expectations; thus she herself called them "slim . . . because the essentials will not relinquish their right to be let alone."[24]

She apparently worked backwards from her most recent experience, psychoanalysis, getting increasingly personal—and correspondingly fanciful—along the way. No less than misleading in their entire autobiographical purport,[q] her memoirs are true to life otherwise, especially as they characterized other people. Midway she quoted a dictum allegedly drawn from an old diary of hers: "To memories

[n] As of Lou→Schoenberner, 25 v 1933, she had just finished adding 100 pages to her memoirs, previously 168 pages long: this was evidently the last substantial addition before the general supplement "Was am 'Grundriss' fehlt" (below, pp. 472-73). As, however, Podach's 1932 transcript of her chapter on Nietzsche (below, pp. 467-69) differs significantly line for line from the text published by Ernst Pfeiffer (*Lebensrückblick*), Lou probably did *some* further revising. And Pfeiffer certainly did some *more* (cf. Pfeiffer, *Leben*, 385)—the validity of my treatment of Lou's memoirs being limited accordingly.

[o] *Mrs. Maria Apel: "She must have rewritten each chapter twenty times."

[p] Beginning (after her inadequate essay "Erleben") in the first entry of her first diary following her 1900 Russian trip and proceeding in consideration of Bergson and Scheler, in exchange with Buber and Spranger, etc.

[q] At least wherever outside evidence is available, that is, and except insofar as documents are quoted or paraphrased.

I shall ever be true, to persons never"[25]/[r]—a perfect motto for her life as against her reminiscences.

Her "Freud experience" came out as a formal appreciation of psychoanalysis, which "admits us into the brotherhood of all Being"[26] (that is, which admitted her into Freud's brother horde). With Rilke she was less formal. She introduced him as the author of anonymous poems supposedly received by her before their first meeting, which she confused with their second by misreading her calendar.[27] Oblivious of his suicidal "other," she represented him as gloriously free of inner tension or conflict during the early months and years of their acquaintance except for a literary conscience so heavy between productive spells that "it seemed to me *any* sort of work . . . were better than empty waiting . . ."[28]/[s] This supreme harmony of body and mind, together with that of person and poet, allegedly climaxed during their second Russian trip as he spoke out his prayers instead of grappling to write them[29]: she herewith refashioned the fable in her *Rainer Maria Rilke* about his having written *The Book of Hours* in Russia, his contradictory diary account having been published in the interim. She presented his human ruination as the counterpart to his poetic self-discipline undertaken after 1900[30]—unmindful of his coincident separation from her. Of that counterpart she affirmed: "Whoever saw it happening had to let it happen. Helpless and reverent"[31]/[t] —with time out, she might have added, for a frantic *no* to his psychoanalysis. She retroactively applauded as, "through Rodin, Rainer achieved unforgettable perfection of his ability. Whoever knows the *New Poems*, which leave even *The Book of Hours* far behind, let alone the earlier lyrics, doubtless experienced that directly."[32]/[u] She construed his poetical imperative as one to supply sense to a Creation senseless by dint of godlessness[33]: her Nietzsche's imperative. Her Nietzsche's was likewise the original of "Rainer's final solitude, which, even atop the mountain peaks, considerably shielded his eyes for him a brief moment with his own hand, covered them before the abyss into which he plunged"[34]/[v]—as someone figuratively stood watching, helpless and reverent . . . a few hundred meters below Sils.

[r] The original for this is Lou→Frieda [1905?]: "To want to keep faith with him as a memory improves nothing at all . . ."

[s] Cf. 1931a:166, however, where the heavy conscience is hysterical "already from youth on" (with body-mind conflict).

[t] Cf. above, p. 455, on his last *days*.

[u] In 1929a she had rectified her hostility to Rilke's Rodin course only sparingly (1929a:88) and had even taxed him with estericism in his late work (*ibid.*, 88-89).

[v] More literally, this evokes Rée's final solitude and, as Lou thought, suicide.

With Nietzsche she went the Louish limit, representing him as an obtruder upon her prototypical "friend-experience." By this account, friend Rée bursts in upon her life at Malwida's one evening in January 1882 coming straight from Monte Carlo, where he has gambled all his money away.[35]/[w] A few days more and he is proposing to her through her mother, "to my angry sorrow."[36] She is just laying plans with him for a housekeeping salon when Nietzsche arrives "unexpectedly"[37]/[x] and, at the first word, counts himself in.[38]/[y] Already in Rome he proposes to her through Rée,[z] only to learn of her "aversion on principle to all marriage whatsoever,"[39] the greater for her claim on a future Imperial Russian pension due to blue-blooded spinsters. Skeptical, Nietzsche talks it out with her in Lucerne[a]—and "at the same time" insists upon that prankish group photo, himself arranging all the particulars.[40] Jenia, despatched by Sasha to lend their mother moral support, accompanies her and Lou from Zurich to Berlin,[b] where "the final battles break out"[41]; thence he escorts Lou to Schneidemühl, where Rée meets them, and "guardian and thief" shake hands.[42]/[c]

Lou sojourns in Stibbe "probably months,"[43] then joins Malwida in Bayreuth, making acquaintances with Wagner and especially Cosima, who seeks her out as Malwida's friend. Lisbeth is missing— but so is Jena thereafter, for Lou next turns up "for several weeks"[44] in Tautenburg,[d] where "quarrels between Nietzsche and me seem to have taken place at first, occasioned by all sorts of gossip that has to this day remained incomprehensible to me because there was no reality whatever behind it."[45] The quarrels yield to an intellectual rapport established virtually from scratch, she having read none of

[w] In fact Rée purchased an interest in a score by Gast in III 1882 right on top of his gambling losses such as they were.

[x] "Unexpectedly from Messina," to be equivocally exact.

[y] ". . . *sich zum Dritten im Bunde machte.*"

[z] An addition to the oral version of 1909.

[a] In the Basel draft, Nietzsche and Rée have meanwhile left Rome with Lou and her mother; in the published version (1931a:99-100), they would have done so except for a last-minute headache of Nietzsche's. (There was in fact no question of their leaving together.)

[b] In the Basel draft, Lou travels with her mother straight from Lucerne to Berlin, where Jenia joins them.

[c] Cf. above, p. 306.

[d] ". . . in a house owned by the local preacher, who proved to be a former pupil of my chief professor in Zurich, Alois Biedermann" (1931a:103): a typical misleading clause, since Nietzsche informed her to this effect (to be exact, that the preacher was a disciple of Biedermann's) only after her departure. Here the misleading was collaterally a vehicle for name-dropping: having had no "university experience" worth a chapter, she had no proper place for Biedermann.

his writings beforehand. Her fascination for his religious mode of thinking stirs "memories or half unconscious feelings deriving from my very earliest yet most personal, indestructible childhood. Only: it was at the same time just this that would never have permitted me to become his disciple, his successor: it would perpetually have given me pause to pursue a course from which I had to extricate myself so as to see clearly. Fascination and inner resistance went together."[46/e] She returns to Stibbe "for the autumn"[47] without incident there.

Then with Rée she meets Nietzsche in Leipzig "for three weeks"[48] during which her "inner orientation toward Nietzsche" is impaired, "primarily" by "the increasing frequency of his insinuations meant to put Paul Rée in bad with me—as also my astonishment that he could regard this procedure as efficacious."[49/f] Such was the single, shadowy showing of those low designs of Nietzsche's so dear to Lou[g] (to which she had pleaded guilty as Margharita)—and her first assertion ever that he had betrayed them to her. As for the fearful repulsion: "What later followed seemed so contrary to Nietzsche's nature and dignity that it can only be ascribed to alien influence."[50/h] More, "only a preliminary letter became known to me" of the whole hateful series, Rée having considerably intercepted the rest![51/i] Behind this invention lay the wish to cancel Nietzsche's adieu,[j] seconded by the knowledge (acquired since her oral version of 1909, which had tended toward her repelling him[k]) that none of her last letters to Nietzsche survived—but not that the drafts of his letters to her (published fragmentarily by Lisbeth) established these as so many *replies*.[l]

[e] She herein not only overintellectualized her erotic interest in Nietzsche but referred it back to a childhood prototype by way of shrugging it off: cf. below, pp. 494-95. As this passage has no counterpart in the Basel draft, it amounts to a disguised, belated concession to the emotional truth.

[f] This reversal of the truth (Nietzsche had thus far been handsome toward Rée, who had backbitten *him*) is also absent from the Basel draft. Its documentary point of departure was presumably Nietzsche's letter of XII 1882 treating Rée as pathetically shiftless (below, p. 544).

[g] Except (displaced) as Nietzsche's "insinuations against Rée and me" by mail (1913a:105)—or, in the Basel draft, "the very insinuations from the danger of which he had helped dissuade my mother because *he* was taking us under his protection."

[h] This sole, discreet allusion to Lisbeth corresponds to the single hint at her in "Geschwister" as against "Zwischenland": the vice squad.

[i] Perhaps the fact distorted by this fantasy was Nietzsche's having left it up to her in late XI 1882 whether to deliver his showdown letter to Rée (above, p. 96—in which case the fantasy was self-reproachful, as her delivering the letter had precipitated the sorry denouement)—unless it was her having concealed from Rée her writ of apology to Nietzsche (above, p. 428).

[j] Her word for *intercept* ("*unterschlagen*") also means *suppress*. (Cf. the "Geschwister" refrain: "He did not repulse her.")

[k] Above, p. 169 and n. *d*.   [l] Cf. above, p. 97 n. *h*.

Thus her final formal word on Nietzsche's repudiation of her—that she knew of none—rejoined her first, the one in her Nietzsche book. With it went a claim to have written that book out of personal loyalty to her misunderstood friend[52]—but it hardly went with her dogged efforts to effect a reconciliation, of which Stein's plea in Sils was avowed almost undistortedly.[53]

Meanwhile, she and Rée, cohabiting for nearly five years,[54]/[m] animate a huge, brilliant circle in Berlin[55]/[n] related to Nietzsche only by contrast—through its "healthy, clear climate" of scientific objectivity.[56] Between times she tosses off *Im Kampf um Gott* so as to acquire a residence permit as authoress by way of resisting forcible repatriation.[57]/[o] Rée takes a room apart because of his early schedule as a medical student.[58] Then, "misunderstanding" her betrothal,[59] he relapses into the suicidal melancholia out of which her friendship had lifted him.[60] In due course he moves "back to Celerina," there to fall to his death.[61]

Upon Gillot's death in 1916 Lou had at long last rendered the earlier of his two imaginary proposals to her—the *Ruth* one rather than the "Ein Wiedersehen" one—nonfictional[p] in a diary passage about how she had defended against noticing the amorous undertone in his voice until, "first, I unconsciously needed it as a 'pretext for a break,' for emancipation, and, second, it was at the same time nullified through the marriage endeavors. . . . Perhaps I most idealized him in the unconscious perception of that very tone, so that the proposal paled him in its decorousness even more than in signifying his wish to bind me fast."[62] Thus the undertone was retroactively relegated to her unconscious, where "the marriage endeavors" did nullify it for purposes of written reminiscence. For that tone was the only nonfictional expression ever given by her on paper to Gillot's putative low designs on her, though after her Jena outburst she went on indulging these orally just as she did Nietzsche's. In fact she confined the Gillot as against the Nietzsche proposal to paper until it had taken final shape in her memoirs.[q]

---

[m] Basel draft: four.

[n] She gave a putative short membership list actually overlong: 1931a:112.

[o] Similarly, on lending her copy to the Göttingen librarian at about this time she alleged concerning "the miserable concoction" that "I am ashamed to send it: at the time it served merely to enable me to complete my studies abroad; it was deliberately thrown together as nothing else by me ever was" (Lou→Selle [early 1930's]).

[p] Cf. above, p. 281 (in 1900 she was tending rather toward the "Wiedersehen" one, which presupposed that there had been none prior).

[q] *Franz Schoenberner (categorically): Lou's oral version of her Gillot experience excluded, indeed *pre*cluded, the proposal. Perhaps coincidentally,

Through its final shape, its point of departure—Gillot's letter to Rome calling her to order in accord with her mother—was visible: ". . . my enduring childlikeness—due to northerly-late bodily development—had obliged him to withhold from me at first that he had already undertaken the familiar preliminaries to a union between us. As, unexpectedly, the decisive moment required me to bring heaven down to earth, I refused"[63]—the *Ruth* finale with, however, a blank in lieu of those specifications of time and place which had proclaimed the fiction such. She improved on *Aus fremder Seele* for the prior romance in that she claimed to have not just inspired his preaching, but prepared sermons that he delivered without even looking them over first.[64] As in "Gottesschöpfung," she was confirmed by him in Holland at his suggestion "before my departure for Zurich" just so as to qualify for a passport of her own.[65] Correspondingly, she distanced her refusal to be confirmed by Dalton from her "love experience." It was, she maintained, "an instinctual *must* not amenable to reason"—one supposedly deriving, however, from loyalty to her dead god.[66] At least she allowed that there was "no fanaticism for truth" to it after all[67]—a concession to Nietzsche fifty years overdue.

The postponement of her confirmation as her father lay dying became a postponement of her "exit from the church" then already intended[68/r]: thus her Lutheran protest against a catechism interposed between the worshipper and God was set back before her father's death, which had in reality been the cue for it.[s] She displaced her god's disappearance in turn so far back into her childhood that the memory of her consequent "struggles of faith"[69] was supposedly long since dormant in the depths when the catechism stirred it. And it supposedly revived in full only after she turned up "a crinkled old scrap of paper" containing some verse "scribbled" in Finland one midsummer night in the thick of her godforsakenness[70]: that same "verselet come back to me" out of the Rongas "moss and seaweed" in 1900[t]— improved. However, not only had she told about her "struggles of faith" already in 1882 from Rome to Tautenburg: the verse could not have been written as late as the summer of 1877 if its mood was to be

---

the literary record affords the same interval between fictional and nonfictional versions of the proposal for Gillot as for Nietzsche before him (respectively 1894-1895 to 1916 and 1883-1884 to 1905).

[r] Bäumer, *Gestalt*, 480, quotes her in oldest age to the effect that, by a happy accident, her parents' change of residence had spared her the need to be confirmed!

[s] However, she gave her age correctly as seventeen at the time of the protest (1931a:24) and even as sixteen (a year too young) at her father's death (*ibid.*, 56).

[t] See above, p. 280.

immemorial the following winter, when her catechism began, or as early as the summer of 1877 given the relative infantility of her "An die Winne," composed the previous winter. Besides, the Salomés' summer of 1879 in Finland was a novelty. *This*, then, was the summer of the original "verselet" (if there was an original)—in which case the mourning was the one then attending her issueless love for Gillot, and her "God-experience" had remained uninterruptedly actual. In terminating her "God-experience" earlier and earlier over the years, she was aiming at having left it behind her at birth—to be resumed after death.

Concerning that birth, her father "passionately wished for a little girl, whereas Mushka would have preferred completing the masculine half dozen"[71]—for those two dead brothers of hers by Freud were now autobiographic.[u] Her father now flirted with her behind her mother's back during her childhood. Yet her mother emerged as the heart and soul of her whole rich "family experience": her mother who, while privately grieving over her youthful licence, yet stood by her "unswervingly" before all the world.[72] Under her father's influence she would have gone Narodnika except that Gillot "de-Russified" her[73]—whereas in her Russian diary he had attracted her just because of his Western orientation.[v] The song of her homeland now sounded anew in tune with her love song for Rainer. Rainer moreover shared honors with the Russians for having predisposed her to Freudianism given his "soul's destiny extraordinary and rare" and their "immediately self-disclosing inwardness"[74]—only not the expectation aroused by him in Russia that his might be "a fate like, say, Garshin's."[w] Her "gateway to Russia" with Rainer was of course Tolstoi: to epitomize their second passage through it she depicted "a brief stroll taken by the three of us" as dominated by Tolstoi's forget-me-nots routine and that Yasnaya pilgrim discovered by her in 1913.[75] Perhaps Rainer's fit following her original epitomization had its share in prompting the projection that followed this one: "Perhaps this hour had its share in prompting Rainer's exaggeration of looking hopefully to every little peasant along his way as to a possible union of simplicity and profundity."[76]

By and large, Lou treated other celebrities just like Tolstoi in not letting on how well or ill she knew them and as if her knowing them were a matter of course—though in fact she ransacked her "Celebrities" file to compile two chapters teeming with them. Typically,

[u] As the first- and fourth-born (grown up since "Geschwister" from the two last-born): 1931a:51.
[v] Cf. above, p. 18.   [w] See above, p. 299.

Strindberg and Hauptmann answered together to a roll call of her suburban neighbors.[77] Harden turned up in Stanislavsky's wings with the rider: "In those days we understood each other at all times, but during the World War I became wholly estranged from him."[78] Her Paris was as much Hermann Bang as Frank Wedekind,[79] with unrenowned Goldmann nowhere in sight. Eduard Keyserling meant most to her in old Munich.[80] Schnitzler dominated her old Vienna even if "later I was potently diverted from him in another direction"[81]: Beer-Hofmann was named only as one of Schnitzler's cronies, and the cult of "the *merely* sweet girl" became Vienna's generally and Schnitzler's specifically[82]—whereupon hermaphroditic Peter Altenberg took over. Another noncelebrity, Zemek came in as simply the "friend" with whom Lou hiked one summer from Vienna to Venice.[83/x]

Before completing her *Grundriss,* Lou began proposing it for publication. "Recently something happened," she mysteriously told Freud, "which will presumably necessitate bringing it out now and not, as I half wished, only after my death (on account of the rectifications concerning Nietzsche and other matters)"[84/y]; Freud replied that his press was out of business. Schoenberner found the work trying,[85] while Lulu von Strauss, widow of Eugen Diederichs and head of his publishing firm, merely complimented its technique.[86] In 1933, having designated it "my *opus posthumus*"[87/z] after all, Lou wrote a first supplement intended to appear "only some time afterwards,"[88] promisingly titled "Was am 'Grundriss' fehlt" (What is Missing From the *Outline*). In it she disclosed that hers had been a sham marriage—only to penalize Andreas for her candor. To his side of the courtship she imputed that insuperable inner dictate[89] avowed on her side in her diary for 1888.[a] She claimed to have yielded to his moral "coercion"[90] culminating in an attempted suicide[91/b]—modeled on Stefan's in "Geschwister."[c] She alleged that even so she consented to marriage in name only, Andreas willing for a start[92]—whereby she diminished the guilt assumed toward Rée in this same context.[93] She put roughly her own words of 1888 about the impossibility of divorce into Andreas's mouth: "I cannot help *knowing* that you are my wife."[94/d] She even put him up to attempting to rape her in her sleep so that she woke

---

[x] "By foot," "foot trip" (ditto Lou→EK, 20 I 1903).

[y] She was evidently alluding to Podach: below, p. 479 and n. *c.*

[z] That is, it was to appear "*als mein Nachlass.*"

[a] See above, p. 135.

[b] "On the eve of our betrothal."

[c] Compare 1933a:260 with 1919g:57-58 ("the doctor intimated to Wienchen that, what with present-day cardiosurgical techniques and the like, death from hemorrhage was not absolutely unavoidable").

[d] Cf. above, p. 142.

up choking him—this being her reverie of "Vor dem Erwachen," bedeviled.[e] She also told of that turning point in her marriage, her love for Ledebour—or rather his for her, since she insisted that any reciprocation on her part was strictly unconscious.[95] She dated their first encounter after his term in prison, with a complex anecdote to match.[96] As for their last, she broke with him to oblige Andreas,[97] who "wanted to stab him but not speak to him."[98] "Many travels followed," she added suggestively[99]—and wondered in compensation: "Who could have thought with what ardor I at all times of my life would have wished my husband . . . the nicest, best, most beautiful mistress?"[100] She left her marital difficulties only to explain away Andreas's scholarly unproductiveness again.[101]

A year or so later she added a new confession beginning: "April, *our* month, Rainer—the month before the one that brought us together"[102]—which makes no other sense than that she met Nietzsche in April. "If I was your wife for years, that was because to me you were something unprecedentedly real, body and person inseparably one"[103]; "we became spouses even before we became friends, which we became hardly by choice but likewise out of a wedding subterraneanly consummated"[104]; "we were siblings, as in olden times before sibling marriage became sacrilege"[105/f]—not quite as in her "last call," according to which "in Wolfratshausen I came to you as a mother."[106] She wilily intimated that he was her first lover,[g] perhaps her *only* one[h]: out of boudoir snobbery she had not so much as named a lesser lover, unless it was Volinsky "of evil memory" in the context of her Rainer and Russia experiences.[107] Serene and timeless, this April romance was insofar a replica of the one in her Nietzsche book, with, however, a full fleshly complement to the spirituality. It ran its extrinsic, terrestrial course through that "inexpressibly cheery

---

[e] It was fictionally semibedeviled in "Abteilung" (where the seducer gets murdered for his pains), "Unterwegs" (where the "Sleeping Beauty" reminiscence prefaces an involuntary murder—that of a farm-hand), and especially "Vaters Kind" (where the murderous rage was displaced onto the father). Wedekind's hapless play for Lou, assimilated to Andreas's, touched it off: see above, p. 185 n. *x*. Schnitzler's diary, 16 XII 1895: "Lou here. Talk about love, how she almost choked her husband" (cf. above, p. 197 n. *l*). *Ellen Delp: Lou's 1933a version departed markedly from her prior oral one.

[f] Cf. 1893a:169, which mocks a couple in Strindberg's *The Creditors* who "play at little brother and sister" so as to mask the simple sensual reality.

[g] 1934e:173: "that stillness and naturalness that joined us . . ."; 1933a:269-70: "love met me beneath a great stillness and naturalness . . ."

[h] Of itself, "Was am 'Grundriss' fehlt" suggests rather a turnover of lovers, though faintly as against her diaries; "April . . ." seems to have superseded it in tending to represent Rilke as a one-and-only, Lou not having lived long enough for this tendency to prevail retroactively.

vacation time,"[108] the summer of 1900, when the lovers lived Russia together in a unison such as "could have been depicted to no one"[109/i] —least of all herself at the time. In or around Kiev "our innocent laughter ceased" at the first premonitory symptoms of Rainer's nervous disorder,[110/j] which came of the tension between his intense hymnic experience and his meager poetic means. To develop these latter, he needed to exchange the cradle that was Lou for the world of man. This "urgent necessity" was first recognized by her in Finland. "I was there—altogether briefly—to visit my family . . . when your letter reached me describing you as almost abject because of the presumption in your prayers"[111]—after two weeks alone in Petersburg without word from her. So she sent the neurotic homunculus packing? Well . . . "Never did you stand before me greater and more admired: your inner complications drew me to you with a ravishment that never abated. Now haste was needed for you to enter free and clear upon the development still before you. And yet—and yet: did they not also draw me away from you? from your realness as of those beginnings in which we had been as if of a single mold. Who fathoms the darkness of ultimate mutual nearness and farness! In ardent, grieving nearness I yet stood outside of that which links man and wife—and never again did that change for me, untouchably cut off from that which remained to grow on into your, into my dying hour. I mean to palliate nothing. My head bowed in my hands, I often grappled for understanding . . ."[112/k] Of Clara, no trace.

Delivering Rainer up to the world, to life and to death, to his fearsome poetic fate, Lou was both bearing and sacrificing him in her best Marian manner, after the fictional precedent set in *Das Haus* as revised. That haste to dispatch him, originally manifest as haste to deliver "Witalii," reechoed Nietzsche's "big hurry" to dispatch her[l] (and, as she now unconsciously construed it, deliver *Zarathustra*[m]). "With the separation of our residences went the requisite pledge not to sustain in writing our absolute habituation to sharing everything with each other—*unless in some hour of highest need*."[113] Highest

---

[i] Cf. 1931a:149: "what happened there happened ever and again to *us*"; *ibid.*, 85: "conjoint experience"; etc. The *Ródinka* revisions fictionally preelaborated Lou's Russian romance with Rilke.

[j] Perhaps faintly anticipated by 1934e:175: "the gush of your letters daily pursuing me" from Wolfratshausen in IX 1897 (in fact his two extant, relatively sober letters from Wolfratshausen to Hallein were obviously within a card or telegram of that whole epistolary story).

[k] Conversely, Rainer's sacrifice of her was the latent sense of 1919a:366 (below, p. 499 n. *w*).

[l] See above, pp. 293 and 417ff.

[m] Between the lines of 1931a:104.

need befell Rainer in Rodin's workshop, whereupon "the occasion for our first reunion" was the manuscript left in Lou's hands[114]—with no time out for his two years of supplication.[n] "Rainer, this was our Whitsun, 1905," and "to me it was like an ascension of the poetry over the poet. . . . My heart stood still as something in me hailed the Elegies unborn for decades to come"—and vindicated her *no* to his psychoanalysis. "In this I became yours again after a second fashion —in a second maidenhood."[115] Ah, me! Elsewhere in her memoirs she had already specified that at their every reunion thereafter they felt "almost as if secret, imaginary correspondence had abrogated the foregoing separation"[116]—1906-1909 presumably included. She owed it to herself and him to make up for her injustice to him during the decade following 1900; instead she made believe there had been none. In the final reckoning Rilke occupied over a fourth of her text, leaving less than a tenth to his closest contender.

That contender was Freud, on whom a brief personal memorandum followed in about another year's time—a truest tissue of falsities big and small. It begins with Freud laughing at her in Weimar "for my zeal about wanting to learn his psychoanalysis,"[117] whereas in actuality he interpreted her presence in Weimar "as a propitious omen" of future interest.[118] "As I then, after a half year of autodidactic study, arrived at Freud's in Vienna, he laughed even more heartily at me in my innocence, for I told him of wanting to work also with Alfred Adler, who had meanwhile turned into his mortal enemy"[119]: it was more than twice "a half year," besides which she was all too privy to the enmity and remiss about informing Freud of her traffic with the enemy. Trebor-like, Freud "good-naturedly" enjoins discretion on both fronts, and "this condition was so well fulfilled that it was months before Freud learned of my break with Adler's study group"[120]—in fact because she neglected to break with it all those months. From Vienna the scene shifts to Tegel in 1928, with Freud gathering an autumnal bouquet for her "before one of our almost daily excursions to Berlin"[121]—though in fact they were in Tegel in March 1929, and she paid him "two visits" there, presumably indoors.[122] They chat away as at all their prior reunions—whereas in reality Freud, too deaf to make out her hushed voice, left the conversation to Anna.[123/o] "On such occasions we often spoke of 1912, my psychoanalytical study year, when I had to leave word of my momentary whereabouts behind in my hotel at all times so as, should Freud come into any free time, to be able to reach him as

[n] Elsewhere—1931a:224-25—Lou managed to work her 1904 Copenhagen postcard prank into a context of abiding oneness with Rilke.

[o] See above, p. 376.

quickly as possible wherever I might be"[124]: her fantasy analysis by Freud, relentlessly pushed by *him!*[p] Arriving for one such session, she finds him reading her "Hymn to Life" in Nietzsche's version, which he promptly slams shut, exclaiming that a good cold would cure him of such life-loving foolishness: thus she arrived early for that Sunday visit of 1913 when, as she then gathered, "he must just have read" the hymn.[125/q] In Tegel the two reminisce about that conversation, whereupon she irrepressibly bursts into tears over his "martyrdom" in the manner of her hymn. "Freud made no reply. I only felt his arm around me"[126]—around the martyr's angel of Orta. Lou's protonarcissistic indifference to return love had lapsed.[r] And her dream of a protonarcissistic revival in old age had come climactically untrue, for her inner dissension was as great as the discrepancy between her memoirs and the memories behind them.

In "a bit of autobiographical scribbling" probably also of 1935 and probably her last, Lou reclaimed—at a close remove—that "fanaticism for truth" which she had lately disavowed in connection with her insistence on being confirmed by Gillot. At long last, she scribbled, it was clear to her why she had rused to bring Gillot to Holland to bless her marriage "without an instant's thought" for how he felt: "probity compulsion"! and fidelity too, for "one can hardly imagine a faith greater than one persisting beyond all personal, passionate experience into most vital decisions so that they must be sanctioned by him who replaced one's childhood god." To be sure, she pursued, she was using Gillot for purposes no longer felt by him to be his own, but "at bottom an identity of 'he' and 'I' remains, and nothing stronger can be said of any love." To live out of such a fundament, she concluded, was "practical prayer" indicating that piety lay at the "start and finish of our humanity."[127]

Lou purged and trimmed her literary estate in the sense of her memoirs,[s] if with some telltale inefficiency. Her Gillot affair and her first years of marriage were hardest hit in the end: merest scraps

[p] This fantasy was already half presaged nonfictionally in 1926a:12 (on the benefits of analysis to "the analyst himself, whom Freud warned way back that one could come no farther with anyone else than one has come with oneself") and 1931a:199-200 ("not for nothing does depth psychology require that he who would analyze others should first have subjected himself to the exigencies of its method"—the upper half of her message here being her self-analysis hoax, maintained collaterally to the last: below, pp. 488-89).

[q] Cf. above, pp. 385, 394.

[r] Already somewhat in Lou→Freud [5? IV 1931] (exultation over some foregoing words of affection from Freud).

[s] *Mrs. Maria Apel: Lou destroyed "much" on each of "several occasions" in the 1930's.

survive.[t] And of her great men, Nietzsche lost out most: gone are his messages to her in Bayreuth except for the close of his reinvitation to Tautenburg (". . . I am suffering too much for having made you suffer . . ."),[u] and those to her and Rée in Berlin except for the beginning of his opium letter (". . . I am sick in the head, a semilunatic . . .").[v] She kept the most precious portion of the rich residue in her bank safe. But whenever she left Göttingen for any length, she would take Nietzsche's letters along: Franz Schoenberner recollects that, on arriving in Munich, she would not let them out of her hands until she was safely at home with him.[128]

Schoenberner was for ages heir designate to Lou's literary estate; however, he became editor-in-chief of the anti-Nazi satirical journal *Simplicissimus* in 1929, then slipped across the Swiss border in March 1933, thus opening the problem of succession at Loufried. Thereupon as if by enchantment Sasha's youngest son, Kolia (Conrad), an emigrant since the civil war, turned up in Göttingen, stateless and penniless. Lou adopted him and, with all her spare capital, set him up as book dealer; his deals fast fell through,[129] though, and he grew so importunate that in time she sought to undo the adoption.[130] Meanwhile a sometime student with income from an East Prussian estate, Ernst Pfeiffer, who had consulted Lou once in the fall of 1931 "on account of a sick friend of his"[131] quite possibly himself, revisited her opportunely on July 10, 1933. Lou called this "an exceedingly important day for me" at the start of a retrospect on 1933, which proceeded with a reminder of her diary piece on Rainer's apparition of twenty years earlier: "of a sudden Pf. was standing before our garden gate."[132] Freud learned from Lou's next birthday letter of this second "splendid acquisition" of hers: "He is a Kleist researcher, yet 'wholly without office or honors,' of peasant stock and likewise a war

---

[t] As far as I know, that is: see below, pp. 557ff. (Toward the last Lou evidently gave a Göttingen "daughter" her Gillot letters to read: Peters, 292.) As regards her diaries specifically, the post-Tautenburg, premarital ones were equally hard hit.

[u] See above, p. 76.

[v] See above, p. 99 (see also above, p. 158 and n. *k*). Rilke took his heaviest toll for 1897-1901 (and took it after 1928: cf. Pfeiffer, *Briefwechsel*, 33n. and 516); his likely letter of late XII 1906 on Clara is also missing. Freud came through virtually intact: even his shocker on Tausk's suicide survives (though not its likely successor). On Hauptmann there exists a late-life notation of Lou's to the effect that she could no longer locate his letters to her except for a paltry few—which, as far as I can tell (see below, pp. 557-60), are the full set. As to the "large correspondence with Tolstoi, Wagner . . ." about which she told Schoenberner (Schoenberner, 44), she must have destroyed it by error.

casualty physically (in his early forties). I find it nice of life to have sent me something so select in companionship even this late."[133] She talked Kleist with him, psychoanalyzed him to the extent of eliciting a colossal transference, and initiated him into her paper world. By the end of 1934 the estate was his "to own and administer" after her death[134]/w on the understanding that he would make it available "to posterity"[x]—a condition presaged in her retrospect on 1933 by a passage about the joys of writing for oneself alone.[135]

"How glorious your work together with your friend must be," Helene once remarked,[136] and again: "Yes, to 'remain preserved, laid out in state,' as you write, a little while longer in another, beloved person when one has shut one's eyes, that is lovely!"[137] There is something at once grandiose and dreadful about old Lou meticulously preparing to meet posterity—about her daily closed sessions with an heir and successor charged with propagating her life's myth on a documentary basis narrowed between times by obliteration and incineration. It was a personalized parody of Nietzsche's intended use of *her*, besides being, in her words on Nietzsche's last productive period, "the mystery of a prodigious self-apotheosis."[138] For by then her impersonation of Nietzsche nearing madness as in her Nietzsche book was strikingly close, beginning with her commitment to the supposed aim of his "optimism" and "religious exaltation"[139]: reciprocal absorption of self and world, anticipated through his sneaking suspicion that "in his essential unity with life's fullness" he was authoring the world divinely and deathlessly.[140] Or perhaps beginning rather with her "frightful leap"[141] into the sandals of Narcissus, her ideal self-image, whose cult she celebrated in the very terms she had earlier employed to disparage Nietzsche's alleged Dionysian cult of himself ("the world of emotional impulses" as "source for a new valuation and estimation of all things,"[142] and so forth[y]). Her own leap is,

---

[w] Lou's will read: "My literary estate I have already given away." She kept her diaries in her bank safe to the last, however, and gave her calendars to Mariechen.

[x] Herbert Bayer (Pfeiffer's lawyer)→Maria Apel, 14 v 1937 (claiming the diaries left in the bank safe).

[y] See above, pp. 152-53, and further 1890a:173 (paraphrasing the late Nietzsche): "Torn from the plain unity of his original animal consciousness through the development of his mental faculties, man has come into conflict with the natural soil in which his strength has its roots . . ."—or Nietzsche himself (*Twilight*: "What I Owe to the Ancients," 4): "What did the Hellene vouch for with these [Dionysian] mysteries? Eternal life, the eternal return of life; the future promised and consecrated in the past; the triumphant yea to life beyond death and beyond change; *true* life as collective survival through propagation, through the mysteries of sex. Hence the *sexual* symbol was to the Greeks the venerable symbol in itself, the deep sense of all ancient piety. Every

incidentally, no easier to date than was his, since she felt a premonitory kinship with her Narcissus from the first just as did her Nietzsche with his overman—and her Jesus the Jew with the Messiah prophesied by him. She had a book of revelation behind her, *Der Teufel und seine Grossmutter*, to match Nietzsche's *Zarathustra*, and now a posthumous "Ecce Mulier" ahead of her to match his posthumous *Ecce Homo*. She meanwhile continued to treat of his madness as psychogenic, indeed as that same old mental split "into all-sufferer and all-dominator—God."[143/z] She paid him the one big tribute of having made psychoanalysis possible by opening up the investigation of thought as instinctual[144]—meaning her reductionism. She quoted him continually, even without quotation marks (especially "a sign language of the affects," "even virtues are avenged," and "only where there are graves are there resurrections"). At Freud's mention of the Roman moon she remarked: "It is especially memorable to me from 1882 and my first walks with Nietzsche, whose presence solemnized the antiquities in every which way."[145/a] Off paper she would nonetheless scream at the sound of Nietzsche's name: "For me, he is *dead!*"[146/b]

With Schoenberner's help, the anti-Nietzsche scholar Erich Podach won her confidence in 1931 to the extent of obtaining the use of her Nietzsche documents for a monograph on Nietzsche and herself.[147/c] With Podach she once even sent greetings to Ida Overbeck[148]—fifty years after. All went smoothly until, as Podach put it to Schoenberner, "she delivered herself and us up to Pfeiffer."[149/d] In 1934 Freud asked whether she might not be willing to spare some advice for "a dear friend, Arnold Zweig," then planning a work on Nietz-

---

particular of the procreative act, of pregnancy, of birth, aroused the most lofty, solemn feelings. In the mystery teachings, *pain* is pronounced holy: 'birth pains' hallow pain . . . procreation as the *holy* way . . ."

[z] Cf. 1929a:62-63 on the "eternal return" as the way to self-deification for him who could stand such monotony in all eternity, and on Nietzsche as having had "to preach nothingness at the last in order thereby to shout it down": cleverest old misconstruals.

[a] Likely she never saw Nietzsche—as against Rée—by moonlight in Rome.

[b] Cf. Pfeiffer, *Leben*, 280: Lou "once wondered in old age whether she could not think him out of her life."

[c] Lou→Freud, 22 v 1932, mentions forthcoming "publications (not mine) that mean to work out the Nietzsche business with the documents in a purely scholarly fashion."

[d] Podach brought out his *FN und LS* upon her death (Lou→Schoenberner, 25 v 1933: "he is so infinitely slow"). It ingenuously honored her fables (except for Gillot's proposal: maybe Podach did not read that part of her memoirs) *and* Lisbeth's forgeries, at Nietzsche's expense—with, however, a nice documentary appendix (to Pfeiffer's annoyance).

sche.[150] "Participation would be *utterly un*thinkable for me," she replied, "even were it ever so slight or lax! For me that is something untouchable. Please tell this to the party concerned most emphatically and for good and all."[151] Lisbeth on her side kept after Lou to the sour end: as of Weimar 1935, Lou had offered Nietzsche secretarial assistance so as to attract his attention, only to learn from the Overbecks that he was a second-rater and exclaim: " 'What! Not famous? not great?' As she saw it, she had troubled to no purpose,"[152] hence she set about calumniating him. After Lisbeth's death, her successors obtained Lou's consent in 1936 to integral publication of the Nietzsche material in Göttingen on the "precondition" that they repudiate Lisbeth's "tendencies" and "testimony. A public declaration in this sense ensued."[153] Lou had won out—as far as she ever knew.

A T F O R T Y Lou had looked forward to senescence as to a fulfillment.[154] At forty-one she had considered: "Perhaps in old age one reattains to a half dreamlike view of things such as belongs to childhood and substantially lightens the pressure of life."[155] And at forty-two she had reflected on the subsidence of erotism: "It is just as strong a renewal of life as puberty: and at the same time a reconquest of the land of our childhood, which spread out well beyond love."[156] Twenty years later she was wavering: "Who would not often like to get out along the way, before old age unhitches the wagon; but again, who would want to forego seeing the shores of his childhood again?"[157] Similarly: "One overflows in positive joy after having long garnered the world thinkingly and lovingly (as it were, nest-building); on the other hand, long experience teaches displeasure with oneself."[158] She added: "It teaches reducing to essentials"[159]— and two years later gave this as her reason for "feeling grateful not to have died young (as if early diers were indeed, as the ready quote runs, the gods' darlings, but were not life's). At the same time, to be sure, purely personal and physical troubles multiply . . ."[160] In another two years she described herself to Freud as "all eagerness about the surprises still in store for me from the wonder packet 'life' "[161] and, in receipt of his low-keyed rejoinder, insisted that as between potency and its aftermath she "truthfully" knew not which she would choose: "For one leaves the narrower erotic life behind like a grand but blind alley with room for just two and enters upon indescribable breadth—to which childhood belonged too, and which we had to forget just awhile. Through our ever more acute and conscious self-differentiation from everything, canceled only temporarily by means of specially constructed vital bridges, we have lost our primal oneness with so much of what made childhood rich, and wise in all its foolishness, and somehow superior. One believes oneself to be reliving something of this—only *something*—and yet by way of compensation to be sated with experience. . . . One finds nests everywhere, lays eggs everywhere, grows continually lighter, and finally flies away. Wherein the body, which in youth helped build the love bridges, is ever more of a hindrance at the last as the outer piece of us: to the devil with it."[162] And she remarked at seventy-three that, as it takes so long to turn the world into "inner experience, . . . it is really good to grow awfully old, despite the less pleasant other side to it. . . . And since so-called life, from youth on, is replete with nuisances, this contradiction of its bestowing a bonus on us through its length so that we shouldn't complain of it too bitterly is almost consoling."[163]

Almost; for the rest, her body overcompensated for its extra long youthfulness. On leaving the clinic in 1930, she was "a heap of pain."[164] As the pain eased over the months, she went back from 100 to 125 pounds[165] even on a limited calorie diet—one permitting her chocolate at night in lieu of bread by day. By mid-1931 she declared herelf "as well as can be wished: gobble what I may like a good girl and am fresh."[166] Later that year she was laid up in plaster with a broken foot. Her proud calligraphy was reduced to a pencil scrawl— as during her prostration of two years before, only this time definitively, for her eyesight was failing. She feared blindness through the insulin treatment for diabetes[167]—and not idly, for at about this time she forcibly ejected a pastor who called at Loufried some weeks after she had quarreled with a different one.[168] Late in 1932 she was obliged to "lie flat as an ironing board" because of "a slight kidney irritation."[169] Another year or so and her chronic heart ailment had set in for the duration,[170] followed by cancer in a breast that was successfully amputated in mid-1935 after she had put her papers in final order and taken leave of the world. And by uremia.

By then Lou was—off the record—torn between renewed temptations to suicide[171] and her fear of death, grown downright "fearful."[172/e] If her official life-loving did not obviate the temptations, neither was the fear palliated by her denials of death dating from that tricky metaphor of 1901 about our stepping back as artists of life to view our completed work[f]—reformulated thirty years later with *us* as *life*'s work of art.[173] Orally she specified in old age: "Come what may, I never lose the certitude that arms are open behind me to receive me."[174] Only for want of such certitude was it her "favorite thought" after 1900 that the individuation leading out of childhood is reversed in old age[175]—but the sudden, full realization that "we die" did not come to her without the escape clause that this very realization "deepens living together forever."[176] Variants of her favorite thought were that it takes a whole lifetime to learn the simplest things "just as if death intervened only so that we might—apply this lesson,"[177] that "what may make it hard to die is no longer lov-

---

e *Mrs. Maria Apel: Lou primarily feared the physical aspect of death.
f See above, p. 303.

ing: love alone joins death and life (shows them to be one),"[178] that if "in the midst of life we are enclosed by death," as the verse ran, so "also vice versa,"[179] that the end term of aging was self-renewal through "upheaval (and this were life's crown, with death merely its bodily symbol),"[180] and that to crave solitude as she did "means nothing other than to be nowhere alone, not even when dead."[181] At seventy-five she declared that, all our rationality notwithstanding, "deep, deep inside us something lies hidden that mutely excepts itself, *feels* itself excepted" from mortality.[182/g] Nor can her writing have resumed in her late years devoid of its aboriginal purpose of warding off death,[h] for all its posthumous orientation.

In April 1933, Lou's memoirs led her beyond themselves into "an almost incomprehensibly good spell of work that just swished along as I snatched at it with joy. (Perhaps it is the strongest joy," she reflected that May—"at least next to spring, which is spread about so gloriously as if there were no darkness.)"[183/i] The matter was "all old stuff" long since "on its way to me"[184]: she conjoined "Jutta" with "Geschwister" to make an incongruous literary hybrid, "which gave me great fun,"[185] then rewrote that "age-old fairy play" *Die Tarn-kappe* when it "of a sudden presented itself as not in the least a fairy thing but a real dramatic occurrence"[186]! The last of 1933, forgetting that she had outgrown Eros, she committed "Am Krötenteich" (At the Toad Pond), a trashy tale in which an elderly widow, alone on a holiday from sorting her late husband's papers, encounters a young naturalist who, at the sound of toads mating, tells her that he has dreaded sex ever since, in his boyhood, a housemaid died in her bed beside him and he simply stole away. That night, as the widow lies half hoping, a "presence" materializes in the dark, "and as it enfolded her in its arms she named it with the last of her dwindling consciousness: death." At dawn it departs, crying: "Morning of life!" She wakes, veils the mirror lest the ex-presence magically glimpse her aged face in it, and wonders whether he is asking himself: "Have I not murdered after all?" Then she leans out to the blossoming foliage beneath her window, her back to the mirror, smiling faintly. "Am

---

[g] ". . . as if a fist were raised in the face of reason"—though in fact, as far as *reason* went, her own mortality remained to be proven.

[h] See above, p. 11.

[i] Similarly, Lou→Schoenberner, 15 v 1933: "Astonishingly, I have never worked so splendidly well as since April, maybe just because without printing possibilities"—an allusion to Nazism (cf. Lou→Schoenberner, 25 v 1933, and 1934a) not wholly plausible since fiction only was involved and since she expected the *Grundriss* (with its many Jews in honor) to be published upon her death (Lou→Hanna, 2 xii 1934).

Krötenteich" was signed on New Year's Eve 1933, the day before the presence rematerialized at the garden gate in nonfictional retrospect.

A few retrospective lines more that New Year's Day and Lou was celebrating her literary "reunion with myself" ("after some twenty years"!) in the first of some new informal essaylets lengthier and more discursive than the old ones. This first one went on to contrast the psychologist Ludwig Klages' abstinent bisexuality with her own perverse genitality by dint of which "the draught from the chalice" was her first taste of a given lover—who always "fell out of existence" at that even before the chalice was empty, since in orgasm she was "good" to herself alone.[187] Then came one on Kleist, "last truly great German literary genius," precursor of psychoanalysis through his "mental investigation of actually experienced sensory facts not for the sake of 'art' but for the dual purpose of *pure* science and *personal* therapy," whose seeming mother-fixation was really a womb-fixation and who inserted Kantian judgments of experience as a damper between his impulsive self and hostile reality.[188] According to the next one, Goethe's art was incidental to his experience, whereas Kleist's was "*absolute*," was "the *other* way into another reality, not just some substitute way into our residual reality or some correction or adornment or reparation of it"—and, because his other reality was not here and now, "he went away."[189]

Next Lou sought to envisage the human species when in due course it will have growing up down pat. The individual will not notice his soul, but will only extrospect. He will know none of our mortal troubles such as the tension between our inner and outer lives (what with our experiencing things first outwardly in their time, then inwardly in ours) or our mounting distress at our lengthening past and dwindling future (our watching life come till middle age, then watching it go). And she added that her own reward from old age with all its ills was an ever-increasing "presentness" as the future elapsed.[190] Next she took the "creaturely commonplace" that our individual existence only gradually emerges from our parents' existence as a cue for considering anew that we humans tend to lose the sense of how "all existence streams together" and to assert our own existence as alone "fully real" over against the rest. And yet, she pursued, our bodies continually pass over into externality if we would feel identical with them, just as they keep intruding upon our selves if we would decorporealize these. "And our consciousness itself? With all its sharp senses and wits, what is it up against more surely than its mere medial position between inner and outer stimuli impinging upon it, amid which it strives to orient and protect itself—far less as their overlord than as their alien subject?" He feels most self-reliant who draws his animus most directly from "the common subsoil of all Being," although on the summits of most personal enjoyment and enthusiasm we all "simply forget that *we* are the great enjoyers, enthusiasts." All metaphysics, ethics, religion is attuned to our recessive awareness of that common subsoil—an awareness which, however, attains to pure, immediate expression only in bold, naïve, self-seeking prayer, "as if to legitimate its drastic wishfulness." Whoever rejects devotion because of its wishful aspect (read: Freud) "deprives himself of the inclusion and exultation in life that is operant within him too and is merely overlain by his ego-consciousness." A problem remains: "that we cannot, for all our selfhood, help identifying this with the more that underlies it. That is: an identity of self-love, self-assurance, *and* devotion—of what is passive in us as alone fully capable of action. Antithetical as these two may seem, they yet converge in our inner attitude: the more egoistic, the less egoistically grounded. In other words: we look upon the ground beneath us as a vault above us"[191] —topsy-turvy.

In her next essaylet, Lou treated of herself outright: as a "psychotic type" and thence "repressionless"—in contrast to Rainer, with whom her "oneness" was consequently only of the deepest. To Rainer, a sudden eruption of repressed infantile material beyond what he could control poetically was "hell." She, however, found it "a sobriety of sorts" to take the stuff of her wishes and dreams for primordial reality just as in her fantasy-ridden childhood.[j] For her lifelong blissful, guiltless imperviousness to the world's judgment she had, she now realized, this "sobriety" to thank and not her permissive childhood god: "on the contrary, his constitution, childlike-reckless, was given by the very audacity with which I created him for myself out of what seemed to me most desirably real and so was indubitable." Likewise, she had perhaps chalked up too much in her life to femininity: her dread of "absolute duration" even in erotic experience now seemed to her rather "a stoppage of elemental breakthrough as a result of its very intensity." She had felt "reverence" for a lover only after bringing him back into steady focus following a moment's passionately contorted view of him. In such warm, neutral perspective alone, as before God's leveling glance, are things ours at large and we theirs; hence any breach in its continuity "so diminishes us that we become

[j] This is unequivocally put (with reference to her *Grundriss* at that)—yet was meant not as a warning against her self-accounting, but as a warrant for its candor.

unsure of our warmth toward ourselves—an alarming symptom. And yet I candidly acknowledge how prone I am to overstate my case here: for somehow (rightly or wrongly) only the convergence of aspirations to communal feeling and to mental clarity comes naturally to me," whence she had ever striven to feel her thoughts and think her feelings. Once Freud had called this unfeminine of her: "to my objection that nothing awakened such tempestuous gratitude in me as someone's power of making me love him, absolutize him as glorious above all, however briefly,[k] Freud replied with his subtle smile: 'Of course, your sort requires being made to love even more than being loved, and that's just what's unfeminine—for do you know what it comes down to? Coldness.' The reply perplexed me at first, yet how right he was"[192] (. . . to have called her narcissistic sort "thirsty for return love and embittered without it"[193/l]).

Lou next considered the thinker: how he goes about taking Being apart even while dreaming "the primal human dream" of unity; doubting his ideas, and himself with them, at every new insight; secretly willing them flesh while shunning the flesh as their solvent; suspect to the community in his time because mindful of the rifts within it and perils surrounding it; feminine and masculine at once in his "unexampled dedication to wholeness, into which his self flows over"; aware at his best that thought at its best "relieves us of our individual, subjective self," being "objective" and also reminiscent of "our common center"; even so, able to reenter "the totality" only the common human way, when suddenly a great joy becomes too much for him alone—an inevitability, since "man strides toward that which overwhelms him, as if only: toward himself."[194] And next she again dealt with the two worlds of the bounded and the boundless self as manifest in diverse activities at diverse ages of man and mankind, concluding awkwardly: "Yet more befalls him whom the good and ill fortune has befallen of becoming a self-aware subject: namely this, that the malignly disconcerting subject-object discrepancy, creating, *decreates* itself."[195]

Her last prose composition followed: a final reconsideration of how one's dim remembrance of having once been contained in the "all" will abide through a lifetime of all-grasping individuation until the "inevitable homecoming." Mightily and exquisitely wrought, with many a beguiling new twist (notably a construal of "activity, action" as modified "playing"), it was especially distinguished by a word of doubt more than merely rhetorical and by a gentle cosmic complaint.

[k] The inconsistency with the passage on "reverence" above was Lou's.
[l] Cf. above, p. 398 and n. *p.*

For, concerning our self-differentiation pending self-reintegration, she declared at the outset: "it may spell a mere kink of mine, as may also my urge to put it in writing."[m] And at the close: "This human folly is at all odds no human doing (hence is far, far clear of all merit or demerit), is only the incidence on us of the recency of our existence. Our ultimate implantedness in that passivity in which everything nonhuman has stayed put. Which is our natural issue, outlet of all action and agitation. Like a hug without arms—even if, to be sure, one must toil one's life long, sorely active enough, for its consummation.—"[196] Who ever signed off more pointedly?

Of her "retired existence" Lou told Freud in January 1935 that, "full and round," it too followed from his vital gift to her "now as ever."[197] A month earlier she had told a daughter that, while still practicing daily, she was accepting no new patients "given the uncertainty of the psychoanalytical future."[198] Financially she was well enough off "now as ever" despite her assuring Emma after Kolia's ruinous deals that "what now remains, if anything does, is perhaps only a few hundred Marks."[199] For she had big medical bills ahead of her then, yet left more Marks than that behind, to say nothing of gems. Besides, she got by "well enough just on the widow's pension, for," as she put it, "I live quite quietly."[200] This was nothing new; indeed, her existence changed little from being suddenly curtailed by illness and thrown back upon Göttingen. She ate calf's foot as did her latest dog, a ghastly mongrel that had once tagged after her.[201] When at work, she would be disturbed on no account[202]; when not, she tended her garden or roamed the woods, with time out for occasional impulsive local friendships and enmities.[203] And for charity: once she volunteered aid to a cripple, only to be plagued by his whole family for weeks.[204] She dressed as starkly as ever, heedless of the figure she cut —which was still a stately, womanly one "with the supple gait of, so to say, a roving young tree,"[205] with her reddish blond hair and fine teeth intact,[206] but with brows discreetly penciled toward the last[207] after a lifelong aversion to cosmetics.[208] While she deplored the Third Reich confidentially, she protested aloud only when ordered to obtain an up-to-date identity photo.[209] Worse, in her "April" memoir she even upbraided Rilke for homelessness, beginning: "Now, Rainer, that the question of our autochthony is so thrust upon us Germans..."[210]

In 1931 the press respectfully noted her seventieth birthday: sharp-witted Helene Stöcker, who visited her for the occasion, reported that

[m] Later again: "But I will not swear to it: possibly my most stubborn kink is speaking here."

she "remains in inner harmony with her sometime friend" Nietz-sche,[211]/[n] adding that the charm but also the limit of her science and art was "her personality."[212] Near oblivion followed. The neurologist Viktor von Weizsäcker, beset with a mystical malaise,[213] addressed himself to her after having been taken by her "very personal refash-ioning" of psychoanalysis in *Mein Dank an Freud.*[o] With "unique flair," he recollects, "she straightaway knew . . . where my needs had their roots."[214] So he visited Loufried: "neither before nor since have I—so helpfully—come up against a like instance of someone's hav-ing grasped this science deeply enough and yet remained a distinct personality. . . . I received the femininity and warmth of her nature with gratitude, and it is perhaps no mistake, though surely a loss, if our contact, so live at first, later ceased: she had discharged a mission upon me, and I probably had little to offer in return still of use to her in old age."[215] For two days early in 1936 Gertrud Bäumer, author of a fine explication of Rilke along Lou's own lines, visited Lou in response to a letter from her calling it "the definitive book on Rilke."[216]/[p] By then Lou, affected by age, solitude, and diabetes, had developed a psychosis for special visitors: striking a sibylline pose, she would speak trancelike as if in communion with the dead. "The chair on which Rilke had always sat was as if drawn into our circle," Gertrud Bäumer related, "and she . . . included him in the conversa-tion in a peculiarly, almost mystically affecting way, so that I instinc-tively asked myself about everything I said whether it should be said that way, if at all, in his presence."[217] Lou, then under orders to lie still because of her heart, kept bobbing up irrepressibly—"the pic-ture of a young girl."[218] Once she remarked: "Strange: whenever I most firmly believed that what I was doing was perfectly sensible and natural, that I was on the straight and narrow path, I brought about the worst catastrophes. How come?"[219] Again, she asked her guest: " 'Did you want children?' 'Yes,' I replied, 'I think every woman does.' 'Not I!' she cried vehemently," and she cited Europe's "ultima ratio of killing" as her reason[220] (though in the thick of the war she had prescribed motherhood as a cure-all for women, caught between ethicality and sensuality[221]). And she related that she had

[n] Nominally as concerned 1890-1910, but cf. Stöcker, "ʟ ᴀ–s" (1931), 51.

[o] Weizsäcker (*Natur*, 187) dates his reading of *Dank* from around Christmas 1931—possibly a year before the fact, as his review of it appeared on 15 ɪ 1933.

[p] Bäumer, *Gestalt*, 504: "I believe she was so delighted with my book only because it presented Rilke as a religious genius." But Bäumer's title and sub-title respectively—*Ich kreise um Gott. Der Beter Rainer Maria Rilke*—suggest Lou's *Im Kampf um Gott* and refer to her hapless tale of how Rilke prayed *The Book of Hours* in Russia (above, pp. 463, 466).

psychoanalyzed herself during her apprenticeship—"astonishing things emerge"—but that when "her teacher" had asked what she proposed to do with all she had learned about herself, she had replied: "Forget it."[222] Gertrud Bäumer observed with wonderment that to Lou, given her quest for the fundamental, "the *historical*" meant just about nothing.[223]

A stepsister-in-law of Andreas's noted that, with the few old acquaintances such as herself who visited Lou toward the last, she would discuss only their very own ways of experiencing the world despite her conviction that these were incommunicable: "as if anything could get across and back," she once commented afterwards.[224] Another such caller was Lulu von Strauss in 1933. Perhaps another was Emma, with whom she corresponded much about gifts and legacies to their relatives in Russia. Faithful Helene could come only by mail. Asked in 1934 to choose a birthday gift, she requested some volume from Lou's possession such as one containing letters by Rainer. Lou explained apologetically that, as Rainer's letters to her were preassigned to the Rilke Archiv, she was sending her dedicated edition of the Elegies instead. "For heavens sake!" cried Helene[225/q] —and one year later all over again: "I meant only the volume of Rainer's letters to all and sundry, not on my life the originals of those addressed to you. Nor can you have believed that either!"[226] In between, Lou had sent back Helene's old letters[r] without clear explanation in the course of a documentary housecleaning, actually for the reason that Helene was a "personal" friend[s] (not famous like a Hauptmann or mythicized like a Gillot). Poor Helene inquired nonplussed: "Are you taking leave of me? . . . I have hesitated these many days to answer you and acknowledge your parcel, as I did not know: may I still write you? And what would the reason be for me not to?—your dear eyes, of which you wrote so gravely, or the desire to withdraw into a final solitude? Whatever it may be, Lou, I defer to every wish of yours. You are and will ever remain actual for me, are an indefeasible, perpetual constituent of my life. What I have you to thank for I can never say, can only impart it through my relations with those close to me. You have made me very rich, Lou! Dear, dear Lou, we have written each other only very seldom of late; but to know that we *could* write was so lovely. The door was open: are you gently closing it?"[227]

Closest to Lou after her husband's death was Mariechen, who thenceforth tended her in lieu of Marie.[228] Lou would take her anti-

---

[q] Cf. above, p. 454 n. *o*.   [r] Of before 1931.
[s] To follow Ernst Pfeiffer's oral usage presumably appropriated from Lou.

diabetic injections from no one else. Freud put his foot in it when, in telling Lou about Anna as his nurse, he quoted Goethe's Mephistopheles on how we wind up dependent upon creatures of our own making.[229/t] Two other intimates came to Lou by turns day after day to the last: Pfeiffer, for whom she discoursed out of the depths of her phantasmagoric past, and Josef König, Pfeiffer's good friend, of whom she related in December 1934 that with him "I work many times weekly very seriously (he teaches the theory of knowledge at the university here)."[230] On February 2, 1937—König was due that evening—Lou felt ill. "Is it death, do you think?" she asked Mariechen, adding: "It's dreadful." She thereupon fell into a death sleep just over three days long.

Lou's wish was to be cremated, then scattered about her garden; the police forbade the scattering, so the urn containing her ashes was set into her husband's grave—to which, being terrified of cemeteries, she had not returned since his burial.[231] The epitaphs on her all bore out the apt one by Andreas's stepsister-in-law: "Whoever came close to her succumbed to the magic of her personality."[232/u] Loufried devolved upon Mariechen, who occupies it to this day, honoring her dead mistress's memory. As to Lou's immortal remains, their custodian has made them available to posterity to the extent of four publications: her memoirs, her correspondence with Rilke and with Freud, and the diary of her psychoanalytical apprenticeship, all deftly annotated to her greater glory. For the rest, he has permitted access to none of them except at his exceeding discretion—not even to the Nietzsche material, and least of all to the originals of his editions. For in regard to Lou's posterity, as he puts it, he now stands in her stead. Goethe's Mephistopheles has been vindicated.

t "*Am Ende hängen wir doch ab / von Kreaturen, die wir machten.*"
u For Freud's obituary see above, p. 374 and n. *q*.

III · A RETROSPECT

OUTWARDLY AND inwardly both, Lou Salomé's life is among the richest on record. She kept company—uncannily stimulating, uncannily receptive—with the cultural elite of her times as judged from ours. She wrote in the widest variety of literary genres, including a couple of her own devising, happy and unhappy respectively: the diary essaylet and the achronological memoir. And by and large she wrote well: her peers among essayists at all odds are numbered (which is not to say that she essayed no nonsense). She also grasped the other business of culture as if from the inside: painting, the performing arts, religious inspiration, even motherhood—only not music. Inclusive as were her cultural concerns, her concerns were that exclusively cultural: nowhere do her own ample annals disclose that, for instance, her life in Germany began under Bismarck and ended under Hitler.[v] Only here again she was in the best of cultural company, especially in Germany.

Seen from afar, hers was a course of continual self-development, even self-renewal, in response to a dynamic historic culture. Nor is this impression quite false. Seen from close up, however, her mind was singularly self-consistent and self-contained along that course. She took little from others on the balance, and that little was as if properly her own: thus she lived down having been caught copying at the Petrischule. Her life's work reads in substance like a running extrapolation from its earliest chapter and verse. It was in this sense as authentic (the fraud inclusive) as anyone's ever.

All her ideas, however dissimilar otherwise, were, psychologically considered, variants of a few *idées fixes*. To these corresponded repetitive experiences, and the two together—her thought and conduct—served the purpose of shock-absorption. The shock was her father's big *no*, traumatized anew by Nietzsche's adieu. Absorbing it, she became a moral monster with redeeming features and secret remorse: a moral monstrosity. Defending against it retroactively, meanwhile, she became a distraught fabler—distraught because she feared madness from this very fabling for dear life. Her choicest gratifications likewise tended to undo that deathly rejection: accord-

[v] D 28 IX 1906 likens politics to death as a permanent background to life and thus something never much thought about.

ingly they were felt as perilously transitory, were overwritten with frantic exulting, were postelaborated beyond recognition. Yet, minus any half of them, her life would still have been enchanted. The truth to her cosmic pathos was that the cosmos itself would have left her wanting—and this, folly apart, was stupendous of her.

rau Lou registers my progress to date with its subject: a mind at work throughout a lifetime. As I wrote it, new lines of inquiry kept opening up, leading to new factual or interpretive discoveries, and therewith to newer lines of inquiry. I refrained as best I could till a full draft was done, then followed up lead after lead left outstanding: huge piecemeal revisions ensued—and my lead list came off only the longer. I am leaving the text discontinuous and inconsistent just so as to underscore its inconclusiveness.

I called an arbitrary halt in the thick of a hapless hunt for a biographic referent: that for Ludin's betrayal of Anjuta's imposture in "Inkognito." Ludin's running into Erwin at the post office suggested a letter from Schnitzler to Beer-Hofmann—and indeed, Beer-Hofmann's verdict that "it is best to travel *alone*" followed fast upon a letter from Schnitzler evidently received that very same Friday the thirteenth in Schönberg for which Lou noted: "Up late, to the post office together. Quarrel."[a] Even the "together" checked, for Erwin was carrying Anjuta's luggage (signifying herself). However, the fictional post office was in Innsbruck, not Patsch. And Schnitzler's letter contained nothing offensive to Lou: it respected her "official" story on Copenhagen. Did Beer-Hofmann, then, *not* show Lou the letter —and Lou *suspect* that he had written the unofficial truth about Copenhagen three mornings previous, when he had sealed a letter to Schnitzler posthaste upon her arrival at table?[b] In this connection, Schnitzler's counterpart in "Mädchenreigen" blurts out to Beer-Hofmann's, who hasn't a notion how come a certain "fair widow" of his acquaintance has turned up at his hotel: "Quite simple—utterly simple: she rode after you. Only I don't get this secretiveness—among ourselves."[1] At least on the face of it, this would attest Beer-Hofmann's discretion. Besides, Anjuta's was no fib about her presence in Erwin's vicinity, but a self-falsification toward Erwin about her sex.

Within Lou's Nietzsche complex, her pretense at *non*femininity toward Nietzsche was implied, Nietzsche having followed up Stein's roadside account of her existence in Berlin with that disabused word about how she rose to the "eternal masculine."[c] But within her Beer-

[a] See above, p. 195
[b] Ditto.
[c] See above, p. 129.

Hofmann complex? Her pretense vis-à-vis Beer-Hofmann was hardly Anjuta's of all-maidenliness. Rather it was the dual one of being a woman with mere comradely intent. Possibly Beer-Hofmann recoiled when it fell through on the womanly count: the half seduction in "Abteilung 'Innere Männer,' " a symbolic understatement in respect of Zemek, may have been the whole truth concerning Beer-Hofmann. The shades are drawn telltale tight that night in "Inkognito." In the first Schönberg tale, meanwhile, Hans's pretense is the exaggerated reverse of Anjuta's: that of being a he-woman of experience. In the third, guileless Jutta fits into one of Lou's shoes, the camaraderie one, but wears the other backwards, as she is half suspected of experience despite her nominal innocence—and mistakenly at that. Was Lou's false pretense, then, her self-introductory one of a continuing, sexless friendship with Goldmann? Or was Ludin's exposure of Anjuta displaced from one by Goldmann in Munich[d] about Lou's Russian giant? Or did "Inkognito" perhaps simply reverse Beer-Hofmann's view—unreversed in "Mädchenreigen"—that Lou loved someone who was not? This last is least likely, given Anjuta's attendant guilt—which, incidentally, is all too plenteous in that Erwin eagerly leaps to his false conclusions about her, which she sustains ever so effortlessly.

But enough! I cried—the louder since numberless other points rated priority anyhow on my probing schedule. The first of these was that of Lou's eventual appropriations from her psychoanalytical lovers—of whether some Bjerre did not brush off onto her "all," some Tausk onto her protonarcissism, some Gebsattel onto her dialectic of lovers' mutual shame.[2/e] The second was that of just how the Siegfried Wilm story affected her, given the crucial fact that her diary evolved in the wake of her grandmother's out of reports to a grandfatherly god. The third was that of whether she did not project backwards from her Nietzsche experience in telling about Gillot or even her god before him—whether in fact Märchen's undeceiving was not the rudest of Lou's life. As concerns her god, she wrote "Gottesschöpfung" and again "Die Stunde ohne Gott" just when the Nietzsche complex was stirring within her (the first between chapters of her Nietzsche book, the second after receiving Freud's letter on dead Tausk), and in "Im Zwischenland" the world turns spectral for Musja after Apollon lets her down just as it does for Ursula in "Die Stunde

---

[d] Goldmann did not write to Beer-Hofmann in Schönberg.

[e] Fragments of Gebsattel→Lou, 7 i 1915 and 18 i 1915, together with an incomplete draft of Lou→Gebsattel, 15 i 1915, constitute the only correspondence between Lou and her psychoanalytical lovers that was available to me: see below, pp. 557ff.

ohne Gott" after God lets her down.[3][f] And primarily, since Lou did project her father romance backwards onto her narcissistic beginnings, perhaps her father romance was itself merely precursive, her Nietzsche romance decisive. And so forth.

This third course of inquiry might well have led to conclusions contradicting Freud's as to the prepotence of the Oedipus complex and, generally, of motives out of childhood. So it is as well I drew the line where I did: I am in enough of a methodological mess as is. I undertook a local application of psychoanalysis to the history of thought, but the results have latterly run counter to one tenet of psychoanalysis after another.

To be sure, results merely supplemental to Freud's or merely at variance with them must be distinguished from results subversive of Freudianism. Perhaps the cosmic pathos does derive from the Oedipus complex rather than from protonarcissism[g]: Freud would stand corrected, but within the terms of Freudianism (even in line with his own derivation of dogmatic, ritualistic religion). Nor would psychoanalysis likely lose out could I explain, say, Lou's flair for god-men having fantasies of anal transmission commensurate with her own, or again the inordinate importance of ambiguity for her mental life. About ambiguity: I chalked it up to bisexuality, though Lou's masculinity evidently followed from her tardy father-identification rather than from her sexual constitution itself, which was feminine at the core what with her prepotent masochism and penis-envy.[h] On another count, Lou's case suggests that we can renounce a pleasure only by dint of tacit self-assurance that it will be restored to us a thousandfold in the fullness of time[i]—suggests, that is, an addendum to Freud's theory of repression. And Lou broke a psychoanalysts' rule, but no rule of psychoanalysis, in developing hysterical symptoms with only the slightest show of oral motivation,[j] as also in identifying

[f] Perhaps Lou's god's disappearance itself (especially as in 1931a:19) was postelaborated according to Nietzsche's parable on God's death (FN, *Science*, 125).

[g] Perhaps womb nostalgia does too: according to Buber, 33 (above, p. 328 and n. *k*), it is really a desire to restore the primal I-Thou.

[h] Besides, penis-envy underlay her mythomania, which her ambiguity chiefly subserved.

[i] This self-assurance perhaps derives from the lesson learned in infancy of drawing out and eventually postponing pleasures (oral, anal) so as to intensify them. (Historically, Christianity both solemnized and disguised the infinite payoff under the name "redemption." Originally the Christian heaven really was heaven: a place where virtues are redeemed. Only Christianity gradually postponed the infinite payoff *sine die*, thereby ruining its credit.)

[j] One nursing reminiscence (pronouncedly anal at that) and a craving for sweets is about the sum of it.

with love-objects through unconscious assimilation on an anal rather than an oral model.[k] Only from persons with whom she identified, moreover, did she ever acquire ideas from without: here, then, is a Freudian answer to a first question of immediate interest for the history of thought, that of how intellectual influence works. Her Spinoza was Gillot's—was in fact Gillot.[l] Her idealism was Malwida's, her positivism Rée's, her postpositivist "realism in religion" Nietzsche's backed by Biedermann's. Her psychoanalysis was Zemek's, then Bjerre's, then Freud's—before she claimed it as primordially hers. Only as Ledebour did she author nothing. Two other questions of influence elude me: that of inspiring (short of supplying ideas) the way young Rilke inspired Lou's golden age, and that of the blinding spell Lou cast over friends such that they simply would not see the warped side of her.[m] As for how ideas originate, my few cases in point (none nearly solid except "original hate") yield no ready generalizations beyond the one that a new idea is a self-confession denied insofar as it is not disguised. On a related point, many an insistent contention of Lou's (that femininity is positive, that marriage thrives on mutual concealment, that "differentiation" is specially masculine, is evil, is canceled by love) countered an earlier assertion by her on the same subject, as if to the end of self-dissuasion. So did many of her set sayings counter the assertions behind them. Through her rhetoric about a woman's first truly becoming a mother upon giving her grown children away "to the world and to death" she was asserting, *I did not kill those children I never actually bore*: thus by that social parturition she meant the earlier, biological one after all. And by that assertion she meant, at a further subjacent remove, the one issued earlier through her pre-rhetorical *Ma*: that, for having declined to bear those children *biologically*, she was the eternal mother that Ma became by declining to deliver *socially*. This all speaks ill for the force of reason, though not for the faculty of reason. I early made it a rule of thumb to look behind any *non sequitur* or nonsense of Lou's for an irrational motive perturbing her train of

---

[k] Possibly the underlying assimilative fantasy went back to an early use of suppositories.

[l] So was her Spinoza's god—and she in turn was the Spinozist in Rilke as well as Rilke's Spinozistic god (before he knew that his religion was Spinoza's: cf. above, p. 294 and n. *b*).

[m] That they chose not to see it is evident not only from Rilke's "midway land" but also from Nietzsche's having called her a sick fraud as soon as the spell broke (ditto Lisbeth, Wedekind). Perhaps Bernecker, 394, provides the key: "She often aroused an oddly ambivalent response from the first, both strongly attracting and strongly repelling": when the ambivalence turned negative side up, her infirmities loomed extra large.

thought, taken to be unerring of itself—and always found one.[n] What more could Freud have asked?

Freud's trouble begins with Lou's fiction—with her fictionalization of her experience. Her tales, I have said, served to dispose of psychic materials pressing upon consciousness against her ego's resistance. Thus her love for Nietzsche or for Beer-Hofmann won no more recognition from her after the brush-off in each case than in *Im Kampf um Gott* or the Schönberg trilogy respectively—which is to say that it won permanent entrée to her conscious system under the thinnest effective disguise. Dreams serve to eliminate tensions between the ego and certain preconscious materials in the very same way, for the dream too remains accessible to consciousness after having been dreamed. Thus Freud mistook the function of dreams, which "protect sleep" only incidentally to their protecting peace of mind in sleep or out like fictionalizations. The three episodes of *Im Kampf um Gott* or again the three installments of the Schönberg serial resemble successive dreams working up the same latent materials.[o] A single night's dreaming, however, will work up "the residues of the previous day" for good and all (as Freud's very term "the residues of the previous day" implies): they do not come unbound years afterwards to mix into new dreams. Moreover, Lou's tales worked up latent materials older at their newest than just the previous day: some weeks old in "Ein Todesfall"[p] (Zemek's gloomy prophecy concerning Rainer) and likely "Eine Nacht"[q] (Zemek's call to the dying man's bedside), but typically some months or years old[r]—and typically off her mind as far as she knew. Besides, to a tale of Lou's there were as a rule many strata of latent materials, whereas to a dream there

[n] I mistakenly inferred from a first few cases in point that we think straighter unconsciously than consciously: thus my unconscious system had sought to assert rational superiority.

[o] The material is no more or less disguised on the balance from one fictional episode or installment to the next (in "Inkognito" as against "Mädchenreigen," Schnitzler and Goldmann are merely caricatured, but Schön[e]berg, Patsch, and Innsbruck are named; etc.)—and yet, since the three tales of amorous escapade to the Alps, like the three heartbreaks over Kuno, were linked literarily, the effect was one of increasing disclosure.

[p] Only some days old in the case of her discussion of the future "Ein Todesfall" with Rainer—so perhaps the lag between precipitating event and first literary *conception* was generally brief.

[q] If, that is, "Eine Nacht" and not "Abteilung" is the "*Spitalnovelle*" of Lou's calendars: see below, p. 566.

[r] Lou evidently responded at once, however, to Gillot's wife's death with the denouement of *Ruth*, the latent stuff of which was age-old, and *Ródinka* registered traces of her current experience with the prototypes for its characters (Nikolai Tolstoi's not answering her letters; Rilke's going off to Clara, his child by her, his 1903 bid to return; Hauptmann's child by Grete).

are as a rule only "the residues of the previous day" backed by an infantile wish.[8] By way of exception, "Am Krötenteich" comes to mind as a two-level, dreamlike piece—and yet what was the original of the old lady's moral holiday if not Anjuta's in "Inkognito"? Strangely, Lou's own thesis of the late 1890's was that recent "undigested emotional residues" of experience entered into a work of art on the strength of some infantile motivation: she skipped the strata in between as if in consideration of dreams.

Some elements of a preconscious complex admitted to consciousness in the form of a story (as also of a dream) may be recognized in the process. So in fact may an entire complex as such: the Gillot complex behind *Ruth* and the Novinky complex behind *Ródinka* are cases in point. Such recognition makes a difference inasmuch as *Ruth* at all odds is unthinkable except as a knowing semimemoir. It makes no difference, however, to the unknowing half of the memoir—to the key propositions "Would I had left Gillot on his knees" or again "Would I had come to Novinky as an intimate." And significantly, there is no identifying Lou's knowing semimemoirs for sure beyond those she identified herself—though *Im Kampf um Gott* does seem almost certainly to have been one, the Schönberg serial less certainly, and "Tor und Ur" almost certainly not. Again, in writing *Das Haus* Lou knew that she was describing her conjugal abodes one after the other, yet surely not that she was idealizing her marriage. In such cases the latent message was distorted just the same—or, if undistorted (that true marriage in *Das Haus* or that spurned suitor in *Ruth* or that summer's sojourn in *Ródinka*), was admitted to consciousness as "fiction only." Possibly she knew the proximate latent identity of every important character or incident in her tales *ironically*—told herself that she was playing around with any old raw materials of her experience as in her childhood (arbitrarily, unmeaningly). For this is how she characterized her fictionalizing in general, though indeed she also spoke of the work of art as elaborated in the depths. Yet even when she knew what autobiographical material she was elaborating, she did not elaborate it *at will*; hers was then rather the situation of the dreamer who knows he is dreaming about his sister Susie without, however, understanding his dream.

But most often, it seems, a screen person concealed even the proximate latent identity of a character from Lou as author after the fashion of dreams: thus the mother in *Das Haus* was ostensibly a Göttingen neighbor and the mother in *Ma* a Petersburg neighbor.

---

[8] Freud took no theoretical account of latent dream materials dating from between the previous day and infancy, though he frequently mentioned such: cf. below, p. 507.

Her semimemoirs may in fact all have screened *current* concerns: she may have meant Märchen's Kuno as Gillot, with Nietzsche then interloping unnoticed, just as Gillot's efforts to extricate her from dreamland in *Ruth* clearly fronted for Ledebour's[t] or again as Novinky clearly fronted for Loufried in the writing of *Ródinka*. At all odds, more recent experiences occasionally lay deeper beneath the surface of her tales than less recent ones. Her controlling tendency was to align not so much newer on older as less on more assimilated experiences: her Ledebour on her Gillot experience in "Das Paradies," her Gillot on her Nietzsche experience in *Ruth* or originally vice versa in the Märchen sequence of *Im Kampf um Gott*. Nor was this a mere matter of like experiences registering as such: if Gillot and Nietzsche went together naturally enough in her unconscious, it took straining to conjoin duplicity vis-à-vis Ledebour with daydreaming vis-à-vis Gillot. She would in fact impress such strained equivalences onto her actual as well as her reminiscent experience. Take her Nietzschefication of Rainer. In "Ein Todesfall" she sent Rainer off into solitude in Italy for want of her love and adulation, there to succumb to a fit of madness[u] (literally: a hemorrhage): his trip to Florence ensued. "Im Zwischenland," which excused Nietzsche's repulsion of her on the ground that madness was threatening him, prefigured her repulsion of Rainer, for which her "last call" then gave this same excuse.[v] And the "Geschwister" legend that Nietzsche had rejected her for her own good, hence had not really rejected her, corresponded to the one in *Das Haus* concerning her rejection of Rainer—a case of pseudoreminiscent alignment as between two stories.[w]

[t] See above, p. 181 n. *d*; cf. "Paradies," in which Ledebour's recalled Gillot's.

[u] Thus the resurrectional bust was also Lou's Nietzsche book: above, p. 219 (and n. *x*).

[v] The relations were of course reversed as between the two cases in that Rainer and Clara stood to her in 1901 as she and Rée had stood to Nietzsche in 1882.

[w] Cf. above, p. 474. Exceptionally, Lou's reminiscent alignment of Rilke's on Nietzsche's creative agony (above, pp. 462, 466) began *non*fictionally, in the infratext of "Des Dichters Erleben" (written at the time of "Geschwister")—to the effect, however, that both had alike renounced *her* (renounced all outer support and comfort), and this so as to save *themselves*! This mechanism of alignment, incidentally, *complements* that by dint of which old unabreacted unconscious materials burst their latest literary bindings through association, however farfetched, with new materials of the sort being bound up literarily for a first permanent acceptance into consciousness (e.g. Nietzsche's conjoined to Freud's "repulsion" in "Geschwister")—with Gillot-Ledebour in "Paradies" as a borderline case (as also perhaps Andreas-Wedekind in "Vor dem Erwachen": above, pp. 184-85 and n. *x*, 472-73 and n. *e*). Further, insofar as Lou did not align Rilke on Nietzsche, she aligned herself vis-à-vis Rilke on Nietzsche vis-à-vis herself: qualified accordingly, the rule stated above, p. 26, for the final sense of her amendments to the past still holds.

By and large Lou's devices for translating a latent into a manifest tale were the same regressive ones in use with dreamers. The big exception is that the literary medium favored the pun and the anagram over the rebus. Nonetheless the rebus is not—as Freud thought it was—primarily a mode of representation called forth by the dreamer's pictorial medium and only incidentally a mode of distortion. Rather it is that variant of the distortion technique of crudification, or naturalistic caricature, most suitable to dreams. Thus in "Geschwister" the representation of disciples as lovers, of psychoanalysis as orthopedics, and of moral as bodily repulsion were all of a kind and were all distortions pure and simple ("psychoanalysis" being as easy to *write* as "orthopedics")—even though, taken in the order stated, they tend increasingly to plastic convenience. Among the lesser technical equivalences between dreaming and—to judge by Lou's case—fictionalizing is the one that to the censoring blurs in dreams correspond narrative obscurities in a story. For the rest, a story interchanges personal attributes or relationships just like a dream—as codetermined by the latent theme of switching sexes in "Geschwister," of reversing Nietzsche's charges in "Im Zwischenland," of a substitution of persons in "Abteilung 'Innere Männer.'" The tale will also condense several latent elements into a single manifest one and, to a far lesser extent, represent one or another latent element many times over. The resultant overall compression certainly approaches that for dreams: my whole lengthy explication of "Geschwister" above merely skims the text underlying the fifteen-page denouement.[x] Much of the condensation in Lou's tales is due to the superposition of latent complexes—and the resultant superposition of persons (as well as the displacement of personal attributes within complexes) was the latent truth to Lou's allegation that she would confect a fictional character by joining one real man's head to another's shoulders in the manner of her childhood street game. Tales avail themselves of the same symbols as do dreams. They also accommodate some latent material (phrases, emotions) undistorted, as do dreams. Finally, the rule holds for Lou's tales as for dreams: symbols apart, to every manifest element corresponds at least one preconscious latent element, and to this in turn at least one element of prior experience—or for short: no manifest element without at least one referent in prior experience. Thus the seizure in "Geschwister" or "Im Zwischenland" or *Aus fremder Seele* perforce designates Nietzsche's—if also remotely Siegfried Wilm's. And virtually every

[x] In point of compression, moreover, "Geschwister" does not seem exceptional among Lou's tales, though of course Lou's may be exceptional tales.

such biographic referent crops up nonfictionally somewhere in Lou's published writings or her literary estate, Nietzsche's seizure being the great exception. Thus also the secondary elaboration of a tale really is secondary, deliberate as it may be: nothing in any of Lou's tales is there by reason of the requirements of plot. "Mädchenreigen," for instance, ends indecisively only because it ends just short of Lou's disappointment over Beer-Hofmann. All Lou's art went into suffusing it with a melancholic mood to the effect that Hans would wind up alone whatever happened next, hence that whatever did happen next was immaterial. That mood was Lou's, elaborated to distract from the occasion for it.

Lou changed off fictionalizing techniques continually, but I could not grasp the sense of the changes. Much less could I discern any pattern of difference in the techniques used by her to fictionalize older as against newer complexes. Certain it is, though, that her techniques varied from one fictionalization of a given complex to the next. And her adult complexes retained their preconscious character through any number of fictionalizations—underwent no archaization over the years and decades. Accordingly, the initiative for her fiction, dominated as it was by associated adult complexes,[y] lay with her ego. The precondition for her fictionalizing seems to have been that more associated preconscious materials be clamoring for expression over and against her ego's objections than ever a dream could have accommodated—though what a nonauthor does in such a case I do not know. Her fiction differed insofar not only from dreams, which can as well originate in the id, but also, it would seem, from her essays, which (except for such occasional pieces as book or play reviews) ordinarily did originate in the id and not the ego, for all the wakeful elaboration that characterized them.[z] Here I am presuming, however, as I could make out precious little of the ego material beneath her essays—and as, worse, I could at least make out that her ego did have a huge secret say in the essay sequence beginning with " 'Anal' und 'Sexual' " (as also that Nietzsche's had one in *The Genealogy of Morals* and Freud's in his late theorizing). "Jesus der Jude" was perhaps an *essai à clef* in that it skipped over Gethsemane (the great seizure) by contrast to the Calvary quite as did "Im Zwischenland" and "Geschwister." "Der Mensch als Weib" for its part may have been compensatory for an abortion undergone in the summer of 1898.

[y] I cannot put this categorically, however, as the proximate biographical sense of some of Lou's fiction has eluded my researches—notably of "Vaters Kind," apparently so infantile.

[z] Lou said this in effect of her essays (D [II] 1919—quoted above, p. 304 n. *x*) as also of her thought complexes (D IX 1919).

It certainly involved self-reassurance on Lou's part that Rainer would come home to her after a trip abroad just then underway[a] and that she could virtually do without him anyhow. And with her sexually coactive Woman she was reacting against Nietzsche's genealogical parable according to which, "physiologically put," the slave's "action is at bottom reaction."[4] Then too, "Gedanken über das Liebesproblem" did signify that the honeymoon with Rainer was over and the one with Andreas, such as it was, perennially on. Again, woman as such sovereignly using men in "Der Mensch als Weib" bore on Lou's incipient erotic practice, as did the prescription in "Gedanken über das Liebesproblem" for short and sweet liaisons: did some essays, then, latently serve to help regulate conduct rather than, like stories, to help assimilate experience? The key to the ego's latent share in formalized thought is wanting. Whatever that share, though, all of "Gedanken über das Liebesproblem" as of "Der Mensch als Weib," of "Jesus der Jude" as of " 'Anal' und 'Sexual,' " indulged childish fancy in disguise—chiefly through ambiguity or denial. One childish motive or another (mostly that ferment of her fantasy play, penis-envy) went into the making of Lou's every tale as well, only quite subordinately. And ego material was often enough wishfully handled in her tales just like childish motives, but this is something else.

Concerning this something else, it is striking that Lou's wishful handling of ego material in her tales was invariably retroactive. She did not, for example, fictionally project a new and prolonged visit to Novinky; instead she prolonged her old visit, prefixing a prior romance to it to boot. Of course this fictional fancy of hers was originally an actual one amounting to: "Would I were here for the summer on a reunion visit (and without Rainer)," for she indulged that fancy by means of ambiguity in her very first diary account of her visit. Similarly, "Wolga" followed up her project of July 1900—abandoned "in tears"—for a new Volga trip. So did the finale of *Ruth* elaborate her semiconscious wishful construction of late March 1882 upon Gillot's letter about having intended her education to be merely transitional. So did Märchen's fatal misunderstanding in *Im Kampf um Gott* indulge (besides exposing) Lou's own precedent misunderstanding of Nietzsche's words about asking her hand and again about wishing to talk with her in the Löwengarten. So did Kuno's seduction of Margharita take off from a fond-fanciful reading of Nietzsche's prankish Genoese greeting to "that Russian girl"—and Kuno's pro-

---

[a] See above, p. 247 (Rilke left for Vienna 22 II 1899; Lou began writing "Mensch" 24 II 1899).

posal to Margharita from such a reading of Nietzsche's Columbus poem. So did Kuno conceivably turn up to deliver Jane from the ennui of her village retreat beside her nameless consort pursuant to some pleasant imaginings of Lou's dating from her Stibbe sojourn of October 1882—from between aphorisms. And was not Lou's splendid hushed excuse to herself for Nietzsche's rejecting her—that madness was threatening him and hence indirectly her too—preconsciously preelaborated eighteen years before "Im Zwischenland" following his own lead: "Consider well . . . that I am sick in the head"? In fact all the amendments to bygone reality latent in Lou's fiction may well only dilate upon old amendments to current reality latent in her thoughts at the time.[b] All daydreaming may even be retroactive at bottom in this sense of disguisedly indulging obsolete wishes. But again, the concept of retroactivity may be misleading here, for these dated fancies of Lou's, like all the other old, repudiated motives that went into her fiction, were there as present-tensed,[c] as actual and urgent, as on the first day—timelessness being thus no prerogative of the unconscious as against the preconscious system.

They were more than actual and urgent: they were creative, and this not only fictionally but autobiographically. For many an autobiographic fable of Lou's was anticipated in her fiction—so many as to make it look as if her chief purpose in writing fiction might have been to fool herself ultimately about the past: as if, that is, the avowed fiction mediated the unavowed.[d] And generally an autobiographic fable in its anticipatory fictional form twisted some phrase drawn from her prior experience. Thus her two brothers dead in childhood by the terms of her memoirs went back, by way of Jutta's two dead brothers and one twin,[e] to Freud's phrase about the six transference brothers in his seminar. Again, her precocious loss of faith in "Gottesschöpfung" went back, by way of Märchen's godlessness, to the label

[b] Those designed to undo past doings must, however, have been retroactive from the first—like Lou's wishfully retracting her Jena outburst (and consequently its consequences) in that it was missing from "Im Zwischenland" and "Geschwister."

[c] Similarly, in *The Sickness unto Death*, B. (b) (I) (i), Søren Kierkegaard wrote of "a present *in praeterito*" upon remarking that "illusion has essentially two forms: that of hope, and that of recollection"—only S. K. did not notice that the two generally went together.

[d] "Avowed" must be qualified, though, in respect of the equivocation implicit in professed semimemoirs such as *Ruth* and *Ródinka* as to just what was fictive and what factual in them.

[e] In "Geschwister," that is. In "Jutta" six transference brothers front for three real ones, originally six: doubtless the extra three real ones date from the 1933 revision (above, p. 422 n. *j* and 483) and thus offset the *Grundriss* two likewise authored then (cf. above, p. 421 and n. *h*, on Freud as odd brother out).

"youthful" that in Tautenburg she had set upon her religious ardor. And again, that pilgrim who in 1914 materialized on the periphery of Yasnaya Polyana "the last time I saw Leo Tolstoi" went back, by way of Dimitrii's prayerful greeting to Ródinka from without through Margot within, to Rainer's naïve account of approaching Tolstoi's house with Lou "like pilgrims": thus the pseudomemoir signified, "No, Rainer, *you* were the mere pilgrim; I was an old friend."[f]

There may be such a phrase behind *every* fictional precedent to an autobiographic fable of Lou's, and a written phrase at that[g]; she might even have preserved to the last all the evidence of this that was hers, the exceptions encountered by me being then due simply to gaps in my documentation. For instance, her memoir of Andreas stabbing himself just before their engagement followed up Stefan's suicide in "Geschwister," which stood for Tausk's of just before his wedding: in the memoir she substituted her fiancé of 1886-1887 for Tausk, after having substituted herself for Tausk's fiancée in the tale. And the phrase preparing the substitution is likely to be found in one of Tausk's letters to Lou, of which I saw none. Unless . . . but of course! It was Tausk's phrase to Lou recollected by her upon his death: "No one will sit down at the same table with a wretch: not even you have done so." For sitting down at the same table symbolizes marriage, and Jutta sat down at the same table with Stefan, and Andreas's suicide knife "had lain on the table at which we sat facing each other."[5] So perhaps the rule is a hard-and-fast one: never the fiction behind an autobiographic fable of Lou's without the prior suggestive phrase as well, and vice versa. And of course never the two behind a memoir without its being deceptive. Given this dual antecedence to Lou's reminiscence concerning her supposed two brothers dead in childhood, their birth and death will be nowhere on record in all the Russias. Similarly, no evidence beyond Lou's say-so will ever turn up that Gillot or Nietzsche proposed to her. And no say-so of hers in either case will ever turn up antedating *Ruth* and *Im Kampf um Gott* respectively—or for that matter antedating either putative suitor's death. Here, then, is a rule of historical necessitation as trivial as the data for which it holds. But what rule of world-historical necessitation holds for specific data—that is, holds at all?

[f] Further: "the last time I saw Witalii in this world" (1901a:256) reduplicates Tolstoi's farewell retreat as in Lou's Russian diary—over the fields and away, fast upon some broken, none too significant discourse. Tolstoi, though, was herein headed back home—so perhaps Witalii's end also owed something to Tolstoi's fatal flight of 1910 from Yasnaya.

[g] Unless Nietzsche's equivocal spoken words about asking Lou's hand rather than his suggestive written ones about talking to her in the Löwengarten underlay Märchen's fatal misunderstanding.

Beyond Frau Lou

Not all Lou's autobiographic fables were preelaborated fictionally. Some were straight reversals of latent memories, such as Nietzsche's backbiting Rée; some were misconstruals of documents, such as Rée's meeting Jenia in Schneidemühl; some were I know not what genetically, such as Rée's coming broke to Malwida's straight from Monte Carlo or the telephone number routine of 1912-1913 with Freud. Nor were all Lou's fictionalizations subsequently autobiographized: none relating to her Beer-Hofmann fiasco ever was. Ordinarily, moreover, in altering her past nonfictionally, she contented herself with misleading statements rather than outright misstatements—rather than "honest-to-goodness lovely lying," to quote her very own Ursula.[6/h] She would mislead through underemphasis, as in underemphasizing her Beer-Hofmann affair in her memoirs; or through simple omission, as in omitting her Pineles affair from her memoirs; or typically through ambiguity, meaning through wordings only an unnatural reading of which squared with the facts, as when she wrote about how she *"could* have stayed" with Gillot or about Tolstoi's not eating that roast "with us" or, in reference to her reunion with Freud at Tegel, about "our almost daily excursions to Berlin." Such verbal trickery was a compromise between truth and untruth[i] struck deliberately in the first instance, after which its recessive, truthful meaning was evidently lost to consciousness except in the form of a limit beyond which the dominant meaning might not be stretched in any reformulation. How her playing with her past registered in her consciousness is, however, irrelevant to a consideration of the rules of her game.[j] In respect of Gillot, her misleading *"could* have stayed" anticipated that fiction—*Ruth*—by dint of which the inhibiting limit was sprung after his death. In respect of Nietzsche, on the contrary, her New Year's diary piece of 1883 was misleading to the effect that he had meant nothing to her, and her Nietzsche book ten years later was misleading to the effect that she had been his perennial girl friend, whereas her figment due to prevail —his proposal as a *pis aller*—was prefigured fictionally in the interim as between Kuno's halfhearted proposal to Margharita and pseudo-proposal to Märchen. At all odds, *every* autobiographic formulation

[h] "Was lying, honest-to-goodness lovely lying, more for girls than for boys?" wondered Ur—and indeed, Lou's lying came of her penis-envy.

[i] Ingenious Brausewetter, 4-5, characterized Lou's mental life generally as a painful struggle to harmonize an acquired impulse to factuality with an underlying impulse to fantasy.

[j] Fortunately—for this problem in particular is complicated by the discrepancy between her written and her oral fabling, which I could not consider systematically given the inadequacy of my data on the latter: see e.g. above, pp. 469 and n. *q*, 473 n. *e*.

of Lou's was misleading in some way or other if not outright false, *none* being outright false that followed immediately upon an event. Moreover, successive autobiographic formulations departed increasingly from the facts. "Honest-to-goodness lovely lying" took time— and yet time was not of the essence here inasmuch as a first reminiscence by Lou decades after the event would invariably check out better than an associated re-reminiscence. Since the corresponding memories meanwhile all survived intact subjacently, it was *the form in which* a given memory was admissible to consciousness that underwent progressive distortion from one reminiscence to the next. All reminiscence may work this way: so-called dulling or fading of recurrent memories would, then, be simply the normal way in which they are vitiated. The one objectively stable order of reality, the past, would then be the one assured of subjective instability.

And what would the sense of such vitiations be—wishful thinking? Certainly not *gross* wishful thinking as a rule. Lou's late pseudo-reminiscences on Freud to the effect that she had been forthright with him about Adler and been psychoanalyzed by him and been embraced by him—all anticipated in "Geschwister"—put small feathers in her cap as against the truths, let alone the lies, she left untold. She merely touched up their common past as it survived in her files and his. But was it *at all* wishful of her to turn his having taken her presence in Weimar for a "propitious omen" in 1911[7] into his having laughed in Weimar at her zeal to study "his psychoanalysis"[8]? This was random distortion—unless all distortion be taken for wishful of necessity, by dint of a tautological pleasure principle. Between the Basel draft and the final copy of her late-life memoir on Nietzsche and Rée, Lou went haphazardly from bad to worse in numerous details. Freud supposed that the pleasure principle does not operate in the case of colossal excitations requiring to be bound first; Lou's handling of lateral recollections not themselves charged with affect suggests that the pleasure principle does not operate for trivial excitations either. And if the tendency to distort memories was not all too singular in Lou's case, a fear of contradiction may be the one sure restraint on an all-human inclination to unreality—which would explain why anchorites go mad.

If the pleasure principle does not govern memory distortion, then my construal of Lou's writing as an operation whereby her pleasure-ego excreted unpleasant residues of experience *sub rosa* and ingested pleasant substitutes falls. It falls also inasmuch as the intact memories, superseded in reminiscence, remain within the ego after all, surviving—*pre*consciously? *Preconscious*, for Freud, meant accessible to consciousness or, in his topographical scheme, this side of the censor's station. And yet Freud held that the preconscious components of a dream or symptom assumed archaic guise in order to gain access to consciousness—to get past the censor's station. But let the censor set up where he will in Freud's scheme: there is no place in it for *strata* of psychic material inaccessible to consciousness. In theorizing, Freud overlooked yester*year*'s nonconscious motives; in analyzing, he assimilated those few that he found operative in dreams or symptoms to the infantile unconscious. However, compensatory mental activity is not all tensed between present frustrations and infantile fixations, for yester*year*'s subjacent motives dominated Lou's fiction and at all odds Freud's late nonfiction after Nietzsche's *The Genealogy of Morals*. To be sure, earliest childhood with its polymorphous perversity, Oedipus complex, and terminal amnesia remains the psychological starting point in all respects: this said lest pre-Freudians misunderstand. As to post-Freudianism, strata may be an ill-advised conceptual image for latent complexes that are not quite regularly the deeper buried—that is, the more taboo—the older they are.[k] Perhaps the taboo is rather a *brand*—and one that is standard from psyche to psyche, like those archaic modes of expression. Long days before detecting the latent sense of "Geschwister" I felt as though it were all spelled out on the nether side of a thick cephalic fog that, stare as I might, I could penetrate only far enough to decipher a few disparate fragments. Then came a sudden breakthrough: for two days and nights and then another two I pursued Lou's latent associations as if driven at dizzying speed in all directions at once. Now, *my* censor had no good grounds for previously barring those latent thoughts of Lou's from my consciousness: on the contrary. So the formalistic fiend must have implicitly honored the ban put upon them by *hers*—or rather the ban*s*, some stronger than others, for after having nearly exhausted the Freud complex I was strung up a few hours before I could penetrate the Nietzsche complex in its turn. The stronger the ban on a set of memories, then, the more drastically their reminiscent form would evolve, whereas memories under no ban would simply dim. And how about binding and unbinding of banned memories? But halt! This scheme of bans is altogether premature. Theorizing comes perilously easier than discovering, which it readily impedes. A new model for the mind is needed, but new insight is needed first, beginning with insight into the latent sense of essays. And by the same token, more investigation of closely documented

[k] Older ones not correspondingly more taboo may, however, be conscious insofar: cf. above, p. 499.

lives is needed, along with fresher, sharper wits on the investigative end.

And these are needed for something beyond schematizing the mind anew—something unconscionably farfetched the possibility of which my experience with Lou nonetheless argues. I mean establishing a science of history on infrapersonal foundations. All historians not merely macrocosmic anecdotalists are after the whys and wherefores of the past—which, formally put, means after a science of history. There is no science, however, without the possibility of inferring specific events from other specific events, and such inference is possible nowhere along the course run by the stock superpersonal or impersonal subjects of our histories—cultures, modes of production, nations, wars, institutions, social groups, techniques, ideas. Maybe the stock subjects are wrong. The stock subjects of intellectual history were extraneous to Lou, who went the *Zeitgeist*'s way with no guidance from the *Zeitgeist*. Commonly ideas and their ilk are chronicled as if they developed somehow one from the other or else in response to conditions and events of public life; they developed neither way, however, through Lou. This, by the way, puts me out on a limb professionally in that my classroom standard has been to account for historic works of the mind as if nothing were known about their composition beyond its place and date.

Is the personal subject perhaps historically law-abiding? Lou of all people would seem to have been so: her life seemingly unfolded all of a piece. About midway through my labors I sought to formulate the course of her adult life integrally along some such line as that she was forever striving to secure her self-identification with her father-god and differentially so as to determine her response to any event given the magnitude of subjective variables such as father-libido bound or unbound. I got nowhere—as was brought home to me at long last by repeated failures to anticipate her experience wherever I was still reconstructing it from documentary remains. Even in her rituals she was unreliable: to be self-consistent, she should, for instance, have defied Freud more drastically. And yet so much *in* her life was repetition! (and so much of the remainder was imitation!) *How* much does not emerge clearly from my chronological exposition: thus I could treat none of her big romances—unconscious epilogues inclusive, that is—unitarily for comparative purposes, since each lasted the rest of her days once it was underway. I violated chronology only to accommodate a few immediate romantic sequels, notably the legend of Nietzsche's proposal and the tales of the Beer-Hofmann/ Zemek continuum. I compared on the side. And am still comparing:

thus Lou abreacted each of these two congruent romances as proximate latent stuff of fiction during the second year after the event and identified intellectually with the sometime beloved as of the middle of the second decade—a timetable that holds, however, for Nietzsche and Beer-Hofmann alone. Lou's abreactions in particular give the impression of an inner fatality at work in that they each ran their pat course rain or shine, war or peace, whatever her conscious occupations or preoccupations, even though they ran it in consideration of externals such as that her last letters to Nietzsche no longer survived or again that Rainer was growing great—of externals known to her unconscious as if through a one-way peephole into consciousness.

While my integral and differential tabulations came to nought, some disparate rules of thumb meanwhile evolved by me to assist my researches wound up as subpersonal rules of necessitation—those cited throughout this conclusion, such as no fictional element without an empirical antecedent. Admittedly, they all work backwards only, like those of the biological sciences (genetics or evolution). Or like those of psychoanalysis: deterministic as were his premises, Freud could tell only how dreams were made, not what anyone was going to dream up next. I likewise can say only that every idea of Lou's was a compromise formation if new with her and, if not, was some self-identified beloved person's beforehand; I cannot say when, alternatively, she was due to compromise on a symptom or appropriate an idiosyncrasy, much less what symptom or which idiosyncrasy. Even my master rule for the antecedents to Lou's every autobiographic fable is irreversible all the way: given Freud's quip about the six big brothers, its reminiscent outcome was by no means a foregone conclusion. Or was it? Even supposing it was, however: could any number of such ultramicrocosmic rules ever yield Lou's whole mental history, let alone the whole history of thought? Not likely. But a microchemistry of history could lead into a new macrophysics of history in ways unforeseeable—not excluding some simple transpositions, as from how we singly to how we collectively reformulate our past. A fascinating scholarly prospect! with madness at the end of it. For men cannot help thinking as if their thoughts were free, but they would be mad to think that way if they knew better.

BIBLIOGRAPHICAL NOTES

PREFACE

1. Lou→EK, 1 VIII 1898.

PART ONE CHILDHOOD

1. 1904a:47.
2. 1901a:21.
3. Cf. Bäumer, *Gestalt*, 477-78.
4. 1891d:171.
5. 1913c:459.
6. *Ibid.*
7. *Ibid.*
8. 1936a.
9. 1919d:17.
10. 1913e:4.
11. 1913a:162.
12. 1911a:86.
13. 1936a.
14. See especially 1927b:30.
15. Lou→Caro [IX 1898] (draft?).
16. *Ibid.*
17. D [early II 1913].
18. Lou→Freud [5? IV 1931].
19. 1913e:3.
20. 1893g:38.
21. 1931a:76.
22. Louise Salomé→FN, 10 XI [1882].
23. 1913a:140; 1931a:14.
24. 1913c:464.
25. D VI 1917.
26. *Ibid.*
27. D V-VI 1923.
28. D VIII 1912.
29. 1913c:461.
30. *Ibid.*, 462.
31. 1891d:174.
32. 1913c:463.
33. 1920b:365.
34. Lou→RMR [12 XII 1925].
35. 1913c:5.
36. *Ibid.*, 464.
37. 1911a:87.
38. 1913c:464.
39. 1911a:87.
40. 1901a:25.
41. D 15 XII 1902.
42. As per Caro→Lou, 5 VI 1879 and other fragments.
43. 1931a:76.
44. Cf. 1893g:23-24, 29 (a wishful rectification).
45. *Ibid.* and 1900b:291.
46. Lou→Caro [2? VI 1898] (draft?).
47. Caro→Lou, 12 X 1878.
48. Podach, *FN und LS*, 133-34 (quoting Dr. Otto Buek).
49. Pfeiffer, *Leben*, 288-89.
50. 1893g:59.
51. *Ibid.*
52. *Ibid.*, 80.
53. *Ibid.*, 81.
54. Caro→Lou, 23 IV 1879.
55. D 15 VIII 1900; cf. 1913e:5, 1931a:32.
56. D [late XII 1912].
57. D [III?] 1918.
58. Caro→Lou, 17 II 1879.
59. Louise Salomé→Caro [early 1879].
60. Caro→Lou, 17 II 1879.
61. Louise Salomé→Caro [early 1879].
62. Caro→Lou, 23 IV 1879.
63. *Ibid.*
64. *Ibid.*
65. *Ibid.*
66. *Ibid.*
67. *Ibid.*
68. Caro→Lou, 5 VI 1879.
69. D 15 VIII 1900.
70. D III 1923.
71. 1891d:title.
72. D [late VIII 1882].
73. Caro→Lou, 23 IV 1879 (evidently quoting Lou).
74. As in 1895f.
75. D 15 VIII 1900.
76. 1931a:76.
77. *Ibid.*, 24.
78. D V 1919.
79. 1913e:6.
80. 1891d:179.
81. D 31 X 1888.
82. *Ibid.*
83. *Ibid.*
84. 1891d:178.
85. *Ibid.*
86. *Ibid.*

87. D I 1919.
88. D 31 X 1888.
89. *Ibid.*
90. D V 1911.
91. D VIII 1917.
92. *Ibid.*
93. D V 1911.
94. D [III?] 1918.
95. *Ibid.*
96. D III 1914.
97. D [III?] 1918.
98. D 1917.
99. D IV 1923.
100. D [III?] 1918.
101. D [mid-III 1913].
102. 1929a:14.
103. Lou→Tönnies (7-)13 XII 1904, draft.
104. D [V? 1913].
105. D [late spring 1913].
106. D VI 1922.
107. 1920b:366 (ditto metaphysicians).
108. Lou→Spranger, 27 V 1914.
109. Lou→Frieda [early 1909].
110. D [8 II 1913].
111. 1913e:6.
112. 1904a:47.
113. *Ellen Delp.
114. 1914c:650.
115. Rée→FN, 20 IV 1882 (below, p. 52).
116. 1920b:363n.
117. 1914a:266ff.; 1920b:363n.; etc.
118. D 20 X 1911.
119. D 2 II 1919.
120. Peter Gast→Cäcilie Gussenbauer, 7 XI 1882.
121. *Ibid.*

PART TWO YOUTH

1. Biedermann→Louise Salomé, 7 VII 1883.
2. Kinkel→Lou, 21 IX 1881.
3. 1935a:212.
4. Kinkel→Lou, 21 IX 1881.
5. D I 1919; cf. 1931a:37.
6. Kinkel→Lou, 17 I 1882.
7. MvM→Lou, 13 VII [1882].
8. MvM→Lou, 25 V [1882].
9. *Ibid.*
10. MvM→Lou [14? III 1882].
11. MvM→Lou, 25 V [1882].
12. *Ibid.*

13. *Ibid.*
14. *Ibid.*
15. Rée→FN, 10 X 1877.
16. Rée→Lisbeth, 8 VI 1879.
17. Rée→FN, X 1879.
18. Rée, *Ursprung*, concluding chapter.
19. MvM→Lou, 2 X [1882].
20. Lou→Tönnies, 1 XII 1904.
21. Rée→FN, 2 VII 1877.
22. Rée→FN, 31 X 1875.
23. FN→Lisbeth and Franziska Nietzsche, 9 X 1876.
24. FN, *HKG:B*, IV, 321.
25. FN, *Human*, II, 52.
26. D 21 VIII [1882].
27. Lou→FN, 4 VI [1882].
28. FN, *Human*, II, 36.
29. *Ibid.*, 37.
30. FN→Rée [late IV] 1878.
31. FN→Rée [10 VIII 1878].
32. FN→Lisbeth, 24 VII 1879; FN→O, 12 VIII 1879.
33. FN→Rée, 31 X 1879.
34. FN→O [late I or early II 1880].
35. FN, *Ecce*, "So Spoke Zarathustra," 1.
36. FN→Rée [20?] VIII 1881.
37. FN→Lisbeth, 18 VIII 1881.
38. Rée→Franziska Nietzsche, 20 XI 1879, quoting FN, *Human*, II, 55.
39. FN→Rohde, VI 1878.
40. Rée→Franziska Nietzsche, 17 VI 1880.
41. FN→Lou [8? IX 1882].
42. FN, *Science*, 342.
43. Rée→Lisbeth, 5 II 1882.
44. FN→Lisbeth, 10 II 1882.
45. Rée→Lisbeth, 11 II 1882.
46. FN→Lisbeth, 10 II 1882.
47. FN→Gast, 4 III 1882.
48. Rée→Lisbeth [mid-III 1882].
49. *Ibid.*
50. *Ibid.*
51. FN→Rée [21 III 1882].
52. FN→Rée [23 III 1882].
53. MvM→Lou, 25 V [1882].
54. MvM→Rée [23 III 1882].
55. Reconstructed from Lou→Gillot, 26 III 1882, copy, in 1931a:96-98.
56. Lou→Gillot, 26 III 1882, copy, in 1931a:96-98.
57. MvM→Lou, 25 V [1882].
58. *Ibid.*
59. *Ibid.*

60. *Ibid.*
61. FN→Louise Salomé [early VIII 1883], draft.
62. FN→Georg Rée [early VIII 1883], draft.
63. MvM→Olga Monod-Herzen [late IV] 1882.
64. 1890a:13.
65. *Ibid.*, 11 and 12n.
66. *Ibid.*, 12.
67. MvM→Olga Monod-Herzen [late IV] 1882.
68. Ida O, in Bernoulli, *FO und FN*, I, 336, quoting Nietzsche.
69. FN MvM [early VII 1882], draft.
70. Halévy, 245n.
71. D [late VIII 1882].
72. D 18 VIII [1882].
73. O→Gast, 25-26 VI 1882.
74. *Ibid.*
75. Ida O, in Bernoulli, *FO und FN*, I, 336.
76. *Ibid.*, 343.
77. *Ibid.*, 336.
78. *Ibid.*, 343.
79. *Ibid.*, 346.
80. *Ibid.*, 336.
81. FN→Rée [8 V 1882].
82. FN→O, 15 V 1882.
83. Bernoulli, *FO und FN*, I, 334, quoting Overbeck.
84. I Thessalonians 4:11 (after Lou's Lutheran version).
85. Ida O, in Bernoulli *FO und FN*, I, 336.
86. Rée→Lou [late V 1882].
87. FN→Lou [10? VI 1882].
88. Rée→Lou [late V 1882].
89. Bernoulli, *FO und FN*, I, 349.
90. CG→Lisbeth, 19 I 1882, echoing Lisbeth.
91. Ida O, in Bernoulli, *FO und FN*, I, 338.
92. Rée→Lou [31 VII 1882].
93. Lisbeth→Ida O, 5 VI 1882.
94. Biedermann→Louise Salomé, 7 VII 1883.
95. Lou→FN, 4 VI [1882].
96. FN→O [7? VI 1882] (foregoing O→FN missing).
97. MvM→Lou, 25 V [1882].
98. MvM→Lou, 6 VI [1882].
99. Lisbeth→Ida O, 5 VI 1882.
100. MvM→Lou, 18 VI [1882] (to Stibbe).
101. Lisbeth→CG, 24 IX/2 X 1882.

102. Hüter's memorandum.
103. Hüter→MvM, 4 VII 1882.
104. Hüter's memorandum.
105. Lou→Frieda [late I 1905].
106. FN→Lou [9 VII 1882].
107. FN→Gast, 13 VII 1882.
108. Halévy, 240.
109. FN, *Untimely*, III, 1.
110. FN→Gast, 13 VII 1882.
111. FN→MvM [early VII 1882], draft.
112. FN→Lou [XII 1882], draft.
113. FN→Ida O, 29 VII 1883, draft.
114. Lou→Ida O [mid-VII 1882]; etc.
115. FN→Rohde [15 VII 1882]; cf. FN→MvM [early VII 1882], draft.
116. FN→O [early XI 1882]; cf. FN→ Lou [26 VI 1882].
117. D 14 VIII [1882].
118. FN→Lou [9 VII 1882].
119. FN→Lou [3? VII 1882].
120. FN→Lou [9 VII 1882].
121. Rée→Lou [4? VIII 1882].
122. Rée→Lou [late V 1882].
123. Rée→Lou [4? VIII 1882].
124. Lou→Tönnies (7-)13 XII 1904, draft.
125. MvM→Lou, 5 VII [1882].
126. MvM→Lou, 13 VII [1882].
127. FN→Lisbeth, 28 VII 1882.
128. Lisbeth→CG, 24 IX/2 X 1882.
129. Rée→Lou [4? VIII 1882].
130. Rée→Lou [6? VIII 1882].
131. FN→Gast, 1 VIII 1882.
132. Lou→Ida O [mid-VII 1882].
133. Lisbeth→CG, 24 IX/2 X 1882.
134. Lisbeth→Gast, 31 I 1883.
135. Ida O, in Bernoulli, *FO und FN*, I, 340.
136. Lisbeth→CG, 24 IX/2 X 1882.
137. *Ibid.*
138. Lou→FN, 2 VIII 1882.
139. Lisbeth→Ida O, 29 I 1883; cf. Lisbeth→Gast, 31 I 1883, and O→Gast, 17 III 1883.
140. Lisbeth→CG, 24 IX/2 X 1882.
141. Lisbeth→Ida O, 29 I 1883.
142. Lisbeth→CG, 24 IX/2 X 1882.
143. *Ibid.*
144. *Ibid.*
145. Lisbeth→Ida O, 29 I 1883.
146. D 14 VIII [1882].
147. Lisbeth→Ida O, 29 I 1883.
148. D 14 VIII [1882].
149. Lisbeth→CG, 24 IX/2 X 1882.

150. D 21 VIII [1882].
151. D [late spring 1913].
152. FN→Lou [16? IX 1882].
153. Follows from FN→Lou [8? IX 1882].
154. Quoted by O, in Bernoulli, *FO und FN*, I, 338.
155. FN→O [7 IV 1884]; FN→MvM [early V 1884], copy.
156. D 18 VIII [1882].
157. FN→O [14?] IX 1882.
158. FN→Gast, 20 VIII 1882.
159. FN→O [14?] IX 1882.
160. D 18 VIII [1882].
161. Lisbeth→CG, 24 IX/2 X 1882.
162. D 18 VIII [1882].
163. Lisbeth→CG, 24 IX/2 X 1882.
164. D [late VIII 1882].
165. D 21 VIII [1882].
166. D 14 VIII [1882].
167. D 21 VIII [1882].
168. D 18 VIII [1882].
169. D [late VIII 1882].
170. FN→O [14?] IX 1882.
171. Lisbeth→CG, 24 IX/2 X 1882.
172. *Ibid.*
173. FN→Gast, 20 VIII 1882.
174. FN→Lou [3? IX 1882].
175. Lisbeth→CG, 24 IX/2 X 1882.
176. FN→Lou [3? IX 1882].
177. FN→O [14?] IX 1882.
178. *Ibid.*; cf. FN→Rée [15? IX 1882].
179. FN→Lisbeth [6?] IX 1882.
180. FN→O [14?] IX 1882.
181. FN→O [9? II 1883].
182. FN→O [14?] IX 1882.
183. FN→Lou [3? IX 1882].
184. FN→Rée [3? IX 1882].
185. Follows from FN→Rée [15? IX 1882].
186. Quoted in FN→Lisbeth [6?] IX 1882 and in FN→O [14?] IX 1882.
187. Ditto.
188. FN→O [14?] IX 1882.
189. FN→Lou [8? IX 1882].
190. FN→Rée [15? IX 1882].
191. Rée→FN [17? IX 1882].
192. Quoted in FN→Lou [16? IX 1882].
193. FN→Lou [16? IX 1882].
194. *Ibid.*
195. Inferred from FN→Lou [26? IX 1882].
196. FN→Lou [26? IX 1882].
197. Lisbeth→CG, 24 IX/2 X 1882.
198. *Ibid.*
199. *Ibid.*
200. FN→O [14?] IX 1882.
201. FN→Gast, 2 X 1882 and 3 X 1882.
202. Gast→Cäcilie Gussenbauer, 16 [X] 1882 and 7 XI 1882.
203. Lou→Stein, 24 X 1882.
204. FN→Romundt [early XI 1882].
205. FN, *Human*, I, 390.
206. Explicit in D 21 VIII [1882].
207. FN→Lisbeth and Franziska Nietzsche, 17 X 1882.
208. Gast→O, 14 XI 1883.
209. FN→Georg Rée [early VIII 1883], draft.
210. *Ibid.*
211. FN→O [early XI 1882].
212. MvM→Lou, 2 X [1882].
213. Lou→Hüter [14 X 1882].
214. Louise Salomé→FN, 10 XI [1882].
215. FN→Rée [XII 1882], draft.
216. Inferred from Gast→Cäcilie Gussenbauer, 7 XI 1882.
217. Quoted in Lisbeth→Gast, 10 II 1883; cf. FN→Lou, 8 XI 1882.
218. Letter missing.
219. Ida O, in Bernoulli, *FO und FN*, I, 338.
220. FN→Gast, 23 XI 1882.
221. Letter missing.
222. Quoted in FN→Georg Rée [early VIII 1883], draft.
223. Ditto.
224. FN→Hans von Bülow [XII 1882].
225. FN→Gast, 19 II 1883.
226. FN, *Ecce*, "So Spoke Zarathustra," 1.
227. Quoted in FN→Georg Rée [early VIII 1883], draft; cf. FN→Rée [early VIII 1883], draft.
228. FN→O [early III 1883].
229. FN→O [9? II 1883].
230. FN→Gast, 19 II 1883.
231. FN→O [22 II 1883].
232. FN→O [early III 1883].
233. FN→Gast, 24 III 1883.
234. FN→O [22? III 1883].
235. FN→Gast, 19 II 1883.
236. FN→O [22 II 1883].
237. FN→O [early III 1883].
238. FN→MvM [late III 1883].
239. FN→MvM [early IV 1883].

240. Ida O, in Bernoulli, *FO und FN*, I, 341.
241. FN→Gast, 27 IV 1883.
242. FN→Lisbeth, 27 IV 1883.
243. FN→O [29 IV 1883].
244. Gast→O, 27 III 1883.
245. FN→O [27? VIII 1883].
246. FN→Ida O, 29 VII 1883, draft.
247. FN→O, VII 1883.
248. FN→O [25 XII 1882].
249. FN→Ida O, 29 VII 1883, draft.
250. FN→MVM, VIII 1883.
251. FN→O, VII 1883.
252. FN→Ida O [mid-VIII 1883].
253. Bernoulli, *FO und FN*, I, 270, quoting Overbeck.
254. FN→O [27? VIII 1883].
255. FN→Franziska Nietzsche [II 1884], draft.
256. Lisbeth→Gast, 26 IV 1884.
257. Hüter's memorandum.
258. Hüter→MVM, 31 III 1883.
259. MVM→Hüter, 8 I 1883.
260. Deussen, 221.
261. 1931a:111.
262. *Ibid.*
263. Lou→Tönnies (7-)13 XII 1904, draft.
264. Tönnies→Paulsen, 31 V 1883.
265. *Ibid.*
266. Paulsen→Tönnies, 3 VI 1883.
267. Biedermann→Louise Salomé, 7 VII 1883.
268. Lou→Emma, VII 1883.
269. *Ibid.*
270. Tönnies→Paulsen, 11 VII 1883.
271. Tönnies, "Rée," 672.
272. Tönnies→Paulsen, 11 VII 1883.
273. Rée, *Entstehung*, 175 (meaning uncertain).
274. Tönnies→Paulsen, 6 III 1885.
275. Rée, *Entstehung*, 32.
276. Tönnies, "Rée," 670.
277. Tönnies→Paulsen, 4 VIII 1883.
278. Lou→Emma, VII 1883.
279. Lou→Tönnies (7-)13 XII 1904, draft.
280. Tönnies→Paulsen, 4 VIII 1883.
281. Tönnies, "Selbstdarstellung," 16/218.
282. Tönnies→Lou, 23 IX 1883.
283. Tönnies→Lisbeth, 1 IX 1900.
284. Tönnies→Paulsen, 26 VIII 1883.
285. Tönnies→Paulsen, 8 IX 1883.
286. Tönnies→Lou, 23 IX 1883.
287. Tönnies→Paulsen, 3 X 1883.
288. Tönnies, "Selbstdarstellung," 16/218.
289. Lou→Tönnies, 5 XI [1886].
290. Lou→Caro [1 I 1884].
291. FN→O [7 IV 1884]; FN→MVM [early V 1884], copy.
292. 1883a:*passim*.
293. *Ibid.*, 239ff.
294. *Ibid.*, 87.
295. *Ibid.*, 72-73 and *passim*.
296. *Ibid.*, 76.
297. *Ibid.*, 210.
298. *Ibid.*, 76.
299. *Ibid.*, 208.
300. *Ibid.*, 187.
301. D [late VIII 1882].
302. 1883a:86.
303. *Ibid.*, 130.
304. *Ibid.*, 109.
305. *Ibid.*
306. *Ibid.*
307. *Ibid.*, 113.
308. *Ibid.*, 113-14.
309. *Ibid.*, 114.
310. *Ibid.*, 119f.
311. *Ibid.*, 120.
312. *Ibid.*, 125.
313. *Ibid.*, 126.
314. *Ibid.*, 128.
315. *Ibid.*
316. *Ibid.*, 130.
317. *Ibid.*
318. *Ibid.*, 110.
319. *Ibid.*
320. *Ibid.*, 133.
321. *Ibid.*, 138.
322. *Ibid.*, 226.
323. *Ibid.*, 262.
324. *Ibid.*, 257.
325. *Ibid.*, 275.
326. *Ibid.*, 267.
327. *Ibid.*, 278.
328. *Ibid.*, 279.
329. *Ibid.*, 286.
330. *Ibid.*, 298.
331. *Ibid.*, 302.
332. *Ibid.*, 316.
333. *Ibid.*
334. *Ibid.*, 212.
335. Lou→Caro [1 I 1884].
336. *Ibid.*
337. 1883a:313.
338. 1920b:379.
339. FN→MVM [early V 1884] draft.
340. FN→O [7 IV 1884].
341. Stein→FN, 28 V 1884.

342. Stein→FN, 7 XII 1884 (misdated 1 XII 1884 in FN, *GB*, III).
343. FN→Lisbeth [mid-XII 1884].
344. Lou→Emma [summer 1884].
345. Lou→Emma [summer 1884], "letter fragment," quoted by Pfeiffer, *Leben*, 323.
346. Deussen, *Leben*, 140.
347. *Ibid.*, 221.
348. FN→O, 4 V 1885, quoting Ida; cf. FN→O, XII 1885.
349. O→FN, 29 XI 1885.
350. Rohde→O, 8 XI 1891.
351. Andler, 306.
352. FN→O, 4 V 1885.
353. FN→O, 17 X 1885.
354. *Ibid.*
355. FN→Stein, 15 X 1885.
356. FN→O, 17 X 1885; cf. FN→ Stein, 15 X 1885.
357. FN, *Beyond*, 86.
358. *Ibid.*, 232.
359. *Ibid.*, 85.
360. *Ibid.*, 144.
361. *Ibid.*, 79.
362. *Ibid.*, 74.
363. *Ibid.*, 157.
364. *Ibid.*, 92.
365. *Ibid.*, 236.
366. FN, *Beyond*, 6.
367. Deussen, *Leben*, 221.
368. Gersdorff→O, 18 IV 1885.
369. Hartmann, 143.
370. 1931a:119.
371. Rée→Lou [1883?].
372. FN→Stein, 15 X 1885.
373. Lou→Tönnies [7 IV 1886].
374. Kolle, 169.
375. Schulz→Lou, 13 I 1886.
376. Lou→Tönnies [7 IV 1886], [late spring 1886], and 5 XI [1886].
377. Gildemeister→Lou, 22 VII 1886.
378. Gildemeister→Hugo Göring, 2 VIII 1886.
379. Gildemeister→Lou, 13 VIII 1886.
380. Lou→Emma, 22 IX 1886, copy.
381. Schulz→Lou, 2 IX 1886.
382. D XII 1911.
383. Romundt→O, 13 XI 1898.
384. D 31 X 1888.
385. FN→MVM [12 V 1887].
386. FN, *Ecce*, "Human, All Too Human," 6.
387. FN→Franziska Nietzsche, 23 VII 1888; cf. Deussen, *Leben*, 94.
388. FN→Stein, 15 X 1885.
389. FN, *Genealogy*, I: 8.
390. *Ibid.*, I: 8.
391. *Ibid.*, III: 8.
392. FN, *Ecce*, "Why I Write Such Good Books," 5.
393. FN, *Ecce*, "So Spoke Zarathustra," 1.
394. Gersdorff→FN [30] XI 1897.
395. Kolle, 169-70.
396. D [III?] 1918; 1931a:255-56.
397. Rée, *Philosophie*, 362-63.
398. Lessing, 73-74.
399. Rée, *Philosophie*, Preface.
400. Kolle, 170.
401. Hüter's memorandum.
402. Louise Salomé→Lou [21 V 1887].
403. 1935c.
404. *Ibid.*
405. D 23 VI 1904.
406. Lou→Lollo, 17 II [1890].
407. Lou→Tönnies, 5 IV 1889.
408. Lou→Lollo, 17 II [1890].
409. 1889a:84.
410. *Ibid.*, 70.
411. *Ibid.*, 71-72.
412. *Ibid.*, 72.
413. *Ibid.*, 84.
414. Brausewetter, 9.
415. 1889a:87.
416. *Ibid.*, 171.
417. *Ibid.*
418. *Ibid.*, 159, 180.
419. *Ibid.*, 162.
420. *Ibid.*, 162-63.
421. *Ibid.*, 161.
422. *Ibid.*
423. *Ibid.*, 162.
424. *Ibid.*, 173.
425. 1889a:131-32n.; cf. 1893a:162, 1907a:199.
426. 1891b:1005.
427. *Ibid.*, 1027-29.
428. *Ibid.*, 1004.
429. *Ibid.*
430. *Ibid.*, 1027.
431. *Ibid.*, 1030.
432. *Ibid.*, 1082.
433. *Ibid.*, 1081.
434. *Ibid.*, 1082.
435. *Ibid.*
436. *Ibid.*, 1083.

437. *Ibid.*, 1082; also 1058, 1079-80, etc.
438. 1890a:17.
439. *Ibid.*, 20.
440. *Ibid.*, 31.
441. *Ibid.*, 32.
442. *Ibid.*
443. *Ibid.*, 29.
444. *Ibid.*, 33.
445. *Ibid.*, 34.
446. *Ibid.*, 35.
447. *Ibid.*, 48.
448. *Ibid.*
449. *Ibid.*, 39.
450. *Ibid.*, 117.
451. *Ibid.*
452. *Ibid.*, 118.
453. *Ibid.*, 125.
454. *Ibid.*, 147.
455. *Ibid.*
456. *Ibid.*, 254.
457. *Ibid.*
458. *Ibid.*, 197.
459. *Ibid.*, 48.
460. *Ibid.*, 49.
461. *Ibid.*, 48.
462. *Ibid.*, 55.
463. *Ibid.*, 138.
464. *Ibid.*, 229 and *passim*.
465. *Ibid.*, 153.
466. *Ibid.*
467. *Ibid.*, 131.
468. *Ibid.*, 184.
469. *Ibid.*, 161.
470. *Ibid.*, 154.
471. *Ibid.*, 168.
472. *Ibid.*, 23.
473. *Ibid.*, 144.
474. *Ibid.*, 192-93.
475. *Ibid.*, 193.
476. *Ibid.*
477. *Ibid.*, 192-93.
478. *Ibid.*, 197.
479. *Ibid.*, 227.
480. *Ibid.*, 43n., cf. 43, 259.
481. *Ibid.*, 43.
482. *Ibid.*, 102.
483. *Ibid.*, 120.
484. *Ibid.*, 101.
485. *Ibid.*, 120.
486. *Ibid.*
487. *Ibid.*
488. *Ibid.*, 122.
489. *Ibid.*, 120.
490. *Ibid.*, 259.
491. *Ibid.*, 43n.
492. *Ibid.*, 5.
493. *Ibid.*, 3, 125, 127.
494. *Ibid.*, 127.
495. *Ibid.*, 55.
496. *Ibid.*, 22.
497. *Ibid.*, 223.
498. *Ibid.*
499. *Ibid.*
500. *Ibid.*, 14-15.
501. *Ibid.*, 11ff.
502. Lou→Frieda [late I 1905].
503. 1890a:222.
504. *Ibid.*, 224.
505. *Ibid.*, 53ff.
506. *Ibid.*, 87.
507. *Ibid.*, 223.
508. *Ibid.*, 141, 224, and *passim*.
509. *Ibid.*, 142.
510. *Ibid.*, 224.
511. *Ibid.*, 10.
512. *Ibid.*, 47.
513. *Ibid.*, 41.
514. 1891d:173.
515. *Ibid.*, 172.
516. *Ibid.*, 170.
517. *Ibid.*, 171-72.
518. *Ibid.*, 175.
519. 1890a:5.
520. *Ibid.*, 4n.
521. Heilborn, "L A–S," 25-26; etc.
522. Hofmiller, "Lehrjahre," 602.
523. Rohde→o, 13 III 1891.
524. Rohde→o, 17 III 1895.
525. o→Rohde, 31 XII 1894.
526. Bernoulli, *FO und FN*, II, 389.
527. Quoted *ibid.*, I, 87 (with assent).
528. Gast, Introduction, xvi.
529. *Ibid.*, x; xvff.
530. *Ibid.*, xv.
531. Gast→Hofmiller, 13 VII 1894.
532. Gast→Hofmiller, 17 IX 1894.
533. Gast→Hofmiller, 21 V 1908.
534. Kögel, 235.
535. *Ibid.*, 234.
536. *Ibid.*, 233.
537. *Ibid.*, 234-35.
538. Gersdorff→Lisbeth, 10 IV 1895.
539. Romundt→o, 10 II 1895, 16 II 1895, 21 II 1895, IV 1895, and 20 V 1895.
540. Romundt, "Noch," 524.
541. *Ibid.*, 526.
542. Kögel→Hofmiller, 8 II 1896.
543. Hofmiller, "Lehrjahre," 605.
544. Kögel→Hofmiller, 8 II 1896.
545. Gast→Hofmiller, 10 XI 1896.

546. Kögel→Hofmiller, 25 ix 1897.
547. Bernoulli, "Erlebnis," 26, quoting Mrs. Kögel.
548. See Hofmiller, *FN*, 46f.
549. Gast→Hofmiller, 21 v 1908.
550. E F-N, Introduction, lxv.
551. E F-N, *Leben*, 402-18 and *passim* (also anticipations in the preceding volumes).
552. *Ibid.*, 403.
553. *Ibid.*, 408.
554. *Ibid.*, 403.
555. *Ibid.*, 411.
556. E F-N, "Legenden," 171.
557. *Ibid.*, 172.
558. *Ibid.*, 173.
559. 1931a:106; etc.
560. Pfeiffer, *Leben*, 106n.; Lou→ Frieda [late I 1905].
561. Lou→Frieda [late I 1905].
562. *Ibid.*
563. Halévy, 243-59.
564. Bernoulli, "Erlebnis."
565. Andler, 280.
566. *Ibid.*, 282.
567. D 13 viii 1900.
568. D [summer?] 1911.
569. Bäumer, *Gestalt*, 488-89.
570. Klingenberg, 237.
571. *Ibid.*, 252.

PART THREE

WOMANHOOD

1. D [1892-1893].
2. *Ibid.*
3. *Ibid.*
4. *Ibid.*
5. *Ibid.*
6. Siemsen, 8.
7. 1931a:122.
8. D VI 1917.
9. D 17 viii 1903.
10. Lou→Frieda [1901].
11. 1892b:1220.
12. *Ibid.*, 1217.
13. *Ibid.*, 1220.
14. *Ibid.*, 1221.
15. *Ibid.*, 1222.
16. *Ibid.*
17. 1893a:154, 168.
18. *Ibid.*, 171.
19. *Ibid.*, 169.
20. 1893b:325.
21. 1893c: *passim.*

22. 1893d:575.
23. *Ibid.*, 576.
24. 1893e:1167.
25. 1893h:1348.
26. *Ibid.*
27. Hauptmann's diary, 14 ii 1937.
28. D 26-28 xii 1893.
29. 1893g:292.
30. D 31 x 1888.
31. 1893g:115.
32. Pauli, "Frauen," 277.
33. Hamann, 1901.
34. Romundt→o, 22 i 1896.
35. Romundt→o, 5 vii 1896.
36. Hamann, 1901.
37. D 9 viii 1894.
38. Quoted in Wedekind, 369n. (undated but apparently from Paris).
39. D 22-23 iv 1894.
40. D 24 ix 1894.
41. D 31 x 1894.
42. D 26 x 1894.
43. D 1 xi 1894.
44. D 17 xi 1894.
45. D 11-13 xi 1894.
46. D ii 1895.
47. Ricarda Huch→Lou [answering Lou's of mid-summer 1895?].
48. 1895a:42.
49. 1920b:385n.
50. 1894b:343.
51. *Ibid.*, 344.
52. *Ibid.*
53. *Ibid.*, 347.
54. *Ibid.*
55. *Ibid.*, 348.
56. *Ibid.*, 349.
57. *Ibid.*, 350.
58. *Ibid.*, 351.
59. *Ibid.*
60. *Ibid.*
61. *Ibid.*
62. *Ibid.*, 350.
63. *Ibid.*
64. *Ibid.*, 351.
65. Lou→RMR, 13 i 1913.
66. FN, *Antichrist*, 24 (first published early 1895); anticipated in FN, *Genealogy*, i: 8.
67. D [late 1910]; cf. 1904a:294ff., etc.
68. D 12 v 1901.
69. Lou→Caro [ix 1898] (draft?).
70. D 23 iv 1895.
71. 1931a:123.

72. Lou→Johanna Niemann, 16 III 1895.
73. Lou→Schnitzler, 15 v 1894.
74. Lou→Schnitzler, 28 IV 1895.
75. Lou→Schnitzler, 1 v 1895.
76. D 27 IV 1895.
77. Lou→B-H, 17 VII 1895.
78. Lou→B-H, 7 [VI] 1913.
79. D [late XII 1912].
80. B-H, *Novellen*, 79.
81. Schnitzler's diary, 11 v 1895.
82. *Ibid.*, 21 v 1895.
83. B-H→HVH, 22 v 1895.
84. Lou→B-H, 17 VII 1895.
85. D 30 IV 1895—in the future tense.
86. D 15-16, 19, 21 VI 1895.
87. D 8 VI 1895.
88. D 15-16 VI 1895.
89. 1895f:138.
90. Lou→B-H, 17 VII 1895.
91. *Ibid.*
92. HVH→Schnitzler, 21 VIII 1895.
93. Schnitzler→HVH, 1 IX 1895.
94. *Ibid.*
95. Schnitzler→B-H, 11 IX 1895 (postmarked 12 IX 1895).
96. D 14 IX 1895.
97. D 15 IX 1895.
98. Schnitzler→B-H, 15 IX 1895.
99. B-H→Schnitzler, 17 IX 1895.
100. D 11-13 XI 1895.
101. D 23 XI 1895.
102. D 24 XI 1895.
103. Lou→Schnitzler [25 XI 1895].
104. D 26 XI 1895.
105. D 27 XI 1895.
106. D 28 XI 1895.
107. D 29 XI 1895.
108. D 3 XII 1895.
109. B-H, *Paula*, 76.
110. *Ibid.*, 79ff.
111. *Ibid.*, 85.
112. B-H, *Tod*, 22.
113. Lou→B-H [late XII 1895 or I 1896].
114. Peters, 200.
115. D 31 XII 1895.
116. D 12 II 1896.
117. D 17 v 1896.
118. D 28 v 1896.
119. D 31 v 1896.
120. 1897a:99.
121. *Ibid.*, 101.
122. *Ibid.*, 121.
123. *Ibid.*, 124.
124. 1897h:271.
125. *Ibid.*, 267.
126. *Ibid.*, 270.
127. 1896c:68.
128. 1897e:147.
129. *Ibid.*
130. D III 1923.
131. D 4 I 1904.
132. D 3 IV 1903.
133. Lou→Frieda [1905?].
134. 1909b:52.
135. *Ibid.*, 20.
136. *Ibid.*, 55.
137. *Ibid.*, 54.
138. *Ibid.*, 18.
139. *Ibid.*, 52.
140. 1914c:650.
141. 1913e:11.
142. D I 1915.
143. D [early XI 1913].
144. D [III?] 1918.
145. 1931a:27-28.
146. 1909b:28.
147. D [summer?] 1911.
148. 1913c:467.
149. 1909b:50.
150. *Ibid.*, 14.
151. FN, *Beyond*, 64.
152. 1882 aphorism.
153. 1893c:469.
154. 1913e:5.
155. Lou→Frieda [1900?].
156. 1909b:45.
157. 1913e:13; cf. 1899f, etc.
158. 1909b:45.
159. *Ibid.*, 45, 48.
160. 1893g:210.
161. 1896a.
162. 1897k:1218.
163. 1909b:63.
164. Lou→EK [VIII 1901].
165. 1931a:137.
166. D 31 v 1903.
167. 1896d:20.
168. D 12 XII 1896.
169. 1896d:97.
170. D 11 v 1913.
171. RMR→Lou [6 VI 1897].
172. RMR→Lou [8 VI 1897].
173. *Ibid.*
174. RMR→Lou [9 VI 1897].
175. D 15 VI 1897.
176. D [VII 1913].
177. Lou→RMR [26 II 1901].
178. RMR, *Tagebücher*, 117.
179. Lou→Freud, 19 X 1917; 1920b: 370n.

180. Lou→RMR [26 II 1901].
181. D 13 VII 1897.
182. D 14 VII 1897.
183. RMR→Lou [17 VII 1897].
184. 1897g:179.
185. Lou→RMR [26 II 1901].
186. 1898b:181.
187. D 18 IX 1897.
188. 1897j:113.
189. *Ibid.*, 134.
190. *Ibid.*, 104.
191. Engel, *passim.*
192. Stöcker, "Frauentypen," 630.
193. 1898a:325.
194. *Ibid.*, 341.
195. 1897k:1219.
196. *Ibid.*, 1220.
197. 1898c:6.
198. *Ibid.*, 7.
199. 1898d:154.
200. 1898b:178.
201. *Ibid.*, 179.
202. *Ibid.*
203. *Ibid.*, 182.
204. *Ibid.*, 181.
205. D 1917.
206. D [1916] (Munich supplement).
207. 1898e:515.
208. RMR, *Tagebücher*, 22.
209. *Ibid.*, 30.
210. *Ibid.*, 87.
211. *Ibid.*, 87-88.
212. Lou→Caro [2? VI 1898] (draft?).
213. Lou→Caro [6? VI 1898] (draft?).
214. Lou→EK, 29 X 1899.
215. RMR, *Tagebücher*, 138.
216. *Ibid.*, 36.
217. *Ibid.*, 37.
218. *Ibid.*, 53.
219. *Ibid.*
220. *Ibid.*, 118.
221. *Ibid.*, 134.
222. 1904a:26, 45-47.
223. 1900b:*passim.*
224. RMR, *Tagebücher*, 135.
225. *Ibid.*
226. *Ibid.*, 137.
227. Butler, 25.
228. RMR, *Tagebücher*, 150-51.
229. Lou→EK, 1 VIII [1898].
230. Lou→EK, 30 IX 1898.
231. Lou→EK, 1 VIII [1898].
232. Lou→Caro [IX 1898] (draft?).
233. Lou→EK, 30 IX 1898.

234. 1898g:1148.
235. *Ibid.*, 1153.
236. *Ibid.*, 1155.
237. 1898h:222.
238. *Ibid.*
239. *Ibid.*
240. "Aphorismen . . ."
241. "Der dritte Bruder . . ."
242. "Sehnsucht . . ."
243. "Bilder . . ."
244. "Die eherne Schlange . . ."
245. Lou→EK, 29 X 1899.
246. 1898i:402.
247. Lou→EK, 1 VIII [1898].
248. 1899c:239.
249. *Ibid.*, 238.
250. *Ibid.*, 239.
251. *Ibid.*
252. 1899a:225.
253. *Ibid.*, 226.
254. *Ibid.*, 228.
255. *Ibid.*
256. *Ibid.*, 229.
257. *Ibid.*
258. *Ibid.*
259. *Ibid.*, 230.
260. *Ibid.*
261. *Ibid.*
262. *Ibid.*
263. *Ibid.*
264. *Ibid.*
265. *Ibid.*, 231.
266. *Ibid.*, 233.
267. *Ibid.*, 237.
268. *Ibid.*, 238-39.
269. *Ibid.*, 235.
270. D [1912?].
271. Buber→Lou, 28 III 1906.
272. Dohm, 280.
273. *Ibid.*, 279.
274. *Ibid.*, 280.
275. *Ibid.*, 282.
276. *Ibid.*, 283.
277. *Ibid.*, 285.
278. *Ibid.*, 290.
279. *Ibid.*, 287.
280. *Ibid.*
281. *Ibid.*, 290.
282. *Ibid.*, 291.
283. *Ibid.*
284. EK→Lou, 16 IV 1900.
285. Lou→EK, 22 IV 1900.
286. 1899a:235.
287. FN, *Beyond*, 232.
288. D [21 XI 1912].
289. 1899a:240-41.

290. *Ibid.*, 230.
291. 1899b:368.
292. *Ibid.*
293. *Ibid.*, 369.
294. *Ibid.*
295. *Ibid.*
296. *Ibid.*, 370.
297. *Ibid.*
298. *Ibid.*, 370-71.
299. *Ibid.*, 371.
300. *Ibid.*, 372.
301. *Ibid.*
302. *Ibid.*
303. *Ibid.*
304. D 21 VIII [1882].
305. FN, *Genealogy*, II: 17.
306. D IX 1919.
307. 1918b:330.
308. 1899d:122.
309. Romundt→o, 22 I 1897.
310. Romundt→o, 13 VIII 1899.
311. Romundt, 28 and *passim.*
312. *Ibid.*, 44.
313. Romundt→o, 13 XI 1898.
314. Romundt→o, 13 VIII 1899.
315. RMR→Lou, 18 III 1899.
316. 1899a:228.
317. RMR→Frieda, 28 I 1899.
318. RMR→Elena, 28 XII 1898.
319. RMR→Elena, 9 III 1899.
320. RMR→Frieda, 22 IV 1899.
321. D 28 IV 1899.
322. RMR→Hugo Salus, 19 V 1899.
323. RMR→Elena, 10 V 1899.
324. Boutchik, 130.
325. RMR→Elena, 11 V 1899, 16 V 1899.
326. RMR→Elena, 17 IX 1899.
327. RMR→Frieda, 7 VI 1899.
328. Lou→EK, 29 X 1899.
329. D 16 VI 1899.
330. EK→Lou, 25 X 1899.
331. Lou→EK, 29 X 1899.
332. *Ibid.*
333. Quoted in RMR, *Briefe und Tagebücher*, 420.
334. D 30 VII 1899.
335. D 12 VIII 1899, 25 VIII 1899.
336. D 3 VIII 1899.
337. D 30 VIII 1899.
338. Quoted in RMR, *Briefe und Tagebücher*, 420.
339. Lou→Frieda [late 1908].
340. D 12 IX 1899.
341. D 13 IX 1899.
342. D 15 IX 1899.
343. Lou→EK, 29 X 1899.
344. 1913e:12-13.
345. *Ibid.*, 13.
346. Lou→Broncia, XI 1898 (Peters, 257).
347. Lou→EK, 29 X 1899.
348. D VI 1917.
349. 1899f:200.
350. Lou→EK, 29 X 1899.
351. Lou→RMR [26 II 1901].
352. RMR, *Tagebücher*, 160-61.
353. *Ibid.*, 203.
354. *Ibid.*, 204.
355. D 1 I 1900.
356. 1900a:1010.
357. *Ibid.*
358. *Ibid.*
359. *Ibid.*, 1011.
360. *Ibid.*
361. *Ibid.*
362. *Ibid.*, 1012.
363. *Ibid.*
364. *Ibid.*
365. *Ibid.*, 1012-13.
366. *Ibid.*, 1014.
367. *Ibid.*
368. *Ibid.*
369. *Ibid.*
370. *Ibid.*, 1015.
371. *Ibid.*
372. *Ibid.*
373. *Ibid.*, 1016.
374. *Ibid.*, 1015.
375. *Ibid.*, 1017.
376. *Ibid.*
377. *Ibid.*
378. *Ibid.*
379. *Ibid.*, 1018.
380. *Ibid.*
381. *Ibid.*, 1019.
382. *Ibid.*
383. *Ibid.*, 1020.
384. *Ibid.*
385. *Ibid.*
386. *Ibid.*
387. *Ibid.*
388. *Ibid.*
389. *Ibid.*
390. *Ibid.*
391. *Ibid.*, 1020-21.
392. *Ibid.*, 1021.
393. *Ibid.*
394. *Ibid.*
395. *Ibid.*
396. *Ibid.*
397. *Ibid.*

398. *Ibid.*
399. *Ibid.*
400. *Ibid.*, 1022.
401. *Ibid.*
402. *Ibid.*
403. *Ibid.*
404. *Ibid.*, 1023.
405. *Ibid.*
406. *Ibid.*
407. *Ibid.*
408. *Ibid.*, 1024.
409. *Ibid.*, 1025.
410. *Ibid.*
411. *Ibid.*, 1026.
412. *Ibid.*, 1025.
413. *Ibid.*, 1026.
414. *Ibid.*
415. *Ibid.*
416. *Ibid.*
417. *Ibid.*, 1027.
418. *Ibid.*, 1020.
419. 1931a:44-45.
420. D 16 I 1904; cf. D 8 III 1903, etc.
421. 1900a:1024.
422. *Ibid.*
423. *Ibid.*, 1025.
424. 1920b:title.
425. FN, *Tragedy*, I.
426. RMR, *Tagebücher*, 204 (2 XII 1899).
427. Lou→B-H, 11 III 1900.
428. D 24 III 1904.
429. D 24 XI 1900.
430. 1905a:290.
431. FN, Zarathustra I ("Von der schenkenden Tugend")—quoted 1919c:138.
432. B-H, *Tod*, closing lines.
433. Kahler, 231.
434. 1931a:27.
435. D [late 1910] (close of a diary).
436. Implicit in Lou→B-H, 1 I 1919.
437. D [late 1910], re "Das Kind."
438. 1905a:288 and *passim.*
439. B-H, *Tod*, 209.
440. *Ibid.*, 213.
441. *Ibid.*, 219.
442. 1900a:1010.
443. 1900b:313.
444. *Ibid.*, 334.
445. *Ibid.*, 263.
446. *Ibid.*, 331.
447. D [late 1910].
448. "Vom Bazillus . . ."
449. Lou→EK, 29 X 1899.
450. D [early V] 1900.

451. RMR→Schill, 23 II 1900.
452. Schill→Drojjin, 8 III 1900.
453. RMR→Schill, 16 III 1900.
454. RMR→Pasternak, 5 II 1900.
455. Lou→EK, 22 IV 1900.
456. RMR→Pasternak, 5 II 1900.
457. RMR→Schill, 16 III 1900.
458. D 20 V 1900.
459. Quoted in RMR, *Tagebücher*, 7.
460. D 11 V 1900.
461. Pasternak, 13.
462. *Ibid.*, 14.
463. Betz, 155.
464. RMR, *Tagebücher*, 282.
465. 1913d:7.
466. *Ibid.*
467. RMR, *Tagebücher*, 279-82.
468. Betz, 154-59.
469. D 10 VI 1900.
470. *Ibid.*
471. D 20 VI 1900.
472. *Ibid.*
473. *Ibid.*
474. RMR, *Tagebücher*, 233.
475. D [24 VI] 1900.
476. D [27 VI] 1900.
477. *Ibid.*
478. *Ibid.*
479. *Ibid.*
480. RMR, *Tagebücher*, 233-34.
481. D [early VII] 1900.
482. *Ibid.*
483. *Ibid.*
484. D 7 VII 1900.
485. D [early VII] 1900.
486. D 7 VII 1900.
487. *Ibid.*
488. D 6 VII 1900.
489. D 7 VII 1900.
490. RMR, *Tagebücher*, 434.
491. Droshshin, 226.
492. *Ibid.*, 227.
493. *Ibid.*, 228.
494. *Ibid.*
495. D [21 VII] 1900.
496. Droshshin, 228.
497. *Ibid.*, 230.
498. *Ibid.*
499. *Ibid.*, 231.
500. *Ibid.*
501. D [21 VII] 1900.
502. *Ibid.*
503. *Ibid.*
504. Lou→RMR [26 II 1901].
505. Lou→Tönnies (7-)13 XII 1904, draft; etc.

506. RMR→Lou [11 VIII 1900]—misdated 4 VIII 1900 by Pfeiffer,
Briefwechsel ("for two weeks
. . .").
507. *Ibid.*
508. RMR→Frieda, 24 X 1900.
509. *Ibid.*
510. Hauptmann archive reference:
A2, 151.
511. RMR, *Tagebücher*, 406.
512. *Ibid.*, 409-11.
513. *Ibid.*, 415-19.
514. *Ibid.*, 420-21.
515. *Ibid.*, 429.
516. *Ibid.*, 422.
517. RMR→Hauptmann, 16 XII 1901.
518. RMR, *Tagebücher*, 429.
519. *Ibid.*, 429, 430.
520. 1901b:73.
521. *Ibid.*, 71.
522. D [21 VII] 1900.
523. 1900d:94.
524. D 3 I 1901.
525. D 9 I 1901.
526. *Ibid.*
527. 1900d:409.
528. Bülow, 475.
529. Lou→B-H, 17 VII 1895.
530. D 10 I 1901.
531. D 15 I 1901.
532. *Ibid.*
533. 1901b:73.
534. *Ibid.*, 74.
535. *Ibid.*, 73.
536. *Ibid.*, 79.
537. *Ibid.*, 71.
538. D 16 I 1901.
539. D 17 I 1901.
540. D 3 I 1901.
541. D 15 I 1901.
542. D 19 I 1901.
543. D 10 I 1901.
544. RMR→Lou, 23 VI 1903; cf. Lou
→RMR [26 II 1901] and 1904a:
223.
545. D 13 VIII 1900.
546. RMR, *Tagebücher*, 233.
547. D [9-21 VII 1913].
548. D 7 IV 1902.
549. D 8 IV 1902.
550. RMR→Marie Thurn und Taxis,
24 V 1924.
551. Cf. Bab, 128.
552. Mövius, 27-28, 41.
553. 1901a:59.
554. D VIII 1900 ("Finnish supplement").
555. 1901a:71.
556. *Ibid.*, 106.
557. *Ibid.*, 107.
558. D VIII 1900 ("Finnish supplement").
559. D 21 III 1901.
560. D 10, 20, 21 I and 21 III 1901.
561. D 8 V 1901.
562. D 12 V 1901.
563. Meyer-Benfey, "L A-S," 304. Cf.
"Stöcker, "L A-S" (1904); etc.
564. 1901c:146.
565. *Ibid.*
566. *Ibid.*
567. *Ibid.*
568. *Ibid.*, 147.
569. *Ibid.*
570. *Ibid.*, 149.
571. *Ibid.*, 150.
572. *Ibid.*
573. D 6 V 1902.
574. Lou→RMR, 16 IX 1904.
575. D 23 X 1901.
576. D XI 1901 (an ostensibly obliterated fragment).
577. D [III?] 1918.
578. Lou→Tönnies, 1 XII 1904, draft.
579. Lou→Tönnies (7-)13 XII 1904,
draft.
580. 1889a:72.
581. D 1922.
582. Bühler, 362.
583. Hug-Hellmuth, *passim.*
584. Spranger→Lou, 25 V 1914.
585. Lou→Spranger, 17 VIII 1914.
586. Lou→EK, 20 I 1903.
587. *Ibid.* (anticipating the move).
588. D 2 IV 1903.
589. D 4 VI 1903.
590. *Ibid.*
591. D 30 VI 1903.
592. D 23 VI 1903.
593. *Mrs. Maria Apel.
594. D 23 VI 1903.
595. D 27 VII 1903.
596. RMR→Lou, 23 VI 1903.
597. Lou→RMR, 27 VI 1903.
598. RMR→Lou, 30 VI 1903.
599. See 1904a:251-57 in conjunction
with Lou→RMR, 5 VII 1903.
600. Lou→RMR, 5 VII 1903.
601. Lou→RMR, 22 VII 1903.
602. *Ibid.*

603. D 17 VII 1903.
604. D 22 VII 1903.
605. RMR→Lou, 25 VII 1903.
606. Lou→RMR, 7 VIII 1903; D 6 VIII 1903.
607. RMR→Lou, 10 VIII 1903.
608. Lou→RMR, 8 VIII 1903.
609. RMR→Lou, 11 VIII 1903.
610. Lou→RMR, 8 VIII 1903.
611. D [IX] 1903.
612. D [X] 1903.
613. Lou→Tönnies (7-)13 XII 1904, draft.
614. D 2 II 1904 (supplement to D 1900-1903).
615. D 31 XII 1903.
616. Lou→Frieda [late 1903].
617. Stöcker, "L A-S" (1904), 29.
618. *Ibid.*, 30.
619. D 2 II 1904.
620. 1901a:193-95 ("Auf dem Heimweg").
621. *Ibid.*, 199-200.
622. *Ibid.*, 107.
623. D 25 I 1904.
624. RMR→Lou, 15 I 1904.
625. Lou→RMR, 9 XI 1903.
626. 1904a:280.
627. *Ibid.*, 291-96.
628. *Ibid.*, 296.
629. *Ibid.*, 297.
630. Lou→Tönnies (7-)13 XII 1904, draft.
631. 1904a:74.
632. *Ibid.*, 76.
633. RMR→Lou, 13 XII 1903.
634. Lou→RMR [early V 1904].
635. D 8 III 1904.
636. RMR→Lou, 30 V 1904.
637. *Ibid.*
638. Lou→RMR [early VI 1904].
639. D 19 VI 1904.
640. D [end VII] 1904.
641. D 3 VIII 1904.
642. D 7 VIII 1904.
643. D [8 IX] 1904.
644. D 18 IX 1904; cf. Lou→RMR, 16 IX 1904.
645. D 21 IX 1904.
646. Lou→RMR, 16 IX 1904; D 18 IX 1904.
647. D 4 X 1904.
648. Lou→Caro, 13 I 1905.
649. Lou→RMR, 16 IX 1904.
650. RMR→Lou, 17 X 1904.
651. RMR→Lou, 19 X 1904.
652. D 31 XII 1904.
653. Lou→B-H, 2 I 1905.
654. Lou→Caro, 13 I 1905.
655. 1905a:289.
656. *Ibid.*, 292-93.
657. Lou→Harden, 13 I 1905.
658. Harden→Lou, 14 I 1905 (letter withheld from me).
659. D Easter 1911.
660. Schoenberner, 50.
661. D 23 IV 1905.
662. D 15 V 1905.
663. EK→B-H, 4 V 1905.
664. Lou/EK→RMR, 16 IV 1905.
665. RMR→Lou [7 I] 1905.
666. RMR→Lou, 19 V 1905.
667. Lou→RMR, 21 V 1905.
668. D VII 1904.
669. RMR→Clara, 18 VII 1905.
670. 1906a:400.
671. Lou→Harden, 8 II 1906.
672. D 27 I 1906.
673. Lou→Harden, 5 III 1906.
674. Lou→Harden [9? III 1906].
675. Lou→Harden, 19 III 1906, [21 III 1906], [28 III 1906].
676. D X 1913.
677. D 1919.
678. D 30 V 1906.
679. 1906b:305.
680. Lou→EK, 1 VIII 1906.
681. D 25 VIII 1906.
682. 1907a:200.
683. Lou→Harden, 14 XII 1906.
684. See RMR→Clara, 17 XII 1906.
685. 1906c:98.
686. D 14 II 1907.
687. D 4 II 1907.
688. 1907a:199.
689. Lou→Dehmel, 19 XII 1907.
690. Lou→Schnitzler, VI 1908.
691. EK→Lou, 20 XI 1908.
692. D [late 1909 or early 1910].
693. Quotations from Lou's journal of her Balkan trip.
694. Quoted in Pfeiffer, *Leben*, 339-43.
695. Not quoted *ibid*.
696. EK→Lou, 20 XI 1908.
697. Lou→EK, 27 VII 1909.
698. EK→Lou, 21 XII 1912.
699. 1927a:43.
700. D [late 1910 or early 1911].
701. *Ibid.*
702. D [9-12 VII 1913].

703. Reconstructed from EK→Lou, 15 VII 1909.
704. EK→Lou, 15 VII 1909.
705. Lou→EK, 27 VII 1909.
706. Reply to EK→Lou, 23 III [1910].
707. Reply to preceding.
708. Missing.
709. EK→Lou, 30 VII 1910.
710. Lou→EK, 27 VII 1909.
711. Lou→RMR [VIII 1909].
712. Reply to EK→Lou, 15 I 1910.
713. EK→Lou, 23 III [1910], [V 1910]; D III 1911, IV 1911.
714. Lou→RMR [28 XII 1909].
715. Buber→Lou, 28 III 1906.
716. 1909b:22.
717. *Ibid.*, 21.
718. *Ibid.*, 23.
719. *Ibid.*, 32.
720. *Ibid.*, 52-53.
721. Buber→Lou, 10 II 1910.
722. Reply to EK→Lou, 23 III [1910].
723. D [III 1910].
724. Lou→EK, 27 VII 1909.
725. EK→Lou [V 1910].
726. D 1916.
727. Buber→Lou, 10 II 1910.
728. D [25 IV 1911].
729. D 20 X 1911.
730. D VI 1911.
731. *Ibid.*
732. Buber, 57.
733. Pfeiffer, *Briefwechsel*, 244 and n.
734. *Ellen Delp (dating only probable).
735. D [IX] 1911.
736. *Ibid.*
737. Lou→EK, 20 V 1914.
738. "Das Kindlein . . ."
739. D 20 X 1911.
740. D [XI] 1911.
741. *Ibid.*
742. Spranger→Lou, 7 VII 1914.
743. Lou→Spranger, 18 VII 1914.
744. 1909a:chapter III.
745. *Ibid.*, chapter VI.
746. *Ibid.*, chapter IV.
747. *Ibid.*
748. *Ibid.*
749. *Ibid.*, chapter V: 1.
750. *Ibid.*, chapter V: 2.
751. *Ibid.*, chapter VI.
752. Heine, "L A-S," 81.
753. 1909a:chapter II.
754. *Ibid.*, chapter V: 2.
755. *Ibid.*, chapter I.
756. *Ibid.*
757. *Ibid.*

PART FOUR

MATURITY

1. Abraham→Freud, 28 IV 1912.
2. 1912b:1692.
3. Indirectly through Abraham→ Freud, 28 IV 1912, and Freud→ Abraham, 2 V 1912; directly through Lou→Freud, 27 IX 1912, and Freud→Lou, 1 X 1912.
4. Adler→Lou, 1 VII 1912 (Pfeiffer, *Schule*, 227-28); Lou→Adler, 12 VIII 1913 (*ibid.*, 175).
5. D [28 X 1912]; Lou→Adler, 12 VIII 1913 (Pfeiffer, *Schule*, 177).
6. Lou→Freud, 3 XI 1912.
7. Freud→Lou, 4 XI 1912.
8. Lou→Adler, 12 VIII 1913.
9. Freud→Lou, 2 III 1913; cf. Freud→Lou, 10 XI 1912.
10. Lou→Freud [9 XI 1912].
11. Freud→Lou, 10 XI 1912.
12. D [22 I 1913].
13. D [11 XII 1912].
14. D [26 X 1912].
15. D [30 XI 1912].
16. D [2 XI 1912].
17. D [7-9 IV 1913].
18. D [6 IV 1913].
19. D [21 XI 1912].
20. D [25 I 1913].
21. D [30 X 1912], [2 XI 1912], [21 XI 1912].
22. D [late XI 1912]; etc.
23. D [29 I 1913].
24. D [4 XII 1912].
25. 1920b:363n.
26. Lou→Adler, 12 VIII 1913 (Pfeiffer, *Schule*, 178).
27. *Ibid.*; see also D 1912-1913, *passim*.
28. Adler→Lou, 16 VIII 1913 (Pfeiffer, *Schule*, 178-80).
29. Freud→Lou, 5 VII 1914.
30. D [28 I 1913]; cf. D 1912-1913, *passim*.
31. 1914a:267.
32. *Ibid.*, 266.
33. *Ibid.*, 267-68.
34. D [7-8 IX 1913].
35. D VI 1922.
36. D [26 XI 1912].

37. D [early summer 1913].
38. D [30 XI 1912]; etc.
39. D 7 VII 1900 (see above, p. 303 and n. *v*).
40. D [8 XII 1912]; cf. 1929a:105-06, etc.
41. 1920b:363.
42. 1929a:40.
43. See e.g. D [26 XI 1912].
44. 1936a.
45. 1919a:358.
46. Lou→Freud, 15 VII 1915.
47. D 1912.
48. See 1914b:13-14; D [22 II 1913]; 1931a:198.
49. D [8 II 1913]; 1913e:11; 1931a:198.
50. D [mid-III 1913].
51. 1919a:359.
52. *Ibid.*, 359ff.
53. *Ibid.*
54. D [25 I 1913].
55. D [late spring 1913].
56. D [17-21 X 1913].
57. *Ibid.*
58. Søren Kierkegaard, *Concluding Unscientific Postscript*, "The Subjective Thinker," 2.
59. D [17-21 X 1913].
60. 1882a.
61. D [X 1913].
62. D [late spring 1913]; etc.
63. 1890a:242.
64. 1936b.
65. D [30 IX 1913].
66. Lou→Freud, 14 VII 1929.
67. Freud→Lou, 14 VII 1916.
68. D [2 IV 1913].
69. Lou→Freud, 30 VI 1916, enclosure (introduction to 1914b); cf. D [2 IV 1913], 1926a:finale.
70. Freud→Lou, 7 VII 1914, 14 VII 1916.
71. D [27 XI 1912].
72. *Ibid.*
73. D [30 XI 1912].
74. *Ibid.*
75. D [mid-II 1913].
76. 1914a:251.
77. D [VII?] 1911.
78. D [mid-II 1913].
79. 1912c:43-47.
80. Cf. Freud, VII, 203-09.
81. Lou→Freud, 5 VII 1914.
82. Lou→Freud, 14 XI 1915.
83. Lou→Freud, 15 VII 1915.
84. Freud→Lou, 30 VII 1915.
85. Lou→Freud, 7 XI 1915.
86. Lou→Freud, 15 VII 1915.
87. Freud→Lou, 18 XI 1915.
88. Freud, *An Introduction to Psychoanalysis*, chapter XX.
89. Freud, X, 409-10.
90. 1914a:258.
91. Freud, *Discomfort*, chapter IV, first note.
92. FN, *Beyond*, 187.
93. D VII 1917.
94. Freud, VII, 246n.
95. D [5 III 1913].
96. *Ibid.*
97. *Ibid.*; D [late VIII 1913].
98. D [late VIII 1913].
99. *Ibid.*
100. 1913c:460.
101. D [early XI 1913].
102. 1913e:9.
103. D 11 IX 1914.
104. 1914a:252-53.
105. D 28 XI 1914.
106. Lou→Freud, 4 XII 1914.
107. Lou→Freud, 10 I 1915.
108. *Ibid.*
109. *Ibid.*
110. *Ibid.*
111. Freud→Lou, 31 I 1915.
112. *Ibid.*
113. Lou→Freud, 30 III 1915.
114. 1914b:11.
115. 1914a:273.
116. D [XII 1915].
117. D [19 XI 1912] ("precious above all theory"); also D [26 X 1912], [30 X 1912], [2 XI 1912], [5 II 1913]; Lou→Freud, 9 IV 1916; etc.
118. Lou→Freud, 30 VI 1916.
119. Lou→Freud [21?] V 1916.
120. Freud→Lou, 29 V 1916.
121. Freud→Lou, 4 I 1917; cf. Freud →Lou, 3 XII 1916.
122. Freud→Lou, 22 XI 1917.
123. Freud→Lou, 9 III 1919.
124. Lou→Freud, 18 III 1919.
125. Freud→Lou, 9 V 1920.
126. 1920b:364.
127. *Ibid.*, 363.
128. *Ibid.*, 366-67.
129. *Ibid.*, 364.
130. D [2 II 1913].
131. Lou→Freud, 14 VI 1917.
132. 1931a:200.

133. D [11 XII 1912].
134. Lou→RMR, 28 X 1913.
135. Lou→EK, 20 V 1914.
136. *Ibid.*; D V 1914.
137. D VIII 1914.
138. Lou→Freud, 3 V 1930; Freud→ Lou, 8 V 1930.
139. Lou→Freud, 30 IV 1928, 23 V 1928.
140. Lou→Freud, 6 V 1929.
141. Freud→Lou, 17 II 1918.
142. Lou→Freud, 15 III 1923; Freud →Lou, 23 III 1923.
143. Freud→Lou, 1 VIII 1919.
144. Freud→Lou, 23 III 1923.
145. Freud→Lou, 13 III 1922.
146. D 31 XII 1921.
147. Lou→Freud, 10 VIII 1913; etc.
148. Freud→Lou, 5 VIII 1923.
149. Lou→Freud, 10 VIII 1923.
150. Freud→Lou, 28 I 1925.
151. Freud→Lou, 11 XII 1927.
152. Freud→Lou, 5 VIII 1923.
153. Freud→Lou, 9 III 1919.
154. Lou→Freud, 18 III 1919.
155. Lou→Freud, 16 VI 1920, 20 VII 1920.
156. Lou→Ferenczi, 31 VIII 1921; cf. Lou→Freud, 6 IX 1921.
157. Lou→RMR, 18 I 1923.
158. Lou→Freud, 11 XI 1923, 25 II 1924; Lou→RMR, 16 III 1924.
159. D 18 II 1915.
160. Lou→Freud, 20 VII 1920.
161. Rank→Die Zentrale, 15 V 1922.
162. Lou→Freud, 26 VI 1922.
163. Freud→Lou, 2 VII 1922.
164. Lou→Freud, 26 VI 1922.
165. Lou→Freud [summer 1925].
166. Lou→Freud, 23 V 1928.
167. Lou→Freud [early VIII? 1929].
168. Lou→Freud [early VI 1925].
169. Freud→Lou, 14 VI 1925.
170. Lou→Freud [summer 1925].
171. 1929a:13.
172. Lou→Freud, 10 VIII 1923.
173. Lou→Freud, 19 XI 1914; cf. D 20 XI 1914.
174. Freud→Lou, 25 XI 1914.
175. Freud→Lou, 1 X 1918.
176. Lou→Freud, 25 VIII 1919.
177. Freud→Lou, 9 V 1920.
178. Freud→Lou, 2 VIII 1920; cf. Freud→Lou, 3 VII 1922.
179. Lou→Freud, 16 VI 1920; cf.
180. Lou→Freud, 20 VII 1920, 26 XII 1920.
181. Lou→Freud, 6 IX 1921; cf. Lou →Ferenczi, 31 VIII 1921.
181. Letter (of circa 10 IX 1921) missing; inferable from Lou→ Freud, 13 IX 1921.
182. Freud→Lou, 20 X 1921.
183. Lou→Freud, 24 X 1921.
184. D [late 1921].
185. *Ibid.*
186. *Ibid.*
187. Lou→Freud, 2 III 1922; D [late 1921].
188. D [late 1921].
189. Freud→Ernst and Lucie Freud, 20 XII 1921.
190. Freud→Lou, 3 VII 1922.
191. Freud→Lou, 3 VII 1922, 13 V 1924, 11 VIII[?] 1924, 10 V 1925, 11 V 1927, 11 XII 1927, 6 I 1935.
192. Freud→Lou, 13 III 1922; cf. Freud→Lou, 3 VII 1922.
193. Freud→Lou, 10 V 1925; cf. Freud→Lou, 11 V 1927.
194. Lou→Freud, 3 IX[?] [1924]; cf. Lou→Freud, 18 V 1925.
195. Lou→Freud [4? V 1925]; cf. Lou→Freud, IX 1923; etc.
196. Lou→Freud, 16 VI 1920.
197. Lou→Freud [4? V 1922].
198. Lou→Freud, 5 XII 1924.
199. Freud→Lou, 13 V 1924.
200. Freud→Lou, 11 V 1927; cf. Freud→Abraham, 22 VII 1916.
201. Jones, II, 421.
202. Freud→Lou, 11 V 1927; cf. Freud→Lou, 31 I 1915.
203. Freud, *GW*, XVI, 270.
204. Freud→Lou, 2 VIII 1920.
205. Freud→Lou, 30 VII 1915, 9 XI 1915, 13 VIII 1917, 11 XII 1927, etc.
206. Freud→Lou, 23 III 1930.
207. Freud→Lou, 9 V 1931.
208. Freud→Lou, 9 II 1919.
209. Freud→Lou, 30 VII 1915.
210. Lou→Freud, 11 V 1916, [21? V 1916]; Freud→Lou, 18, V 1916, 25 V 1916.
211. Freud→Lou, 13 VII 1917.
212. Freud→Lou, 25 X 1916; cf. Freud→Lou, 22 X 1917, 17 XI 1924, etc.
213. Freud→Lou, 3 IV 1931.
214. Lou→Freud [5? IV 1931].

215. Freud→Lou, 9 v 1929.
216. Lou→Freud, 14 vii 1929.
217. Lou→Freud, 4 v 1931; Freud→ Lou, 9 ii 1931.
218. Lou→Freud, 23 xii 1932.
219. Lou→Freud [4? v 1933].
220. Lou→Freud, 3 v 1934.
221. Lou→Freud, 4 v 1935.
222. D [17-20 viii 1913].
223. Freud→Lou, 28 vii 1929.
224. Freud→Lou, 1 iv 1915.
225. 1935b:195.
226. 1931a:203.
227. *Ibid.*, 204.
228. D [27 xi 1912].
229. D [13 ii 1913].
230. *Ibid.*
231. D [7-9 iv 1913].
232. D [7-8 ix 1913].
233. Freud→Lou, 7 vii 1914.
234. Lou→Freud [mid-xi 1924].
235. Lou→Freud, 3 v 1924.
236. Lou→Freud [mid-xi 1924]; cf. Lou→Freud, 21 ix 1924.
237. 1929a:47.
238. D [14 iii 1913]; cf. D 1912-1913, *passim.*
239. D [late x 1913].
240. D [25 i 1913].
241. *Ibid.*; D [early summer 1913].
242. 1931a:197-99.
243. *Ibid.*, 193.
244. See especially Lou→Freud, 9 iv 1916; also Lou→Freud, 20 vi 1918, etc.
245. D [23 ii 1913].
246. *Ibid.*
247. *Ibid.*
248. *Ibid.*
249. Freud→Lou, 28 vii 1929.
250. Freud→Lou, 30 vii 1915.
251. 1920b:373.
252. D [late xii 1921].
253. D iv 1923.
254. D [5 iii 1913].
255. *Ibid.*
256. Lou→Freud, 6 xi 1927.
257. Freud→Lou, 11 xii 1927.
258. Freud→Lou, 17 xi 1924.
259. Freud→Lou, 30 vii 1915.
260. Freud, *Discomfort*, chapter i.
261. Freud→Lou, 7 x 1917.
262. Lou→Freud, 15 x 1917; D [x 1917].
263. Lou→Freud, 5 xii 1924; 1929a: 19; etc.

264. 1929a:41; etc.
265. Lou→Freud, 26 xii 1920.
266. 1929a:41.
267. Lou→Freud, 26 xii 1920; etc.
268. Lou→Freud, 5 xii 1924; etc.
269. 1929a:39; cf. *ibid.*, 41.
270. *Ibid.*, 38-39.
271. Lou→Freud, 26 xii 1920.
272. Freud→Lou, 13 vii 1917.
273. D [10-11 ix 1913].
274. 1929a:41.
275. Freud, *Discomfort*, chapter vi.
276. Freud, *GW*, xiii, 21.
277. D [23 ii 1913].
278. 1890a:222.
279. D i 1919.
280. *Ibid.*
281. *Ibid.*
282. Lou→Freud, 30 i 1919.
283. Freud→Lou, 9 ii 1919.
284. 1929a:76-77.
285. 1920b:380.
286. *Ibid.*, 381.
287. *Ibid.*, 379-80.
288. *Ibid.*, 381.
289. *Ibid.*
290. D [17-20 viii 1913].
291. Lou→Freud [early viii? 1929].
292. 1914c:648.
293. *Ibid.*; cf. Lou→Freud, 17 vii 1916.
294. D vii 1917.
295. D v 1919.
296. D 5 i 1917.
297. 1917a:789.
298. *Ibid.*
299. D [15 i 1913].
300. D [23 ii 1913].
301. D [early iii 1913].
302. 1913c:469.
303. *Ibid.*, 461-62.
304. *Ibid.*, 465.
305. D [early xi 1913].
306. 1914b:19.
307. 1920b:376.
308. D iii 1923.
309. 1929a:65.
310. *Ibid.*
311. *Ibid.*, 67-68.
312. Lou→Freud [late 1927].
313. Freud→Lou, 11 xii 1927.
314. Freud, *Discomfort*, chapter i.
315. Lou→Freud, 4 i 1930.
316. Freud→Lou, 15 i 1915.
317. Freud→Lou, 10 v 1923.
318. Freud→Lou, 25 xi 1904.

319. Freud→Lou, 6 I 1935.
320. Exodus 5:21.
321. Freud→Lou, 6 I 1935.
322. *Ibid.*
323. FN, *Genealogy*, II: 21.
324. D [23 II 1913].
325. *Ibid.*
326. Lou→Freud [8? I 1935].
327. *Ibid.*
328. Lou→Freud, 4 V 1935.
329. D [23 II 1913]; cf. Lou→Freud [late XI 1927]; etc.
330. D [11 XII 1912].
331. *Ibid.*
332. Lou→Freud, 5 VII 1914.
333. D [V-VI 1913].
334. *Ibid.*
335. 1914b:10-11.
336. Lou→Freud, 3 IX [1924].
337. Freud→Lou, 11 VIII 1924.
338. D [2 XI 1912]; cf. Lou→Freud, 9 IV 1916; 1929a:105.
339. D [XII 1912 or I 1913]; cf. D [III 1913]; etc.
340. D [2 XI 1912].
341. D [8 IX 1913].
342. 1931a:201, 203 (point not quite explicit).
343. 1914c:650; cf. D [17-21 X 1913]; 1927b:29, 30.
344. 1914a:272-73; etc.
345. 1914b:section 3; etc.
346. 1927b:28.
347. D [mid-III 1913].
348. 1913e:8; cf. 1919b:693.
349. 1927b:27-28.
350. *Ibid.*, 29-30; cf. D [early XII 1912].
351. 1913e:11-12; cf. D [mid-III 1913], etc.
352. 1927b:30.
353. *Ibid.*
354. D [early XII 1912].
355. D [9 II 1913]; 1913e:11; 1920b: 367-72; 1922a:4; etc.
356. D VI 1922.
357. D [early summer 1913]; 1912c: 77-78 (passage penned late 1913); 1913e:11; etc.
358. D VI 1922.
359. 1917b.
360. D [5 III 1913].
361. D [mid-III 1913].
362. D [10-16 X 1913].
363. D *passim.*
364. Bjerre, *Wahnsinn*, 15-19 and *passim.*
365. EK→Lou, 1 XII 1911.
366. D V, VI 1912.
367. D XII 1911 and reading notes 1911-1912.
368. D 11 V 1913.
369. D [7-8 IX 1913].
370. Quoted by Peters, 271.
371. Freud→Lou, 12 I 1914.
372. Lou→Freud, 15 I 1914.
373. EK→Lou, 21 XII 1914; further EK→Lou, 4 XI 1916.
374. Bernecker, 394.
375. *Ibid.*, 389.
376. D [21 VIII to 5 IX 1913].
377. *Ibid.*
378. D [27 XI 1912], [29 I 1913], [12 II 1913], etc.
379. D [13 II 1913].
380. D [14 III 1913].
381. D [22 II 1913].
382. RMR→Lou, 2 XII [1913]; D [late XII 1912 or early I 1913].
383. D [8 XII 1912].
384. D [mid-III 1913].
385. *Ibid.* (and Goethe's *Faust*).
386. D [V? 1913].
387. D [21 VIII to 5 IX 1913].
388. *Ibid.*
389. D [7-8 IX 1913].
390. Freud→Lou, 1 VIII 1919.
391. Lou→Freud, 25 VIII 1919.
392. Gebsattel→Lou, 7 I 1915.
393. D 12 III 1906.
394. Weizsäcker, 170-71.
395. Gebsattel→Lou, 18 I 1915.
396. D [17-20 VIII 1913].
397. Gebsattel→Lou, 18 I 1915.
398. D [7-8 IX 1913].
399. *Ibid.*
400. D [17 IX 1913].
401. Gebsattel→Lou, 18 I 1915.
402. EK→Lou, 28 I 1914; Lou→EK, 20 V 1914.
403. Gebsattel→Lou, 23 VII 1914.
404. Gebsattel→Lou, 18 I 1915.
405. *Ibid.*
406. *Ibid.*
407. *Ibid.*
408. D 28 XI 1914.
409. D [early] I 1915.
410. Inferred from Gebsattel→Lou, 7 I 1915.
411. *Ibid.*
412. *Ibid.*

413. Lou→Gebsattel, 15 I 1915, draft
    (fragmentary).
414. Gebsattel→Lou, 18 I 1915.
415. *Ibid.*
416. *Ibid.*
417. *Ibid.*
418. D 1916.
419. D 4 VIII 1914; cf. Lou→Spran-
    ger, 8 VIII 1914.
420. D 8 VIII 1914.
421. D 9 VIII 1914.
422. D 10 VIII 1914.
423. D 22 VIII 1914.
424. D 24 VIII 1914.
425. D 18 IX 1914.
426. D 17 X 1914.
427. D 24 X 1914.
428. Lou→EK, 2 XI 1914.
429. Freud→Lou, 14 XI 1914.
430. Lou→Freud, 19 XI 1914.
431. Freud→Lou, 25 XI 1914.
432. Lou→Freud, 4 XII 1914.
433. Freud→Abraham, 11 XII 1914
    (Jones, III, 145).
434. D 4 XII 1914.
435. Lou→Freud, 15 VII 1915.
436. Freud→Lou, 30 VII 1915.
437. D [early] I 1915.
438. Quoted in Gebsattel→Lou, 7 I
    1915.
439. Lou→Gebsattel, 15 I 1915,
    draft.
440. Lou→Freud, 10 I 1915.
441. D 1916.
442. 1917b:52-53.
443. Lou→EK, 10 VIII 1917.
444. D [IX] 1917.
445. D XI 1917.
446. D XII 1917.
447. D 12 II 1918.
448. Lou→Freud, 18 V 1918.
449. Freud→Lou, 29 V 1918.
450. D XI 1914.
451. D 20 II 1915.
452. D 28 II 1915.
453. Lou→Freud [8? X] 1918.
454. D I 1919.
455. D 2 II 1919.
456. D I 1919.
457. D 2 II 1919.
458. D [VIII?] 1919.
459. 1919e:386.
460. Lou→RMR, 22 IX 1921; cf. Lou
    →RMR, 18 I 1923; 1931a:61-62.
461. Lou→RMR, 18 I 1923.
462. 1912c:32.

463. Lou→Kurt Wolff, 18 VIII 1917;
    cf. 1912c:58n.
464. Lou→Spranger, 2 VII 1914.
465. 1901d:223, 257.
466. D II 1913.
467. Lou→EK, 2 XI[=I] 1920, and
    collaterally Lou→RMR, 16 I
    1919.
468. D VI 1917.
469. D VIII 1917.
470. Bab, 128.
471. 1901a:255.
472. 1931a:171.
473. D VIII 1917.
474. 1901a:22-23.
475. *Ibid.*, 21-23.
476. D V 1919.
477. D IX 1919.
478. 1919g:46.
479. *Ibid.*, 47.
480. *Ibid.*, 48.
481. *Ibid.*, 50.
482. *Ibid.*, 52.
483. *Ibid.*, 56.
484. *Ibid.*, 59.
485. *Ibid.*, 56.
486. *Ibid.*
487. *Ibid.*, 57.
488. Freud→Lou, 1 VIII 1919.
489. *Ibid.*
490. *Ibid.*
491. 1919g:46, 52, and *passim*.
492. D [17-20 VIII 1913].
493. *Ibid.*
494. 1919g:46.
495. *Ibid.*, 52.
496. *Ibid.*
497. D [II 1913].
498. 1919g:57.
499. 1929a:8ff. (also published as
    "Der Kranke hat immer recht");
    1931a:192-93.
500. See e.g. 1931a:52-54.
501. 1919g:25.
502. *Ibid.*, 50.
503. *Ibid.*, 34.
504. *Ibid.*
505. *Ibid.*, 28.
506. *Ibid.*, 34.
507. *Ibid.*, 44.
508. D [2 II 1913].
509. 1919g:56.
510. *Ibid.*, 34.
511. *Ibid.*, 45.
512. Lou→Freud, 7 VII 1919.
513. 1919g:41.

514. Freud→Lou, 1 VIII 1919.
515. *Ibid.*
516. Lou→Freud, 25 VIII 1919.
517. 1919g:51.
518. Freud→Lou, 1 VIII 1919.
519. 1919g:60.
520. *Ibid.*, 59.
521. 1900d:93.
522. *Ibid.*, 95.
523. *Ibid.*, 80.
524. *Ibid.*, 74.
525. FN→Lou [26 VI 1882].
526. 1900d:76.
527. *Ibid.*, 85.
528. *Ibid.*, 86.
529. D 3 I 1901.
530. 1919g:47.
531. *Ibid.*, 48.
532. 1900d:74.
533. *Ibid.*, 76-77.
534. 1919g:51.
535. *Ibid.*, 57.
536. 1900d:92.
537. *Ibid.*, 94.
538. 1919g:56.
539. *Ibid.*, 59.
540. *Ibid.*, 48.
541. *Ibid.*, 44.
542. *Ibid.*, 63.
543. *Ibid.*, 34.
544. 1931a:101.
545. 1897h:268.
546. *Ibid.*, 267.
547. *Ibid.*, 270.
548. *Ibid.*, 271.
549. 1931a:132.
550. 1897h:256.
551. *Ibid.*, 249; cf. *ibid.*, 264.
552. 1919g:52.
553. *Ibid.*, 45.
554. Lou→Gebsattel, 15 I 1915, draft.
555. 1919g:48.
556. *Ibid.*, 46.
557. *Ibid.*, 34.
558. *Ibid.*, 32.
559. *Ibid.*, 47.
560. Lou→RMR, 16 I 1919.
561. D VII 1917.
562. *Ibid.*
563. Lou→Freud, 18 III 1919.
564. Lou→RMR, 16 I 1919.
565. Lou→Freud, 18 III 1919.
566. Lou→EK, 21 XI[=I] 1920.
567. 1909c (above, p. 327).
568. Lou→Schoenberner, 25 V 1933.

569. Lou→Martersteig, 4 IV 1921.
570. Follows from Lou→Martersteig, 26 IV 1921.
571. 1913d:5.
572. 1918a:1276.
573. 1918c:127.
574. *Ibid.*, 138.
575. *Ibid.*
576. *Ibid.*, 138-39.
577. 1921a.
578. 1918b.
579. 1912b.
580. 1919f.
581. 1920c; cf. Lou, "Eros und die Evangelien."
582. 1916b:331.
583. 1917c:213.
584. *Ibid.*, 210.
585. D 17 IV 1919.
586. Delp, 108.
587. Carossa, 106.
588. D [17 IX 1913].
589. D 26 III and 2, 3, 4, 10, 13, 16 IV 1919.
590. D V 1919; cf. D 12 IV 1919.
591. Delp, 157.
592. Lou→B-H, 21 X 1917.
593. D 26 III 1919.
594. Lou→B-H, 28 X 1912.
595. Lou→B-H, 21 XII 1912.
596. Lou→B-H, 22 XII 1913.
597. D [late XII 1912].
598. *Ibid.*
599. *Mrs. Mirjam Beer-Hofmann Lens.
600. Ditto.
601. Lou→B-H, 21 X 1917 (and 7 [VI] 1913).
602. D 8 II 1913.
603. Lou→B-H [1 IV 1913].
604. Lou→Paula, 9 IV 1913.
605. Lou→B-H, 7 [VI] 1913.
606. Lou→B-H, 11 IV 1913.
607. Lou→B-H, 7 [VI] 1913.
608. Lou→B-H, 1 I 1919.
609. D [late 1921].
610. D [V?] 1923.
611. Lou→B-H, 22 XII 1913; cf. Lou →B-H, 12 VII 1914.
612. D 15 II 1913.
613. Lou→B-H, 3 III 1913, [15 III 1913], 1 IV 1913.
614. D [late 1921].
615. Wedekind→Tilly Wedekind, 31 X 1911.
616. D [15 II 1913].

617. D 22 IV 1919.
618. D 10 III 1915.
619. D [9 XI 1912].
620. D 18 X 1914; cf. D 4 XII 1914.
621. Lou→Harden, 11 VII 1917.
622. Lou→Harden, 14 XI 1922.
623. D 25 II 1915.
624. Behl and Voigt, 78.
625. D 2 II 1919.
626. Lou (and Else Heims)→B-H, 21 X 1917.
627. D [V?] 1923.
628. D 7 IV 1919, 10 IV 1919.
629. Schoenberner, 131.
630. D 1923.
631. Lou→RMR, 5 I 1921.
632. Lou→EK, 2 XI 1920.
633. Lou→Martersteig, 4 and 26 IV 1921.
634. D [late 1921].
635. Schoenberner, 44.
636. D 18 II 1915.
637. Inferred from Lou→Ferenczi, 31 VIII 1921.
638. Lou→Freud, 18 X 1921.
639. D 1926.
640. D [29-30 IX 1913].
641. D 18 II 1915.
642. Lou→Spranger, 10 VI 1914; cf. Lou→Spranger, 18 VI 1914.
643. Spranger→Lou, 28 VI 1914.
644. Lou→Spranger, 2 VII 1914.
645. Spranger→Lou, 7 VII 1914.
646. Lou→Spranger, 18 VII 1914.
647. D 7 VIII 1914; cf. Lou→Spranger, 8 VIII 1914.
648. Blüher, 350.
649. *Ibid.*, 355.
650. D 4 III 1915.
651. D 15 III 1915.
652. D XII 1915.
653. D [I] 1917.
654. Lou→RMR, 26 V 1924.
655. D [29 III 1913].
656. D 11-12 III 1916.
657. Lou→Freud, 17 VII 1916.
658. D 1916.
659. EK→Lou, 28 I 1914; Lou→EK, 20 V 1914.
660. EK→Lou, 18 V 1914; Lou→B-H, 12 VII 1914; EK→Lou, 28 VIII 1914; Lou→EK, X 1914.
661. Lou→EK, 2 XI 1914.
662. Lou→EK, 10 VIII 1917.
663. EK→Lou, 17 I 1920.
664. RMR→Lou, 28 XII 1911.

665. RMR→Lou, 10 I 1912.
666. RMR→Lou, 20 I 1912.
667. D [early 1912].
668. Lou→RMR, 13 I 1913.
669. E.g. 1920b:385n.—and, at the last, Bäumer, "L A-S," 310.
670. RMR→Lou, 24 I 1912.
671. D VII 1913.
672. *Ibid.*
673. D [VII 1913] (improved version: see text immediately below).
674. *Ibid.*
675. D VII 1913.
676. D [VII 1913].
677. D [17-20 VIII 1913].
678. Ullmann, Introduction, 7.
679. RMR→Benvenuta, 21 II 1914.
680. D [7-8 IX 1913].
681. RMR→Marie Thurn und Taxis, 15 IX 1913.
682. D [early X 1913] (but dated 1917 in Pfeiffer, *Briefwechsel*, 143n.).
683. Lou→B-H, 22 XII 1913; cf. Lou (and RMR)→B-H, 2 X 1913.
684. D [5-7 X 1913].
685. Lou→RMR, 18 X 1913.
686. D 19 VIII 1914.
687. D [III-V] 1915.
688. D 1916.
689. D [III?] 1918.
690. D 15 I 1919.
691. Addended to D [IV-VI] 1919.
692. D 21 IV 1919 (Easter Sunday).
693. D [summer] 1919.
694. *Ibid.*
695. RMR→Lou, 11 II 1922.
696. Lou→RMR [16 II 1922]; cf. Lou→RMR, 6 III 1922.
697. RMR→Lou, 19 II 1922.
698. *Ibid.*
699. Lou→RMR, 24 II 1922.
700. RMR→Lou, 27 II 1922.
701. Lou→RMR [6 III 1922].
702. Lou→RMR, 16 II 1922.
703. RMR→Lou, 31 X/8 XII 1925.
704. Lou→RMR, 12 XII 1925 (following a copy made by Dieter Bassermann and communicated to Ernst Pfeiffer by Max Niehans).
705. RMR→Lou, 16 III 1912.
706. 1927a:112.
707. RMR→Lou [13 XII 1926].
708. Quoted in Pfeiffer, *Briefwechsel*, 640.
709. Ditto.

710. Ditto.
711. Ditto.
712. Lou→Freud, 26 VI 1922.
713. Lou→Freud, 25 XI 1918.
714. Lou→Freud, 30 I 1919.
715. Lou→Freud, 2 III 1922.
716. *Mrs. Maria Apel.
717. Lou→RMR, 16 III 1924.
718. Lou→Freud, 10 VIII 1923.
719. Lou→RMR, 16 III 1924.
720. Lou→Freud, 24 V 1926.
721. Lou→Freud, 4 V 1927.
722. Lou→Freud, 3 V 1930.
723. *Ibid.*
724. Lou→Freud [mid-x 1930].
725. D XI 1930; cf. Lou→Freud [mid-x 1930].
726. 1933a:273.
727. 1931a:246.
728. Lentz, 9-10.
729. Selle, 375-76.
730. Lentz, 7.
731. Lou→Freud [mid-x 1930] in conjunction with D 7 XI 1930.
732. 1931a:219.
733. Freud→Lou, 22 X 1930.
734. Lou→Freud [mid-x 1930].
735. D [early] 1931.

PART FIVE

OLD AGE

1. Bäumer, *Gestalt*, 474; etc.
2. 1926a:9.
3. 1927b (above, p. 397).
4. 1927a:5-6.
5. Lou→Freud, 20 V 1927.
6. D [mid-]1919.
7. 1927a:102.
8. *Ibid.*, 103.
9. *Ibid.*, 111.
10. *Ibid.*, 19.
11. *Ibid.*, 20.
12. Lou→Freud [5? IV 1931], 28 IV 1931, 10 VII 1931.
13. 1929a:50-54.
14. Freud→Lou [10? VII 1931].
15. Lou→Freud [12? VII 1931].
16. Freud→Lou, 9 V 1931; cf. Freud →Lou [10? VII 1931].
17. Lou→Freud [12? VII 1931]; cf. Lou→Freud [late V 1931].
18. Sarasin, 548.
19. *Ibid.*
20. 1931a:241.

21. *Ibid.*, 241-42, 245.
22. 1933a:262.
23. D [mid-XI 1912].
24. Lou→Hanna, 2 XII 1934.
25. 1934e:184.
26. 1931a:206.
27. *Ibid.*, 141.
28. *Ibid.*, 144.
29. *Ibid.*, 152-53.
30. Also 1929a:82-83.
31. 1931a:71.
32. *Ibid.*, 162.
33. *Ibid.*, 154-55.
34. *Ibid.*, 171.
35. *Ibid.*, 93.
36. *Ibid.*, 94.
37. *Ibid.*, 98.
38. *Ibid.*
39. *Ibid.*, 99.
40. *Ibid.*, 100.
41. *Ibid.*, 101.
42. *Ibid.*
43. *Ibid.*
44. *Ibid.*, 103.
45. *Ibid.*
46. *Ibid.*, 104-05.
47. *Ibid.*, 105.
48. *Ibid.*
49. *Ibid.*
50. *Ibid.*
51. *Ibid.*
52. *Ibid.*, 106-07.
53. *Ibid.*, 106.
54. *Ibid.*, 94.
55. *Ibid.*, 107, 112.
56. *Ibid.*, 110-12 (above, pp. 113-14 and n. *m*).
57. *Ibid.*, 108.
58. *Ibid.*, 114.
59. *Ibid.*
60. *Ibid.*, 113-15.
61. *Ibid.*, 116.
62. D V 1916.
63. 1931a:33-34.
64. *Ibid.*, 35.
65. *Ibid.*
66. *Ibid.*, 24.
67. *Ibid.*
68. *Ibid.*
69. *Ibid.*
70. *Ibid.*, 22.
71. *Ibid.*, 56.
72. *Ibid.*, 66.
73. *Ibid.*, 76; cf. *ibid.*, 84.
74. *Ibid.*, 191.
75. *Ibid.*, 146-48.

76. *Ibid.*, 148.
77. *Ibid.*, 120.
78. *Ibid.*, 224.
79. *Ibid.*, 123-26.
80. *Ibid.*, 138
81. *Ibid.*, 132.
82. *Ibid.*, 132-33.
83. *Ibid.*, 134.
84. Lou→Freud, 9 v 1932.
85. *Franz Schoenberner.
86. *Ernst Pfeiffer, concerning a letter of 1933 from Lulu von Strauss to Lou: cf. below, p. 559.
87. Lou→Hanna, 2 xii 1934.
88. *Ibid.*
89. 1933a:256.
90. *Ibid.*
91. *Ibid.*, 260.
92. *Ibid.*, 255-58.
93. *Ibid.*, 255.
94. *Ibid.*, 268.
95. *Ibid.*, 266-67.
96. *Ibid.*, 266.
97. *Ibid.*, 268.
98. *Ibid.*, 267.
99. *Ibid.*, 268.
100. *Ibid.*, 269.
101. *Ibid.*, 271-74.
102. 1934e:173.
103. *Ibid.*
104. *Ibid.*
105. *Ibid.*, 174.
106. Lou→RMR [26 ii 1901].
107. 1931a:142.
108. 1934e:179.
109. *Ibid.*
110. *Ibid.*, 180.
111. *Ibid.*, 182.
112. *Ibid.*, 183.
113. *Ibid.*, 184.
114. *Ibid.*
115. *Ibid.*, 185.
116. 1931a:225.
117. 1935a:209.
118. Freud→Lou, 1 x 1912.
119. 1935a:209.
120. *Ibid.*
121. *Ibid.*, 212.
122. Freud→Lou, 9 v 1929.
123. *Ibid.*
124. 1935a:212.
125. D [23 ii 1913].
126. 1935a:213.
127. 1935b.
128. *Franz Schoenberner.

129. Lou→Emma, 22 ii 1934; *Mrs. Maria Apel.
130. *Mrs. Maria Apel.
131. 1934a.
132. *Ibid.*
133. Lou→Freud, 3 v 1934.
134. Lou→Hanna, 2 xii 1934.
135. 1934a.
136. Helene→Lou, 11 v 1935.
137. Helene→Lou [1935?].
138. 1890a:154.
139. *Ibid.*, 230.
140. *Ibid.*, 231.
141. *Ibid.*, 147.
142. *Ibid.*, 153.
143. 1931a:111-12.
144. 1926a:10.
145. Lou→Freud [22 ix?] 1923.
146. *Mrs. Maria Apel.
147. Podach, *FN und LS*, 130.
148. Podach (and Lou)→Ida O, 16 v 1932.
149. Podach→Schoenberner, 4 ix 1938.
150. Freud→Lou, 16 v 1934.
151. Lou→Freud, 20 v 1934.
152. E F-N, *Frauen*, 118.
153. Schlechta, Appendix, 1372n.
154. 1901c:*passim*.
155. D 6 v 1902.
156. D 4 vi 1903.
157. D iii 1923.
158. D v 1923.
159. *Ibid.*
160. Lou→Freud, 18 v 1925.
161. Lou→Freud, 4 v 1927.
162. Lou→Freud, 20 v 1927.
163. Lou→Freud, 3 v 1934.
164. Lou→Freud, 3 v 1930.
165. Lou→Freud, 22 x 1930.
166. Lou→Freud, 10 vii 1931.
167. *Franz Schoenberner.
168. *Mrs. Maria Apel.
169. Lou→Freud, 23 xii 1932.
170. Bäumer, "L A-S," 305.
171. *Ernst Pfeiffer.
172. *Mrs. Maria Apel.
173. 1929a:14.
174. Pfeiffer, *Leben,* 379.
175. D 13 i 1905.
176. D 23 vi 1904.
177. D 1 i 1906.
178. D [1910?].
179. *Ibid.*
180. D [vii?] 1919.
181. D iii 1923.

182. 1936a.
183. Lou→Freud [4? v 1933].
184. 1934a.
185. Lou→Schoenberner, 25 v 1933.
186. *Ibid.*
187. 1934a.
188. 1934b.
189. 1934c.
190. 1934d.
191. 1935b.
192. 1935c.
193. D [5 III 1913].
194. 1935d.
195. 1936a.
196. 1936b.
197. Lou→Freud, 2 I 1935.
198. Lou→Hanna, 2 XII 1934; cf. Bäumer, "L A-S," 307.
199. Lou→Emma, 22 II 1934.
200. Lou→Freud [mid-x 1930].
201. Hermann.
202. *Mrs. Maria Apel.
203. Ditto.
204. Ditto.
205. Weizsäcker, *Natur*, 187.
206. *Mrs. Maria Apel; Bäumer, "L A-S," 305.
207. *Mrs. Maria Apel.
208. *Franz Schoenberner.
209. *Mrs. Maria Apel; cf. Lou→ Freud, 4 v 1935.
210. 1934e:185-86.
211. Stöcker, "L A-S" (1931), 51.
212. *Ibid.*, 53.

213. Weizsäcker, *Natur*, 187.
214. *Ibid.*, 186.
215. *Ibid.*, 187.
216. Bäumer, "L A-S," 308.
217. Bäumer, *Gestalt*, 499.
218. Bäumer, "L A-S," 305.
219. *Ibid.*, 306.
220. *Ibid.*, 306-07.
221. 1916b:333.
222. Bäumer, "L A-S," 308-09.
223. *Ibid.*, 308.
224. Hermann.
225. Helene→Lou, 6 v 1934.
226. Helene→Lou, 7 v 1935.
227. Helene→Lou, 16 I 1935.
228. Helene→Lou, 12 II 1931.
229. Freud→Lou, 16 v 1935.
230. Lou→Hanna, 2 XII 1934.
231. *Mrs. Maria Apel.
232. Hermann.

BEYOND *FRAU LOU*

1. 1897a:84.
2. 1941a:260-61 (below, pp. 557ff.).
3. 1900d:85-88; 1919d:62-65.
4. FN, *Genealogy*, I: 10.
5. 1933a:260.
6. 1913a:144.
7. Freud→Lou, 1 x 1912.
8. 1935a:209.

APPENDIX A

Lou's Literary Expression (from "Dichterischer Ausdruck,"
Das literarische Echo, December 15, 1918: 325-27)

Als der unmittelbare
dichterische Ausdruck er-
scheint der lyrische: vom
Berufenen herab bis zum
herzerleichternden Verslein
eines vom Leben bewegten
Menschenkindes. Im Lyrischen
scheinen wir die ganze Fülle
der Ausseneindrücke mit der
reinsten Gefühlshingebung zu
umfangen, die sich unbe-
schränkt und unbedenklich mit
ihnen einlässt, dadurch im
Ausdruck weltumspannend:
jedoch eben am Gefühlsmä-
ssigen ist er am festesten
gebannt in die Schranken des
Personellen. In der Art,
wie wir lyrisch hinaus-
greifen ins Weite, liegt
doch eine Kunst des sofort-
igen Sichausstreckens, um
sich wieder in sich zurück-
zuziehen, ohne dass die Or-
ganisation sich dem dauern-
den Gefüge des Aussen ange-
passt, Glieder dafür ange-
setzt hätte. Hängen wir
mit derartigem Fühlen am
Nebenmenschen, so reissen
wir ihn leicht in unsere
dichterische Verfassung
herein, machen uns an ihm
produktiv anstatt ihm zu
dienen,—wofür der Verlieb-
te, seiner Liebe-Lyrik
Überantwortete, das Schul-
beispiel gibt; am Dichter
ist es sogar der schönste
Teil seiner Treue gegen
Menschen, die sie so schöp-
ferisch für ihn erhöht, wäh-

Lyricism appears
to be literary expres-
sion pure: from the
inspired lyric down to the
little rhyme with which the simplest man, when moved by life, un-
burdens his heart. In lyricism
we seem to embrace the totality of outer impressions
with the sheerest emotional
abandon of which they un-
restrictedly and unrestrain-
edly admit, thereby encompassing the world in expression—
which is most strictly confined within personal limits,
however, as regards emotionality
in particular. For in our
way of lyrically reaching
into the distance lies
an art of stretching
out all at once only
to contract back
again, without our or-
ganism's having adapted itself to the permanent structure
of outer reality, sprouted **limbs**
to fit in with it. If with
suchlike feeling we fasten onto
a fellow creature, we easily
pull him into our
poetical constitu-
tion, produce due to
him instead of serv-
ing him—for which the lover, delivered up to his
love lyric, provides the
classic example. In the poet's
case this is even the loveliest
aspect of his loyalty to
men, which exalts them for
him so creatively even

rend die Personen selbst
ihm meist dabei um so
gründlicher entschweben.
Weil aber die Folge Ent-
täuschung am Wirklichen
sein muss, ergibt das ty-
pisch lyrische Verhalten
eine letzte Sehnsucht nach
dem Erlöstwerden von sich
selbst, nach einem Aufge-
nommensein im Positiven,
nach etwas ausserhalb so-
wohl des Schöpferischen als
auch des Geniesserischen,
wenn es nur, streng und
bescheiden, dem Zufälligen
wie dem Zügellosen enthebt
und unterkommen lässt als
"Ding unter Dingen". Ge-
rade vom Lyrischen geht,
wo es mächtig die Seele
bestimmt, auch selbst-
rettend eine ästhetische
Freude aus an allem Ge-
haltenen, Zurückhaltenden,
am Sinn aller Konventionen,
und die "interessante Ver-
wilderung", die eine solche
zu sein sich's noch leisten
kann, kommt aus geringerer
Tiefe herauf, als manche
Korrektheit, ja heimliche
Pedanterie, womit ein Poet
wider Willen verrät, was
alles er zu kompensieren
hatte, und was dann in seine
flachern, toten Stunden mit
emporgespült wurde, wie
Muscheln, die die Ebbe zu-
rückliess: wunderlich wich-
tig und winzig. Steht doch
sogar die grössere Strenge
und Mannigfaltigkeit der
Formen, deren die Lyrik im
Vergleich mit sonstigen
Dichtungen sich befleissigt,
ganz gewiss ebenfalls im
gleichen Zusammenhang,—
mit der Gefahr der Entwirk-
lichung; dem Zwang sich
formell zu bändigen; dem

as the particular persons
by and large lapse the more
thoroughly from his sight.
But because the result must
be disappointment with
reality, the typical
lyrical attitude yields
an ultimate yearning
for deliverance from the
self, for being absorbed
in that which is positive,
for something beyond
creativity as well
as pleasurableness—
if only, austere and modest,
it provides release from
whatever is fortuitous or
impulsive, and accommodation as
a "thing among things." From
lyricism in particular,
when it powerfully
activates the soul,
emanates a saving aes-
thetic joy in everything
contained, restraining,
in the spirit of all conventions,
and the "instructive running
riot" that such
joy can further afford
to be arises out of lesser
depths than much of the
punctiliousness, indeed covert
pedantry, by which a poet
involuntarily discloses all
that he had to compensate
for and that was then
washed up into his shal-
lower, dead hours like
sea shells deposited by
the tide: wondrously
weighty and wee. Surely
even the greater strictness
and variety of the
forms assumed by
lyrism as compared
with other creative
writing belong in
this same context too—
along with the danger of loss
of reality, the compulsion to
fetter oneself with formalism, the

Antrieb, über das Allzusub-
jektive damit einen Schleier
zu breiten, der nur durch-
scheinen lässt, was im
Grunde in Einsamkeit, in
Selbstgenuss, sich voll-
zog und eine Scham ab-
werfen muss, um öffent-
lich zu werden.

Eine ganz natürliche
Ergänzung unseres
lyrischen Verhaltens zum
Leben ist in uns allen
deshalb das Stück dra-
matischen Temperaments,
desjenigen, wodurch wir
uns auf die Seite der
Dinge werfen, in ihre
objektive Gliederung und
Gestaltung. Um wieviel
materieller gerichtet
sich das auch gebe, um
soviel ist es doch ent-
selbstender, entmateriali-
lisierender sozusagen, in
bezug auf uns. Weit un-
mittelbarer übergehend
aus einer bloss dichte-
rischen in die positive
Einigung mit jeglichem;
ohne poetische Über-
schätzung schärfer blik-
kend, doch auch blutwärmer
liebend und der lyrischen
Enttäuschung drum nicht
ebenso zugänglich. Dafür
die andere Gefahr: sich
am einzelnen zu ver-
stricken, anstatt das
Viele und Ganze zu um-
fassen, wie wir es ja
auch menschlich er-
reichen möchten, und wie
es dem Dichter in uns das
wesentliche Lieben ist:
denn in und hinter allem
Geschauten ist er dem
allein verbunden, woran
alle Mannigfaltigkeit zu
ewiger Wandlung, Spiel
und Maske wird. Wonach

urge thus to spread a
veil over that which is all too
subjective so that
what came about essen-
tially in solitude, in
self-indulgence, and must
cast off its shameful-
ness before becoming pub-
lic, can only glimmer through.

A quite natural
complement to our
lyrical approach to
life is therefore the
dash of dramatic tem-
perament in us all—
of that by dint of which we
leap over to the side
of things, into their
objective composition and
configuration. The more
materially
this comes off, the
more depersonalizing,
immaterializing so
to say, it is
for us. Much more
directly passing over
from a merely poet-
ic into positive
union with everything;
without poetic over-
estimation looking more
sharply, yet also loving more
warm-bloodedly and thus not
so susceptible to lyrical
disappointment. Instead,
the other danger: getting
entangled in partic-
ulars rather than com-
prehending the much and the
whole, which indeed we
should like to get at hu-
manly too, and which
to the poet in us
is basic loving:
for he is united, in and
behind everything seen,
to that alone through
which all multiplicity becomes eternal change, game,
and mask. The object

seine Sehnsucht geht,
während er sich drama-
tisch dazu einstellt, das
ist drum die Lösung im
Allgemeinsamen, das jedes
Ding durchströmt und aus-
füllt, jedes gerade da-
durch erst rundend und
legitimierend zu einer
Welt für sich. *Ihm* liegt
nicht daran, und sei es
durch Formhüllen, einen
feinsten Schleier der
Scham zu wahren über
seinem Einsamsein; ab-
zuwerfen strebt er alle
Verschleierung, bis Blick
auf Blick trifft und er
im Auge des andern, wie
in Heimat aufgenommen,
sich wiedererkennt, der
hinausgestreut war in die
Welt der Dinge und—in
sich selber bedrängt mit
allen ihren Gegensätzen
oder Möglichkeiten,—
nicht nach Hause fände
ohne diesen Richtblick.
So möchte man auch sagen:
ein anderes noch, als der
Leser oder Hörer dem
Lyriker ist, sei dem
Dramatiker der Zuschauer
vor der Bühne, über die
sein Werk sich ausbreitete,
—als erfolge die wahre,
eigentliche Handlung erst
auf dessen und seiner
eigenen Seelenbühne; als
bliebe darin noch etwas übrig
von der geheimen Bedeutung
jenes ursprünglichen, jenes
sakralen Schauspiels, wo das
mythische Geschehen als
solches den Zuschauenden als
Handelnden mit in sich ein-
schloss, und erst so zum
Vollzug des Dargestellten
wurde. Wäre es auch wunderlich, derartige Masstäbe an
unsere Dramen legen zu

of *his* yearning,
as he attunes himself
to it dramatically, is
thus to dissolve in the
universality that flows
through and fills out each
thing, only thereby
first rounding it off and
legitimating it as a
world unto itself. *His* concern is not, even
through sheaths of form, to
preserve a finest
veil of shame over
his aloneness; he
strives to cast off all
veiling, till glance
meets glance and he
recognizes himself again
in the other's eyes, as if
received home after
having been scattered out into the
world of things and—in-
wardly oppressed by
all its contradictions
or possibilities—
unable to find his way home
without this guiding glance.
So one might also say:
something different from what the
reader or listener is to the
lyricist, is to the
dramatist the spectator
before the stage on which
his work unfolded—
as if the true, authentic
performance first took place
on both their
souls' stage, as if
herein something survived
of the secret meaning
of that original, that
sacral spectacle in which the
mythic happening as
such involved the
onlooker as partici-
pator, thus alone becoming
the fulfillment of what was represented. If it would be
strange to try apply-
ing such standards to our

wollen, so doch nur deshalb,
weil diese sich seitdem be-
gnügen, entweder natura-
listische Abbilder zu sein
(was ihnen die Methoden
ihrer Formung ja nahelegen),
oder beim lyrischen Sinn-
bild Ergänzung zu suchen.
Nur durch das aber, was
vom religiösen Ursinn der
dramatischen Handlung noch
in ihnen nachwirken mag,
ist ein Drama mehr als ein
Lied (sonst ist es weniger).
Denn nur dadurch ist der
Breite seiner Gestaltung
auch alle Lyrik noch ein-
gesenkt; Poesie, stumm
untergründend was Wort
wurde, latent darunter
verharrend, und dann doch
gelöst zwischen Mensch und
Mensch als ein Erlebnis
letzter Gemeinschaft.

Es gäbe nun noch
den dritten Weg, der be-
schritten wird nach Dich-
terland: in Poesie und
Prosa den des Epischen.
Aber zunächst steigt er an
vom Ausserdichterischen,
von der berichtenden, er-
zählenden Mitteilung prak-
tisch-logischer Sprache,
und dann, höher hinauf,
durchschreitet er jedesmal
das lyrische sowie das
dramatische Gebiet. Frei-
lich soll das nicht heissen:
widerrechtlich oder zu Miss-
brauch, er bringt damit nur
eine neue, seine eigene,
Poesie in Trab und Gang.
Wie mir scheint, auf
folgende Weise: der
Lyrik geht das Epische
nicht so weit nach, dass
die Selbständigkeit der
Gestalten sich an sie
verlöre; andrerseits je-
doch entspringen ihm diese

dramas, that is only be-
cause these confine them-
selves either to being
naturalistic replicas
(as indeed the methods of fashioning them incline them to be)
or to seeking comple-
tion in lyrical imagery.
But only by virtue of whatever
may persist in them of
the primal religious
sense of dramatic action
is a drama more than a
song (otherwise it is less).
For only by virtue of that is
any lyricism still implanted in
the breadth of its composition
either: poetry, mutely
underlying that which has become
word, enduring beneath it
latently, only to be dis-
solved after all between man and
man as an experience
of ultimate fellowship.

There would now remain
the third route that is
taken to authors'
land: the epical one
in poetry and prose.
But it first rises
outside authordom,
out of the informative, narrative communication of prac-
tical-logical parlance,
and then, higher up,
it every time traverses
the lyric as well as the
dramatic province. Of
course that should not mean
illicitly or abu-
sively; it therewith only brings
a new, its own,
poetry into play.
As I see it, in
the following way:
epic does not follow
up lyric so far that
the individuality of the
characters gets
lost; but
again, neither do these

auch nicht weit genug ins
dramatisch Leibhafte, um
aus dem Bereich des Erzäh-
lenden hinauszufallen. Er,
der Erzählende, ob auch un-
sichtbar geworden wie der
Gott hinter seiner Schöp-
fung, überwölbt sie dennoch
mit sich wie mit einem
Himmel, aus dem ihr all
ihr Licht und Schatten
kommt. Es ist ebenso
richtig zu sagen: die
epische Haltung sei die
des Zurücktretens, allein
darum sorgend, dass das
Sachliche selbständig sich
heraushebe, als auch: es
erstehe erst zu einer Welt
für sich, indem es unmerk-
lich eingebettet sei in
die Denk- und Fühlsweise
des Dichters, der es zu
umgreifen weiss. Von da-
her die grosse Spannungs-
weite des Epischen: vom
simpelsten Bericht bis zur
grandiosesten Dichtung;
von daher auch das Urteil:
dass sein Wert zunehme mit
der Weite des Umfassten,
des sachlich wie geistig
Bewältigten, und sein Ziel
irgendwie das Weltenepos
selber sei: gleichsam die
Erzählung Gottes an uns.

deviate far enough into
dramatic lifelikeness to
fall outside the nar-
rative sphere. He,
the narrator, although become invisible, like
God behind his crea-
tion, overarches it nonetheless
with himself as with a
sky from which its
light and shadow all come
to it. It is just as
correct to say: the
epic posture is one
of detachedness, concerned
only that the
matter should stand out
on its own, as also: it
only emerges as a world
unto itself through being imper-
ceptibly embedded in
the mode of thought and feeling
of the writer able
to encompass it. Thence
the great scope
of the epic: from the
simplest report to the
most grandiose fiction.
Thence also the judgment
that its value increases with
the scope of what it takes in,
what it factually as also mentally
controls, and that its aim
is somehow the world
epos itself: as it were,
God's narration to us.

APPENDIX B

I

Some of Nietzsche's fragmentary drafts for letters of XII 1882 to Rée: "Strange! I have a preconceived opinion about Lou: and though I must say that all my experience this summer contradicts it, it will not leave me. A whole row of higher feelings, most *rare* and distinguishing, must either be or have been present in her. . . . Really, though, no one has behaved so nastily toward me in my life. To this day she has not retracted that odious defamation of my whole character and purpose with which she introduced herself in Jena and Tautenburg, and this even though she knows that it has done me considerable harm in its aftereffects (particularly in Basel). Whoever does not break off relations with a girl that says such things must be I don't know what: that is the inference drawn. That I did not do so was the consequence of that preconceived opinion: moreover it cost me a *good bit* of self-control. . . . How I would deal with a man who spoke that way about me to my sister there is no doubt. For I am a soldier and always will be, I can handle weapons. But a girl! And *Lou*! I did not at all doubt but that she would at some time cleanse herself of those ignominious deeds in a heavenly way. Dirt! Any other man would have turned away from such a girl with disgust: I too felt disgust, but overcame it again and again. It moved me to pity to see a nobly endowed nature in its momentary degeneration; and, to tell the truth, I spilled countless tears in Tautenburg—not on my own account, but on Lou's. This trick pity played on me. I lost the little I still possessed: my good name, the confidence of a few people—perhaps I shall yet lose a friend: you . . . and what pains me most: my whole philosophy is laid base by   [*sic*] I truly need have no shame before myself in this whole matter: the strongest and warmest feeling of this year I had for Lou, and there was nothing partaking of erotism in this love. At most I might have made the Good Lord jealous. . . . Can't you straighten these things out? I have never wanted to speak about them with Lou, except for a single point you know about. On the main point I wanted to leave her free to make amends *on her own*: everything *forced* between two people is gruesome to me. . . . Dear friend, I call Lou my sirocco incarnate: not one minute have I had with her that clear sky that I need above me, with or without people. She combines all the human qualities repulsive and hateful to me, and since Tautenburg I have for that very reason put myself to the *torture of loving* her! But in the long run I am torturing her to death. . . . Odd! I thought an angel was being sent to me as I turned to men and life again—an angel who would soften much in me that had grown too hard through anguish and solitude, and above all an angel of courage and hope for everything still *before me*. It was no angel. . . . I thought you had persuaded her to come to my help: now I see that she is out for amusement and good mental entertainment. And when I think that questions of morality come in there too I am, to put it mildly, revolted. She took it very ill of me that I denied her the right to

543

the term 'heroism of knowledge,' but she should be honest and say: 'I am heavens away from just that.' Heroism is a matter of sacrifice and duty, and this by the day and hour, and *much more* besides: the whole soul must be full of a thing, and life and happiness of no account alongside. . . . Listen, friend, to how I see things today! She is an utter misfortune—and I am its victim. In the spring I thought I had found someone able *to help me*: for which not only a good intellect but a first-rate morality is needed. I discovered instead a being who wants to have fun and is shameless enough to believe that the most distinguished minds on earth are just good enough for her fun. As a result of this mistake I more than ever lack the *means* of finding such a person. I am writing this in clearest weather: do not confuse my sense with the nonsense of my recent opium letter. I am certainly not crazy, nor do I suffer from delusions of grandeur. But I should have friends who warn me in good time about such desperate things as those of last summer. Who could suspect that her talk of 'heroism,' of 'fighting for a principle,' her poem 'To Pain,' her tales of struggles for knowledge, are simply fraud? . . . Or is it otherwise? The Lou in Orta *was* a different person from the one I found again—from that being without ideals, without goals, without duties, without shame, in a word without morality, on the lowest rung of humanity despite her good head. She herself told me she has no morality—and I thought she, like me, had a stricter morality than anyone else, and brought to it frequently, daily and hourly, some personal sacrifice, and had a right to think about morality. . . . I should like the most painful recollection of this year to be taken from my soul—painful not because it offends me but because it offends *Lou* in me. . . . What is more, I want nothing more to do with her. It was a *completely futile* waste of love and heart—though in truth I can afford it. . . . Lou debases the whole dignity of our striving: she should have nothing further to do with your name and mine. I no longer understand you, dear friend. How can you stand being near such a creature? For heaven's sake, pure air and highest mutual esteem! Otherwise [*sic*]"

And one of Nietzsche's drafts of XII 1882 apparently meant for Lou reads: "As for friend Rée, it was the same as every time, even after Genoa: I cannot watch that slow ruination of an extraordinary nature without becoming *furious*! That lack of *purpose*! And thence that lack of pleasure in work, of diligence, even of scholarly conscientiousness. That perpetual waste! If at least it were waste from joy in squandering! But he has such a look of bad conscience."

II

According to " 'Anal' und 'Sexual,' " just as the regulation of feeding first gives an infant to understand that the world is not his body, so does his original act of asceticism, the renunciation of anal licence, lead him to recognize that his self is distinct from his bodily processes and drives. In resisting the outside pressure for renunciation, he is still at one with his drives and hates the outside world as their opponent. By contrast, the earlier oral experience, periodically restoring his [felt] identity with the outside world, is all incestuous "sunshine and blessedness" [251], as free of inner discord as of outgoing hate (though these may be superadded in retrospect, magnified by neurotic guilt); it is the prototype for later object-cathexes and the basis for such piety as amounts to the assurance of being God's child [!]. Conversely the anal situation, in which child and parents are at odds, is the source of all satanism and blasphemy. Yet through it the world, by becoming hateful, first becomes truly objective. By parental inducement, part of this hate is transferred to the drive itself, the rest taking the form of spite. In the ensuing struggle between indulgence and abstinence, the distinctive anal pleasure, over and beyond mere anal licence, is aroused. And anal curiosity is heightened. Already the child has come to know himself in his anal activity as a parental power, excreting part of himself without diminishing himself—so "that the severed world is restored in an intenser reunion than would be thinkable the other way round, from object to subject" [252].

Here is the starting point for all productivity, even intellectual and artistic, as well as the source of all curiosity, which thus does begin as curiosity about generation, as Freud said, only about *anal* generation rather than childbirth. Now, though, having been linked back up with the world positively through (oral) joy and negatively through (anal) spite, the child is made contentious toward it through learning shame and disgust before his anal products. And all this before he knows how to verbalize—which is perhaps why psychoses originating then are incurable. Shame and disgust may convert his nascent self-love—the libidinal counterpart to his siding defiantly with his drives against the outside world—into inchoate self-loathing in consideration of his past naughtiness. They need have no damaging effect, though, if only he can smoothly transfer his defiant love of his nascent self inclusive of all its drives to a potential self pure of reprehensible drives—if he can see himself as a developing individual instead of merely the author of his past deeds and misdeeds. Indeed, the idealism of youth involves the feeling that one is truly identifiable only by his finest prospects. The confidence underlying this feeling derives from the infant's belief in the omnipotence of thought: it would long since have been shaken had he not sanguinely pulled his first "trace" of a self [251] together over and beyond his rejection of its undesirable incidences. He does later transfer his self-love onto his ego ideal, as Freud says—only Freud was wrong to refer the self-satisfaction and vanity of later life to protonarcissism, where self-world identity holds sway, instead of to this ulterior love of one's potential self, the libidinal basis for obeying commands and renouncing gratifications.

Conscience develops differently according as parental authority is introjected as a domineering and reproachful or as a sympathetic and affectionate instance: it tends toward the limiting forms of moral rigorism in the first case and of devotional ecstasy in the second, the degenerative extremes being respectively paraphrenia, with its projection outward of hostile claims on the ego, and hysteria, with its plethora of object-cathexes and self-identifications. To be healthful, however, this compensatory love of the ideal self in the making as against the real self in the unmaking during the period of anal adjustment must not go too far in the way of fantasy idealizings or of denials or repudiations of the real self's defects and deficiencies; instead it should foster sober self-awareness through the whole course of postanal surmountings even if some repressions be therewith left imperfect or incomplete. The impulse to psychic self-renovation through introjection and elimination is provided by the prior experience of oral and anal pleasure, the paradigm for self-denial being the anal pleasure itself, which "derives originally from a tension of self-restraint" [254]. Such self-renewal is the psychic analogue to an organism's ingesting and excreting [cf. above, p. 349 n. z]—and what we mean by *life* biologically is that which manifests itself in this very turnover.

As erotic impulses go, the anal is not only distinctive for being sublimated so early; it is unique in that the shame and disgust it arouses afterwards, which derive their pungency from that of the precedent pleasure, are wholly displaced from the activity, thereafter discounted as strictly physiological and nonmoral, onto its product, with the likes of which we would have nothing further to do could we help it. Excrement comes to symbolize whatever is execrable, degrading, unlike us. Its very "blackness" [254] makes it emotionally harmless: whatever we may happen to besmirch with it, we are disgusted with *it* and not *ourselves*; it becomes, like death, something we issue into physically, extrinsically, unavoidably —the no-longer-us, the eternally alien, inanimate, inorganic. Emptied of erotic content, the activity signifies elimination pure and simple after the affect has been transferred to riper sexual modes. However, "if this splitting miscarries at a single point" [256]—if, because the original prohibition is too emphatic or menacing, some of the taboo slips over from the activity with its dirty product onto the erotic affect generally in the form of dread or disgust, or if conversely something of the infantile activity works its way inhibitingly into later sexual development or even only into morbid fantasy—then what should be a source of joy is perverted into its opposite: *unclean* links up with *alluring*, the beautiful becomes suspect because beautiful, "the eternally dead infests the eternally live with inexpungeable blotches of rot" [256].

If a component impulse is sustained intact, it cannot but clash with its successors; if it is rejected *in toto*, we are so much the poorer. Generally a sly symptomatic compromise develops between the impulse and the defense against it. The typical compromise is neurotic guilt, which is singular in that its repressed instinctual basis is conscious, attended, however, by disgust—that is, expelled from the self, which seeks to cleanse itself and atone. Neurotic guilt begins with the anal experience, in which the self comes to be at the cost of instinctual unison with the world; it can emerge, though, only when the guilty wish or deed is repudiated and denigrated in the anal manner as a thing "in which we dare not recognize ourselves" [257]. Unable to face the internal enemy in "fair battle" because unwilling to sully ourselves by so much as acknowledging him, we are "morbidly halved" [257]. Great pagan transgressors, assured of natural retribution, could feel guilt heroically, with the pride of defiance; Christianity, however, by instituting atonement, made sins into mere dirt to be cast off. Beasts know none of man's enmity toward his instincts, which has developed historically—none of his ability to fall ill of instinctual conflicts or to progress by surmounting them. Man's whole historic task of adapting his nature to a self-given moral law began as he set up " 'disgust' as monitor over 'dirt'—that is, over that which is found in the wrong place" and is accordingly "excreted" into inner unconsciousness and death [258].

Appendix B

Like animals, primitive humans evidence how close genital and anal erotism lie. These both stagger the ego as they emerge; both are stimulated by external prohibition and by internal conflict; they employ similar means in bodily proximity; anal regressions find genital support. Genital sexuality overruns all other kinds, however, whereas anal erotism is forcibly retired in its time. Also, genitality is object-directed, anality self-directed: whereas anality issues in "pleasurable separation in protest against the surrounding world," genitality "fulfills itself . . . in a creating through the coupling embrace" [260]. "Reversals" occur too, though: the feces as a child's token of tenderness and "onanism without fantasies of partnership" [260]. Since what first arouses anal shame and disgust is the presence of a witness, if they do carry over to genital love [D [30 XI 1912]: they *perforce* carry over] they do so all the more just because genital love involves a partner—in fact involves pleasure (the word itself faintly connotes shame!) in the same bodily area as formerly the anal, in another's presence, with his cooperation, by means of his own tabooed parts. Even the new mode of overcoming the shame—making an accomplice of the witness—is shameful (which is why the genital act, should it satisfy one party only, will mostly shame him as well by turning his accomplice into "judge and victim both" [261]). As this psychic use to which partners are put is reciprocal, "the earliest shame, bodily licence, crosses . . . with the ultimate intimacy, ego surrender" [261]. Thus shame, by dint of which the ego emerged, pervades the genital passion unto the final ego fusion, be it piquantly or souringly—"as if lovers possessed each other not so much by means of as in spite of the body" [261]. Insofar as the (other's) body is thus felt as a final hindrance to personal intimacy, it retains a little of its anal connotation (the "non-us," the "dead")—"and perhaps just in such supreme moments of love, as in some dark memory, we confront it once again as a piece of life extracted from us, a 'beloved corpse' " [261-62].

Afterwards only the sense of smell helps sustain an illusion of mutual penetration. This most animalic sense is the one least developed by humans for purposes of differentiation. Its growing up on "anal soil" perverts its natural erotic significance, so that odor passes over into odium—though it does serve as that final reminder of aboriginal self-world unity, "the primal anal experience" [262]. The other senses early acquire more seemly erotic specializations while also subserving the ego. "Precise border regulations" between their two "overlordships" [262] being slow to develop, however, abiding permutations and conflicts ensue, whence in their specialized sexual obedience they have fallen into disrepute as perverse upstarts and would-be usurpers. Yet their choral accompaniment to the Song of Songs is a delightful one. They animate mature sexuality the more for bearing the ego's impress in their "every tenderness of hand or mouth or glance" even as, marvelous, they hark back to "the very infancy of sexual experience," when they each still acted for the whole person [263 (cf. 1909b:19)]. With more of the infantile-primitive but also more of the adult-intellectual about them, stopping short of sexual consummation themselves yet enabling more of the person to attain it, they recapitulate on a small scale "the completed love process itself" [263]. The genital function meanwhile, in centralizing them erotically, appropriates the ego's stake in them—a transaction often mistaken for sublimation. In fact, if their libidinal means are curtailed, their ends are in no wise desexualized for being harmonized.

No such frenzied confluence is thinkable in the instrumental use of our specialized organs (indeed, it would mean their sexualization); none such and the genital act reduces to "an analogue of the anal" [263]—regressive, fragmentary, cryptoneurotic—or at all odds the capacity for full natural gratification is stunted. Sexual cripples of this sort are "surprisingly often" the most outstanding individuals, thus stunted "as if to pay the price for their mind's overweening pretension to be as little body as possible" [264]. Here is true sublimation. The ego, lacking earthly sensuality, is joyless and vulnerable; it scales the heights till a dizzy spell brings it back to earth—or lures it into the abyss. Their imbalance shows in their work, on which they expend themselves. The deeper their trouble, the less their work relieves them. For the urge to restore the primal union with the object world may be sublimated into productive labor before genital sexuality—its readiest outlet—develops, in which case the libidinal input is younger, richer, and less personalized, while the creative output (beyond its earliest "presophisticated form" and "infantile-subjective" contents) tends toward the most comprehensive transsubjective relations of thought, deed, and art [265]. Because to sublimate is to bury an impulse in part and substitute another as different as is the resurrection from the grave, the tabooed and the highest values—the sub- and the superhuman— are mutually dependent, in fact covertly equivalent, and the grandest transmutations befall those objects or instincts most reviled, which then, when their hour strikes, ride the golden coach like that cloacal heroine Cinderella to a dignity and glory far exceeding their once worthier sisters'. [An addendum on Adler and Jung (above, p. 361) concludes the essay. And D [I–III 1915] supplements it: ". . . born into the world out of protonarcissism, we first hit up against corporeality as against 'ourselves.' *Whence the odium attaching to materiality: that in it the barrier between beings becomes positive.*"]

III

"Psychosexualität" begins by distinguishing (as Freud purportedly did "with great emphasis" [5]) an aboriginal phase of psychosexual development during which the infant, feeling no difference at all between himself as subject and himself as object, seeks pleasure simply in every bodily occurrence and activity, from narcissism proper, the psychosexual sequel, during which the infant's diverse desires converge on an object that is "his own person"—construed by him, however, as inclusive of the whole outside world. In other words, he sees himself everywhere and loves what he sees. Grammatically put, to his unspoken *I* have been added a likewise unspoken *myself* and *me*, but as yet no *you*, let alone an *it*. Narcissism thus constitutes a psychic analogue to the newborn infant's nestling up against his mother as if still bound up with her: autoerotism is really promiscuous erotism, and narcissism is its psychic expression, the original psychic condition.

Throughout, the bodily processes and sensory functions continue to be sexualized—that is, to be governed by the uncontradicted pleasure principle, which is what is meant by the original identity of ego and libido. This psychic orientation is to be distinguished from a mere directing of libido to one's own body to the exclusion of one's "ego-person" [5], which one may insofar despise, as likewise from a pleasurable adoring of one's self as distinct from the world, or egoism: both belie that interpenetration of subject and object which betokens the true Narcissus, who sees himself and the world as one. [Lou here (5n.)—ineptly—quoted Freud for authority on how a parent, in caressing as in rearing his child, narcissistically fondles a former part of his own body and strives to reduplicate his own best self.] Whatever shows itself the least bit refractory to our erotic demands we at first expel from our greater selves as unreal; then, as it persists, we repel it from our lesser selves with hate and thereby externalize—objectify—it definitively. Such are the origins of the outside world, for which, once it is constituted, we would have no further use except that certain urgent new sexual impulses cannot very well be discharged autoerotically.

Meanwhile, just as the organism stores protoplasm in every cell as a "lasting reserve behind all of its differentiations" [6], so does narcissism remain as the unitary unconscious basis of all later sexual or egoistic strivings whether object- or self-directed, and this though it can never be "expressed in firm forms of consciousness" [6]. So too does the original pattern persist of projecting uncongenial inner realities outward and of extrojecting from all reality whatever stands in the way of our pleasure: our every convenient oversight or even tolerant disapprobation is an unconscious death sentence. In the Oedipal situation the child makes a show of both narcissistic determinations in wishing to fuse with the one parent and to extroject the other from the world. At the same time, in learning to regulate or renounce his instinctual activity, he excludes from his self his own body, with which, however, he still feels identical during erotic indulgence; these two contradictory attitudes find acute simultaneous expression in the case of undischarged sexual excitation, more still in hypochondria, and most of all in organic illness as one's body, deemed hostile, yet absorbs one's total interest [cf. Lou→Freud, 10 i 1915].

Sexual partnership tends to reestablish the narcissistic "confluence of 'I and Thou' as of body and soul" [12]. Object-love is felt as ego-impoverishing only where, neurotically, it is nourished by libido previously repressed. Otherwise, only as long as love goes unrequited is it felt unpleasantly as excessive; when requited, it is felt as insufficient given the longing to make the I-Thou identity absolute. The child, after first focusing his excess libido outward, strives to resume possession of it by aping his beloved, whom he thereby introjects into the self in the form of an ego ideal [as if little girls did not ape their mothers in flirting with their fathers]. Only through fulfilling this ideal can he thereafter satisfy his narcissist nostalgia. As the ideal is originally a prohibitory authority, its fulfillment entails instinctual renunciation. This is accomplished most narcissistically through sublimation, which, when flawless and total, yields a wholly sexualized ego—and then "our past is triumphantly at one with our mental future" [14].

The reason why the component sexual instincts all have an active and a passive purpose (sadism-masochism, voyeurism-exhibitionism, oral aggression and reception, etc.) is their underlying narcissistic determination with its subject-object unity (and not, as Freud held, bisexuality). At first both purposes go together, but insofar as they are separable the active one generally comes to prevail before puberty (even in girls) because better suited to the childish-aggressive ego, the passive one turning purely reactive. [Having desexualized her infantile masochism, Lou was denying it for good measure.] Once separated, the two purposes are manifested alternately in some cases of perversion, simultaneously only in sublimation (e.g. the artist is sadomasochistically both master and slave of his work). Yet even then, just as at the time of their postnarcissistic emergence (within the pleasure-pain complex of infantile "prepleasure," precursive of sadomasochism), they are manifested disjunctively: in sadomasochism one part of the self suffers pleasurably at the other's pleasure. Not only pain but all the ego's enemies (fright, need, shame) and even ego-extinction can become sources of sexual pleasure. And in this, "what is primal in sexuality is right on the job again: narcissism, which was able to unite pleasure and pain within itself, wishing to know nothing of ego-bounds—and an ember of narcissistic voluptuousness blazes up even in the final ecstasy of genital love like a flame feeding itself, however much it seems to be kindled by the partner" [16].

Another "emissary of narcissism," which confounds the sexes, is homosexuality: it makes possible loving even enemies as sons of the womb just like oneself. Women, being physiologically obliged to repress clitoris sexuality at puberty, readily sublimate their homosexuality; thus they sooner couple sexuality and spirituality (narcissistically) than do men, who experience sex and sublimation as rivals when the homosexual option finally confronts them. Women moreover can discharge their unsublimated homosexuality within marriage by bearing and bossing children, whereas men have been victimized in their homosexuality to the extent that, in our times, the " 'freefloating' quantum of religiosity" has gone to sanctify the ideal of a marriage monopolizing the husband's as well as the wife's affective interests [19].

"Psychosexualität" concludes with a rhapsodic, nebulous celebration of life as most mysteriously grandiose just when most banal—and as at first concentrated in a mother's egoistically-autoerotically enfolding her babe before and after delivery, then dispersed into manifold guises only to return and confront its parent as creature, beggar, yea enemy. [Lest that mother-womb mislead: according to 1917b:52, men would achieve peace through primal solidarity as children of One Father rather than simply of One Womb.]

IV

According to "Narzissmus als Doppelrichtung," Freud applied the concept *narcissism*, originally synonymous with autoerotism, to the phase of libidinal development that follows original self-world confusion and in which the self is singled out from the world as a first love-object; in addition, he considered that this original self-love persists thereafter as egoism, subsequent object-cathexes being effected only over and beyond it (by means of supplementary libido subsequently generated), and that while psychoanalyses, to be therapeutically effective, must go back this far, adjusting ego to sex all the way down the line, they can go no farther, for within narcissism ego and sex cannot be distinguished. Now—Lou pursued on her own—the original self-world fusion remains the libido's basic tendency as distinct from its ego-syntonic tendency, narcissism proper, and the first is subjacently coactive with the second within "the narcissistic double phenomenon" [362]. The ego's emergence spells a painful loss of snug embeddedness within one's milieu only slowly superseded by robust self-delight; out of resentment at individuation arises sadism, the impulse to restore "the lost identity" [364] through a community of pain—with the Oedipus complex "astonishingly close" [364]. The forced restricting of the contours of the self releases anxiety; psychotics reverse this development, making the recessive side of narcissism dominant, but can enunciate it no better than nurselings or metaphysicians. If narcissism is too one-sidedly taken to be "ego-happy erotism" [366], the "mirror hero Narcissus" [366] is a little to blame, though indeed he may have seen not only himself reflected in his pool "but also himself as still everything" [366–67] —and "besides ravishment, does not melancholy too show in his visage from way back" [367]?

The inception of object-love due to a surfeit of libido betokens the libido's basic despisal of ego boundaries, which it would therewith redissolve. It first comes into its own in self-oblivious love of someone else overvalued to the point of symbolizing the all. Thus love's joy is "narcissistically produced and nourished at bottom" [368], the prototypical love-objects being already sustitutive through transference "out of still unimpaired subject-object unity onto a detached outer image" [368] [!].

Women's passive sexuality after puberty puts them closer to the anti-egoistic side of narcissism, so that they are less prone to feel fearsomely bereft of ego-libido when in love and thence to crave love's requital. Their joy in the ego's being overwhelmed by the libido may well be heightened masochistically through their assenting to bodily pain and to "the humiliating situation" [369], which is narcissistic not only in that the ego "cooperates" [369] at its own expense in realizing a primal pleasure-pain composite, but also in that "the reversion to passivity restores their original free play to the erotogenic zones" [369-70], ever more infantile-sensitive than men's. Woman's performance in bearing, nourishing, and rearing children is, moreover, "almost two-sexed, hence again rounded out protonarcissistically as in the whole world only the image of the mother, who, giving of herself, holds herself to her own breast, can be" [370]. Conversely, as men's egos are overwhelmed by genital libido at puberty, their "narcissistic self-love" [370] suffers until they discharge the surplus upon objects.

But if object-love does not impair narcissism, narcissism menaces object-love continually: in making the object personally stand for the superpersonal and physically for the superphysical, it builds up to a big let-down, this build-up and let-down being, however, a contrapuntal accompaniment to love's ecstasy itself. Friendship too is rooted in proto-narcissism, being a "sociable self-world confusion *à deux*" [372]—a "compensation for the genital-libidinal narrowness of that other embrace" [372] by way of displacement upwards (to heart and *mind*), but one which, like all sublimations out of narcissism, winds up in "the world of objective emphases" [372], for "objectivity is the glorious human goal that finally beckons to narcissism as metamorphosed Eros in the service of research or progress, art or culture, as if out of childhood dreams" [372].

Like amorous overvaluing, all valuing is itself narcissistic-libidinal cathexis: value denotes quintessence transcending limitations and particularities, so that all valuing tends toward overvaluing, toward the definitive and absolute. We are never sold on values for good reasons, but out of deep-lying faith in our own feeling for what is right and fit. Metaphysics, "insofar as it aims at according 'Being' with 'God' (as highest value), . . . is the philosophically sublimated effigy of the bond between narcissism and objectivity" [373], while an ecstatic valuing of life is but narcissism asserting itself. The vehicle for valuation is the ego ideal, a repository for self-love, inflated through protonarcissistic giganticizing of the parental images. Its extreme form is the overvaluing of valuing—"our narcissism's highest achievement" [375]. [Lou here saddled Freud with a view of the ego ideal as the self's substitute for the world lost to it, hence of protonarcissism and not utility or inculcation as the source of all values.] "All ethical autonomy doubtless constitutes a compromise between command and desire: . . . while it renders what is desired unattainable given the ideal strictness of the value demanded, it draws what is commanded from the depths of the dream of all-encompassing, all-substantiating Being" [376] [cf. 1936b: at the point of choice in action, inner merges with outer reality]. Every religious promise of transcendental wish-fulfillment has its ethical strain, every system of moral imperatives its strain of delight— and just as overvalued mortal love-objects are depersonalized, so the ultimate in love and value, God, divinely commanding and divinely intimate, is personalized, becoming the "symbol of all love symbols" [376].

If duty's lording it over desire is preneurotic, its symptoms being guilt and self-despisal, so is it prepsychotic to set conscience aside, to de-inhibit desires, if only in fantasy (in detachment from reality). The normal counterparts to neurotic and psychotic are feeling pain at the ego's shortcomings and at the world's respectively. The latter, expressive of the "narcissistically surviving primal union" [378], is the more infantile, but can survive alongside the former. Absolutist ethics are as protonarcissistic as they are pragmatic, for they would cover every case; ascetical ethics are narcissistic in both senses in that they turn away from the world but embrace the ego ideal; etc. In putting the unconditional across from case to case, ethics is creative "par excellence" [379]: a poet of the deed, the ethicist "risks his dream in reality, against affliction, through experience, amidst contingency and chaos. Therein lies the dignity of that very fragmentariness, incompleteness of his possible successes as compared with finished works of art. . . . Ethics is risk, narcissism's boldest venture, its exemplary adventure, its sublimest bravado, its ultimate outburst of spirit and spiritedness in life" [379].

Inner and outer experience are immediately identical in artistic creation, which draws on memory traces—prearticulated composites of inner and outer, feeling and fact, thought and deed: "poetry is memory become perfect" [380]. Art is, as Freud called it, a specific against the toxic effects of repression: release of repressed materials will excite joy or anxiety according as they are of protonarcissistic or ulterior derivation. Neurotical when inhibited, artists are psychotical when creating (indulging desires in fantasy behind the ego's back). Their impulse to fashion their idle visions derives from the protonarcissistic "undividedness of active and passive" [385]. This would be blissful child's play but for the overexcitement and for the danger of sudden repression or regression. "In creativity, if anywhere, we find the colors and images with which the almost godlike is painted earthlike. And if man imagines a god as creator of worlds, he does so to explain not only the world but also the god's—narcissistic—nature: may evil galore inhere in such a world, pious faith would fail only in a god that did not dare become work, world" [386].

v

"Des Dichters Erleben" was addressed to the general public, with Freud named only in a note expressing indebtedness. Nominally it rests on evidence from Hermann von Boetticher's *Erlebnisse aus Freiheit und Gefangenschaft* (about Boetticher's trying to write while in and out of captivity during the war), which also putatively inspired the paragraphs quoted above, pp. 537-42. In fact it notably differed from its prepsychoanalytical forerunners only in that it drew more on Rilke's (backed by Nietzsche's) creative anguish and bliss than on Lou's own—in confirmation whereof D [summer] 1919 cited her "Boetticher essay" to explain Rilke's pedantry.

According to "Des Dichters Erleben," we call that man creative who, living most immediately out of protonarcissism [explained but not named], draws closer to it with his every "heightening of consciousness" [359]. True, what stimulates art is inhibited wishing, but not of the more or less conscious, realistic sort, which can only disturb or damage it. Art begins rather where the desire for practical gratification leaves off. Nor is it of merely subjective any more than of merely objective validity. Rather, it restores the simple unity of subject and object behind which lies only somatic darkness: its effectiveness derives from its reviving this original mode of consciousness within us.

Great art "lives" [360] because it is a message from the artist's vital fundament to that of all men, making them feel supremely solitary *and* supremely brotherly as nothing else can. Of such a grand unitary emotion, however, the artist, trembling between the bliss of creating and the despair of not creating, knows nothing. If his work does not come off, he feels himself cast out from all he stood for, stranded "over bottomless emptiness" [361], God's vanquished rival; if it does, he is visited by joy as if in embraceable, unbroken, all-containing totality. "He who does not enter into the very heart of this joy of taking up residence in the primal paradise innocent of prohibitions and valuations, where all began and all was still ours and the lion rested beside the lamb, enters into the surrounding darkness . . ." [361]. Old self-reproaches, fears long stilled, pains out of childhood, revive, looming gigantic. Infantile sexual desires reawaken in turn, but as the taboos against them do not relax, the artist is exhausted nervously and overwhelmed with guilt—and yet these very desires are the source of his joy in finally producing.

This regression to what once was makes him feel that his fantasy product preexists and that on completion it will at last be his securely. A potent anticipatory joy may beset him, growing even as he instinctively combats it lest it disrupt that productive organization of his psyche within which creation has meant torment. In this he behaves like a woman in labor, her constitution attuned to pain—and upon delivery he too feels alleviated, restored to life in all its laxity, yet also robbed and emptied. For till then raw longing itself spells consummation for him, contemplation conjoins with action, dreaming and waking merge, as at the outset of individual development, before disjunction sets in. Likewise, the creating artist has made a world center out of himself just as he has given himself up altogether to his impending creation: the acute subjectivity out of which he creates fuses with acute objectivity toward that which he is creating. Only in boldly risking pathological regression does creative genius come into its own. Much of this same venturesomeness and inventiveness goes to waste in neuroses and psychoses, just as the making of many a masterwork was almost that of madness instead . . .

Illustrative material from Boetticher follows, involving three new points: how the artist in labor, ethicizing his abstinence from direct indulgence of reactivated infantile desires, may perilously sacrifice every outer support and comfort as a bribe to the fates for his artistic salvation (as when a hallucinatory Christ bade Boetticher: "Sell all you have and follow me" [366]); how his experience of artistic triumph, with its consummate instinctual fullness, is so unimaginably at variance with what is normally expected of experience that even he may feel bitterness afterwards over all he had missed out on for its sake (asking scornfully with Boetticher: "What—write, suffer, lie some more?" [366]); and how on its successful issue the creative process, after having revived and intensified the artist's old guilt and remorse, relieves him of it all at once, as if by high dispensation, even as it lifts him out of his everyday perspective on the world around him upon readmitting him to "all-motherly goodness" [367] (as a poetic parable of Boetticher's more or less discloses).

"Narzissmus" in turn harked back to the late 1890's what with the artist's emerging from production as from possession, or again his slipping into infantile sexuality as if to renew himself when his productive effort breaks down (but castigating himself for breakdown and slip, and so turning a child's heaven into a child's hell). The relative novelties in "Narzissmus" concerning art were protonarcissistic: anxiety or joy attends artistic release according as more or less postnarcissistic repressed matter separates the artist from the great source; "the artist has his public within himself, beside himself, and the more so, the more completely he ignores it, consumed by the creative process itself" [381]; the felt need to put the artistic vision into durable, definitive, universally intelligible shape arises out of the original identities of passive and active, of subject and object, even of form and content; except for the anxious hypertension due to the formal requirement that a unitary artistic vision be actualized piece by piece before it fades, except also for the resultant struggle against inhibition and risk of regression, art would be blissful child's play, a reveling in primality, whence its approach is ever heralded by joy; lastly, if work stoppages feel like the loss of the world, resumptions of work feel like its recovery.

Appendix B

Autobiographical to start, "Typus" in its theoretical part first singled out the renunciation of clitoris sexuality at puberty as determinative of "the specifically feminine virtues one and all," which "are those of abnegation: where women assert themselves in competition with men, those are the very virtues from which they would emancipate themselves" [7]. It pursued: "The lesser differentiatedness implicit in that involution draws around the increasingly dispersive instinctual life a sort of limitative circle, which keeps it all closer to the common point of departure; this circumstance represents no mere backsliding, though, but a revival on a higher level of what once was" [7]. Emasculated, woman's sexuality is less ego-like than man's, so that, with its narcissistic reversion at puberty, woman "can pull off the paradox of separating ego and sex by uniting them. Thus femininity is equivocal where masculinity remains unequivocally aggressive, but is unitary where the latter's uninhibited aggressiveness comes apart in the opposite directions of ego and sex" [7]. Since the father sets the ego ideal, only for woman can it conveniently coalesce with the love-object. Man contrasts with woman as enterprising achiever with indolent receiver snug in her "joy-egoism" [8]. More unitary and rudimentary, woman does not so readily disjoin tenderness from sensuality. Devoted idealistically even as sexually, she puts across her "second and deepest paradox: to experience what is most vital as most sublimated. This mentalizing, idealizing, draws its spontaneity from the fact that, in the transferences of love, their point of departure remains more palpably present for the feminine-unitary nature throughout life—that aboriginal fusion with the totality in which we rested before we were given to ourselves and before the world broke up into individual formations" [11]. Thus woman will idealize so far as to depersonalize: "The individual [beloved] person in all his factuality becomes for her so to say transparent in all directions, a diaphane with human contour through which the fullness of the whole gleams, unbroken and unforgotten" [11]—and this even while she prizes and overprizes not the virtually unattainable, but the already obtained, "her devotion to which destroys her before herself if it does not exalt her before herself" [11]. When man and man-imago come apart, woman typically turns frigid—"a concealed hardness in all specifically female love (often well exceeding all male hardness)" [11-12]. For woman, whose lover is person and superperson at once, love's bondage is no tragic fate, but a grace of nature. In her self-surrender, her sensuality is also her holiness. And yet the very lushness of her love feast may well overtax her means, leaving little "for a reasonable, durable arrangement" [12]. To be sure, woman deserves love's elaborate ethical and matrimonial trimmings, "superadded out of false shame to begin with, then out of will to compensate and desire for approbation" [12]—but all this just because mating is the existential focal point of "her native greatness as well as her acquired pettiness" [12]. Mating is in fact her one cultural act, given its natural outcome: childbirth. This first leads her outside of herself through "tender self-identification" with her child [12], who in due course grows into a person in his own right, whom she must let go. Man's cultural task is intellectual as distinct from erotic, even as against erotic, which two unite for him only dreamily in dim memory or else, by virtue of his femininity, in his creative works, which disclose "how much for him too the final sense of culture lies in grasping that unity anew—how much on its account he creates the world over again from out of himself in all spheres as his own, so as to feel palpably and see graphically that the same pulse beats in the 'other' outside, that it is one with him" [13]. His lot being duality, "the goal is never attained by him in things, only in superpersonal values and images" [13]. What this mental goal is for him, the bodily embrace is for woman. A cultural value in herself, she is warranted to expand beyond herself culturally in concentric circles only. The sole image appropriate to this "female Narcissus" [14] is that "of the plant at the high noon" of culture [14—Nietzsche's "high noon"!] cooling itself in its own shadow lest it be singed before its time.

BIBLIOGRAPHY

I. UNPUBLISHED SOURCES

My chief source of unpublished material for this study was Lou's literary estate in Göttingen insofar as its proprietor, Ernst Pfeiffer, permitted. In January 1960, I wrote Mr. Pfeiffer asking whether I might utilize Lou's papers for a biographical study of her mind. He replied that he was loath to divulge what he still proposed to publish but that, as he also aimed to conceal nothing, a middle course could surely be found if, as he hoped, I came to Göttingen. This I did in July 1961. It ensued that Mr. Pfeiffer insisted upon mediating the materials personally—talking about them, reading aloud from some, displaying a letter or notation now and again. Because of my wish to obtain direct access to them I was charged with presuming to push him aside. His purpose of defending his vicarious ground in the world of letters concealed another, that of covering up for Lou's autobiographical aberrations—and concealed it from *him* in the first instance. For in his official estimate Lou was all candor, self-awareness, selflessness, as incapable of a mean motive as of an intellectual error, her every word a blessing and her every act a reverence.

Early in September 1961, having completed my research into published sources as far as I could then tell, I notified Mr. Pfeiffer that I would base my work on these alone unless he privileged me forthwith to utilize Lou's entire literary estate, in which case I would cover the costs of typewritten transcripts of it for his use as well as my own. He thereupon quite solemnly granted me full and free access to it for my documentary purposes provided only that some few "personal" items not be typed out and that he alone arrange for the typing. I never saw his typists, who prepared copies of several diaries under his supervision. Nor were Lou's papers put at my disposal readily and without restriction: such originals as passed through my hands were almost wrested from his, until late in October, with the typing completed for his projected edition of her diaries, he denounced our working arrangement. I left Göttingen with my duplicate copies. He sent after me denying my right to utilize any of the unpublished Lou materials at issue. I offered to share future royalties with him in return for his good will about my utilizing such materials as I had seen. He replied in due course that he agreed in principle, adding, however, that he wished to see my manuscript first. By then I had realized what he was up against keeping Lou's autobiographic record clean.

In all, I gained cognizance of the following unpublished materials in Mr. Pfeiffer's possession.

Lou's WORKS:
Four poems ("Lebensgebet," "Wellen," "Unflüggem Vöglein gleich . . . ," "In Streit und Sieg . . .": [late 1881] manuscript); just over 180 aphorisms (interspersed with 5 or 6 by Rée and corrected, annotated, and numbered by Nietzsche: 1882 notebook, severely mutilated);

"Jutta" (1933 typescript copy); *Der Stiefvater* (old typescript); *Die Tarnkappe* (typescript); *Der Gott* (typescript prepared by Mr. Pfeiffer); "Die Liebende" (typescript); "Am Krötenteich" (typescript); nine late essaylets (four in typescript, five dictated by Mr. Pfeiffer from manuscript)—excluding at least one on Josef König and another on Mariechen and her husband.

Lou's NOTEBOOKS, ORIGINALS:
School compositions, German (x 1876 to II 1877, 25-odd pages, corrected in red ink); school assignments, French (50-odd pages, lightly corrected); catechism (50-odd pages); Zurich course notes, winter term 1880-1881 ("Logik und Metaphysik I" 42 pages, "Die Griechen" 80-odd pages, diverse reading notes 10 pages); notes on Biedermann's courses (29 plus 24 pages); résumés (of *Les Âmes mortes* 20 sides that follow forwards, of Gillot's "lectures" 37 sides that follow backwards, of unidentified texts 8 loose sides); reading notes (90-odd sides that follow forwards from Bergson, 45-odd that follow backwards from Jung); more reading notes (84 sides that follow forwards from Freud, 22 that follow backwards from Adler).

Lou's DIARIES, ORIGINALS:
Tautenburg [VIII 1882] (severely mutilated); 20-odd single pages or scraps [1882-1892]; Ledebour retrospect (fragmentary); calendar notations (XI-XII 1893; I-XII 1894; 31 I, II-VI, VIII-IX, XI-XII 1895; I-II, V, X, XII 1896; IV-XII 1897; I-II, X 1898; I-II, 25-30 IV, V-VI, 27-31 VII, VIII-IX 1899; I, V-VI 1900); Russian journal, summer 1900; diary 29 XI 1900 to 2 II 1904; Balkan journal, fall 1908. These allegedly constituted all of Lou's diary leavings except for those covered by the transcripts described next; however, notations of Lou's for 14 and 26 V 1898 and 24 II 1899 cited in Pfeiffer, *Briefwechsel*, 33 and 517 respectively, indicate that further sources exist.

Lou's DIARIES IN TRANSCRIPT:
31 XII 1903 to 1 I 1907 and 1910, in typescript versions of 40 and 14 pages respectively, prepared before my sojourn in Göttingen (given to me along with a like version of the 1900-1904 diary which proved one long, omissive rewrite); 1907 and 1910-1931, in respectively 1 and some 235 typescript pages prepared during my sojourn (too rapidly, I think, for significant rewriting) except for some 15 of them *passim*. These latter transcripts together with the preexisting 1910 one and the Balkan journal supposedly represent all of Lou's diary leavings of after 1906 apart from those covered by Lou Andreas-Salomé, *In der Schule bei Freud* (doubtless also a selective rewrite, as a comparison with the two excerpts from the 1912-1913 diary in Rainer Maria Rilke and Lou Andreas-Salomé, *Briefwechsel*, 309 and 591-92, suggests) and except for some "personal matter," especially notations on day-to-day activities—supplied for Berlin early 1907 through selective, top-speed dictation (but not for at least Munich spring 1915 as quoted in the *Briefwechsel*, 389, and the 1930's as available in an appointments book once displayed to me from afar).

Bibliography

LETTERS (including cards, telegrams, notes, etc., and counting fragments):

Originals to Lou: from Ellen Key 62, Helene Klingenberg 24, "Lotte" 6, Eduard Spranger 5, "Caro" 4, Ferdinand Tönnies 2, Gottfried Kinkel 2, Julius Gildemeister 2, Carl von Schulz 2, Emil von Gebsattel 2 (?), Martin Buber 2, young Hamburger (13 VI 1882) 1, Hanna Bormann 1, Hermann Conrad 1, Lou's mother 1.

Originals from Lou: to Sigmund Freud 131 (photocopies), Ellen Key 25 (microfilm), Frieda von Bülow 18, Eduard Spranger 18, Ferdinand Tönnies 9, Emma Flörke 7, "Caro" 6, Paul Rée 2, Sandor Ferenczi 1 (photocopy), Johanna Niemann 1, young Hamburger [1884] 1, "Lollo" 1, Götz von Selle 1, Hanna Bormann 1, plus drafts to Sigmund Freud, Ferdinand Tönnies, Emil von Gebsattel, Emma Flörke.

Originals: from Julius Gildemeister to Hugo Göring 2, from Lou's mother to "Caro" 1.

Additionally, in Ernst Pfeiffer's and Karl Schlechta's transcription of 1937-1939 (see Karl Schlechta, in Friedrich Nietzsche, *Werke*, III, 1372n.): from Friedrich Nietzsche to Paul Rée 34, to Lou 24, and to Rée and Lou 1, to Franz Overbeck 4 and to Ida Overbeck 1, to Elisabeth Nietzsche 2, to Peter Gast 1, to Malwida von Meysenbug 1 (plus some 15 drafts to Lou and/or Paul Rée, 3 to Malwida von Meysenbug, 2 to Franz Overbeck and 2 to Ida Overbeck, 1 to Lou's mother, 1 to Georg Rée, 1 to Elisabeth Nietzsche, as well as fragments addressed to Elisabeth and others, diverse jottings of late 1882, a two-page rewrite of Lou's 1882 essay on woman, and an outline for her projected full-scale study of woman); from Paul Rée to Friedrich Nietzsche 27, Lou 25, Elisabeth Nietzsche 20, Franziska Nietzsche 13, Franz Overbeck 2, Georg Rée 1; Malwida von Meysenbug to Lou 12, Paul Rée 2; Elisabeth Nietzsche to Ida Overbeck 5, Peter Gast 4, Clara Gelzer 1; Lou to Friedrich Nietzsche 2, Paul Rée 1, Franz Overbeck 1, Ida Overbeck 1, Hendrik Gillot 1 (from Lou's copy); Franz Overbeck to Peter Gast 3; Peter Gast to Franz Overbeck 3; Lou's mother to Friedrich Nietzsche 1; Rée's mother to Lou 1; Alois Biedermann to Franz Overbeck 1, Lou's mother 1; Clara Gelzer to Elisabeth Nietzsche 1—and a memorandum by Ludwig Hüter on Lou including a letter from Lou to himself plus two each way between Malwida von Meysenbug and himself. Additionally, in Mr. Pfeiffer's transcription: to Lou from Sigmund Freud 85, Paul Rée 4, Sandor Ferenczi 1; from Lou to a Karlsruhe student (Rée period) 1.

Mentioned but withheld: to Lou from Gerhart Hauptmann 5, Carl Hauptmann 2, Marie Hauptmann 1, Margarete Hauptmann 2, and Benvenuto Hauptmann 1, Maximilian Harden 5, Max Reinhardt 4 or more plus one from his troupe, Lulu von Strauss 4, Ricarda Huch 3, Verner von Heidenstam 2, Georg Simmel 1 and Simmel's wife 1, Heinrich von Stein 1 (plus some from Stein to Rée), Arne and Hulda Garborg 1, Hegeler 1, Henrik Ibsen 1, Emil Milan 1, Hugo von Hofmannsthal 1, Peter Altenberg 1 (plus a manuscript by him on Lou), Sophia Goudstikker 1, Agnes Miegen 1, Heinrich Vogeler 1, Käthe Kollwitz 1, Alexander Moissi 1, Herbert Eulenburg 1, Lucia Dora

Frost 1, Eduard von Keyserling 1, Ina Seidel 1, plus an unspecified number to Lou from Poul Bjerre (two glimpsed) and Viktor Tausk, from Frieda von Bülow (additional) and Gertrud Eysoldt (one sighted), from fans and publishers, and from Andreas—as also Lou's to Andreas.

Mr. Pfeiffer formally and emphatically denied possessing any further letters to, from, or about Lou—though in fact he draws on letters to Lou from Marie von Ebner-Eschenbach, Max Eitingon, Otto Rank, Mrs. Sandor Ferenczi, Anna Freud, and Karl Abraham in his annotation to *Lebensrückblick* (345) and to *Sigmund Freud, Lou Andreas-Salomé, Briefwechsel* (239; 245-46; 258; 274; 277; 286; 285). All Rée's originals were lent to me, but I could not decipher them—and I glimpsed the Nietzsche and Freud originals.

FINALLY:

I saw two notations by Lou (on her 1882 itinerary, on her Hauptmann letters) and was able to rummage part of her library, besides which one line was read to me from an appointments book of Andreas's (on his meeting *Töchterchen*'s train).

Lou's Nietzsche materials were also available to me in Erich Podach's typescript at the Basel University Library, which put the following unpublished materials at my disposal as well.

ORIGINAL LETTERS, ETC. (the Pfeiffer-Schlechta transcriptions mentioned above include the first 19):

Lou to Franz Overbeck 1, to Ida Overbeck 1; Friedrich Nietzsche to Franz Overbeck 4, to Ida Overbeck 1; Elisabeth Nietzsche to Ida Overbeck 5, to Clara Gelzer 1; Paul Rée to Franz Overbeck 2; Peter Gast to Franz Overbeck 3; Alois Biedermann to Franz Overbeck 1; Heinrich Romundt to Franz Overbeck 15; Carl von Gersdorff to Franz Overbeck 1; Erwin Rohde to Franz Overbeck 1; Franz Overbeck to Erwin Rohde 4; Peter Gast to Josef Hofmiller 5; Fritz Kögel to Josef Hofmiller 4; Erich Podach to Ida Overbeck 1; Erich Podach and Lou to Ida Overbeck 1.

OTHER:

Fritz Kögel's excerpts from Friedrich Nietzsche's notebooks; an unpublished 48-page manuscript by Carl Albrecht Bernoulli, "Nietzsche's Lou-Erlebnis," dated 1931.

The Goethe- und Schiller-Archiv in Weimar replied most painstakingly to my queries by mail concerning its Nietzscheana pertaining to Lou (all covered by the Pfeiffer-Schlechta transcriptions cited above) and further provided me with photocopies of two letters from Lou to Max Martersteig. Benvenuto Hauptmann gave me the run of his father's diaries housed at Ronco sopra Ascona, where Martin Machatzke helped me through them: they yielded two entries concerning Lou. The Deutsche Akademie der Künste, Berlin, sent me a photocopy of one letter from Lou to Gerhart Hauptmann. The Stadtbibliothek in Munich provided a note from Lou to Henry von Heiseler dated 23 ɪɪ 1912 and the printer's copy of Lou's *Drei Briefe an einen Knaben* for my use. Dr. Olaf Klose of the Schleswig-Holsteinische Landesbibliothek, Kiel, deciphered for me the passages concerning Lou deleted from Ferdinand Tönnies' letters to Friedrich Paulsen as published. Mrs. Maria Apel of Loufried provided me with an extract from Lou's will and a photocopy of a letter to herself from Herbert Beyer (Ernst Pfeiffer's lawyer)—besides showing me about Loufried and lending me Simon Glücklich's portrait of Lou to be photographed (incidentally, D 17 I 1900: "Thanked Glücklich for the picture" —likely just then received by mail). The Bundesarchiv, Koblenz, microfilmed Lou's twelve letters to Maximilian Harden for my use. Hamburg University sent me copies of Lou's two notes to Richard Dehmel. Zurich University communicated the record of Lou's studies there. At the Misani hotel in Celerina I was shown the registration book containing Lou's entries for 1883 and 1885 and Paul Rée's for 1900 and 1901. The University Library, Cambridge, furnished me with copies of letters to Arthur Schnitzler as follows: 21 from Lou and 16 of between V 1895 and I 1896 from Richard Beer-Hofmann. Yale University prepared copies of Beer-Hofmann's nine letters to Schnitzler relating to Lou and of three from Lou to Kurt Wolff. Mrs. Mirjam Beer-Hofmann Lens accorded me free use of the letters to her father still in her possession: I drew on 32 from Lou, one from Ellen Key, and one from Helene Klingenberg. Heinrich Schnitzler readily excerpted his father's diaries for my purposes. Franz Schoenberner contributed three letters to himself from Lou and one from Erich Podach concerning her. I utilized the following items held by Columbia University: one letter each from Lou, Sigmund Freud, and Anna Freud to Otto Rank, and two of Rank's circulars to the Central Committee of the International Psychoanalytical Association.

Of my oral sources, finally, the most important were Ernst Pfeiffer, whose readiness to reminisce about Lou contrasted pointedly and pleasantly with his reluctance to divulge her papers; Mrs. Maria Apel, who informed me abundantly of Lou's domestic existence; Ellen Delp, who told enchantedly and enchantingly of her friendship with Lou; Franz Schoenberner, who plugged countless gaps in the documentary records, particularly with regard to Lou's family background and her Munich acqaintanceships; and Mrs. Mirjam Beer-Hofmann Lens, who recollected Lou's visits of 1912–1913 with flabbergasting exactitude and who, spiritedly seconded by Miss Naëmah Beer-Hofmann, filled me in authoritatively on Lou's Austria.

II. LOU'S PUBLICATIONS

VZ(S) = *Vossische Zeitung* (Sonntagsbeilage)
FB   = *Freie Bühne für modernes Leben*
NDR = *Neue deutsche Rundschau*
NR   = *Die neue Rundschau*
DR   = *Deutsche Rundschau*
LE   = *Das lit(t)erarische Echo*
APV = *Almanach des Internationalen Psychoanalytischen Verlages*
*Not available to me.

The publications are listed in chronological order; only the first place and date of each are shown.

Bibliography

Im Kampf um Gott. Leipzig, 1885.
"Die Wildente," *FB*, 1890: 849-52, 873-75. (Chapter of *Henrik Ibsens Frauen-Gestalten.*)
Henrik Ibsens Frauen-Gestalten. Nach seinen sechs Familiendramen. Ein Puppenheim/Gespenster/Die Wildente/Rosmersholm/Die Frau vom Meere/Hedda Gabler. Jena, 1891.
"Zum Bilde Friedrich Nietzsches," *FB*, 1891: 64-68, 81-91, 109-12.
*"Friedrich Nietzsche," *VZ*(S), January 11 and 25, 1891: 7-10 and 7-12.
"Ein holländisches Urteil über moderne deutsche Dramen," *FB*, 1891: 521-24, 541-46, 571-78, 592-95, 670-73, 696-701.
"Der Realismus in der Religion," *FB*, 1891: 1004-09, 1025-30, 1057-59, 1079-1083.
*"Ossip Schubin," *VZ*(S), January 10 and 17, 1892: 10-12 and 11-12.
"Gottesschöpfung," *FB*, 1892: 169-79.
"Zum Bilde Friedrich Nietzsches," *FB*, 1892: 249-51, 285-96.
*"Emil Marriot," *VZ*(S), August 7 and 21, 1892: 4-7 and 9-12.
"Harnack und das Apostolikum," *FB*, 1892: 1214-22.
"Ein Apokalyptiker," *Das Magazin für Litteratur*, September 19 and 26, 1892: 753-55 and 777-79.
"Die Duse," *FB*, 1893: 76-81.
"Ibsen, Strindberg, Sudermann," *FB*, 1893: 149-72.
"Der Talisman," *FB*, 1893: 323-25.
"Hanna Jagert," *FB*, 1893: 467-71.
"Ein Frühlingsdrama," *FB*, 1893: 572-77.
*"Ideal und Askese," *Zeitgeist*, No. 20, 1893.
"Hartlebens 'Erziehung zur Ehe,' " *FB*, 1893: 1165-67.
"Hannele," *FB*, 1893: 1343-49.
Friedrich Nietzsche in seinen Werken. Vienna, 1894.
"Von der Bestie bis zum Gott. Über Totemismus bei den Ursemiten," *NDR*, 1894: 398-402.
*"Das Problem des Islams," *VZ*(S), July 22 and 29, 1894: 4-8 and 3-6.
Ruth. Eine Erzählung. Stuttgart, 1895.
"Durch Dich," *Die Frau*, February 1895: 268.
"Winterlaub," *Die Frau*, April 1895: 401.
"Rote Rosen," *Die Frau*, July 1895: 590.
"Ricarda Huch: Erinnerungen von Ludolf Ursleu dem Jüngeren," *Die Frau*, October 1895: 32-36.
*"Vom Ursprung des Christentums," *VZ*(S), December 22, 1895: 7-10.
Aus fremder Seele. Eine Spätherbstgeschichte. Stuttgart, 1896.
"Kampfruf," *Die Frau*, February 1896: 297.
"Jesus der Jude," *NDR*, 1896: 342-51.
"Scandinavische Dichter," *Cosmopolis*, November 1896: 552-69.
"Abteilung 'Innere Männer,' " *Cosmopolis*, February 1897: 513-36.
"Russische Dichtung und Kultur," *Cosmopolis*, August and September 1897: 571-80 and 872-85.
"Aus der Geschichte Gottes," *NDR*, 1897: 1211-20.
Fenitschka. Eine Ausschweifung. Stuttgart, 1898.
"Vor dem Erwachen," *Meisternovellen deutscher Frauen.* Edited by Ernst Brausewetter. Berlin, 1898. (Included in *Menschenkinder*.)

Bibliography

*"Das russische Heiligenbild und sein Dichter," *VZ*, January 1, 1898.

"Russische Philosophie und semitischer Geist," *Die Zeit*, January 15, 1898: 40.

"Grundformen der Kunst," *Pan*, February 1898: 177-82.

"Ein Todesfall," *Cosmopolis*, April 1898: 197-225. (Included in *Menschenkinder*.)

"Religion und Cultur," *Die Zeit*, April 2, 1898: 5-7.

"Vom religiösen Affekt," *Die Zukunft*, April 23, 1898: 149-54.

"Missbrauchte Frauenkraft," *Die Frau*, June 1898: 513-16.

"Mädchenreigen," *Cosmopolis*, September 1898: 803-28. (Included in *Menschenkinder*.)

"Physische Liebe," *Die Zukunft*, October 29, 1898: 218-22.

"Der dritte Bruder. Novellen von Adine Gemberg," *LE*, November 1, 1898: 189.

"Aphorismen. Von Paul Nikolaus Cossmann," *LE*, November 1, 1898: 194-95.

"Bilder aus der Geschichte und Litteratur Russlands. Von Fürst Sergei Wolkonskij," *LE*, November 15, 1898: 255.

"Sehnsucht, Schönheit, Dämmerung. Die Geschichte einer Jugend. Roman von S. Hochsteller," *LE*, November 15, 1898: 248.

"Leo Tolstoi, unser Zeitgenosse," *NDR*, 1898: 1145-55.

"Zurück ans All," *Die Romanwelt*, January, February, and March 1899. (Included in *Menschenkinder*.)

Menschenkinder. Stuttgart, 1899. ("Vor dem Erwachen"; "Abteilung 'Innere Männer' "; "Mädchenreigen"; "Eine Nacht"; "Unterwegs"; "Ein Wiedersehen"; "Das Paradies"; "Inkognito"; "Ein Todesfall"; "Zurück ans All.")

"Die eherne Schlange. Von Thomas P. Krag," *LE*, January 1, 1899: 461.

"Der Egoismus in der Religion," *Der Egoismus*. Edited by Arthur Dix. Leipzig, 1899: 383-402.

"Ketzereien gegen die moderne Frau," *Die Zukunft*, February 11, 1899: 237-40.

"Ein Wiedersehen," *Die Frau*, February 1899: 257-64. (Included in *Menschenkinder*.)

"Der Mensch als Weib. Ein Bild im Umriss," *NDR*, 1899: 225-43.

"Vom Kunstaffekt," *Die Zukunft*, May 27, 1899: 366-72.

"Erleben," *Die Zeit*, August 19, 1899: 120-22.

"Essais. Von Ellen Key," *LE*, October 1, 1899: 66-67.

"Russische Geschichten," *Die Zeit*, December 9, 1899: 153.

"Vom Bazillus zum Affenmenschen. Naturwissenschaftliche Plaudereien von Wilhelm Bölsche," *LE*, January 15, 1900: 583.

"Die Schwester," *Die Romanwelt*, October 1900. (Included in *Im Zwischenland*.)

"Gedanken über das Liebesproblem," *NDR*, 1900: 1009-27.

Ma. Ein Porträt. Stuttgart, 1901.

"Ein Dank an einen Dichter. Zur Würdigung des 'Michael Kramer' von Gerhart Hauptmann," *Der Lotse*, April 20, 1901: 71-79.

"Alter und Ewigkeit," *Die Zukunft*, October 26, 1901: 146-50.

"Wolga," *Deutsche Roman-Bibliothek*, 1901: 657-88. (Included in *Im Zwischenland*.)

Bibliography

Im Zwischenland. Fünf Geschichten aus dem Seelenleben halbwüchsiger Mädchen. Stuttgart, 1902. ("Im Zwischenland"; "Vaters Kind"; "Eine erste Erfahrung"; "Die Schwester"; "Wolga.")

"Der Graf von Charolais," *Die Zukunft*, February 18, 1905: 286-93.

"Das Glashüttenmärchen," *Die Zukunft*, March 17, 1906: 399-404.

"Frühlings Erwachen," *Die Zukunft*, January 19, 1907: 97-100.

"Vier Kammerspiele," *Die Schaubühne*, February 20 and 27, March 5, 1908: 199-203, 225-27, 250-54.

"Lebende Dichtung," *Die Zukunft*, February 22, 1908: 262-67.

"Die Russen," *Die Schaubühne*, September 23, 1909: 305-08.

Die Erotik. "Die Gesellschaft," edited by Martin Buber. Berlin, 1910.

"Der Lebensbund," *Die neue Generation*, October 1910: 391-98. (Chapter of *Die Erotik*.)

"Das Kindlein von Erika Rhenisch," *LE*, October 15, 1911: 143-45.

"Im Spiegel," *LE*, October 15, 1911: 86-88.

*"Eine Nacht," *Geistiges Leben*, May 1912.

"Vom Kunstaffekt," *Deutsche Monatschrift für Russen*, July 1912: 595-601. (Reprint.)

"Realität und Gesetzlichkeit im Geschlechtsleben. Von Marie Louise Enkendorff," *LE*, September 1, 1912: 1672-76.

"Elisabeth Siewert," *LE*, September 15, 1912: 1690-95.

"Von Paul zu Pedro," *Die neue Generation*, October 1912: 529-33.

"Aus dem Briefwechsel Leo Tolstois," *LE*, October 1, 1913: 1-8.

"Von frühem Gottesdienst," *Imago*, 1913: 457-67.

"Das Bündnis zwischen Tor und Ur," *Velhagen und Klasings Monatshefte*, December 1913: 529-40. (Included in *Die Stunde ohne Gott und andere Kindergeschichten*.)

"Zum Typus Weib," *Imago*, 1914: 1-14.

"Seelchen," *Velhagen und Klasings Monatshefte*, April 1914: 529-36.

"Kind und Kunst," *LE*, October 1, 1914: 1-4.

"Zum Bilde Strindbergs," *LE*, March 1, 1915: 645-53.

"Bericht über einen Weihnachtsmann," *Velhagen und Klasings Monatshefte*, December 1915: 509-15. (Included in *Drei Briefe an einen Knaben*.)

" 'Anal' und 'Sexual,' " *Imago*, 1916: 249-73.

"Angela Langer," *LE*, December 15, 1916: 329-33.

Drei Briefe an einen Knaben. Leipzig, 1917.

" 'Expression,' " *LE*, April 1, 1917: 783-90.

"Insekt und Krieg," *Die Tat*, April 1917: 48-53.

"Psychosexualität," *Zeitschrift für Sexualwissenschaft*, April and May/June 1917: 1-12 and 49-57.

"Luzifer. Eine Phantasie über Ricarda Huchs Buch 'Luthers Glaube,' " *Die neue Generation*, May 1917: 210-15.

"Nadja Strassers 'Russin,' " *NR*, August 1917: 1148-49.

"Karl Nötzels Tolstoi," *LE*, August 1, 1918: 1269-76.

"Dichterischer Ausdruck," *LE*, December 15, 1918: 325-31.

"Der russische Intelligent," *NR*, 1919: 127-28.

"Strindberg. Ein Beitrag zur Soziologie der Geschlechter. Von Leopold v. Wiese," *LE*, March 1, 1919: 692-93.

Bibliography

"Des Dichters Erleben," *NR*, 1919: 358-67.

"Tolstois Jugendtagebuch," *Der neue Merkur*, May 1919: 137-39.

"Der geistliche Russe," *Der neue Merkur*, November 1919: 380-86.

"Agnes Henningsen," *LE*, January 15, 1920: 456-64.

"Die Klerisei. Roman. Von Nikolaus Leskow," *LE*, April 15, 1920: 879-80.

"Spiegelzauber. Von Geza Roheim," *LE*, May 15, 1920: 1011-12.

"Im Traumland. Von Isolde Kurz," *LE*, May 15, 1920: 1011-12.

*"Unser Anteil an Dostoevski und Tolstoi," *VZ*, July 23, 1920.

"Diekmanns Denkwürdigkeiten und Erinnerungsbücherei. Band I. 'Die Liebe' von Kurt Engelbrecht," *LE*, August 1, 1920: 1332.

"Tagebuch eines halbwüchsigen Mädchens," *LE*, September 1, 1920: 1463-64.

"Waldemar Bonsels," *LE*, October 1, 1920: 8-17.

"Satiren von Michael Saltykow Schtschedrin," *LE*, November 1, 1920: 181.

Das Haus. Berlin, 1921.

"Eros und die Evangelien. Aus den Notizen eines Vagabunden," *LE*, March 1, 1921: 684-85.

"Russische Romantik," *Romantik*, No. 5, 1921: 67.

"Kranke Liebe. Von Hans Jäger," *LE*, October 15, 1921: 121.

"Geschwister," *DR*, October 19, 1921: 24-63.

"Die Diktatur der Liebe. Von Theodor Zell," *LE*, November 1, 1921: 178.

"Narzissmus als Doppelrichtung," *Imago*, 1921: 361-86. English translation by Stanley A. Leavy in *Psychoanalytic Quarterly*, XIII (1962): 1-30.

"Der werdende Mensch. Von Gustav Landauer," *LE*, December 1, 1921: 307.

Die Stunde ohne Gott und andere Kindergeschichten. Jena, 1922.

Der Teufel und seine Grossmutter. Jena, 1922.

"Tendenz und Form russischer Dichtung," *LE*, January 1, 1922: 398-401.

"Eros," *Faust*, Heft 9, 1922/1923: 1-6.

Ródinka. Russische Errinnerung. Jena, 1923.

"Zum sechsten Mai 1926," *APV*, 1927: 9-14.

Rainer Maria Rilke. Leipzig, 1928.

"Was daraus folgt, dass es nicht die Frau gewesen ist, die den Vater totgeschlagen hat," *APV*, 1928: 25-30.

"Rilke in Russland," *Russische Blätter*, October 1928: 86-88. (Part of *Rainer Maria Rilke*.)

Mein Dank an Freud. Vienna, 1931.

"Der Kranke hat immer recht," *APV*, 1928: 36-45. (Chapter from *Mein Dank an Freud*.)

Lebensrückblick. Edited by Ernst Pfeiffer. Zurich, 1951.

Rainer Maria Rilke, Lou Andreas-Salomé. Briefwechsel. Edited by Ernst Pfeiffer. Zurich, 1952.

In der Schule bei Freud. Tagebuch eines Jahres. 1912-1913. Edited by Ernst Pfeiffer. Zurich, 1958. English translation by Stanley A. Leavy: *The Freud Journal of Lou Andreas-Salomé*. New York, 1964.

Sigmund Freud, Lou Andreas-Salomé. Briefwechsel. Edited by Ernst Pfeiffer. Frankfurt am Main, 1966.

Bibliography

III. LOU'S LITERARY OUTPUT

1882a (Aphorisms. Unpublished.)
1883a Im Kampf um Gott: [1883 to mid-1884].
1889a Henrik Ibsens Frauen-Gestalten: [1889-1890].
1890a Friedrich Nietzsche in seinen Werken (based on "Zum Bilde Friedrich Nietzsches," "Friedrich Nietzsche," "Ein Apokalyptiker," "Ideal und Askese"): [1890-1893].
1891a Ein holländisches Urteil über moderne deutsche Dramen: [late spring 1891].
1891b Der Realismus in der Religion: [IX 1891].
1891c Ossip Schubin: [XII 1891].
1891d Gottesschöpfung: [XII 1891].
1892a Emil Marriot: [summer 1892].
1892b Harnack und das Apostolikum: [fall 1892].
1892c Die Duse: [XII 1892].
1893a Ibsen, Strindberg, Sudermann: [I 1893].
1893b *Der Talisman*: [II 1893].
1893c *Hanna Jagert*: [early spring 1893].
1893d Ein Frühlingsdrama: 23 IV 1893.
1893e Hartlebens *Erziehung zur Ehe*: [early fall 1893].
1893f Von der Bestie bis zum Gott: [fall 1893].
1893g Ruth: 18 23 24 XI, 21-31 XII 1893; 1-11 13 18 19-28 30 I, 1-10 II 1894.
1893h *Hannele*: 25 27 28 XI, 4 5 XII 1893.
1894a Das Problem des Islams: 14-16 18 20 22 II 1894.
1894b Jesus der Jude: 10 12 26 X, 16 17 XI 1894; 17 21 23 II, 11 12 VIII 1895.
1894c Das Paradies: [XII 1894 to I 1895].
1895a Durch Dich: [I 1895].
1895b Winterlaub: [I 1895].
1895c Vor dem Erwachen: 8-13 26 27 II 1895.
1895d Ricarda Huch: *Erinnerungen von Ludolf Ursleu dem Jüngeren*: 16-18 20 II 1895.
1895e Rote Rosen: [IV 1895].
1895f Aus fremder Seele ("Himmelspastor": 1 26-30 VI 1895): 15-24 26 II 1896.
1895g Vom Ursprung des Christentums: [late 1895].
1896a Kampfruf: [I 1896].
1896b Scandinavische Dichter: 1 3 4 V 1896.
1896c Abteilung 'Innere Männer' ("Unzeitgemäss": 4-7 16 22 XII 1896).
1896d Fenitschka: 7-12 14-16 30 31 XII 1896.
1896e Eine Nacht ("Spitalnovelle": 25-26 29-30 XII 1896).
1897a Mädchenreigen: [spring 1897].
1897b Russische Dichtung und Kultur, Part I ("essay": 20-23 VI 1897).
1897c Das russische Heiligenbild und sein Dichter ("Leskow": 25-30 VI 1897).
1897d Russische Philosophie und semitischer Geist: 4-7 VII 1897.
1897e Unterwegs ("Amor": 18 22 26 27 VII, 5 VIII 1897).

1897f   Russische Dichtung und Kultur, Part II ("Volinsky essay": 2-4 VIII 1897).

1897g   Ein Wiedersehen: 14-16 18-19 VIII 1897; 1-4 I, 22-23 X 1898.

1897h   Inkognito: 20-22 VIII, 26 IX, 21 23-26 30 XII 1897.

1897i   Ein Todesfall ("Der Sieger": 18 24 IX, 26 29 XI, 1 3 15-16): 28-30 XII 1897.

1897j   Eine Ausschweifung ("Sklavenglück": 30 X, 4-9 11 XI 1897): 17 21 26-31 I 1898.

1897k   Aus der Geschichte Gottes ("Volinsky essay": 11 13 15-17 XI 1897).

1898a   Zurück ans All: 7-10 12-14 I 1898.

1898b   Grundformen der Kunst: 31 I, 1-2 4-6 II 1898.

1898c   Religion und Cultur: 7-10 II 1898.

1898d   Vom religiösen Affekt: 12 14-15 II 1898.

1898e   *Missbrauchte Frauenkraft*: 23 26 II 1898.

1898f   Jutta: [1898?]; IV 1933. Unpublished.

1898g   Leo Tolstoi, unser Zeitgenosse: 1-6 X 1898.

1898h   Physische Liebe: 10-11 13 X 1898.

1898i   Der Egoismus in der Religion: 26-29 X to XII 1898.

1899a   Der Mensch als Weib: 2-4 6 9-11 21 I, 24-28 II . . . 1899.

1899b   Vom Kunstaffekt: 16 I, II . . . 1899.

1899c   Ketzereien gegen die moderne Frau: 7 I 1899.

1899d   Erleben: [III to early IV] 1899.

1899e   *Essais* von Ellen Key: 25 VI 1899.

1899f   Ma ("Neige": 11 12 14 16-18 20-22 24-26 IX, [X-XII] 1899): 1-3 9 I 1900.

1900a   Gedanken über das Liebesproblem: 8 9 11 12 22 I [II-IV] 1900.

1900b   Die Schwester: 22 23 25-28 30 I 1900.

1900c   Wolga: late XII 1900; 4 5 7 9 10 I 1901.

1900d   Im Zwischenland: XII 1900; 2 3 I 1901.

1901a   Ródinka ("Witalii": 1 I to late III 1901): XII 1903 to 25 I 1904; VIII 1917 [to 1922].

1901b   Ein Dank an einen Dichter: 10 13 14 I 1901.

1901c   Alter und Ewigkeit: V to 15 VI 1901.

1901d   Eine erste Erfahrung: [winter 1901-1902].

1901e   Vaters Kind: [winter 1901-1902].

1904a   Das Haus ("Ehe": 28 I to [IV] 1904): [mid-1904 to 1905]; [summer 1910]; VI 1917 . . .

1905a   *Der Graf von Charolais*: 11 12 I 1905.

1906a   *Das Glashüttenmärchen*: 27 I, 15 II 1906.

1906b   Die Russen: 13 VI to 25 VIII 1906.

1906c   *Frühlings Erwachen*: [late XII 1906].

1907a   Vier Kammerspiele: [late spring 1907].

1907b   Lebende Dichtung: [late XII 1907 to II 1908].

1908a   Die Tarnkappe: [1908?]; late IV to 2 V 1933. Unpublished.

1908b   Der Stiefvater: [1908?]. Unpublished.

1909a   Der Gott: VII 1909 to III 1910; XII 1911. Unpublished.

1909b   Die Erotik: X 1909 to II 1910.

1909c   Die Geschichten von der Gänseblume und von den Wolken: 28 XII 1909.

1911a   Im Spiegel: [early fall 1911].

1912a   Kind und Kunst: [early 1912?]; late VI 1914.

1912b   Elisabeth Siewert: VI 1912.

1912c   Drei Briefe an einen Knaben: VI 1912; XI to 5 XII 1913; early 1917.

1912d   *Realität und Gesetzlichkeit im Geschlechtsleben*: [late summer 1912].

1913a   Das Bündnis zwischen Tor und Ur: [late IV–V 1913].

1913b   Seelchen: [V–VI] 1913.

1913c   Von frühem Gottesdienst: [VI 1913].

1913d   Aus dem Briefwechsel Leo Tolstois: [early fall 1913].

1913e   Zum Typus Weib: late XII 1913; early I 1914.

1914a   'Anal' und 'Sexual': VI–VII 1914; fall 1915; . . . 14 XI 1915.

1914b   Ubw.: [7-11 X 1914 to mid-1915; early 1916; I 1917]. (Page references are to "Psychosexualität," the second of three sections; otherwise only the introduction and table of contents survive— as enclosures in Lou→Freud, 30 VI 1916.)

1914c   Zum Bilde Strindbergs: [XI 1914; I 1915].

1915a   Der Teufel und seine Grossmutter: [1915?].

1916a   Die Liebende: [1916?]. Unpublished.

1916b   Angela Langer: [XII 1916].

1917a   'Expression': [mid-I 1917].

1917b   Insekt und Krieg: IV 1917.

1917c   Luzifer: [V 1917].

1917d   Geschlecht: [VII 1917]. Lost?

1918a   Karl Nötzels *Tolstoi*: [summer 1918].

1918b   Dichterischer Ausdruck: [late 1918].

1918c   Der russische Intelligent: [late 1918].

1919a   Des Dichters Erleben: [mid-I to III 1919].

1919b   *Strindberg*: [II 1919].

1919c   Tolstois Jugendtagebuch: [IV 1919].

1919d   Die Stunde ohne Gott: [VIII]-IX 1919.

1919e   Der geistliche Russe: [fall 1919].

1919f   Agnes Henningsen: [late 1919 or early 1920].

1919g   Geschwister: [25 XII 1919? to early 1920]; IV 1933.

1920a   Unser Anteil an Dostoevski und Tolstoi: [late spring 1920].

1920b   Narzissmus als Doppelrichtung: [1920-1921].

1920c   Waldemar Bonsels: [IX 1920].

1921a   Tendenz und Form russischer Dichtung: XII 1921.

1922a   Eros: [late summer 1922].

1926a   Zum sechsten Mai 1926: [1926].

1927a   Rainer Maria Rilke: [1927].

1927b   Was daraus folgt, dass es nicht die Frau gewesen ist, die den Vater totgeschlagen hat: [1927].

1929a   Mein Dank an Freud: fall 1929 to VII 1931.

1931a   Grundriss einiger Lebenserinnerungen: [1931] to V 1933. Published in *Lebensrückblick*.

1933a   Was am 'Grundriss' fehlt: [latter 1933?]. Published in *Lebensrückblick*.

1933b   Am Krötenteich: XII 1933. Unpublished.

1934a "In 1933 . . .": I 1934. Unpublished.
1934b "Des Menschen tiefste Wünsche . . .": v 1934. Unpublished.
1934c "Mal las ich doch . . .": vi 1934. Unpublished.
1934d "Aus meinem Königsberger Aufenthalt . . .": [1934]. Unpublished.
1934e "April, unser Monat, Rainer . . .": [1934?]. Published in *Lebensrückblick*.
1935a "Als ich, aus einem Aufenthalt . . .": [1935?]. Published in *Lebensrückblick*.
1935b Ein Versuch: [1935]. Unpublished.
1935c "Innerhalb der sogenannten Normalität . . .": [1935]. Unpublished.
1935d "Unser menschliches Bewusstwerden . . .": 1 xii 1935. Unpublished.
1936a "Sinne ich an Frühestes . . .": ii [1936]. Unpublished.
1936b Nachträge: v-vi 1936. Unpublished.

I was unable to identify the following notations by Lou with completed works by her: "the drama" 7 x 1894; "Verjährt" 1 xi 1894; "Knecht-gestalt" 17 xi 1894; "Novelle(n)" 16-18 30 xii 1894; "Stuttgarter Novelle" [= "Das Paradies"?] 4-7 ii 1895; "Gegen den Strom" 7 9 vi, 3 viii, 6 7 9-13 15 16 ("ended") ix 1895; "Totentanz" 3 viii 1895; "Eine fixe Idée" 2 3 6 ("ended") xi 1895; "essay for Heilborn" and "second essay" 20 iv 1897 (cf. above, p. 213 n. *g*); "Die russische Legende" (with Volinsky) 16-19 vi 1897; "essay for Yassinky" (with Volinsky) 17 vii 1897; "second essay" 8 10 11 viii 1897; "put finishing touches, wrote Vol. and package" 10 x 1897; "Deutsche Dramatik" (for Volinsky) 28 31 x, 1 3 xi 1897; " 'Zeit' proofs" 10 i 1898; "Letzte Schönheit" 7 ii 1898; "new essay for Bahr" 7 ii 1898; "Apostolikum" [for God book?] 17 ii 1898; "Novelle" 18 19 ii 1898; "Am Abend" 7 8 x 1898; "Am Brunnenrand" 24 i 1899; "proofs from Fischer" 11 ii 1899; "*Pan* revision" 13 ii 1899; "notes for new essay in connection with Muther" 12 i 1900 [= "Gedanken über das Liebesproblem"?]; "a drama, a story, and the novel" conceived 22 xii 1901; "Novellchen" 28 ii 1907. Moreover, Klingenberg, 249, mentions a short story by Lou, "Haus," about a seductive young man of God who moralistically incites young girls to immorality, and according to Freud→Abraham, 2 v 1912, "she is said to have sent Jung a paper for the *Jahrbuch*."

IV. OTHER PUBLISHED WORKS (those utilized by me plus a few of related interest)

FB = *Freie Bühne für modernes Leben*
NDR = *Neue Deutsche Rundschau*
NR = *Die Neue Rundschau*
DR = *Deutsche Rundschau*
LE = *Das lit(t)erarische Echo*
ML = *Das Magazin für Literatur*
SM = *Süddeutsche Monatshefte*

Andler, Charles. *Nietzsche*. Vol. IV. Paris, 1928.
Anonymous. "Notizen," *Die Gegenwart*, July 11, 1903: 31.

Bibliography

Antisthenes. "Menschenkinder," *Der Lotse*, May 24, 1902: 235-38.

Bab, Hans Jürgen. *Lou Andreas-Salomé. Dichtung und Persönlichkeit.* Inaugural-Dissertation zur Erlangung des Doktorgrades vorgelegt der Philosophischen Fakultät der Freien Universität zu Berlin. 1955. (Typescript.)

Bachman, H. "Andreas-Salomé, Lou: Rainer Maria Rilke," *Literarischer Handweiser*, August 1928: 858.

Bartels, Adolf. "Romane und Erzählungen," *Literarisches Centralblatt für Deutschland*, January 6, 1900: 81-84.

Bassermann, Dieter. *Der späte Rilke.* Essen, 1948.

Bäumer, Gertrud. "Lou Andreas-Salomé," *Die Frau*, March 1937: 305-11.

————. *Gestalt und Wandel.* Berlin, 1939.

Beer-Hofmann, Richard. *Novellen.* Berlin, 1893.

————. *Der Tod Georgs.* Berlin, 1900.

————. *Der Graf von Charolais.* Berlin, 1904.

————. *Paula.* New York, 1949.

————. Four letters printed in *Neue Zürcher Zeitung* (Sonntagsausgabe), October 2, 1955: 4.

————. *Gesammelte Werke.* Berlin, 1963.

Behl, Carl F. W., and Felix A. Voigt. *Chronik von Gerhart Hauptmanns Leben und Schaffen.* Munich, 1957.

Bernecker, Santa. *Frauen im Hintergrund.* Berlin, 1943.

Bernoulli, Carl Albrecht. *Franz Overbeck und Friedrich Nietzsche.* 2 vols. Jena, 1908.

————. "Nietzsches Lou-Erlebnis," *Raschers Jahrbuch I*, 1910.

Betz, Maurice. *Rilke vivant.* Paris, 1936.

Binder, Elsa. *Malwida von Meysenbug und Friedrich Nietzsche.* Berlin, 1917.

Bjerre, Poul. *Der geniale Wahnsinn.* Translator unnamed. Leipzig [1903?].

————. *The History and Practice of Psychoanalysis.* Translated by Elizabeth N. Barrow. Boston, 1916.

————. *The Remaking of Marriage.* Translated by T. H. Winslow. New York, 1931.

Blüher, Hans. *Werke und Tage.* Munich, 1953.

Blunck, Richard. *Friedrich Nietzsche, Kindheit und Jugend.* Munich, 1953.

Bölsche, Wilhelm. "Sechs Kapitel Psychologie nach Ibsen," *FB*, 1891: 1272-74.

————. "Das Geheimnis Friedrich Nietzsches," *NDR*, 1894: 1026-33.

Bonus, Arthur. "Glossen zu allerhand Büchern," *Die Christliche Welt*, March 6, 1924: 140-41.

Boutchik, Vladimir. "Helene and Rilke," *Oxford Slavonic Papers.* Vol. IX, 1960: 129-32.

————. E. L. Stahl and Stanley Mitchell. "R. M. Rilke's Letters to Helene," *Oxford Slavonic Papers.* Vol. IX, 1960: 146-64.

Brandes, Georg. *Friedrich Nietzsche.* Translated by A. G. Chater. London, 1914.

————. "Aristokratischer Radikalismus," *NDR*, 1890: 52-89.

————. *Menschen und Werke.* Frankfurt am Main, 1894.

Bibliography

Brausewetter, Ernst (editor). *Meisternovellen Deutscher Frauen*: "Charakterskizze," 3-14. Berlin, 1898.

Brockdorff, Cay von. *Zu Tönnies' Entwicklungsgeschichte*. Kiel, 1937.

Buber, Martin. *Ich und Du*. Berlin, 1936.

Bühler, Charlotte. *Kindheit und Jugend*. Leipzig, 1931.

Bülow, Frieda von. "Neue Bücher," *Vom Fels zum Meer*, Heft 7, 1902: 474-75.

Busse, Carl. "Literarische Monatsberichte," *Deutsche Monatsschrift für das gesamte Leben der Gegenwart*, October 1902–March 1903: 598-605.

Butler, E. M. *Rainer Maria Rilke*. Cambridge, 1941.

Carossa, Hans. *Führung und Geleit*. Leipzig, 1933.

Christaller, Helene. "Rodinka," *Die christliche Welt*, November 18, 1926: 1144-45.

Delp, Ellen. *Regina Ullmann*. Einsiedeln, 1960.

Deussen, Paul. *Erinnerungen an Friedrich Nietzsche*. Leipzig, 1901.

―――. *Mein Leben*. Leipzig, 1922.

Dohm, Hedwig. "Reaktion in der Frauenbewegung," *Die Zukunft*, November 18, 1899: 279-91.

Droshshin, Spiridon Dmitrijewitsch. "Der deutsche Dichter Rainer Maria Rilke. Erinnerungen," *Das Inselschiff*, summer 1929: 225-33.

Eloesser, Arthur. "Neue Bücher," *NDR*, 1901: 652-62.

―――. "Neue Bücher," *NDR*, 1903: 259-72.

Engel, Eduard. "Fenitschka. Eine Ausschweifung," *LE*, December 15, 1898: 390-91.

Essl, Karl. "Neue Bücher über Rainer Maria Rilke," *Witiko*. Vol. II, 1929: 266-67.

Festschrift. Friedrich Carl Andreas zur Vollendung des siebzigsten Lebensjahres am 14. April 1916, dargebracht von Freunden und Schülern. Leipzig, 1916.

Förster-Nietzsche, Elisabeth. Introduction to Henri Lichtenberger, *Die Philosophie Friedrich Nietzsches*. Dresden, 1899.

―――. *Das Leben Friedrich Nietzsches*, Band II, zweiter Halbband. Leipzig, 1904.

―――. "Nietzsche-Legenden," *Die Zukunft*, January 28, 1905: 170-79.

―――. Notes to: *Friedrich Nietzsches Gesammelte Briefe*. 5 vols. Berlin, 1900-1909.

―――. *Der einsame Nietzsche*. Leipzig, 1913.

―――. *Friedrich Nietzsche und die Frauen seiner Zeit*. Munich, 1935.

Freud, Sigmund. *Gesammelte Werke*. 17 vols. London, 1940-1952. (*The Standard Edition of the Complete Psychological Works*. London, 1953-1964.)

―――. *Letters*. Selected and edited by Ernst L. Freud. Translated by Tania and James Stern. New York [1960].

――― and Karl Abraham. *A Psycho-Analytic Dialogue*. The Letters of Sigmund Freud and Karl Abraham 1907-1926. Edited by Hilda C. Abraham and Ernst L. Freud. Translated by Bernard Marsh and Hilda C. Abraham. New York, 1965.

Gallwitz, S. D. "Die Freundin von Nietzsche und Rilke," *Die Frau*, October 1928: 12-16.

Bibliography

Gast, Peter. Introduction to Friedrich Nietzsche, *Menschliches, Allzumenschliches*. Leipzig, 1893.

————. *Briefe Peter Gasts an Friedrich Nietzsche*. Munich, 1924.

Gersdorff, Carl von. *Die Briefe des Freiherrn Carl von Gersdorff an Friedrich Nietzsche*. Weimar, 1937.

Halévy, Daniel. *La Vie de Frédéric Nietzsche*. Paris [1909].

Hamann, E. M. "Ruth," *Allgemeines Litteraturblatt*, July 1, 1901: 413.

Harden, Maximilian. "Notizbuch," *Die Zukunft*, August 13, 1904: 272-78.

Hartmann, Eduard von. *Kritische Wanderungen durch die Philosophie der Gegenwart*. Leipzig, 1890.

Heilborn, Ernst. "Frauen in ihrem Schaffen," *Die Frau*, April 1897: 389-91.

————. "Lou Andreas-Salomé," *Die Frau*, October 1898: 25-29.

Heine, Anselma. "Lou Andreas-Salomé," *LE*, October 15, 1911: 80-86.

————. "Drei Briefe an einen Knaben," *LE*, May 1, 1918: 940-41.

————. "Die Stunde ohne Gott und andere Kindergeschichten," *LE*, June 15, 1922: 1131.

A. H. [Hermann, Adele]. "Lou Andreas-Salomé, Erinnerung an eine Freundin," obituary from unidentified newspaper: clipping in Göttingen.

Hessel, Franz. "Lou Andreas-Salomé: Rainer Maria Rilke," *Die Literarische Welt*, August 3, 1928: 5.

Heuss, Theodor. "Lou Andreas-Salomé," *Der Kunstwart*, January 1908: 9-13.

Hofmiller, Josef. "Nietzsches Lehrjahre," *Die Zukunft*, December 28, 1895: 602-05.

————. "Nietzsche," *SM*, November 1931: 73-131.

————. *Friedrich Nietzsche*. Lübeck, 1933.

Houben, Heinrich H. (editor). *Bibliographisches Repertorium II*. Die Sonntagsbeilage der Vossischen Zeitung 1858-1903. Berlin, 1904.

Hug-Hellmuth, H. von. "Lou Andreas-Salomé. Im Zwischenland," *Imago*, 1914: 85-90.

Jancke, Oskar. "Literaturwissenschaft," *Die Tat*, August 1929: 386-91.

Jones, Ernest. *The Life and Work of Sigmund Freud*. 3 vols. New York, 1957.

Kahler, Erich. "Richard Beer-Hofmann (1866-1945)," *NR*, January 1946: 227-37.

Klingenberg, Helene. "Lou Andreas-Salomé," *Deutsche Monatsschrift für Russland*, March 15, 1912: 237-52.

Kögel, Fritz. "Friedrich Nietzsche und Frau Lou Andreas-Salomé," *ML*, February 23, 1895: 225-35.

Kolle, Kurt. "Notizen über Paul Rée," *Zeitschrift für Menschenkunde*, September 1927: 168-74.

Krug, Walther. "Zwölf Briefe Nietzsches an einen Jugendfreund," *SM*, August 1930, 788-98.

Landsberger, Fritz. "Menschen, Leben, Existenz. Eine Buchchronik," *NR*, 1928: 310-19.

Lentz, Wolfgang. "F. C. Andreas†," *Zeitschrift für Indologie und Iranistik*. Vol. VIII, 1931: 1-17.

Lepsius, Sabine. *Stefan George*. Berlin, 1935.

Lessing, Theodor. *Jüdischer Selbsthass*. Berlin, 1930.

Lichtenberger, Henri. *La Philosophie de Nietzsche*. Paris, 1898.

Mackey, Ilonka Schmidt, *Lou Salomé*. Inspiratrice et interprète de Nietzsche, Rilke, et Freud. Paris, 1956.

Mahrholz, Werner. *Deutsche Literatur der Gegenwart*. Berlin, 1930.

Martini, Fritz. *Deutsche Literaturgeschichte von den Anfängen bis zur Gegenwart*. Stuttgart, 1958.

Mauthner, Fritz. "Lou Andreas-Salomé: 'Ibsens Frauen-Gestalten,' " *ML*, February 20, 1892: 134-35.

Meyer-Benfey, Heinrich. "Lou Andreas-Salomé: Die Erotik," *Die neue Generation*, November 14, 1910: 465-66.

————. "Lou Andreas-Salomé," *Die Frau*, February 1931: 304-07.

Meysenbug, Malwida von. *Im Anfang war die Liebe*. Edited by Berta Schleicher. Munich, 1926.

Mörchen, Hermann. *Rilkes Sonette an Orpheus*. Stuttgart, 1958.

Mövius, Ruth. *Rainer Maria Rilkes Stundenbuch*. Leipzig, 1937.

Nadler, Josef. *Literaturgeschichte der deutschen Stämme und Landschaften*. Vol. IV: *Der deutsche Staat*. Regensburg, 1928.

Naumann, Gustav. *Zarathustra-Commentar*. Leipzig, 1899-1901.

Nietzsche, Friedrich. *Friedrich Nietzsches Gesammelte Briefe*. 5 vols. Berlin, 1900-1909.

————. *Friedrich Nietzsches Briefwechsel mit Franz Overbeck*. Edited by Dr. Richard Oehler and Carl Albrecht Bernoulli. Leipzig, 1916.

————. *Historisch-kritische Gesamtausgabe: Werke*. 5 vols. *Briefe*. 4 vols. Munich, 1933-1942.

————. *Werke*. 3 vols. Munich, 1954-1956.

Oehlke, Waldemar. *Die deutsche Literatur seit Goethes Tode*. Halle, 1921.

Pasternak, Boris. *Safe Conduct*. "Selected Writings." Translated by Beatrice Scott. New York, 1949.

Pauli, Hans. "Frauen-Literatur," *NDR*, 1896: 276-81.

————. "Ein literarischer Streifzug," *NR*, 1897: 414-22.

Peters, H. F. *My Sister, My Spouse*. A Biography of Lou Andreas-Salomé. New York, 1962.

Pfeiffer, Ernst. Notes to: Lou Andreas-Salomé, *Lebensrückblick*. Zurich, 1951.

————. Notes to: *Rainer Maria Rilke, Lou Andreas-Salomé. Briefwechsel*. Zurich, 1952.

————. Notes to: Lou Andreas-Salomé, *In der Schule bei Freud*. Zurich, 1958.

Platzhoff, Eduard. "Ma," *LE*, August 1901: 1573-74.

————. "Im Zwischenland," *LE*, August 15, 1903: 1583-84.

Podach, Erich F. *Gestalten um Nietzsche*. Weimar, 1932.

————. *Friedrich Nietzsche und Lou Salomé*. Zurich, 1937.

Rée, Paul. *Der Ursprung der moralischen Empfindungen*. Chemnitz, 1877.

————. *Die Entstehung des Gewissens*. Berlin, 1885.

————. *Die Illusion der Willensfreiheit*. Berlin, 1885.

————. *Philosophie*. Berlin, 1903.

R. [Regener, E. A.]. "Mosaikbilder VI. Lou Andreas-Salomé," *Revue franco-allemande. Deutsch-französische Rundschau*. December 1901: 768-70.

Bibliography

Rilke, Rainer Maria. *Gesammelte Werke*. 6 vols. Leipzig, 1927.

————. *Briefe*. 6 vols. Edited by Carl Sieber and Ruth Sieber-Rilke. Leipzig, 1929-1937.

————. *Briefe und Tagebücher aus der Frühzeit*. Edited by Carl Sieber and Ruth Sieber-Rilke. Leipzig, 1931.

————. *Tagebücher aus der Frühzeit*. Edited by Carl Sieber and Ruth Sieber-Rilke. Leipzig, 1942.

————. *Briefe*. 2 vols. Edited by Carl Sieber and Ruth Sieber-Rilke. Wiesbaden, 1950.

———— and Marie Thurn und Taxis. *Briefwechsel*. 2 vols. Zurich, 1951.

———— and Katharina Kippenberg. *Briefwechsel*. Wiesbaden, 1954.

————. *Briefwechsel mit Benvenuta*. Esslingen, 1954.

Romundt, Heinrich. "Noch einmal Friedrich Nietzsche und Frau Lou Andreas-Salomé," *ML*, April 27, 1895: 523-26.

————. *Eine Gesellschaft auf dem Lande*. Leipzig, 1897.

Rostosky, Fritz. "Andreas-Salomé, Lou: Rainer Maria Rilke," *Die schöne Literatur*, February 1929.

Sarasin, [Philipp]. "Andreas-Salomé, Lou: 'Mein Dank an Freud,' " *Internationale Zeitschrift für Psychoanalyse*, 1932: 548-49.

Schlechta, Karl. *Nietzsches Grosser Mittag*. Frankfurt am Main, 1954.

————. Appendix to Friedrich Nietzsche, *Werke*, Vol. III. Munich, 1956.

————. *Der Fall Nietzsche*. Munich, 1959.

Schnitzler, Arthur and Hugo von Hofmannsthal. *Briefwechsel*. Frankfurt am Main, 1964.

Schnitzler, Olga. *Spiegelbild der Freundschaft*. Salzburg, 1962.

Schoenberner, Franz. *Confessions of a European Intellectual*. New York, 1946.

Selle, Götz von. "F. C. Andreas," *Indogermanisches Jahrbuch*, 1931: 366-76.

Siemsen, Anna. "Georg Ledebour," *Georg Ledebour*. Assembled by Minna Ledebour. Zurich, 1954: 7-31.

Simmel, Georg. *Die Religion*. "Die Gesellschaft," edited by Martin Buber. Frankfurt am Main [1906].

Soergel, Albert. *Dichtung und Dichter der Zeit*. Leipzig, 1916.

Sonns, Stefan. *Das Gewissen in der Philosophie Nietzsches*. Winterthur, 1955.

Stahl, E. L. "Rilke's Letters to Helene," *Oxford Slavonic Papers*. Vol. IX, 1960: 133-37.

Stein, Heinrich von. *Idee und Welt*. Stuttgart, 1940.

Steiner, Rudolf. *Friedrich Nietzsche*. Dornach (Switzerland), 1926.

Stöcker, Helene. "Neue Frauentypen," *ML*, July 8, 1899: 630-33.

————. "Lou Andreas-Salomé," *Frauen-Rundschau*, Heft 1, 1904: 29-30.

————. "Lou Andreas-Salomé, der Dichterin und Denkerin zum 70. Geburtstag," *Die neue Generation*, January-March 1931: 50-53.

————. "Lou Andreas-Salomé (zum 70. Geburtstag)," *Die Literatur*, October 1930–September 1931: 393.

Thiel, Rudolf. "Zwei Bücher über Rainer Maria Rilke," *Der Gral*, November 1928: 138-39.

Tönnies, Ferdinand. *Der Nietzsche Kultus*. Leipzig, 1897.

————. "Paul Rée," *Das freie Wort*, IV (1904-1905), 666-73.

Bibliography

————. *Die Philosophie der Gegenwart in Selbstdarstellungen.* Edited by Raymund Schmidt. III: 1-36 (also numbered 199-234). Leipzig, 1922.

———— and Friedrich Paulsen. *Briefwechsel 1876-1908.* Kiel, 1961.

Ullmann, Regina. *Erinnerungen an Rilke.* Sankt Gallen [1945?].

————. Introduction to Ellen Delp, *Vergeltung durch Engel und andere Erzählungen.* Freiburg, 1952.

Wedekind, Frank. *Gesammelte Briefe.* Vol. II. Edited by Fritz Strich. Munich, 1924.

Weizsäcker, Viktor von. "Mein Dank an Freud. Von L. Andreas-Salomé," *Der Nervenarzt,* January 15, 1933.

————. *Natur und Geist.* Göttingen, 1954.

Wurmb, Agnes. "Lou Andreas-Salomé: Rodinka," *Die Frau,* March 1925: 164-66.

Zepler, Wally. "Die neue Frau in der neuen Frauendichtung," *Sozialistische Monatshefte,* January 1914: 53-65.

In addition, the Lenin State Library extracted all data on the Salomés from the *Petersburgskii Nekropol* for me at the request of the Soviet Institute of Columbia University. My chief sources of published material were Lou's own estate as enlarged by Ernst Pfeiffer; Göttingen University and the German libraries system; Basel University; the New York Public Library and Columbia University.

INDEX

This index is designed for the reader rather than the skimmer. That is, any of its entries may help the reader to refresh his memory or to investigate thematic connections, but some of the entries (those for certain places or things or fictional characters of special significance in Lou's life) serve no other purpose. Subheads have been kept at a minimum except for authors' works; but the several entries amount to subheads in relation to Lou herself, who accordingly appears as author only. Sources have not been indexed where they are merely cited without being mentioned in their own right. "Adler" covers "Adlerian," "Darwin" covers "Darwinism," and so forth. Inexplicit references are signaled by parentheses.

Abraham (patriarch), 393

Abraham, Karl, 335, 368, 447n

Adler, Alfred, ixn, 331, 335-39, 358, 361, 363n, 368, 378n, 382n, 383-84, 389, 400n, 418n, 423-24, 428, 433, 475, 506, 548

Albert, Henri, 162n, 182

Alex (character in "Mädchenreigen"), 200-201, 202n, 258n

Alexander II (czar), 18, 415

Altenberg, Peter (pen name of Richard Engländer), 197, 472

Andler, Charles, 128, 168-69

Andreas, Friedrich Carl, 22n, 133-35, 139n, 141-46, 165n, 175-77, 182n, 184, 185n, 194, 205n, 207, 209, 217-18, 221, 225, 246-50, 252, 265, 284n, 292, 293n, 300-301, 305, 307n, 309-12, 313n, 314-15, 317-20, 323n, 373n, 376, 411, 432, 438, 456-57, 464, 472-73, 489, 490, 499n, 502, 504

Andreas-Salomé, Lou: "Abteilung 'Innere Männer'" (1896c), 29n, (199), 203-04, 212, 218, 220, (415), 435n, 473n, 494, 497n, 500; "Agnes Henningsen," 441-42; "Als ich, aus einem Aufenthalt . . ." (1935a), 380n, 475-76; "Alter und Ewigkeit" (1901c), 301-03, 329n; "Am Krötenteich," 483-84, 498; "'Anal' und 'Sexual'" (1914a), 185n, 351-54, 356, 357n, 360-61, 365n, 379n, 384n, 395, 422n, 501-02, 544-48; "An die Winne," 12, (28), 471; "Angela Langer," 442; "April, unser Monat, Rainer . . ."

(1934e), 473n, 474n, 487; "Aus dem Briefwechsel Leo Tolstois" (1918a), (269), (440), (504); "Aus der Geschichte Gottes," 221-22, 356; Aus fremder Seele, 192-93, 199, 213, 429, 435, 470, 500; "Aus meinem Königsberger Aufenthalt . . .," (484); "Eine Ausschweifung" (1897j), 213n, 220, 229n, 430n; "Das Bündnis zwischen Tor und Ur," 415-16, 419n, 424-25, 436, 439, 498, 505; "Ein Dank an einen Dichter," (286), (290), 291-92, 305n; "Dichterischer Ausdruck," (441), 537-42; "Des Dichters Erleben," 388, 413, 441, 499n, 553-54; "Diekmanns Denkwürdigkeiten," 442n; "Die Diktatur der Liebe," 442n; Drei Briefe an einen Knaben, (350), 412, 413n, 439, 454n; "Durch Dich," 184; "Die Duse," (179); "Der Egoismus in der Religion," 232-33; "Ehe," see Das Haus; "Elisabeth Siewert," (335), (441); "Emil Marriot," (146); "Erleben" (1899d), 246, 389n, 465n; "Eros," 375n, 399; Die Erotik (1909b), 259n, 327, 329, 330n, 362n, 395, 396, 397n, 398, 413, 463; "Eine erste Erfahrung," 307, (308), 413; "Essais. Von Ellen Key," (249); "'Expression,'" 389; "Fenitschka," (210), 212-13, 220; Friedrich Nietzsche in seinen Werken (1890a), 55n, 90n, 148-64, (166), (176), (177n), (182), (229), (363n), (385), (426), (428), (431), (435),

(440), (462), (463), (469), (473), (478-79), (499*n*), (505); "Ein Frühlingsdrama," (179); "Frühlings Erwachen," (323); "Gedanken über das Liebesproblem," 252-60, 263, 397, 398, 399*n*, 418*n*, 502; "Der geistliche Russe" (1919e), 189*n*, 441*n*; "Die Geschichten von der Gänseblume und von den Wolken," (327), (439); "Geschlecht," 438, 439; "Geschwister" (1919g), 226*n*, 264*n*, 364*n*, 416-38, 439, 453*n*, 468*n*, 471*n*, 472, 483, 499, 500, 501, 503*n*, 504, 506, 507; "Das Glashüttenmärchen," (321); *Der Gott*, (327), 329-31, 395, 413, 439, 463; "Gottesschöpfung," 158*n*, 160-62, 192*n*, 470, 494, 503-04; "Der Graf von Charolais" (1905a), 262*n*, (318); "Grundformen der Kunst," 223-25; *Grundriss einiger Lebenserinnerungen*, 464-72, 483*n*, 485*n*, 503*n*; "Hanna Jagert," (179); "Hannele," (180-81); "Harnack und das Apostolikum," (178); "Hartlebens 'Erziehung zur Ehe,'" (179); *Das Haus* (also "Ehe": 1904a), 203*n*, 226-27*n*, 305*n*, 313-16, 319, 325*n*, 328, 380*n*, 414, 439, 450, 474, 498, 499; *Henrik Ibsens Frauen-Gestalten* (1889a), 144-46, 150*n*, (259), (308), (440); "Ein holländisches Urteil über moderne deutsche Dramen," (146); "Ibsen, Strindberg, Sudermann," (179); *Im Kampf um Gott*, 118-29, 147*n*, 159, 160*n*, 161*n*, 168*n*, 170, (181), 193, 220*n*, 428, 429, 430, 469, 488*n*, 497, 498, 499, 502, 504; "Im Spiegel" (1911a), 439*n*; "Im Traumland," 442*n*; "Im Zwischenland" (1900d), 226*n*, 287-90, 293*n*, 308, 415, 421, 426-33, 436, 468*n*, 494, 499, 500, 501, 503; *Im Zwischenland*, 308-09; "Inkognito," 199-203, 218, 219*n*, 239*n*, 434-35, 436*n*, 493-94, (497), 498; "Innerhalb der sogenannten Normalität . . . ," (485-86); "Insekt und Krieg," (409-10); "In 1933 . . . ," (484); "Jesus der Jude," (183), (184), 185-89, (193), (214), (223), 232*n*, (479), 501, 502; "Jutta" (1898f), 199-203, 209, 226*n*, 229*n*, 416*n*, 422n, 439, 483, (494), (497), (498), 503*n*; "Kampf-

ruf," (210); "Karl Nötzels Tolstoi," (440); "Ketzereien gegen die moderne Frau," (233-34), (243); "Kind und Kunst," 413; "Das Kindlein von Erika Rhenisch," (329); "Die Klerisei," 441*n*; "Knechtgestalt," 183; "Kranke Liebe," 442*n*; "Lebende Dichtung," (323); "Lebensgebet," (37-38), (55-56), (85), (86*n*), (101), (120), (138), (139*n*), (156), (169*n*), (385), (394), (476), (544); "Leo Tolstoi, unser Zeitgenosse," (230-31); "Die Liebende," 438, 439, 456; "Luzifer," (442); *Ma* (1899f), 28*n*, 227*n*, 230*n*, 250-52, 260*n*, 263, 301, 316, 496, 498; "Mädchenreigen," 199-203, 212, 493, 494, (497), (498), 501; "Mal las ich doch . . . ," (484); *Mein Dank an Freud* (1929a), 342*n*, 353*n*, 364*n*, 369*n*, 382*n*, 384*n*, 387*n*, 391*n*, 463-64, 488; "Der Mensch als Weib" (1899a), 230*n*, 234-43, 246, 247, 251, 258, (397), 501-02; *Menschenkinder*, 199*n*, 230; "Des Menschen tiefste Wünsche . . . ," (484); "Missbrauchte Frauenkraft," (225); "Eine Nacht," 212, 264, 315, 497; "Nachträge" (1936b), 308*n*, 361*n*, 383*n*, 391*n*, (486-87); "Nadja Strassers 'Russin,'" 441*n*; "Narzissmus als Doppelrichtung" (1920b), 364-65, 375, 380-81, 384*n*, 387, 390-91, 432*n*, 454*n*, 550-53, 554; "Ossip Schubin," (146); "Das Paradies," 181-82*n*, 184, 209*n*, 315*n*, 435*n*, 499; "Physische Liebe," (231), (234), (239), (245-46), (259); "Das Problem des Islams" (1894a), 179*n*; "Psychosexualität," *see Ubw.*; *Rainer Maria Rilke*, 461-63, 466; "Der Realismus in der Religion," 146-47, 178*n*, 221*n*; "Religion und Cultur," 222; "Ricarda Huch: Erinnerungen von Ludolf Ursleu dem Jüngeren," (184); *Ródinka* (also "Witalii": 1901a), 227*n*, (289), 290, (293), 294*n*, 295-98, 307*n*, 312-13, 331, 413*n*, 414-15, 439, 440, 441, 454*n*, 474, 497*n*, 498, 499, (502), 503*n*; "Rote Rosen" (1895e), 189*n*; "Die Russen," (322); "Russische Dichtung und Kultur," (215-16), 229; "Das russische Heiligenbild und sein Dichter,"

Index

(215); "Der russische Intelligent," (440); "Russische Philosophie und semitischer Geist," (215); *Ruth* (1893g), 15*n*, 17*n*, 180-82, 198*n*, 214, 218*n*, 220*n*, 328, 469, 470, 497*n*, 498, 499, 502, 503*n*, 504, 505; "Satiren von Michael Saltykow Schtschedrin," 441*n*; "Scandinavische Dichter," (199); "Die Schwester" (1900b), 29*n*, 205*n*, 226-27*n*, 263-64, 308; "Seelchen," 416, 439; "Sinne ich an Frühestes . . ." (1936a), 245*n*, (486); "Die Stadt der Toten," 183; *Der Stiefvater*, 324, 439-40; *"Strindberg"* (1919b), 388*n*; "Die Stunde ohne Gott" (1919d), 11*n*, 160*n*, 364*n*, 416, 439, 494-95; "Tagebuch eines halbwüchsigen Mädchens," 442*n*; "Der Talisman," (179); *Die Tarnkappe* (1908a), 264*n*, 324, 418*n*, 439-40, 483; "Tendenz und Form russischer Dichtung," (441); *Der Teufel und seine Grossmutter*, 413, (415*n*), 438*n*, 439, 479; "Ein Todesfall," 219, 225, 264, 284-86, 291, 416, 497, 499; "Tolstois Jugendtagebuch," (440-41); *Ubw.* (including "Psychosexualität": 1914b), 351*n*, 360-63, 365, 384*n*, 390, 395, 421-22*n*, 548-50; "Unser menschliches Bewusstwerden . . . ," (486); "Unterwegs," (199), 204, 211*n*, 217, (218), 473*n*; "Vaters Kind," 307-08, 473*n*, 501*n*; "Verjährt," 183; "Ein Versuch," (476), (484-85); "Vier Kammerspiele," 323; "Vom Bazillus zum Affenmenschen," (264); "Vom Kunstaffekt" (1899b), 230*n*, 243-46; "Vom religiösen Affekt," 222, 223; "Vom Ursprung des Christentums" (1895g), 193*n*; "Von der Bestie bis zum Gott," 178, 179*n*; "Von frühem Gottesdienst," 390, 439*n*; "Von Paul zu Pedro," 442*n*; "Vor dem Erwachen," 184-85, 209*n*, 473, 499n; "Waldemar Bonsels," (442); "Was am 'Grundriss' fehlt," 465*n*, 472, 473*n*; "Was daraus folgt, dass es nicht die Frau gewesen ist, die den Vater totgeschlagen hat," (354), 397-98, (461); "Der werdende Mensch," 442*n*; "Ein Wiedersehen," 218, 219*n*, 287*n*, 289*n*, 296, 433, 436*n*, 469; "Die Wildente," (144); "Winterlaub," (184); "Witalii," *see Ródinka*; "Wolga" (1900c), 227*n*, 286-87, 288, 290, 296, 308, 309, 502; "Zum Bilde Strindbergs," (388); "Zum sechsten Mai 1926," (461); "Zum Typus Weib," (350-51), 397, 555-56; "Zurück ans All" (1898a), 28*n*, 220-21, 229*n*, 314*n*, 442*n*

Anjuta (character in "Inkognito"), 200, 201-02, 239*n*, 258*n*, 434-35, 493-94, 498

Apel, Maria (Mariechen), 319, 478*n*, 489-90

Apollon (character in "Im Zwischenland"), (287-88), 415, 426-27, 428, 430, 436*n*, 494

Aristotle, 40

Avenarius, Richard, 35

Babuschka (character in *Ródinka*), 289, 297, 298, 312, 313*n*

Babushka (Nikolai Tolstoi's mother), 276-79

Bach, Johann Sebastian, 284

Bagehot, Walter, 44, 136

Bahr, Hermann, 322

Bain, Alexander, *The Emotions and the Will*, 45*n*

Bang, Hermann, 182, 472

Barrès, Maurice, 182

Bäumer, Gertrud, 488-89; *Ich kreise um Gott*, 488

Baur, Ferdinand Christian, 14, 37

Bayreuth (place), 56, 59, 60, 61, 62, 63, 64, 65, 66, 67, 68, 72-76, 85, 93, 98, 99, 127*n*, 169*n*, 170*n*, 467, 477

Beer-Hofmann, Gabriel, 444

Beer-Hofmann, Mirjam, (260), 444

Beer-Hofmann, Naëmah, 444

Beer-Hofmann, Paula, 196-97, 202, 203*n*, 434, 444, 445, 448*n*

Beer-Hofmann, Richard, 23*n*, 144*n*, 190-92, 193*n*, 194-204, 207, 208-09, 212, 218, 220, 221, 239*n*, 258, 260-63, 290, 292, 293, 299*n*, 303, 315, 318, 319, 331, 380*n*, 415, 434-36, 444-45, 448*n*, 461, 462, 472, 493-94, 497, 501, 505, 508-09; "Camelias," 190-91, (197); *Der Graf von Charolais*, 262, 318, 324, 444; *Jaákobs Traum*, 262, 444; "Das Kind," 191, (197), 261, 262, 264; *Novellen*, 191*n*; "Schlaflied für Mirjam," 260; *Der Tod Georgs*, (191),

Index

260-62, 290*n*, 303*n*, 315*n*, 406*n*
Benfey, Meta, 317
Bergson, Henri, 465*n*
Bernhardt, Sarah, 49
Bernoulli, Carl Albrecht, 168, 169*n*
Berthold (character in "Eine Nacht"), 212, 315, 436*n*
Biedermann, Alois, 35-36, 38*n*, 61, 81, 115, 160*n*, 188, 467*n*, 496
Bismarck, Otto von, 491
Bjerre, Poul, 208*n*, 294*n*, 329, 331, 349, 366*n*, 388*n*, 400-401, 402, 422, (428), (432), 451, 494, 496
Blüher, Hans, 448
Boetticher, Hermann von, *Erlebnisse aus Freiheit und Gefangenschaft*, 553-54
Böhme, Jakob, 37
Bölsche, Wilhelm, 143, 144*n*, 162*n*, 175, 183*n*, 231, 233, 234*n*, 264, 362
Bonsels, Waldemar, 442
Boris (character in "Im Zwischenland"), 287-88, 289*n*, 426-31, 463
Bourget, Paul, 155*n*, 184
Brahm, Otto, 143, 321
Brandes, Georg, 115, 134, 136*n*, 145*n*, 148*n*, 162*n*
Brandt family, 35, 38, 39, 51, 53, 56
Brausewetter, Ernst, 210*n*, 505*n*
Brenner, Albert, 43*n*, 47*n*
Breuer, Josef, 242*n*
Breysig, Maria, 329*n*
Buber, Martin, 237, 327, 328, 329, 446; *Ich und Du*, 328*n*, 465*n*
Bülow, Frieda von, 167-68, 177, 178*n*, 182, 184, 189-90, 192, 195-96, 197, 212, 213, 215, 216, 217, 219, 233-34, 243, 247, 248, 249-50, 290, 293, 308*n*, 309, 311, 315, 316*n*, 318, 319, 320, 321, 323, 325, 326
Bülow, Sophie von, 182, 293
Burckhardt, Jakob, 62

"Caro," 11-12, 13, 15, 16-17, 18, 31, 72, 125, 145, 189, 226*n*, 227-28, 230, 248-49, 318, 336, 361, 433
Carossa, Hans, 443
Celerina (place), 112*n*, 117, 126, 131, 132*n*, 140, 429*n*, 469
Chekhov, Anton, 216*n*
Christ, *see* Jesus
Claus, Carl, 234*n*
Columbus, Christopher, 51, 94, 95, 131*n*, 152, 154*n*
Comte, Auguste, 40

Confucius, 37

Dalton, Hermann, 12, 16, 470
d'Annunzio, Gabriele, 192, 197, 260*n*, 292*n*, 406*n*
Darwin, Charles, 40, 42, 44, 136, 379*n*
Dehmel, Richard, 143, 321, 408*n*
Delp, Ellen, 328, 335, 337, 401, 443-44, 446, 447, 448, 451, 452
Deronda, Daniel (George Eliot's character), 95*n*
Deussen, Paul, 113, 128, 131, 136
Deutsches Theater, 322. *See also* Freie Bühne
Dickens, Charles, 193
Diderot, Denis, 393*n*
Diederichs, Eugen, 322, 472
Dimitrii (character in *Ródinka*), 289, 294*n*, 295-96, 297-98, 312-13, 414*n*, 504
Diotima (of Mantinea), 464
Dohm, Hedwig, 237-39
Dostoevsky, Feodor, 154*n*, 293, 354*n*
Drojjin, Spiridon, 248*n*, 264, 275-78, 287*n*, 288, 289, 297, 415, 425-26, 429, 430, 431, 432*n*
Drujok (dog), 409, 411, 444, 445, 452, 454*n*
Duse, Eleonora, 179, 323

Ebbinghaus, Hermann, 115, 128
Ebner-Eschenbach, Marie von, 192, 197, 233, 449
Eitingon, Max, 368, 373*n*, 376, 446, 449
"Elena," 226, 247, 248
Emma, *see* Flörke
Empedocles, 385-86*n*, 393*n*, 448
Endell, August, 213, 214, 216, 217, 218, 249, 264, 321, 323, 449
Engländer, Richard, *see* Altenberg
Erdmann, Ilse, 444*n*
Erik (character in *Ruth*), 17*n*, 28*n*, 180-82, 209, 433
Erwin (character in "Geschwister"), 422, 423, 425, 435-36, 472*n*
Erwin von Stein (character in "Inkognito"), 200, 201-02, 258, 434, (436), 493-94
Eysoldt, Gertrud, 320, 324*n*, 446

Federn, Paul, 383*n*, 450
Ferenczi, Sandor, 337, 360*n*, 368, 371*n*, 373*n*, 382*n*, 384*n*, 385*n*, 447

Feuerbach, Ludwig, 37, 42, 328, 331, 342*n*
Fiedler, Friedrich, 248*n*
Fischer, Samuel, 321, 322
Flaubert, Gustave, 143, 155*n*; *Madame Bovary*, 125*n*
Fliess, Wilhelm, 337*n*
Flörke, Emma (née Wilm), 9, 11, 15, 25, 127, 133, 227*n*, 251, 307*n*, 312, 322, 487, 489
Förster, Bernhard, 65, 109, 110-11*n*, 164
Förster-Nietzsche, Elisabeth, (32), (46), (47), 48, 49, 51-52, 54*n*, 57, 60, 61, 62, 63, 66, 67, 68, 71, 72, 74-79, 82, 84-85, 86-87, 88, 89-90, 94*n*, 95, 97*n*, 98-99, 100*n*, 103, 104-05, 106, 107-08, 109-11, 115*n*, 117*n*, 118, 127*n*, 162, 163*n*, 164, 165, 167, 168, 169, 170*n*, 318, 322, 352*n*, 427, 467, 468, 479*n*, 480, 496*n*, 543
Die Frau (review), 213*n*
Freie Bühne, 143, 213. *See also* Deutsches Theater
Die freie Bühne (review), 143, 144, 146, 162*n*, 177, 179
Freud, Anna, 308*n*, 371, 372-73, 374*n*, 376, 381, 440, 445, 475, 490
Freud, Sigmund, ix, x, 22*n*, 23*n*, 38*n*, 198, 217*n*, 218, 236*n*, 241-42, 260, 286*n*, 299, 327*n*, 329, 331, 335-39, 340, 346-403, 404*n*, 408-09, 410, 411*n*, 412, 415, 416, 417-25, 427-29, 431-33, 436, 437-38, 440, 443, 444, 445, 446, 447, 449, 451, 456-57, 461, 463-64, 466, 471, 472, 475-76, 477, 479, 481, 485, 486, 487, 490, 495-97, 498*n*, 499*n*, 500, 501, 503, 505, 506-07, 508, 509, 545, 548, 549, 550, 552, 553; *Beyond the Pleasure Principle*, 383-85; *Discomfort in Civilization*, 392; *The Ego and the Id*, 365*n*; *The Future of an Illusion*, (391); "Instincts and their Vicissitudes," 351*n*, (352-53), 360*n*; *An Introduction to Psychoanalysis*, (353); *Moses and Monotheism*, (393*n*); "Narcissism: An Introduction," (356-59); *An Outline of Psychoanalysis*, 359*n*, 384*n*; *Three Essays on Sexual Theory*, 353; *Totem and Taboo*, 393*n*
Frost, Lucia Dora, 328
Fulda, Ludwig, 179

Gammelskagen (place), 305, 316
Garborg, Arne, 128, 143, 146*n*
Garborg, Hulda, 128, 143, 146*n*
Garshin, Vsevolod, 216, 299, 471
Gast, Peter, 49, 56*n*, 68, 69, 75, 80, 81, 85, 89, 90, 92, 95, 97*n*, 98*n*, 103, 104, 111, 118*n*, 130*n*, 138-39*n*, 163-64, 166, 467*n*
Gebsattel, Victor Emil von, 404-07, 409, 413, 419-20, 422, 428, 432, 436, 437, 443*n*, 447, 448, 449, 450, 451, 452, 494
Gelzer, Clara, 76, 78, 89, 162*n*
Gelzer, Heinrich, 76, 78, 104*n*
George, Stefan, 218-19, 224
Gersdorff, Carl von, 43, 48, 131, 139, 164
Gildemeister, J., 133
Gillot, Hendrik, 13-21, 25, 28, 38, 39, 49-51, 71, 81, 83, 84*n*, 122-23, 124-25, 126*n*, 127, 141, 142, 144*n*, 146, 171, 180-81, 182*n*, 185*n*, 188, 189, 192, 204*n*, 211, 218, 220, 272-73, 281, 287, 289, 294*n*, 296, 303, 304*n*, 310, 340*n*, 345, 351-52, 365, 429, 433, 435, 461, 469-71, 476, 477*n*, 479*n*, 489, 494, 496, 497*n*, 498, 499, 502, 504, 505
Glücklich, Simon, 199, 212, 213, 561
Goethe, Johann Wolfgang von, 37, 38, 56, 129-30, 310, 484; *Faust*, 401, 449, (490)
Goldmann, Paul, 182, 183, 190, 192*n*, 194, 200, 204*n*, 209, 322*n*, 494, 497*n*
Gorky, Maxim, 275, 321; *The Lower Depths*, 320
Gottlieb (character in "Geschwister"), 416-25, 429, 430, 431, 437*n*, 438, 453*n*
Goudstikker, Sophia, *see* "Puck"
Grabbe, Christian, *Hannibal*, 381
Griensteidl (café), 190, 196, 197, 198, 202, 434
Grimm, Jacob and Wilhelm, "Der Teufel und seine Grossmutter," 413*n*
Groddeck, Georg, 382
Grunewald (forest), and Nietzsche, 54*n*, 61, 63, 65, 68, (126*n*), 434*n*; otherwise, 291
Günzburg, Elias, 268

Haeckel, Ernst, 154*n*, 234*n*
Halbe, Max, 143, 197*n*, 198*n*; *Jugend*, 179

Halévy, Daniel, 168, 169*n*, 327*n*
Haller, Ludwig, 131
Hamsun, Knut, 182, 199
Hans (character in "Mädchenreigen"), 199-200, 201-02, 258, 494, 501
Hansson, Ola, 143
Harden, Maximilian, 167-68, 318-19, 321, 322, 446, 472
Harnack, Adolf von, 178*n*
Hart, Heinrich, 143
Hart, Julius, 143
Hartleben, Otto Erich, 177, 182, 184; *Die Erziehung zur Ehe*, 179; *Hanna Jagert*, 179
Hauptmann, Benvenuto, (282), (283*n*), (313)
Hauptmann, Carl, 144*n*, 282*n*, 284*n*
Hauptmann, Gerhart, 144, 180, 184, 192, 213, 282-86, 291-92, 298, 300, 305, 307, 313, 319*n*, 320-21, 322*n*, 323, 362-63, 416, 446, 461, 472, 477*n*, 489, 497*n*; *Einsame 'Menschen*, 144*n*; *Friedensfest*, 291, 323; *Greek Springtime*, 446; *Hannele*, 179-80, 189, 192, 196, 282, 292*n*; *Das Hirtenlied*, 291, 300, 312; *Michael Kramer*, 282, 284-86, 290, 291-92, 300, 321*n*, 362, 363*n*, 416; *Und Pippa tanzt*, 320-21, 322; *Vor Sonnenaufgang*, 143
Hauptmann, Margarete (née Marschalk), 282, 283-84, 291, 298, 300, 305*n*, 319*n*, 323, 497*n*
Hauptmann, Marie, 144, 184, (282), (283), 323
Hegel, Georg Wilhelm Friedrich, 14, 35, 37, 135*n*, 154*n*, 342*n*, 350*n*
Heilborn, Ernst, 213*n*, 221*n*
Heims, Else, 323, 446
Heine, Heinrich, 188*n*
Heinemann, Max, 131
Heinze, Max, and wife, 76, 93
Heiseler, Emmy von, 321, 323, 446, 447, 449
Heiseler, Henry von, 321, 322, 323, 446
Henningsen, Agnes, 441-42
Herder, Johann Gottfried von, 14, 310
Hermann, Adele, (489), (490)
Herwegh, Georg, 183
Hitler, Adolf, 176, 491
Hitz, Dora, 322
Hofmannsthal, Hugo von (Loris), 190, 191-92, 194, 195, 196, 247, 250, 292*n*
Hofmiller, Josef, 162, 165-66

Holz, Arno, 143
Huch, Ricarda, 184, 250, 443; *Ludolf Ursleu*, 184
Hugo, Victor, 37
Hume, David, 40
Hüter, Ludwig, 66-67, 112-13, 140
Huysmans, Joris Karl, 182

Ibsen, Henrik, 143, 144*n*, 145*n*, 146, 193, 323, 377; *A Doll's House*, 145, 150*n*; *Ghosts*, 143, 193; *Hedda Gabler*, 145; *The Master Builder*, 179; *Rosmersholm*, 145; *The Wild Duck*, 144-45, 193; *The Woman of the Sea*, 145, (146), (315)
Iḥtišam-ed-daule (sultan), 134
Ikhnaton, 392, 394
Imago (review), 363, 365, 390, 397, 454*n*
Innsbruck, 117-18, 194, 195, 200, 434, 493, 497*n*
Ischl (place), 194, 199, 203, 204

Jahweh, 11*n*, 392
Jakobsen, Peter, 399*n*
Jane (character in *Im Kampf um Gott*), 120-22, 124, 125, 128, 160*n*, 161*n*, 225, 428, 503
Jeanne d'Arc, 211
Jena, and Lou, 75, 76-77, 84, 89, 90, 92, 93, 95, 97, 99, 104*n*, 107, 168*n*, 169*n*, 170*n*, 258, 427, 467, 469, 503*n*, 543; otherwise, 46
Jesus Christ, 10*n*, (11), 13*n*, 14, 21*n*, 31*n*, 37, 54, 72*n*, 119*n*, 121, 137, 144, 153, 183, 184, 185-89, 193, 219, 221-22, 262, 323, 420-21, 427, 431, 554
Joseph (Jesus' father), 10*n*, 209*n*, 243*n*
Jukovsky, Paul von, 73
Jung, Carl J., 338-39, 361, 363*n*, 378, 451, 548
Jutta (character in "Geschwister"), 416-25, 428-34, 436, 437, 503, 504; (character in "Jutta"), 201-02, 221*n*, 416*n*, 494

Kahler, Erich, 261
Kant, Immanuel, 15, 35*n*, 37, 43, 246, 484
Kayssler, Friedrich, 445
Keim, Theodor, 37
Kerr, Alfred, 320, 321, 322, 323
Key, Ellen, 168, 169*n*, 225, 228, 229, 230, 232, 233, 238, 239, 240, 248, 249-50, 265, 305, 317, 319-20, 324,

Index

325-26, 327, 329, 388*n*, 400, 408, 449
Keyserling, Eduard, 472
Keyserling, Hermann, 321, 322
Kierkegaard, Søren, 344, 503*n*
Kinkel, Gottfried, 37, 38
Kirchbach, Wolfgang, *Das Buch Jesu*, 222*n*
Kirschner, Lola, (146)
Klages, Ludwig, 484
Kleist, Heinrich von, 447*n*, 477, 478, 484
Klimt, Gustav, 325
Klingenberg, Helene (née von Klot-Heydenfeldt), and family, 212, 213, 216, 264, 282, 309, 311, 318, 320, 321, 323, 327-28, 329, 331, 412, 439*n*, 440, 448-49, 454*n*, 478, 489
Kögel, Fritz, 164-66, 168, 169*n*
Kollwitz, Käthe, 322
König, Josef, 490
Kresta (place), 274, 297
Krug, Gustav, (85*n*)
Krügel, Hanna, 132*n*
Krüger, Therese, 177, 182, 184, 219
Kuno (character in *Im Kampf um Gott*), 119-25, 128, 147*n*, 160*n*, 161*n*, 211, 218*n*, 326, 386, 433, 497*n*, 499, 502-03, 505
Kym, Andreas Ludwig, 35

La Bruyère, Jean de, 82
Landauer, Gustav, 322, 442*n*
Langen, Albert, 182
Langer, Angela, 442
La Rochefoucauld, François de, 41
Laurent, Walt, 389, 452
Lazard, Loulou, 443, 452
Ledebour, Georg, 22*n*, 175-76, 180*n*, 181, 182*n*, 184-85, 209*n*, 268, 435, 441, 473, 496, 499
Leipzig, and Nietzsche or Lou, 48, 64-66, 72, 76, 86-95, 96, 98, 103*n*, 119-20, 122, 124, 154, 158, 160, 168*n*, 169*n*, 170*n*, 404*n*, 427, 428, 434, 443*n*, 468; otherwise, 328, 439, 447-48
Leistikow, Walter, 144, 321, 322
Lenin, Nikolai, 410
Lepsius, Sabine, (219)
Leskov, Nicolai, 215*n*, 230-31, 441*n*
Lessing, Gotthold Ephraim, 90, 93; *Nathan the Wise*, 90
Lessing, Theodor, *Jüdischer Selbsthass*, 307
Lisbeth, *see* Förster-Nietzsche

Liszt, Franz, 74*n*
Loris, *see* Hofmannsthal
"Lotte," 324
Löwengarten (in Lucerne), 55, 168*n*, 326, 502, 504*n*
Lucerne, 54-56, 57, 74, 99, 101, 114, 158, 168, 169*n*, 183*n*, 433, 467
Luther, Martin, 13, 442, 470

Mackay, John Henry, 144
Maeterlinck, Maurice, 144*n*, 249*n*, 292*n*; *Aglavaine et Sélysette*, 323
Das Magazin für Literatur, 164
Mallarmé, Stéphane, 330*n*
Märchen (character in *Im Kampf um Gott*), 122-25, 144*n*, 161*n*, 181, 221, 263, 287, 345, 428, 494, 499, 502, 503, 504*n*, 505
Marcinowski, Johannes, and wife, 368-69
Margharita (character in *Im Kampf um Gott*), 119-20, 121, 124, 125, 209, 218*n*, 220*n*, 326, 428, 433, 468, 502-03, 505
Margot (character in *Ródinka*), 289, 293, 294*n*, 295-98, 307*n*, 312, 414, 415, 504
Marholm, Laura, 144, 225, 237, 239
Marie, 306, 311, 312, 317, 318, 319, 451, 489
Mariechen, *see* Apel
Marriot, Emil, *see* Mataja
Martersteig, Max, (439-40)
Mary (Jesus's mother), 10*n*, 11, 209, 215, 243, 474
Mataja, Emilie, (146), 192, 197*n*
Maupassant, Guy de, 184, 203
Mauthner, Fritz, 167*n*, 177, 182, 184, 192, 219, 445
Mendelssohn, Moses, 37
Meran (place), 118, 124, 126, 132*n*
Meyer, Amelie, 317
Meyer, Conrad Ferdinand, 250
Meysenbug, Malwida von, 38-40, 42, 43, 45*n*, 47, 49-52, 53, 54, 56, 62, 63, 64, 66, 67, 68, 69, 72, 73, 75, 78*n*, 85, 94, 98, 103-04, 105-06, 108, 110*n*, 112, 113, 116*n*, 135, 140, 141*n*, 167, 168*n*, 169*n*, 467, 496, 505
Mill, John Stuart, 41*n*
Misani (hotel in Celerina), 112*n*, 117, 126*n*, 131, 140
Mohl, Emma von, 251
Moissi, Alexander, 321, 446
Monod-Herzen, Olga, 39*n*

monte sacro, 54, 79, 80, 114, 433
Moses, 392-95
Musja (character in "Im Zwischenland"), 287-88, 289*n*, 293*n*, 415,
426-27, 428, 430, 433, 494

Nansen, Peter, 199
Naumburg (place), 46, 48, 56, 57,
60, 61, 64, 65, 68*n*, 74*n*, 75, 86,
89, 90, 92, 98, 100, 109, 111, 132,
164, 322*n*, 434
Nemethy, Countess, 182
Niemann, Johanna, 184, 226, 249,
309, 310
Nietzsche, Elisabeth, *see* Förster-
Nietzsche
Nietzsche, Franziska (Friedrich's
mother), 46, 48, 54*n*, 57, 60, 61,
(63), 66, 85, 86, 87*n*, 89, 99, 100,
103, 104, 109, 127, 136, 164, 166
Nietzsche, Friedrich, ix, x, 37*n*, 40*n*,
43-132, 135-39, 141*n*, 142, 145, 146-
71, 181, 183, 185*n*, 188, 189*n*, 193,
198, 200*n*, (201), 203n, 205, 207,
211*n*, 216-17, 229, 232, 235*n*, 239-
40, 242, 244-45, 246, 252, 258, 260,
265, 271*n*, 275, 280-81, 282, 289,
292*n*, 303, 307, 313, 322, 325, 326,
327*n*, 337*n*, 345, 346, 352*n*, 353-
54, 363*n*, 366*n*, 374n, 377, 379*n*,
380*n*, 382*n*, 385-86, 394, 395, 400,
404, 406*n*, 416, 425-37, 448, 456*n*,
462, 465, 466-70, 472, 473-74, 476,
477, 478, 479-80, 488, 490, 491,
493, 494-95, 496, 497, 499, 500,
501, 502-03, 504, 505, 506, 507,
508-09, 543-44, 553, 556; *The Antichrist*, 152*n*; *Beyond Good and
Evil*, 129-30, 136*n*, 137, 148*n*, 151*n*,
152, 363*n*; *The Birth of Tragedy*,
44*n*, 346; *Ecce Homo*, 102*n*, 136,
138, 139*n*, 152*n*, 240, 479; *Flush
of Dawn*, 62, 84, 151*n*, 157*n*; *The
Gay Science*, 48, 60, 63, (64), (65),
70, 71, 84-85*n*, 87, 89, 130*n*, 137*n*,
151*n*, 158; *The Genealogy of Morals*, 44*n*, 135-39, 152, 171*n*, (188*n*)
215*n*, 246*n*, 282*n*, 341*n*, (354),
(394), (416), 501, (502), 507;
Human, All Too Human, 43-44, 46,
47, 57, 70, 72, 89, 94, 102, 136,
151*n*, 163; "Idyllen aus Messina,"
130*n*; "Lieder des Prinzen Vogelfrei," 130*n*; "Nach neuen Meeren,"
94*n*, 130-31*n*; "Der neue Kolumbus," (94), (120), (130*n*), (503);

"Richard Wagner in Bayreuth"
(*Untimely Reflections*), 72; "Schopenhauer as Educator" (*Untimely
Reflections*), 56, 68, (101); "Sils-
Maria," 130*n; So Spoke Zarathustra*, (81), 102, 103, 104, 118,
130*n*, 150*n*, 152, 158*n*, (260), 474,
479; *The Twilight of the Idols*,
152*n*, 478-79*n*; *Untimely Reflections*, 48*n*, 56, 72, 155*n*
Nonne, Else, 312*n*, 317
Nötzel, Karl, 440-41, 446-47
Novinky (estate), 276-79, 288, 289,
297-98, 313, 498, 499, 502

Oberwaltersdorf (place), 198-99, 305,
309, 325
Orta (place), 54, 68, 70, 96, 99, 114,
119, 258, 435, 476, 544
Ott, Louise, 85
Overbeck, Franz, 54-55, 56, 57, 61-
62, 63, 66, 68, 74, 81, 84, 85*n*,
86, 87, 90, 92, 94-95, 98*n*, 100,
103, 104*n*, 105, 106, 107, 109, 117,
128, 162, 163, 165, 168*n*, 169*n*,
182, 480
Overbeck, Ida, 54-55, 56, 57, 60, 61-
62, 63, 68, 74-75, 81*n*, 90, 95, 98*n*,
101, 103*n*, 104, 105, 106, 108-09,
128, 130, 169*n*, 479, 480

Pasternak, Boris, 266
Pasternak, Leonid, 247, 264-65, 266,
321
Paul (of Tarsus), 37, 56
Paul (character in Richard Beer-Hof-
mann, "Das Kind"), 191, 193, 261,
262, 264; (character in Richard
Beer-Hofmann, *Der Tod Georgs*),
191, 193*n*, 197, 260-63
Paulsen, Friedrich, 112, 115, 118,
128*n*, 307
Peterhof (place), 6, 10, 22*n*, 206*n*,
249, 449
Peters, Carl, 177, 250, 315, 316*n*
Petrischule, 12, 434, 491
Pfeiffer, Ernst, 465*n*, 477-78, 479,
(484), 490
Pfleiderer, Otto, 14*n*
Pindar, 64
Pineles, Broncia, 198-99, 212, 218,
219, 230, 251*n*
Pineles, Friedrich (Zemek), 22*n*, 198-
99, 201-04, 205*n*, 208-09, 211, 212,
213*n*, 217*n*, 218, 219, 220, 221*n*,
227*n*, 230, 236*n*, 251, 281, 299,

301, 305-06, 309, 310, 311, 315, 316, 317, 318, 324-25, 326, 335, 362, 366*n*, 369, 445*n*, 461, 472, 494, 496, 497, 505, 508
Podach, Erich, 465*n*, 472*n*, 479
Proust, Marcel, *Swann's Way*, 308
"Puck" (Sophia Goudstikker), 213, 216
Pushkin, Alexander, 216, 230, 273
Pygmalion, 100*n*
Pythagoras, 48*n*, 61, 155*n*, 386*n*

Racine, Jean, *Phèdre*, 123
Rank, Otto, 375-76*n*, 377-78, 381
Ranke, Johannes, 234*n*
Rathenau, Walther, 322
Rée, Georg, 42, 90, 107-08, 117
Rée, Paul, 22*n*, 40-128, 131-32, 135-37, 139-40, 141, 153-54*n*, 155, 157-58, 161*n*, 163, 164, 165, 166-68, 169, 177*n*, 181*n*, 182, 192-93, 209, 225, 237*n*, 246, 287*n*, 306-07, 315, 366*n*, 367, 395, 406*n*, 414*n*, 416, 427, 428, 432, 433, 435, 466*n*, 467-69, 472, 477, 479*n*, 496, 499*n*, 505, 506, 543-44; *Die Entstehung des Gewissens*, (40-41), (59), (71), 87*n*, (103), 116, 128, (132), 137*n*; *Philosophie*, 40*n*, 139-40; *Psychologische Beobachtungen*, 40, (43); *Der Ursprung der moralischen Empfindungen*, 40, (43-44), 87*n*, 137*n*
Reinhardt, Max, 320, 322, 323, 324*n*, 444*n*, 446
Repin, Ilya, 248*n*
Reuter, Gabriele, 321
Rig- Veda, 37
Rilke, Clara (née Westhoff), 300*n*, 310, 317, 320, 321-23, 404, 414*n*, 452, 474, 477*n*, 497*n*, 499*n*
Rilke, Rainer Maria, ix, 5*n*, 27*n*, 30*n*, 170*n*, 177*n*, 205*n*, 208*n*, 209*n*, 213-19, (224), 225-31, 235*n*, 245, 247-50, 251, 252, 259, 260, 263-79, 281-301, 303, 307, 308*n*, 310-26, 384*n*, 400, 404*n*, 414-15, 426, 430, 431, 432, 439*n*, 442, 443, 444, 447*n*, 449-55, 456, 461-63, 466, 471, 473-75, 477, 485, 487, 488, 489, 490, 496, 497, 499, 502, 504, 509, 553; *The Book of Hours* (including the "monk's songs"), 252, 294, 295-96, 300, 313*n*, 320, 462, 463, 466, (475), 488*n*; *Cornet*, 252; *The Duino Elegies*, (295), (451), (453-54), (462), (475), (489); "Florence diary," 225-27, 228-30, 231, 235*n*, 245, 308*n*, 405*n*; "monk's songs," *see The Book of Hours*; *New Poems*, 324, 466; *The Notebooks of Malte Laurids Brigge*, 217*n*, 264, 294*n*, 311; *Rodin*, 311; *Sonnets to Orpheus*, 294*n*, 453-54
Rilke, Ruth, 310, 313
Robertson, George Croom, 44*n*
Rodin, Auguste, 295, 310, 311, 321, 326, 466, 475
Rohde, Erwin, 100, 128, 135, 162, 163*n*, 165; *Psyche*, 193*n*
Rolland, Romain, 381*n*
Rome, 38-40, 42-43, 49-54, 55, 56, 62*n*, 67, 96, 104, 114, 121*n*, 122-24, 137, 158, 181, 188*n*, 220*n*, 313, 467*n*, 470, 479
Romundt, Heinrich, 43, 48, 90, 95*n*, 113, 126, 131, 132, 157*n*, 182, 246; *Eine Gesellschaft auf dem Lande*, 246
Rongas (place), 17-18, 279-81, 294*n*, 307*n*, 470
Rosen, Friedrich, 142*n*
Ruskin, John, 250
Ruth (character in *Ruth*), 17*n*, 180-82, 209, 433

Sacher-Masoch, Leopold von, 322
Sachs, Hanns, 369
Salomé, Alexander (Sasha), (6), 9, 226*n*, 279, 307*n*, 410-11, (421), (422), (430), (432), (434), 437, 467, 477
Salomé, Conrad (Kolia), 477, 487
Salomé, Eugene (Jenia), (6), 8, 11, 13, 21, 58, 62, 131, 133, 182, 183*n*, 189-90, 199, 208, 225, 226, 227-28, 230, 306, 307*n*, 421, (422), 427, 430, 432, 433, 434, 436-37, 467, 505
Salomé, Gustav Ludwig in person, 5-9, 10*n*, 11, 12-13, 16*n*, 23, 37*n*, 205*n*, 281, 284*n*, 293-94*n*, 470-71, 491; as Lou's lost love, 6-8, 21-26, 29*n*, 100, 124, 206, 207, 240, 241, 307, 345, 347, 349, 351-52, 365, 366, 375, 386, 398, 433-34, 471, 491, 495
Salomé, Louise (Lou), *see* Andreas-Salomé, Lou
Salomé, Louise (Lou's mother), 5-9, 10*n*, 11, 12, 16-17, 19, 22*n*, 32, 35, 37*n*, 38-39, 49, 51, 53, 56, 58,

62, 68*n*, 95, 106, 114, 115*n*, 117*n*, 121, 141, 169*n*, 189-90, 199*n*, 226*n*, 227-28, 230, 247-48, 251, 287, 317, 327, 329, 347-52, 410-11, 433, 467, 468*n*, 470, 471

Salomé, Robert (Roba), (6), 9, 12, 192, 226*n*, 228, 317, 412, (421), (422), (430), (432), (436)

Salten, Felix, 190, 194, 196, 197, 198, 321, 445

Salzburg, and Beer-Hofmann, 194, 202*n*, 445; otherwise, 63, 378, 443*n*

Sand, George, 155*n*

Scheler, Max, 447, 465*n*

Schill, Sophia, 264, 266, 269, 271, 275, 277, 415

Schleiermacher, Friedrich, 37

Schnitzler, Arthur, 190, 191-92, 194-98, 200, 201*n*, 202, 247, 284*n*, 321, 324, 434, 445, 472, 473*n*, 493, 497*n*; "Halb Zwei," 190; *Liebelei*, 190, 194, 195, 196; *Reigen*, 201*n*; *Ruf des Lebens*, 321; "Eine überspannte Person," 190

Schoenberner, Franz, 446, 447, 472, 477, 479

Schönberg (place), 194-95, 199, 200*n*, (201-04), 493-94, 497, 498

Schopenhauer, Arthur, 40, 43, 44*n*, 69, 72, 73, 101, 105, 113, 148, 151, 211*n*

Schubin, Ossip, *see* Kirschner

Schuhmann, Professor, 133

Schulz, Carl von, 132-33, 184

Schwarz, Eduard, 309

Siewert, Elisabeth, 322, 323, 441

Sils-Maria (place), 47, 104, 117, 118*n*, 126, 127*n*, 429*n*, 466, 469

Simmel, Georg, 188*n*, 218, 237, 321, 322, 404

Simplicissimus, 477

Socrates, 464

Solf, Wilhelm, 142*n*

Sombart, Werner, 321

Spinoza, Baruch, 15-16, 28*n*, 88*n*, 294, 337, 379*n*, 382*n*, 396, 401, 496

Spranger, Eduard, 309, 447-48, 449, 465*n*

Ssavely, (183), (204*n*), (494)

Stanislavsky, Constantin, 320, 321, 322, 472

Stefan (character in "Geschwister"), 416-17, 419-25, 427-29, 432-37, 472, 504

Stefansdom (cathedral in Vienna), 192. *See also* Stefansplatz

Stefansplatz (square in Vienna), 196*n*, 218, 325, 436

Stein, Heinrich von, 73, 85, 90, 113, 126-27, 131, 132, 434-35, 469, 493

Stekel, Wilhelm, 369

Stibbe (manor), 42, 48, 55*n*, 56, 58, 59, 60, 61, 64, 67-72, 76, 78*n*, 79*n*, 85, (87-)89, 102, 114, 118, 139-40, 192, 306, 467, 468, 503

Stöcker, Helene, 210*n*, 220, 309, 312, 320, 321, 323, 447, 487-88

Stolze, Franz, 143

Strauss, David Friedrich, 14

Strauss und Torney, Lulu von, 322, 323, 324, 472, 489

Strindberg, August, 143, 177, 179, 190*n*, 388, 400, 442*n*, 447*n*, 472; "Corinna," 145*n*; *The Creditors*, 473*n*; *The Ghost Sonata*, 388*n*

Sudermann, Hermann, 194*n*; *Heimat*, 179

Swift, Jonathan, 441*n*

Swoboda, Hermann, 336

Tao-teh-king, 37

Tausk, Jelka, 403, 419, 424

Tausk, Viktor, 208*n*, 336, 339, 348, 355, 358-59, 379*n*, 380*n*, 401-04, 415-16, 417-21, 424-25, 427-28, 432, 436, 437-38, 494, 504

Tautenburg (place), 67-68, 73, 74, 75, 76, 77-85, 86, 87, 88*n*, 89, 91, 105, 107, 118*n*, 120-22, 124, 128, 129, 130, 138, 147, 151, 154, 156, 157*n*, 158, 159-60, 161*n*, 168*n*, 169*n*, 171, 240, 245, 427, 467, 470, 477, 504, 543

Tegel (place), 367*n*, 376, 475, 476, 505

"Théâtre Antoine" (Théâtre libre"), 182

Tolstoi, Leo, 189, 212, 216, 230, 231, 247, 266-71, 275, 278*n*, 288, 440-41, 463, 471, 477*n*, 504, 505; *Anna Karenina*, 298

Tolstoi, Nadesha Alexandrovna, *see* Babushka

Tolstoi, Nikolai, 275-79, 289, 296-98, 414, 497*n*

Tönnies, Ferdinand, 27*n*, 40*n*, 115-18, 129*n*, 133, 143*n*, 209, 213*n*, 306-07; *Der Nietzsche Kultus*, 213*n*

Trebor (character in "Geschwister"), 416-25, 427-29, 431-34, 436-37, 475

Trotsky, Leon, 410

Troubetzkoy, Paul, 247, 268

Ullmann, Regina, 443

Verlaine, Paul, 182
Virchow, Rudolf, 234n
Vogeler, Heinrich, 247n, 251n, 284n, 323
Volinsky, Akim L'vovich, 213, 215-18, 219n, 249, 260, 280, 473
Volkonsky, Sergei, 232
Voltaire, 78, 118

Wagner, Cosima, 43n, 73-74, 102, 467
Wagner, Richard, 43n, 55, 72, 73, 74, 87n, 102, 127n, 148, 151, 169n, 183, 467, 477n; *Parsifal*, 56, 72, 74, 103, 108
Wagner, Siegfried, 73
Wassermann, Jakob, 213, 217, 321, 445
Wedekind, Frank, 182-83, 185n, 209, 212-13, 320, 322, 323, 329n, 446, 472, 473n, 496n, 499n; *Frühlings Erwachen*, 183, 323; *Lulu*, 183n; *Pandora's Box*, 446; *Salomé*, 311
Wedekind, Tilly, (322), (323), (446)
Weizsäcker Viktor, von, 488
Wenneberg, Gunnar, 400n
Werfel, Franz, 452
Westhoff, Clara, *see* Rilke, Clara
Wille, Bruno, 143
Wilm, Eduard, 5n, 9n
Wilm, Emma, *see* Flörke
Wilm, Louise, *see* Salomé, Louise (Lou's mother)

Wilm, Louise (Lou's cousin), 446
Wilm, Siegfried, 5, 27n, 494, 500
Witalii (character in *Ródinka*), 289-90, 293, 294n, 295-98, 312-13, 414-15, 441, 504n
Wolff, Kurt, 439n
Wolfratshausen (place), 214-18, 229, 281, 299, 314, 473, 474n
Worpswede (place), 247, 281, 282n, 294, 295, 310, 323

Zemek, *see* Pineles, Friedrich
Die Zukunft (review), 167, 168, 318, 446
Zurich, 35-38, 56, 58, 59-61, (115), 180n, 183, 184, 275, 306, 378, 467, 470; University of, 17, 32, 35-38, 46, 56, 60, 161n
Zweig, Arnold, 479

Postscript: While preparing this index, I realized that "Jane" is an anagram of "Jena" (cf. above, p. 92 n. z), that "Anjuta" at "Schöneberg" is an anagram of "Jane" inasmuch as *jut* is the letter "j" as pronounced in German (cf. above, pp. 120, 200), and thence that the unhappy end of Anjuta's Schöneberg idyll was *inter alia* the unhappy beginning of Lou's Tautenburg idyll, with Anjuta-Lou's unladylikeness exposed when her luggage alias herself is fetched in Innsbruck alias Jena (cf. above, pp. 198, 200, 434-35, 493).